HISTORICAL GEOGRAPHY OF ANCIENT INDIA

HISTORICAL GEOGRAPHY OF ANCIENT INDIA

BY

BIMALA CHURN LAW

M.A., LL.B., Ph.D., D.Litt.

Membre d'Honneur de la Societe Asiatique de Paris; Hony. Fellow, Royal Asiatic Society of Great Britain and Ireland; Hony. Member, Royal Asiatic Society, Ceylon Branch; Fellow, Royal Asiatic Society of Bengal; Author, Tribes in Ancient India; History of Pali Literature; Geography of Early Buddhism; Geographical Essays; The Magadhas in Ancient India, etc.

WITH A PREFACE BY PROF. LOUIS RENOU

GYAN

Published by

GYAN

Gyan Publishing House
5, Ansari Road
Daryaganj, New Delhi-110002
Phone: 011-47034999, 9811692060
E-mail: books@gyanbooks.com

Distribution Network
gyanbooks.com
India, USA, Canada, UK, Australia, France

ISBN : 978-81-212-2466-6 (HB)
First Published, 1954

2nd Impression 2021

Printed at: Gyan Press, Delhi.

Historical Geography of Ancient India
Author: Bimala Churn Law

HISTORICAL GEOGRAPHY OF ANCIENT INDIA

By BIMALA CHURN LAW

M.A., LL.B., Ph.D., D.Litt.

Membre d'Honneur de la Société Asiatique de Paris; Hony. Fellow, Royal Asiatic Society of Great Britain and Ireland; Hony. Member, Royal Asiatic Society, Ceylon Branch; Fellow, Royal Asiatic Society of Bengal; Author, *Tribes in Ancient India; History of Pali Literature; Geography of Early Buddhism; Geographical Essays; The Magadhas in Ancient India*, etc.

With a Preface by Prof. Louis Renou

Published by
Société Asiatique de Paris
1, rue de Seine
Paris–VIe
FRANCE

AVANT-PROPOS

Permi les travaux de M. Bimala Churn Law—dont le nombre défie presque l'énumération—une grande partie a été consacrée à extraire des textes de l'Inde ancienne, en les présentant de manière dûment classifiée, les informations concrètes sur la géographie, l'histoire, la société, bref tous les *realia* que ces textes peuvent contenir. L'entreprise n'est pas aisée, quand on mesure les déformations, intentionnelles ou non, que des sources littéraires ou religieuses ont souvent fait subir aux faits élémentaires que les auteurs avaient sous les yeux et qu'ils étaient tentés d'enrober sous quelque parure mythique.

Le travail de dépouillement, de classification, n'en est que plus urgent. Malgré bien des travaux d'approche, des synthèses parfois prématurées, la compilation des sources, effectuée sans parti-pris de système, demeure indispensable. Elle a trouvé un ouvrier diligent et compétent, éloigné de tout esprit d'aventure et d'hypothèse, en la personne de M. B. Ch. Law. Celui-ci a déjà abordé à plusieurs reprises la géographie historique de l'Inde ; il a notamment porté son attention sur les sources bouddhiques, qui demeurent les plus 'parlantes'.

Le présent ouvrage résume ses travaux antérieurs sur ce sujet et apporte nombre de données nouvelles. Il embrasse en somme l'ensemble de notre documentation, depuis le Véda jusqu' aux *Purāṇa* les plus récents, en passant par les textes canoniques du bouddhisme et du jainisme, les épopées, la *smṛti*, l'épigraphie sanskrite, sans négliger ces éléments d'information connus depuis les origines de l'indianisme, mais auxquels chaque recherche nouvelle conduit à attacher un prix nouveau : les historiens ou géographes grecs, les pélerins chinois, les voyageurs arabes.

M. B. Ch. Law a souhaité que cette publication parût sous le patronage de la *Société Asiatique de Paris :* celle-ci est heureuse de l'accueillir.

LOUIS RENOU

AUTHOR'S NOTE

A systematic and comprehensive historical geography of ancient India is undoubtedly a great necessity. It is indeed a long-felt want to have such a geography especially based on epigraphic data. With this object in view I have attempted to prepare the present book which is the outcome of my continued study of ancient Indian geography. I have arranged the geographical names in an alphabetical order and fully dealt with them under proper divisions to which they belong. I have utilized original works in Sanskrit (Vedic and Classical), Pali, Prakrit, Sinhalese, Burmese, Tibetan, and Chinese and I have received an invaluable help from other sources such as epigraphy, archaeology, numismatics, accounts of Greek travellers and Chinese pilgrims. Due attention has been paid to modern literature and modern researches on the subject. The investigations made in the line by Sir Alexander Cunningham, Sir William Jones, Lassen, Vivien-de St. Martin, Stanislas Julien, Buchanan Hamilton, Mackenzie, Sir Aurel Stein, Kirfel, Dey, S. N. Majumdar, Raychaudhuri and others are noteworthy, but they now require careful revision in order to make them thorough and up-to-date. My previous publications have given me an immense help to prepare this detailed treatise. The task is no doubt, fraught with difficulties, but I have tried my utmost to avert them as far as possible. I have spared no pains to make my treatment systematic, exhaustive, lucid, and useful. Three sketch-maps are given in this book for the guidance of the readers. I shall consider my labour amply rewarded, if this book greatly helps the geographers engaged in researches on ancient Indian geography.

I am highly grateful to Prof. Dr. Louis Renou for his *Avant-propos*. The Société Asiatique of Paris has laid me under a deep debt of obligation by accepting this book as their publication.

43 Kailas Bose Street,
Calcutta 6,
India.
1st August, 1954.

B. C. LAW.

CONTENTS

INTRODUCTION

I. Sources

To reconstruct a systematic geography of ancient India Vedic literature, *Brāhmaṇas*, *Upaniṣads*, *Dharmasūtras* and *Dharmaśāstras* render us some help. Of the geographical names in the *Ṛgveda* those of the rivers alone permit of easy and certain identifications. The Epics and the Purāṇas are recognized as a rich mine of geographical information about ancient India. They contain some chapters giving a fairly accurate account of not only the different territorial divisions of India but also of her rivers, mountains, lakes, forests, deserts, towns, countries and peoples. The Tīrthayātrā-Digvijaya sections of the *Mahābhārata*, the *Jambukhaṇḍavinirmāṇaparva* of the same epic, and the *Kiṣkindhyā-kāṇḍa* of the *Rāmāyaṇa* are rich in geographical information. The *Bhuvanakoṣa*, the *Jambudvīpavarṇanā*, the Kūrmavibhāga sections of the *Purāṇas*, the *Bṛhatsaṃhitā*, the *Parāśaratantra* and the *Atharvapariśiṣṭa* are equally important in eliciting valuable geographical information. No less important are Pāṇini's *Aṣṭādhyāyī* (4.1.173, 178; 4.2.76; 4.2.133; 5.3. 116-117, etc.), Patañjali's *Mahābhāṣya*, Kauṭilīya *Arthaśāstra* and the *Yoginītantra* for a study of early Indian geography.

The geographical accounts in the different Purāṇas are more or less identical, and the account in one is often repeated in another; in some cases a larger account is summarized into a shorter one. The list in the *Vāyu*, *Matsya* and *Mārkaṇḍeya Purāṇas* is a long one, while that in the *Viṣṇu* is very short. The Pauranic lists of countries and peoples occur also in the *Mahābhārata*, sometimes in a more detailed form. The particulars of the country of Bharata as given in the *Bhīṣmaparva* of the *Mahābhārata* (ślokas 317–78) are almost the same as in the *Purāṇas*, but in some cases additional information can be gathered. It is obvious that these lists are framed in pursuance of a traditional account handed down from earlier times. But it must be admitted that the accounts are substantially correct. The fabulous element as pointed out by Cunningham is confined, as a rule, to outside lands, and their allusions to purely Indian topography are generally sober.

The *Viṣṇu Purāṇa* list of countries is very meagre; the *Mahābhārata* has a much longer catalogue without any arrangement; so also in the *Padmapurāṇa*. The longest list of countries and peoples of India is, however, contained in the *Mārkaṇḍeya*, the *Skanda*, the *Brahmāṇḍa* and the *Vāyu Purāṇas*. The *Mārkaṇḍeya Purāṇa* contains a description of Jambudvīpa and mentions the forests, lakes and mountains around Meru. It mentions the nine divisions of Bhārata, the seven mountain ranges in India and twenty-two separate hills. It describes the course of the Ganges and refers to the famous rivers in India, grouping them according to the mountain ranges out of which they arise. The principal peoples in India and on its borders are also mentioned in it, arranged according to the natural regions of the country. The majority of the names of countries and peoples found in the *Purāṇas* is very much the same as we find in the *Nadyādivarṇanā* section of the *Mārkaṇḍeya Purāṇa*, but there is also quite a good lot of names that are entirely new and original. The *Mārkaṇḍeya Purāṇa* (Ch. 57) which really contains the strictly geographical information of other major *Purāṇas*, has a section called the *Kūrmavibhāga* containing a list of countries and peoples of India arranged according to the position of the country conceived as a tortoise, as it lies on water resting upon Viṣṇu and looking eastwards.[1] This arrangement is based on earlier astronomical works, like those of Parāśara and Varāhamihira. This chapter is invaluable from the topographical standpoint. The *Bhāgavatapurāṇa* also contains some geographical information. So we find that the *Purāṇas* are really very important for a geographical study of ancient India.

The innumerable *Māhātmyas* require to be carefully studied from the geographical standpoint. The extensive *Māhātmya* literature which contains portions from the *Purāṇas* or *Saṃhitās*, deals with the topography of the various *tīrthas* or holy places. Their geographical importance is very great in the sense that evidences may be adduced from them to enable us to locate important sites. One finds it tedious to read the legendary history of *tīrthas* or holy places, but to a geographer it will never be a fruitless study.

The later Sanskrit literature abounds with geographical information. As for example, Rājaśekhara's *Kāvya-mīmāṃsā* (p. 93) clearly states the five traditional divisions of India. It contains some useful geographical information about Utkala, Sumha, Niṣadha, and Kāśmīra (Ch. 17), Aṅga, Vaṅga, Puṇḍra, Vālhīka, Pañcāla, Śūrasena, etc. (Ch. 3). The *Raghuvaṃśa* (4th sarga, śls. 35, 38), the *Naiṣadhīyacarita* by Śrīharṣa (5th sarga, śls. 50, 98), the *Meghadūta* by Kālidāsa (Pūrvamegha, śls. 24, 25, 26), the *Daśakumāracarita* by Daṇḍin (6th *ucchvāsa*), the *Harṣacarita* by Bāṇabhaṭṭa (6th and 7th *ucchvāsas*), Dhoyī's *Pavanandūta* (27) may be utilized for our geographical knowledge. A fairly good idea of Kālidāsa's knowledge of geography may be gathered from his works.

To present a complete geographical picture of India in the Buddha's time and later, Pali literature is undoubtedly the most important. From about the time of the Buddha to about the time of Aśoka the great literature of the early Buddhists is certainly the main source of the historical and geographical information of ancient India, supplemented by Jaina and Brahmanical sources here and there. Texts or narratives of purely historical or geographical nature are altogether absent in the literature of the early Buddhists, and whatever historical or geographical information can be gathered is incidental and very much reliable. Thus for the history of the rise and vicissitudes as well as for the geographical situation and other details of the sixteen *Mahājanapadas*, the most important chapter of the Indian history and geography before and after the time of the Buddha, the Pali *Aṅguttara Nikāya* is the main source of information which is supplemented by the Jaina *Bhagavatīsūtra* and the Karṇaparva of the *Mahābhārata*. For later periods when we have abundant epigraphical and archaeological sources and literary sources, too, which are mainly Brahmanical, as well as the accounts of the classical geographers and the itineraries of the Chinese pilgrims, the geographical information contained in Pali and Sanskrit Buddhist literature is considerably important.[2] Some geographical information may also be available from Tibetan texts.

The *Pāli Piṭaka*, specially the *Vinaya* and the *Sutta*, contains incidental references to cities and places connected with the gradual spread of Buddhism. They supply us with an abundant information concerning the *Madhyadeśa* or the Middle country and the localities bordering it. The *Milindapañha* which is an important non-canonical Pali text, and the *Mahāvastu*, a Buddhist Sanskrit work of great importance, contain many

---

[1] This conception fits well with our present knowledge of the topography of India.
[2] Vide Law, *Geography of Early Buddhism* and *Geographical Essays*, Ch. I.

important geographical notices. The Pali commentaries, specially those of Buddhaghosa, and the chronicles of Ceylon, specially the *Dīpavaṃsa* and the *Mahāvaṃsa*, furnish us with chips of information as to the geographical knowledge of the Buddhists.

The Sanskrit Buddhist texts which are later in date than the Pali texts, have some geographical information. Cities of fiction which are not part of the real world, are found in them. Countries like Ratnadvīpa and Khaṇḍadvīpa, cities like Vandhumatī and Puṇyavatī, and mountains like Triśaṅku and Dhūmanetra, mentioned in them, admit hardly of any identification and help only to add to the legendary element pervading most of the accounts of the Sanskrit Buddhist texts. The Sanskrit Buddhist texts which are very important from religious and philosophical points of view, do not elicit much information of a historical or geographical character. The *Mahāvastu* speaks mostly of the life of the Buddha; the *Lalitavistara* and the *Buddhacaritakāvya* also refer to the Master's life. The *Bodhisattvāvadānakalpalatā* gives a number of stories relating to the former existences of the Buddha, while the *Aśokāvadāna* speaks of Aśoka and his times. Very few Sanskrit Buddhist texts have a great corroborative value. Really speaking, they are not important from geographical standpoint. They were mostly written from the 6th century onwards to the 12th and 13th centuries of the Christian era. They no doubt contain the most important contemporary evidence as to the religious history, but geographically they speak of very remote times. For already by the 6th and 7th centuries of the Christian era the whole of the Indian continent with its major divisions and sub-divisions, cities, countries, provinces, rivers, mountains, etc., had become too widely known to its people. Contemporary epigraphic, literary and monumental evidences abound with information regarding many geographical details. Moreover, the Indians of those centuries had also planted their political, cultural and commercial outposts and colonies not only in Suvarṇabhūmi (Lower Burma) but also in Java and Sumatra, Campā and Kamboj. Their priests and missionaries had already travelled to China and Central Asia carrying with them Sanskrit Buddhist texts. But it is difficult to find in them any idea of far wider geographical knowledge and outlook of the times. Even the Indian continent is not fully represented in its contemporary geographical information.

The earlier texts of the Jainas have many geographical and topographical references. The *Acārāṅgusūtra*, *Bhagavatīviyāhapaṇṇatti*, *Nāyādhammakahāo*, *Uvāsagadasāo*, *Aṃtagaḍadasāo*, *Aṇuttarovavāiyadasāo*, *Paṇhāvāgaraṇāiṃ*, *Vivāga-sūya*, *Ovavāiya-sūya*, *Rāyapasenaiya-sūya*, *Paṇṇavaṇā*, *Jambuddīvapaṇṇatti*, *Nirayāvaliya-sūya*, *Nisīha-mahānisīha-sūyas*, *Kalpasūtra*, *Uttarādhyayanasūtra*, and the *Āvaśyakasūtra* contain geographical data. The *Jambuddīvapaṇṇatti* which is the sixth *upāṅga* of the Jainas, contains a description of Jambudvīpa as well as that of Bhāratavarṣa. It speaks of seven *varṣas* or countries constituting seven main divisions of Jambudvīpa. Although it gives us the mythical geography of the Jainas, there is much that is of great value to geographers of ancient India. It is no doubt an interesting Jaina treatise on geography and it should be studied along with the *Vividhatīrthakalpa* which is not included in the Jaina canon. The *Vividhatīrthakalpa* of Jinaprabha Sūri contains legends mixed up with facts. Great care should be taken to separate fact from fiction in order to present a true geographical picture.[1]

[1] Law, *Some Jaina Canonical Sūtras*, Appendix II.

The inscriptions of Aśoka and those at the Khaṇḍagiri and Udayagiri hills of Orissa also help us greatly. Coins too sometimes enable us to locate a particular nation or tribe. As for example, the discovery of some copper coins at Nāgri, a small town 11 miles north of Chitor, enables us to locate the kingdom of king Sivi of the *Sivi Jātaka*.

Among the early classical geographers Hecataeus of Miletus (B.C. 549–486) was the first Greek geographer whose knowledge stopped on the frontier of the Persian empire, the river Indus. He knew the people called Gandhāri on the upper Indus. He was acquainted with the names of other Indian peoples of the frontier hills (*Cambridge History of India*, I, 394). Herodotus (B.C. 484–431) wrote about India, much of which was drawn from Hacataeus. He knew that the population of India was great.[1] In fact, most of his allusions to India refer to the times of Darius and Xerxes (*Ibid.*, I, 329). From a passage in Herodotus (IV. 44) it appears that the valley of the Indus from its upper course to the sea including the Punjab and Sind, was annexed by the Persians or was brought under their control (*Ibid.*, I, 336). Regarding minor states in India in the period from 325 B.C. to 300 A.D. some information has been supplied by him (B. C. Law, *Indological Studies*, Pt. I, 11). Ktesias (B.C. 398) collected materials during his stay for a treatise on India. His account was unfortunately vitiated by a large number of fables and it was left to the followers of Alexander to give to the Western world for the first time fairly accurate accounts of India and its inhabitants.

The great conqueror carried scientific men with him to chronicle his achievements, and described the countries invaded by him. Some of his officers were men of literary culture. Of his companions three men enriched the Greek conception of India by their writings. Nearchus was one of them. His book contained a good deal of incidental information about India (*C.H.I.*, I, 398). Alexander's Indian expedition produced quite a large number of narratives and memoirs relating to India. All these works are lost, and their substance is found in brief in Strabo, Pliny and Arrian. Some subsequent writers made considerable additions to the stock of information concerning India, among whom may be mentioned Diodorus, Strabo, Curtius, Arrian, who was the best of Alexander's historians, and Justinus.[2] The Greek and Roman historians of Alexander carry on geographical knowledge eastwards beyond the Jhelum (Hydaspes), the eastern limit of Gandhāra to the Beas (Hyphasis) (*Cambridge History of India*, I, 58-59).

Strabo's geography furnishes us with some information about the well-known Assaka or Aśmaka tribe. Though Strabo speaks of the country of the Gandarai, the name of the Gandhāra country is not mentioned by any of Alexander's historians. According to Strabo Taxila lay between the Indus and Hydaspes (the Jhelum). It was a large city which was governed by good laws. According to him the country of the elder Poros, the Kekaya country, was extensive and fertile, having in it some 300 cities. The principality of the younger Poros was called Gandaris. But this name is not to be taken as conclusive. He says that the region where Sophytes ruled was marked by the presence of a mountain composed of rock salt of sedimentary origin, yielding enough salt to meet the demands of the people of India as a whole. He further says that in the realm of Sophytes dogs were characterized by remarkable courage. He gives an interesting account of the inhabitants of the territory of

---

[1] *Cambridge History of India*, I, 395.

[2] McCrindle, *Ancient India as described by Megasthenes and Arrian*, pp. 5ff.

Mousikanos. The king of the territory of Oxykanos was called by him and Diodoros as Portikanos. He tells us that the Parthians deprived Eukratides of a part of Bactriana. The conquests by the Bactrian Greeks were, according to him, partly achieved by Menander (middle of the 2nd century B.C.) and partly by Demetrios, son of Euthydemos (*cir.* 190 B.C.). Such historico-geographical information, among other details, is found in his geography.

Megasthenes who lived long in India gives us topographical matters of great value. He came to the court of Candragupta Maurya on an embassy. He himself said that he had often visited Sandrokottos, the greatest king of the Indians. According to Arrian he also visited king Poros. The fragments of his *Indika* furnish us with invaluable materials concerning India, her inhabitants, rivers, countries, cities, size, fertility of the soils, wild animals, horses and elephants, Indian trees, peoples, castes, tribes, races, occupations, Indian philosophers, Śramaṇas and Brāhmaṇas, etc.

Arrian who distinguished himself as a historian, was the famous author of the account of the Asiatic expedition of Alexander the great. He also gave us a fine description of India. His *Indika* consists of three parts: the first part deals with the general description of India chiefly based on the accounts of the country given by Megasthenes and Eratosthenes; the second part gives an account of the voyage made by Nearchos the Cretan from the Indus to the Pasitigris, chiefly based on the narrative of the voyage written by Nearchos himself; and the third part gives ample evidence to prove that the southern parts of the world are uninhabitable on account of excessive insolation. In his *Indika* he refers to the regions beyond the river Indus on the west inhabited by the two Indian tribes, Astakenoi and Assakenoi. He mentions the countries lying to the east of the Indus as denoting India proper. He states the dimensions of India, and deals with her rivers, tribes, etc. He divides the Indian people into about seven castes and describes the hunting of wild animals by the Indians, etc.

Eratosthenes wrote a scientific geography. He described India on the authority of Alexander's historians.

Pliny treats of the geography of India in his *Natural History*, which was dedicated to Titus, son of Vespasian and his successor as emperor. The first ten books of this history were probably published in A.D. 77. Books III–VI are devoted to geography and ethnography. His treatment is uncritical but extremely valuable judging from the incidental facts presented by him.

The *Periplus of the Erythræan Sea* by an anonymous writer is a guide-book containing an account of trade and commerce carried on from the Red Sea and the coast of Africa to the East Indies (modern Indonesia). It is really a guide-book to the Indian ocean including its bordering seas, the Red Sea and the Persian Gulf. The articles of trade, which were handled by the ports, are mentioned in the *Periplus* (Translated by W. H. Schoff, 1912, pp. 284–288). According to the *Periplus* tin was shipped from Egypt to Somaliland and India. Ebony came to Rome from both India and Egypt. Minnagara was the name given temporarily to some cities in India during the period of the Scythian occupation. After the collapse of the Indo-Scythian power these cities resumed their former names with their autonomy. This guide-book contains some information about the Indus, Syrastrene (Surāṣṭra), Barygaza (modern Broach), the river Mahī (Mais), the river Narmadā (Nammadus), Arachosii (the country around the modern Kandahar), Gandaraei (Gandhāra), Ozene (Ujjain),

Tagara (modern Ter), Suppāra (modern Sopara), Calliene (modern Kalyāna), Pandian Kingdom (Pāṇḍya), etc.

Ptolemy's *Geography* is a work of great importance. Ptolemy was indebted to Marinus of Tyre for his materials. His treatise is divided into eight books. His description of India within the Ganges Valley, and his account of the countries, cities, towns, rivers, mountains, hills, etc., deserve to be studied with great care. The position of India beyond the Ganges, inland towns and villages of the trans-Gangetic India, seven mountain ranges, rivers of the Indus system, and the territories and peoples of India classified according to the river-basins, are some of the topics ably treated by him. His *Geography* is undoubtedly very helpful to the geographers of ancient India.

The itineraries of Chinese pilgrims are of inestimable value as sources of the ancient Indian geography. The accounts of Fa-Hien and Yuan Chwang who toured all over Northern India are very important. The account of Yuan Chwang who visited India in the 7th century A.D., is fuller and more exhaustive. For an accurate and exhaustive geography of Northern India during the 5th and 7th centuries of the Christian era, the accounts of these two pilgrims are the most important sources of information. There was another Chinese pilgrim who visited India in the 8th century A.D. He was U-Kong (*Calcutta Review*, August, 1922). The accounts of other Chinese pilgrims, Song Yun and Hwiseng, are short and describe only a few places in north-west India. I-tsing who visited many important places in ancient India in 673 A.D. gives us a detailed account. Another Chinese pilgrim named Wang-hiuen-t'se who came to India in 643 A.D., wandered over and visited the countries of the Lord Buddha, as he himself said in his account.[1] He visited Magadha and ascended the Gṛdhrakūṭa hill (Ki-tche-Kiu) and left there an inscription. He also went to Mahābodhi at Gayā. As related in his account he visited five Indies. At the head of the Tibetan and Nepalese cavalry he marched on Magadha, defeated the Indian troops, captured the capital, siezed the king and took him triumphantly to China. He himself visited Nepal and Tibet. His description of Tibet (Tou-fan) is interesting. This Chinese pilgrim in his leisure time wrote a book entitled *Account of the Voyage*. He narrates an interesting account of the law of Magadha which was then prevalent. If someone was guilty, he was not beaten by a rod, but recourse was taken to a wonderful weighing. His inscriptions engraved on the Gṛdhrakūṭa and at Mahābodhi have been translated by Chavannes. His account of the places in India visited by him is very useful from geographical standpoint.

The geographical accounts of Muslim writers are equally helpful. Alberuni, who was in the territory of modern Khiva in A.D. 973, distinguished himself in science and literature. In his book on *India* he deals with its geography which is sure to render some help to geographers. India as far as known to him was Brahmanic and not Buddhistic. In the first half of the 11th century A.D. all traces of Buddhism in Central Asia, Khurashan, Afghanistan and North-Western India seem to have disappeared. There his notes on Buddhism were very scanty. Benares and Kashmir were then two centres of Indian learning. He had not the same opportunity for travelling in India as Hiuen Tsang had. Hence his geographical notes are not so very exhaustive. In his book on *India* (English

---

[1] It is related in Sylvain Levi's article *Les Missions de Wang-Hiuen-T'se dans l'Inde*, published in the *Journal Asiatique*, 1900. This paper has been recently translated into English by Dr. S. P. Chatterjee.

edition by Dr. E. C. Sachau, Ch. XVIII) he deals with the Madhyadeśa, Prayāga, Sthāneśvara, Kānyakubja, Pāṭaliputra, Nepal, Kashmir and other countries and towns, rivers, animals, the western and southern frontiers of India, the western frontier mountains of India, islands, rainfall, etc. He also refers to the Hindu method of determining distances between the various parts of India.

Kalhaṇa's *Rājataraṅgiṇī*, the well-known Kashmir Chronicle of the 12th century A.D., should be used with caution as it contains a large number of confused ancient traditions. It is valuable, says Vincent Smith, as it gives a trustworthy account of local events (*Early History of India*, 4th Ed., p. 10).

Marco Polo, the famous Venetian traveller, visited South India and Central Asia in the 13th century A.D. The account of his travels may be found useful. (Vide *Travels of Marco Polo* by L. R. Fawcus published in the *Introducing India*, Pt. I, R.A.S.B. publication.)

There are other means of approach to the historical geography of India, such as, the early surveys contained in the Imperial and Provincial Gazetteers, which are really mines of information. The *Reports of the Archaeological Survey of India*, and the geographical references in the *Epigraphia Indica*, *Corpus Inscriptionum Indicarum*, *South Indian Inscriptions* and *Epigraphia Carnatica*, contain detailed geographical knowledge of the most definite character. The *Census Reports of India* are equally important.

In the *Imperial Gazetteer of India* (New Edition, Vol. II, Historical, The Indian Empire, pp. 76–87), Dr. J. F. Fleet's attractive note on Geography will no doubt be helpful to researchers. He has shown the importance of the study of early Indian Geography and has traced the principal sources of this interesting branch of study.

The Annual Reports of the Archaeological Survey of India contain detailed accounts of the excavations carried out by the Archaeological Department at different sites of historical importance, and they dwell at length upon the topography of places of geographical interest, e.g., Besnagar, Bhiṭā, Kāsiā, Pāṭaliputra, Rājagṛha, Sārnāth, Vaiśālī, Takṣaśilā. The Annual Report for 1907-08 contains an account of the ancient temples of Aihole with the topography of the site. In the Report for 1915-16, M. B. Garde writes a paper on the site of Padmāvatī, which is mentioned in the *Viṣṇupurāṇa* as one of the three capitals of the Nāgas and described in Bhavabhūti's *Mālatī-mādhava* as the place where the hero of the poem, Mādhava, was sent by his father from Kuṇḍinapura in Vidarbha. Padmāvatī is identified with modern Pawaya on the confluence of the Sind and the Pārvatī. The Report for 1927-28 contains a note by K. N. Dikshit on the identification of Puṣkaraṇa in the Susunia inscription of Candravarman. Puṣkaraṇa of the inscription (ed. H. P. Śāstrī, *Ep. Ind.*, XIII, p. 133) is identified with the village of Pokharan, 25 miles to the northwest of Susunia. The Reports for 1925-26, 1927-28 and 1928-29, contain accounts of the excavations at Paharpur in the Rajshahi district, while the Report for 1928-29 contains an account of the excavations at Mahāsthān in the Bogra district of north Bengal,[1] identified with the ancient site of Puṇḍravardhana.

'*The Buddhist Antiquities of Nāgārjunakoṇḍa, Madras Presidency*', by A. H. Longhurst, published by the Archaeological Survey of India as their Memoir No. 64, gives an interesting account of the Buddhist antiquities discovered at the Nagarjuna's hill on the right bank of the Kṛṣṇā river in

[1] Now in East Pakistan.

the Palnāḍ taluk of the Guṇṭur district. Most of the scenes in the beautiful bas-reliefs recovered from the ruined stūpas at the site illustrate well-known stories connected with the life of the Buddha. The author has taken much pains to identify the different scenes portrayed in the sculptures. He has given us a very readable account of the locality and an interesting history of the site. The chief buildings and antiquities discovered during the explorations have not escaped the careful attention of the author, and he has furnished us with a very good account of them. The fruitful result of his careful investigation embodied in this monograph will surely be appreciated by every student of early Indian geography.

Explorations in Sind by N. G. Mazumdar published as a Memoir No. 48 by the Archaeological Survey of India is a valuable contribution to ancient Indian geography. It contains prominent topographical features of Sind and its climate. It also gives an account of the excavations carried out at the site during the years 1927-28, 1929-30 and 1930-31.

II. Different Names of India

Bounded on the north by stupendous mountain ranges and on the other three sides by the mighty seas and ocean, India constitutes a distinct geographical unit. The vastness of the country with its infinite variety of fauna and flora, races and languages, religions and culture justly entitles it to be called a great sub-continent. The remote parts of this great country revealed themselves to the observers and explorers of ancient times only gradually and by stages. It is for this reason therefore that we do not meet with any comprehensive term to designate the whole country in the earliest records. The word 'India' is derived from the name of the river Sindhu or the Indus.[1] The Chinese also knew the ancient name of India as Shin-tuh or Sindhu.[2] In the *Rigveda* (VIII. 24. 27) it is referred to as Sapta Sindhavas or 'the Seven Rivers'. The designation doubtless corresponds to the term Hapta Hindu found in the *Avestan Vendīdād.*[3] In the famous inscriptions of Darius at Persepolis and Naksh-i-Rustam the entire territory watered by the Indus and its affluents is styled simply Hi(n)du.[4] Herodotus calls it 'India' which was the twentieth division of the Persian empire. It should, however, be noted that the Vedic Sapta Sindhavaḥ and the Persian Hi(n)du corresponded only to a particular part of India lying to the north-west. But 'India' of Herodotus was already acquiring a wider denotation, for the Greek historian speaks of the Indians who 'are situated very far from the Persians, towards the south, and were never subject to Darius'.[5]

The exploration of practically the whole country had been completed in or about the fourth century B.C. The literature of the period, both Greek and Indian, shows acquaintance not only with the realm of the Pāṇḍyas in the south, but also with the island of Tāmraparṇī or Ceylon.[6] The people felt the necessity of a comprehensive term for the territory extending from the Himalayas in the north to the sea in the south. The term was Jambudvīpa which was then used. In Buddhist literature Jambudvīpa figures as one of the four Mahādvīpas or the four great con-

---

[1] *Cambridge History of India*, I, p. 324.
[2] Law, *Geography of Early Buddhism*, p. xvi; Legge, *Fahien*, p. 26.
[3] *Cambridge History of India*, I, p. 324.
[4] *Ibid.*, p. 335.
[5] Raychaudhuri, *Studies in the Indian Antiquities*, p. 81.
[6] Bhandarkar, *Carmichael Lectures* (1918), pp. 6ff.; *Cambridge History of India*, Vol. I, pp. 423ff.

tinents including India with Mt. Sineru (Sumeru) in the centre of them. A portion of Jambudvīpa known as the Aṅgadvīpa was inhabited by the Mlecchas according to the *Vāyupurāṇa* (48. 14–18).

Childers (*Pali Dictionary*, p. 165) points out that when opposed to Sīhaladīpa, Jambudvīpa means the continent of India.[1] It is difficult to be definite on this point. In Sanskrit Buddhist texts we have references to Jambudvīpa.[2] The Minor Rock Edict No. 1 of Aśoka mentions Jambudvīpa [3] which denotes the vast country ruled by that great emperor. In the Epics and Purāṇas Jambudvīpa is described as one of the seven concentric islands, encircled by seven *samudras*.[4] Of these seven islands the Jambudvīpa is the most alluded to in various sources and is one which is in its narrower sense identified with Bhāratavarṣa[5] or the Indian peninsula.

An interesting account of Jambudvīpa (*Pali* Jambudīpa) is found in Pali-Buddhist texts and commentaries. Jambudvīpa has been named after the Jambu tree. (*Visuddhimagga*, I, 205-206; cf. *Vinaya Texts*, I, 127; *Atthasālinī*, p. 298). According to the *Papañcasūdanī*, the commentary on the *Majjhima Nikāya*, it is called Vana or forest (Vol. II, p. 423). It is also called Sudarśanadvīpa which is said to derive its name from a tree growing in it, the branches of which extend over 1,000 yojanas. (*Brahmāṇḍapurāṇa* 37. 28–34; 50. 25-26; *Matsya*, 114. 74-75; cf. *Mahābh.* VI. 5. 13–15; VI. 7. 19-20). The Sineru which is the highest of the mountain peaks, was encompassed by seven celestial ranges, named Yugandhara, Īsadhara, Kāravika, Sudassana, Nemindhara, Vinataka and Assakaṇṇa. The Jambudvīpa looks like a lotus with Meru as its *karṇika* (pericarp of a lotus) and the *varṣas* or *mahādvīpas*, *Bhadrāśva*, *Bhārata*, *Ketumāla* and *Uttarakuru* as its four petals.[6] Buddhaghosa, the celebrated Pali commentator, points out that Jambudīpa was 10,000 yojanas in extent and it was called Great (*mahā*).[7] The five great rivers, Gaṅgā, Yamunā, Sarabhu, Aciravatī and Mahī, after watering Jambudīpa fell into the sea.[8] The Buddha, while relating the *Cakkavattisīhanāda Suttanta*, predicted thus: 'Jambudīpa will be mighty and prosperous, the villages, towns and royal cities will be so close that a cock would fly from each one to the next'. According to the *Sumaṅgalavilāsinī* Jambudīpa had 500 islands (Vol. II, p. 449). In Jambudīpa there were pleasant parks, pleasant groves, pleasant grounds and lakes, but their number was not great. Moreover, there were many steep precipitous cliffs, unfordable rivers, inaccessible mountains and dense thickets of stakes and thorns.[9] Gold was collected from the whole of Jambudīpa.[10] Aśoka built 84,000 monasteries in the whole of Jambudīpa.[11] The Sāṃkhya, Yoga, Nyāya and Vaiśeṣika systems of philosophy, arithmetic, music, medicine, the four Vedas, the *Purāṇas* and the *Itihāsas*, astronomy, magic, spells, the art of war, poetry and conveyancing were taught here.[12] There were disputants here in arts and sciences.[13] The importance of Jambudīpa was very great as it was often

---

[1] Law, *Geography of Early Buddhism*, p. xvi; *Geographical Essays*, p. 5.

[2] *Mahāvastu*, III, 67; *Lalitavistara*, Ch. XII; *Bodhisattvāvadānakalpalatā*, 78th Pallava, 9.

[3] R. K. Mookerjee, *Aśoka*, p. 110.

[4] Law, *Geography of Early Buddhism*, p. xvi; Cunningham, *Ancient Geography of India*, p. xxxvi.

[5] *Mahābhārata*, VI. 6. 13; *Brahmāṇḍapurāṇa*, 37. 27–46; 43. 32.

[6] Nīlakaṇṭha's commentary on the *Mahābhārata*, .VI. 6. 3–5; *Mārkaṇḍeya*, 55, 20ff.; *Brahmāṇḍa*, 35. 41; 44-45.

[7] *Sumaṅgalavilāsinī*, II, 429.

[8] *Ibid.*, p. 17.

[9] *Aṅg. Nik.*, I, 35.

[10] *Papañcasūdanī*, II, 123.

[11] *Dīpavaṃsa*, p. 49; *Visuddhimagga*, I, 201.

[12] *Milinda*, p. 3.

[13] *Therīgāthā Commy.*, p. 87.

visited by Gautama the Buddha besides Mahinda.[1] The people of Jambudīpa led a virtuous life according to the *Kathāvatthu* (p. 99). The whole of Jambudīpa was stirred up by Sānu, the only son of a female lay disciple who mastered the Tripiṭaka.[2] The *Cūḷavaṃsa* refers to the great Bo-tree at Jambudīpa (Vol. I, p. 36). There were heretics and monks here and the unruliness of the heretics was so very great that the monks stopped holding the *uposatha* ceremony for seven years.[3] A dreadful famine once visited it.[4]

Bhāratavarṣa was just one of the nine *varṣas* or countries constituting the nine main divisions of Jambudvīpa. The Jaina work *Jambuddīvapaṇṇatti* speaks of seven *varṣas* as constituent parts of Jambudvīpa. According to the Epic and Puranic authors Jambudvīpa was originally divided into seven *varṣas*. Two other *varṣas* were added later to the original seven and the total number of *varṣas* was raised to nine.[5] Thus with the Jaina and Brahmin writers Jambudvīpa as a continent was thought of as of much wider extension than Jambudvīpa as known to the Buddhists. Among the *varṣas* of Jambudvīpa Bhāratavarṣa lay most to the south. In agreement with the Great Epic[6] and the *Purāṇas*, the *Jambuddīvapaṇṇatti* derives the name Bhāratavarṣa from King Bharata, a descendant of Priyavrata, son of Manu Svyambhava,[7] whose sovereignty was established over it.[8] Bhāratavarṣa, according to Pauranic cosmology, was divided into nava-khaṇḍas or nine divisions 'separated by seas and as being mutually inaccessible'.[9] But Bhāratavarṣa, as we now know it, is not separated by seas within itself, nor are its component parts 'mutually inaccessible'. It is not thus our India, covering present geographical area. Of the nine khaṇḍas eight have been shown to be divisions not of India proper. They are not so many provinces of India, but of Greater India, and are islands and countries that encircle the Indian Peninsula.[10] This fact was also noted long ago by scholars like Alberuni and Abul Fazl.[11] The ninth *dvīpa* or *khaṇḍa*, i.e., Kumārī or Kumārikādvīpa, which is described in the *Purāṇas* to have been girt by sea (*sāgarasaṃvritaḥ*) and to have been inhabited by the Kirātas at its eastern extremity, and the Yavanas at its western, with the Brāhmaṇas, Kṣatriyas, Vaiśyas and Śūdras thrown within, seems to be identical with India proper.[12]

The early Greek writers regarded the Indus as the western boundary of India, but they knew of Indian settlements in the valley of the Kabul and its tributaries. Accordingly some regarded the Cophes, i.e., the river Kabul, as the furthest limit of India on its west.[13] The inclusion of Yonas or Yavanas, who probably occupied the place near Kabul, and of the Gandhāras, who were located in the region comprising the modern districts of Peshawar in the North-Western Frontier Province and Rawalpindi in the Punjab, both in Pakistan, among the peoples of *Uttarāpatha* in the Great Epic and the *Purāṇas*, suggests that India at one time embraced

---

[1] *Dīpavaṃsa*, p. 65.
[2] *Dhammapada Commy.*, IV, 25.
[3] *Mahāvaṃsa*, p. 51.
[4] *Dhammapada Commy.*, III, 368, 370, 374.
[5] Law, *India as described in early texts of Buddhism and Jainism*, p. 1 n; Law, *Geographical Essays*, 119ff.; Cunningham, *Ancient Geography of India*, pp. 8, 749ff.
[6] *Mahābh.*, Bhīṣmap., III. 41.
[7] *Bhāgavatapurāṇa*, XI, 2. 15ff.
[8] B. C. Law, *India as described in early texts of Buddhism and Jainism*, p. 14.
[9] Cunningham, *Ancient Geography of India*, p. 751; Law, *Geographical Essays*, p. 121; *Markaṇḍeya*, 575—*nine dvīpas*.
[10] Cunningham, *Ancient Geography of India*, Appendix I, pp. 749–754.
[11] Raychaudhuri, *op. cit.*, p. 78, f.n. 4.
[12] Law, *Geographical Essays*, p. 121.
[13] McCrindle, *Ancient India as described by Megasthenes and Arrian*, p. 156.

within its boundaries not only the land lying immediately to the west of the Indus but also the north-eastern corner of the Iranian Tableland. The mango-shaped island of Ceylon,[1] which does not form part of India proper, is both geographically and culturally closely connected with it.

III. Shape and Divisions of India

The ancient Indians had a very accurate knowledge of the true shape and size of their country. Alexander's informants gathered their knowledge from the people of the country and described India as a rhomboid or unequal quadrilateral in shape with the Indus on the west, the mountains on the north and the sea on the east and south.[2] In the *Mahābhārata*, the shape of India has been described as an equilateral triangle divided into four smaller equal triangles.[3] Cunningham observes, 'The shape corresponds very well with the general form of the country, if we extend the limits of India to Ghazni on the north-west, and fix the other two points of the triangle at Cape Comorin, and Sadiya in Assam'. (*C.A.G.I.*, p. 6.) That India was divided into nine portions was first pointed out by Parāśara and Varāhamihira. It was afterwards adopted by the authors of some of the *Purāṇas*.[4] In the *Kūrmaniveśa* section the surface of India is made to conform to the convex shape of the upper shell of a tortoise 'lying outspread and facing eastwards'. Some Pauranic passages suggest that the ancient Indians were acquainted with the four-fold conformation of India. This is also borne out by the early Greek accounts of the country. We learn from Strabo that Alexander caused the whole of the country to be described by men well acquainted with it. They were undoubtedly of Indian origin. Not long afterwards the Hellenistic ambassadors who were accredited to the court of the great Maurya kings at Pāṭaliputra also wrote accounts of India based partly on their own observations and partly on the information derived from the Indian sources. In the Geography of Ptolemy we find that the acute angle formed by the meeting of the two coasts of the Peninsula at the Cape Comorin, is changed to a single coast line running almost straight from the mouth of the Indus to the mouth of the Ganges.[5] According to the early Buddhists, India is broad on the north whereas in the south it has the form of the front portion of a cart and is divided into seven equal parts.[6] This shape of India corresponds to a great extent to the actual shape of the country which is broad on the north having the Himalayas extending from east to west and triangular towards the south. It agrees wonderfully with the description of the shape given by the Chinese author Fah-kai-lih-to. According to him the country is broad towards the north and narrow towards the south. The Chinese traveller, Hiuen Tsang, who visited India in the 7th century A.D., describes the shape of the country as a half-moon with the diameter or broadside to the north and the narrow end to the south. His travels were mainly confined to the north of India which may be said to resemble a half-moon with the Vindhyas as its base and the Himalayas spreading its two arms on two sides as the diameter. About the size of India Megasthenes and Deimachos consider the distance from the southern sea to the Caucasus to be over 20,000 stadia.[7] According to Megasthenes the breadth of India at the shortest is 16,000 stadia and its length is at the

---

1 *Āmradvīpa* in the Inscription of Mahānāman, II (*C.I.I.*, Vol. III).
2 *C.A.G.I.*, p. 2.
3 *Ibid.*, p. 5.
4 *Ibid.*, pp. 6-7.
5 *Ibid.*, p. 9.
6 *Dīgha*, II, p. 235.
7 McCrindle, *Ancient India as described by Megasthenes and Arrian*, p. 49.

narrowest 22,300 stadia.[1] The Sanskrit Buddhist texts give us no glimpse as to the size and shape of India.

We have five traditional divisions of India according to the early Indian texts. The *Kāvyamīmāṃsā* (p. 93) clearly states that the eastern country lies to the east of Benaras; to the south of Māhiṣmatī (identified with Māndhātā on the Narmadā) is the Deccan or the Dakṣiṇāpatha; to the west of Devasabhā is the western country; to the north of Pṛthudaka, (modern Pehoa, about 14 miles west of Thaneswar) is the northern country (Uttarāpatha), and the tract lying between the confluence of the Jumna and the Ganges is called the Antarvedī. By the time when the *Kāvyamīmāṃsā* came to be written the Aryans had already outstripped the older limits of the Madhyadeśa, and Aryandom had extended up to Benaras.

As with the Brahmanical Aryans, so with the Buddhists, Āryāvarta to which Patañjali refers in his *Mahābhāṣya* (12. 4. 1, p. 244) is described in the Dharmasūtras and the Dharmaśāstras to have extended from the region where the river Sarasvatī disappears in the west, to the Black Forest in the east and from the Himalayas in the north to the Pāripātra in the south. Almost all the Brahmanical sources give a description of Madhyadeśa or Āryāvarta, the most important division of India. The Middle country was the cradle on which the Brahmanical Aryans or the Buddhists staged the entire drama of their career. The five divisions, as indicated in the *Bhuvanakoṣa* section of the *Purāṇas*, are identical with those given in the *Kāvyamīmāṃsā*. They are as follows:—

(*a*) Madhyadeśa (Middle Country),
(*b*) Udīcya or Uttarāpatha (Northern India),
(*c*) Prācya (Eastern India),
(*d*) Dakṣiṇāpatha (Deccan), and
(*e*) Aparānta (Western India).

Pāṇini in his *Aṣṭādhyāyī* mentions Prācya-Bhāratadeśa (8. 3. 75). The boundaries of Madhyadeśa or Majjhimadesa have been referred to and explained in early Brahmanical and Buddhist texts. As early as the age of the Sūtras the country of the Aryans, which is practically identical with the country later on known as Madhyadeśa, is described in the *Dharmasūtra* of Baudhāyana as lying to the east of the region where the river Sarasvatī vanishes, to the west of the Kālakavana which is identified with a tract somewhere near Prayāga,[2] to the north of Pāripātra and to the south of the Himalayas[3] as already pointed out. The eastern boundary thus excluded not only the country now known as Bengal but also Behar which in ancient times included the entire Magadha country. The *Dharmaśāstra* of Manu calls the Āryāvarta of the *Sūtras* to be the Madhyadeśa. He defines it as extending from the Himalayas in the north to the Vindhyas in the south and from Vinaśana in the west to Prayāga in the east.[4] The Āryāvarta of the *Sūtras* and the Madhyadeśa of Manu are, according to the *Kāvyamīmāṃsā* (p. 93), known as Antarvedī which extends up to Benaras in the east. The eastern boundary of the Madhyadeśa gradually expanded itself with the progress of time so as to include places which acquired sanctity within the Brahmanical fold. The boundaries of the Buddhist Majjhimadesa as given in the *Mahāvagga* (Vol. V, pp. 12-13), may be described as having extended in the east to the town of Kajaṅgala

---

[1] McCrindle, *Ancient India as described by Megasthenes and Arrian*, p. 50.
[2] *C.A.G.I.*, Intro., pp. xli and xli, f.n. 1.
[3] Baudhāyana, I. 1, 2. 9; Vaśiṣṭha, I. 8.
[4] *Himavad-Vindhyayor-madhyaṃ yat prāk Vinasanādapi pratyageva Prayāgāśca Madhyadeśaḥ.*

(identified with *Ka-chu-wen-ki-lo* of Yuan Chwang) beyond which was the city of Mahāsāla; in the south-east to the river Salalavatī (Śarāvatī); in the south to the town of Śatakarṇika; in the west to the Brāhmaṇa district of Thūna (identified with Sthāniśvara); in the north to the Usīradhaja mountain (identified with Usīragiri, a mountain to the north of Kaṅkhal, Hardwar). The *Divyāvadāna* (pp. 21-22), however, extends the eastern boundary of the Majjhimadesa still further to the east so as to include Puṇḍravardhana which in ancient times included Varendra, roughly identical with north Bengal. The other boundaries as given in the *Divyāvadāna* are identical with those as in the *Mahāvagga*. Madhyadeśa, which is mentioned in the Belāva copper-plate of Bhojavarman and the Barrackpore copper-plate of Vijayasena (N. G. Majumdar, *Inscriptions of Bengal*, III, 16ff.), is, according to Aśvaghoṣa, said to have been situated between the Himalayas and the Pāripātra mountain which formed the southern boundary line of the Madhyadeśa (*Saundaranandakāvya*, II, v. 62). The four boundaries of the Uttarāpatha are nowhere mentioned in the Brahmanical or Buddhist texts. According to the Brahmanical tradition recorded in the *Kāvyamīmāṃsā* the Uttarāpatha or northern India lay to the western side of Pṛthudaka (*Prithudakātparataḥ Uttarāpathaḥ*). The Brahmanical definition of Āryāvarta excludes the greater portion of the land of the Ṛgvedic Aryans, which, however, is included in the Uttarāpatha. The entire Indus Valley, which was the cradle of the Ṛgvedic culture and civilization, is included in the Uttarāpatha according to the *Kāvyamīmāṃsā*. The *Dharmasūtras* of Vaśiṣṭha and Baudhāyana and the *Dharmaśāstra* of Manu point out that the Uttarāpatha lies to the west of the place where the river Sarasvatī disappears. The Buddhist northern division is also to be located to the west of the Brāhmaṇa district of Thūna or Thāneśwar. The Uttarāpatha mentioned in the Hāthigumphā Inscription of Khāravela probably signifies the region including Mathurā in its south-eastern extension up to Magadha. The Uttarāpatha may be supposed to have been originally a great trade-route—the northern high road, so to say, which extended from Sāvatthī to Takkasilā in Gandhāra. It is not at all improbable that the Uttarāpatha in Pali literature might have also signified the entire northern India from Aṅga in the east to Gandhāra in the north-west and from the Himalayas in the north to the Vindhyas in the south. Bāṇabhaṭṭa, the author of the *Harṣacarita*, seems to include within Uttarāpatha the western part of the Uttara Pradeśa, the Punjab and the North-Western Frontier Provinces of India and Pakistan.

According to the *Kāvyamīmāṃsā* (93) the country lying to the west of Devasabhā was called the Paścāddeśa[1] or the western country. According to the Pali *Sāsanavaṃsa* (p. 11) Aparāntaka or western India lies to the west of the upper Irawady. Sir R. G. Bhandarkar points out that Aparānta was the northern Konkan whose capital was Surpāraka, modern Sopara. The western sea-board of India was called Aparāntaka or Aparāntika according to Bhagavanlal Indraji. Aparānta is often mentioned in the *Mahābhārata* (Bhīṣmaparva, IX. 335; Vanaparva, CCXVII. 7885-6; Śāntiparva, XLIX, 1780–82). According to the *Mārkaṇḍeya Purāṇa* (Ch. 58) Aparānta seems to have been located north of the Sindhu-Sauvīra country. According to D. R. Bhandarkar Ariake is Aparāntika. Aparānta is referred to in Aśoka's Rock Edict V. It is also mentioned in Luders' List No. 965. From the Nasik record of Gautamī Balaśrī we learn that her son extended his sway over Aparānta which was reconquered later by

---

[1] *Devasabhāyāḥ parataḥ Paścātdeśaḥ, tatra Devasabhā-Surāṣṭra Daseraka-Travana-Bhrigukaccha Kacchīya-Ānarta brāhmaṇavāha Yavana-prabhṛtayo janapadāḥ.*

Śaka satrap Rudradāman of Western India as evidenced by the Junāgadh Rock Inscription of 150 A.D. For further details vide Law, *Tribes in Ancient India*, p. 392; Law, *Indological Studies*, I, 53.

Dakṣiṇāpatha is the region lying to the south of Māhiṣmatī identified with Māndhātā according to the *Kāvyamīmāṃsā*, as already pointed out. Some hold that it is situated between the Bridge of Rāma and the river Narmadā (Hultzsch, *S.I.I.*, I, p. 58; cf. Fleet, *I.A.*, VII, 245). The *Dharmasūtras* testify to the fact that Dakṣiṇāpatha lay to the south of Pāripātra, generally identified with a portion of the Vindhyas. The *Mahāvagga of the Vinaya Piṭaka* and the *Divyāvadāna* seem to record that the Dakṣiṇajanapada lay to the south of the town of Śatakarṇika. Buddhaghosa, the celebrated Buddhist commentator, defines Dakṣiṇāpatha or the Deccan as the tract of land lying to the south of the Ganges (*Sumaṅgalavilāsinī*, I, 265). The whole tract of land lying to the south of the Ganges and to the north of the Godāvarī is known as Dakṣiṇāpatha according to the *Suttanipāta* (Prologue of Bk. V; *Vinaya-Mahāvagga*, V, 13; *Vinaya-Cullavagga*, XII. 1). The Sanskrit Buddhist texts refer to Dakṣiṇāpatha as having extended southwards beyond the Śarāvatī river and the Pāripātra mountain.

The Damiḷas who had two settlements on both sides of the Ganges are identified with the Tamils. They were warlike, and the island of Laṅkā was very much troubled by them from time to time. They are described as uncultured (*anariyā*). 'Might is right' was their policy which they rigidly followed, with the result that they were defeated and mercilessly massacred in almost all the battles with the Ceylonese (*Mahāvaṃsaṭīkā*, 482; Law, *Tribes in Ancient India*, 168ff.; Law, *Geographical Essays*, Ch. IV). They were disrespectful to the Buddhist *Stūpas* (*Mahāvaṃsa-Ṭīkā*, 447).

The Prācya or the eastern country lay to the east of the Madhyadeśa, but as the eastern boundary of the Madhyadeśa changed from time to time, the western boundary of the Prācya country consequently diminished. According to the *Dharmasūtras* the eastern country lay to the east of Prayāga. The *Kāvyamīmāṃsā* points out that it was to the east of Benaras, while according to the commentary on the *Vātsyāyana sūtra* it lay to the east of Aṅga. The western boundary of the Pūrvadeśa shrinked still more and extended to Kajaṅgala according to the *Vinaya Mahāvagga*, or to Puṇḍravardhana according to the *Divyāvadāna*.

The Sanskrit Buddhist texts refer to the three divisions of India, namely, Madhyadeśa, Uttarāpatha and Dakṣiṇāpatha. Pāṇini refers to Uttarāpatha in his *Aṣṭādhyāyī* (5. 1. 77). Patañjali also mentions it in his *Mahābhāṣya*. Daṇḍin in his *Kāvyādarśa* (I. 60; I. 80) refers to the people of Dākṣiṇātya and Adākṣiṇātya. The last two divisions are mentioned in name only; there is no defining of their boundaries nor is there any description of the countries or regions that constitute the divisions. Two other divisions, namely, the Aparānta or western and the Prācya or eastern are not referred to even in name, but are suggested by the boundary of the Madhyadeśa as given in the *Divyāvadāna*.

The division of India into five provinces was also adopted by the Chinese. India is described in the official records of the Thang dynasty of the 7th century A.D. as consisting of five divisions called the East, West, North, South and Central, which are generally styled as the Five Indies. (*C.A.G.I.*, p. 11). The Chinese system of the five divisions was directly borrowed from the Hindu Brahmanical system as described in the Purāṇas with slight modifications. Modern India and adjacent countries may thus be divided for our purpose into: (1) Northern India, comprising the Punjab proper including Kashmir and the adjoining hill states with the whole of Eastern Afghanistan beyond the Indus and the present Cis-Sutlej states to the West of the Sarasvatī river. The entire Indus Valley is included in Northern India.

(2) Western India comprising Sind and Western Rajputana with Cutch and Gujarat and a portion of the adjoining coast on the lower course of the Narmadā river.

(3) Mid-India or Central India comprising the whole of the Gangetic provinces from Thanesvar to the head of the Delta and from the Himalayan mountain to the banks of the Narmadā.

(4) Eastern India comprising Assam and Bengal proper including the whole of the Gangetic Delta together with Sambalpur, Orissa and Ganjam.

(5) Southern India comprising the whole of the Peninsula from Nasik on the west and Ganjam on the east of Cape Comorin (Kumārī) on the south including the modern districts of Berar and Telengana, Mahārāṣṭra and Konkan with the separate states of Hyderabad, Mysore and Travancore-Cochin or very nearly the whole of the Peninsula to the south of the Narmadā and the Mahānadī rivers. (*C.A.G.I.*, pp. 13-14.)

South India is an inverted triangle in shape with its apex in the south at Cape Comorin, 8 degrees north of the equator. The two sides of the Peninsula are bounded by the Arabian Sea on the west and the Bay of Bengal on the east. The base of the triangle, i.e., the northern boundary consists of the Vindhya mountains. Along with the Vindhyas and the Satpuras mention may be made of the Ajantas and Aravallis. South of the Ajantas lies the country of Hyderabad. South of the Satpura and other hills there was once a belt of impenetrable jungle called the Daṇḍakāraṇya. In the extreme south there are the Tamil land, the Andhra territory and the Malayalam region. North of the Malayalam region is the Kannada country proper and beyond that is the Mahārāṣṭra country.

These traditional regions of India will be most helpful in working out any new scheme for dividing the country into various regions.

IV. Physical Features

Geographically India occupies a position of great advantage. It lies in the centre of the eastern hemisphere and forms the central peninsula of Southern Asia. Its sea position is thus well adapted for trade with lands around the Indian ocean. No country, again, has been favoured more by nature than India in providing it with well-marked natural boundaries. Its three sides on the east, west and south are washed by the waters of the Bay of Bengal, the Arabian Sea and the Indian Ocean respectively. On its north, north-west and north-east the country is cut off by a huge mountain-wall from the Chinese Turkestan and Tibet, the Iranian Plateau and Baluchistan and from the Chindwin and the Irrawaddy Valleys of Burma. The entire area comprised within the boundaries of the pre-partitioned India is about a million and a half square miles, which is more than one-third of the size of Europe. The surf-beaten coast extends over nearly 3,000 miles. It is almost unbroken and there are very few bays or gulfs which can be used as natural harbours.

The enormity of the size of India is quite in keeping with the extraordinary variety of its physical features. Along with the climatic variations that can be marked from the majestic heights of the Himalayas to the low-lands imperceptibly merging into the sea, and from the dripping hills of Assam to the waterless desert of Sind, India has been favoured with a luxuriant variety of flora and fauna. No less remarkable are the numerous races of mankind inhabiting this historic land and speaking countless languages. India is really the epitome of the whole world. The history of India, like that of other countries, has been affected by its geography. It is therefore necessary to notice in detail some of the major physical features.

A. *Mountains*

The mountain wall in the north to which we have referred above includes the Himalayas, the Trans-Himalayas and their eastern and western offshoots.

Hemavata (Pali Himavā, Himācala and Himavantapadesa, Sanskrit Haimavata).—This mountain which is called Nagādhirāja by Kālidāsa (*Kumārasaṃbhava*, I) is mentioned in the *Atharvaveda* (XII. 1. II) as well as in the *Ṛgveda* (X. 121. 4). The *Taittirīya Saṃhitā* (V. 5. 11. 1), *Vājasaneyi Saṃhitā* (XXIV. 30; XXV, 12) and *Aitareya Brāhmana* (VIII. 14. 3) also refer to it. According to the Great Epic (*Mahābhārata*, Vanaparva, Ch. 253) the Haimavata region was situated just to the west in Nepal (*Nepal-viṣaya*) and according to the same Epic it mainly comprised the *Kulindaviṣaya* (Ptolemy's *Kunindrae*), representing the region of high mountains in which the sources of the Ganges, Jumna and Sutlej lay. It may thus be taken to include the Himachal Pradesh and some parts of Dehra Dun. The *Bhāgavata Purāṇa* and the *Kūrmapurāṇa* (30. 45–48) refer to it. The *Yoginītantra* mentions this mountain (1/16). The *Kālikā-purāṇa* (Ch. 14. 1) also refers to it. It is described as the king of mountains according to the *Kālikāpurāṇa* (Ch. 14. 51). In the Epics and *Purāṇas* the Himavanta is classed both as a *Varṣaparvata* and a *Maryādāparvata*. The author of the *Mārkaṇḍeyapurāṇa* knew the Himavat to have stretched from the eastern to the western sea like the string of a bow (*Kārmukasya Yathāguṇaḥ* 54, 24; 57, 59). The statement of the *Mārkaṇḍeya Purāṇa* is supported by the *Mahābhārata* (VI. 6. 3) and *Kumārasambhava* (I. 1). The eastern Himalayan region extending up to Assam and Manipur roughly constituted the Haimavata division of the Jambudvīpa in respect of which Aśoka introduced the Nābhakas and Nābhapaṃtis in his Rock Edict XIII (Barua, *Asoka and His Inscriptions*, Pt. I, p. 101). The Himalayan region (*Himavantapadesa* in Pāli) of the Jambudvīpa extended northward, according to the Pali accounts, as far as the south side of the Mount Sumeru (Pali *Sineru*). The southern boundary of the Haimavata division of India is indicated by the Kālsi set of Rock Edicts, the Asokan monoliths at Niglīva, Lumbinī, and those in the district of Champaran (*Ibid.*, pp. 81-82). The Haimavatapadesa has been identified by some with Tibet, by Fergusson with Nepal, and by Rhys Davids with the Central Himalayas. According to ancient geographers the name Himavanta was applied to the entire mountain range stretching from Sulaiman along the west of the Punjab and the whole of the northern boundary of India up to the Assam and Arakan hill ranges in the east. The Śākyas and the Koliyas were transported by the Buddha to the Himalayas, and the Buddha pointed out to them the various mountains in the Himalayan region. The Kailāsa mountain formed a part of the Himalayan mountain but the *Mārkaṇḍeya-purāṇa* takes it to be a separate mountain. According to Alberuni Meru and Niṣadha were connected with the Himalayan chain. The Himalayan mountain is the source from which the ten rivers have their rise (*Milinda*, 114). Ptolemy points out that the Imaos (the Himalayan mountain) is the source of the Ganges and the Indus as well as the Koa and the Swat rivers. The *Apadāna* mentions a few other mountains in the neighbourhood of the Himavanta which is also called the *parvatarāja* (*Ang.*, I, 152):

Kadamba (p. 382), Kukkura or Kukkuṭa (p. 178), Bhūtagaṇa (p. 179), Kosika (p. 381), Gotama (p. 162), Paduma (p. 362), Bharika (p. 440), Lambaka (p. 15), Vasabha (p. 166), Samaṅga (p. 437) and Sobhita (p. 328). The Himalayan mountain is the only *varṣaparvata* which is placed within the geographical limits of Bhāratavarṣa. (Vide B. C. Law, *Geography of Early Buddhism*, 27, 41-42; for further details, vide B. C. Law, *India as described in the Early Texts of Buddhism and Jainism*, pp. 5ff.; B. C. Law, *Geographical Essays*, p. 82; B. C. Law, *Mountains of India*, pp. 4ff.) The Himavanta mountain occurs in Luders' List, No. 834. The Monghyr grant of Devapāla refers to Kedāra, which is situated in the Himalayas. The *Kālikāpurāṇa* (Ch. 14. 31) says that Śiva and Pārvatī went to the fall of the Mahākauśikī river in the Himalaya mountain.

The Himalaya which is the loftiest mountain range in the world forms a circular arc with its convexity turned towards India in between the banks of the Indus and the Brahmaputra in the west and the east. It consists of three almost parallel ridges of varying altitude, viz., the Great Himalaya, the Lesser Himalaya, and the Outer Himalaya. The Great Himalaya comprises the northernmost high range and rises to over 20,000 feet above the sea-level, i.e., above the limits of the perpetual snow. More than 100 peaks exceed this limit, and the most famous among them are the Nagnaparvata or the Bare Hill (26,620 ft.), Numkum (23,410 ft.), Nandadevī (25,645 ft.), Triśūl (23,360 ft.), Nandakoṭ (22,510 ft.), Dunagiri (23,184 ft.), Badrināth (23,190 ft.), Kedārnāth (22,770 ft.), Nīlakaṇṭa (21,640 ft.), Gaṅgotrī (21,700 ft.), Śrīkaṇṭa (20,120 ft.), Brandarpunch (20,720 ft.), Gaurīśṛṅga or the Mount Everest (29,002 ft.), which is the loftiest peak in the whole world, Kāñcanjaṅgā (28,146 ft.), Dhaulagiri (26,795 ft.), Makalu (22,790 ft.), Gosainthan (26,291 ft.), and Namcha Barwa (25,445 ft.). The Gauriśriṅga or Gauriśaṅkar, Kāñcanjaṅgā and Dhaulagiri are the highest peaks of the Nepal Himalaya which extends as far as the Tista river from the eastern boundary of the Kumaon Himalaya. Namcha Barwa is included in the Assam Himalaya which extends from the Tista to the easternmost frontier of India. The Gaurīśaṅkara is really situated on the Nepal Tibet border. It is known by various names, e.g., Devadhuṅga, Como Kankar, Como Lungma, Como Uri, Chelungon and Mi-ti-gu-ti-ca-pu Longnga. This Himalayan peak has defied any attempt at finality both as regards its height and local name. Opinions differ as to the real discoverer of this highest mountain peak. Some claim Radhanath Sikdar to be the discoverer, but others hold that the discovery was due to the combined effort of the department of the Survey of India. Tenzing, an Indian and Hillary, a Newzealander, both members of the British Mt. Everest Expedition Party, were the first to climb to the top of Mt. Everest in 1953.

The Lesser Himalaya consists of the southern spurs of the Great Himalaya, and the ranges of lower elevations which run parallel to the Great Himalayan range extending as far as the outer Siwalik ranges. Its average width is 50 miles. The Pir Panjal extends eastward from south of the Kashmir Valley across the source of the Beas joining with the Great Himalayan range a little farther east. The Dhaoladhar range is situated to the south of the Pir Panjal range extending from near Udampur in Jammu to the Simla Hills in the West, joining the Great Himalayan range near Badrināth. The Outer Himalaya consists of low hills which run almost parallel to the Great Himalayan range from the Indus to the Brahmaputra. On the west it is known as the Siwalik hills which extend for about 200 miles from the Beas to the Ganges and were known to the ancient geographers as Mainākaparvata. Beyond the foot-hills there are belts of low land and behind the Siwalik lies the well-known Dehra Dun district of the Uttara Pradeśa. The Trans-Himalayan zone comprises the Hindukush, the Kārākoram and the Kailāsa mountains. The Hindukush mountain, known to the ancient Indians as the Mālyavat and as the Indian Caucasus to the Greeks, starts from the north-western extremity of the Himalayas and extends south-westwards, first dividing India from Afghanistan, and then through north-eastern Afghanistan. A number of spurs run from the main range, such as the Badakhshan spur separating the Oxus from the Kokcha, and the Kokcha spur dividing the Kokcha range from that of the Kunduz. The height of the Hindukush varies between 14,000 and 18,000 ft. in the eastern section. The Karakoram, known as the Kṛṣṇagiri to ancient geographers, is continuous with the Hindukush in the west. It forms the northern boundary of Kashmir. It nestles within it the lofty peak of Godwin Austen (28,250 ft.). Following a spur of the Karakoram to the south-east we come to the Mount Kailāsa overlooking the Mānasa Sarovara. According to the modern geographers this mountain was uplifted earlier, and hence is older than the Himalaya proper. It is of Hercynian age and got considerably folded and faulted subsequent to its uplift. To the east of the Mānasa Sarovara lake there runs a lofty range known as the Ladakh range parallel to the Greater Himalaya. It is composed mainly of granite and is separated from the Greater Himalaya by a valley some fifty miles wide. The Kailāsa range runs parallel to the Ladakh range 50 miles behind the latter. It contains a number of groups of joint peaks. One such group stands near the Mānasa Sarovara, the highest of the groups being Kailāsa (22,028 ft.), known to the ancient geographers as the Vaidyūtaparvata. The Zaskar range bifurcates from the great Himalayan range near Nampa. It contains the Kamet peak (25,447 ft.). There are other peaks, too, and this range extends across the Indus north-westwards.

In the north-west of India, a lofty range runs dividing the Indus Valley from the hills of Baluchistan and extending from the west of Dehra-Ismail Khan to the sea-coast. The northern portion of this range is called the Sulaiman mountain, known to the ancient geographers as Añjana, and the southern part, the Kirthār mountain, extends southwards from Mūla river gorge in a series of parallel ridges for 190 miles.

In the north-east of India an almost continuous ridge of folded mountains, similar in structure to the Himalaya, extends right up to the coast of the Bay of Bengal, and separates Burma from India. From north to south it consists of the Mishmi mountain, the Patkai hills, the Naga hills, the Barail range, the Lushai hills and the Arakan Yoma. We do not find reference to these hills and mountains in ancient Indian literature, as these were not thoroughly explored by the geographers of the olden times. The mountain-wall in the north-east sends out a great branch westward into Assam. This branch forms the Jaintia, Khasi and Garo hills.

Since the main crest rises above the line of perpetual snow, the name Himavanta or Himalaya was well conceived by the ancient geographers of India. The comparison of the shape of the Himalaya with the string of a gigantic bow fits admirably with our modern knowledge of the trend of the Himalaya. This arcuate disposition of the Himalaya, the convex side facing towards the Indian plains, can be ascribed to the main tangential thrust coming from the south.

The Himalayan rivers are seen cutting through the main chains in deep transverse gorges after long flowing parallel to the trend of the chain. The Indus and the Brahmaputra are the best examples of this.

Some Mountains and Rivers of India

Geologically the Himalaya may be divided into three zones: the Tibetan zone, the Himalayan zone and the Sub-Himalayan zone. The fossiliferous beds of the Palaeozoic and Mesozoic ages are well developed in the Tibetan zone. The Himalayan zone is composed chiefly of crystalline and metamorphic rocks. The Sub-Himalayan zone consists entirely of tertiary beds.

On the north side of the Everest the Rongbuk glacier ends at about 16,500 ft. In the Kanchengunga group the glacier may come down to 13,000 ft., while in Kumaon they reach 12,000 ft. and in Kashmere under special circumstances they may come as low as 8,000 ft.

A valuable study may be made of the Himalayan plants and animals. The European flora of the Mediterranean reaches the Himalaya. The observations made by the Everest expeditions have added much to our knowledge of the plant-life of the Himalayan region. The bird-life of the Himalayas is rich. The butterflies are renowned for their beauty and grandeur. The python, the cobra, the lizard and the frog are found in various kinds.

The importance of the Himalayan system in shaping the destiny of India seems to be great. It shuts off the country from other parts of Asia and acts as an effective barrier against the outside world on land. There are several passes in the north which may be divided into three groups, viz., the Shipki group, the Almora group and the Darjeeling-Sikkim group. These allow trade to be carried on between India and Tibet. In the north-east there are several back-doors to Burma leading through the north-eastern corner of Assam, Manipur State and the Arakans. Chief among the numerous passes that lead across the north-western frontier to India are the Khyber, Kurram, Tochi, Gomal and Bolan.

A group of forest-clad hills forming themselves into a wide plateau runs obliquely along the west of India from the Gulf of Cambay to Rajmahal in the east, and divides the country into two separate parts, viz., the Indo-Gangetic basin in the north and the Deccan tableland in the south. The northern section of them from west to east consists of the Vindhyas, and the connected ranges of Bharner and Kaimur which passing through the neighbourhood of Gayā, terminate near Rājmahal. In the south and in the same direction stretch almost in a parallel line the Satpurā, the Mahādeva hill, the Maikāl range and the hills of Chota Nagpur. Beyond the Vindhyan ranges in the west in the centre of the Kathiawar Peninsula is situated mount Girnar also known as Raivataka near Junagarh in Gujarat. The Aravalli range, which runs across Rajputana in the west-easterly direction and cuts the country into two halves is closely connected with the Vindhyan system by the rocky ridges of Southern Rajputana and Central India. Although regarded as a part of the Aravalli range, but completely detached from it by a narrow valley in the south-west stands the rock-island of Abu also known as Arbuda in the Sirohi State of Rajputana. According to Megasthenes and Arrian Mt. Abu is identical with Capitalia which attains an elevation of 6,500 ft. It rises far above any other summit in the Aravalli range.[1]

The Pāripātra or Pāriyātra, the Ṛkṣavat, and the Vindhya are the mountains of Central India. The earliest mention of the Pāripātra is found in the *Dharmasūtra* of Baudhāyana[2] who refers to it as being situated on the southern limit of Āryāvarta. The *Skanda Purāṇa* refers to it as the farthest limit of Kumārīkhaṇḍa, the centre of Bhāratavarṣa.

---

[1] McCrindle, *Ancient India as described by Megasthenes and Arrian*, p. 147.
[2] *Baudhāyana*, I. 1. 25.

Pargiter identifies the Pāripātra with that portion of the modern Vindhya range which is situated west of Bhopal in Central India together with the Aravalli mountains identified with the Apokopa by Ptolemy.[1]

The Ṛkṣavat has been identified with the Ouxenton of Ptolemy. It is the source of the rivers Toundis, Dosaran and Adamas. The Dosaran has been identified with the river Daśārṇa (modern Dhasan near Saugar in C.P.) which is said to have issued from the Ṛkṣa according to Ptolemy. By the Ṛkṣa or the Ṛkṣavant he meant the central region of the modern Vindhya range north of the Narmadā.

The Vindhya corresponds to Ptolemy's Ouindon, the source of the Namados and Nanagouna identified with the Narmadā and the Tāpti. According to Ptolemy the Ouindon stands for only that portion of the Vindhya wherefrom rise the Narmadā and the Tāpti. Different parts of the Vindhya mountain are known under different names. The Vindhyapāda-parvata is the mountain Sardonyx of Ptolemy. It may be identified with the Satpurā range from which rises the Tāpti.

The Satpurā is the Vaidūrya Parvata which is associated with the rivers Payoṣṇī (an affluent of the Tāpti) and the Narmadā in the *Mahābhārata*.[2] The mountain which runs south of the Narmadā is at present known as the Sātpurā. The Maikāl range stands for the ancient Mekala-parvata in Gondwana in Central Provinces. Hence the Narmadā is called the Mekalasutā.[3] Its eastern peak Amarakaṇṭaka is also known as the Soma-parvata and Surathādri or Surathagiri.[4] The Amarakaṇṭaka is the source of three great rivers, viz., Narmadā, Śoṇa and Mahānadī.

The Citrakūṭa mountain has been identified with Kāmptānāth-giri in Bundelkhand. It is an isolated hill on a river called the Paisuni or Mandākinī. It is about four miles from the Citrakūṭa Station of the G.I.P. Railway. The Kālañjara identified with Kalinjar, a hill fort in the Banda district, Bundelkhand, was located between the Ganges and the Vindhya mountain. The Jain texts refer to it (*Āvaśyaka Cūrṇī*, p. 461).

The forest-clad mountains of Central India stood as a serious obstacle to the unification of the whole country in ancient times, for it was not easy in those days to lead an invading army across this wide belt of stone and jungles.

The Gayāśīrṣa (Gayāsīra, Gayāsisa) is the principal hill of Gayā. Gayāsisa, the chief hill of Gaya, according to the *Vinaya Piṭaka*[5] is the modern Brahmayoni and identical with what is called Gayāśīra in the *Mahābhārata*[6] and in the Purāṇas.[7] The early Buddhist commentators account for the origin of its name by the striking resemblance of its shape with that of the head of an elephant (*gajasisa*).

A group of five hills encircling the ancient capital of Magadha is known to the early Pali texts as Isigili (Ṛṣigiri), Vebhāra (Vaihāra), Paṇḍava, Vepulla (Vipula) and Gijjhakūṭa (Gṛdhrakūṭa) which stood to the south of Vepulla. In the *Mahābhārata* we have two lists, one naming the hills as Vaihāra, Vārāha, Vṛṣabha, Ṛṣigiri and Subhacaityaka,[8] and the other as Pāṇḍara, Vipula, Vārāhaka, Caityaka and Mātaṅga.[9] To the north of Gayā and west of Rājagṛha stands the Gorathagiri (modern Barabar hills)[10]

---

1 McCrindle, *Ancient India as described by Ptolemy*, S. N. Majumdar's ed., p. 355.

2 III, 121, pp. 16–19.

3 *Padma Purāṇa*, Ch. 6.

4 *Mārkaṇḍeya Purāṇa*, Ch. 57.

5 *Vinaya Piṭaka*, I, 35ff.; II, 199.

6 *Mbh.*, III. 95. 9.

7 Barua, *Gayā and Buddha Gayā*, I, 68.

8 Sabhāparva, Ch. XXI, v. 2.

9 *Ibid.*, Ch. XXI, v. 11.

10 Vide Jackson's identification of Goradhagiri in *J.B.O.R.S.*, Vol. I, Pt. II, p. 162; B. M. Barua, *Old Brāhmī Inscriptions on the Udayagiri and Khaṇḍagiri Caves*, p. 224.

mentioned as the Khalatika Parvata in the Cave Inscriptions II and III of Aśoka and the Mahābhāṣya of Patañjali.[1] From the Gorathagiri or Goradhagiri one could have a view of Girivraja, the earlier capital of Magadha.[2] The Śuktimat range, according to Beglar, lies to the north of the Hazaribagh district.[3] There is a difference of opinion as to its location. Cunningham identifies it with the hills south of Sehoa and Kanker separating Chattisgarh from Bastar.[4] According to Pargiter it may be identified with Garo, Khasi and Tippera hills.[5] Some have located it in Western India and identified it with Kāthiāwāḍ range.[6] Others have identified it with the Sulaiman range.[7] Rai Chaudhuri applies the name with the chain of hills, extending from Sakti in Raigarh in C.P. to the Dalma hills in Manbhum drained by the Kumārī river and perhaps even to the hills in the Santal Parganas washed by the affluents of the Bāblā.[8] The Kukkuṭapādagiri or the Gurupāda mountain has been identified by Stein with Sobhanath peak. Some have identified it with Gurpa hill, above 100 miles from Bodh-Gayā.[9] The Antaragiri identified with the Rajmahal hills in the Santal Parganas, the Makulaparvata identified with the Kaluhā hill, about 26 miles to the south of Buddhagayā, and about 16 miles to the north of Chātrā in the Hazaribagh district, the Pātharghāṭā hill which was ancient *Śilā-saṅgama* or *Vikramaśilā-saṅghārāma*, the Mallaparvata identified with the Pareshnath hill in Chota Nagpur also known as the Mount Maleus[10] by the Greeks, and the Mandara hill known to Megasthenes and Arrian as Mallus in the Bāṅkā sub-division of the Bhagalpur district are some other hills and mountains in Eastern India, worthy of notice.

The South Indian mountain system consists of the Western Ghats, the Eastern Ghats and the Nilgiris. The Western Ghats run close to the west coast almost without a break for about 1,000 miles from the pass of Kundaibari in Khandesh to Cape Comorin with an average elevation of 4,000 ft. above the sea-level. They send several spurs into the interior of the Deccan Plateau, the most important of which are the Ajantā and the Bālāghāt ranges. The sea side is extremely steep and of difficult ascent. Communication with the interior is carried on through the passes of the Thal Ghat near Nasik, the Bor Ghat near Poona and the Palghat or the Coimbatore gap below the Nilgiris. The continuity of the mountain to the Cape after the southern gap is carried through the Annamalai and the Cardamom hills.

The Western Ghats above the Coimbatore gap were known to the ancient geographers of India as the Sahyādri. The Sahyādri hills run almost parallel to the west coast from the Cape Comorin to the Tapti Valley. Ptolemy divides it into two parts, the northern part is called the Oroudian (identified with the Vaiḍūryaparvata) and the southern part, the Adeisathron. Among the hills associated with the Western Ghats mention may be made of Trikūṭa (from which the Traikūṭakas derive their name), Govardhana (Nasik Hill),[11] Kṛṣṇagiri[12] (modern Kaṇheri), Ṛṣyamūka (overlooking Pampā which has been identified with Hampe), Mālyavat in the Kiṣkindhyā country (identified by Pargiter with the hills

---

[1] I. ii, 2.

[2] *Mbh.*, Sabhāp., Ch. XX, vv. 29-30: *Goratham girim āsādya dadṛśur Magadhampuram*; cf. Beal, *Records of the Western World*, II, p. 104.

[3] *A.S.R.*, VIII, 124-5.

[4] *Ibid.*, XVII, 24, 26.

[5] *Mārkaṇḍeya Purāṇa*, 285, 306 notes.

[6] C. V. Vaidya, *Epic India*, 276.

[7] *Z.D.M.G.*, 1922, p. 281 note.

[8] *Studies in Indian Antiquities*, 113–20.

[9] *J.A.S.B.*, 1906, p. 77.

[10] McCrindle, *Megasthenes and Arrian*, pp. 62, 139.

[11] Rapson, *Andhra Coins*, pp. xxix, xlvii, lvi.

[12] *Rāmāyaṇa*, VI, 26, 30.

near Kupal, Mudgal and Raichur), Praśravaṇa (associated with the Godāvarī and the Mandākinī[1]) and Gomanta. Ṛṣyamūka and Gomanta may also be associated with the Sahya mountain. Pargiter identifies the former with the range of hills stretching from Ahmadnagar to beyond Naldrug and Kalyāṇi. He identifies the Gomanta with the hills south or south-east of Nasik.[2] According to Rai Chaudhuri to the north of Gomanta was Vanavāsī so that the hill might be placed in the Mysore region.[3]

The Eastern Ghats run as detached hills, more or less parallel to the eastern coast of India, with an average elevation of about 2,000 ft. The detached hills are known by different names in different parts of the country. In their northern extremity the hills are known as the Maliahs, which approach the sea. The Maliahs in Ganjam, Vizagapatam and Godāvarī regions are much dissected and widened considerably in the district of Kurnool. In the latter district the Eastern Ghats are known as the Nallamalai hills. Further south the Eastern Ghats take the name of Palkonda hills, and the southern extremity of the Eastern Ghats joins the Nilgiri plateau in the Coimbatore district of the Madras State. This extremity is locally known as the Biligiri Rangan hills. The Shevaroy hills are a detached range in the Salem district.

It appears from the *Rāmāyaṇa*[4] that the Eastern Ghats are known as the Mahendraparvata. The Mahendra range seems to indicate the whole range of mountains extending from Ganjam as far south as the Pāṇḍya country to the whole of the Eastern Ghat range. The Mahendrādrī or the Mahendra mountain is situated between the Gaṅgāsāgara-saṅgama and the Saptagodāvarī.[5] A portion of the Eastern Ghats near Ganjam is still called the Mahendra hill. There is also a Mahendragiri in the Tinnevelly district.[6] Pargiter thinks that the name should be limited to the hills between the Mahānadī, Godāvarī, and Wain-Gaṅgā, and may perhaps comprise the portion of the Eastern Ghats north of the Godāvarī.[7] According to Pargiter the Mahendra hills of the *Rāmāyaṇa* and those of the *Purāṇas* are the two different ranges. But Rai Chaudhuri thinks that the same range of hills is meant by the authors of the *Rāmayāṇa* and the *Purāṇas*.[8] Some minor hills associated with the Mahendra mountain are the Śrīparvata overhanging the river Kṛṣṇā in the Kurnool district,[9] Puṣpagiri (north of Cuddapah), Venkaṭādri (Tirumalai mountain near Tripati or Tirupati in the North Arcot district, about 72 miles to the north-west of Madras), Aruṇācala (on the river Kampā)[10] and Ṛṣabha (in the Pāṇḍya country according to the *Mahābhārata*).[11]

The Eastern and the Western Ghats meet in the south in a knot of rocks known as the Nilgiris. The ancient Malayaparvata has been correctly identified by Pargiter with the portion of the Western Ghats from the Nilgiris to the Cape Comorin. The southern extension of the Western Ghats below the Kāverī, now known as the Travancore hills, really forms the western side of the Malayagiri. That the Malayagiri was joined by the Mahendra hills which extended as far south as Madura is

1 *Rāmāyaṇa*, Āraṇyakāṇḍa, 64. 10–14.
2 *Mārkaṇḍeya Purāṇa*, p. 289 note.
3 *Studies in the Indian Antiquities*, p. 133.
4 Kiṣkindhyākāṇḍa, 41. 18–20; Laṅkākāṇḍa, 4. 92–94.
5 Cf. *Bhāgavata Purāṇa*, X, 79.
6 *Tinnevelly District Gazetteer*, I, p. 4.
7 *Mārkaṇḍeya Purāṇa*, p. 305 note.
8 *Studies in Indian Antiquities*, pp. 108-109.
9 *Agni Purāṇa*, CXIII, 3-4; Pargiter, *Mārkaṇḍeya Purāṇa*, p. 290 notes.
10 *Skanda Purāṇa*, Ch. III, 59–61; IV, 9, 13, 21, 37.
11 *Mahābhārata*, III, 85. 21; *Bhāgavata Purāṇa*, X, 79.

proved by the *Caitanya-caritāmṛta* and the *Harṣacarita*[1] respectively. The Malayaparvata was also known as the Śrīkhaṇḍādri and Candanādri.[2] It is the same as Tamil Podigei or Podigai, the Bettigo of Ptolemy. On the summit of the Malayakūṭa or the Malaya range there was the hermitage of the sage Agastya.[3] Associated with the Malaya is the hill called Dardura[4] which is identical with the Nilgiris or the Palni hills.

The group of mountains known as Mahendra, Malaya, Sahya, Śuktimat, Ṛkṣa, Vindhya and Pāripātra is known to ancient Indian geographers as the Kulācalas.[5] They were so called because each of them was associated with one particular country or tribe. 'Thus Mahendra is the mountain *par excellence* of the Kaliṅgas, Malaya of the Pāṇḍyas, Sahya of the Aparāntas, Śuktimat of the people of Bhallāṭa,[6] Ṛkṣa of the people of Māhiṣmatī,[7] Vindhya of the Āṭavyas and other forest folks of Central India, and Pāripātra or Pāriyātra of the Niṣādas.'[8]

The *Bhāgavata Purāṇa*[9] refers to some mountains which are difficult to be identified. They are as follows: Surasa, Śata, Śṛṅga, Vāmadeva, Kuṇḍa, Kumuda, Puṣpa, Varṣa, Sahośra, Devānīka, Kapila, Īśāna, Śatakeśara, Devapāla and Sahasraśrota.

B. *Caves*

The caves in prehistoric times discovered all over the world, mostly represent natural caves partly improved by human hand. Some of them contain ante-chambers and the walls of many of them are decorated with pictures of animals and natural objects. These caves served as shelters of men in life and death. It was in them that our remote ancestors developed in different ways our culture and civilization. The caves as religious retreats are referred to for the first time in the early texts of Buddhism. The cave (*guhā*) of the *Upaniṣads* is not a religious retreat but the cavity of the heart. The forests, open spaces, roads, tree-shades, deserted houses, cemeteries and mountain caves (*giriguhā*) became important as temporary shelters and retreats of the Indian 'runaways', the recluses, and wanderers as distinguished from the hermits (*tāpasas*). The caves also served as suitable places for meditation of the recluses. They were really the means of protection against heat and cold, wind and sunlight, ferocious animals and showers of rain.[10] The early caves and caverns are mostly associated with the hills around the ancient city of Rājagriha. Only one of them is located in the neighbourhood of Kauśāmbī. The Indrasāla-guhā and the Saptaparṇī cave are the most noted among the caves and caverns of Rājagriha. According to the *Vinayapiṭaka* a natural cave deserves to be called a *leṇa* when it is touched by human hand and improved by human skill. It is difficult to take the early caves to be the examples of cave architecture. The Indian caves acquired an architectural significance from the days of Aśoka. They continued to be so up till the reign of King Khāravela of Orissa. The four caves dedicated by Aśoka to the Ājīvikas in the Khalatika or Barabar hills, about 20 miles north of the town of Gayā, the three caves dedicated by Daśaratha in the Nāgārjuni hills, and

1 *Harṣacarita*, VII.
2 Cf. Dhoyi's *Pavanadūta*.
3 *Bhāgavata Purāṇa*, XI, 79.
4 *Mahābhārata*, II, 52, 34; *Ibid.*, XIII, 165, 32; *Rāmāyaṇa*, Laṅkākāṇḍa, 26, 42; *Raghuvaṃśa*, IV, 51.
5 *Mārkaṇḍeya Purāṇa*, 57. 10.
6 *Mahābhārata*, II, 30. 5f.
7 *Harivaṃśa*, 38. 19.
8 Rai Chaudhuri, *Studies in Indian Antiquities*, pp. 105-106.
9 Skandha V, Ch. 20.
10 *Vinaya Cullavagga*, VI. 1. 3-4.

the caves dedicated to the Jain recluses on the twin hills of Udayagiri and Khaṇḍagiri, were all intended to serve as shelters during the rains, while some of them in South India came to serve the sepulchral purpose in mediaeval times. From the time of the Śātakarṇis of the Andhra dynasty the Indian caves began to develop as *vihāras* (monastic abodes) and *caityas* or shrines. This observation holds true of the caves of Kārle, Bhāja, Ajantā, Ellorā, Aurangabad, Elephanta and Bāgh. The Kailāsa temple of Ellora was a magnificent rock-cut temple which developed in the tradition of the caves as religious shrines. As compared and contrasted with the caves of India, the *leṇas* of Ceylon which do not strictly deserve the name of *guhā*, are nothing but the slanting slopes of rocks barely touched and rudely dressed by human hand. It is worthwhile to give a short account of some important Indian caves.

Indasālaguhā.—As explained by Buddhaghosa[1] this cave took its name from an Indasāla tree marking its entrance. The cave with this tree is represented in one of the Barhut sculptures. Later it also became known by the name of Indraśailaguhā evidently for the reason that it is made the scene of action of the famous Pali discourse called *Sakkapañha Sutta*, the discourse in which Sakka or Inda, the king of the gods, interviewed the Buddha to have satisfactory replies to his questions. In the *Dīgha Nikāya* we find that this cave is located in the Vediyaka mountain situated at a short distance to the north of the village of Ambasaṇḍa (Mango-grove).[2] The Vediyaka mountain is now identified with the Giriyak Hill, six miles from the city of Rājagaha, modern Rājgir.[3] According to Buddhaghosa it was a pre-existing cave between two hills with an Indrasāla tree at its door. The particular hill with which it was connected was called Vediyaka or Vediya since it was surrounded by altar-shaped blue rocks.[4]

We read in the Pali text[5] that at the time when the Buddha stepped into it, the cave which was uneven became even, which was narrow became wide, and which was dark became lighted as if by the supernatural power of the gods. The element of the miracle is altogether dispensed with by Buddhaghosa when he describes that cave as being surrounded by a wall fitted with doors and windows covered with *chunam* plaster decorated with scrolls and floral designs, done up on the whole into picturesque cave-dwelling.[6] The Barhut medallion represents it as a mountain cave with a rocky floor and open-mouthed hall inside having an arched roof. It is polished inside. The Indrasāla tree is shown above it. The monkeys sit on cubical rocks, while two bears peep out through the piled up rocks.[7] On the Bodh-Gayā stone railings the cave has an open mouth and an arched hall inside,[8] and it is enclosed by a Buddhist railing. It is difficult to infer from the description given in the Pali text that the cave received any improvement by human hand.

Pipphali guhā.—This solitary cave which took its name from a Pippali or Pipphali tree[9] near its entrance was a favourite resort of Thera Mahā-Kassapa.[10] It was used for the purpose of lonely meditation.[11] According to Fa-Hien this rocky cave was regularly resorted to by the Buddha for silent meditation after his midday meal.[12] It is known to the Chinese

---

1 *Sumaṅgalavilāsinī*, III, 697.
2 *Dīgha*, II. 263-4.
3 Cunningham, *Ancient Geography of India*, pp. 540-41.
4 *Sumaṅgalavilāsinī*, III, 967.
5 *Dīgha N.*, II. 269-70.
6 *Sumaṅgalavilāsinī*, III, 697.
7 Cunningham, *Stupa of Bhārhut*, plate XXVII, 4, pp. 88-89.
8 Barua, *Gayā and Buddha Gayā*, II, figs. 55, 73, 73A.
9 *Udānavaṇṇanā* (Siamese ed.), p. 77.
10 *Udāna*, I, p. 4.
11 *Dhammapada Commentary*, II, 19–21.
12 Legge, *Fa-hien*, p. 85.

travellers as Pipphala cave and to the author of the *Mañjuśrīmūlakalpa*[1] as Paipala guhā. The location of the cave is open to dispute. There is no evidence as yet to show that the cave was fashioned in any way by human hand.

Sattapaṇṇi cave.—It is also known as Sattapaṇṇa (*Sapta-parṇa*) guhā. It apparently derived its name from saptaparṇī creeper serving as its cognizance. All traditions connected with the Vebhāra or Vaihāra mountain, the *Mahāvastu*[2] and the Chinese pilgrims[3] definitely locate it on the north side of this hill. The later accounts represent this spacious cave as the venue of the First Buddhist Council. The Vinaa yaccount does not however refer particularly to any single cave as the place where the *theras* (Elders) of the First Council met. On the other hand, it suggests that while the Council was in session, its five hundred delegates were required to stay in Rājagaha and in all the retreats, *vihāras*, *guhās* and *kandaras* which were then available. We are also told that these retreats were caused to be repaired so as to make them serve as shelters during the rainy season. According to Ceylon chronicles the Saptaparṇī cave alone was repaired for the purpose. The location of this cave is still doubtful. Fa-hien places it about a mile to the west of the Pippala or Pipphala cave.[4] Cunningham identifies it with the Son-Bhāṇḍār cave on the southern side of the Vaihāra mountain.[5] The Pali evidence in support of this identification is to be found in the *Dīgha Nikāya*[6] in which the cave is placed adjacent to the Isigili (Rishigiri) mountain. Although the Pali account connects the cave with the Vaihāra mountain and locates it on a side of it (*Vebhārapasse*), it does not definitely mention on which side the cave stood. The present situation of the Son-Bhāṇḍār cave is ideal for the purpose of a Council. It is moreover a commodious cave-dwelling with clear signs of construction by human skill. There is no other cave in Rājagriha which is so ideally situated and so beautifully made.

Varāha guhā.—This was a natural cave (*Sukarakhāta*) on the Gijjhakūṭa mountain, which served as the retreat to the wandering ascetics including the Buddhist recluses. The wanderer named Dīghanakha met the Buddha in this cave.[7] It came to be known as the boar's cave evidently for the reason that it was a place for the boars to live in.

The *Kandaras* were all natural caverns in the rocks. The *Tinduka Kandara* was marked out by a Tinduka tree[8] standing near it. The *Tapoda kandara* received its name from its proximity to the *Tapodas* or hot springs. Why *Gomata Kandara* was so called is not known. The *Kapota Kandara* was undoubtedly a favourite resort of the pigeons.[9] The *Udāna*[10] locates it at some distance from Rājagaha while Hiuen Tsang places it about 9 or 10 miles north-east of the Indraśaila cave.[11]

---

1 Paṭala liii, p. 588: Magadhānaṃ jane śreṣṭhe Kuśāgrapurīvāsīnaṃ parvataṃ tatsamīpan tu varāhaṃ nāma nāmataḥ. Tatrāsau dhyāyate bhikṣuḥ guhālino 'tha paipale.

2 Vol. I, p. 70.

3 Legge, *Fa-hien*, p. 85; Watters, *On Yuan Chwang*, II, 160.

4 *Ibid.*, pp. 84-5.

5 Cunningham, *Ancient Geography of India* (S. N. Majumdar's ed.), p. 531.

6 *Mahāparinibbāna Suttanta.* (*Dīgha*, II.)

7 *Majjhima Nikāya* I, *Dīghanakha Sutta*; Malalasekera, *Dictionary of Pali Proper Names*, II, pp. 1271-1272; *Papañcasūdanī*, III, p. 203; *Sāratthappakāsinī*, III, p. 249.

8 This tree cannot be accurately identified. It may be *Diospyros embryopteris* or *Strychnos Nux Vomica*.

9 *Udānavaṇṇanā* (Siamese ed.), p. 307.

10 IV. 4.

11 Watters, *On Yuan Chwang*, II, p. 175.

The Pali canonical texts refer to the *Pilakkhaguhā* or a cave which was marked by the Pilakkha tree (Plakṣa, the wave-leaved fig tree, *Ficus Infectoria*). It is said to have been a pit or hollow in the earth caused by rain water. The water accumulated there during the rains made it look like a pool which became dried up in summer. A wanderer named Sandaka used to live in it with his 500 followers in summer by providing it with a temporary roof supported on pillars or posts.[1]

We then meet with several rock-cut caves, some of which are situated in Orissa, and some in southern and western India. Those in eastern India are associated with king Khāravela, the great Jain Emperor of Kaliṅga, his chief queen, son, other royal personages, and officers. Those in western and southern India are associated with the name of the Śātakarṇī rulers. Almost to the same age may be relegated the Pabhosā cave, about two miles west of Kosam, the site of ancient Kauśāmbī dedicated to the Kāśyapiyas, a religious community of the time, by king Āṣāḍhasena of Ahicchatra.

The evidence of the religious faith of the donors of the Jain caves in the twin hills of Udayagiri and Khaṇḍagiri lies in the dedicatory inscriptions as also in the mediæval cult statues of the *Tīrthāṅkaras* in two of the Khaṇḍagiri caves. Some 35 excavations are now visible. The Anantagumphā on the Khaṇḍagiri and the Rāṇīgumphā, Ganeśagumphā and Jayavijaya caves on the Udayagiri hills are the most remarkable from the architectural and artistic points of view. The Hāthigumphā which was caused to be excavated by Khāravela himself is a natural cavern enlarged by an artificial cutting. It is a wide-mouthed slanting slope of a big boulder. On its left side stands the two-storied Mañcapurī cave. The lower storey has a pillared verandah with chambers hollowed out at the back. Its upper storey is of similar design and dimension. The verandah of the ground floor contains a frieze representing a flying angel. The verandah of the upper storey has a pent-roof, which served the purpose of a shelf. A complete *leṇa* consisted of *pāsāda*, meaning a verandah or façade, pillared or not, *koṭhā*, meaning chamber or chambers hollowed out at the back and at one end, and *jiyā* or pent-roof. At the left wing of the lower storey there are two caves donated by Prince Vaḍukha. The courtyard has a wall in front. Near about the Hāthigumphā there are a few small caves. One of them, called Vyāghragumphā, looks like the face of a tiger with its distended jaws. Another known as Sarpagumphā shows a snakehood carved on its upper edge. Two of them are called Ajagaragumphā and Bhekagumphā for similar reasons. On the slope of the Udayagiri hills there is to be seen a single-storied and building-like cave called Choṭahāthigumphā having two small figures of elephants in its courtyard. The Anantagumphā of the Khaṇḍagiri group is a single storied cave planned on the model of the Mañcapurī. The ornamental arches in the doorways of the cave show various reliefs. The Rāṇīgumphā on the Udayagiri is most elaborately decorated.

The Nasik caves, described as *paṇḍuleṇas*, are situated about 300 ft. above the road level. They were excavated for the Bhadrayānikas, a Hīnayāna sect of the Buddhists. We see altogether 23 excavations. The earliest of them is the *Caitya* cave. The cave No. 1 is an unfinished *vihāra*. The cave No. 2 is an excavation with many later additions. It has a verandah with two wooden pillars. The cave No. 3 is a big *Vihāra* with many cells and a big hall. The entrance is sculptured in the style of the Sāñcī gate. It was an excavation of Śātakarṇi Gautamīputra. The cave No. 10,

[1] *Papañcasūdanī* (Sinhalese ed.), II, p. 687.

too, is a *vihāra*. It has a pillared verandah. The cave No. 17 contains a hall 23 ft. wide and 32 ft. deep. Its verandah is reached by half a dozen steps in front between the two central octagonal pillars. Its back wall shows a standing figure of the Buddha.

The Kārli and Bhāja caves are the well-known Buddhist cave temples in the Borghata hills between Bombay and Poona. The inscriptions in the caves go to show that they were donated at the time of Nahapāṇa and Uṣavadāta. The Karle caves have at their entrance a pillar which, like the Sarnath pillar of Aśoka, is surmounted by four lions with gaping mouths and facing four quarters. There is on their right side a Śiva temple, and close to it there is a second pillar surmounted by a wheel, the symbol of *Dharmacakra*. Its entrance consists of three doorways under a gallery. The Bhāja cave No. 1 is a natural cavern. The caves Nos. 2–6 are all plain *vihāras*. There is a caitya which is one of the finest specimens of cave architecture. Buddhist emblems are distinctly traceable in four of the pillars. The roof is arched. There are decorated arches in front and double railings and many small *vihāras*.

The caves of Ellora which are located in the north-west of the Nizam's territory about 16 miles from Aurangabad and 10 miles to the north-west of Daulatabad are important Buddhist caves. Three different religions are represented here: the southern group comprising 14 caves is Buddhist, the middle one belongs to Brahmanism and the northernmost to Jainism. The Buddhist group contains one real temple, a large caitya hall which is a large caitya temple of the same type as the two halls of Ajantā (Nos. 19 and 26). Some of the Buddhist caves contain distinct signs of later Mahayanism. The cave No. 3 is a vihāra cave. The cave No. 5 is of the type of a large vihāra. There are Brahmanical and Jain caves also. The cave No. 10 is a beautiful caitya cave. The façade is highly ornamental and the carvings are very beautiful. The caves Nos. 11 and 12 have cells in the wall and show signs of Mahayanism.

The Bagh caves form an interesting group of Buddhist caves, situated about 40 miles west of Dhar in Malwa. They were excavations of the Gupta period. They are all monastic caves hewn out of the rocky slope of a hill-side which rises on the north from the valley of the Narmadā. The images of the Buddha found here and there in these caves are evidently of a later age. The architecture is not of the same type as that of Nāsik caves.

The Ajantā caves form another notable group of Buddhist rockcut caves situated 60 miles north-west of Aurangabad in the Nizam's territory. All the 26 caves were not excavated and decorated at one and the same time. The seven of them forming a central group are the primitive type, while the rest display a wealth of ornament in sharp contrast to the simplicity of older days. According to V. A. Smith, the bulk of the Ajantā paintings must be assigned to the sixth century A.D., i.e., the time of the great Chālukya kings. The earliest caves, Nos. 9 and 10, may be dated at the first and second century B.C. The caves of Ajantā belong to the *Caitya* and *Vihāra* types.

The caves of Aurangabad represent, according to Dr. Vogel, the final phase in the long development through which monastic cave-temple architecture has passed. With the exception of one dilapidated Caitya-temple of a primitive type, these little known monastery caves are evidently synchronous in point of time with the latest caves of Ajantā. A striking feature of these later caves is the increasing prominence of the *Bodhisattvas* who take their place beside the numberless Buddha images.

The Elephanta caves, which are situated about six miles to the north-east of the Appollo Bunder, show the influence of Buddhism and Brahmanism. *Trimūrti* or Brahmanical Trinity has been carved on the wall of the main hall. One of the caves contains a Buddhist *caitya*.

Though the caves were no longer used for the purpose for which they were built or donated, they still stand with full memories of the glorious past of India.

C. *Rivers*

Innumerable are the rivers of India which are really the arteries that carry and distribute the water or life-blood of a country. They flow down in various directions seeking the level, cutting valleys sometimes through the mountain ranges, sometimes on land and occasionally changing their beds. They form diverse streams of water (*sarit*), producing ripples (*taraṅginī*) and murmuring sounds (*kalanādinī*) and create waterfalls, lakes and islands. The prosperity of India to a large extent depends upon her river systems. It is along the banks of the rivers and in close proximity to them that we can trace the growth of tribal settlements and mighty kingdoms, prosperous towns and fertile villages, religious shrines and peaceful hermitages. India owes much of her productiveness to her rivers and many of them also constitute highways of trade and commerce. Not unnaturally the *Mārkaṇḍeya Purāṇa* (LVII. 30) says, 'All the rivers are sacred, all flow towards the sea. All are like mothers to the world, all purge away sins.' The *Bhāgavata Purāṇa* (Skandha V, Ch. 20) mentions some rivers which seem difficult to be identified. They are as follows:—*Anumatī, Sinivālī, Kuhu, Rajanī, Nandā, Madhukulyā, Mitravindā, Mantramālā, Āyurdā, Aparājitā, Śrutavindā, Sahasraśruti* and *Devagarbhā*.

It is interesting to note that since the Vedic times it became almost a convention to describe the gradually widening Aryandom by the seven rivers called *Sindhus, Sarasvatis, Gaṅgās* or *Nadīs*. Thus the entire country occupied by the Ṛgvedic Aryans has been described in the Ṛgveda[1] as *Saptasindhavaḥ*, 'the land of seven rivers', namely, the five rivers of the Punjab together with Sindhu (Indus) and another river whether it be the Sarasvatī or the Kubhā (Kābul) or even the Oxus. When the Aryandom embraced the whole of India it came to be represented by the seven principal streams called the Gaṅgā, Yamunā, Godāvarī, Sarasvatī, Narmadā, Sindhu and Kāverī.[2] The seven sacred rivers of the Buddhist Midland are enumerated as Bāhukā (Bāhudā), Adhikakkā, Gayā (Phalgu), Sundarikā, Sarassatī, Payāgā (confluence of the Ganges and the Yamunā), and Bāhumatī.[3] Another version has Gaṅgā, Yamunā, Sarabhū (Sarajū), Sarassatī, Aciravatī, Mahī and Mahānadī.[4]

It is interesting to note what Kālidāsa has said in his *Raghuvaṃśa*. In the far east lay the eastern sea (*Pūrvasāgara*), the modern Bay of Bengal (*Raghuvaṃśa*, IV, 32). Its coast was bordered by the eastern peoples of the lower Ganges, the Suhmas and the Vaṅgas (*Ibid.*, IV, 35-36). It extended to the Great Indian Ocean (*Mahodadhi*) which lay spread to the far south, thus hemming in almost the three southern sides of the Indian continent, and creating the great Indian peninsula (*prāpa tālīvanaśyāmam-upakaṇṭham mahodadhe—Raghuvaṃśa*, IV. 34). The ocean in the south-east and the extreme south was lined with extensive forests of palm trees

[1] *Ṛgveda*, X. 75. 4.
[2] *Gaṅgā ca Yamunā caiva Godāvarī Sarasvatī |*
Narmadā Sindhu Kāverī jale'smin sannidhiṃ kuru ||
[3] *Majjhima Nikāya*, I, p. 39.
[4] *Visuddhimagga*, I, p. 10.

(*Ibid.*, IV. 34). The eastern coast-line running to the south was inhabited by some of the mightiest peoples of India, the Kaliṅgas and the Pāṇḍyas (*Ibid.*, IV. 49). Along the south-west coast of the ocean were settled the Keralas (*Ibid.*, IV. 54). The entire western coast was the region of Aparānta.

(i) *The Indus Group.*—The Indus is known to the Indians as Sindhu since the Ṛgvedic times. It is also called Saṃbheda and Saṅgama. It is counted among the seven streams of the Divyagaṅgā or celestial Gaṅgā. The Indus at the start is a united flow of two streams, one flowing north-west from the north-west side of the Kailāsaparvata and the other in a north-westerly and then in a south-westerly direction from a lake situated to the north-east of the Kailāsa. Beginning from this confluence it flows north-west over a long distance to turn south below the Karakoram range. From this point it follows a slightly meandering and south-westerly course till it falls into the Arabian Sea forming two well-known deltas at its mouth. The Sindhu group as known to Pliny was constituted of the Sindhu (Indus) and nineteen other rivers of which the most famous was the Hydaspes with its four tributaries. The Indus was generally regarded as the western boundary of India.[1] We are informed by Arrian that the Indus spread out in many places into lakes with the result that where the country happened to be flat, its shores appeared far apart. The Sindhu is the greatest known river of Uttarāpatha after which the Indus group is named. To the Vedic Aryans this river stood unsurpassed, while in the opinion of Megasthenes and other classical writers, it was rivalled by no other river than the Ganges. As described in the *Ṛgveda* (X. 75) the Sindhu surpassed all the flowing streams in might. It speeded over the precipitous ridges of the earth and was the 'lord and leader of the moving floods'.

According to Alberuni only the upper course of the Indus above the junction with the Chenab (Candrabhāgā) was known as the Sindhu; lower that point to Aror, it was known by the name of Pañcnād, while its course from Aror down to the sea was called Mihran.[2] In the Behistun Inscription of Darius it is referred to as Hindu and in the *Vendidad* as Hendu. The Sindhu lent its name to the country through which it flowed.[3]

Quite a good number of the tributaries of the Indus finds mention in the *Nadī-stuti* hymn of the *Ṛgveda.*[4] It is not difficult to recognize some of the most important tributaries the Indus receives on the west. The Kubhā is undoubtedly the modern Kabul, the Kophes of Arrian, the Kophen of Pliny, the Koa of Ptolemy, and the Kuhu of the *Purāṇas*. It flows into the Indus a little above Attock (Skt. Hāṭaka), receives at Prang the joint flow of its two tributaries called the Suvāstu or Svāt (Soastos of Arrian) and Gaurī (Garroia of Arrian), identified with the modern Panjkorā, and brings with it another river called Malamantos by Arrian probably represented by the Kameh or Khonar, the largest of the tributaries of the Kabul river. The Vedic Krumu is the modern Kuram which is fed by the tributary called Tachi. The Gomatī which is a tributary of the Indus, is the modern Gomal. There are other western tributaries.[5]

Among the four main eastern tributaries of the Indus, which flow together under the name of the Candrabhāgā or Chenāb, the most western is the Vitastā or Vitaṃsā or Jhelum. The Candrabhāgā or Chenāb appears

---

[1] McCrindle, *Ancient India*, pp. 28, 43.
[2] *India*, I, 260.
[3] Cf. Beal, *Buddhist Records of the Western World*, I, 69; *J.A.S.B.*, 1886, ii, p. 323.
[4] B. C. Law, *Rivers of India*, pp. 9-10.
[5] For their details vide B. C. Law, *Rivers of India*, pp. 15-16.

to flow just above Kishtwar as a confluence of two hill streams. From Kishtwar to Rishtwar its course is southerly. It flows past Jammu, wherefrom it flows in a south-westerly direction forming a doab between it and the Jhelum. This river is the same as the Ṛgvedic Asikṇī, Arrian's Akesines and the Sandabaga or Sandabal of Ptolemy. The Candra and the Bhāga issue on opposite sides of the Bāra Lācha Pass in the Kangra district. The Rāvī or the Irāvatī, known to the Greeks as the Hydraotis, Adris or Rhonadis, appears first to our view at the south-west corner of Chambā in Kashmir as the confluence of two streams. From Chambā it flows past Lahore, flowing a south-westerly course and meets the Chenab or the united flow of the Vitastā and the Candrabhāgā. The Beas (Vipāśā) rises in the Pir Panjal range at the Rhotang Pass near the source of the Rāvī. It appears first to our view at the south-west corner of Chambā in Kashmir as the confluence of two streams, one flowing from north-east and other from south-east and both having their origin in the Himalayan range. From Chambā it flows in a south-westerly direction to meet the Śatadru (Sutlej) at the south-west corner of Kapurtala. It is identical with the Greek Hypases or Hyphasis.

The source of the Śatadru or the Sutlej is traceable to the western region of the western lake of the Mānas Sarovara. The Sutlej which is the Zaradros of Ptolemy and the Hesydrus of Pliny is the most important feeder of the Indus in the east. It turns a little towards south-west above the Mount Kamet as well as the Simla hills to follow a zigzag but south-westerly course through Bilaspur, at the north-west corner of which it turns south, and then from Rupar it takes a westerly course till it receives the Beas at the south-west corner of Kapurtala. The united streams then flow south-west and join the Chenab between Alipur and Uch. The combined flow of four or five rivers proceeds south-west under the name of Chenab to meet the Indus at Panjnad. In ancient times it took an independent course to the confines of Sind (Pargiter, *Mārkaṇḍeya Purāṇa*, p. 291, notes).

(ii) *The Sarasvatī-Dṛṣadvatī* group (the Desert river system).—The Sarasvatī and the Dṛṣadvatī are the two historical rivers of Uttarāpatha that flow down independently without having any connection with the Indus group. Between these two sacred streams lies the region of Brahmāvarta according to Manu. The Sarasvatī, which is the holy stream of early Vedic India, is described in the *Milindapañha* as a Himalayan river. Its source may be traced to the Himalayan range above the Simla hills. It flows southwards through the Simla and Sirmur States forming a bulge. It flows down past Patiala to lose itself in the northern part of the desert of Rajputana at some distance from Sirsā. Manu applies the name of Vinaśana to the place where it disappears from view. The Sarasvatī is correctly described as a river which is visible at one place and invisible in another (*Siddhānta-śiromaṇi*, Golādhyāya, Bhuvanakoṣa). It disappears for a time in the sand near the village of Chalaur and re-appears at Bhavānīpur. At Bālchāpar it again disappears, but re-appears again at Barakhera; at Urnai near Pehoa it is joined by the Mārkaṇḍa, and the united stream bearing still the name of Sarasvatī ultimately joins the Ghaggar or Gharghar which is the lower part of the Sarasvatī. The *Mahābhārata*[1] also says that after disappearing the river re-appears again at three places, viz., at Chamasodbheda, Śirodbheda and Nāgodbheda.[2]

[1] *Vanaparva*, Ch. 82; N. L. Dey, *Geographical Dictionary*, 180ff.; *Punjab Gazetteer*, Ambala District, Ch. I.

[2] Mahābhārata, Vanaparva, 82.

This river which still survives flows between the Sutlej and the Jumna. The Sarasvatī, as known to the Vedic Aryans, was a mighty river which flowed into the sea.[1] The *Kātyāyana Śrautasūtra*,[2] the *Lāṭyāyana Śrautasūtra*,[3] the *Āśvalāyana Śrautasūtra*,[4] and the *Sāṅkhyāyana Śrautasūtra*[5] mention sacrifices held on its banks as of great importance and sanctity.

The sacred river called Dṛṣadvatī flows nearer the Yamunā. Its origin may be traced to the hills of Sirmur. Up to Naham it has a westerly course and then it changes its course towards the south and lies through the districts of Ambala and Shahabad. It tends to meet the Sarasvatī at Sirsā, the place below which both the streams disappear. The ancient town of Pṛthudaka (modern Pehoa) is situated on this river. According to the *Manusaṃhitā* (II. 17) this river formed the eastern and southern boundaries of the Brahmāvarta, while its western boundary was the Sarasvatī. In the Vanaparva of the *Mahābhārata* the confluence of the Dṛṣadvatī and the Kauśikī is considered very sacred. The *Vāmana Purāṇa* (34) considers the Kauśikī to be a branch of the Dṛṣadvatī. Cunningham identifies the Dṛṣadvatī with the modern Rākshi that flows by the south-west of Thanesvar. Elphinstone and Todd identify it with the Ghaggar flowing through Ambala and Sind. According to Rapson it may be identified with the Citrang, Chantang or Citang running parallel to the Sarasvatī. The *Ṛgveda* (III. 23. 4) mentions a river named Āpayā between the Dṛṣadvatī and the Sarasvatī. Ludwig is inclined to identify it with the Āpagā as a name for the Ganges, but Zimmer correctly places it near the Sarasvatī (*Altindisches Leben*, 18), while Pischel assigns it to Kurukṣetra of which the Āpayā is a famous river.[6]

(iii) *The Gaṅgā-Yamunā Group*.—The Ganges is one of the most important sacred rivers of India. The rivers of Mid-land (Madhyadeśa), as known to the early Buddhists, go to constitute the Ganges system. The number of its tributaries, as known to the classical writers, was nineteen.[7] Though the Ganges and the Indus were known to them as the two largest rivers in India, the former was taken as the greater of the two. The Ganges is known by various other names such as Viṣṇupadī, Jāhnavī,[8] Mandākinī, Bhāgīrathī, etc. The *Mahābhārata* traces the source of the Ganges to Bindusara, while the Jaina *Jambudiva-paṇṇatti* to the Padmahrada. The Pali works refer to the southern face of the Anotatta lake as the source of the Ganges. According to modern geographers the Bhāgīrathī first comes to light near Gaṅgotrī in the territory of Garhwal. At Devaprāg it is joined on the left side by the Alakanandā. From Devaprāg the united stream is called the Ganges. Its descent by the Dehra Dun is rather rapid to Haridvār, also called the Gaṅgādvār or the Gate of the Ganges. From Hardwar down to Bulandshahr the Ganges has a southerly course, after which it flows in a south-easterly direction up to Prayāga (Allahabad) where it is joined by the Yamunā. From Allahabad down to Rājmahal she has an easterly course, after which it follows again south-easterly direction. The Alakanandā represents the upper course of the Ganges. The Mandākinī is one of the tributaries of the Alakanandā, and it may be identified with the Kāligaṅgā or Mandākinī rising in the mountains of Kedāra in Garhwal. The Ganges may be supposed to have assumed the name of the Gaṅgā-Bhāgīrathī from the point where it is met

---

[1] Max Müller, *Ṛgveda Saṃ.*, p. 46.
[2] XII. 3. 20; XXIV. 6. 22.
[3] X. 15. 1; 18. 13; 19. 4.
[4] XII. 6, 2. 3.
[5] XIII, 29.
[6] *Mahābhārata*, III, 83, 68.
[7] McCrindle, *Ancient India*, 136ff.
[8] *Yoginītantra*, 2. 3, pp. 122ff.; 2. 7. 8, pp. 186ff.

by the Mandākinī. The Ganges receives a tributary called Nuta just above Farukkabad. Between Farukkabad and Hardai the Ganges receives another tributary called the Rāmagaṅgā. The Gomatī (modern Gumti) joins the Ganges between Benaras and Ghazipur. The Dhutapāpā of the Pauranic fame was a tributary of the eastern Gomatī. The Tamasā or east Tons joins the Ganges to the west of Bālliā after flowing through Azamgarh. The Sarayū, a tributary of the Ganges, joins the Ganges in the district of Chāprā. This great historical river is now known as Ghargharā (Gogrā). Some unimportant tributaries join the Ghargharā in the Gonda district flowing from the district of Bahraich. The little Gandak joins the Ghargharā (Sarayū) on the western border of the district of Sārā. The ancient city of Ayodhyā stood on the Sarayū. The little Gandak also known as the Hiraṇyavatī or Ajitavatī flows through the district of Gorakhpur and falls into the Gogrā or Ghargharā (Sarayū). The Aciravatī, the great tributary of the Sarayū, flows through the districts of Bahraich, Gonda and Basti, and joins the Sarayū or Ghargharā west of Burhāj in the district of Gorakhpur. The Kakutthā was a tributary of the Hiraṇyavatī or the little Gandak. The Gaṇḍakī (modern Gaṇḍak) is an upper tributary of the Ganges. The main stream of the Gaṇḍak flows into the Ganges between Sonpur in the Sara district and Hazipur in the district of Muzaffarpur. The Sadānirā of the *Śatapatha-Brāhmaṇa*[1] has been sought to be identified with the Gaṇḍak by some and with the Tāpti by others. Some have also identified it with the Karatoyā. According to the *Mahābhārata* it has been placed between the Gaṇḍakī and the Sarayū. Pargiter identifies it with the river Rāpti.[2] The Buri-Gaṇḍak which is an upper tributary of the Ganges, meets the Ganges west of Gogrā in the Monghyr district. The Bāhumatī or Bāgmatī is a sacred river of the Buddhists in Nepal. Its junction with the seven rivers goes to form the *tīrthas* or holy places.[3] The Kamalā is an upper tributary of the Ganges. The Kauśikī (modern Kuśī) flows through the districts of Bhagalpur and Purnea and meets the Ganges south-east of Mānhari in the district of Purnea. The Tamasā (modern south Tons), a historical river of the Rāmāyaṇa fame, flows north-east from the Ṛkṣa mountain to fall into the Ganges below Allahabad. The greatest known lower tributary of the Ganges is the Sona (Arrian's Sonos, the modern Son) which takes its rise in the Mekala range (Maikāl) in the district of Jubbalpore and flowing north-east through Bāghelkhaṇḍ, Mirzapur and Shahabad districts, joins the Ganges at Patna. The Son is fed by five tributaries. The Punappuna (modern Punpun), a southern tributary, meets the Ganges just below Patna. The Phalgu, another southern tributary, joins the Ganges in the district of Monghyr north-east of Lakhisarai. The Sakuti, identified with Sakri, flows into the Ganges between Patna and Monghyr. The Campā forming the boundary between Aṅga in the east and Magadha in the west, is probably the same river as one to the west of Campānagara and Nāthnagar in the suburb of the town of Bhagalpur.

The Ganges in its lower course is known as the Bhāgīrathī-Hughli in West Bengal and the Padmā-Meghnā in East Bengal. The Ganges enters Bengal between Rajmahal and Malda and bifurcates a little above Jangipur in the district of Murshidabad.

The Bhāgīrathī branch of the Ganges is met on the right side by the first tributary called Bansloi in the district of Murshidabad. The Ajaya

---

[1] Eggeling, *Introduction to the Śatapatha Brāhmaṇa*, S.B.E., Vol. XII, p. 104.
[2] *Mārkaṇḍeya Purāṇa*, p. 294.
[3] *Svayambhū Purāṇa*, Ch. V; *Varāha Purāṇa*, 215.

which is an important tributary joins the Bhāgīrathī at Katwa in the district of Burdwan and forms a natural boundary between the districts of Burdwan and Birbhum. The Bhāgīrathī in its lower course receives on the right side the well-known tributary called the Damodar which flows into the Hughli in several streams in the district of Midnapore. The Damodar takes its rise in the hills near Bagodar in the district of Hazaribagh, and flows through the districts of Manbhum and Santal Parganas and then through the districts of Burdwan and Hughli. The Rūpnārāyaṇ, another important tributary of the Bhāgīrathī branch of the Ganges, flows through the districts of Bankura, Hughli, and Midnapur to join the Hughli river near Tamluk. The Hughli is joined on the right side by the united flow of the Haldi and Kashai. The Panar which is the first upper tributary of the main stream of the Ganges in Bengal, joins the Ganges below Nawabganj.

The Kaṃsavatī and Pūrṇabhava are the two tributaries of the Panar in the district of Malda. The Ātrai (Atreyī) and the lesser Yamunā meet together in the district of Rajshahi. These are also the tributaries of the Panar. At Goalundo the Ganges receives the greater Yamunā which is nothing but the main stream of the Brahmaputra as it flows through East Bengal. The united stream is now known as the Padmā. It joins the estuary of the Meghnā to the east of the Faridpur district. The Garāi issuing from the Gaṅgā above Pānsā in the district of Faridpur flows down under the name of the Madhumatī and reaches the Bay a little above Pirojpur in the district of Backergunj under the name of the Haringhāṭā.

The Āriyālkhāl river, which is a distributary of the Ganges, issues from the right side of the Padmā, below the town of Faridpur, and flows down into the Bay through the Madaripur sub-division of Faridpur and the district of Backergunge. The Āriyālkhāl and the Madhumatī are connected by a small river which flows from the former a little above the town of Madaripur and joins the latter a little above Gopalgunge in Madaripur sub-division. The lower course of the Padmā becomes known as the Kīrtināśā or Destroyer of memorable works from the ravages wrought amongst the monuments and buildings of Rājā Rāj Vallabh at Rājnagar in the district of Faridpur.

Besides the Bhāgīrathī and the Padmā, the water of the Ganges is carried to the sea through numerous other channels. The seaward end of the delta of the Ganges encloses the large swampy area covered with jungles called the Sundarbans.

The first and great western tributary of the Ganges is the Yamunā proper which is mentioned in the *Yoginītantra* (2. 5, pp. 139-40). It takes its rise in the Himalayan range below Mount Kamet. It cuts a valley through the Siwalik range and Gharwal before it enters the plains of northern India to flow south parallel to the Ganges. From Mathurā downwards it follows a south-eastern course till it meets the Ganges forming the famous confluence of Prayāga or Allahabad. In the district of Dehra Dun it receives two tributaries on the western side, one of which is known as the Northern Tons. Between Agra and Allahabad it is joined on the left side by four tributaries. Many holy places of India are situated on this river. The Yamunā is called by the Chinese as Yen-mou-na. It is one of the five great rivers according to the Buddhists. It serves as a boundary between Śūrasena and Kośala, and further down between Kośala and Vaṃśa. The Yamunotrī which is eight miles from Kursoli is considered to be the source of the river Yamunā. It is identical with the Greek Erannaboas (Hiraṇyavāha or Hiraṇyavāhu). The Vāluvāhinī is mentioned in the *Skanda Purāṇa* as a tributary of this river.

(iv) *The Brahmaputra-Meghna System.*—The origin of the Brahmaputra, otherwise known as the Lauhitya (Rohita), is traceable, according to the modern geographical exploration, to the eastern region of the Mānas Sarovara. The Brahmaputra maintains its easterly course from the Mānas Sarovara to Namcha Barwa and at the latter place it turns south and flows down through the eastern extremity of the Himalayan range to enter the valley of Assam in the north-eastern frontier district of Sadiyā. It flows in a south-westerly direction from Sadiyā down to the place above the Garo hills, and it flows south again to meet the Ganges at a little above the Goalundo Ghat. The course of the Brahmaputra through the tableland of southern Tibet is known by the name of Tsangpo. At a distance of about 200 miles from the Mānas Sarovara it receives an important upper tributary. Further east it is joined by another upper tributary. Further down it receives three lower tributaries, all having their origin in the Himalayan range. The great tributary which meets the Brahmaputra in the district of Sadiyā is the Lohit. The next important tributary on the left is the Buridihing which meets the Brahmaputra south of Lakhimpur. Further down on the left the Disarā which takes its rise in the Patkai hills, flows north-west and west to join the Brahmaputra, north-west of the town of Sibsagar. Between Lakhimpur and Sibsagar districts the Brahmaputra forms a large island called Majuli. The Brahmaputra receives the tributary called Dhansrī which takes its rise from the Nāgā hills north of Manipur. Further down on the left the Brahmaputra receives two streams of the Kalang as its tributaries in the district of Nowgong. On the right two streams flow into the Brahmaputra above and below Tejpur. The Krishnāi flowing from the Garo hills flows into the Brahmaputra, a little above Dāmrā in the district of Goalpara. On the right side the Brahmaputra is joined by the great tributary called Mānas.

The Gaṅgā assumes the name of Padmā after its confluence with the greater Yamunā a little above the Goalundo Ghat. This Yamunā is nothing but the present main stream of the Brahmaputra as it flows through East Bengal, while its older course flows past the town of Mymensingh to meet the Meghnā representing the united stream of the three Assam rivers called Surmā, Barāka and Puinī. The meeting of the older course of the Brahmaputra with the Meghnā takes place a little below Bhairab Bazar in the Kishoreganj sub-division of the district of Mymensingh. The combined waters of the Meghnā and the Brahmaputra flow together under the name of Meghnā. The bifurcation of the Brahmaputra takes place after it enters Bengal. The Yamunā branch of the Brahmaputra receives near Ghorāghāṭ the Tistā (Trisrota) as a tributary on the right. Farther down on the right the Yamunā branch of the Brahmaputra receives another important tributary called Karatoyā which once formed the boundary between Bengal and Kāmarūpa (*Mahābhārata*, Vanaparva, Ch. 85). The Karatoyā has its origin above Domār in the district of Rungpur. The Dhaleśvarī which is a tributary of the lower Brahmaputra is a river of great importance in the district of Dacca. It receives the waters of Lakshyā below Habiganj before it flows into the Meghnā as a river of great breadth. The Burigaṅgā is one of the offshoots of the Dhaleśvarī. The Ichāmatī which is one of the oldest rivers in the district of Dacca, lies between the Dhaleśvarī and the Padmā. Formerly it flowed into the Brahmaputra near Rampal. Now it finds its way into the Dhaleśvarī by several winding routes.

The Lakshyā which is regarded as the prettiest river in the district of Dacca, is found to have been formed by the three streams that took off from the old Brahmaputra. The Surmā which is the second important river of Assam, represents the upper course of the Meghnā, the famous river of East Bengal. It is joined on the right by five tributaries before forming a confluence with the Barāka, West of Habiganj. The Barāka has a westerly course till it joins the Surmā. The Manu issues from the Hill Tipperah, flows north to join the Barāka in Sylhet. The Meghnā is the name by which the lower course of the Surmā river flowing through the district of Dacca is generally known. It joins the mighty Padmā near Rājābāri. The minor stream of the Brahmaputra which was formerly the main stream and which now flows past the town of Mymensingh under the name of Brahmaputra flows into the Meghnā in Kishoreganj sub-division. The Meghnā takes a tortuous course between the districts of Dacca and Tipperah till it joins the Dhaleśvarī a little below Munshiganj. The united waters of the Padmā and the Meghnā flow together into the Bay of Bengal in a southerly direction under the name of Meghnā between the districts of Noakhali and Backerganj and form a few doabs at the estuary. The two great rivers represent 'a most awe-striking sight of an all-engulfing expanse' at the point where they form the confluence.

There are some coastal rivers to the east of the Brahmaputra-Meghnā system. The Feni forming the boundary in its upper course between the Hill Tipperah in the north and the district of Chittagong in the south and in its lower course between the districts of Chittagong and Noakhali takes its rise in the hills of Hill Tipperah and empties itself into the Bay opposite the island of Sandvīp. The Naf is also a boundary river which separates the Cox's Bazar sub-division of Chittagong from the district of Arakan. The Karṇaphuli is the largest of the three main rivers of Chittagong and Chittagong Hill Tracts. It rises from the Lushai Hills that connect the Chittagong Hill Tracts with the south-western part of Assam and flows south-west down to Rāṅgāmāṭī, the headquarters of the Chittagong Hill Tracts. It turns west and follows a straight course down to the mouth of the Hāldā and then takes a southerly course and flows past the town of Chittagong which lies on its right bank. Between Rāṅgāmāṭī and Chittagong town the Karṇaphuli is fed by a few small tributaries. The Sangu rises from the extreme south of the eastern part of the Chittagong Hill Tracts. It reaches the Bay not far from the mouth of the Karṇaphuli. The Mātāmurī is a small internal river of the Cox's Bazar sub-division, which flows into the Bay opposite to the island of Kutubdiā.

It may be noted here that the Suvarṇarekhā in Midnapore is an important river of eastern India, which rises in the district of Manbhum and flows past Jamshedpur and farther down through the districts of Dhalbhum and Midnapore to fall into the Bay.

(v) *The Luni-Chambal Group.*— The Luni is the only important river west of the Aravalli range. It takes its rise in the hills of Ajmer and flows down in a south-westerly direction to reach the border between Rajputana and the Cutch Peninsula. The river then runs direct south to meet the sea by forming a large delta at its mouth. It is fed by no less than six tributaries. A streamlet meets the Luni on the right side. The first left tributary of the Luni is the Bandi which issues from the Aravalli range. The Banas is a notable left tributary which joins the Luni south of Varahai. The Luni in its course towards the Gulf of Cutch is joined on the left by the Sarasvatī flowing down from the Aravalli range.

The Chambal or the Carmanvatī rises from the Aravalli range north-west of Indore and flows north-east through eastern Rajputana into the Yamunā. The Kālisindh flows north from the Vindhya range to join the Chambal on the right a little north of Piparda. The Pārvatī is a local river of Indore which flows north-west to join the Chambal on the right.

According to Cunningham it is the Pārā of the *Purāṇas*. The Kunu is a right lower tributary of the Chambal, and the Mej is its first left tributary. The Berach, a tributary of the Chambal, rises from the Aravalli range. The point where the Berach receives the Dhund, becomes known as the Banas (Skt. Varṇāśā). The Gambhīra is a tributary of the Yamunā above the Chambal flowing east from Gaṅgāpur. The Vetravatī (modern Betwa) rises from the Pāripātra mountains. In its course towards the Yamunā it is joined by many tributaries. The Ken (Cainas according to Arrian) is an important tributary of the Yamunā below the Vetravatī. The Mahī is the most important of the lesser rivers that issue from the Pāripātra mountains and flow into the Arabian sea. It empties itself into the Gulf of Cambay. It has a south-westerly course up to Banswara and then it turns south to pass through Guzrat. The Sabarmatī flows from the Pāripātra mountains and finds its way into the Gulf of Cambay through Ahmedabad. The Vihalā and the Vegavatī are associated with the Mount Ūrjayanta in Surāṣṭra. The river Bhadar of Kathiawar flows into the Arabian Sea. Its source is traceable to the Mandab hills in Kathiawar. The Daśārṇa is a tributary of the Vetravatī. The Nirbindhyā is the river between Vidiśā and Ujjayinī, that is to say, between the Daśārṇā (Dhasan) and the Siprā, according to Kālidāsa. It is identified with the modern Kālisindh which forms a tributary to the Chambal. The Siprā is a local river of the Gwalior State flowing into the Chambal a little below Sitaman. It is the historical river on which stands the ancient city of Ujjayinī. It is immortalized by Kālidāsa.

(vi) *The Narmadā-Tāpti Group.*—The Narmadā which is the most important river of Central and Western India, rises from the Maikal range and flows in a south-westerly direction forming the natural boundary between Bhopal and the Central Provinces. Then this river runs through Indore and flows past Revākaṇṭha of Bombay and meets the sea at Broach. As this river takes its course in between the two great mountain ranges of the Vindhya and the Satpurā, it is fed by a large number of small tributaries. Before the river enters Indore it is joined by not less than thirteen tributaries. This river is further fed by seven tributaries, four on the left and three on the right, as it flows through Indore. It receives no more tributary in the rest of its course up to the sea. The Narmadā (Namados of Ptolemy) is otherwise known as Revā, Samodbhavā and Mekalasutā. The last name is important as indicating its source, namely, the modern Maikal range preserving the name of the ancient territory of Mekala. The Maikal range, evidently a portion of the Ṛkṣa, is also the source of the great river Son. The source of the Revā is traceable to the Amarakaṇṭaka hills adjoining the Vindhya range. The Narmadā and the Revā form a confluence a little above Māndlā to flow down under either name. According to the *Mahābhārata* the Narmadā formed the southern boundary of the ancient kingdom of Avantī. According to the *Matsya Purāṇa* (Ch. 193) the place where the Narmadā falls into the sea is a *tīrtha* or a holy place.

The Tāptī or Tāpī has its source in the Multai plateau to the west of the Mahādeva hills and flows westward forming the natural boundary between the Central Provinces and the north-western tip of Berar. This river passes through Burhanpur and crosses the boundary of the Central Provinces before it enters the Bombay Presidency to meet the sea at Surat. Within the Central Provinces (Madhya Pradeśa) it is met by four tributaries, all flowing from the Mahādeva hills. In eastern Khandesh this river is met by a very important river called the Pūrṇa. Six more rivers meet the Tāptī on the left before it empties itself into the sea. It takes only two tributaries on the right. The Pūrṇa rises from the Satpura branch of the Vindhya range and meets the Tāptī a little below Burhanpur. It is an ancient river according to the *Padma Purāṇa* (Ch. XLI). The Girṇā rises from the Sahya or Western Ghats and flows north-east to join the Tāptī below Chopdā in Khandesh. It is fed by two streams. The Bori rises from the Western Ghats and joins the Tāptī a little above Amalner. The Panjhra is an important lower tributary which rises from Western Ghats and flows into the Tāptī a little below Shirpur in Khandesh.

(vii) *The Mahānadī Group.*—The Mahānadī is the largest river in Orissa which rises from the hills at the south-east corner of Berar. It flows past Sihoa and passes through Bastar in Madhya Pradeśa. It also flows through Bilaspur and Raigarh before it enters Orissa in Sambalpur. It then follows a south-easterly course and flows past the town of Cuttack and reaches the Bay at Falls Point, forming a large delta. It is fed by five tributaries. The Devī and Prochī are the two affluents of the Mahānadī on its right side forming two deltaic rivers in the district of Puri. The Choṭa-Mahānadī rises in the hills north of the district Ganjam and meets the Bay at Candrapur. The Vaṃśadharā which is an internal river of Ganjam, falls into the Bay at Kaliṅgapatam. The Lāṅgulinī (modern Lāṅguliyā) rises in the hills at Kālāhandi and flows south through the district of Ganjam to empty itself into the Bay below Chicacole. The Ṛṣikulyā is the northernmost river in the district of Ganjam which flows into the Bay past the town of Ganjam. The Trisāmā (also called the Tribhāgā or Pitrisomā) and the Ṛṣikulyā are mentioned in the *Purāṇas* as two separate rivers, but it seems that they are one and the same river, the Ṛṣikulyā bearing the descriptive name of Trisāmā-Ṛṣikulyā signifying that the name Ṛṣikulyā was applied to the united flow of three upper streams. The Burbalang which represents the lower course of the Karkai, flows through the district of Balasore. The Salandi issues from the hills in the Keonjhar State and flows through the district of Balasore above the Vaitaraṇī. The Kumārī which is identified with the modern Kumārī, waters the Dalma hills in Manbhum. The Palāsinī (modern Parās) is a tributary of the Koel in Chota Nagpur.

The Vaitaraṇī which is one of the most sacred rivers in India, rises in the hills in the southern part of the district of Singhbhum. It follows a course from north-west to south-east through the district of Balasore and reaches the Bay at Dhāmrā. It receives two tributaries a little below the point where it enters Orissa. The Brāhmaṇī is equally sacred, according to the Hindus, and it flows, like the Vaitaraṇī, through the district of Balasore from north-west to south-east. It is joined east of Angul by an important tributary called the Tikkirā (identified with Antaḥśirā or Antyāgirā).

(viii) *The Godāvarī Group.*—The Godāvarī is the largest and longest river in South India. It rises from the Western Ghats. It takes its source in the Nasik hills of the Bombay Presidency and cuts through the Hyderabad State and a good portion of the Madras Presidency. It is about 900 miles in length. It flows in a south-easterly direction below the Vindhya range cutting a valley through the Eastern Ghats. It falls in three main streams into the Bay of Bengal in the district of Godāvarī forming a large delta at its mouth. In its course through Hyderabad and Madras State it is joined by ten tributaries on the left and by eleven on the right, the important among which are the *Pūrṇa*, *Kadaṃ*, *Pranhitā*, *Indravatī* on the left, and the *Mañjirā*, *Sindphanā*, *Maner* and *Kinarsani* on the right. The Pūrṇa flows south-east from the Sahyādri mountain to meet the Godāvarī on the western boundary of the Nander district, Hyderabad.

The Kadam takes its rise in the Nirmal range of the Vindhya hills and flows into the Godāvarī north of Koratla. The *Pranhitā* is one of the two uppermost tributaries of the Godāvarī, which represents the united flow of the Waingaṅgā and the combined waters of the Varadā and the Pengaṅgā (Pennar). The Indravatī takes its rise in the hills of Kālāhandi in Orissa. It follows a south-westerly course and joins the Godāvarī below Bhopalpatnam. The Sindphanā is a western lower tributary of the Godāvarī. The Mañjirā is also a lower tributary which rises from the Bālāghāt range and flows south-east and north to join the Godāvarī. The Maner flows north-east to meet the Godāvarī east of Manthani. The Kinarsani is received by the Godāvarī opposite to Bhadrachalan in the Bastar State.

(ix) *The Kriṣṇā System.*—The Kriṣṇā is a famous river in South India which has its source in the Western Ghats; flowing east through the Deccan plateau and breaking through the Eastern Ghats in a gorge, it falls into the Bay of Bengal. Its course lies through the Bombay State, the State of Hyderabad and the State of Madras. From the north-east of Alampur to a place below Jaggayyapeta the Kriṣṇā flows forming the southern natural boundary of Hyderabad. In its course through Hyderabad and Madras it is joined by fifteen tributaries on the left and four on the right. It takes its source near Mahabalesvara. The Dhon, a tributary of the Kriṣṇā, rises from the Western Ghats hills and joins the Kriṣṇā. The Bhīmā which figures prominently as the Sahya river in the *Purāṇas*, takes a south-easterly course and flows into the Kriṣṇā north of the district of Raichur, Hyderabad. The Palar rises from the hills north of Nalgondā and flows into the Kriṣṇā. The Munar is the most eastern upper tributary of the Kriṣṇā. It joins the Kriṣṇā opposite Amarāvatī. The Tuṅgabhadrā is the most important among the lower tributaries of the Kriṣṇā. The Tuṅgā and the Bhadrā rise from the Western Ghats on the western border of Mysore and combine to flow together under the name of Tuṅgabhadrā. The Varadā which is a tributary of the Tuṅgabhadrā rises from the Western Ghats north of Anantapur and meets the Tuṅgabhadrā. The Hindri which is a lower tributary of the Tuṅgabhadrā, meets the Tuṅgabhadrā, at the town of Karnool. The Coleroon issues from Trichinopoly and falls into the Bay. The North Pennar flows north, north-east up to Pamidi in the district of Anantapur, Madras, and then it turns south-east and reaches the Bay of Bengal in the district of Nellore on the Coromandel coast. The South Pennar flows into the Bay of Bengal at Fort St. David. Its lower course is known by the name of Ponnaiyār.

(x) *The Kāverī System.*—The Kāverī which is a famous river in South India rises in the Western Ghats hills of Coorg, flows south-east through Mysore and falls into the Bay of Bengal in the district of Tanjore in the Madras State. It forms a large delta at its mouth. It is met by ten streams on the left and eight on the right. In ancient times the Kāverī, noted for its pearl-fishery, flowed down into the sea through the southern portion of the ancient kingdom of Coḷa. Uragapura (modern Uraiyur), the ancient capital of Coḷa, was situated on the south bank of the Kāverī. The Kāverī flows through such sacred spots as Śrīraṅgapatnam, Śivasamudram in the Mysore State and Śrīraṅgam near Trichinopoly.

The four important Malaya rivers in south India are noteworthy. They are the *Kritamālā* (Ṛtumālā of the *Kūrmapurāṇa* and the Śatamālā of the *Varāhapurāṇa*), the *Tāmraparṇī* (Tāmravarṇā of the *Brahmapurāṇa*), the *Puṣpajā* and *Sutpalāvatī* (*Utpalāvatī*). The Pāṇḍyakapāṭa and the Tāmraparṇī are the two rivers noted for pearl-fishery. The Tāmraparṇī is a large Malaya river which must have flowed below the southern boundary of the kingdom of Pāṇḍya. It may be identified with the modern Tāmbravarī or with the combined stream of this river and the Chittar. The port of Korkai stood at the mouth of this river according to Ptolemy. The Kritamālā may be identified with the Vaigai which flows past the town of Madoura (ancient Madhurā, the capital of the Pāṇḍya kingdom). The Vaigai is the principal river in the Madura district. It takes its source in two streams draining the two valleys of Cumbum and Varushanad. It flows through Madura town. Eight rivers flowing east and eleven flowing west from the Malaya range are noticed in the modern atlas.

D. *Lakes*

India, ancient or modern, cannot boast of lakes of such immense dimensions or awful grandeur as are found in some parts of Asia, Africa, Europe or America. Yet the sheets of water, both great and small, known as lakes are by no means rare in India. Some of them in modern times are natural depressions fed by the drainage of the surrounding districts; some are artificially constructed by putting dams in river-beds; and some again are mere expansions of river-channels, as pointed out by Arrian. According to him, the Indus, like the Ganges, its only rival, spread out in many places into lakes.

There was a lake in Madhyadeśa known by the name of Kuṇāla.[1] This lake still remains unidentified. There was a lake at Vaiśālī called Markaṭa which was visited by the Buddha.[2] In the Uttarāpatha there was a lake called Anotatta which was visited by the Buddha several times. This lake is generally supposed to be the same as Rawanhrad or Langa. It was one of the seven great lakes of the Himalayas.[3] According to the *Mahāvaṃsa Commentary* (p. 306) the holy water of the Anotatta lake was used during the coronation ceremony.

The most lovely lakes in modern India are found in Kashmir. The Wular, the Dal and the Manasbal are the most beautiful. The Wular lake has an area of 12½ square miles. Its ancient name, according to some, is Mahāpadmasara. The name Wular is supposed to be a corruption of the Sanskrit word *Ullola*, meaning turbulent. The Dal is situated close to Srinagar, the capital city of Kashmir. Its scenery is lovely. The Moghal emperors greatly enhanced the beauty of this spot by planting terraced gardens round it. In the chronicle of Śrīvara the lake is called Dala. There are two small islands in this lake. Among other lakes of Kashmir we may mention the Anchar near Srinagar, the Kosa Nāg, the Nandan Sar, the Nil Nāg, the Sarbal Nāg, and the Kyum.

There are a few lakes in Gharwal. The Ghona is important. The beautiful lake of Kollar Kahar stands in the midst of the Salt range of the Punjab. The Manchar lake in the Larkana district of Sind is formed by the expansion of the western Nara and fed by several hill-streams.

A number of salt lakes are found scattered in Rajputana, the important of which are the Sambhar, the Didwana and the Puṣkara. The Sambhar is situated on the borders of Jodhpur and Jaipur States. The sanctity of the Puṣkara lake is great. Even the greatest sinner by bathing in it is able to remove his sins. There are some artificial lakes in Rajputana. The Debar or Jai Samand, the Raj Samand, the Pichola in the Udaipur State, the Gundolao in Kishengang, and the Machkund in Dholpur are important artificial lakes.

---

[1] *Jāt.*, V, 419; *Aṅguttara*, IV, 101.
[2] *Divyāvadāna*, p. 200.
[3] *Aṅguttara*, IV, 101.

Some natural lakes and depressions, formed in the old beds of rivers, are found in the Uttara Pradeśa. The valley of Nainital contains a pear-shaped lake. The Sagartal is a fine lake. The Talbahat of the Jhanshi district has a lake covering 528 acres formed by two small dams. A crescent-shaped lake is found four miles to the north of Balia town (Balia district). There are some lakes in the Basti district (U.P.). The Bakhira Tal is the finest piece of fresh water in India. Some of the chief perennial lakes are situated in the Gorakhpur district, namely, the Nandaur, the Rangarh, the Narhar, the Chillera and the Beori Tal.

The Lalsarya, the Seraha and the Tataria are all located in the Champaran district of Bihar. The Ramakri of the Chittagong Hill Tracts, the Chalan Bil on the borders of Rajshahi and Pabna districts, the Dhol-samudra marsh of Faridpur district of Bengal, the Pakaria, the Pota, and the Kalang lakes of the Nowgong district and the Saras lake of the Goalpara district of Assam as well as the Logtak lake of Manipur deserve mention.

In the far-west of India, in Gujrat and the Bombay Presidency mention may be made of the Nal about 37 miles south-west of Ahmedabad, the Karambai lake, the Koregaon and the Pangaon lakes of the Solapur district, and the Bhatodi lake of Ahmednagar. There is an embanked lake near Godhra in the Panch Mahals.

In Central India the city of Bhopal stands on a great lake called the Pukhta-pul Talao. There is another lake called the Bara Talao. At Mahoba there are two artificial lakes called the Kirat Sagar and the Rahilya Sagar. There are also lakes in Maihar.

On the eastern coast of the Deccan plateau there is the Chilka lake. A long sandy ridge separates it from the Bay of Bengal. The scenery of the Chilka lake in parts is exceedingly picturesque. The Colair (the Kolleru or Kolar) lake is the only natural fresh water lake in the Madras State. It lies in the Kitsna district, and roughly elliptical in shape. Most of the Coromandel coast is fringed with lagoons, the largest being the Pilicat lake situated just to the north of Madras. In the Hyderabad State there are artificial sheets of water known as lakes, the largest and most important is the Pakhal lake in the Narsampet taluk of the Warangal district. The Lonar lake occupies a circular depression amidst the Deccan traps of the Buldana district in Berar. On the western coast of the Deccan plateau one of the most striking physical features is the continuous chain of lagoons or back waters near Cochin, which run almost parallel to the sea and receive the drainage of the numerous streams descending from the Western Ghats. There are two fresh water lakes in this region, namely, the Enamakkal and the Manakoddi.

E. *Forests*

In ancient times there were forests all over India. Trees were cut for wood and timber. A number of people liked animal hunting in forests. There existed a regular industry of catching birds by means of snares. Some natural forests (sayaṃjātavanā) existed in the Middle Country (Madhyadeśa) in the 6th century B.C. The Kurujāṅgala, for instance, was a wild region in the Kuru realm, which extended as far north as the Kāmyaka forest. The kingdom of Uttara-Pañcāla was founded in this jungle tract. The Añjanavana at Sāketa, the Mahāvana at Vaiśālī and the Mahāvana at Kapilavastu were natural forests. The Mahāvana outside the town of Vaiśālī lay in one stretch up to the Himalayas. It was so called because of the large area covered by it.[1] The Mahāvana at Kapilavastu also lay in one stretch up to the foot of the Himalaya.[2] The Pārileyyakavana was an elephant forest at some distance from Kauśāmbī and on the way to Śrāvastī.[3] The Lumbinīvana situated on the bank of the Rohiṇī river, was also a natural forest.[4] The Nāgavana in the Vajji kingdom, the Śālavana of the Mallas at Kusinārā, the Bhesakaḷāvana in the Bharga kingdom, the Siṃsapāvana at Kauśāmbī, the one to the north of Setavyā in Kośala, the one near Āḷavi and the Pipphalivana of the Moriyas may be cited as typical instances of natural forests.[5] The Vinjhāṭavi represented the forests surrounding the Vindhya range through which lay the way from Pāṭaliputra to Tāmralipti.[6] It was a forest without any human habitation (*agāmakaṃ araññaṃ*).[7] The *Dīpavaṁsa* refers to the Vindhya forest which one had to cross while going to Pāṭaliputra (XV, 87).

There was a reserve-forest of Pārileyyaka in Vatsa (rather in Ceti), the way to which from Kauśāmbī lay through two villages.[8] As pointed out by the Chinese pilgrim, Hiuen Tsang, the way from Prayāga to Kauśāmbī lay through a forest.[9]

According to the *Devīpurāṇa* (Ch. 74) there were nine sacred forests (*araṇyas*), namely, Saindhava, Daṇḍakāraṇya, Naimiṣa, Kurujāṅgala, Utpalāraṇya (or Upalāvrita-araṇya), Jambumārga, Puṣkara and Himālaya. The Daṇḍakāraṇya, according to Pargiter, comprised all the forests from Bundelkhand to the Kriṣṇā.[10] According to the *Rāmāyāṇa* (Uttarakāṇḍa, Ch. 81) it was situated between the Vindhya and the Saivala mountains; a part of it was called Janasthāna. Rāmacandra lived here for a long time. According to the *Uttara-Rāmacarita* (Act 1) it was placed to the west of Janasthāna. Some hold this forest to be the same as Mahārāṣtra including Nagpur.[11] The *Lalitavistara* (p. 316) refers to the Daṇḍakavana in the Dakṣiṇāpatha. This forest remained burnt for many years. Even the grass did not grow there.

The Naimiṣāraṇya was the holy forest where sixty thousand sages (Ṛṣis) lived. Many *Purāṇas* were written here. It is the modern Nimsar, 20 miles from Sitapur and 45 miles to the north-west of Lucknow. It is a holy place of the Hindus frequented by pilgrims from all parts of India. According to the *Rāmāyaṇa* (Uttarakāṇḍa, Ch. 91) it is situated on the left bank of the Gomatī. The Kurujāṅgala was a forest-country situated in Sirhind north-west of Hastināpura. According to the *Mahābhārata* (Ādiparva, Ch. 26), Hastināpura, the capital of the Kurus, was situated in Kurujāṅgala. The entire Kurudeśa was called by this name, as we find in the *Mahābhārata* (Ādiparva, Ch. 201) and *Vāmana Purāṇa* (Ch. 32). The Utpalāraṇya, according to the *Mahābhārata* (Vanaparva, Ch. 87) was situated in Pañcāla. It was also known as Utpalavana. Here Sītā gave birth to Lava and Kuśa. Some have identified it with Bithoor, 14 miles from Cawnpore, where the hermitage of Vālmīki was situated.

---

1 *Sumaṅgalavilāsinī*, I, 309; *Saṃyutta*, I, 29-30.
2 *Sumaṅgalavilāsinī*, I, 309.
3 *Saṃyutta*, III, 95; *Vinaya*, I, 352; *Udāna*, IV, 5.
4 *Jātaka*, I, 52ff.; *Kathāvatthu*, 97, 559; *Manorathapūranī*, I, 10.
5 *Aṅg.*, IV, 213; *Dīgha*, II, 146ff.; *Majjhima*, I, 95; *Ibid.*, II, 91; *Saṃ.*, V, 437; *Dīgha*, II, 316; II, 164ff.
6 *Mahāvaṃsa*, XIX, 6; *Dīpavaṃsa*, XVI, 2.
7 *Samantapāsādikā*, III, 655.
8 B. C. Law, *India as described in early texts of Buddhism and Jainism*, p. 39.
9 Watters, *On Yuan Chwang*, I, 366.
10 *J.R.A.S.*, 1894, 242; cf. *Milinda*, 130.
11 R. G. Bhandarkar, *Early History of the Dekkan*, Sec. II.

The Jambumārga was situated between Puṣkara and Mount Abu according to the *Agni Purāṇa* (Ch. 109). The Puṣkara forest is situated at a distance of six miles from Ajmere. At the time of the *Mahābhārata* some Mleccha tribes lived near Puṣkara and the Himalaya (Sabhāparva, Ch. 27, 32).

The Himalayan forests were infested with wild animals. They are said to have abounded in elephants[1] living in herds, reptiles, pythons, snakes, birds, etc. The hollows in the mountains and hills served as dens for them.[2] The Kaliṅgāraṇya lay between the Godāvarī river on the south-west and Gaoliya branch of the Indravatī river on the north-west.[3] According to Rapson it existed between the Mahānadī and the Godāvarī.[4]

SIXTEEN GREAT STATES (*MAHAJANAPADAS*)

An account of sixteen great states in Jambudīpa is one of the most important topics of the historical geography of Ancient India. Here an attempt has been made to give a succinct and systematic account of them.

The *Aṅguttara Nikāya*[5] of the Pali *Sutta Piṭaka* mentions sixteen *Mahājanapadas* in Jambudīpa. They are as follows:—Aṅga, Magadha, Kāśī, Kośala, Vajji, Malla, Ceti, Vaṃsa, Kuru, Pañcāla, Maccha, Sūrasena, Assaka, Avantī,[6] Gandhāra and Kamboja, each named after the people who settled there or colonized it. As many as fourteen of these great states may be said to have been included in the Madhyadeśa, and the remaining two countries, Gandhāra and Kamboja, may be said to have been located in Uttarāpatha or Northern Division. The *Dīgha Nikāya*[7] gives a list of twelve only, omitting the last four, while the *Cullaniddesa*[8] adds Kaliṅga to the list and substitutes Yona for Gandhāra. The *Indriya-Jātaka*[9] mentions the following *janapadas*: Suraṭṭha (Surat), Lambacūḷaka, Avantī, Dakkhiṇāpatha, Daṇḍaka forest (Daṇḍakirañño), Kumbhavatī-nagara and the hill tract of Arañjara (Arañjaragiri) in the Majjhima-padesa.

It is interesting to note that according to the *Mārkaṇḍeya Purāṇa* (Ch. 57, 32–35) the countries in Madhyadeśa were Matsya, Kuśula, Kulya, Kuntala, Kāśī, Kośala, Arvuda, Pulinda, Samaka, Vṛka and Govardhana-pura. Avantī is included in Aparānta.

The Jaina *Bhagavatī Sūtra* (otherwise called *Vyākhyāprajñapti*) gives a slightly different list. They are as follows:—Aṅga, Baṅga (Vaṅga), Magaha (Magadha), Malaya, Mālava, Accha, Vaccha (Pali: Vaṃsa), Koccha, Pāḍha (?), Lāḍha (Rāḍha), Bajji (Pali: Vajjī), Moli (Malla ?), Kāsī,[10] Kosala, Avaha (Avāha ?) and Sambhuttara or Subhuttara (Sumhottara ?). The Jaina list seems to be later than the Buddhist list given in the *Aṅguttara Nikāya*.

---

1 Cf. McCrindle, *Ancient India as described by Megasthenes and Arrian*, p. 42.

2 B. C. Law, *India as described in early texts of Buddhism and Jainism*, 64ff.

3 Cunningham, *Ancient Geography*, p. 591.

4 *Ancient India*, p. 116.

5 *Aṅguttara*, Vol. I, p. 213; Vol. IV, 252, 256, 260.

6 Strictly speaking, Assaka at least, if not Avantī, as mentioned in early Buddhist texts, should be considered as situated in Dakkhiṇāpatha or the Deccan, for both the settlements found mentioned in Buddhist sources, lay outside the borders of the Majjhimadesa.

7 *Dīgha*, II, pp. 202-203; *Aṅga-Magadha, Kāsi-Kosala, Vajji-Malla, Ceti-Vaṃsa, Kuru-Pañcāla* and *Maccha-Sūrasena*.

8 *Niddesa*, P.T.S. ed., II, p. 37—*Aṅgā ca Magadhā ca Kaliṅgā ca Kāsī ca Kosalā ca Vajjī ca Mallā ca Cetī ca Vaṃsā ca Kurū ca Pañcālā ca Macchā ca Śūrasenā ca Assakā ca Avantī ca Yonā ca Kambojā ca.*

9 *Jātaka*, III, 463.

10 According to Weber's *Berlin Catalogue*, Vol. II, p. 439, No. 2, No. 13 will be *Kosī*.

The *Mahāvastu* has the traditional record of the sixteen big states of Jambudvīpa, but there is no enumeration of the list (*Jambudvīpe soḍaśahi mahājanapadehi*).[1] A similar reference is also found in the *Lalitavistara* without the traditional list (*sarvasmin Jambudvīpe soḍaśajānapadeṣu*—p. 22). A careful study of the *Mahāvastu* shows that in a different connection it enumerates a list of sixteen big states.[2] It is stated there that Gautama distributed knowledge among the people of Aṅga, Magadha, Vajjī, Malla, Kāśī, Kośala, Cedi, Vatsa, Matsya, Śūrasena, Kuru, Pañcāla, Sivi, Daśārṇa, Assaka and Avantī. This list differs from the Pali list inasmuch as it excludes Gandhāra and Kamboja but includes Sivi and Daśārṇa. The order of the enumeration is also somewhat different.

An interesting account of the tribal characteristics of the peoples of different *janapadas* is given in the Karṇaparva of the *Mahābhārata*. There the following tribes are mentioned to have been inhabitants of their respective *janapadas* named after them: the Kauravas, the Pañcālas, the Śālvas, the Matsyas, the Naimiṣas, the Cedis, the Śūrasenas, the Magadhas, the Kośalas, the Aṅgas, the Gandharvas, and the Madrakas.

Aṅga.—The kingdom of Aṅga had its capital named Campā, situated on the river of the same name[3] (modern Chāndan) and the Ganges[4] at a distance of 60 yojanas from the Videhan capital named Mithilā.[5] The ancient name of Campā was Mālinī or Mālina.[6] It was built by Mahāgovinda.[7] Its actual site is marked by the villages named Campānagara and Campāpurī which still exist near Bhagalpur. Campā gradually increased in wealth, and traders sailed from here to Suvarṇabhūmi (Lower Burma) for the purpose of trade. It was one of the six great cities of India. It was a big town and not a village, as it was mentioned as such by Ānanda while requesting the Master to obtain *parinirvāṇa* in one of the big cities.[8] It had a watch-tower, walls and gates.[9] The kingdom of Aṅga had 80,000 villages and Campā was one of them.[10] Among the seven political divisions into which India was divided according to the *Dīgha-Nikāya* (II, 235), Aṅga was one of them having Campā as its capital. Campā was ruled by Aśoka's son Mahinda, his sons and grandsons.[11] It was here the Master prescribed the use of slippers by monks.[12]

According to the *Mahābhārata* Aṅga may be supposed to have comprised the districts of Bhagalpur and Monghyr, and extended northwards up to the river Kośī. At one time the kingdom of Aṅga included Magadha and probably extended up to the sea. The *Mahābhārata*, however, further tells us that Aṅga was so called after its king Aṅga,[13] who seems to be identical with Aṅga Vairocanī mentioned in the *Aitareya Brāhmaṇa* (VIII. 4, 22). According to the *Rāmāyaṇa* Aṅga or body of Kāmadeva (love god) was consumed here and the country was therefore called Aṅga. Āpana is mentioned as a township in Aṅguttarāpa, a tract which lay north of the river Mahī, evidently a part of Aṅga on the other side of that river (*Paramatthajotikā*, II, 437; Malalasekera, *Dict. of Pali Proper Names*, p. 22). The way from Bhaddiya to Āpana lay through Aṅguttarāpa (*Vinaya*, I, 243ff.; *Dhammapada Commy.*, III, 363).

Aṅga was a powerful kingdom before the time of the Buddha. Once Magadha came under the sway of Aṅga (*Jāt.*, VI, 272). There was a river

---

1 Vol. II, p. 2. 2 Vol. I, p. 34. 3 *Jātaka*, No. 506.
4 Watters, *On Yuan Chwang*, II, 181; *Daśakumāracarita*, II, 2.
5 *Jātaka*, VII, 32.
6 *Mbh.*, XII, 5, 6-7; *Matsya*, 48, 97; *Vāyu*, 99, 105-6; *Hariv.*, 32, 49.
7 *Dīgha*, II, 235. 8 *Ibid.*, II, 146. 9 *Jātaka*, No. 539.
10 *Vinaya Piṭaka*, I, 179. 11 *Dīpavaṃsa*, 28. 12 *Vinaya*, I, 179ff.
13 Ādiparva, CIV, 4179ff.

between Aṅga and Magadha, inhabitated by a Nāgarājā who helped the Magadhan king to bring Aṅga under his sway by defeating and killing the King of Aṅga. King Manoja of Brahmavaḍḍhana (another name of Benaras) conquered Aṅga and Magadha. In Buddha's time Aṅga lost her political power for good. Aṅga and Magadha were constantly at war during this period (*Jāt.*, IV, 454-5). That Aṅga became subject to Śreṇiya Bimbisāra is proved by the fact that a certain brahmin named Sonadaṇḍa lived at Campā on the grant made by king Bimbisāra and enjoyed the revenues of the town which was given to him by the king (*Dīgha Nikāya*, I, 111).

Queen Gaggarā of Campā dug a tank called Gaggarāpokkharaṇī (*Sumaṅgalavilāsinī*, I, p. 279). The Buddha dwelt on its bank with a large company of monks while he was at Campā (*Dīgha*, I, 111ff.). His activities in Aṅga and Campā may be known from the *Vinaya Piṭaka* (I, 312–15). The Master while dwelling in the city of Assapura belonging to the kingdom of Aṅga, preached the *Mahā* and *Culla Assapura Suttantas* to the monks (*Majjhima*, I, 281ff.). In course of his journey from Rājagṛha to Kapilavastu the Master was followed by many sons of the householders of Aṅga and Magadha (*Jāt.*, I, 87). The Himalayan sages came to the city of Kāḷa-Campā in Aṅga to enjoy cooked food (*Jāt.*, VI, 256). Aggidatta, the chaplain of king Mahākosala, father of Pasenadi-Kosala, lived in Aṅga and Magadha after giving up his household life and he was given charities by the people of these two kingdoms (*Dhammapada Commy.*, III, 241ff.).

Aṅga was a prosperous country inhabitated by many merchants who used to go to trade with many caravans full of merchandise to Sindhu-Sovīradesa (*Vimānavatthu Commy.*, 332, 337).

According to the *Aśokāvadāna* (R. L. Mitra, *Nepalese Buddhist Literature*, p. 8) a brahmin of Campāpurī presented king Bindusāra, while he was ruling at Pāṭaliputra, with a daughter named Subhadrāṅgī. The *Lalitavistara* (pp. 125-26) refers to a script or alphabet of the Aṅga country which the Bodhisattva is said to have mastered.

Magadha.—Magadha roughly corresponds to the modern Patna and Gaya districts of Bihar. It is described as a beautiful city with all kinds of gems.[1] In Vedic, Brāhmaṇa and Sūtra periods Magadha was considered to have been outside the pale of Aryan and Brahmanical culture, and was therefore looked down upon by Brahmanical writers, but Magadha has always been included in the Madhyadeśa as the Buddhist holy land.

Girivraja or ancient Rājagṛha was the earliest capital. It was also known as Vasumatī,[2] Bārhadrathapura,[3] Māgadhapura,[4] Varāha, Vṛsabha, Ṛṣigiri, Caityaka,[5] Bimbisārapurī,[6] and Kuśāgārapura.[7] The Ṛgveda mentions a territory called Kīkaṭa which has been alluded to as identical with Magadha in later works.[8]

The Magadha country seems to have had a separate alphabet which the Bodhisattva is said to have mastered.[9]

Giribbaja (Skt. Girivraja) was encircled by five hills, namely, Isigili, Vepulla (Vaṅkaka and Supana),[10] Vebhāra, Paṇḍava and Gijjhakūṭa.[11]

---

1 *Divyāvadāna*, 425.
2 *Rāmāyaṇa*, I, 32, 7.
3 *Mahābhārata*, II, 24–44.
4 *Mbh.*, II, 20, 30.
5 *P.H.A.I.*, p. 70.
6 B. C. Law, *The Life and Work of Buddhaghosa*, p. 87 n.
7 Beal, *The Life of Yuan Chwang*, p. 113.
8 *Bhāgavata Purāṇa*, I, 3, 24; Cf. *Abhidhānacintāmaṇi*, *Kīkaṭā-Magadhāḥ-vayāḥ*.
9 *Lalitavistara*, 125-126.
10 *Saṃyutta*, II, 191-92.
11 *Vimānavatthu Commy.*, p. 82.

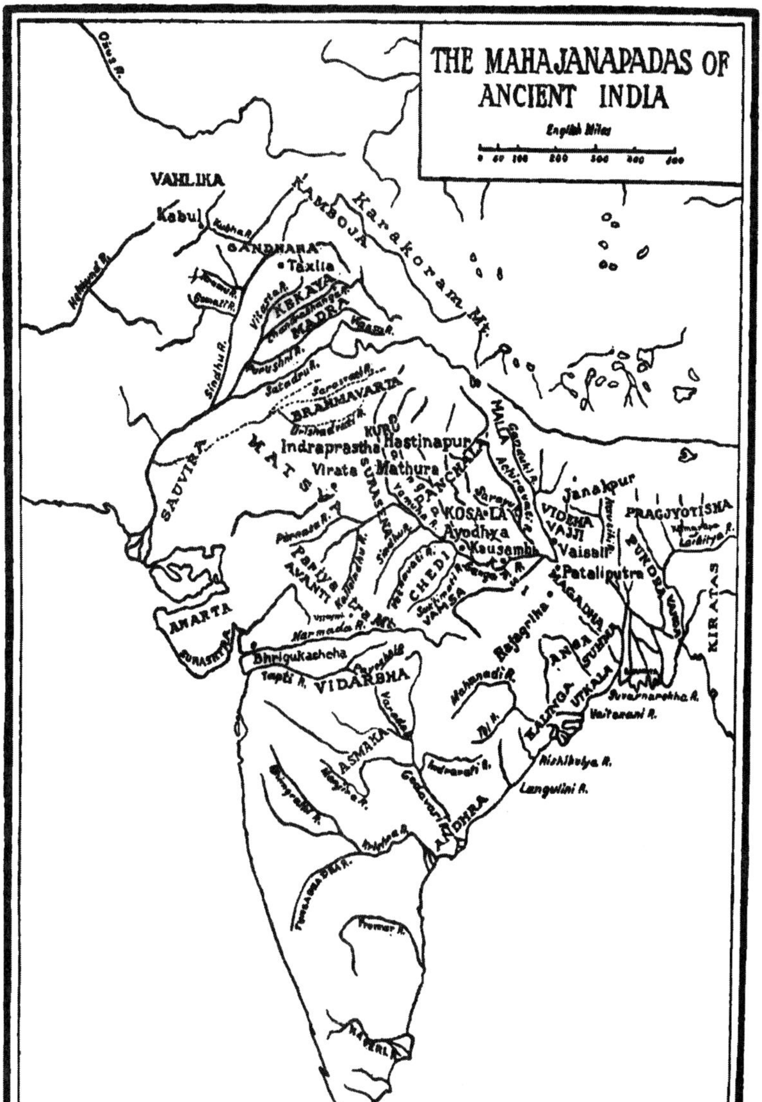
THE MAHAJANAPADAS OF ANCIENT INDIA
English Miles
VAHLIKA
Kabul
KAMBOJA
Karakoram Mt.
GANDHARA
Taxila
KEKAYA
MADRA
BRAHMAVARTA
KURU
Indraprastha
Hastinapur
MATSYA
Virata
Mathura
SURASENA
PANCHALA
MALLA
KOSALA
Ayodhya
Kausambi
Janakpur
VIDEHA
VAJJI
Vaisali
PRAGJYOTISHA
PUNDRA
Pataliputra
MAGADHA
KIRATAS
SAUVIRA
AVANTI
CHEDI
VAMSA
ANARTA
SURASHTRA
Bhrigukachcha
Narmada R.
Rajagriha
ANGA
VIDARBHA
Tapti R.
Mahanadi R.
KALINGA
UTKALA
ASMAKA
Godavari R.
ANDHRA
Krishna R.
Indravati R.
Langulini R.
KERALA

During the reign of king Bimbisāra Magadha contained 80,000 villages, and the river Tapodā flowed by this ancient city.[1] Senānigāma[2] which was a very nice village of Magadha, Ekanālā[3] inhabited by brahmins including Bhāradvāja who was later converted by the Buddha, Nālakagāma[4] where Sāriputta delivered a discourse to a wandering ascetic named Jambukhādaka, Khānumata[5] which was also inhabited by brahmins, and Siddhattagāma[6] were some of the villages of Magadha.

Magadha was an important centre of Buddhism. Here Sāriputta and Moggallāna were converted by the Buddha to his faith.[7] Almost all the missionaries who were sent to different places to preach Aśoka's *Dhamma*, belonged to Magadha.[8] Bimbisāra was a staunch follower of the Buddha. The Buddha while he was at Rājagṛha told the king that he would pay a visit to Vaiśālī. The king then prepared a road for the Buddha and caused the ground from Rājagṛha to the Ganges to be made smooth.[9]

Rājagriha was burnt down by fire during the reign of Bimbisāra when another new capital city called the new Rājagṛha was built. Yuan Chwang points out that when Kuśāgārapura or Kuśāgrapura (probably named after the early Magadha king Kuśāgra),[10] was afflicted by fires, the king went to the cemetery and built the new city of Rājagṛha. Fa-Hien, however, says that it was Ajātaśatru, and not Bimbisāra, who built the new city.

A Buddhist Council was held at Rājagṛha.[11] Rājagriha had a gate which used to be closed in the evening, and nobody, not even the king, was allowed to enter it.[12] It had also a fort which was once repaired by Ajātaśatru's minister Vassakāra. Really speaking Rājagriha was provided with 64 gates.[13]

Veluvana and Kalandakanivāpa which belonged to Rājagaha have often been referred to as dwelling places of the Master. The Nāradagrāma,[14] Kukkuṭārāmavihāra,[15] Gṛdhrakūṭa hill, Yaṣṭivana,[16] Uruvilvagrāma, Prabhāsavana,[17] and Kolitagrāma—all these important localities in and around the city of Rājagṛha are intimately connected with the Buddha and Buddhism.

In Aśoka's time Pāṭaliputra was the Magadhan capital. He is said to have a daily income of four hundred thousand Kahāpaṇas from the four gates of this city.[18]

During the early Buddhist period Magadha was an important political and commercial centre, and the people from all parts of Northern India flocked to this city for trade and commerce. Many merchants passed through this city or dwelt in it for trade.

Magadha can rightfully claim Jīvaka as its citizen, who became the court physician of king Bimbisāra,[19] after qualifying himself as a physician from the university of Taxila.[20] He cured the jaundice of king Pradyota of Avantī being sent by king Bimbisāra of Magadha.

---

1 *Vinaya Piṭaka*, I, 29; IV, 116-17.
2 *Majjhima*, I, 166-67.
3 *Saṃyutta*, I, 172-73.
4 *Ibid.*, IV, 251–260.
5 *Dīgha*, I, 127ff.
6 Rockhill, *Life of the Buddha*, 250.
7 *Kathāvatthu*, I, 89.
8 *Samantapāsādikā*, I, 63.
9 *Dhammapada Commy.*, III, 439-40.
10 Pargiter, *A.I.H.T.*, p. 149.
11 Cullavagga, 11th Khandhaka.
12 *Vinaya Piṭaka*, IV, 116-17.
13 B. C. Law, *Rājagriha in Ancient Literature*, 8ff.
14 R. L. Mitra, *N.B.L.*, p. 45.
15 *Ibid.*, pp. 9-10.
16 *Mahāvastu*, III, 441.
17 R. L. Mitra, *N.B.L.*, p. 166.
18 *Samantapāsādikā*, I, 52.
19 *Vinaya Piṭaka*, II, 184-85.
20 *Vinaya Texts*, S.B.E., II, 174.

The Ganges formed the boundary between the kingdom of Magadha and the republican country of the Licchavis. Both the Magadhas and the Licchavis had equal rights over this river.[1] The river Campā flowing between Aṅga and Magadha formed the boundary between the two kingdoms.[2]

The two kingdoms of Aṅga and Magadha were engaged in battles from time to time.[3] Once the king of Benaras conquered both Aṅga and Magadha.[4] The Magadhan kingdom once came under the suzerainty of Aṅga.[5] There was a war between Pasenadi of Kosala and Ajātasattu of Magadha with the result that Ajātasattu succeeded in extending his sway over the Magadhas with the help of the Licchavis.[6] During the reign of Ajātasattu Magadha also came into conflict with Vesālī of the Vajjis. Under Bimbisāra and Ajātasattu Magadha rose to such eminence that centuries later till Aśoka's Kaliṅga war the history of Northern India is practically the history of Magadha.

Magadha maintained friendly relations by marriage and other alliances not only with the northern neighbours but also with the *mahājanapada* of Gandhāra from whose king Pakkusāti she received an embassy and a letter.

Kāśī.—Kāśī was one of the sixteen *mahājanapadas.* Bārāṇasī was the capital of the people of Kāśī. It was known by various other names, namely, Surundhana, Sudassana, Brahmavaḍḍhana, Pupphavatī, Ramma and Molinī.[7] It was twelve yojanas in extent.[8] Bārāṇasī is said to have been situated on the bank of the river Varaṇā.[9] The city is described as prosperous, extensive and populous.[10] It was not troubled by deceitful and quarrelsome people.[11]

The earliest mention of the Kāśīs as a tribal people seems to be met with in the Paippalāda recension of the *Atharvaveda*. Patañjali in his *Mahābhāṣya* (Ed. Kielhorn, Vol. II, p. 413) mentions Kāśī cloth. The city of Kāśī is stated to have been situated on the Varaṇāvatī river.[12] According to the *Rāmāyaṇa* it was not a city, but a kingdom.[13] According to the *Vāyu Purāṇa*, the kingdom of Kāśī seems to have been extended up to the river Gomatī. Before the Buddha's time Kāśī was a great political power. It was the most powerful kingdom in the whole of Northern India.[14] Sometimes Kāśī extended its suzerain power over Kośala, and sometimes Kośala conquered Kāśī, but in the Buddha's time Kāśī lost its political power. It was incorporated into the Kosalan kingdom for some time and for sometime into the Magadhan kingdom. There were fights between Pasenadi of Kośala and Ajātasattu of Magadha for the possession of Kāśī. Kāśī was finally conquered and incorporated into the Magadhan kingdom. Ajātasattu became the most powerful king of Northern India after defeating the Kosalans.[15]

The city of Benaras was hallowed by the feet of the Buddha who came here to preach his excellent doctrine. Here he gave his first discourse on the *Dhammacakka* or the Wheel of Law in the Deer Park near Benaras (*Majjhima*, I, 170ff.; *Saṃyutta*, V, 420ff.; *Kathāvatthu*, 97, 559; *Saundaranandakāvya*, III, vs. 10-11; *Buddhacaritak.*, XV, v. 87; *Lalitavistara*,

---

[1] *Divyāvadāna*, p. 55.
[2] *Jātaka*, IV, 454.
[3] *Ibid.*, IV, 454-55.
[4] *Jātaka*, V, 315ff.
[5] *Jāt.*, VI, 272; *Dīgha Nikāya*, I,—Sonadaṇḍa Suttanta.
[6] *Saṃyutta Nikāya*, I, 83–85.
[7] *Jātaka*, IV, 119-20; IV, 15.
[8] *Ibid.*, VI, 160.
[9] *Mahāvastu*, III, 402.
[10] *Divyāvadāna*, p. 73.
[11] *Ibid.*, p. 98.
[12] *C.H.I.*, p. 117.
[13] Ādikāṇḍa, XII, 20.
[14] *Jātaka*, III, 115ff.; *Vinaya Texts*, Pt. II, 30ff.; *Jāt.*, I, 262ff.
[15] *Saṃyutta*, I, 82–85.

412-13). The Buddha spent a great part of his life at Benaras, and here he delivered some of the most important discourses and converted many people (*Aṅg.*, I, 110ff., 279-280; III, 320–322, 392, 399ff.; *Saṃ.*, I, 105-106; *Vin. Texts*, I, 102–108, 110–112).

Benaras was a great centre of trade and commerce. Rich merchants of the city used to cross high seas with ships, laden with merchandise (cf. *Mahāvastu*, III, 286). A wealthy merchant came to Benaras with the object of trade (*Mahāvastu*, II, 166-167). There existed trade relations between Benaras and Śrāvastī, and between Benaras and Taxila (*Dhammapada Commy.*, III, 429; I, 123). The people of Benaras used to go to Taxila to learn arts and sciences (*Jāt.*, II, 47).

Kośala.—Kośala, during the time of early Buddhism, was an important kingdom. The ancient Kośala kingdom was divided into two divisions, the river Sarayū serving as the wedge between the two: that to the north was called the Uttarakośala and the one to the south was called Dakṣiṇa Kośala. (R. L. Mitra, *N.B.L.*, p. 20.) The Buddha spent much of his time at Śrāvastī, the capital of Kośala. He delivered a series of sermons at Sālā, a brahmin village of Kośala, and the brahmin householders were converted to the new faith (*Majjhima*, I, 285ff.). The brahmins of Nagaravinda, another brahmin village of Kośala, were also converted by the Master (*Majjhima*, III, 290ff.). The brahmin householders of the brahmin village of Venāgapura also accepted the Master's creed (*Aṅg.*, I, 180ff.). A famous Kosalan teacher named Bāvarī built a hermitage on the bank of the river Godāvarī in the kingdom of Assaka. He went to the Buddha who was then in Kośala with another brahmin to have his dispute settled by the Master (*Suttanipāta*, 190–192).

Kośala had matrimonial alliances with the neighbouring powers. A Kosalan prince married a daughter of the king of Benaras (*Jāt.*, III, 211–213). Mahākośala, father of Pasenadi, gave his daughter in marriage to Bimbisāra of Magadha (*Jāt.*, II, 237; IV, 342ff.). A fierce fight took place between the sons of Mahākośala and Bimbisāra, Pasenadi and Ajātasattu respectively. But the two kings came into a sort of agreement. Ajātasattu married Vajirā, daughter of Pasenadi and got possession of Kāśī (*Saṃ*, I, 82–85; *Jāt.*, IV, 342ff.). The Śākyas of Kapilavastu became the vassals of king Pasenadi of Kośala (*Dialogues of the Buddha*, Pt. III, p. 80).

The capital cities of Kośala were Śrāvastī and Sāketa. According to the Epics and some Buddhist works Ayodhyā seems to have been the earliest capital, and Sāketa the next. In the Buddha's time Ayodhyā became an unimportant town (*Buddhist India*, p. 34), but Sāketa and Śrāvastī were two of the six great cities of India (Cf. *Mahāparinibbāna Suttanta*). Some think that Sāketa and Ayodhyā were identical but Rhys Davids points out that both the cities existed in the Buddha's time. Besides Sāketa and Śrāvastī there were other minor towns like Setavya and Ukkaṭṭha in Kośala proper. It was at Śrāvastī that the Buddha permitted the womenfolk to enter the Buddhist Saṃgha (*Majjhima*, III, 270ff.). The great banker named Anāthapiṇḍika and Visākhā-Migāramātā, the most liberal-hearted lady, were inhabitants of Śrāvastī. Anāthapiṇḍika made a gift of his Jetavana grove to the Lord. The Master is said to have once taken up his residence there (*Mahāvastu*, III, 101).

A good number of famous monks and nuns belonged to Śrāvastī (*Dhammapada Commentary*, II, 260ff., 270ff., *Ibid.*, I, 115; *Theragāthā*, p. 2; *Therīgāthā*, p. 124).

Vajjis.—The Vajjis were included into the eight confederate clans (*aṭṭhakulakā*) among whom the Videhans, the Licchavis and the Vajjis themselves became famous. The other confederate clans were probably the Jñātrikas, Ugras, Bhojas and Aikshvākas. The eighth one is unknown. The Vajji (Vriji) is referred to by Pāṇini in his *Aṣṭādhyāyī* (IV. 2. 131). Kauṭilya distinghishes the Vrijikas from the Licchavikas. The Vrijika was not only the name of the confederacy but also of one of the constituent clans. The Vajjīs like the Licchavis are often associated with the city of Vaiśālī which was not only the capital of the Licchavis but also the metropolis of the entire confederacy. It was so called because of its extensiveness.[1] It had three districts. It may be identified with Besarh in the Muzaffarpur district of Bihar. In Buddha's time this city was encompassed by three walls at a distance of a *gāvuta* from one another and at three places there were gates with watch towers and buildings. The Buddha once visited it being invited by the Licchavis. This city was gay, opulent, prosperous and populous, charming and delightful. It had many buildings, pinnacled buildings, pleasure grounds and lotus ponds,[2] triumphal arches, covered courtyards, etc. The city really rivalled the domain of the immortals in beauty.[3] It was well provided with food. Alms were easily obtainable, harvest was good, and one could earn his living by gleaning or through favour.[4] The inhabitants of Vaiśālī made a rule that daughters of individuals should be enjoyed by *gaṇas* and should not therefore be married.[5]

A road lay from Vaiśālī to Rājagṛha, and another from Vaiśālī to Kapilavastu. Many Śākya ladies from Kapilavastu came to receive ordination from the Buddha who was then dwelling in the Mahāvana.[6] The Buddhist Council held at Vaiśālī is important in the history of Buddhism.[7]

The Licchavis of Vaiśālī made a gift of many *caityas* or shrines to the Buddha and the Buddhist Church. Ambapālī, the famous courtezan of Vaiśālī, also presented her extensive mango-grove to the Buddhist congregation.[8]

Buddha's activities were not only confined to Magadha and Kośala but also to Vaiśālī. Many of his discourses were delivered here either at the mango-grove of Ambapālī or at the Kūṭāgārasālā in the Mahāvana.

The Vajjīs formed the *saṃgha* or *gaṇa*. In other words, they were governed by organized corporation.[9] There existed concord and amity among the Licchavis.[10] The Buddha prophesied that as long as the Licchavis would remain strenuous, diligent, zealous and active, prosperity would be with them, and not adversity. He further foretold that if the Licchavis would be given to luxury and indolence, they were sure to be conquered by the Magadhan king Ajātasattu.[11]

The Political relation between Magadha and Vaiśālī was friendly. That Ajātasattu is called Vaidehīputra goes to show that Bimbisāra established matrimonial alliance with the Licchavis by marrying a Licchavi girl.[12] The Licchavis were also on friendly terms with king Prasenajit of Kośala.[13]

The Magadhan king Ajātasattu made up his mind to destroy the Vajjian power. The immediate cause that led to the outbreak of the war

---

1 *Papañcasūdanī*, II, p. 19.
2 *Vinaya Texts*, S.B.E., II, 171; *Lalitavistara*, Ed. Lefmann, Ch. III, p. 21.
3 *Mahāvastu*, I, 253ff.
4 *Vinaya Texts*, II, p. 117.
5 *Bodhisattvāvadāna-kalpalatā*, 20 pallava, p. 38.
6 *Vinaya Texts*, II, 210-11; III, 321ff.
7 *Ibid.*, III, 386ff.
8 Law, *Mahāvastu*, p. 44.
9 *Majjhima*, I, 231.
10 *Buddhist Suttas*, S.B.E., Vol. XI, pp. 3-4.
11 *Samyutta*, II, pp. 267-68.
12 *Samyutta*, II, 268; *Sumaṅgalavilāsinī*, I, 47; *Papañcasūdanī*, I, 125; *Sāratthappakāsinī*, II, 215; *Divyāvadāna*, p. 55.
13 *Majjhima*, II, pp. 100-101.

between him and the Licchavis was that there existed a port near the Ganges, half of which belonged to Ajātasattu and half to the Licchavis. There was a mine of precious substance at the foot of the mountain standing not far from it. Ajātasattu found the Licchavis too powerful to crush. So he sent his ministers, Sunīdha and Vassakāra, to sow the seed of dissension among them. Vassakāra was successful in bringing about disunion among the Licchavi princes. Thus the Licchavis were destroyed by Ajātasattu.[1]

Malla.—The kingdom of the Mallas was divided into two parts which had Kuśāvatī or Kuśīnārā and Pāvā as their capital cities. Kuśīnārā may be identified with Kasia on the smaller Gandak and in the east of the Gorakhpur district, and Pāvā with a village named Padaraona, twelve miles to the north-east of Kāsiā. The Śāla grove of the Mallas where the Buddha died, was situated near Hiraṇyavatī, identified probably with Gandak.[2] When the Mallas had a monarchial constitution, their capital city was known as Kuśāvatī, but in the Buddha's time when the monarchy was replaced by a republican constitution, the name of the city was changed to Kuśīnārā. The *Mahāparinibbāna Suttanta* refers to Kuśīnārā as a small town, but the Blessed One selected it as the place of his passing away by narrating the former glories of Kuśāvatī. He himself said that Kuśīnārā was ancient Kuśāvatī.[3]

The Mallas had a *Saṃgharājya*. The political relation between the Mallas and the Licchavis was on the whole friendly, but there were occasional rivalries.[4] Buddhism appears to have attracted many followers among the Mallas.[5]

Cedi.—The ancient Cedi country lay near the Jumna. It corresponds roughly to the modern Bundelkhand and the adjoining region. The capital of the Cedi country was Sotthivatīnagara, probably identical with the city of Śuktimati of the *Mahābhārata*.[6] Sahajāti and Tripurī were other important towns of the Cedi kingdom.[7] The road from Kāśī to Cedi was unsafe.[8] The *Cetaràṣṭra* was 30 yojanas distant from Jetuttaranagara, the birthplace of Vessantara.[9] It was an important centre of Buddhism.[10] Anuruddha while dwelling among the Cedis won Arahatship.[11] The Buddha went to the Cedis to preach his doctrine.[12]

Vaṃsa.—The kingdom of the Vaṃsas or Vatsas had Kauśāmbī as their capital, identical with modern Kosam near Allahabad. It had the Bharga state of Sumsumāragiri as its dependency.[13] The city of Kauśāmbī was built at the site of the hermitage of one Kuśāmba.[14] The origin of the Vatsa people is traced to a king of Kāśī.[15] Kauśāmbī is mentioned as one of the great cities where the Blessed One should attain the *Mahāparinibbāna*. The city of Kauśāmbī was visited by the followers of Bāvarī, a leader of the Jaṭilas.[16] Piṇḍola Bhāradvāja dwelt at Ghositārāma at Kauśāmbī. He was the son of the chaplain to king Udena of Kauśāmbī.[17]

---

1 *Dīgha Nikāya*, II, 72ff.

2 Smith, *E.H.I.*, 167 n.

3 *Dīgha*, II, pp. 146-47.

4 Cf. The story of Bandhula; Law, *Some Kṣatriya Tribes of Ancient India*, pp. 160-61.

5 *Vinaya Texts*, III, 4ff.; II, 139; *Psalms of the Brethren*, 80, 90.

6 *Mbh.*, III, 20, 50 and XIV, 83. 2.

7 *Aṅg.*, III, 355.

8 *Jāt.*, No. 48.

9 *Jāt.*, VI, 514-15.

10 *Aṅg.*, III, 355-56; V, 41ff.; 157-61.

11 *Ibid.*, IV, 228ff.

12 *Dīgha*, II, 200, 201, 203.

13 Bhandarkar, *Carmichael Lectures*, 1918, p. 63; *Jāt.*, No. 353.

14 Law, *Saundarananda-Kāvya*, Tr. into Bengali, p. 9.

15 *Hariv.*, 29, 73; *Mbh.*, XII, 49, 80.

16 *Suttani. Commy.*, II, 584.

17 *Psalms of the Brethren*, pp. 110-11.

A conversation on religious subjects took place between king Udena of Kosambī and Piṇḍola Bhāradvāja.[1] The Buddha while he was at Ghositārāma gave discourses on *Dhamma*, *Vinaya*, etc.[2]

Kuru.—There was a janapada named Kuru and its kings used to be called Kurus.[3] The ancient literature refers to two Kuru countries, Uttarakuru and Dakṣiṇakuru. The Buddha delivered some profound discourses to the Kurus in one of the Kuru towns named Kammāsadhamma. The thera Raṭṭhapāla was a Kuru noble who is mentioned in the *Majjhima Nikāya* as holding a religious discussion with king Koravya.[4] As to the origin of the Kurus a Cakkavattī king of Jambudīpa named Mandhātā conquered Pubba Videha, Aparagoyāna and Uttarakuru. While returning from Uttarakuru a large number of the inhabitants of that country followed Mandhātā to Jambudīpa, and the place in Jambudīpa where they settled became known as Kururāṣṭra.[5] A large number of people in the Kuru country embraced Buddhism after listening to a number of religious discourses delivered by the Buddha.[6]

The ancient Kuru country may be said to have comprised Kurukṣetra or Thaneswar. The district included Sonapat, Amin, Karnal and Panipat, and was situated between the Sarasvatī on the north and the Dṛṣadvatī on the south. The Kuru country was 300 leagues in extent and the capital city of Indraprastha extended over 7 leagues.[7]

The *Bodhisattvāvadāna-Kalpalatā*[8] definitely states that Hastināpura was the capital of Kuru kings. King Arjuna of Hastināpura was in the habit of killing those holy men who were unable to satisfy him by answers to the questions put by him.[9] Sudhanu, son of Suvāhu, another king of Hastināpura, fell in love with a *kinnarī* in a distant country and came back with her to the capital where he had long been associated with his father in the government of the kingdom.[10]

Pañcāla.—The Pañcāla country was divided into two divisions, northern Pañcāla and southern Pañcāla, the Bhāgīrathī forming the dividing line. The Vedic texts refer to the eastern (Prācya Pañcāla) and western divisions of the country.[11] The Pañcālas were known as Krivis in the *Śatapatha Brāhmaṇa*. According to the *Divyāvadāna* (p. 435) the capital of Uttara Pañcāla was Hastināpura, but the *Kumbhakāra Jātaka* mentions Kāmpilyanagara (Kampillanagara) as its capital.[12] According to *Mahābhārata* (138, 73-74) northern Pañcāla had its capital at Ahicchatra, identical with modern Ramnagar in the Bareilly district, while southern Pañcāla had its capital at Kāmpilya, identical with modern Kampil in the Farukhabad district. Sometimes Uttara Pañcāla was included in the Kururāṣṭra,[13] and had its capital at Hastināpura; at other times it formed a part of the Kāmpilyarāṣṭra.[14] Sometimes kings of Kāmpilyarāṣṭra had court at Uttara Pañcālanagara; at other times kings of Uttara Pañcālarāṣṭra had court at Kāmpilya.[15] Visākha who was the son of the daughter of the king of the Pañcālas, succeeded in his title on the death of his father.

---

1 *Sam.*, IV, pp. 110–12.
2 *Vinaya Texts*, III, p. 233.
3 *Papañcasūdanī*, I, 25.
4 *Majjhima*, II, 65ff.
5 *Papañcasūdanī*, I, 225-26.
6 *Aṅguttara*, V, 29–32; *Saṃyutta*, II, 92-93, 107ff.; *Majjhima*, I, 55ff., 501ff.; II, 261ff.; *Dīgha*, II, 55ff.
7 *Jātaka*, No. 537.
8 3rd pallava, 116; 64th pallava, p. 9.
9 *Mahāvastu*, III, 361.
10 *Mahāvastu*, II, 94-95.
11 *Vedic Index*, I, 469—*Saṃhitopaniṣad Brāhmaṇa*.
12 Cowell, *Jātaka*, III, 230.
13 *Jātaka*, No. 505.
14 *Jātaka*, Nos. 323, 513, 520.
15 *Ibid.*, No. 408; *P.H.A.I.*, p. 85.

He renounced the world after listening to the Buddha's discourse on *Dhamma.*[1]

Pañcāla was originally the country north and west of Delhi from the foot of the Himalayas to the Chambal. It roughly corresponds to modern Budaun, Farukhabad and the adjoining districts.

Matsya.—The Matsya country comprises the modern territory of Jaipur. It included the whole of the present territory of Alwar with a portion of Bharatpur. According to the *Ṛgveda,*[2] the country of the Matsyas lay to the south or south-west of Indraprastha and to the south of Śūrasena. Virāṭanagara or Vairāṭa was its capital, so-called because it was the capital of Virāṭa, king of the Matsyas.

Śūrasena.—The Śūrasenas had Mathurā as their capital on the Jumna. Mathurā is generally identified with Maholi, 5 miles to the south-west of the present town of Mathurā, which should be distinguished from Madhurā or Madurā, the second capital of the Pandyan kingdom on the river Vaigi in Madras. They witnessed a dice-play between Dhanañjaya Korabba and Puṇṇaka Yakkha.[3] The ancient Greek writers refer to the Śūrasena country as Sourasenoi and its capital as Methora. Buddhism was predominant in Mathurā for several centuries. Mahākaccāyana delivered a discourse on caste in Mathurā.[4] The Buddha while proceeding from Mathurā to Verañji halted under a tree and he was worshipped by many householders there.

Mathurā was built by Śatrughna, the brother of Rāma. A son of Śatrughna was Śūrasena after whom the country was so called.[5] The Epic and Pauranic story of Kamsa's attempt to make himself a tyrant of Mathurā by overpowering the Yādavas and his death at the hands of Śrīkṛṣṇa is not only mentioned by Patañjali but also in the Ghata-Jātaka.[6]

Mathurā must have formed a part of the Maurya empire when Megasthenes wrote about the Śūrasenas. It again became important as a centre of Buddhist religion and culture during the Kuṣāṇa supremacy. Many images of Buddhas and Bodhisattvas have been unearthed here.[7]

Assaka.—Assaka was a *mahājanapada* of Jambudvīpa, which had Potana or Potali as its capital. Potana was the Paudanya of the *Mahābhārata* (I. 77, 47). There is a mention in the *Suttanipāta* (V. 977) of another Assaka country in the Dakṣiṇāpatha. The brahmin Bāvarī lived on the banks of the Godāvarī in the Assaka territory in close proximity to Aḷaka or Muḷaka. King Kāliṅga of Dantapura and king Assaka of Potana were not on friendly terms, but they later lived amicably.[8] A king of the Assaka territory was ordained by Mahākaccāyana.[9] In the Hāthigumphā Inscription of king Khāravela we find that king Khāravela caused a large army to move towards the west and strike terror into Asaka or Asikanagara. The Assaka of the Cullakāliṅga Jātaka and the Asikanagara of the Hāthigumphā Inscription are probably identical with the Assaka of the *Suttanipāta*, which is located on the Godāvarī. Assaka represents the Sanskrit Aśmaka or Aśvaka which is mentioned by Asaṅga in his *Sūtrālaṅkāra* as a country in the basin of the Indus.

Asaṅga's Aśmaka seems therefore to be identical with the kingdom Assakenus of the Greek writers, which lay to the east of the Sarasvatī at

---

[1] *Psalms of the Brethren*, pp. 152-53; cf. *Thera-therīgāthā*, (P.T.S.), p. 27.
[2] VII, 18, 6; cf. Gopatha-Brāhmaṇa, 1, 2, 9. (*Bibliotheca Indica Series*, p. 30—R. L. Mitra's Ed.).
[3] Cowell, *Jātaka*, VI, 137.
[4] *Majjhima Nikāya*, II, 83ff.
[5] *C.A.G.I.*, p. 706.
[6] *Jātaka*, No. 454.
[7] Law, 'Mathurā in Ancient India,' *J.R.A.S.B., Letters*, Vol. XIII, No. 1, 1947.
[8] *Jātaka*, III, 3-5.
[9] *Vimānavatthu Commy.*, 259ff.

a distance of about 25 miles from the sea on the Swat Valley. The Aśmakas are placed in the north-west by the authors of the *Mārkaṇḍeya Purāṇa* and *Bṛhat Saṃhitā*. In early Pali texts Assaka has always been associated with Avantī. Bhaṭṭasvāmī, the commentator of the Kauṭilīya Arthaśāstra, identifies Aśmaka with Mahārāṣṭra. Really speaking the Assaka country of the Buddhists, whether it be identical with Mahārāṣṭra or located on the Godāvarī, lay outside the pale of the Madhyadeśa.

Avantī.—The capital of Avantī which was one of the sixteen great *janapadas*, was Ujjayinī which was built by Accutagāmī.[1] Avantī roughly corresponds to modern Mālwā, Nimār and adjoining parts of the Central Provinces. D. R. Bhandarkar rightly points out that ancient Avantī was divided into two parts: the northern part had its capital at Ujjayinī and the southern part called Avantī-Dakṣiṇāpatha had its capital at Māhiṣmatī.[2] According to the Mahāgovinda Suttanta of the *Dīgha Nikāya* Māhissati was the capital of Avantī with Vessabhu as its king. This apparently refers to the Avantī country in the Dakṣiṇāpatha. In the *Mahābhārata* (II, 31, 10) Avantī and Māhiṣmatī are stated to be two different countries.

Avantī was an important centre of Buddhism. Many leading *theras* (elders) and *therīs* (female elders) were either born or lived there.[3] Mahākaccāyana was born at Ujjayinī in the family of the Chaplain of king Caṇḍapajjota. He converted the king to the Buddhist faith. Isidatta was one of the converts of Mahākaccāyana.[4] He belonged to Avantī. Soṇa Kuṭikaṇṇa was also ordained by him.[5] In the Buddha's time India was divided into small independent kingdoms. Of these kingdoms Magadha under Bimbisāra and Ajātasattu, Kosala under Pasenadi, Avantī under Pajjota, and Kosambī under Udena, played important rôles in the political drama of India in the sixth and fifth centuries B.C. There was rivalry among these powers, each trying to extend his supremacy at the cost of another. Pajjota tried to extend his supremacy over Udena, but he could not achieve his object. He gave his daughter Vāsabhadattā in marriage to Udena. This matrimonial alliance saved Kosambī from being conquered by Pajjota. Udena also established a matrimonial alliance with the king of Magadha. These two royal marriages were necessary for the maintenance of the political independence of Kauśāmbī which served as a buffer state between Avantī and Magadha.

Gandhāra.—It is included in the list of sixteen great countries. The Gandhāras were an ancient people whose capital was Takkasilā. Moggaliputta Tissa sent the thera Majjhantika to Kasmīra-Gandhāra for propagating Buddhism.[6] Gandhāra comprises the districts of Peshwar and Rawalpindi in the north Punjab.

Trade relationship existed between Kasmīra-Gandhāra and Videha.[7] Pukkusāti, the king of Gandhāra, was a contemporary of king Bimbisāra of Magadha. He is said to have sent an embassy and a letter to his Magadhan contemporary as a mark of friendship. He waged war against king Pradyota of Avantī who was defeated.

The Behistun inscription of Darius (*cir.* 516 B.C.) refers to Gadara or Gandhāra which was one of the kingdoms subject to the Persian Empire. In the latter half of the 6th century B.C., the Gandhāra kingdom was

---

1 *Dīpavaṃsa*, 57.

2 *Carmichael Lectures*, 1918, p. 54.

3 *Theragāthā Commentary*, 39; *Therīgāthā Commy.*, 261–264; *Theragāthā*, 120; *Udāna*, V. 6; *Saṃ.*, III, 9; IV, 117; *Aṅg.*, I, 23; V, 46; *Majjhima*, III, 194, 223; *Vinaya Texts*, Pt. II, p. 32; *Theragāthā*, 369.

4 *Psalms of the Brethren*, p. 107.

5 *Dhammapada Commentary*, IV, 101.

6 *Mahāvaṃsa*, Ch. XII, V, 3.

7 *Jātaka*, III, pp. 363–69.

conquered by the Achæmenid kings. In Aśoka's time Gandhāra formed a part of his empire. The Gandhāras are mentioned in Aśoka's Rock Edict V.

Kamboja.—It was one of the sixteen *mahājanapadas*. It was noted for good horses.[1] The Kambojas occupied roughly the province round about Rajaori or ancient Rājapura including the Hazara district of the North-Western Frontier Province. The Thera Mahārakkhita established the Buddha's religion at Kamboja and other places.[2]

Dvārakā occurs along with Kamboja. It is not expressly stated if it was the capital of the Kamboja country. In early or later Pali texts there is no mention of the capital city of the Kambojas. It is certain that Kamboja must be located in north-west India, not far from Gandhāra. The Kambojas had a city called Nandipura mentioned in Luders' inscriptions Nos. 176 and 472.

The Kambojas were supposed to have lost their original Aryan customs and to have become barbarous.[3] From the *Bhuridatta Jātaka*,[4] we learn that many Kambojas who were not Aryans told that people were purified by killing insects, flies, snakes, bees, frogs, etc. The Jātaka tradition is corroborated by Yāska's *Nirukta* and Yuan Chwang's account of Rājapura and the adjoining countries of the north-western India.[5]

IMPORTANT PUBLICATIONS ON ANCIENT INDIAN GEOGRAPHY

We have at present some useful works on the early geography of India. Cunningham's *Ancient Geography of India* is mainly based upon the accounts of Fa-Hien and Hiuen Tsang, and on those of the Greek writers. The author's own great archaeological discoveries have also been embodied. This work has been re-edited with introduction and notes by S. N. Majumdar (Calcutta, 1924). N. L. Dey's *Geographical Dictionary of Ancient and Mediaeval India* is not a systematic treatise, but a dictionary and a very useful hand-book. It is defective because it omits in general the grounds of identification. In it the geography of southern India has been neglected. The first edition of the book appeared in Calcutta in 1899, and a second edition was published in 1927, by Messrs. Luzac & Co., London. Both these works are wanting in relevant inscriptional data. B. C. Law's *Geography of Early Buddhism* attempts for the first time at presenting a geographical picture of ancient India drawn from Pali Buddhist Texts. It may be added here that the same author has also written, by way of a supplement to the above work, an article entitled *Geographical Data from Sanskrit Buddhist Literature* published in the *Annals of the Bhandarkar Oriental Research Institute* (XV, 1934, Oct.–Jany.) and later incorporated into his *Geographical Essays* published by Messrs. Luzac & Co., in 1937. *Geographical Essays*, Vol. I, is a collection of articles eliciting geographical and topographical information which will be of value especially to geographers of ancient India.

The *Vedic Index of Names and Subjects* by the late Professors A. A. Macdonell and A. B. Keith incorporates all the geographical information contained in the most ancient Sanskrit works. Sorensens' *Index to the Mahābhārata* and Malalasekera's *Dictionary of Pali Proper Names* are very useful from geographical standpoint.

---

[1] *Sumaṅgalavilāsinī*, I, 124.
[2] *Sāsanavaṃsa*, 49.
[3] *Jātaka*, Ed. Cowell, VI, 110 f.n. 2.
[4] *Jātaka*, VI, 208, 210.
[5] Watters, *On Yuan Chwang*, I, 284ff.

B. C. Law's *Some Kṣatriya Tribes of Ancient India* (1923), *Ancient Mid-Indian Kṣatriya Tribes* (1924), *Ancient Indian Tribes*, Vols. I and II, and *Tribes of Ancient India* (1941) deal with the history and historical geography of a large number of Kṣatriya tribes. The location of the place occupied by each tribe and the extent of its kingdom at different periods of time have been dealt with in detail.

B. C. Law's *Historical Gleanings* (1922) may be found useful for a geographical study of ancient India.

B. C. Law's *Holy Places of India*, published by the Calcutta Geographical Society in 1940, contains a brief account of almost all the important sacred places belonging to the Hindus, Buddhists and Jains, arranged regionally and illustrated with maps and sketches.

B. C. Law's *Mountains of India and Rivers of India* published in 1944 by the Geographical Society of Calcutta, are the historico-geographical studies which present a systematic account of the mountains and rivers of India based on the materials available from Indian literature, the accounts of the Greek geographers, and the itineraries of the Chinese pilgrims.

B. C. Law's *Ujjayinī in Ancient India* published by the Archæological Department of the Gwalior Government in 1944 gives a connected account of the ancient city of Ujjayinī based on the original literary sources, the itineraries of the Chinese pilgrims, and the relevant epigraphic and numismatic evidences.

B. C. Law's *India as described in early texts of Buddhism and Jainism* published in 1941 and his book entitled *Some Jaina Canonical Sūtras* published by the B.B.R.A.S. in 1949 will be of great value to geographers.

B. C. Law's *Śrāvastī in Indian Literature*, *Rājagriha in Ancient Literature*, *Kauśāmbī in Ancient Literature* and *Panchālas and their capital Ahicchatra* published by the Archæological Department of the Government of India as their Memoirs Nos. 50, 58, 60 and 67 contain exhaustive and systematic accounts of the four ancient Indian cities based on literary, epigraphic and numismatic materials as well as on the accounts of the Greek and Chinese travellers in a handy form so as to render them useful to the archæologists and historians.

Indological Studies, Pt. I, by B. C. Law is a helpful aid to the study of ancient Indian geography.

Pargiter's *Ancient Indian Historical Tradition*, his translation of the *Mārkaṇḍeya Purāṇa* and Wilson's translation of the *Viṣṇupurāṇa* elicit geographical information from the *Purāṇas*.

Studies in Indian Antiquities by H. C. Raichaudhuri (Calcutta University, 1932) is a collection of detached essays, of which five are geographical.

Die Kosmographie der Inder by Prof. Kirfel is a valuable work which is so much interwoven with geography and which is not unrepresented in the Buddhist Piṭakas.

Pre-Aryan and Pre-Dravidian in India is the title given to a book consisting of French articles by Sylvain Levi, Jean Przyluski and Jules Bloch, translated into English by P. C. Bagchi (University of Calcutta, 1929). *Pre-Aryan and Pre-Dravidian in India* is an article by Prof. Levi included in this book, which originally appeared in the *Journal Asiatique*, Tome CCIII (1923). It begins: 'The geographical nomenclature of ancient India presents a certain number of terms constituting almost identical pairs, differentiated between themselves only by the nature of their initial consonants. I propose to examine some of them here: (1) *Kosala-Tosala*, (2) *Anga-Vanga*, (3) *Kaliṅga-Triliṅga*, (4) *Utkala-Mekala*, (5) *Pulinda-Kulinda*, (6) *Kāmarūpa-Nāmarūpa*, etc.'

The paper entitled *Names of Indian Towns in the Geography of Ptolemy* by Jean Przyluski was first published in the *Bulletin de la Societe de Linguistique*, 1926. Kodumbara or Odumbara was taken from J. Przyluski's article: Un ancien peuple du Punjab: les Udumbara, *Journal Asiatique*, 1926. *Paloura-Dantapura* by Sylvain Levi was first published in the *Journal Asiatique*, CCVI, 1925, (Notes Indiennes). Pithuṇḍa, Pithuḍa, Pituṇḍra by Sylvain Levi (*J.A.*, CCVI, 1925-26) is also included in this book. *The History of Bengal*, Vol. I, published by the Dacca University (1943) contains much geographical information concerning Vaṅga.

For a systematic study of our ancient geography we find the works of classical writers very much useful. They are as follows:

Notes on the Indica of Ctesias by H. H. Wilson (Oxford, 1836).

Etude sur la Geographie Grecque et Latine de l'Inde, et en particulier sur l'Inde de Ptolemee, by Vivien De Saint-Matin.

Ancient India as described by Megasthenes and Arrian by J. W. McCrindle (reprinted from *Ind. And.*, 1876-77; Calcutta 1877; new ed. Calcutta, 1926).

The Commerce and Navigation of the Erythraean Sea by J. W. McCrindle (reprinted from *Ind. Ant.*, Calcutta, 1879).

Ancient India as described by Ptolemy by J. W. McCrindle (reprinted from *Ind. Ant.*, 1884; Calcutta, 1885).

Two notes on Ptolemy's *Geography of India* by E. H. Johnston (*J.R.A.S.*, 1941).

Notes on Ptolemy by J. Ph. Vogel (*B.S.O.A.S.*, xii, xiii and xiv, Pt. I).

Ancient India as described by Ktesias the Knidian by J. W. McCrindle (reprinted from *Ind. Ant.*, 1881; Calcutta, 1882).

The Invasion of Alexander the Great by J. W. McCrindle, new ed., 1896.

Alexander's passage of the Jhelum by Sir Aurel Stein (*The Times* dated the 5th April, 1932).

The Sangala of Alexander's Historians by Hutchison (*Journal of the Punjab University Historical Society*, Vol. I).

Ancient India as described in Classical Literature by J. W. McCrindle, 1901.

The Periplus of the Erythraean Sea, translated and annotated by W. H. Schoff, London, 1912.

La geographie de Ptolémeé l'Inde (VII, 1–4) by L. Renou, Paris, 1925.

In this connection mention must be made of The *Gates of India* by T. Holdich (London, 1910), and Sir Aurel Stein's *On Alexander's Track to the Indus* (London, 1929), and his paper on *Alexander's Campaign on the North-West Frontier* in the *Geographical Journal*, London (Vol. LXX, 1927, Nov.-Dec., pp. 417ff., 515ff.).

A list of noteworthy contributions published in different periodicals is given below:

Journal of The Royal Asiatic Society

1873. Hiouen-Tsang's Journey from Patna to Ballabhi by J. Fergusson.
1893. The Sarasvatī and the Lost River of the Indian desert by Oldham.
1894. Geography of Rāma's exile by F. E. Pargiter.
1897. The birthplace of Gautama Buddha by V. A. Smith.
1897. Piṣṭapura, Mahendragiri, and Acyuta by V. A. Smith.
1898. The kingdom of Kartṛpura by Oldham.
1898. Kauśāmbī and Śrāvastī by V. A. Smith.
1898. Kapilavastu in the Buddhist books by T. Watters.
1898. The Geography of the Kandahar Inscription by J. Beames.
1902. Vaiśālī by V. A. Smith.

1902. Kuśinārā or Kuśīnagara and other Buddhist holy places by V. A. Smith.
1903. Kauśāmbī, Kāśapura, and Vaiśālī by W. Vost.
1903. Rāmagāma to Kuśīnārā by W. Vost.
1903. Setavyā or To-wa by W. Vost.
1903. Where was Malwa? by A. F. R. Hoernle.
1904. Kauśāmbī by W. Vost and V. A. Smith.
1904. The Middle country of Ancient India by T. W. Rhys Davids.
1905. Sāketa, Sha-chi or Pi-so-kia by W. Vost.
1905. Mo-la-p'o by R. Burn.
1906. Gauḍadeśa by B. C. Mazumdar.
1906. Kapilavastu by W. Hoey.
1907. The Five Rivers of the Buddhists by W. Hoey.
1907. Veṭhadīpa by G. A. Grierson.
1907. Dimensions of Indian cities and countries by J. F. Fleet.
1908. Śrāvastī by J. Ph. Vogel.
1909. The Modern Name of Nālandā by T. Bloch.
1910. Mahiṣamaṇḍala and Māhiṣmatī by J. F. Fleet.
1912. The Kambojas by Grierson.
1913. Proposed identification of two South Indian place-names in the Periplus by W. H. Schoff.
1916. Some notes on the Periplus of the Erythræan Sea by J. Kennedy.
1917. Some river-names in the Ṛg-Veda by M. A. Stein.

Sir Aurel Stein discusses the identification of the rivers mentioned in Ṛg-Veda (X, 75), the famous *Nadī-stuti*. He identifies the Marudvṛdhā with the Maruwardwan, the Asiknī with the Ans, and the Suṣomā with the Sohān.

F. W. Thomas writes a short note on *Udyāna and Urdi*, the latter being derived from the form 'Aurdāyānī' as in Patañjali (1918).

Magadha and Videha by Pargiter (1918).

Mr. S. V. Venkaṭeśwara makes Satiyaputa, mentioned in the second Rock-Edict of Aśoka, equivalent to Satyavrata-Kṣetra, the ceremonial designation of Kāñcī or Conjeevaram (1918). S. Krishnaswami Aiyangar refutes the above identification, and concludes that 'these Satiyaputras were a Western people, and have to be looked for between the Keralas and the Rāṣṭrikas along the Western hills, and that it is likely that the Satpute are their modern representatives. If so, could it not be the collective name of the various matriarchal communities like the Tulus and the Nayars of the Malabar and Kanara districts of today?' (1919).

V. A. Smith accepts that Satiyaputra should be identified with the Satyamangalam Taluk in Coimbatore, which adjoins Coorg in the Western Ghats (1919).

Sagara and the Haihayas, Vaśiṣṭha and Aurva by F. E. Pargiter. The author discusses geographical locations of the Haihayas, Māhiṣikas, Dārvas, Khasas, Colas, Culikas, Śakas, Yavanas, Pahlavas, Kambojas, Druhyus, etc. (1919).

Identification of the 'Ka-p'i-li country' of Chinese authors by V. A. Smith (1920).

An unidentified Territory of Southern India by K. V. Subrahmanya Aiyer (1922). It identifies the ancient Mūṣaka kingdom as mentioned in the *Mahābhārata*, *Viṣṇupurāṇa*, *Bhārata-Nāṭya-Śāstra* and in the inscription of Khāravela, in the Mahākūṭa pillar inscription of the Western Cālukya king, Maṅgaliśa Raṇavikrānta, etc., with Irāmakuḍam on the west Coast of the Deccan extending from Tulu or South Canara to the Kerala dominions.

S. Krishnaswami Aiyangar denies that in the days of Aśoka the Kosar were a people so closely associated with the Tulu country that they gave their name to the region (1923).

Kauśāmbī by Dayaram Sahni (1927). The identification of the ancient Kauśāmbī with the village of Kosam in the district of Allahabad, which was first proposed by Sir Alexander Cunningham, is finally proved.

Kauśāmbī by Sita Ram (1928).

Two Notes on the Ancient Geography of India by J. Ph. Vogel (1929).

Hathur and Arura by Jwala Sahai (1932). Hathur near Ludhiana is identified with Arhatpur of Jaina fame and Arura near Hathur identified with Ahicchatra.

Indian Antiquary

Note on Pauṇḍravardhana by E. V. Westmacott (1874).
The Geography of Ibn Batuta's Travels in India by Col. H. Yule (1874).
On the identification of places in the Sanskrit Geography of India by J. Burgess (1885).
The Topographical List of the Brihat-Saṃhitā by J. F. Fleet (1893).
The Topographical List of the Bhāgavata Purāṇa by J. E. Abbott (1899).
Four villages mentioned in the Nasik Cave Inscriptions by Y. R. Gupte (1912).
Kollipaka by Lewis Rice (1915).
Some literary references to the Isipatana Migadāya (Sarnath) by B. C. Bhattacharyya (1916).
The extent of Gautamīputra's territory as described in the Nasik cave Inscription by D. R. Bhandarkar (1918).
Contributions to the study of the Ancient Geography of India by S. N. Majumdar (1919 and 1921).
Deccan of the Sātavāhana period by D. R. Bhandarkar (1920).
The early course of the Ganges by N. L. Dey (1921).
The Māhiṣmatī of Kārtavīrya by Munshi Kanaiyalal (1922).
Geographical Position of certain places in India by Y. M. Kale (1923).
History of Important ancient towns and cities of Gujarat and Kathiawaḍ by A. S. Altekar (1924).
Triliṅga and Kuliṅga by G. Ramdas (1925).
The capital of Nahapāna by V. S. Bakhle (1926).
A possible identification of Mount Devagiri mentioned in Kālidāsa's Meghadūta by A. S. Bhandarkar (1928).
To the East of Samataṭa by N. N. Das Gupta (1932).
The river courses of the Punjab and Sind by R. B. Whitehead (1932).
Mandāra Hill by R. Bose (Vol. I).
Frescoes and architecture of the Ajanta caves (Vols. I, II, III, XXII, XXXII, XL).
Nilgiri Hills (Vols. II and IV).
Ramgarh Hill (Vols. II and XXXIV).
Kumbhakonam (Vol. III).
Khandesh (Vol. IV).
Account of Champā (Vol. VI).
Nepal (Vols. XIII, XIX, XXII).
A note on Ptolemy's Geography by V. Ball (Vol. XIV).
Identity of Nandikeśvara (Vol. XIX).
Proposed identification of Kong-Kin-na-pu-lo with Karnul (Vol. XXIII).
Antiquities at Mandasor (Vol. XXXVII).

Ramtek, Nagpur Dist. (Vol. XXXVII).
Buddhist caves in Malwa (Vol. XXXIX).
The Mandasor Praśasti of Vatsabhaṭṭi (Vol. XLII).
A note on a few localities in the Nasik Dist. mentioned in the ancient copper-plate grants by Y. R. Gupte (Vol. XLII).
Chandra's conquest of Bengal by R. G. Basak (Vol. XLVIII).
Contributions to the study of the ancient geography of India by S. K. Bhuyan (Vol. XLIX).

Asiatic Researches

Description of the caves or excavations near Ellora by C. Mallet (Vol. I).
Remarks on the city of Tagara by Lieut. F. Wilford (Vol. I).
Some account of the caves in the island of Elephanta by J. Goldingham (Vol. IV).
On the course of the Ganges through Bengal by Major R. H. Colebrooke (Vol. VII).
The principal peaks of the Himalayas by J. Hodgson and J. D. Herbert (Vol. XIV).
Geography of Assam by J. B. Neufville (Vol. XVI).

Journal of The Asiatic Society of Bengal

Geographical notice of Tibet by Csoma de Koros (*J.A.S.B.*, Vol. I).
Further account of the remains of ancient town discovered at Behut near Saharanpur by Capt. P. T. Cautley (Vol. III).
Notes on the locality of Rājagriha of the town of that name in Behar by T. R. (Lt. T. Renny) (Vol. III).
H. P. Śāstrī's identification of the names of places ruled over by the allies and feudatories of Rāmapala as mentioned at the beginning of the second chapter of Sandhyākara Nandi's *Rāmacarita* (Vol. III) is noteworthy. R. D. Banerjee's identification of those places (Vol. IV).
Excursions to the ruins and site of an ancient city at Bakhra 13 Cos north of Patna and 6 north from Singhea by J. Stephenson (Vol. IV).
Note on the above by James Prinsep (Vol. IV).
Some account of the sculptures at Mahabalipuram usually called the seven Pagodas by J. Goldingham (Vol. V).
Observations upon the past and present condition of Oujein or Ujjayinī by Lt. Edward Conolly (Vol. VI).
The course of the Narmadā by Lt. Col. Ouseley (Vol. XIV).
Notes on the vihāras and chaityas of Bihar (Vol. XVI).
A comparative essay on the ancient geography of India by Col. F. Wilford (Vol. XX).
The Rajmahal hills by W. S. Sherwill (Vol. XX).
An account of the Antiquities of Jaipur in Orissa by C. S. Banerjee (Vol. XL).
Independent Sikkim by W. T. Blauford (Vol. XL).
Contributions to the geography and history of Bengal by H. Blochmann (Vol. XLII and XLIII).
Note on Mahāsthān near Bagura, Eastern Bengal by C. J. O'Donnell (Vol. XLIV).
The Kaimur range by C. S. Banerjee (Vol. XLVI).
On the temples of Deoghar by Dr. Rajendralal Mitra (Vol. LII).
Antiquities of Gayā by T. F. Peppe and C. Horne (*J.P.A.S.B.*, 1865).
Antiquities at Bairāṭ, Ajmir, Gwalior, Khajuraha and Mahoba by Major Genl. A. Cunningham (1865).
Remarks on some temples in Kashmir by Bishop Cotton (1865).

Note on Māhiṣmatī or Maheśvara (Mahesar) on the Narmadā and the identification of Hiouen Thsang's Maheśvarapura by P. N. Bose (1873).
Notes on Sunargaon, Eastern Bengal by James Wise (1874).
Ancient dwellings and tombs in Baluchistan by Capt. E. Mockler (1876).
Antiquities of Bagura (Bogra) by H. Beveridge (1878).
Ancient Countries in Eastern India by F. E. Pargiter (1897).
Notes on Chirānd in the district of Saran by N. L. Dey (1903).
Notes on the history of the district of Hughli or the ancient Rāḍha by N. L. Dey (1910).
A forgotten kingdom of East Bengal by N. K. Bhaṭṭasāli (1914).
Notes on ancient Aṅga or the District of Bhagalpore by N. L. Dey (1914).
Aṅga and Campā in Pali Literature by B. C. Law (1915).

Journal of The Bombay Branch Royal Asiatic Society

Notes on the Shrine of Mahābāleśvara by V. N. Mandlik (1871–74).
Notes on the History of Antiquities of Chaul by J. Gerson Da Cunha (1876).
The Sudarśana or Lake Beautiful of the Girnar Inscriptions (B.C. 300–A.D. 450) by Ardeseer Jamsedji (1890).
Besnagar by H. H. Lake (1914).
Ancient Pāṭaliputra by J. J. Modi (1916-17).
The antiquity of the Poona District by D. R. Bhandarkar (1930).

Journal of The Bihar and Orissa Research Society

The Magadhapura of Mahābhārata by Sir George Grierson (Vol. II).
Sites in Rajgir associated with Buddha and his disciples by D. N. Sen (Vol. III).
Hiuen Tsang's Route in South Bihar: an identification of the Buddhavana Mountain and a discussion of the most probable site of the Kukkuṭapādagiri by V. H. Jackson (Vol. IV).
A Note on the Koṅgoda Country by Binayaka Misra (Vol. XII).
Ajapura of Skandagupta, and the area round Bihar by P. C. Chaudhuri (Vol. XIX).

Indian Historical Quarterly

Rāḍha or the Ancient Gaṅgārāṣṭra by N. L. Dey.
The Rāmāyaṇa of Vālmīki mentions two Kosalas by L. P. Pandeya Sarma (Vol. III).
The Study of Ancient Indian Geography by H. C. Ray Chaudhuri (Vol. IV).
The Study of Ancient Geography by H. V. Trivedi (Vol. IV).
Eastern India and Āryāvarta by H. C. Chakladar (Vol. IV).
The Karoura of Ptolemy by K. V. Krishna Ayyar (Vol. V).
Identification of Brahmottara by K. M. Gupta (Vol. VII).
Some Janapadas of Ancient Rāḍha by P. C. Sen (Vol. VIII).
Udayapura-nagara by D. C. Sircar (Vol. IX).
Puṇḍravardhana—its site by P. C. Sen (Vol. IX).
Uḍḍiyana and Sāhore by N. N. Das Gupta (Vol. XI).

Indian Culture

The Vaṅgas by B. C. Law (Vol. I, No. 1).
The Geography of Kauṭilya by Harihar V. Trivedi (Vol. I, No. 2).
Some Notes on Tribes of Ancient India by B. C. Law (Vol. I, No. 2).
Yavanas in early Indian Inscriptions by O. Stein (Vol. I, No. 3).

Some Ancient Indian Tribes by B. C. Law (Vol. I, No. 3).
Kauśikā and Kuśiārā by K. L. Barua (Vol. I, No. 3).
Kośala by B. C. Law (Vol. I, No. 3).
Geographical Data of the Dekhan and South India as gathered from the Rāmāyaṇa by V. R. Ramachandra Dikshitar (Vol. I, No. 4).
The identification of Satiyaputa by B. A. Saletore (Vol. I, No. 4).
Candradvīpa by N. N. Das Gupta (Vol. II, No. 1).
Notes on the Śakas by Sten Konow (Vol. II, No. 2).

Quarterly Journal of The Andhra Research Society

The Pathless countries of the Lāḍhas by B. Singh Deo (Vol. II).
Tosali and Tosala by B. Singh Deo (Vol. III).
Hippokoura and Sātakarṇī by Jean Przyluski (Vol. IV).
Capital of Bṛhatphalāyanas by D. C. Sircar (Vol. VII).

Quarterly Journal of The Mythic Society

The Seven Dwīpas of the Purāṇas by V. Venkatachellam Iyer (Vols. XVI and XVII).
The Sringeri Mutt by K. Ramavarma Raja (Vol. XVI).
Identification of Sopatma and Phrourion of the Greek writers by S. Soma Sundara Desikar (Vol. XXI).

Ceylon Historical Review (April 1952, Vol. I, No. 4)

The Geographical aspect of the Pāli Chronicles by B. C. Law.

Chapter I

NORTHERN INDIA

Abastanoi.—The Abastanoi corresponded to the Sanskrit Ambaṣṭhas, who were the same as the Sambastai of Diodorus, Sabarcae of Curtius and Sabagrae of Orosius. In Alexander's time the lower Akesines (*Asiknī*) was their territory and they had a democratic government. They submitted to Alexander (McCrindle, *Invasion of India*, pp. 292ff.; Law, *Indological Studies*, I, 31ff.).

Aciravatī.—The river Aciravatī was also known as the Ajiravatī or the Airāvatī.[1] It was known to the Chinese pilgrim Yuan Chwang as A-chi-lo, flowing south-eastwards past the city of Śrāvastī.[2] According to I-Tsing Ajiravatī means the river of the Aji (dragon).[3] This river is mentioned in the Jain texts as Erāvai.[4] It has been identified with the modern Rapti in Oudh, on the western bank of which stood the ancient city of Śrāvastī,[5] the third or the last capital of Kośala. If Saheṭh-Maheṭh on the south bank of the Rāpti be the modern site of Śrāvastī, it is positive that the Aciravatī of the Buddhist fame is no other than the modern Rāpti. The author of the *Daśakumāracaritam* knew this city as situated on a river which seems presumably to have been the Aciravatī or the Rāpti, though our author does not unfortunately name the river.[6]

The Aciravatī is a tributary of the Sarayū which has its origin in the Himalayan range. The long description of the origin of the five rivers Gaṅgā, Yamunā, Aciravatī, Sarabhū and Mahī from the Anotatta lake, is given in the Pali commentaries.[7] Some five hundred rivers are mentioned in the *Suttanipāta Commentary*.[8] Only ten of them were to be reckoned according to the *Milinda-Pañho*.[9] Of the ten rivers [10] the Aciravatī was one of the five great rivers,[11] which constituted the Ganges group and the rest constituted the Sindhu group. The Aciravatī was one of the sacred rivers of the Buddhist Midland.[12] As it fell into the sea, it lost its former name and was known as the sea.[13] According to the *Saṃyutta Nikāya* [14] the Aciravatī along with the Gaṅgā, Yamunā, Sarabhū and Mahī flowed, slided and tended to the east. It was a deep river as its water was immeasurable.[15]

The Buddha stayed in a mango grove at Manasākaṭa, a Brahmin village of Kośala, situated on the bank of the Aciravatī, to the north of

---

1 *Avadānaśataka*, I, 63; II. 60; Pāṇini's *Aṣṭādhyāyī*, IV. 3. 119.

2 Watters, *On Yuan Chwang*, I, 398-399.

3 *Travels*, p. 156.

4 *Kalpasūtra*, p. 12; *Brihat-Kalpasūtra*, 4. 33.

5 Identified with modern Saheṭh-Maheṭh.

6 Weber, *Ueber Das Daśakumāracaritaṃ in Indische Streifen*, Berlin, 1868.

7 *Papañcasūdanī*, Sinhalese Ed., II, 586; *Manorathapūraṇī*, Sinhalese Ed., ii, 759-60; *Suttanipāta Commy.*, P.T.S., 437–439.

8 *Paramatthajotikā*, II, 437.

9 Ed. Trenckner, p. 110.

10 *Mārkaṇḍeyapurāṇa*, 57. 16–18.

11 *Pancamahānadiyo.*

12 *Vinaya*, II, p. 239; *Visuddhimagga*, I, p. 10.

13 *Vinaya*, II, p. 239; *Aṅg.*, V, p. 22; *Ibid.*, IV, 198-199, 202—Gaṅgā Yamunā Aciravatī Sarabhū Mahī tā mahāsamuddampattā jahanti purimāni nāmagottāni mahāsamuddo tveva saṃkhaṃ gacchanti.

14 II, 135; cf. *Saṃ.*, V, 39, 134.

15 *na sukaram udakassa pamāṇaṃ gaṇetuṃ*—*Sam.*, V, 401.

Manasākaṭa, inhabited by many distinguished and wealthy Brahmins.[1] There was a grove of fig trees on the bank of this river.[2] A small stream at Śrāvastī called the Sutanu, which was visited by the Buddha's disciple, Anuruddha, must have fallen into this river.[3]

The river Aciravatī flows through the districts of Bahraich, Gonda, and Basti and joins the Sarayū or Ghargharā (Gogrā), west of Barhaj in the district of Gorakhpur. According to the Chinese pilgrim Yuan Chwang it flows south-eastwards past the city of Śrāvastī.[4] It is fed by no less than three tributaries on the left side, all in the district of Gorakhpur, and by a small tributary on the right in the same district. During the hot season it ran dry leaving a bed of sand.[5] Two Sāvatthians, who adopted the religious life, came to this river. After a bath they stood on the sand enjoying the sunshine and talking pleasantly together.[6] This river was crossed in rafts.[7] It nourished wheatfields on its bank.[8] A Sāvatthian Brahmin cut trees on its bank in order to cultivate the land. Crops grew on it but the whole crop was carried to the sea by a flood.[9] The revered Ānanda came to this river with some monks to bathe. After his bath he stood in one garment drying his limbs.[10] A Sāvatthian householder, who gave up his household life, went to the river Aciravatī, took his bath, and saw two white swans flying by.[11] A fisherman belonging to the village of Paṇḍupura on his way to Śrāvastī saw some tortoise-eggs (*kacchapa-aṇḍāni*) lying on the bank of this river.[12] The Chabbaggiya monks used to catch hold of the cows crossing this river by their horns or ears or necks or tails or spring up upon their backs.[13] The people on the bank of this river were in the habit of casting nets for fishing.[14] The early Buddhist records refer to the swimming of the cattle across it.[15]

Sāriputta, one of the famous disciples of the Buddha, took his bath in this river.[16] Four daughters of a rich merchant also bathed in this river before entering into a mango-grove.[17] Nuns were in the habit of bathing in this river with prostitutes being naked.[18]

A certain country monk came to the ferry on the Aciravatī and expressed his desire to cross this river before a ferryman with the help of his boat. The ferryman asked him to wait but he refused. At last he was put into his boat. Due to bad steering his robe was wet and it became dark before he reached the farther shore.[19] This river could be seen from the terrace of the Kosalan king Pasenadī's palace.[20] Five hundred lads who used to visit this river engaged themselves in wrestling on its bank.[21] Viḍūḍabha, the son of king Pasenadī, met the Śākyas on its bank and

---

1 *Dīgha* I, 235ff.

2 *Suttanipāta Commy.*, I, p. 19.

3 *Samyutta*, V, 297.

4 Watters, *On Yuan Chwang*, I, 398-99.

5 *Aṅg.*, IV, 101.

6 *Jātaka*, II, 366—*Aciravatīṃ gantvā nahātvā vālikapuline ātapaṃ tappamānā sāraṇīyakathaṃ kathentā aṭṭhaṃsu.*

7 *Vinaya*, III, 63.

8 *Suttanipāta Commentary*, P.T.S., p. 511—*Acīravatīnadītīre yavaṃ vapissāmīti khettaṃ kasati.*

9 *Jāt.*, IV, p. 167—*Sabbaṃ sassaṃ samuddaṃ pavesesi.*

10 *Aṅguttara*, III, p. 402.

11 *Jātaka*, I, p. 418.

12 *Dhammapada Commy.*, III, 449.

13 *Vinaya*, I, pp. 190-91—Chabbaggiyā bhikkhū Aciravatīyā nadiyā gāvīnaṃ tarantīnaṃ visāṇesu pi gaṇhanti, kaṇṇesu pi gaṇhanti, gīvāya pi gaṇhanti, cheppāya pi gaṇhanti, piṭṭhim pi abhirūhanti.

14 *Udāna Commy.*, p. 366.

15 *Vinaya*, I, 191.

16 *Aṅg. Commy.*, Sinhalese Ed., p. 315.

17 *Jāt.*, III, p. 137.

18 *Vinaya*, I, 293—*Idha bhante bhikkhuṇiyo Aciravatīyānadiyā vesiyāhi saddhiṃ naggā ekatitthe nahāyanti.*

19 *Jātaka*, III, 228.

20 *Vinaya*, IV, 111-12.

21 *Jātaka*, II, p. 96.

completely routed them.[1] Sometimes this river became so full that disastrous floods occurred, in one of which Viḍūḍabha and his army were swept into the sea.[2] Anāthapiṇḍika, the great banker of Sāvatthī, lost eighteen crores of his wealth by the destructive floods of this river which swept away his hoarding on its bank.[3] A merchant had a treasure buried in the bank of this river. When the bank was eroded away, the treasure was carried into the sea.[4]

Adraisti Country.—It was situated on the eastern side of the Hydraotes (Rāvī). Pimprāmā was their stronghold. The Adrijas mentioned in the Droṇaparva of the *Mahābhārata* (Ch. 159, 5) are supposed to be identical with the Adraistai of the Greeks. The Adraistai or Adhṛṣṭas are said to have bowed down before Alexander's army (*Cambridge History of India*, I, 371 and n. 2; B. C. Law, *Indological Studies*, I, pp. 21-22).

Agaru.—It is a forest lying in the Kuru country between the Candrakānta and Sūryakānta mountains (*Vāyu*, 45. 31).

Agrohā.—It is situated on the metalled road between Hissar and Fatehabad at a distance of 14 miles from the former. It appears to have been mentioned by Ptolemy who calls it Agara. As a result of the excavation at the site, coins, beads, fragments of sculptures and terracottas have been discovered. (For details vide *Excavation at Agrohā*, Punjab, by H. L. Srivastava, *M.A.S.I.*, No. 61).

Ahicchatra.—It was the capital of northern Pañcāla (*Mahābhārata*, Ādiparva, Ch. 140; cf. Rapson, *Ancient India*, p. 167). The river Bhāgīrathī formed the dividing line between the northern and southern Pañcāla. The Vedic texts refer to an eastern and western division of the country (*Vedic Index*, I, 469). Patañjali refers to it in his *Mahābhāṣya* (II, p. 233, Kielhorn's ed.). The *Yoginītantra* mentions it (2/4, pp. 128-129). According to the *Divyāvadāna* (p. 435) the capital of northern Pañcāla was Hastināpura, but the Kumbhakāra Jātaka (Cowell, *Jātaka*, III, 230) states that the capital of northern Pañcāla was Kampillanagara.

Pañcāla was originally the country, north and west of Delhi, from the foot of the Himalayas to the river Chambal (cf. Cunningham, *A.G.I.*, p. 413, 1924 Ed.). The capital of southern Pañcāla was Kāmpilya[5] (*Mahābhārata*, 138, 73-74) identical with modern Kampil in the Farrukhabad district, U.P. In the Pabhosā Cave Inscription of the time of Udāka (?), Bahasatimitra appears to be the king whose coins have been discovered at Ramnagar (Ancient Ahicchatra, capital of Pañcāla, Bareilly District, U.P.) and Kosam (Ancient Kauśāmbī, capital of the Vatsas, Allahabad District, U.P.). In the same inscriptions we find that Ahicchatra was ruled by Saunakāyani. The Allahabad Pillar Inscription of Samudragupta refers to a powerful king named Acyuta whose coins have been found at Ahicchatra, modern Ramnagar, in the Bareilly district, U.P. It was still a considerable town when visited by Hiuen Tsang in the 7th century A.D.[6] This country, according to the Chinese pilgrim, was more than 3,000 li in circuit, and its capital was 17 or 18 li in circuit. The country yielded grain and had many woods and springs and a genial climate. The people were honest and diligent in learning. There were more than ten Buddhist monasteries. Deva-temples were nine in number

---

[1] *Dhammapada Commy.*, I, 359-60.

[2] *Dīgha*, I, 244-245; *Jāt.*, IV, 167; *Dhammapada Commy.*, I, 360.

[3] *Dhammapada Commy.*, III, p. 10—*aṭṭhārasakoṭi-dhanaṃ*.

[4] *Jātaka*, I, 230—*Aciravatīnadītīre nihitadhanaṃ nadīkule bhinne samuddaṃ paviṭṭhaṃ atthi*.

[5] *B. C. Law Volume*, Part II, 1946, pp. 239–42.

[6] Smith, *Early History of India*, 4th Ed., pp. 391-392.

(Watters, *On Yuan Chwang*, I, 331). According to Cunningham the history of Ahicchatra goes back to 1430 A.D.

The name is written as Ahikṣetra as well as Ahicchatra (Serpent-umbrella). Ahicchatra seems to be the correct form.[1] The old name of Ahicchatra is Adhicchatra (preserved in an inscription; Luders' List of Brāhmī Inscriptions, Index) which is nearer to the Greek form of Adisadra of Ptolemy, (McCrindle, *Ancient India as described by Ptolemy*, p. 133). It was also called Chatravatī (*Mahābhārata*, Ādiparva, Ch. 168). Adhicchatrā is the name found in the Pabhosā cave inscription of Āshāḍhasena dated about the beginning of the Christian era (*E.I.*, II, p. 432; Luders' List, Nos. 90 and 905; *Inscription of Gautamīmitra*, N. G. Majumdar, *I.H.Q.*). Arjuna gave the city of Ahicchatra together with that of Kāmpilya to Droṇa after having defeated Drupada in battle. Having accepted both the cities, Droṇa, the foremost of victors, gave away Kāmpilya to Drupada (*Harivaṃśa*, Ch. XX, 74-75). According to the *Vividhatīrthakalpa* (p. 14), Saṃkhyāvatī was the earlier name of Ahicchatra. Pārśvanātha wandered about in this town. Kamaṭhāsura, inimical to Pārśvanātha, caused an incessant shower of rains inundating the entire earth. Pārśvanātha was immersed in water up to his neck. To protect him the Nāgarājā of the place, accompanied by his queens, appeared on the scene, held a canopy of his thousand hoods over his head and coiled himself round his body. That is the reason why the town was named Ahicchatra.

In modern times Ahicchatra was first visited by Capt. Hodgson who describes it as the ruins of an ancient fortress several miles in circumference, which appears to have had 34 bastions and is known as the Pāṇḍu's Fort. (McCrindle, *Ancient India as described by Ptolemy*, p. 134). For an identification of this place, see *E.I.*, XXVI, Pt. 2, April, 1941, p. 90. For further details see B. C. Law, *Pañchālas and their capital Ahicchatra*, *M.A.S.I.*, No. 67; *A.S.I.R.*, I, pp. 255ff.; *Progress Report of the Epigraphical* and *Architectural branches of North-western Provinces and Oudh*, 1891-92, 1ff.; B. C. Law, *Some Jaina Canonical Sūtras*, 169-170; B. C. Law, *Tribes in Ancient India*, p. 34; Beal, *Buddhist Records of the Western World*, I, pp. 200-201; McCrindle, *Ancient India as described by Ptolemy*, p. 134.

Ajayagaḍh.—It is identical with Banda district, U.P. (*Inscriptions of Northern India revised by D. R. Bhandarkar*, No. 408, V. 1243).

Ajudhan.—This ancient town is situated on the bank of the old Sutlej, 28 miles to the south-west of Depālpura and 10 miles from the present course of the river (*C.A.G.I.*, 1924, p. 245).

Alakanandā.—A river in the Garhwal Himalaya, a headwater of the Ganges. Her course can be traced from the Gandhamādana mountain (*Bhāgavatapurāṇa*, IV, 6. 24; *Brahmāṇḍapurāṇa*, III, 41. 21; 56. 12; *Viṣṇupurāṇa*, II, 2. 34. 36; *Vāyupurāṇa*, 41. 18; 42. 25–35). It represents the upper course of the Ganges. Its upper tributary is constituted of the Piṇḍā and another stream at the confluence of which is situated Śrīnagara in Garhwal. Mandākinī is one of its tributaries, which may be identified with Kālī-Gaṅgā or Mandāgnī, rising in the mountains of Kedāra in Garhwal. The Bhāgīrathī-Gaṅgā is joined on the left side by the Alakanandā at Devaprayāga (B. C. Law, *Rivers of India*, p. 19). The Ganges may be supposed to have assumed the name of the Gaṅgā-Bhāgīrathī from the point where it is met by the Mandākinī (Law, *Rivers of India*, p. 21; *Imperial Gazetteer of India*, Vol. I, p. 125; regarding the Mandākinī, Cunningham, *Archaeological Survey Report*, XXI, 11).

---

[1] Cunningham, *Ancient Geography*, S. N. Majumdar Ed., p. 412.

Alasanda.—It was the chief city of the Yona territory. Geiger identifies it with the town of Alexandria founded by Alexander near Kabul in the Paropanisadae country (*Mahāvaṃsa*, Geiger's Translation, p. 194). It has been described in the *Milindapañha* as an island where king Milinda was born in the village of Kalasigāma (Trenckner Ed., pp. 82-83; *Cambridge History of India*, I, p. 550).

Amaranātha.—About sixty miles from Islamabad lies Amaranātha, a celebrated shrine of Śiva in a cave in the Bhairavaghāṭi range of the Himalayas. It is considered holy by the Hindus. (For further details, see Law, *Holy Places of India*, p. 31.)

Ambaṣṭha Country.—The country of the Ambaṣṭhas was situated on the lower Chenab. The *Mahābhārata* (II, 48, 14) and the *Bhāgavata Purāṇa* (X. 83, 23) refer to it. It is also mentioned in the *Brahmāṇḍap*. (III. 74, 22), *Matsyap*. (48. 21), *Vāyu* (99. 22), and Viṣṇu (II. 3. 18). Pāṇini also refers to it in one of his *sūtras* (VIII. 3. 97). As early as the time of the *Aitareya Brāhmaṇa* (VII, 21-3) they probably settled themselves in the Punjab. The *Mahābhārata* (II, 52, 14-15) mentions them as north-western tribes. They were intimately connected with the Śivis and the Yaudheyas and were settled on the eastern border of the Punjab (Pargiter, *Ancient Indian Historical Tradition*, 109, 264). During the first quarter of the 2nd century A.D. the Ambaṣṭhas are referred to by the geographer Ptolemy as the tribe which is described as settled in the east of the country of the Paropanisadai (McCrindle, *Ancient India as described by Ptolemy*, pp. 311-12). They seem to have migrated in later times to some place near the Mekala hill which is the source of the Narmadā (B. C. Law, *Tribes in Ancient India*, pp. 97, 374). For further details vide B. C. Law, *Indological Studies*, I, 31ff.

Andhavana.—It was situated at Śrāvastī. The Elder Anuruddha fell ill while he was here. The monks approached him and asked him the cause of his bodily suffering (*Saṃyutta*, V, 302).

Añjana Mountain (*Añjanagiri*).—It was situated in the Mahāvana (*Jātaka*, V, 133). It is mentioned in the *Rāmāyaṇa* (Kiṣkindhyākāṇḍa, 37. 5) and in the *Mārkaṇḍeya Purāṇa* (58. 11). It is also mentioned in the Jaina *Āvaśyaka-cūrṇi*, (p. 516). According to the *Skandapurāṇa* (Chap. I, Śl. 36–48) it was made up of gold. It is the Sulaiman range in the Punjab. The Sulaiman mountain, known to the ancient geographers as the Añjanagiri, separates the N.W.F. Province and the Punjab (P) from Baluchistan. It overlooks the Gomal river on the north and the Indus on the south. The Takht-i-Sulaiman (Solomon's Throne) is the highest peak (11,295 ft.). The southern part of the main range is composed of sandstones, whereas the northern part is built up of limestones. The range is pierced by a number of gorges through which run the main routes from India to Baluchistan.

Añjanavana.—It was a deer park in Sāketa where the Buddha dwelt. When the Master was here, a wanderer named Kuṇḍaliya had a discussion with him on religious and philosophical topics. (*Saṃyutta*, I. 54; V. 73ff.).

Anoma.—This mountain does not seem to have been far off from the Himalaya (*Apadāna*, p. 345).

Anomā—(*Chinese Ho-nan-mo-Ch'iang*).—Anomā is the river Aumi in the Gorakhpur district. Carlleyle identifies this river with the Kudawa nadī in the Basti district of Oudh. The Buddha after leaving Kapilavastu proceeded to the bank of this river and then he adopted the life of a monk (*Dhammapada Commentary*, I, 85).

Anotatta (*Chinese A-nou-ta*).—This lake may be identified with the Rawanhrad or Laṅga. It was visited by the Buddha many times (*Aṅg*.,

IV, 101). According to the *Shui-ching-chu* this lake otherwise known as the Anavatapta (the unheated) was on the top of the Himalaya. Four rivers issued from this lake: the Gaṅgā to the east, the Sindhu to the south, the Vakṣu (Oxus) to the west and the Sītā (Tārim) to the north (*Northern India according to the Shui-Ching-Chu*, p. 14).

Aṅṣumatī.—It is mentioned in the *Ṛgveda* (VI. 27. 5, 6; VIII. 85. 13) as a river in Kurukṣetra.

Antaravedī.—The traditional Antaravedī mentioned in the Indore copperplate inscription of Skandagupta (466 A.D.) is the country lying between the Ganges and the Jumna[1] and between Prayāga and Hardwar. According to this inscription, a lamp was maintained in a temple of the sun (*sūrya*) at Indrapura out of a perpetual endowment made by a Brahmin named Devaviṣṇu (*C.I.I.*, Vol. III). The Bulandshahar district lies actually in this Antaravedī.

Anupiya-ambavana.—It was in the kingdom of the Mallas. Here Gautama spent the first seven days after his renunciation on his way to Rājagriha (*Jāt.*, I, pp. 65-66; *Vinaya*, II, p. 180).

Apava-Vaśiṣṭha-āśrama.—It was situated near the Himalayas (*Yogavāśiṣṭha-Rāmāyaṇa*, I). Apava Vaśiṣṭha is said to have cursed Kārtyavīryārjuna for the latter burnt his hermitage.

Arail.—This ancient village is situated on the right bank of the Jumna at its confluence with the Ganges (*Allahabad District Gazetteer* by Nevill, p. 221).

Ariṣṭapura (Pali Ariṭṭhapura).—Pāṇini mentions it in one of his *sūtras* (VI. 2. 100). It was the capital of the Sivi kingdom. This king was educated at Taxila. He was made viceroy during the lifetime of his father and after his father's death he became king. He ruled his kingdom righteously. He built six alms-halls at the four gates in the midst of the city and at his own door. He used to distribute each day six hundred-thousand pieces of money. On the appointed days he used to visit the alms-halls to see the distribution made.

The Sivi kingdom may be identified with the Shorkot region of the Punjab—the ancient Śivipura or Śivapura (B. C. Law, *Geography of Early Buddhism*, p. 52). Early Greek writers refer to a country in the Punjab as the territory of the Siboi. For further details vide B. C. Law, *Indological Studies*, I, 24ff.

Aruṇācala.—This mountain is situated on the west of the Kailāsa range (Law, *Mountains of India*, p. 3; vide also *Skandhapurāṇa*, Ch. III, 59–61; IV. 9, 13, 21, 37).

Asitañjananagara.—It was in the Kaṃsa district where a king named Mahākamsa reigned (*Jāt.*, IV, p. 79).

Asni.—It is a village situated about 10 miles north of Fatehpur U.P., where a stone pillar inscription has been discovered (*I.A.*, XVI, 173ff.).

Aśoka.—This mountain does not seem to have been far off from the Himalaya (*Apadāna*, p. 342).

Aspasian territory.—It was a minor state in Alexander's time. The Iranian name Aspa corresponds to the Sanskrit Aśva or Aśvaka (Law, *Indological Studies*, I, p. 1). The Aspasians, as they were called by the Greeks, may be regarded as denoting some western branch of the Aśvaka or Aśmaka tribe (*Cambridge History of India*, I, 352, n. 3). Their country

---

[1] Cf. *Bhaviṣyapurāṇa*, Pt. III, Ch. 2. Antaravedī is the doab between these two rivers. The Aryāvarta of the Sūtras and Madhyadeśa of Manu are designated, according to the *Kāvyamīmāṃsā* (93), as Antaravedī which extends up to Benares (*Vinasana Prayāgayoḥ Gaṅgā-Yamunayośca antaraṃ Antaravedī*).

lay in Eastern Afghanistan (Law, *Tribes in Ancient India*, p. 180). According to some it was situated in Suvāstu (modern Swat Valley).[1] The Aśmakas were the first Indian people to bear the brunt of Alexander's invasion. One of the cities of the Aspasian territory is said to have stood on or near the river Euaspla which is supposed to be identical with the Kunar, a tributary of the Kabul river.[2]

Aṣṭāpada.—It is a great Jain *tīrtha*. It may be identified with the Kailāsa mountain. According to the *Vividhatīrthakalpa* many sages and the sons of Ṛṣabha attained perfection.[3]

Audumbara.—Pāṇini refers to it in his Aṣṭādhyāyī (4. 1. 173). This country may be located in the Pāṭhānkoṭ region.[4]

Ayodhyā.—It is one of the seven holy places of the Hindus otherwise known as Ayojjhā or Ayudhā. Vinītā was another name for this city.[5] It was the birthplace of the first and fourth Tīrthaṅkaras.[6] Fa-Hien calls it Sha-che and according to Ptolemy it is known as Sogeda. In Brāhmaṇa literature it is described as a village.[7] This city is also known as Sāketa, Ikṣvākubhūmi (*Āvassaka Nirjjuti* 382), Rāmapurī and Kośala.[8] The *Bhāgavata Purāṇa* refers to it as a city (IX. 8, 19). According to the *Skandapurāṇa*[9] Ayodhyā looks like a fish. It is one yojana in extent in the east, one yojana in the west, one yojana from the Sarayū in the south, and one yojana from Tamasā in the north. The spurious Gayā copper-plate inscription of Samudragupta mentions this ancient city, situated on the river Sarayū,[10] identified with the Ghagrā or the Gogra in Oudh (*C.I.I.*, III) about six miles from the Fyzabad Railway Station. According to this inscription Ayodhyā was the seat of a Gupta *Jayaskandhāvāra* or camp of victory as early as the time of Samudragupta. It was an unimportant town in Buddha's time.[11] It is mentioned in the *Rāmāyaṇa* as the earlier capital of Kośala. Some think that Sāketa and Ayodhyā were identical, but Professor Rhys Davids has been successful in pointing out that both the cities existed in Buddha's time.[12] Ayodhyā was twelve yojanas long and nine yojanas broad according to the Jaina account.[13] It was the birthplace of Ṛṣabha, Ajita, Abhinandana, Sumati, Ananta and Acalabhānu. Here Lord Ādiguru attained enlightenment. Kumārapāla, the king of the Cālukyas, installed a Jaina image in this city. Here still exists the temple of Nābhirāja.[14] According to Alberuni, it is situated about 150 miles south-east from Kanauj. In the Buddhist period Kośala was divided into north and south. The capital of the southern Kośala was Ayodhyā.

Ayodhyā seems to have been included in the kingdom of Puṣyamitra Śuṅga. An inscription found here mentions the fact that Puṣyamitra performed two horse sacrifices or *aśvamedhas* during his reign.[15]

The Chinese pilgrim, Fa-Hien, who visited Ayodhyā in the 5th century A.D., saw the Buddhists and the Brāhmaṇas not in good terms. He also

---

[1] Raychaudhuri, *P.H.A.I.*, 4th Ed., p. 197.
[2] Law, *Indological Studies*, Pt. I, 1ff.
[3] B. C. Law, *Some Jaina Canonical Sūtras*, p. 174.
[4] For further details vide B. C. Law, *Tribes in Ancient India*, p. 355.
[5] *Āvassaka Commy.*, p. 244*a*.
[6] *Āvassaka Nirjjuti*, 382.
[7] *Aitareya Brāh.*, VII, 3ff.; *Sāṅkhyāyana Śrauta Sūtra*, XV, 17–25; cf. *J.R.A.S.*, 1917, 52 note.
[8] *Vividhatīrthakalpa*, p. 24.
[9] Chap. I, 64-65.
[10] Cf. *Vinaya*, II, 237; *Aṅg.*, IV, 101; *Saṃ*, II, 135; *Udāna*, v. 5.
[11] *Buddhist India*, p. 34.
[12] B. C. Law, *Geography of Early Buddhism*, p. 5.
[13] *Vividhatīrthakalpa*, Ch. 34.
[14] B. C. Law, *Some Jaina Canonical Sūtras*, p. 173.
[15] *E.I.*, XX, p. 57.

saw a tope there where the four Buddhas walked and sat.[1] Another Chinese pilgrim, Yuan Chwang, who visited India in the 7th century A.D., after travelling more than 600 li and crossing the Ganges to the south, reached the Ayudha or Ayodhyā country. According to him, Ayodhyā was the temporary residence of Asaṅga and Vasubandhu. He says that Ayudha is Sāketa, i.e., Ayodhyā. The country yielded good crops, was clothed with luxuriant vegetation and had rich fruit orchards and genial climate. The people had good manners and active habits and devoted themselves to practical learning. There were more than 100 Buddhist monasteries and more than 3,000 brethren, who were students of Mahāyāna and Hīnayāna. There were 10 deva temples and the non-Buddhists were few in number. Within the capital was the old monastery in which Vasubandhu composed various *śāstras*. There was a hall in ruins where Vasubandhu explained Buddhism to princes and monks who used to come from other countries. Close to the Ganges was a large Buddhist monastery with an Aśoka tope to mark the place where the Buddha preached his excellent doctrine. Four or five li west from this monastery was a Buddha relic tope and to the north of the tope were the remains of an old monastery where the *Sautrāntika-vibhāsā-śāstra* was composed. In a mango grove 5 or 6 li to the south-west of the city was the old monastery where Asaṅga learnt and taught. The three Buddhist treatises referred to by Yuan Chwang were communicated to Asaṅga by Maitreya. Above 100 paces to the north-west of the mango-grove was a Buddha relic tope. Asaṅga, according to the pilgrim, began his religious career as a *Mahiśāsaka* and afterwards became a Mahāyānist. Vasubandhu began his career in a school of the Sarvāstivādins. After the death of Asaṅga, Vasubandhu who composed several treatises, expounding and defending Mahāyānism, died at Ayodhyā at the age of 83.[2]

According to the *Rāmāyaṇa*, Ayodhyā was a city, full of wealth and granaries of paddy. It had spacious streets and roads, well-watered and decorated with flowers. It had lofty gates furnished with doors and bolts. It was fully protected. It was the home of skilful artisans and craftsmen. It contained palatial buildings, green bowers and mango-groves. The city was rendered impregnable being surrounded by a deep ditch filled with water. A large number of pinnacled houses and lofty seven-storied buildings existed there. It was a crowded city and frequently resounded by musical instruments. This city had Kamboja horses and mighty elephants.[3] In the *Mahābhārata*, it is called 'puṇyalakṣaṇā' that is, endowed with auspicious signs. It was a delightful spot on earth.[4] According to the *Rāmāyaṇa* there were four grades of social order at Ayodhyā, e.g., the Brāhmaṇas, the Kṣatriyas, the Vaiśyas and the Sūdras. They had to fulfil their respective duties and obligations.[5]

Ayodhyā is important in the history of Jainism and Buddhism.[6] The succession to the throne of Ayodhyā was generally determined according to the law of primogeniture in the Ikṣvāku family.[7] Ayodhyā had many well-known kings.[8] The kings of Ayodhyā were connected with the

---

1 Legge, *Travels of Fa-Hien*, pp. 54-55.

2 Watters, *On Yuan Chwang*, I, pp. 354–9.

3 *Rāmāyaṇa*, p. 309, vs. 22–24.

4 *Ibid.*, p. 6, vs. 90–98.

5 *Ibid.*, p. 114, v. 32.

6 S. Stevenson, *Heart of Jainism*, pp. 50-51; *Sam.*, III, 140ff.; *Sāratthappakāsinī*, II, p. 320.

7 *Rāmāyaṇa*, p. 387, v. 36.

8 *Mahābhārata*, 241. 2; *Vāyu*, 99, 270; *Matsya*, 50, 77; *Vāyu*, 85, 3-4; *Agni*, 272, 5–7; *Kūrma*, I, 20, 4–6; *Harivaṃśa*, 11, 660; *Padma*, V. 8, 130–62, etc., etc.

Vaśiṣṭha family. The Vaśiṣṭhas were their hereditary priests.[1] The kingdom of Ayodhyā rose to great eminence under Yuvanāśva II and especially his son Māndhātṛ.[2] The supremacy of Ayodhyā waned and the Kānyakubja kingdom rose into prominence under its king Jahnu. The Haihayas overcame Ayodhyā and the foreign tribes settled there after its conquest. Ayodhyā again became famous under Bhagīratha and Ambarīṣa Nābhāgi.[3] Daśaratha sought the help of the rustic Ṛṣyaśṛṅga from Aṅga.[4] The eastern and southern kings and kings of the distant Punjab were invited to Daśaratha's horse sacrifice at Ayodhyā. Ayodhyā and the Vaśiṣṭhas had no association then with the brahmanically *élite* region, as Pargiter points out.[5] The *Kathāsaritsāgara* refers to the camp of Nanda in Ayodhyā.[6] The *Yoginītantra* mentions this city (2/4, pp. 128-129). The Pali texts refer to some more kings of Ayodhyā.[7] A large number of coins were found at the site of Ayodhyā. For further details vide Law, *Indological Studies*, Pt. III.

Ayomukha.—According to Cunningham it was situated 30 miles south-west of Pratāpgarh.[8]

Āḷavī.—It has been identified by Cunningham and Hoernle with Newal or Nawal in the Unao district in U.P. Some have identified it with Aviwa, 27 miles north-east of Etawah.[9] There was a temple called Aggāḷava close to the town of Āḷavī where the Buddha once dwelt. Many female lay disciples and sisters came here to hear the truth preached.[10]

Āpayā.—It is a river mentioned in the *Ṛgveda* (III. 23, 4) flowing between the Dṛṣadvatī and the Sarasvatī. Some have identified it with the Āpagā as a name for the Ganges. It is near the Sarasvatī, according to Zimmer.[11] It is a small tributary flowing past Thaneswar. It is known to some as a branch of the Chitang river.[12] This river is also mentioned in the *Mahābhārata* (III. 83, 68).

Badarī.—According to the *Varāha Purāṇa* (141. 1) it is a secluded place in the Himalayan region. There are two holy places here called Indraloka and Pañcaśikha (141. 10; 141. 14). The *Padma Purāṇa* (Ch. 133) mentions Sārasvatatīrtha in Badarī.

Badarikārāma.—The Kosam Inscription of the region of Mahārāja Vaiśravaṇa refers to this locality situated in the vicinity of Kauśāmbī (*E.I.*, XXIV, Pt. IV, p. 147). It was a Buddhist retreat where the Master once dwelt. Here the elder Rāhula set his heart on the observance of the rules of monkhood (*Jāt.*, I, 160; III, 64). An elder named Khemaka while dwelling here fell very ill. At this time many elders staying at the Ghositārāma sent one of them named Dāsaka to him, enquiring how he managed to bear pains (*Saṃyutta*, III, 126ff.).

Badarikāśrama.—The *Mahābhārata* (90. 27–34) refers to it. It also mentions Badarikātīrtha (85. 13; cf. *Padma Purāṇa*, Ch. 21; *Tīrthamāhātmya*). The *Yoginītantra* (2. 6. 167ff.) mentions this hermitage. According to Bāṇa's *Kādambarī* Arjuna and Krishṇa visited it (p. 94). According to the *Skanda Purāṇa* (Ch. I, 53–59) a sinner becomes free from sins by visiting this holy place. Here a great *pūjā* (worship) is held, but

---

1 *Viṣṇu*, IV, 3. 18; *Padma*, VI, 219, 44.
2 *Mahābhārata*, III, 126.
3 *Vāyu*, 88, 171-2; *Padma*, VI. 22, 7–18; *Liṅga*, I, 66, 21-22, etc.
4 *Rāmāyaṇa*, I, 9 and 10.
5 *Ancient Indian Historical Tradition*, p. 314.
6 Tawney's Ed., I, p. 37.
7 *Jātaka* (Fausboll), IV, pp. 82-83; *Vaṃsatthappakāsinī* (P.T.S.), Vol. I, p. 127.
8 *C.A.S.R.*, XI, 68; *C.A.G.I.*, pp. 443ff., 708.
9 B. C. Law, *Geography of Early Buddhism*, p. 24.
10 *Jātaka*, I, 160.
11 *Altindisches Leben*, 18.
12 *J.R.A.S.*, 1883, p. 362.

no worship is held for six months every year when it is covered with snow (*Padma Purāṇa*, Uttarakhaṇḍa, 2. 1. 7).

Badrināth.—It is in Garhwal. It is a peak of the main Himalayan range, 55 miles north-east of Śrīnagara. Near the source of the Alakanandā the temple of Nara-Nārāyaṇa was built on the west bank. This temple is said to have been built by Saṅkarācārya in the 8th century A.D. (Law, *Holy Places of India*, p. 18; *Imperial Gazetteers of India* by W. W. Hunter, pp. 287ff.).

Banskhera.—It is about 25 miles from Shajahanpur where a plate of Harṣa was discovered (*E.I.*, IV, 208).

Barbarika (the Barbarei of Ptolemy).—It is evidently the Barbaricum or Barbaricon emporium mentioned in the *Periplus of the Erythraean Sea*. It was a market town and a port situated at the middle mouth of the Indus. It was one of the towns of the islands of the Indus delta (McCrindle's *Ancient India as described by Ptolemy*, Ed. Majumdar, p. 148).

The country of the Barbaras (Barbaradeśa) seems to have extended to the Arabian Sea. The *Mahābhārata* connects the people of Barbaradeśa with the Śakas and Yavanas (*Mahābhārata*, Sabhāparva, XXXI, 1199; Vanaparva, CCLIII, 15254; Śāntiparva, CCVII, 7560-61). The *Mārkaṇḍeya Purāṇa* (LVII. 39) places them in the Sindhu country, and the *Bṛhatsaṃhitā* refers to them as north or north-west tribes. (For further details, see Law, *Tribes in Ancient India*, p. 92).

Basahi.—It is a village two miles to the north-east of the headquarters town of the Bindhuna tahsil in the Etawah district, U.P. An inscription has been found here, which opens with an invocation to Viṣṇu and then gives the genealogy of the family from Mahiālā to Madanapāla (*I.A.*, XIV, 101–4).

Baṭeśvar.—It is a town in the Agra district on the right bank of the Jumna, 35 miles south-east of Agra, containing an ancient mound (*E.I.*, I, 207).

Bāhudā (Bāhukā or Bahukā).—Pargiter identifies this river with the modern Rāmagaṅgā which joins the Ganges on the left near Kanauj (Pargiter, *Mārkaṇḍeya Purāṇa*, pp. 291-92). Some have identified it with the river Dhavalā, now called Dhumela or Burha-Rapti, a feeder of the Rapti in Oudh (N. L. Dey, *Geographical Dictionary*, p. 16). There was another river of this name in the Deccan (*Mahābhārata*, Bhīṣmaparva, 9, 322; Anuśāsanaparva, 165, 7653; *Rāmāyaṇa*, Kiṣkindhyākāṇḍa, 41, 13). The sage named Likhita had his severed arm restored by bathing in this river, which was accordingly named Bāhudā (*Mahābhārata*, Śāntiparva, 22; *Harivaṃśa*, 12). The *Mārkaṇḍeyapurāṇa* (Ch. 57) connects this river with the Himalayas along with the Gaṅgā and Yamunā. According to the Śivapurāṇa Gaurī was turned into the river Bāhudā by the curse of her husband Prasenajit. The Bāhudā is also called the Bāhukā according to the *Majjhima Nikāya* (I, p. 39). The Buddha bathed in this river. Many people could remove their sins by taking their bath in it. (*Ibid.*, I, p. 39). It is also mentioned in the *Jātaka* (V. 388ff.) along with Gayā, Doṇa and Timbaru; the last two cannot be identified.

Bāhumatī.—The Bāhumatī (*Majjhima Nikāya*, I, 39) may be identified with the Bāgmatī, a sacred river of the Buddhists in Nepal. Lassen identifies Kakanthis of Arrian with the river Bāgmatī of Nepal. Bāgmatī is also called Bāchmatī, as it was created by the Buddha Krakucchanda by the word of mouth during his visit to Nepal. Its junction with the rivers Maradārika, Maṇiśrohi, Rājamañjari, Ratnāvalī, Cārumatī, Prabhāvatī and Triveṇī form the *tīrthas* (holy places) called Śāntā, Śaṅkara, Rājamañjarī, Pramodā, Sulakṣaṇā, Jayā and Gokarṇa respectively (*Varāha*-

purāṇa, Ch. 215; cf. *Svayambhūpurāṇa*, Ch. V). On the bank of the Bāgmatī river stands Vatsalā (*Nepālmāhātmya*, Ch. I, 39).

Bārāṇasi.—See *Kāśi.*

Belkhara.—It is a village situated about 12 miles south-east of Chunar in the Mirzapur district, U.P. The Belkhara stone pillar inscription has been discovered in this village, which is incised on a stone pillar, above which there is a small figure of Gaṇeśa.[1]

Bhaddavatikā.—This market-town lay on the way from the Pārileyyaka forest to Śrāvastī. After spending the rainy season at Sāvatthī, the Buddha went out on a begging tour and came here. Near this market-town there was a grove where the Master dwelt. From this town he went to Kosambī.[2]

Bhadraśilā.—It was a rich, prosperous, and populous city. It was 12 *yojanas* in length and breadth and was well-divided with four gates and adorned with high vaults and windows. In this city there was a royal garden.[3] According to the *Bodhisattvāvadāna-Kalpalatā* the city was situated to the north of the Himalayas (5th Pallava, pp. 2 and 6). This city later came to be known as Takṣaśilā because here the head of Candraprabha who was its ruler was severed by a beggar Brahmin.[4]

Bharadvāja-āśrama.—The sage Bharadvāja had his hermitage which was situated at the confluence of the rivers Gaṅgā and Yamunā at Prayāga or Allahabad.[5] Rāma himself admitted that this hermitage was not far from Ayodhyā.[6] It was visited by Rāmacandra on his way to Daṇḍakāraṇya and he sent Hanumān to Bharata.[7] Rāma together with Lakṣmaṇa and Sītā came here. They then duly greeted the sage and informed him that they were going in exile for fourteen years to fulfil the pledge of their father. Bharata in course of his wanderings in quest of Rāma came here with his family-priest Vaśiṣṭha. King Divodāsa being defeated in the fight with the Vītahavyas sought refuge in this hermitage.

Bharga.—The country of the Bhargas became a dependency of Vatsa with Suṃsumāragira as its chief town.[8] Some place it between Vaiśālī and Śrāvastī, but the location of the place is uncertain.

Bhāṣkarakṣetra.—It is mentioned in the inscriptions on the copper-plates from Nutimadugu. It is Hampi in the Bellary district.[9] N. L. Dey has identified it with Prayāga without assigning any definite reason to his identification.[10]

Bhesakaḷāvana.—It was in the neighbourhood of Suṃsumāragiri or Suṃsumāragira of the Bhargas where the Buddha stayed.[11] It was also known as Kesakaḷāvana.[12] It was an important Buddhist retreat and early centre of Buddhist activity in the Vatsa country. This park evidently belonged to Prince Bodhi who became an ardent lay supporter of the Buddha.[13]

Bhitargaon.—It is in the Kanpur district containing a big temple. This village, also known as Bhitrigaon, is situated halfway between Kanpur and Hamirpur, 20 miles to the south of the former place and 10 miles to the north-west of Kora Jāhānābād.[14]

---

1 *A.S.R.*, XI, 128ff.; *J.A.S.B.*, 1911, pp. 763ff.
2 *Jātaka*, I, 360.
3 *Divyāvadāna*, p. 315.
4 R. L. Mitra, *N.B.Lit.*, p. 310.
5 *Rāmāyaṇa*, Ayodhyākāṇḍa, Ch. 54, V. 9.
6 *Ibid.*, Sarga 54, V. 24.
7 *Ibid.*, Ādikāṇḍa, 1 Sarga, V. 87.
8 *Aṅg.*, II, 61; *Vinaya*, II, 127.
9 *E.I.*, XXV, Pt. IV.
10 *Geog. Dict. of Ancient and Mediaeval India*, 2nd ed., 32.
11 *Aṅg.*, II, p. 61; III, p. 295; IV, pp. 85, 228, 232, 268; *Majjhima*, II, 91; *Jātaka*, III, 157; *Majjhima*, I, 513ff.
12 *Majjhima*, II, 91; *Jāt.*, III, 157.
13 *Majjhima*, I, 513ff.
14 *A.S.I.*, *Annual Report*, 1908-9, pp. 5ff.

Bhitarī.—This village, mentioned in the Bhitarī stone pillar inscription of Skandagupta, is situated about five miles to the north-east of Sayyidpur, the chief town of the Sayyidpur tahsil of the Ghazipur district.[1]

Bhiṭā.—It has been identified with the old Biṭbhaya-paṭṭana, a town mentioned in the *Vīracaritra* as having flourished at the time of Mahāvīra. This text refers to Biṭbhayapaṭṭana as the seat of king Udayana who embraced Jainism.[2] The ancient remains of Bhiṭā near Allahabad have been described by Gen. Cunningham who visited the site in 1872.[3] For further details vide *A.S.I.*, *Annual Report*, 1909-10, p. 40; 1911-12, pp. 29–94.

Bhṛgu-āśrama.—The *Mahābhārata* calls it *Bhṛgutīrtha*. The sage had his hermitage at Balia in the Uttara Pradeśa, situated at the confluence of the Ganges and the Sarayū. Here Paraśurāma regained his energy which was taken away by Rāma Dāśarathī.[4] King Vītahavya is said to have fled and taken shelter in this hermitage. Through the good grace of Bhṛgu king Vītahavya became a Brahmin.[5]

Bilsad.—This village otherwise known as Bilasand occurs in the Bilsad stone pillar inscription of Kumāragupta. It consists of three parts, eastern Bilsad, western Bilsad, and Bilsad suburb, situated about four miles towards the north-west of Aligunj in the Etah district.[6]

Bithur.—It is situated 14 miles from Kanpur and contains the hermitage of sage Vālmīki.

Brahmapura.—It is the ancient capital of the Chamba State in the Punjab. It contains three ancient temples of which the largest is of stone and dedicated to Maṇimaheśa, an incarnation of Śiva, the second temple of stone is dedicated to Narasinha or the Lion incarnation of Viṣṇu, and the third, mostly of wood, is dedicated to Lakṣmaṇadevī. According to Cunningham Brahmapura was another name for Vairāṭapaṭṭana. The climate of the place is said to be slightly cold and this also agrees with the position of Vairāṭa. Hiuen Tsang describes the kingdom of Brahmapura as 667 miles in circuit. It must have included the whole of the hilly country between the Alakananda and the Karṇāli rivers.[7] Brahmapura was also known as Po-lo-lih-mo-pu-lo.[8] According to Cunningham Brahmapura existed in the districts of Garhwal and Kumaon. In these districts reigned the Katur or Katuriā rājās connected with Kortripura of Samudragupta's Allahabad Pillar Inscription.[9]

Buri-Gaṇḍak.—It has its origin in the hills of Hariharpur in Nepal. The first western tributary which it receives to the north-east of Matihārī in the district of Champaran, is nothing but a united stream of six rivers. It meets the Ganges west of Gogri in the Monghyr district. For further details, vide B. C. Law, *Rivers of India*, p. 24.

Candapahā.—It is a village in the Kosamba-paṭṭala, which was granted by Karṇadeva to the Paṇḍita Śāntiśarman.[10]

Candrabhāgā.—The *Apadāna*, a Pali canonical text, refers to it[11]. According to the *Milindapañha* (p. 114) this river issues forth from the Himavanta (Himalayan region). The Jaina *Ṭhānaṃga* (5. 470) mentions

---

1 *C.I.I.*, Vol. III.
2 *Allahabad Dist. Gazetteer*, by Nevill, p. 234.
3 *A.S.R.*, Vol. III, 46–52.
4 *Mahābhārata*, III. 99. 8650.
5 Cf. Matin, *Eastern India*, II, 340.
6 *C.I.I.*, Vol. III.
7 *C.A.G.I.*, 407ff.
8 Watters, *On Yuan Chwang*, I, p. 329.
9 *J.R.A.S.*, 1898, 199; *C.A.G.I.*, 704.
10 *E.I.*, XI, pp. 139ff.; see also *J.R.A.S.*, 1927, pp. 694ff.
11 Pp. 277, 291.

it along with other four. The Candrabhāgā or Chenāb appears to flow just above Kishtwar as a confluence of two hill-streams. From Kishtwar to Rishtwar its course is southerly. It flows past Jammu, wherefrom it flows in a south-westerly direction forming a doab between it and the Vitastā (Jhelum). It is the same river as the Ṛgvedic Asikṇī, Arrian's Akesines and Sandabaga or Sandabal of Ptolemy. According to the *Mārkaṇḍeyapurāṇa* there were two rivers of this name. The *Mahābhārata* also seems to support the same contention[1] but it is difficult to identify the second stream. The *Padmapurāṇa*[2] mentions this river.

Candrāvatī.—It is situated in the district of Benares on the left bank of the Gaṅgā, where two copperplates of the Gāhaḍavāla dynasty were discovered.[3]

Cāvala.—This mountain has been described to be not far off from the Himalaya.[4]

Chamba.—This district includes the valleys of all the sources of the Rāvī and a portion of the upper valley of the Chenab between Lāhul and Kāshtwār. The ancient capital was Varmmapura.[5]

Chatarpur.—This village existed near Sheorajpur, 21 miles north-west of Kanpur where a copperplate inscription of Govinda Candradeva was discovered.[6]

Cīna.—The Nāgārjunikoṇḍa Inscription of Vīrapuruṣadatta mentions it. It lay in the Himalayas beyond Cilāta or Kirāta. Himavantapadesa is stated to be the Cīnaraṭṭha in the Pali *Sāsanavaṃsa* (p. 13).

Citrakūṭa (Pali *Cittakūṭa*).—This beautiful mountain finds its place among the holy places mentioned in the *Padmapurāṇa* (Ch. 21—*Tīrtha-māhātmya*). It is known in the Jaina *Bhagavatī-Ṭīkā* (7. 6) as Cittakuḍa. According to Kālidāsa it appears like a wild bull playfully butting against a rock or mound.[7] It stood at a distance of 20 miles (10 *krośas*) from the hermitage of the sage Bharadvāja.[8] The *Uttaracaritaṃ* (Act. I, 24) refers to the road on the bank of the Kālindī leading to the Citrakūṭa mountain. It is the modern Citrakūṭa, a famous hill, lying 65 miles west-south-west of Allahabad.[9] It is situated about four miles from the modern Citrakūṭa railway station. It lay to the south-west of Prayāga. The *Apadāna* (p. 50) vaguely locates it to be not very far off from the Himavanta. The Gaḍhwā stone inscription refers to it.[10] The *Bhāgavatapurāṇa* mentions it as a mountain (v. 19, 16). The *Lalitavistara* (p. 391) refers to it as a hill. It was a pleasant spot.[11] It was a spotless place.[12] It existed in the Himalayan region and it had a golden cave and a natural lake.[13] It was noted for its waterfalls (*Raghuv.*, XIII. 47).

It has been identified with Kāmptānāthgiri in Bundelkhand. It is usually identified with the mountain of the same name in the Banda district, U.P., about 20 miles north-north-east of Kalinjar.[14] The *Mahābhārata* (III. 85. 56) associates it with Kālañjara. As regards its identification we may also refer to *A.S.R.*, XIII and XXI and *J.R.A.S.*, 1894.

According to the Rāmāyaṇa[15] Rāma dwelt on this hill situated on a river called the Payasvinī (Paisunī) or Mandākinī. He came here after

---

[1] Bhīṣmaparva, 9, 322–27.
[2] Uttarakhaṇḍa, vs. 35–38.
[3] *I.H.Q.*, March, 1949.
[4] *Apadāna*, p. 451.
[5] *C.A.G.I.*, pp. 161-162.
[6] *E.I.*, XVIII, p. 224.
[7] *Raghuv.*, XIII, 47.
[8] *Rāmāyaṇa*, Ayodhyākāṇḍa, Sarga 54, v. 28.
[9] *J.R.A.S.*, April, 1894, p. 239.
[10] *C.I.I.*, Vol. III.
[11] *Jātaka*, II, 176.
[12] *Jātaka*, VI, 126.
[13] *Jātaka*, II, 176; III, p. 208.
[14] *J.R.A.S.B.*, Vol. XV, 1949, No. 2, *Letters*, p. 129.
[15] Ayodhyākāṇḍa, Ch. 55.

crossing the Yamunā while returning from the hermitage of Bharadvāja. It was 3 yojanas distant from Bharadvāja-āśrama.[1] This beautiful mountain was an abode of many geese living in the golden cave which it contained,[2] some of which were swift and some golden.[3] A king set out for this mountain being instructed to observe the moral law, to rule the kingdom righteously and to win the hearts of the people.[4] The *Kālikā-purāṇa* (79. 143) points out that a mountain called Kajjala stands to the east of the Citrakūṭa.

There were two rivers at Citrakūṭa called the Mandākinī and Mālinī.[5] The Mandākinī is stated to have been on the north side of this hill. The forest at Citrakūṭa does not appear to have been isolated. The Nīla forest joined the forest on this hill.[6] The *Mahābhārata* (85, 58-59) refers to the Citrakūṭaparvata and the Mandākinī river.

Cukṣa.—Cukṣa occurring in the Taxila Silver Vase Inscription of Johonika, is identified with the plain of Chach near Taxila.[7] Cukṣa, according to Stein, is the present Chach in the north of the Attock district.

Dadhīci-āśrama.—This hermitage lay on the other side of the Sarasvatī. The sage Dadhīci gave up his life for the good of humanity.

Dalmau.—It is the capital of the *pargana* of the same name and the headquarters of the tahsil Dalmau. It is a town of great antiquity and of considerable historical and archaeological interest. It stands on the bank of the Ganges at a distance of 19 miles from Rai Bareli. It contains a fort which really consists of the ruins of two Buddhist stūpas.[8]

Daṇḍakahiraññā.—This mountain seems to have been located in the Himalayan region.[9]

Davālā.—The Khoh copperplate inscription of Mahārāja Samkhoba mentions it, which is the older form of Ḍāhala, which seems to represent the modern Bundelkhand.[10] The Āṭavikarājyas included Āḷavaka (Ghazipur) as well as the forest kingdoms connected with Ḍavālā (Ḍabhālā) or Jabbalpore.[11]

Darvābhisāra.—This place is mentioned in the *Mahābhārata* (VII, 91, 43) which, according to Stein, included the tract of the lower and middle hills lying between the Jhelum and the Chenab. According to some it roughly corresponded to the Punch and Naoshera districts in Kāśmīra and was probably an offshoot of the old kingdom of Kāmboja (Raychaudhuri, *P.H.A.I.*, 4th Ed., p. 200). For further details vide B. C. Law, *Indological Studies*, Pt. I, pp. 17-18.

Deoliā.—It is located in the Partapgarh State in U.P. (*Inscriptions of Northern India* revised by D. R. Bhandarkar, No. 696, V. 1393).

Deoriā.—This village is situated on the south or right bank of the Jumna at a distance of 11 miles south-west from Allahabad and about nine miles west of Karcanā (*Allahabad Dist. Gazetteer* by Nevill, p. 233).

Devikā.—This river is mentioned in Pāṇini's *Aṣṭādhyāyī* (VII. 3. 1), in the *Yoginītantra* (2. 5. 139ff.), and in the *Kālikāpurāṇa* (Ch. 24. 137-138). Pargiter has sought to identify this river with the Deeg, a tributary of the river Rāvī (*Mārkaṇḍeyapurāṇa*, p. 292, note). The *Vāmana*

---

[1] Ayodhyākāṇḍa, LIV, 29-30.
[2] *Jātaka*, V, 337; *Jāt.*, II, 107; V, 381.
[3] *Jātaka*, IV, 212, 423-424.
[4] *Jāt.*, V, 352.
[5] *Rāmāyaṇa*, Ayodhyākāṇḍa, LIV, 39; LVI, 7, 8.
[6] Ayodhyākāṇḍa, LVI, 1-18.
[7] Buhler, *E.I.*, IV. 54; Sten Konow, *C.I.I.*, II, i, 25-28; Raychaudhuri, *P.H.A.I.*, 4th ed., p. 369, f.n. 3.
[8] *Rai Bareli District Gazetteer*, by Nevill, pp. 160ff.
[9] *Jāt.*, II, p. 33.
[10] *C.I.I.*, Vol. III.
[11] *E.I.*, VIII, 284-287.

Purāṇa and the *Matsya Purāṇa* support this identification (Chs. 81, 84, 89; Ch. 113). According to the *Agni Purāṇa* (Ch. 200) it flowed through the Sauvīra country. The *Padmapurāṇa* (uttarakhaṇḍa, vs. 35–38) mentions this river. The *Kālikāpurāṇa* (Ch. 23. 137-138) refers to its source which is in the Maināka hills in the Sewalik range. This river has also been identified with the river Devā or Devikā in U.P., which is another name for the southern course of the Sarayū (*Agra Guide and Gazetteer*, 1841, II, pp. 120, 252). According to the *Kālikāpurāṇa* it flowed between the Gomatī and the Sarayū. The Anuśāsanaparva of the *Mahābhārata* (śls. 7645 and 7647) suggests that the Devikā and the Sarayū were not the one and the same river.

Dhammapālagāma.—This village was included in the kingdom of Kāśī (*Jātaka*, IV, 50).

Dṛṣadvatī.—This river which is mentioned in the *Ṛgveda* (III, 23-4) has been described as the southern and eastern boundary of what was then known as Brahmāvarta (II. 17). According to the *Mahābhārata*, it seems to have formed one of the boundaries of Kurukṣetra (Vanaparva, 5074). In the *Kālikāpurāṇa* (Ch. 51. 77ff.) it is mentioned as looking like the Ganges (Gaṅgā). The confluence of the Dṛṣadvatī and the Kauśikī was of peculiar sanctity. This river has been identified with the modern Citrang which runs parallel to the Sarasvatī (Rapson, *Ancient India*, p. 51; *Imperial Gazetteer of India*, p. 26). The origin of this river may be traced to the hills of Sirmur. Elphinstone and Todd sought to identify it with the Ghagar flowing through Ambala and Sind but now lost in the desert sands of Rajputana (*J.A.S.B.*, VI, 181), while Cunningham found in it the river Rākshi that flows by the south-east of Thaneswar (*Archaeological Survey Report*, XIV). Some have identified this river with the modern Chitang or Chitrung (*J.R.A.S.*, 25, 58). The *Vāmana Purāṇa* (Ch. 34) takes the Kauśikī to be a branch of Dṛṣadvatī. The *Bhāgavata Purāṇa* also refers to it as a river (V. 19, 18; X, 71, 22). The *Yoginītantra* (2. 5. 139ff.) mentions this river.

Dvaitavana.—The Pāṇḍavas lived in this forest during the period of their exile. It was considered to be a free land over which there was no sway of any monarch. It was so called because there was a lake called Dvaita within its boundary. According to the *Mahābhārata* it was close to a desert and the Sarasvatī flowed through it. It was not far from the Himalayas lying between Taṅgana on the north-east and Kurukṣetra and Hastināpura on the south-east. It was from this place the Pāṇḍavas started on a pilgrimage as described in the Vanaparva of the *Mahābhārata*. (*E.I.*, XXVII., Pt. VII, July 1948, pp. 319ff.).

Ekasālā.—It was a Brahmin village where the Buddha once stayed among the Kosalans. He gave instruction on *dhamma* being surrounded by a big assembly of householders. Here Māra suffered a defeat at the hands of the Buddha. (*Saṃyutta*, I, p. 111.)

Gaḍhwā.—The Gaḍhwā stone inscription of Candragupta II refers to this fort comprising several villages in Arail and Bara parganas in the subdivision of the Allahabad district (*C.I.I.*, Vol. III). This inscription locates Gaḍhwā in the Karcanā sub-division of the Allahabad district.

Gaṇḍakī (Gandak).—It is also called Gaṇḍakī and Cakranadī according to the *Bhāgavatapurāṇa* (X. 79, 11; V. 7, 10). The *Padmapurāṇa* (Ch. 21) considers it as holy. The *Yoginītantra* (2/1, pp. 112-113) mentions the river Gaṇḍakī. It is a great upper tributary of the Ganges, which has its origin in the hills in south Tibet. In passing through Nepal it receives four tributaries on the left side and two on the right. The upper tributary of the Gandak on its right side joins it at a place to the north-west of Nayakot in Nepal, and the lower tributary called the Rāpti joins it just above the district of Cāmpārān. Its main stream flows into the Ganges between Sonpur in the Sara district and Hajipur in the district of Muzaffarpur, while its lesser stream bifurcating at Basarh flows down into another river. For details, vide B. C. Law, *Rivers of India*, pp. 23-24.

Gaṇḍaparvata.—It is the Gaṅgotrī mountain at the foot of which Bindusarovara is situated (*Matsyapurāṇa*, Ch. 121).

Gandhamādana.—The *Yoginītantra* (1/15) mentions this *parvata* (mountain). The *Bhāgavatapurāṇa* (IV. I, 58; V. I, 8; X. 52, 3) refers to it as a mountain upon which Brahmā descended. It is described in the *Jātaka* as a rocky mountain, which was visited by king Vessantara with his wife and children (*Jātaka*, VI, p. 519). This mountain forms a part of the Rudra Himalaya and according to the epic writers, a part of the Kailāsa range. It is said to have been watered by the Mandākinī. According to the *Harivaṃśa* (Ch. XXVI. 5–7) King Pururava lived with Urvaśī for ten years at the foot of the Mount Gandhamādana. According to the *Padmapurāṇa* (Ch. 133) there was a *tīrtha* (holy place) here called the Sugandha. This *Purāṇa* (Uttarakhaṇḍa, vs. 35–38) mentions Gandhamādana. Bāṇa describes it as one of the summits of the Himalaya (*Kādambarī*, Ed. Kale, 94). Kālidāsa mentions the Gandhamādana in his *Kumārasambhava* (VIII. 28, 29, 75 and 86). A certain ascetic came to Benaras from this mountain to see the king (*Jāt*., III, 452). There was a cave in this mountain known as the Nandamūla inhabited by the elect (*Sāsanavaṃsa*, P.T.S., p. 68). This mountain had a big *śivaliṅga* (*Kālikāpurāṇa*, 78. 70). To the east of this mountain there existed the Kāma mountain (*Ibid*., 79. 57). According to the *Divyāvadāna* (p. 157) Aśoka's tree was brought from this mountain by Ratnaka, the keeper of a hermitage, and was planted at the place where the Buddha showed miracles. This mountain was visited by the Buddha, when a Brahmin used to live at its foot (*Bodhisattvāvadānakalpalatā*, 5th Pallava, pp. 25, 31).

Gandharva.—The Gandharva country mentioned in the *Mahābhārata* (II, 48, 22-23) has been identified by some with the Gandhāra country. The Gandhāra country mentioned in the *Rāmāyaṇa* is said to be situated on the banks of the Indus (Moti Chandra, *Geo. and Eco. Studies in the Mahābhārata*, p. 115).

Gandhāra.—Gandhāra,[1] which is one of the sixteen *Mahājanapadas* mentioned in the Pali Texts (*Aṅg*., I, p. 213, *Ibid*., IV, 252, 256, and 260), is also mentioned in Pāṇini's *Aṣṭādhyāyī* (4. 1. 169) and in the Nāgārjunikoṇḍa Inscription of Vīrapuruṣadatta. The *Matsyapurāṇa* (114. 41) and the *Vāyupurāṇa* (45. 116) refer to it. It included Rawalpindi and Peshawar districts. It is mentioned in the list of countries given in the Behistun Inscription of Darius I (522–486 B.C.). It is also referred to in the big Susā palace inscription of Darius. The people of Gadāra (Gandhāra) appear to be one of the subject peoples of the Persian empire (*Ancient Persian Lexicon and the Texts of Achaemenian Inscriptions*, by H. C. Tomen, *Vanderbilt Oriental Series*, Vol. VI). The Gandhāras, who were an ancient people known to the Ṛgvedic times (*Ṛgv*., I, 126. 7), are mentioned in Aśoka's Edict V as the inhabitants of Gandhāra, which is equivalent to the North-West Punjab and adjoining regions. Thus it lay on both sides of the Indus (Raychaudhuri, *P.H.A.I.*, 4th edition, p. 50; *Rāmāyaṇa*, VII, 113, 11; 114, 11). Hiuen Tsang found the country of Gandhāra to be above 1,000 li from east to west and above 800 li north to south. The country, according to him, had luxuriant crops of cereals and a profusion

[1] Luders' List, No. 1345.

of fruits and flowers; it produced much sugarcane and prepared sugar-candy. The climate was warm. The people were faint-hearted and fond of the practical arts (Watters, *On Yuan Chwang*, I, 198-99). There were above 1,000 Buddhist monasteries in this country, but they were utterly dilapidated. Many topes were in ruins. There were more than 100 Deva temples and the various sects lived pell-mell (*Ibid.*, I, 202). The most ancient capital of Gandhāra was Puṣkarāvatī, which is said to have been founded by Puṣkara, son of Bharata and nephew of Rāma (*Viṣṇu Purāṇa*, Wilson's ed., Vol. IV, Ch. 4). The early capital cities of Gandhāra were Puṣkarāvatī or Puṣkalāvatī and Takṣaśilā, the former being situated to the west and the latter to the east of the Indus. Some hold that the kingdom of Gandhāra included Kasmira and Takṣaśilā region (Raychaudhuri, *P.H.A.I.*, 4th Ed., p. 124), but this is not corroborated by the evidence of the Jātaka (Vide *Jāt.*, III, 365). It comprises the districts of Peshawar and Rawalpindi in the northern Punjab (*Mahāv.*, Geiger's tr. p. 82, n. 2). Vasubandhu, the famous author of the *Abhidharmakoṣaśāstra*, was a native of Puṣkarāvatī, which was about 14 or 15 li in circuit and was well peopled, according to Hiuen Tsang (Watters, *On Yuan Chwang*, I, 214). For further details see B. C. Law, *Tribes in Ancient India*, pp. 9ff.; *Geography of Early Buddhism*, pp. 49-50; *Indological Studies*, Pt. I, pp. 10ff.

Ganeśrā.—It is near Mathurā. Here a fragmentary inscription was found by Vogel. This inscription reveals the name of a satrap of the Kṣaharāta family called Ghaṭāka.[1]

Gaṅgā.—The Gaṅgā which is also called Alakanandā[2] or Dyudhunī[3] or Dyunadī[4] is mentioned in the *Ṛgveda*[5] and in the *Śatapatha Brāhmaṇa* (XIII, 5, 4, 11). Patañjali's *Mahābhāṣya* mentions it (1, 1, 9. p. 436; 1.4.2. p. 670). It is also mentioned in the *Brahmāṇḍapurāṇa* (II. 18, 26–42; 50–52) as well as in Kālidāsa's *Raghuvaṃśa*.[6] The Gaṅgā is also known as the Bhāgīrathī and Jāhṇavī.[7] The *Yoginītantra* refers to it (1. 6; 2. 1; 2. 7, 8; 2. 5). The victory on the Gaṅgā represents the furthest extent of the Kuru rule (*Vedic Index*, I, 218, f.n. 4). According to the *Taittirīya Āraṇyaka* (II. 20), those who dwelt between the Gaṅgā and the Yamunā were especially honoured. The Varaṇāvatī which is found in the *Atharvaveda* (IV. 7, 1) seems to be the Ganges according to Ludwig.[8] The Gaṅgā or the modern Ganges is said to have issued from the foot of the Nārāyaṇa and followed her course on the Mount Meru; then she bifurcated herself in four streams flowing east, south, west and north; the southern stream was allowed by Śiva through the intercession of king Bharata to flow through India.[9] According to the *Harivaṃśa*[10] king Pururava lived with Urvaśī for five years on the bank of the river Mandākinī which is another name of the Ganges. According to the *Mārkaṇḍeya Purāṇa* (pp. 242-243) the Ganges is described as *Tripathagāminī*, i.e., having three courses. It was visited by Rāma and Lakṣmaṇa.[11] The stream which flows in the east towards the Caitraratha forest is called the Sītā which proceeds towards the Varuṇoda-Sarovara. The stream which flows towards the Gandhamādana mountain from the southern side of the Sumeru

---

1 *J.R.A.S.*, 1912, p. 121.

2 *Bhāgavata Purāṇa*, IV, 6, 24 ; XI, 29, 42.

3 *Bhāgavata Purāṇa*, III, 23, 39.

4 *Bhāgavata Purāṇa*, III, 5. 1; X, 75, 8.

5 X. 75, 5; VI. 45, 21.

6 IV. 73 ; VI. 48 ; VII. 36 ; VIII. 95 ; XIII. 57 ; XIV. 3.

7 *Raghuv.*, VII. 36; VIII. 95; X. 26, 69.

8 *Translation of the Ṛgveda*, 3, 210; Zimmer, *Altindisches Leben*, 20.

9 *Mārkaṇḍeya Purāṇa*, 56. 1–12.

10 Ch. XXVI, 5–7.

11 *Rāmāyaṇa*, Ādikāṇḍa, sarga 23, v. 5.

is called the Alakanandā which falls into the Mānasasarovara in strong currents. The *Vāyu* and *Matsya Purāṇas* give almost the same description as the *Mārkaṇḍeya* of the descent of the Ganges, while the *Viṣṇu, Bhāgavata* and *Padmapurāṇas* as well as the *Mahābhārata* (85. 88–98; 87. 14) agree substantially. According to Bāṇa's *Kādambarī* (p. 75) the Ganges while being brought down by Bhagīratha happened to wash off the altar of Jahṇu who was performing a sacrifice. The *Padmapurāṇa* (Ch. 21) mentions *Gaṅgāsāgara-saṅgama* which is considered holy. According to the *Brahmapurāṇa* (Ch. 78, v. 77) the Ganges which flows to the south of the Vindhya mountain is called the Gautamīgaṅgā and the Ganges flowing to the north of it is called the Bhāgirathīgaṅgā. (For the interesting account given in the *Vāyu Purāṇa*, vide B. C. Law, *Geographical Essays*, Vol. I, p. 85). The *Padmapurāṇa* (Ch. 4, v. 107) mentions the confluence of the Ganges and the Sindhu as a holy spot. This *Purāṇa* refers to the seven branches into which the Ganges is divided, namely, Vaṭodakā, Nalinī, Sarasvatī, Jambunadī, Sītā, Gaṅgā and Sindhu (Svargakhaṇḍa, Ch. 2, v. 68). Some useful information is supplied by Arrian regarding the Ganges and its tributaries when he observes: 'Megasthenes states that of the two (the Ganges and the Indus), the Ganges is much the larger. . . . It receives, besides, the river Sonos and the Sittokatis and the Solomatis which are also navigable and also the Kondochates and the Sambos and the Magon and the Agoranis and the Omalis. Moreover there fall into it the Kommenases, a great river, and the Kakouthis and the Andomatis . . . .' (McCrindle, *Ancient India*, pp. 190-91). According to the *Jambudīvapaṇṇatti* the Ganges flows eastwards with 14,000 other streams joining it. The Great Epic traces the source of this stream to Bindusāra, while the Pali works to the southern face of the Anotatta lake. The Bhāgīrathīgaṅgā comes to light in the Gaṅgotrī in the district of Garhwal. From Hardwar down to Bulandshahar the Ganges has a southerly course after which she flows in a south-easterly direction up to Allahabad where she is joined by the Yamunā. From Allahabad down to Rajmahal she has an easterly course. She enters Bengal below Rajmahal. From Hardwar to Allahabad she flows almost parallel to the Yamunā. The *Mahābhārata* (84. 29) refers to Saptagaṅgā. (For further details, vide Law, *Rivers of India*, 17ff.; Law, *Geographical Essays*, 84ff.)

Gargarā.—It is the name of a river. The Gaṅgdhar Inscription of Viśvavarman mentions this river Gargarā, the ancient name of the modern river Kālisindh, a tributary of the Chambal (*C.I.I.*, Vol. III).

Garhmukhteśvara.—It is a town in the Meerut district situated on the right bank of the Ganges. It is a holy place of the Hindus and is famous for its Gaṅgā temple.

Garjapur (*Garjapatipura*).—It was a town on the Ganges, 50 miles east of Benaras, identified with the modern Ghazipur. It was also known as Garjanapati. Its Chinese name is Chen-chu. It was 2,000 li in circuit. The soil was rich and fertile, and the land was regularly cultivated. The climate was temperate, and the people were honest. There were ten *Saṅghārāmas* and twenty Deva temples (Beal, *Buddhist Records of the Western World*, II, 61).

Gaurīśaṅkara.—It is the Mount Everest in Nepal. This Himalayan peak which is really situated on the Nepal-Tibet border is regarded as the highest mountain-peak on earth. It is 29,002 ft. high. (Law, *Mountains of India*, pp. 2, 6). It is known by various names, e.g. Devadhuṅga, Como Kaṅkar, Como Lungma, Como Uri, Chelungbu and Mi-ti-Gu-ti-Ca-pu Longnga. Some hold that Radhanath Sikdar was not the discoverer of the Mount Everest. The discovery of the Mount was due to the combined efforts of the department of the Survey of India (*Mount Everest—*its name and height by B. T. Gulatee, Survey of India—Technical paper No. 4). Gulatee has pointed out that the Mount Everest has defied any attempt at finality both as regards its height and local name. In 1953 Hillary and Tenzing reached its summit and found it to be a perfect cone covered with snow on which they were free to move about.

Gavidhumat.—It may be identified with Kudarkote, 24 miles to the north-east of Etawah and 36 miles from Sankisa in the district of Farrukhabad (N. L. Dey, *Geographical Dictionary,* p. 59). Patañjali in his *Mahābhāṣya* mentions it (2. 3. 21, p. 194).

Ghositārāma.—This monastery was at Kauśāmbī built by a banker named Ghosita. (*Dīgha,* I, 157, 159; *Saṃ.,* II, 115; *Papañcasūdanī* II. 390). It was named after him (*Samantapāsādikā,* III, 574). The recent excavation at this site has resulted in the discovery of an inscription which helps us in locating this famous *ārāma,* which was situated on the outskirts of Kauśāmbī in the south-east corner. This site seems to be not far off from the Jumna. This *ārāma* was a favourite resort of the venerable Ānanda even after the Buddha's demise (*Saṃyutta,* III, 133ff.). It was occasionally visited by Sāriputta, Mahākaccāyana and Upavāṇa (*Ibid.,* V, 76-77; *Paramatthadīpanī on the Petavatthu,* 140–144). The Buddha after leaving Anupiyā came to Kauśāmbī where he stayed in this *ārāma* (*Vinaya,* II, p. 184). Here Ānanda was met by Channa (*Ibid.,* II, p. 292). A monk named Channa was an inmate of this *ārāma.* The Buddha prescribed the *Brahmadaṇḍa* for him at the time of his demise (*Vinaya Texts,* II, 370). Here two wanderers named Maṇḍissa and Jāliya interviewed the Buddha (*Dīgha,* I, 157, 159-60). Piṇḍola Bhāradvāja, who was instrumental in the conversion of Udayana to the Buddhist faith, used to reside here (cf. *Psalms of the Brethren,* p. 111). Some thirty thousand monks of this *ārāma* headed by Thera Urudhammarakkhita visited Ceylon in about the 1st century B.C. during the reign of king Duṭṭhagāmaṇi (*Mahāvamsa,* P.T.S., p. 228). When Fa-Hien visited Kauśāmbī in the 5th century A.D., the Ghositārāma was tenanted by Buddhist priests 'mostly of the Lesser Vehicle' (Legge, *Travels of Fa-Hien,* p. 96). Hiuen Tsang who visited Kauśāmbī in the 7th century A.D. saw more than ten *saṅghārāmas* all in utter ruin (Watters, *On Yuan Chwang,* I, 366). Out of the ten monasteries one was the famous Ghositārāma situated to the south-east of Kauśāmbī. The Kukkuṭārāma and the Pāvārika (Pāvāriya)—ambavana stood to its south-east and east respectively (*Ibid.,* 370-71). Aśoka built a *stūpa* above 200 ft. high near the Ghositārāma.

Goharwa.—This village is situated in the Manjhanpur tahsil of the Allahabad district where the two copper plates of Karṇadeva were found (*E.I.,* XI, pp. 139–146).

Gokarṇa.—According to the *Svayambhūpurāṇa* Svayambhū produced eight holy men. One of them was Gokarṇeśvara in Gokarṇa, which is identified with the river Bāgmatī (R. L. Mitra, *N.B. Lit.,* p. 253; Law, *Geographical Essays,* p. 46).

Gokula.—The *Bhāgavata Purāṇa* mentions it as a village (X. 2, 7; X. 5, 32). It is situated on the left bank of the Yamunā. It is famous in the history of Vaiṣṇavism. It contains the temple of Gokulanāthaji. Vāsudeva being afraid of Kaṃsa crossed the river Yamunā and left Śrī Kṛṣṇa in charge of Nanda who used to live here. Vallabhācārya who was a contemporary of Śrīcaitanya and who founded the Vallabhacāri sect of the Vaiṣṇavas, built new Gokula in imitation of Mahāvana. There was a forest near Gokula known as the Bṛhadvana (*Bhāgavata P.,* X. 5, 26; X 7, 38).

Gomatī.—This river is almost certainly identical with the Ṛgvedic Gomatī (*Ṛgveda*, X. 75, 6) which is probably the modern Gomal, a western tributary of the Indus. It has also been sought to be identified with the modern Gumtī which joins the Ganges below Benaras and which is described in the *Rāmāyaṇa* as situated in Ayodhyā, and as being crowded with cattle (Ayodhyākāṇḍa, Ch. 49). It rises in the Shāhjāhānpur district and flows into the Ganges about half-way between Benaras and Ghazipur (*I.A.*, Vol. XXII, 1893, p. 178). The *Mahābhārata* (Ch. 84, 73) and the *Bhāgavata Purāṇa* (V. 19, 18; X. 79, 11) mention this river. The *Padmapurāṇa* (Uttarakhaṇḍa, vs. 35–38) also mentions it. The *Skanda Purāṇa* mentions another river of the same name (Avantīkhaṇḍa, Ch. 60); evidently it flowed through Gujarat with Dwārakā on its bank. Some have attempted to identify the Dhutapāpā as a separate river with the modern Dhopāp on the Gumtī, 18 miles south-east of Sultanpur in Oudh. According to the *Skanda Purāṇa* (Kāśīkhaṇḍa, Uttara, Ch. 59), it was a tributary of the Ganges near Benaras (N. L. Dey, *Geographical Dict.*, pp. 57 and 231; B. C. Law, *Rivers of India*, p. 21).

Gomatikoṭṭaka.—The Deo Baranark Inscription of Jīvitagupta refers to it. It must be looked for somewhere along the river Gomatī (modern Gumtī), which, rising in the Shahjahanpur district, passes Lucknow and Jaunpur and flows into the Ganges about half-way between Benaras and Ghazipur (*C.I.I.*, Vol. III).

Gomukhi.—It may be identified with the Gokarṇa of the *Rāmāyaṇa* (I. 42).

Gotama.—This mountain does not seem to be far from the Himalaya (*Apadāna*, p. 162).

Govardhana (*Govaḍḍhana—Jāt.*, IV, 80).—This hill is situated 18 miles from Brindaban in the district of Mathurā. In the village called Paitho Kṛṣṇa is said to have taken this hill on his little finger and held it as an umbrella over the heads of his cattle and townsmen to protect them from rains poured upon them by Indra (*Mahābhārata*, Udyogaparva, Ch. 129). It is also mentioned in the *Bhāgavatapurāṇa* (V. 19, 16; X. 11, 36; 13, 29) and *Harivaṃśa* (Ch. 55) that Govardhanagiri contains the temples of Harideva and Cakreśvaramahādeva and also the image of Śrīnāthaji, formerly known as Gopāla. Kālidāsa in his *Raghuvaṃśa* (VI. 51) mentions this hill. The *Yoginītantra* refers to it (1/14).

Govisanā.—It was situated somewhere north of Moradabad. The old fort near the village of Ujain represents the ancient city of Govisanā which was visited by Hiuen Tsang in the 7th century A. D. The district of Govisanā was 333 miles in circuit. It was also known as Govisanna (Watters, *On Yuan Chwang*, I, 331). It was confined on the north by Brahmapura, on the west by Madāwar, and on the south and east by Ahicchatra. The modern districts of Kāśīpur, Rāmpur and Pilibhit extending from the Rām Gaṅgā on the west to Ghāgra on the east and towards Bareilly on the south represent the district of Govisanā (*C.A.G.I.*, pp. 409ff.).

Haliddavasana.—It was a village in the Koliya country visited by the Buddha (*Sam.*, V, 115).

Harappā.—The ruins at Harappā are situated in the Montgomery district of the Western Punjab (P). The Harappā culture extended much beyond the Indus valley proper. The excavations in 1946 at the site have brought to light a ceramic industry which lay under the mud-brick defences. The people of Harappā used to bury their dead in graves dug into the earth. The 'AB' mound at Harappā, the defensive wall, etc. show that the Harappā civilization was much advanced. The people used to lead a happy life. Trade and commerce had considerably advanced. For details vide M. S. Vats, *Excavations at Harappā*, 1–11, 1940.

Harāhā.—It lies in the Barabanki district where a stone slab containing the inscription of the reign of Īśānavarman Maukhari was found (*E.I.*, XIV, p. 110).

Haridvāra.—It is a holy place of the Vaiṣṇavas in Northern India. According to the *Mahābhārata* it is called Gaṅgādvāra, and according to Vaiṣṇava literature it is known as Māyāpurī. On the bank of the Ganges Vidura listened to the *Śrīmad-Bhāgavata* read out by the sage Maitreya. Here the Ganges descends from the Himalayas. It is in the Saharanpur district.

According to Hiuen Tsang this town was known as Mo-yu-lo or Mayūra situated on the north-west frontier of Madāwar and on the eastern bank of the Ganges. Mayūra was the ruined site of Māyāpura at the head of the Ganges canal. According to the Chinese pilgrim it was 3½ miles in circuit and very populous. According to Cunningham this town may have been called Mayūrapura, as many peacocks were found in the neighbourhood.[1] For details vide *Imperial Gazetteers of India*, Vol. XIII, 51ff.

Hastināpura.—It was the ancient capital of the Kurus, situated on the Ganges in the Meerut district of the United Provinces. It has been traditionally identified with an old town in Mawāna tahsil, Merat.[2] It was ruled by King Dhṛtarāṣṭra. The Pāṇḍus were reconciled to the aged Dhṛtarāṣṭra, who retired to the forest after remaining at Hastināpura for fifteen years, and he and his queens finally perished in a forest conflagration. Parīkṣit, grandson of Arjuna, was the ruler of Hastināpura. He was highly intelligent and a great hero. He was a powerful bowman. He possessed all the noble qualities of a dutiful king. During the reign of Nicakṣu, son of Adhisīma Kṛṣṇa, this city is said to have been carried away by the Ganges, and the king is said to have transferred his residence to Kauśāmbī.[3] The *Mārkaṇḍeyapurāṇa* (LVIII, 9) and the *Bhāgavata Purāṇa* (1. 3. 6; I, 8. 45; IV, 31, 30; X, 57, 8) refer to the Gajāhvayas, who were connected with Hastināpura, the Kuru capital. This city is also called Gajāhvaya according to the *Bhāgavata Purāṇa* (I. 9, 48; I, 15, 38; I. 17, 44; III, 1, 17; IX. 22. 40; X. 68. 16). Ṛṣabha, the first Tīrthaṅkara, was an inhabitant of Hastināpura. He installed Bharata on the throne. He divided his kingdom among his relations. King Hasti founded Hastināpura on the bank of the Bhāgīrathī according to the *Vividhatīrthakalpa*. This city was often visited by Mahāvīra, the founder of Jainism.[4] The *Harivaṃśa* (20, 1053-4) and the *Bhāgavatapurāṇa* (IX, 21, 20) lend support to this fact. Hasti or Hastin had two sons, Ajamiḍha and Dvimiḍha. Ajamiḍha continued the main Paurava line at Hastināpura. He had three sons, and they originated separate dynasties.[5] For further details, vide B. C. Law, *Some Jaina Canonical Sūtras*, p. 172.

Hemavata.—The Himalaya mountain was known in ancient times as Himavān, Himācala,[6] Himavantapadesa, Himādri, Haimavata and Himavat. It is mentioned in ancient Indian texts.[7] It is called the

---

[1] *A.G.I.*, pp. 402ff., 703.
[2] Cunningham, *A.G.I.*, p. 702.
[3] Pargiter, *Dynasties of the Kali Age*, p. 5; cf. *Rāmāyaṇa*, II, 68. 13; *Mahābhārata*, I, 128.
[4] *Bhagavatīsūtra*, II. 9; *Ṭhānamga*, 9. 691.
[5] Pargiter, *A.I.H.T.*, p. 111.
[6] *Padmapurāṇa*, Uttarakhaṇḍa (vs. 35–38) which gives a list of geographical names; Pāṇini's *Aṣṭādhyāyī* (IV. 4. 112).
[7] *Atharvaveda*, XII, 1, 11; *Ṛgveda*, X, 121, 4; *Taittirīya Saṃhitā*, V, 5, 11, 1; *Vājasaneyī Saṃhitā*, XXIV, 30; XXV, 12; *Aitareya Brāhmaṇa*, VIII, 14, 3; *Bhāgavatapurāṇa*, 1, 13, 29; I, 13, 50; *Kūrmapurāṇa*, 30, 45–48; *Yoginītantra*, I, 16.

6

Parvatarāja[1] and *Nagādhirāja*.[2] According to the Great Epic,[3] the Haimavata region was situated just to the west of Nepal (*Nepāla-viṣaya*). According to the same Epic, it mainly comprised the Kulinda-viṣaya (Ptolemy's Kunindrae), representing the region of high mountains in which the sources of the Ganges, Jumna and Sutlej lay. It may thus be taken to include parts of the modern Himachal Pradesh and adjoining tracts, and some parts of Dehra Dun. The author of the *Mārkaṇḍeyapurāṇa* (54, 24; 57, 59) knew the Himalayan mountain (Himavat) to have stretched from sea to sea like the string of a bow (*Kārmukasya yathā guṇaḥ*). The statement of the *Mārkaṇḍeyapurāṇa* is supported by the *Mahābhārata* (VI. 6. 3) and *Kumārasambhava* (1, 1). The two loftiest mountains the Kailāsa[4] and the Himalaya (Himavān) stand to the south of the Meru mountain.[5] These two mountains stretch east and west and extend into the ocean.[6] The Kailāsa mountain frequently mentioned in Sanskrit literature was on the north of the middle portion of the Himalayan range.[7] According to Bāṇa's *Harṣacarita* (Ch. VII) Arjuna subdued the Mount Hemakūṭa in order to complete the Rājasūya sacrifice. In Bāṇa's *Kādambarī* (śl. 16) this mountain was white with crystals or made up of crystal rocks. The Himalaya is described in the *Kuṇāla Jātaka*[8] as a vast region, 500 leagues in height, and 3,000 leagues in breadth. Aśvaghoṣa refers to the Himalaya (Himavān) and places the Madhyadeśa between this mountain and the Pāripātra.[9] The Lord Śiva who dwelt on the peaks of the Kailāsa and the Himalaya was propitiated by the songs of the two *nāgas*.[10]

The Mainākmountain was a part of the great Himalayan range. It was near Kailāsa.[11] In the Himalayan region there also existed a mountain called the Daddara.[12] In it there were four ranges of mountains with a forest and a natural lake.[13] Near the Himalaya there was another mountain called the Dhammaka where a hermitage was built with a cottage for the first Buddha Dīpaṃkara.[14] By the side of the Himalayas a mountain named Caṇḍagiri stood and close by there was a great forest.[15]

The eastern Himalayan region extending up to Assam and Manipur roughly constituted the Haimavata division of the Jambudvīpa in respect of which Aśoka introduced the Nābhakas and Nābhapaṃtis in his R.E. XIII.[16] The Elder Majjhima was sent to the Himalaya to propagate Buddhism.[17] He converted the hordes of *Yakkhas* living in this mountain. The people mostly used to worship the violent and most powerful *Yakkhas*. They were given to understand the doctrine of the Buddha as explained by the five Elders.[18] The *Paulastya rākṣasas* are connected with the Himalaya mountain.[19] According to the *Mārkaṇḍeyapurāṇa*,[20] the *Rākṣasas* were found on the top of the Kailāsa. The Himalayan region (*Himavantapadesa*) of the Jambudvīpa (continent of India) extended northwards,

---

1 *Aṅguttara*, I, 152; cf. *Kālikāpurāṇa*, Ch. 14, 51.
2 *Kumārasambhava*, 1, 1.
3 *Mahābhārata*, Vanaparva, Ch. 253.
4 *Yoginītantra*, 1. 1; 1. 12.
5 *Mārkaṇḍeyapurāṇa*, Ch. 54, v. 23.
6 Pargiter, *Mārkaṇḍeyapurāṇa*, p. 277.
7 *Ibid*., p. 376.
8 *Jātaka*, No. 536.
9 *Saundarananda Kāvya*, II, v. 62.
10 Pargiter, *Mārkaṇḍeyapurāṇa*, p. 132.
11 *Mbh*., Sabhāp. III, 58–60; Vanaparva, CXXXV. 10,694-5.
12 *Jātaka*, III, p. 16.
13 *Ibid*., IV, p. 338.
14 *Buddhavaṃsa*, II, v. 29.
15 *Mahāvastu*, III, 130.
16 Barua, *Aśoka and His Inscriptions*, Pt. I, p. 101.
17 *Mahāv*., XII, 6; *Thūpav*., 43; *Mahābodhiv*., 114-115.
18 *Sāsanavaṃsa*, p. 169; cf. *Samantapāsādikā*, I, 68.
19 *Mahābh*., III, 274, 15,901; V, 110, 3,830; *Rāmāyaṇa*, III, 32, 14–16.
20 Pargiter's Tr., p. 6.

according to the Pali accounts, as far as the south side of the Mt. Sumeru (Pali Sineru). Haimavata division of India is indicated by the Kālsi set of Rock Edicts, the Asokan monoliths at Niglīva, Lumbinī, and those in the district of Champaran. The Himalayan region (*Haimavata-padesa*) has been identified by some with Tibet, by Fergusson with Nepal, and by Rhys Davids with the Central Himalayas. According to ancient geographers the name Himavata was applied to the entire mountain range stretching from Sulaiman along the west of the Punjab and the whole of the northern boundary of India up to the Assam and Arakan hill ranges in the east. The two ancient Indian tribes, viz., the Śākyas and the Koliyas, were transported by the Buddha to the Himalayas and the Buddha pointed out to them the various mountains in the Himalayan region.[1] The Kailāsa mountain formed a part of the Himalayan mountain,[2] but the *Mārkaṇḍeyapurāṇa* takes it to be a separate mountain. The Kailāsa was a mountain with high peaks. It was of pure white colour (*Mahābodhiv.* 13, 26, 45 and 79). From the monastery on this mountain the elder Suriyagutta came to Ceylon with 96,000 monks (*Thūpav.* 73). On the top of the Kailāsa mountain which is the Kangrinpoche of the Tibetans, situated about 25 miles to the north of the Mānasasarovara, stood Sudhammapura (*Sāsanavaṃsa*, p. 38).

According to Alberuni, Meru and Niṣadha which are described as *Varṣaparvatas* in the *Purāṇas*, were connected with the Himalayan chain. The Himalayan mountain is the source from which the ten rivers, namely, Gaṅgā, Yamunā, Aciravatī, Sarabhu, Mahī, Sindhu, Sarasvatī, Vetravatī, Vitaṃsā and Candabhāgā[3] take their rise (*Milinda*, 114), but the *Purāṇas* mention more than ten rivers issuing from the Himavat, viz., the Gaṅgā, Sarasvatī, Sindhu, Candrabhāgā, Yamunā, Śatadru, Vitastā, Irāvatī, Kuhu, Gomatī, Dhutapāpā, Bāhudā, Dṛṣadvatī, Vipāśā, Devikā, Raṅkṣu, Niścirā, Gaṇḍakī and Kauśikī (cf. *Mārkaṇḍeyapurāṇa*, 57, 16–18; *Ibid.*, Vaṅgabāsī ed., Ch. 61, v. 16 E; for details of these rivers, vide Law, *Geographical Essays*, pp. 84–95). Ptolemy points out that the Imaos (the Himalayan mountain) is the source of the Ganges and the Indus as well as the Koa and the Swat rivers. The river Migasammatā flows down from the Himalaya and enters the Ganges (*Jāt.*, VI, 72). The river Ūhā is stated in the *Milinda-Pañho* (p. 70) to have been located in the Himalaya. A few other mountains in the neighbourhood of the Himalaya are mentioned in the *Apadāna*, a Pali canonical text: Kadamba (p. 382), Kukkuta (178), Kosika, (p. 381), Gotama (p. 162), Paduma (p. 362), Bhārika (440), Lambaka (15), Vasabha (p. 166), Samaṅga (p. 437), and Sobhita (p. 328). The Himalayan mountain is the only *Varṣaparvata* which is placed within the geographical limits of *Bhāratavarṣa*. The Monghyr grant of Devapāla refers to Kedāra which is situated in the Himalayas. The *Kālikāpurāṇa* (Ch. 14, 31) points out that Śiva and Pārvatī went to the fall of the Mahā-Kauśikī river in the Himalaya mountain. It refers to a small river called Darpaṭ flowing from the same mountain (*Kālikā Purāṇa*, 79, 3). According to the *Kumārasaṃbhava* (I. 1) the excellent Himalaya mountain stands on the north of Bhāratavarṣa and it is engulfed by the sea on the east and west. The beauty of this mountain, which is a mine of various kinds of gems, is not marred by the glacier (*Kumārasam.* I, 3). It contains various kinds of minerals on its summit (I. 4). The sages take shelter on the sunny summits of the Himalaya (I. 5), the caves of which are covered by clouds (I. 14). The Kirātas, the wild tribe of hunters, can trace the course of the

[1] *Jātaka*, V. 412ff. [2] *Matsya Purāṇa*, 121. 2.
[3] These are important rivers out of 500 rivers issuing forth from the Himalaya.

lions on this mountain, which kill elephants, although the mark of blood is washed away by the water from the ice (I. 6). The self-luminous roots and herbs give light to the Kirātas at night living with their wives in the dark caves of the Himalaya (I. 10). The chief territory of the Kirātas was among the mountains: Kailāsa, Mandāra and Haima, i.e., the region around the Mānasasarovara.[1] The Himalayan tract which is thickly covered with snow is troublesome to those who walk on it (I. 11). The rays of the sun cannot dispel darkness with which this mountain is enveloped (I. 12). The Himalaya is noted for the yak having white fur (I. 13). The nymphs, when asked, replied that they would wait for the king on the Hemakūṭa (*Hemakūṭaśikhare*) which is the Himalaya mountain.[2]

The Buddhist texts mention seven great Himalayan lakes: Anotatta,[3] Kaṇṇamuṇḍa, Rathakāra, Chaddanta, Kuṇāla, Mandākinī and Sīhappapāta.[4] Each of them is fifty leagues in length, breadth and depth. Their names are such as to defy all attempts at a correct identification, and the description of their length, breadth and depth is too symmetrical to inspire confidence. Among the Himalayan peaks mention may be made of the Maṇiparvata, Hiṅgulaparvata, Añjanaparvata, Sānuparvata and Phaḷikaparvata.[5] None of them can be satisfactorily identified.

In between Bhāratavarṣa and Harivarṣa are placed the Himalayan range and the Hemakūṭa, the former lying to the south of the latter. This is the setting of the countries and mountain ranges to be found in the Jaina text called the *Jambudīvapaṇṇatti* and the Great Epic, *Mahābhārata*. The Hemakūṭa region is also known as Kiṃpuruṣavarṣa and the Haimavata region as Kinnara-khaṇḍa. According to the southern Buddhist conception the Himalayan region extended to the north up to the Gandhamādana range, which is a part of the Rudra Himalaya, but the Epic writers take it as a part of the Kailāsa range. The Anotatta (Anavatapta) lake or the Mānasasarovara, which was one of the seven great lakes situated in the Himalaya mountain,[6] was associated with the Kailāsa and Citrakūṭa peaks. The *Jambudīvappaṇṇatti* seems to be right in pointing out that there were two lakes each called Mahāpadmahrada, one connected with the Western Himalayan range (*Kṣudra-Himavanta*) and the other connected with the Eastern Himalayan range (*Mahā-Himavanta*). The Himalayan lake called the Chaddanta was 50 leagues long and 50 leagues broad. This lake contained white and red lotuses, red and white lilies and white esculent lilies.[7] The Himalayan region had fair women who brought utter ruin on all that fell into their power.[8]

The Himalayan mountain was the home of wild animals. Elephants, deer, rhinoceros, buffaloes, frogs, peacocks and peahens were found on this mountain. The Himalayan forests are said to have abounded in elephants living in herds or as rogues.[9] They contained horses of diverse breed, reptiles, pythons, water-snakes, etc. A lion dwelt in a cave of the Himalayas, killed a buffalo and ate its flesh. It then took a draught of water and came back to its cave.[10] A full-grown goose, which lived in a cave in the Citrakūṭa mountain in the Himalayan region, took the wild paddy that grew on a natural lake.[11] The rivers and lakes were full of fish and the birds were numerous. This mountain was resounded by the songs of

---

1 Pargiter, *Mārkaṇḍeyapurāṇa*, p. 322 f.n.
2 *Vikramorvaśī*, Act I.
3 *Mahāv.*, I, 18; *Mahābodhiv.*, 36, 100-101; 152, 155, etc.
4 *Aṅguttara*, IV, p. 101; *Manorathapūraṇī*, II, p. 759; *Paramatthajotikā*, II, p. 443.
5 *Jātaka*, V, p. 451.
6 *Mahāvaṃsa*, I, 18.
7 *Jātaka*, V, 37.
8 *Ibid.*, V, 152.
9 *Ibid.*, VI, 497.
10 *Ibid.*, III, 113.
11 *Ibid.*, III, 208.

birds.[1] In winter trees were found all flowering as well as the blooming lotuses.[2] Edible lily-seeds could be procured from the Himalaya.[3]

This mountain region was penetrated by the hermits, hunters, and kings on hunting expeditions. The hermits and ascetics built many hermitages there. The examples are too numerous,[4] but we may cite a few of them. The hermitage of Kapila was by the side of the Himalayas not far from the river Bhāgīrathī.[5] The famous hermitage known as Vṛṣaparvan's hermitage existed near the Mount Kailāsa in the Himalayas.[6] An ascetic named Nārada who dwelt in a cave in the Himalaya spent seven days in meditation, possessed supernatural faculties and at last realized what was bliss.[7] Four rich householders of Benaras, realizing the misery resulting from desire, went into this mountain and embraced the ascetic life. There they lived for a long time on the forest roots and fruits.[8] A wealthy Brahmin adopted the life of an ascetic and took up his abode in the Himalaya after developing supernatural power.[9] Five hundred ascetics came down from the Himalaya to procure salt and vinegar from Benaras.[10] A Brahmin belonging to the Kāśī country adopted the religious life of an ascetic in the Himalaya after his mother's death.[11] The king of Videha gave up his rule in the city of Mithilā, went to the Himalayan region, where he took up the religious life. He dwelt there peacefully, living on fruits only.[12]

A king of Benaras after having entrusted his kingdom to his mother entered into the Himalayan region for killing deer and eating their flesh.[13] Another king of Benaras went to hunt deer in the Himalayan region with a pack of well-trained hounds. There he killed deer and pigs and ate up their flesh. He then climbed to a great height of this mountain. There when the pleasant stream ran full, the water was breast-high.[14]

Hiṅgula Mountain (*Hiṅgalaparvata*).—It is in the Himalayan region (*Jātaka*, V, 415). Hinglāj is situated at the extremity of the range of mountains in Baluchistan, called by the name of Hiṅgula or Hingulā, about 20 miles from the sea-coast on the bank of the Aghor or the Hiṅgulā river. (N. L. Dey, *Geographical Dictionary*, p. 75).

Hiraññavatī (*Hiraṇyavatī*).—It is the little Gandak and the same as the Ajitavatī near Kuśīnārā. It flows through the district of Gorakhpur about eight miles to the west of the great Gandak and falls into the Gogrā or Ghogrā (Sarayū). The Śāla-grove of the Mallas of Kuśīnārā existed on the bank of this river (*Dīgha*, II, 137).

Hṛṣikeśa.—This mountain is situated 24 miles to the north of Hardwar, which was the hermitage of Devadatta (*Varāhapurāṇa*, Ch. 146). It is situated on the Ganges on the road from Hardwar to Badrināth. According to some this holy city of the Vaiṣṇavas is situated on the Ganges, about 20 miles from Haridvāra.

Icchānaṅgala.—It was a Brahmin village in Kośala. The Buddha once stayed here in the Icchānaṅgalavanasaṇḍa (*Aṅg. Nikāya*, III, 30, 341; *Ibid.*, IV, 340). The name of the village is given as Icchānaṅkala in the *Suttanipāta* (p. 115).

---

1 *Jātaka*, VI, 272. 2 *Ibid.*, VI, 497. 3 *Ibid.*, VI, 390.

4 *Jātaka*, III, 37, 79, 143; IV, 74, 423; I, 361, 371, 406, 431; II, 101, 41, 53, 57, 65, 72, 85, 131, 171, 230, 258, 262, 269, 395, 411, 417, 430, 437, 447, etc.; cf. *Mahāvastu*, I, 232, 272, 284, 351, 353; III, 41, 130, 143, etc.

5 *Saundaranandakāvya*, I, 5; *Divyāvadāna*, p. 548.

6 *Mahābh.*, Vanaparva, CLVIII, 11,541–3; CLXXVII, 12,340–44.

7 *Jātaka*, VI, 58. 8 *Ibid.*, VI, 256. 9 *Ibid.*, V, 193.

10 *Ibid.*, V, 465. 11 *Ibid.*, III, 37. 12 *Ibid.*, III, 365.

13 *Ibid.*, VI, 77. 14 *Ibid.*, IV, 437.

Ikṣumatī.—It is a river in Kurukṣetra (*Bhāgavatapurāṇa*, V, 10. 1).

Indrapura.—This large and lofty mountain mentioned in the Indore copperplate inscription of Skandagupta stands about five miles to the north-west of Dibhai, the chief town of the Dibhai pargana in the sub-division of the Bulandshahar district (*C.I.I.*, Vol. III).

Indrasthāna.—The *Bhāgavatapurāṇa* mentions it as a city (X. 58, 1; X. 73, 33; XI. 30, 48; XI. 31, 25). According to the *Padmapurāṇa* (200. 17-18) Indra performed many religious sacrifices in this city, worshipped Ramāpati several times and offered many treasures to the Brahmins in the presence of Nārāyaṇa. Since then this place became famous as Indraprastha. It is mentioned in the Kamauli plate of Govindachandra (V.S., 1,184). It has been identified with Indraprastha (*E.I.*, XXVI, Pt. II, p. 71; *I.A.*, XV, p. 8, f.n. 46), built on the bank of the Jumna about two miles south of modern Delhi. It extended over seven leagues (*Sattayojanike Indapattanagare—Jātaka*, No. 537; B. C. Law, *Geography of Early Buddhism*, p. 18). It is also called Bṛhatsthala in the *Mahābhārata*. It was the capital of Yudhiṣṭhira, the first Pāṇḍava brother. Indraprastha (the modern Indrapat near Delhi) was the second capital of the Kurus, the first being Hastināpura, situated on the Ganges, identified with the present Meerut district of the United Provinces. The blind king Dhṛtarāṣṭra ruled the old capital Hastināpura, while he assigned to his nephews, the five Pāṇḍus, a district on the Jumna, where they founded Indraprastha. The ancient capital of the Kurus became insignificant in course of time, and the new city erected by the Pāṇḍavas has now become the seat of the government of India. (For further details, vide N. L. Dey, *Geographical Dictionary*, pp. 77-78).

Irāvatī.—Patañjali refers to it in his *Mahābhāṣya* (2. 1. 2, p. 53). It is the modern Rāvī, the Greek Hydraotis or Adris or Rhonadis. This river rises in the rock-basin of Bāṅgahal and drains the southern slopes of the Pir Pañjal and the northern slopes of the Dhaulā Dhar. According to the *Kālikāpurāṇa* (Ch. 24. 140) this river has its origin in the Irā lake. The length of the course of this river in the Himalayas is 130 miles. This river appears first to our view at the south-west corner of Chamba in Kashmir. From Chamba it flows past Lahore, following a south-westerly course, and meets the Chenab or the united flow of the Vitastā and Chandrabhāgā between Ahmadpur and Saraisidhu (Law, *Rivers of India*, p. 13).

Isipatana-Migadāya (*Ṛṣipatana-Mrigadāva*).—Same as Sārnāth.

Isukāra (Riṣukāra).—This wealthy, famous, and beautiful town existed in the Kuru kingdom (*Uttarādhyayana Sūtra*, XIV, I).

Jawalāmukhī.—It is an ancient site in the Dera Gopipur tahsil of the Kangra district in the Punjab, situated on the road from Kangra town to Nadaun. It was once a considerable and opulent town, as its ruins testify. It is now chiefly famous for the temple of the goddess Jawalāmukhī, which lies in the Beas Valley. (For further details, see Law, *Holy Places of India*, p. 24).

Jālandhara.—The *Yoginītantra* mentions it (1/11, 2/2, 2/9). Jālandhara included the state of Chamba on the north, Mandi and Sukhet on the east and Śatadru on the south-east. It was 1,000 li or 167 miles in length from east to west, and 800 li or 133 miles in breadth from north to south. According to the *Padmapurāṇa* (Uttarakhaṇḍa) it was the capital of the great *daitya* king Jālandhara (*C.A.G.I.*, pp. 156ff.).

Jānkhaṭ.—It is in the Tirwa tahsil of the Farrukhabad district of the United Provinces where an inscription of the time of Vīrasena has been discovered (*E.I.*, XI, p. 85).

Jetavana.—It was one of the royal gardens in Northern India which became a favourite retreat of the Buddha (*Dīgha*, I, 178) and an early centre of Buddhism. It was situated at a distance of one mile to the south of Śrāvastī (modern Saheth-Maheth). It was a Buddhist monastic establishment in the suburb of Śrāvastī, which perpetuates the noble deeds of Prince Jeta, who is said to have laid out the Jetavana garden, according to the *Mahāvaṃsa Commentary* (P.T.S., p. 102). This monastic institution is represented as Anāthapiṇḍika's *ārāma* to perpetuate the memory of Anāthapiṇḍika, the purchaser of the site (*Papañcasūdanī*, 1, 60-61). With the construction of the Jetavana monastery and the formal dedication of the same to the Buddha by Anāthapiṇḍika was erected the first permanent centre of Buddhism in Kośala proper, particularly in Śrāvastī. After his return to Śrāvastī from Rājagṛha the banker Anāthapiṇḍika was on a look-out for a suitable site for constructing the *ārāma*. Prince Jeta's garden appeared to be the desired site. As soon as the Prince agreed to sell it, the banker employed his men to cut down the trees and clear the site. The whole of the site was laid with gold. According to the *Vinaya* account the banker caused to be built therein a number of buildings, e.g., dwelling rooms (*vihāras*), retiring rooms (*pariveṇas*), store-rooms (*koṭṭhakas*), service halls (*upaṭṭhānasālās*), halls with fire-places in them (*aggisālās*), closets, cloisters, wells, bath-rooms, tanks, pavilions, etc. To complete this work of piety a huge amount of money had to be spent. It is interesting to note that all the stages in the process of construction of this monastery consummated by the ceremony of dedication, are represented in the Barhut bas-relief, while the Bodh-gaya relief illustrates only the scene of fulfilment of the term of purchase (Barua, *Gayā and Buddhagayā*, II, 104-5; Barua, *Barhut*, II, 27–31). The Karerikūṭi, the Kosambakūṭi, the Gandhakūṭi and the Salalaghara were the four main buildings in the Jetavana (*Sumaṅgalavilāsinī*, II, 407). This locality at Śrāvastī occurs in Luders' List, No. 731 as well as in the Jātaka Label No. 5 (Barua and Sinha, *Barhut Inscriptions*, p. 59). It was at this place that king Prasenajit of Kośala became the Buddha's disciple (*Samyutta Nikāya*, I, 68ff.). A Buddhist inscription from Bodhgayā of the reign of Jayacandradeva points out that Govindacandra, the Gāhaḍavāla king of Kanauj, who was married to a Buddhist princess named Kumāradevī, set apart several villages for the support of the monks living in the Jetavana Vihāra (*E.I.*, XI, 20ff.). In this *vihāra* the Buddha lived for some time (*Dīpavaṃsa*, p. 21; *Mahāvaṃsa*, p. 7). For further details vide B. C. Law, *Śrāvastī in Indian Literature*, *M.A.S.I.*, No. 50, pp. 22ff.

Jhusi.—The ancient town of Jhusi stands on the left bank of the Ganges at a distance of 14 miles south-west from Phulpur (*Allahabad District Gazetteer*, by Nevill, p. 245).

Kadamba.—This mountain does not seem to be far from the Himalaya (*Apadāna*, p. 382).

Kahaum.—The Kahaum stone pillar inscription of Skandagupta mentions this village, which is also known as Kakubha or Kakubhagrāma, situated about five miles to the west by south of Salampur-Majhauli, the chief town of the Salampur-Majhauli pargana, in the Dewaria tahsil in the Gorakhpur district (*C.I.I.*, Vol. III).

Kahror.—This ancient town is situated on the southern bank of the old Bias river, 50 miles to the south-east of Multan and 20 miles to the north-east of Bahawalpur (*C.A.G.I.*, 1924, p. 277). According to Alberuni the great battle between Vikramāditya and the Śakas was fought here.

Kailāsa.—It is mentioned in the *Yoginītantra* (1/1, 1/12). The Puruṣottamapurī plates of Rāmacandra refer to this mountain (*E.I.*, XXV,

Pt. V). It is called a king of mountains. It is also known as Bhūteśagiri surrounded by the river Nandā also called Gaṅgā (*Bhāgavatapurāṇa*, IV. 5, 22; V. 16, 27). The *Kālikāpurāṇa* (Vaṅgabāsī Ed.) refers to Kailāsa (Ch. 13. 23). It was visited by Śiva and Pārvatī (*Ibid.*, Ch. 14. 31). Śāntanu lived on this mountain and also on the Gandhamādana (Ch. 82. 7). The *Mahābhārata* (Vanaparva, Chs. 144, 156) includes the Kumaun and Garwal mountains in the Kailāsa range. It is also called Hemakūṭa according to the *Mahābhārata* (Bhīṣmaparva, Ch. 6). This mountain, also known as the Śaṅkaragiri was visited by Vīraśekhara, son of Mānasavega and grandson of Vegavat, a king of Ikṣvāku's line (*Daśakumāracaritam*, p. 54). Kālidāsa refers to Kailāsa in his *Kumārasambhava* (Nirṇayasāgar Ed., viii, 24). It is known to the Jainas by the name of the Aṣṭāpada mountain where the sons of Ṛṣabha and many sages attained perfection. Indra erected three *stūpas*. Bharata built a *caitya* called Siṃhaniṣadya, and twenty-four Jina images together with his own. Rāvaṇa was attacked by Bālī.[1] The Kailāsa range runs parallel to the Ladakh range, 50 miles behind the latter. It contains a number of groups of giant peaks. It may be identified with the Vaidyūtaparvata. It is the Kangrinpoche of the Tibetans, situated about 25 miles to the north of Mānasasarovara. Badarikāśrama is said to be situated on this mountain.[2]

Kakutthā.—It is a small stream called Barhi which falls into the little Gandak, eight miles below *Kāsiā*. Carlleyle has identified it with the river Ghāgī, 1½ miles to the west of Chitiyaon in the Gorakhpur district. The Buddha while going from Rājagriha to Kuśīnārā had to cross this river which was near Kuśīnārā.[3] He then arrived at the mango-grove and then proceeded to the Śāla-grove of the Mallas near Kuśīnārā.[4]

Kalasigāma.—It was situated in the island of Alasanda or Alexandria. It was the birthplace of king Menander.[5]

Kamalā.—It is an upper tributary of the Ganges, the lower course of which is known as the Ghugrī. It takes its rise in the Mahābhārata range in Nepal, and joins the Ganges at Karagolā in south Purnea. The Kamalā receives two tributaries on the right side and five on the left. For further details, vide B. C. Law, *Rivers of India*, p. 25.

Kamauli.—This village stands near the confluence of the Barṇā and the Ganges at Benaras. An inscription has been found here which records that Mahārājaputra Govindacandra from his victorious camp at Viṣṇupura granted the village of Usītha to a Brahmin.[6] It was Govindacandra who re-established the supremacy of his line over Kānyakubja and the territories depending on it. He assumed the ambitious titles of *Aśvapati-Gajapati-Narapati-rājatrayādhipati* originally used by the Kalacuri kings of Ḍāhala.[7] Twenty-one copperplates of the kings of Kanauj together with four other inscriptions are said to have been found in this village.[8]

Kamboja (Kāmboja).—The Kambojas are supposed to have occupied the Western Himalayas. Geographically they are located in the north.[9] They are referred to in Pāṇini's *Aṣṭadhyāyī* (4. 1. 175) and in Patañjali's *Mahābhāṣya* (1. 1. 1, p. 317; 4. 1. 175) as well as in Aśoka's Rock Edict, V.[10]

---

1 B. C. Law, *Some Jaina Canonical Sūtras*, p. 174.

2 For further details, vide N. L. Dey, *Geographical Dictionary*, pp. 82, 83; B. C. Law, *Geography of Early Buddhism*, p. 39; Law, *Mountains of India*, p. 7.

3 *Dīgha*, II, 129, 134ff.; *Udāna*, VIII. 5.

4 Law, *Geography of Early Buddhism*, p. 37; Law, *Rivers of India*, p. 23.

5 *Milinda-Pañha*, p. 83.

6 *E.I.*, II, 358–61.

7 *E.I.*, XXVI, Pt. II, p. 71 and f.n. 6.

8 *E.I.*, IV, 97ff.

9 *Mahābhārata*, Bhīṣmaparva, Ch. 9.

10 B. M. Barua, *Aśoka and His Inscriptions*, pp. 92–94.

The Kambojas appear to have been one of the early Vedic tribes. They were settled to the north-west of the Indus and were the same as Kambujiya of the old Persian inscriptions. The *Bhāgavatapurāṇa* refers to it as a country (II. 7, 35; X. 75, 12; X. 82, 13). Some have placed them in Rājapura. Speaking of Rājapura Yuan Chwang says, 'From Lampa to Rājapura the inhabitants are coarse and plain in personal appearance, of rude violent dispositions, ... they do not belong to India proper but are inferior peoples of frontier stocks'.[1] V. A. Smith has placed this country among the mountains either of Tibet or of the Hindu Kush. Some have assigned it to the country round modern Sindh and Gujrat. Kamboja was famous for its horses which were speedy and were of perfect form.[2] For further details, vide B. C. Law, *Tribes of Ancient India*, Ch. I; B. C. Law, *Indological Studies*, Vol. I, pp. 9-10; *Geography of Early Buddhism*, pp. 50-51.

Kañcana Mountain.—It is the Uttara Himalaya (*Jātaka*, II. 396, 397, 399; VI. 101).

Kaṇhagiri.—This is same as Kṛṣṇagiri mountain (Kanheri) (Luders' List, No. 1123). It is the Karakorum or the Black mountain (*Vāyu Purāṇa*, Ch. 36). This mountain is continuous with the Hindu Kush on the west. According to modern geographers the Karakorum mountain was uplifted earlier, and is hence older than the Himalayan proper. This mountain is of Hercynian age, and got considerably folded and faulted subsequent to its uplift (B. C. Law, *Mountains of India*, pp. 4, 7)

Kaṅkhala (*Kanakhala*).—It is situated two miles to the east of Hardwar at the junction of the Ganges and the Nīladhārā. It was the scene of Dakṣa-yajña of the Purāṇas (*Kūrmap.*, Ch. 36; *Vāmanap.*, Chs. 4 and 34; *Liṅgap.*, Pt. 1, Ch. 100). The *Padmapurāṇa* (Ch. 14—*Tīrthamāhātmya*) mentions it as a *tīrtha* or a holy place (cf. *Mahābhārata*, Vanaparva, 84, 30). The *Yoginītantra* (2–6) mentions it.

Kāṇva(*Kaṇva*)-*āśrama.*—The hermitage of the sage Kāṇva who adopted Śakuntalā as his daughter was called Dharmāraṇya, situated on the bank of the river Mālinī, flowing through the districts of Saharanpur and Oudh. According to some it was situated on the river Chambal (*Mahābhārata*, Vanaparva, Ch. 82; *Agnip.*, Ch. 109) while in the opinion of others it existed on the bank of the river Narmadā (*Padmap.*, Ch. 94).

Kapilavastu (*Chia-Wei-lo-Yueh*).—It was the capital of the Śākyas among whom the Buddha was born. It is also known as Kapilavastu (*Divyāvadāna*, p. 67), Kapilapura (*Lalitavistara*, p. 243) or Kapilāhvayapura (*Ibid.*, p. 28). The *Divyāvadāna* connects Kapilavastu with the sage Kapila (p. 548). In the *Buddhacaritakāvya*, the city is described as *Kapilasya vastu* (*B.K.*, I, v. 2). It was surrounded by seven walls according to the *Mahāvastu* (Vol. II, p. 75). According to the *Shui-Ching-Chu* the city contained some *Upāsakas* (lay disciples) and about 20 householders belonging to the Śākya family. The people of this city highly cultivated religious energy and still maintained the old spirit. They completely repaired the dilapidated *stūpas* (*Northern India according to the Shui-Ching-Chu* by L. Petech, p. 33). The famous Rummindei Pillar marks the site of the ancient Lumbinī garden, the traditional scene of Śākyamuni's birth. Vincent Smith is inclined to identify Kapilavastu, which lay not far from the Lumbinīgrāma, with Piprāwā in the north of the Basti district of the Nepal frontier. Rhys Davids takes Tilaura Kot to be the old Kapilavastu.

---

[1] Watters, *On Yuan Chwang*, I, pp. 284ff.
[2] *Jaina Sūtras* (S.B.E.), II. 47.

P. C. Mukherji agrees with Rhys Davids and identifies Kapilavastu with Tilaura, two miles north of Tauliva, which is the headquarters of the Provincial Government of Tarai, and 3½ miles to the south-west of the Nepalese village of Nigliva, north of Gorakhpura, situated in the Nepal Tarai. Rummindei is only 10 miles to the east of Kapilavastu and two miles north of Bhagavānpura. The *Mahāvastu* (I. pp. 348ff.) gives a story of the foundation of Kapilavastu.

According to the Chinese pilgrim Fa-Hien, the city was thinly populated.[1] Here he saw towers set up at various places. According to Hiuen Tsang, it was about 4,000 li in circuit. The villages were few and desolate, and the monasteries were more than 1,000 in number. There were Deva temples where different sectarians worshipped. After the passing away of the Buddha topes and shrines were built at or near Kapilavastu (Watters, *On Yuan Chwang*, II, p. 4). This town which was known to the Chinese as Kie-pi-lo-fa-sse-ti, had no supreme ruler. It was rich and fertile and was cultivated according to the regular season. The climate was uniform and the manners of the people soft and obliging (Beal, *Buddhist Records of the Western World*, II, 14). In this city there was the Mote Hall (*Santhāgāra*) where the administrative and judicial business was carried out (*Buddhist India*, p. 19). Between this city and that of Koliya the water of the river Rohiṇī was caused to be confined by a single dam (*Dhammapada Commentary*, Vol. III, p. 254). According to the *Lalitavistara* (pp. 58, 77, 98, 101, 102, 113, 123) Kapilavastu was a great city, full of gardens, avenues and market-places. There were four city gates and towers all over the city. It was an abode of the learned and a resort of the virtuous. With arched gateways and pinnacles it was surrounded by the beauty of a lofty table-land (*Buddhacarita*, I, vv. 2, 5). The city had intelligent ministers (*Saundaranandakāvya*, I). As there was no improper taxation, poverty could not find any place there, where prosperity alone shone resplendently (*Buddhacaritakāvya*, I, v. 4).

According to the Rummindei Inscription, king Aśoka personally came and honoured this city because the Buddha was born here. He erected a stone pillar to mark the site of the Buddha's birth. He made Lumbinīgrāma free from taxes, and the villagers had to pay an eighth share of their produce (*C.I.I.*, III, 264-65). For further details, vide B. C. Law, *Geographical Essays*, Vol. I, pp. 182ff.; *Tribes in Ancient India*, pp. 248-49; *Geography of Early Buddhism*, pp. 28ff.; *Indological Studies*, pt. III.

Kapiśa.—Kapiśa (Chinese *Kia-pi-shi*) is the Capissa of Pliny and the Caphusa of Solinus. According to Ptolemy it was situated 155 miles north-east from Kabul. Julien supposes this place to have occupied the Panjshir and the Tagao valleys in the north border of Kohistan. According to Hiuen Tsang this country was 10 li in circuit. It produced various kinds of cereals and fruit trees. The Shen horses were bred here. The climate was cold and windy. The inhabitants of the place were cruel and fierce, and the language was rude. The inhabitants used hair garments and garments trimmed with fur. They used gold, silver and copper coins. The king of the place was a Kṣatriya. He loved his subjects very much. Every year he used to make a silver figure of the Buddha 18 ft. high and convoked an assembly called the *Mokṣamahāpariṣad* when alms were distributed to the poor and the wretched. There were one hundred convents, stūpas, *saṅghārāmas* and deva temples (Beal, *Buddhist Records of the Western World*, I, 54ff.).

---

[1] *Travels of Fa-Hien*, by Legge, pp. 64, 68.

Kara.—This place of historical importance is situated at a distance of about five miles north-east from Sirathu and 41 miles from Allahabad (*E.I.*, XXII, p. 37).

Karmāsadharma.—It was a small town in the Kuru country visited by the Buddha (*Aṅg.*, V, 29-30).

Karṇikācala.—It is one of the names of the Meru mountain.

Kauśāmyapura.—The Ajayagaḍh stone inscription (vs. 1345, *E.I.*, Vol. XXVIII, Pt. III, July, 1949) refers to Kauśāmyapura which seems to be identical with Kauśāmbī or Kosaṃ in the Allahabad district.

Kauśikī (Pali: *Kosikī*, *Jāt.*, V. 2).—It is the modern river Kuśī, which flows into the Ganges through the district of Purnea in Behar (*Rāmāyaṇa*, Ādikāṇḍa, 34; *Varāhapurāṇa*, 140). This river is mentioned in the *Rāmāyaṇa* (Ādik., v. 8) as a great river issuing from the Himalaya. The *Bhāgavatapurāṇa* mentions this river (I. 18, 36; V. 19, 18; IX. 15, 12; X. 79, 9). It is also mentioned in the *Yoginītantra* (2/4, pp. 128-129). It seems to have largely shifted its course (Pargiter, *Mārkaṇḍeyapurāṇa*, p. 292, note). It appears to view under this name in the southern part of eastern Nepal as the united flow of four rivers, three of which have their origin in Tibet. This river, also known as Kośī, is probably the river Cos Soanas mentioned by Arrian in his *Indika* (Ch. IV) on the authority of Megasthenes as being one of the navigable tributaries of the Ganges. It is remarkable for the rapidity of its stream, the dangerous and uncertain nature of its bed and chiefly for its constant westerly movement, as pointed out by W. W. Hunter in his *Statistical Account of Bengal* (Purnea) 1877. In its eastward course it meets the river Karatoyā having the Atrai and the Tista for its affluents (vide F. A. Shillingford, 'On changes in the course of the Kuśī river and the probable dangers arising from them', published in *J.A.S.B.*, Vol. LXIV, Pt. I, 1895, pp. 1ff.). For further details, vide B. C. Law, *Geographical Essays*, I, 94-95.

Kaviḷāsa.—It is Mount Kailāśa, the abode of Śiva (*Siṅgur Inscription of Yādava Mahādeva-raya, Daṅgur Inscription of Devaraya Mahāraya*, Śaka 1329, *E.I.*, XXIII, Pt. V, p. 194).

Kākaṃdī.—This is the same as Kākandī of the Jaina Paṭṭāvalī and of Buddhist literature. The location of this place is unknown. Kākandī was originally the abode of Ṛṣi Kākanda (*Kākandassa nivāso Kākandī*), that is to say, it was like Mākandī, Sāvatthī, Kosambī, and Kapilavastu (Barua and Sinha, *Barhut Inscriptions*, p. 18).

Kālakārāma.—This monastery was at Sāketa where the Buddha once dwelt. This park was given to the Buddha by a banker of Sāketa named Kālaka. (*Dhammapada Commy.*, Sinhalese Ed., III, 465ff.; *Aṅguttara Commy.*, Sinhalese Ed., II, 482ff.).

Kālindī.—See Yamunā.

Kāma-āśrama.—This hermitage was situated at the confluence of the Sarayū and the Ganges. Mahādeva is said to have destroyed Madana in this hermitage with the fire of his third eye on his forehead. (*Rāmāyaṇa*, Bālakāṇḍa, Ch. 23; cf. *Raghuvaṃśa*, Ch. II, v. 13; *Skandap.*, Avantī-Khaṇḍa, Ch. 34).

Kāmagāma.—It was the capital of the Koliya country which lay to the east of the Śākya territory (*Jātaka*, Cowell, Vol. V, pp. 219ff.).

Kāmpilya (Vedic *Kāmpīla*; Pali *Kampilla*).—It was the capital of southern Pañcāla. The *Rāmāyaṇa* (Ādikāṇḍa, Sarga 33, v. 19) describes it as beautiful as the abode of Indra. The *Mahābhārata* (138, 73-74) definitely mentions Kāmpilya as the capital of southern Pañcāla. But the Jātakas erroneously locate it in Uttarapañcāla.[1] It was an ancient city of India to which Pāṇini refers.[2] It was a sacred place of the Jainas. The epithet Kāmpīlavāsinī which is applied to a woman, occurs in the *Taittirīya Saṃhitā* (VII, 4, 19, 1), *Maitrāyanī Saṃhitā* (III, 12, 20), *Taittirīya Brāhmaṇa* (III. 9, 6), and *Śatapatha Brāhmaṇa* (XIII, 2, 8, 3). Weber and Zimmer take Kāmpīla as the name of a town known as Kāmpilya in later literature, which was the the capital of Pañcāla.[3] The Jaina *Ovavāiya sūya* (39) mentions it. The *Āvassaka Nirjjuti* (383) also mentions it as the birthplace of the thirteenth Tīrthaṅkara. The *Yoginītantra* (2/4, pp. 128-129) mentions it.

Kāmpilya is identical with modern Kampil on the old Ganges between Budaon and Farrukhabad.[4] The *Mahābhārata* (1,138,73) and the Jaina *Vividhatīrthakalpa* (p. 50) definitely locate it on the bank of the Ganges. According to N. L. Dey it was situated at a distance of 28 miles north-east of Fathgaḍ in the district of Farrukhabad, U.P. (*Geographical Dictionary*, 88). It is only five miles distant from the railway station of Kaimganj (B.B.C.I. Railway).

Kāmpilya was a very rich town [5] and prosperous.[6] A highly artistic tunnel (*Ummagga*) was dug out from the Ganges to the royal palace at Kāmpilya. The mouth of the greater tunnel was on the bank of the Ganges. It was dug out by many warriors and the lesser tunnel was dug out by seven hundred men. The entrance into the greater tunnel was provided with a door fitted with a machinery. The tunnel was built up with bricks and worked with *stucco*. There were many chambers and lamp-cells in it. It was well decorated (for details vide *Jātaka*, II, 329ff.; *Ibid.*, VI, 410).

This city witnessed *Svayamvara* ceremony of king Drupada's daughter named Draupadī who chose of her own accord the five Pāṇḍava brothers as her husbands (*Mahābh.*, Ādiparva, Ch. 138; *Rāmāyaṇa*, Ādi., Ch. 23). It was hallowed by the five auspicious incidents in the life of Vimalanātha, the thirteenth Tīrthaṅkara, who was a son of king Kṛtavarman by his queen Somadevī. On account of the happening of these five incidents, namely, the descent, the nativity, the coronation, the initiation and the Jinahood, this city was also known as the Pañcakalyāṇaka. It also claimed Ārṣamitra, the disciple of Kauṇḍinya and Gardavāli, the Jaina saint, who renounced the world and attained liberation here. Here in Kāmpilya Gāgalī, the king of Pṛṣthi Campā, was converted to Jainism by Gautama. According to some the renowned astronomer Śrī Varāhamihira was born in this city (*B. C. Law Volume*, Part II, 240).

This city was ruled by many important kings. Drupada, father of Draupadī, the wife of the five Pāṇḍava brothers of the *Mahābhārata* fame, Brahmadatta,[7] Kāmpilya,[8] son of king Haryaśva, who was celebrated as Pañcāla, and Samara,[9] son of Nīpa of the Ajamīḍa dynasty, were the rulers of Kāmpilya. King Cūḷaṇi Brahmadatta was instructed by the learned Brahmins in religious and secular matters (*Jātaka*, VI, 391ff.). There was a king named Pañcāla who gave shelter to a learned Brahmin in his royal garden. The Brahmin, before he left for the Himalayan region, instructed

---

1 *Jātaka*, II, 214; *Ibid.*, VI, 391; *Ibid.*, V, 21; *Ibid.*, III, 79, 379, etc.
2 *Kāśikāvṛtti*, 4, 2, 121.
3 *Indische Studien*, I, 184; *Altindisches Leben*, 36, 37.
4 Cunningham, *A.G.I.*, 413; *A.S.R.*, I, 255.
5 Hariṣeṇa, *Kathākoṣa*, Nos. 104 and 115.
6 *Jātaka*, VI, 433.
7 *Rāmāyaṇa*, Ādikāṇḍa, Sarga 33.
8 *Viṣṇupurāṇa*, Ch. II; *Bhāgavatapurāṇa*, Ch. 22.
9 *Viṣṇupurāṇa*, IV, 19.

the king to keep the moral law, observe the fast days and to be religious (*Jātaka*, III, 79ff.). King Dummukha, who was a contemporary of king Naggaji of Gandhāra, renounced the world after having listened to the religious discourse delivered by the four *Paccekabuddhas*.[1] The *Bodhisattvāvadāna-Kalpalatā* of Kṣemendra[2] mentions king Satyarata who was very pious, and king Brahmadatta to whom the *Mahāvastu* also refers (Vol. I, p. 283). King Sañjaya of Kāmpilya gave up his kingly power and adopted Jainism being instructed by a monk not to indulge in life-slaughter.[3] Dharmaruci was a very pious king of Kāmpilya who carried his whole army to Kāśī through the air by virtue of his piety when the king of Benaras picked up a quarrel with him.[4]

Kāmpilya was ruled by good and bad kings. An unrighteous king of this city oppressed his subjects by heavy taxation. His ministers were also unrighteous. The subjects were also oppressed by the royal officers who used to plunder them by day and the robbers robbed them of their wealth at night.[5]

The modern town of Kampil contains two Jain temples which are frequented by visitors from all parts of the globe.

Kānyakubja.—It was also known as Gādhipura, Kuśasthala and Mahadaya.[6] It is modern Kanauj. It was visited by Viśvāmitra as related in the *Mahābhārata* (Ch. 87, 17). According to the *Vinayapiṭaka* (Vol. II, p. 299) Kaṇṇakujja or Kānyakubja was visited by the venerable elder Revata from Saṅkassa (Saṃkāśya). It is also mentioned in the *Bhāgavatapurāṇa* (VI, 1, 21) as a city of Ajāmila. The *Yoginītantra* (2. 4) refers to it. Bāṇa in his *Harṣacarita* (Ch. VI) mentions a princess of Kānyakubja named Rājyaśrī who was cast into prison. The city of Kānyakubja existed in the kingdom of Pañcāla (*E.I.*, IV, 246). The Ratnapur Stone Inscription of Jājalladeva of the Cedi year 866 mentions that Jājalla was allied with the ruler of Cedi and honoured by the prince of Kānyakubja Jejābhuktika (*E.I.*, I, 33). A copperplate discovered at Khalimpura points out that the kings of the Bhojas, Matsyas, Kurus, Yadus and Yavanas were forced to acknowledge Cakrāyudha as the king of Kānyakubja (R. D. Banerjee, *Vāṅgālār Itihāsa*, Pt. I, pp. 167–69). Towards the close of the 11th century A.D. Kānyakubja came under the sway of Karṇadeva (C. 1040–1070 A.D.), son of Gāṅgeyadeva (R. D. Banerjee, *Prācīna Mudrā*, p. 215). Kānyakubja was under the rulers named Avantivarman and Grahavarman, who were the descendants of Susthitavarman Maukhari (*Gupta Inscriptions*, Intro., p. 15). The old capital of Kānyakubja was originally called Kusumapura (vide *the Allahabad posthumous stone pillar inscription of Samudragupta—C.I.I.*, Vol. III). It was the birthplace of Viśvāmitra (*Rāmāyaṇa*, Bālakāṇḍa). When the Chinese pilgrim Hiuen Tsang visited it in the 7th century A.D., Harṣavardhana was the reigning sovereign. Hiuen Tsang saw 100 Buddhist establishments at Kānyakubja. According to him the Ganges was on the west side of Kanauj and not on the east, as held by Cunningham. This kingdom was about 4,000 li in circuit. It had a dry ditch around it with strong and lofty towers. It contained flowers and woods, lakes and ponds. The people were well off and contented. The climate was agreeable and soft. The people were honest and sincere, noble and gracious in appearance. For clothings they used ornamented and bright-shining

---

1 *Jātaka*, III, 379ff.
2 66th pallava, p. 4 and 68th pallava, p. 9.
3 *Uttarādhyayana Sūtra*, XVIII.
4 *Vividhatīrthakalpa*, p. 50.
5 *Jāt.*, V, 98ff.
6 *Abhidhāna-Rājendra*, IV, 39-40.

fabrics. They were fond of learning. There were believers in the Buddha and heretics equal in number (Beal, *Buddhist Records of the Western World*, I, 206-207). The reigning king of Kanauj in his time named Harṣavardhana was just in his administration and punctilious in the discharge of his duties. He devoted his heart and soul to the performance of good works. He erected many topes on the bank of the Ganges and also Buddhist monasteries. He brought the monks together for examination and discussion, giving reward and punishment according to merit and demerit. The king also made visits of inspection throughout his dominion. The king's day was divided into three periods, of which one was given up to affairs of government, and two were devoted to religious works. He was an indefatigable worker (Watters, *On Yuan Chwang*, I, 343-44). Kanauj was the capital of the Maukhari kings before the time of Harṣavardhana. The Surat grant of Trilocanapāla contains the earliest reference to a Rāṣṭrakūṭa family at Kanauj. That the Rāṣṭrakūṭas lived in the vicinity of Kanauj is definitely proved by the Budaun Stone Inscription of Lakṣmaṇapāla (*E.I.*, I, 61–66). The territories of the Mālavas, Kośalas and Kurus appear to have been under the Gurjara rulers of Kanauj. Dhaṅga obtained exalted sovereignty after defeating the king of Kanauj (*Kānyakubjanarendra*, *E.I.*, I, 197). Five copperplate inscriptions of the Gahaḍavāla king Govindacandra were discovered at Kanauj (*E.I.*, VIII, 149ff.). Two copperplate inscriptions refer to the reign of the Mahārājādhirāja Mahendrapāla of Kanauj (*E.I.*, IX, 1ff.).

The Gwalior Praśasti tells us that Pratihāra Vatsarāja wrested the sovereignty of Kanauj from Bhaṇḍikula (*E.I.*, XVIII, 101). The Wani and Randhanpur plates inform us that Rāṣṭrakūṭa Dhruva defeated Vatsarāja, who in his turn inflicted a defeat on the Gauḍa king. Dharmapāla, who was his rival, did not give up his ambition to occupy Kanauj even though his first attempt was foiled (*E.I.*, VI, 244). The Kamauli Plate of Govindacandra, King of Kanauj, of 1184 V.S., refers to Kuśika, Gādhipura and Kānyakubja, which have been generally identified with one and the same place, namely, the modern Kanauj (*E.I.*, XXVI, Pt. II, April, 1941, p. 71). It was Govindacandra who re-established the supremacy of his line over Kānyakubja and the territories depending on it.

Kāritalāi.—This is a small village, 29 miles north by east of Murwārā, the headquarters of a tahsil of the same name in the Jabbalpur district (*E.I.*, XXIII, Pt. V—*Karitalāi Stone Inscription of Lakṣmaṇarāja*).

Kāśi.—Among the holy places of India Kāśī or Vārāṇasī stands preeminent (*Saurapurāṇa*, Ch. IV, v. 5; *Kālikāpurāṇa*, 51, 53; 58, 35; cf. *Mahābhārata*, 84, 78). Kāśī is included in the list of sixteen *Mahājanapadas* (*Aṅg.*, I. 213; IV, 252, 256, 260). Pāṇini in his *Aṣṭādhyāyī* (4. 2. 116), and Patañjali, in his *Mahābhāṣya* (2. 1. 1., p. 32), mention Kāśī. The *Bhāgavatapurāṇa* (IX. 22, 23; X. 57, 32; X. 66, 10; X. 84, 55 and XII. 13, 17) also mentions this city. The *Skandapurāṇa* (Ch. I, 19–23) and the *Yoginītantra* (1/2; 2/4) make mention of this holy city. The Kamauli plate of Govindacandra (V.S. 1184) refers to it (*E.I.*, XXVI, Pt. II, p. 71; *I.A.*, XV, p. 8, f.n. 46). Vārāṇasī, which was the chief city of the ancient kingdom of Kāśī, occurs in Lüders' List, No. 925, as a town. It was an important town like Kampillapura, Palāsapura and Ālabhi within the kingdom of Jiyasattu according to the Jaina *Uvāsagadasāo* (pp. 84-85, 90, 95, 105, 160, 163). It was known by different names in different ages; Surundhana, Sudassana, Brahmavaḍḍhana, Pupphavatī, Ramma and Molinī (*Jātaka*, IV, pp. 15, 199; *Cariyāpiṭaka*, p. 7). According to the *Kūrmapurāṇa* (Pūrvabhāga, Ch. 30, śl. 63) it lies in the midst of the rivers Varaṇā and Asī. It is situated 80 miles below Allahabad on the north bank of the Ganges. From the joint name of the two streams, the Varaṇā and Asī, which bound the city to the north and the south, the name Vārāṇasī is derived. The Varaṇā which is undoubtedly a considerable rivulet may be identified with the river Varaṇāvatī mentioned in the *Atharvaveda* (IV. 7. 1). Vārāṇasī is also called Kāśīnagara and Kāśīpura (*Jātaka*, V, 54; VI, 115; *Dhammapada Commentary*, I, 87). The extent of the city as mentioned in the *Jātaka* (IV, 377; VI, 160; cf. *Majjhima Commy.*, II, 608) was 12 yojanas. It was built by Śūlapāṇi Mahādeva. It was visited by king Hariścandra accompanied by his wife Śaivyā and son (*Mārkaṇḍeya-purāṇa*, Vaṅgavāsī Ed., p. 34). It could be reached from Śrāvastī by convenient roads. It stood on the left bank of the Ganges. It was a great centre of trade and industry and trade relation existed between it and Śrāvastī and Takṣaśilā. (*Dhammapada Commy.*, III, p. 429; I, p. 123). It was a most populous and prosperous country (*Dham. Commy.*, III, 445; *Suttanipāta Commy.*, II, 523ff.; *Jāt.*, II, 109, 287, 338; III, 198; V, 377; VI, 151, 450; *Jāt.*, I, 355; *Aṅg.*, III, 391; *Jāt.*, II, 197; I, 478; VI, 71). Vārāṇasī, which features fairly in Hindu, Buddhist and Jain literature, was included in the list of great cities suggested by Ānanda as a suitable place for the *parinirvāṇa* of the Buddha (*Dīgha*, II, 146). An inscription from Sarnath refers to the repair of some religious buildings in this city (*I.A.*, XIV, pp. 139-140).

According to the Jaina *Vividhatīrthakalpa* Vārāṇasī is divided into four parts: (1) Deva-Vārāṇasī—here stands the temple of Viśvanāth wherein are to be seen twenty-four Jinapaṭṭas; (2) Rājadhānī-Vārāṇasī—here lived the Yavanas; (3) Madana-Vārāṇasī; and (4) Vijaya-Vārāṇasī (Law, *Some Jaina Canonical Sūtras*, pp. 174-175).

Vārāṇasī was known to the Chinese as P'o-lo-ni-sse. It was 4,000 li in circuit and was very densely populated. The climate was soft, the crops abundant, the trees flourishing, and the underwood thick in every place. There were about 30 *saṅghārāmas* and 100 *deva-temples*. The people were humane and were earnestly given to study. They were mostly unbelievers and a few paid reverence to the Buddha (Beal, *Buddhist Records of the Western World*, II, 44ff.). Near Benaras there was a locality named Cundaṭṭhila (Cundavīla) which finds mention in the Barhut Inscriptions (Barua and Sinha, *Barhut Inscriptions*, pp. 7, 18).

From some of the Gāhaḍavāla records (e.g., Rawian Grant, *Bhandarkar's List of Northern Inscriptions*, No. 222) we find that the Ādikeśava-ghaṭṭa near the confluence of the Varuṇā and the Ganges to the north of Benaras was then regarded as a part of Benaras. The southern boundary of the city of Benaras extended at least up to the confluence of the Asī and the Ganges (*I.C.*, II, 148). A Buddhist inscription from Bodh-Gayā of the reign of Jayacandradeva refers to Kāśī. A king of Kāśī is stated to have been defeated by Lakṣmaṇasena according to the Mādhāinagar Grant (*J.P.A.S.B.*, N.S., Vol. V, pp. 467ff.; cf. *E.I.*, XXVI, Pt. I, *India Office Plate of Lakṣmaṇasena*). The Candrāvatī Grant of Candradeva (*E.I.*, XIV, 193) shows the extension of Gāhaḍavāla dominions from Benaras and Kanauj to the confluence of the Sarayū and Gharghārā (Gogra) in Ayodhyā (Fyzabad district). The kingdom of Kāśī was bordered by Kośala on the north, Magadha on the east, and Vatsa on the west (*Cambridge History of India*, I, 316). It was a wealthy and prosperous city (*Aṅguttara*, I, 213; *Dīgha*, II, 75). Kāśī is mentioned several times in the Vedic literature and in the Epics (*Śāṅkhyāyana Śrautasūtra*. XVI, 29, 5; *Bṛhadāraṇyaka Upaniṣad*, III, 8, 2; *Śatapatha Brāhmaṇa*, XIII, 5, 4, 19; *Kauśitakī Upaniṣad*, IV, 1; *Baudhāyana Śrautasūtra*, XVIII, 44; *Rāmāyaṇa*,

Uttarakāṇḍa, 56, 25; 59, 19; Ādikāṇḍa, 13th sarga, Kiṣkindhyākāṇḍa, 40th sarga). This city figures prominently in the *Mahābhārata*. Divodāsa who was the founder of the city of Benaras, fled to a forest after being defeated according to the Anuśāsanaparva of the *Mahābhārata* (Ch. 30, pp. 1899-1900). According to the Udyogaparva of the *Mahābhārata* (Ch. 117, p. 746) Divodāsa, son of Bhīmasena, king of Kāsī, had a son named Pratardana. We have another version of Divodāsa's life-story in the *Harivaṃśa* (Ch. 31; cf. *Vāyupurāṇa*, Ch. 92; *Brahmapurāṇa*, Ch. 13, 75). The *Mahābhārata* and the Purāṇas contain several stories about the kings of Kāśī (Ādiparva, 95, 105; Udyogaparva, Chs. 172–94, pp. 791–806; Sabhāparva, 30, 241-2; Virāṭaparva, 72, 16; Udyogaparva, 72, 714; Droṇaparva, 22, 38; Bhīṣmaparva, 50, 924, *Vāyupurāṇa*, Ch. 92; *Viṣṇupurāṇa*, 5th Aṃśa, Ch. 34). The Udyogaparva of the *Mahābhārata* alludes to Kṛṣṇa's repeated burning of the city. According to the Jainas Pārśvanātha was born in Benaras. Kāśī also figures in the stories of Mahāvīra, the founder of Jainism and his disciples.[1] Although Kāśī and Benaras feature fairly prominently in the Hindu and Jaina sources, it is the Buddhist books and particularly the Jātakas that give us a fuller information on the subject.[2] In the time of the Buddha Kāśī lost its political power. Kāśī's absorption into Kośala was an accomplished fact before the accession of Prasenajit of Kośala. His father Mahākośala gave his daughter named Kośaladevī a village of Kāśī (Kāsīgāma) as bath money on the occasion of her marriage with Bimbisāra of Magadha.[3] Kāśī was finally conquered and incorporated into the Magadhan kingdom, when Ajātaśatru, king of Magadha, defeated the Kośalans and became the most powerful king of northern India.[4]

In spite of good government the country was not entirely free from crime.[5] Kāśī was ruled with justice and equity. The ministers of the king were just and honest. No false suit was brought to court, and sometimes real cases were so scanty that ministers had to remain idle for lack of litigants. The king of Benaras was always on the alert to know his own faults.[6]

Enthusiastic youngmen of Benaras used to go to Taxila for their education (*Dhammapada Commy.*, I, 251ff.; *Khuddakapāṭha Commy.*, 198). The place which was most intimately associated with the several visits of the Buddha was the famous Deer Park (*Isipatanamigadāva*) near the city. It was here that the Buddha preached his first sermon after his enlightenment (*Dīgha*, III, 141; *Majjhima*, I, 170ff.; *Saṃyutta*, V, 420ff., pp. 97, 559). The Buddha converted many people of Benaras, and he preached here several sermons. (*Vinaya*, I, 15, 19; *Aṅguttara N.*, I, 110ff., 270ff.; III, 392ff., 399ff.; *Saṃyutta*, I, 105; V, 406; *Vinaya*, I, 189, 216, 289; *Samantapāsādikā*, I, 201). This city was visited by many venerable Buddhist monks (*Vinaya Texts*, S.B.E., II, 359-60; *Therīgāthā Commy.*, pp. 30-31; *Vinaya Texts*, III, 360, n. 3; 195-96, n. 3).

Kāsiā.—The Kāsiā stone image inscription mentions this village, situated 34 miles east of Gorakhpur in the Padrauna tahsil of the Gorakhpur district (*C.I.I.*, Vol. III). The headquarters of the Kāsiā sub-division are located in a big village at a distance of 34 miles east from Gorakhpur,

---

[1] B. C. Law, *Mahāvīra: His Life and Teachings*, Sec. 1; *Uvāsagadasāo*, Vol. II, 90–8; *Jaina Sūtras*, S.B.E., Vol. II, pp. 136-7; *Sūtrakṛtāṅga*, *Jaina Sūtras*, II, p. 87; S. Stevenson, *Heart of Jainism*, pp. 48-49.

[2] *Aṅguttara*, I, 213; *Dīgha*, II, 146; *Vinaya*, I, 343ff.; *Dhammapada Commy.*, I, 56ff; *Jātaka*, III, 211ff.; 406ff., 452, 487; *Jātaka*, I, 262ff.; *Aṅguttara*, V, 59.

[3] *Jātaka*, II, 237; IV, 342ff.

[4] *Samyutta*, I, 82–85.

[5] *Dhammapada Commy.*, I, 20; *Jātaka*, II, 387-88.

[6] *Jātaka*, II, 1–5.

21 miles north-east from Deoria, and 12 miles south-south-west from Padrauna (*Gorakhpur District Gazetteer* by Nevill, p. 261). The kingdom of the Mallas was divided into two parts having the capital cities of Kuśīnārā and Pāvā. According to some Pāvā may probably be identified with Kāsiā on the smaller Gandak and on the east of the Gorakhpur district (B. C. Law, *Geography of Early Buddhism*, p. 14). The ruins at Kāsiā were explored in 1876 when the main *Nirvāṇa* stūpa was completely exposed. The excavations at the ancient Buddhist site at Kāsiā have revealed the remains of many ancient buildings and other antiquities of great interest (*A.S.I.*, Annual Report, 1911/12, pp. 134ff.; *A.S.R.*, 1904/5, 43ff.; 1905/6, 6ff.; 1906/7, 44ff.; 1910/11, 62ff.; 1911/12, 134ff.).

Kāśmīra (Kaśmīra).—Kāśmīra, the Kasperia of Ptolemy, is mentioned in the Nāgārjunikoṇḍa Inscriptions of Vīrapuruṣadatta. This city was known to Pāṇini (4. 2. 133) and to Patañjali (3. 2. 2., pp. 188-189, 1. 1. 6, p. 276). It is also mentioned in the *Yoginītantra* (1/3, 2/9, p. 77). The *Bṛhat-saṃhitā* also mentions it as a country (xiv. 29). It lies to the north of the Punjab. It saw interesting developments in literature, religion and philosophy The *Divyāvadāna* (p. 399) refers to this beautiful city. In the *Avadānaśataka* (p. 67) and in the *Bodhisattvāvadānakalpalatā* (70th pallava), this city was peopled solely by the Nāgas. The author of the *Sragdharāstotram* was a Buddhist monk of Kāśmīra. A monk named Madhyantika was sent to this place as a missionary by his spiritual guide Ānanda (B. C. Law, *Geographical Essays*, p. 45). According to the *Kauṭilīya-Arthaśāstra*, diamond (*vajra*) was available in this city.

The kingdom of Kāśmīra was about 7,000 li in circuit and was enclosed on all sides by high mountains. The capital of the country on the west side was bordered by a great river which was evidently the Vitastā. The soil was fertile, and hence cereals and fruits, and flowers could be grown profusely. The medicinal plants were found here. The climate was cold and stern. The people were handsome in appearance. They were fond of learning. There were heretics and believers among them. The *stūpas* and *saṅghārāmas* were also found here (Beal, *Buddhist Records of the Western World*, I, 148ff.). It was included in the Gandhāra kingdom. After the dissolution of the Third Buddhist Council Moggaliputta Tissa was sent to Kāśmīra for the propagation of Buddhism. In Aśoka's time it was included in the Maurya dominion (see Watters, *On Yuan Chwang*, I, pp. 267-71).

Among the numerous temples in Kāśmīra, two may be mentioned, Mārtāṇḍa and Payech. Mārtāṇḍa, also called the temple of the Sun, stands on a slope about three miles east of Islamabad overlooking the finest view in Kāśmīr. The great structure was built by Lalitāditya in the 8th century A.D. Payech, which lies about 19 miles from Śrīnagar under the Naunagri Karewa, about six miles from the left bank of the Jhelum river, contains an ancient temple which, in intrinsic beauty and elegance of outline, is superior to all existing temples in Kāśmīra. Kāśmīra was the home of a separate school of Śaivism having a philosophy similar to that of Advaita as developed by Śaṅkara. (For further details, vide B. C. Law, *Holy Places of India*, pp. 30-31.)

Kātripura.—Kātripura, mentioned in the Allahabad Pillar Inscription, seems to have included Kumaun, Almorah, Garwal, and Kangra.[1]

Kedāra.—The *Mahābhārata* (Ch. 83, śl. 72) refers to Kedāratīrtha.[2] It is mentioned in the *Yoginītantra* (1. 8; 1. 11).

---

[1] *J.R.A.S.*, 1898, p. 198.

[2] Cf. *Kūrmapurāṇa*, 30. 45–48; *Saurapurāṇa*, Ch. 69, v. 23.

Kekaya.—This country, which is mentioned in the *Mahābhārata* (II. 48, 13; VI. 61. 12; VII, 19. 7) as well as in the *Bhāgavatapurāṇa* (X. 2. 3; X. 75, 12; X. 84, 55; X. 86, 20) has been identified with the present district of Shahpur in the Punjab. The Kekaya territory, according to the *Rāmāyaṇa* (II. 68, 19–22; VII. 113-114) lay beyond the Vipāśā or Beas and abutted on the Gandhāra territory. Cunningham identifies the capital of the Kekayadeśa with Girjak or Jalalpur on the Jhelum (*J.A.S.B.*, 1895, 250ff.; *A.G.I.*, 1924, 188; *Rāmāyaṇa*, I. 69, 7; II, 71. 18). Pāṇini in his *Aṣṭādhyāyī* (7. 3. 2) and Patañjali in his *Mahābhāṣya* (7. 2. 3) refer to it. Rājaśekhara in his *Kāvyamīmāṃsā* places the Kekaya country in the northern division of India along with the Śakas, Hūṇas, Kāmbojas, Vāhlīkas, etc. According to Strabo it was extensive and fertile having in it some 300 cities (H. and F.'s Tr. III, p. 91). For further details vide Law, *Indological Studies*, Pt. I, pp. 18-19.

Kesaputta.—The *Aṅguttara* (I, 188) mentions Kesaputta in Kosala. The Kālāmas who belonged to this place, were a republican people at the time of Bimbisāra. The philosopher Āḷāra belonged to Kesaputta (*Buddhacarita*, XII, 2; Law, *Geography of Early Buddhism*, p. 30).

Ketakavana.—It was in Kosala near the village of Naḷakapāna (*Jātaka*, I, 170).

Ketumatī.—King Vessantara with his wife and children rested on the bank of this river (*Jātaka*, VI, 518). He crossed the stream and then went to the Nālika hill. He then reached the lake Mucalinda moving towards the north.

Khāṇḍava.—According to the *Taittirīya Āraṇyaka* (V. I. 1.), it formed one of the boundaries of Kurukṣetra. It may be identified with the famous Khāṇḍava forest of the *Mahābhārata*. This name also occurs in the *Pañcaviṃśa Brāhmaṇa* (XXV. 3, 6).

Kīra.—The Khalimpur copperplate of Dharmapāla refers to this country, which, according to Kielhorn, belongs to north-east India (*E.I.*, IV, 243, 246). The people of this country were defeated by Dharmapāla of the Pāla dynasty, and the Kīra king, in order to do homage to the Pāla emperor, came to the Imperial assembly at Kanauj (*E.I.*, IV, 243). According to the Khajuraho Inscription of Yaśovarman, the king of Kīra received the image of Vaikuṇṭha from the Lord of Bhoṭa (*E.I.*, I, 122). The Rewah Stone Inscription of Karṇa refers to Kīra near Baijnāth in the Kangra valley (*E.I.*, XXIV, Pt. III, p. 110).

Kīragrāma.—It has been identified with Baijnāth in the Kangra district containing the *Liṅga* shrine which is picturesquely situated on the south bank of the ancient Binduka stream (Modern Binnu) (*A.S.I.*, Annual Report, 1929/30, pp. 15ff.).

Kirāta.—It is in the Himalayas and is possibly Tibet. According to Ptolemy the Kirātas were located in the Uttarāpatha (cf. McCrindle, *Ancient India*, p. 277). They had their settlements in the eastern region as well. The land of the Kirātas is called Kirrhadia by Ptolemy. Kirrhadia, the country of Kirrhadai, is mentioned in the *Periplus of the Erythraean Sea* as lying west from the mouth of the Ganges. Ptolemy's Kirrhadoi or Airrhadoi spread widely not only over Gangetic India but also over countries further east. Pliny and Megasthenes also mention the Kirātas under the name Skyrites. According to Megasthenes they were a nomadic people. For further remarks on the location of the Kirātas, see Lassen, *Indisches Alterthum*, Vol. III, pp. 235–237. They are referred to in the *Mahābhārata* (XII, 207, 43) together with the Yavanas, Kāmbojas, Gandhāras and Barbaras who all dwelt in the northern region or *Uttarāpatha*. The *Śrīmad-Bhāgavatam* (II, 4, 18) refers to them as living outside the Aryan fold. They are mentioned in the Nāgārjunikoṇḍa Inscription of Vīrapuruṣadatta. The Kirātas of the Uttarāpatha are castigated as peoples, who lived as criminal tribes with predatory habits like those of the hunters and vultures (B. M. Barua, *Aśoka and His Inscriptions*, p. 100). For references from literature see B. C. Law, *Tribes in Ancient India*, pp. 282-83.

Kirthār.—This mountain runs to the south of the Sulaiman between Singh and Jhalawan country of Baluchistan. It extends southwards from the Mūla river gorge in a series of parallel ridges for 190 miles. (For further details see Law, *Mountains of India*, p. 8.)

Kośala.—Kośala, which is mentioned in Pāṇini's *Aṣṭādhyāyī* (4. 1. 171) was one of the sixteen great countries of India (*Aṅguttara Nikāya*, I, 213; cf. *Viṣṇupurāṇa*, Ch. 4, Aṃśa 4). The *Bhāgavatapurāṇa* refers to it as a country (IX. 10, 29; IX. 11, 22; X. 2, 3; X. 58, 52; X. 86, 20; XII. 12, 24). It lay to the east of the Kurus and Pañcālas and to the west of the Videhas from whom it was separated by the river Sadānīrā, probably the great Gandak (*Cambridge History of India*, I, 308; Rapson, *Ancient India*, p. 164; cf. *Śatapatha Brāhmaṇa*, 1, 4, 11). The Kośalans belonged to the solar race and were supposed to have derived directly from Manu through Ikṣvāku. The *Daśakumāracaritaṃ* (p. 195) refers to Kośala under its ruler Kusumadhanvā whose wife was Sāgaradattā, the daughter of Vaiśravaṇa, a merchant of Pāṭaliputra. Kośala is known to the Buddhists as the land of the Kośalan princes, tracing their descent from Ikṣvāku (*Sumaṅgalavilāsinī*, I, 239). In the Epic period Kośala emerges into importance. From the story of Rāma's exile the extent of the Kośala country in the epic period may be known. After Rāma the extensive Kośalan empire is said to have been divided amongst his own sons as well as those of his three brothers. The Kośala country proper is said to have been divided into two. Rāma's elder son named Kuśa became the king of the southern Kośala and transferred his capital from Ayodhyā to Kuśasthalī which he built on the Vindhya range (*Vāyupurāṇa*, 88, 198). Lava, the younger son, became the ruler of northern Kośala and set up his capital at the city of Śrāvastī. The history of Kośala in later times is known chiefly from Jaina and Buddhist literature. There was rivalry between Kāśī and Kośala. Kāśī and Kośala appear as two equally powerful kingdoms flourishing side by side, each with its inner circles, outer districts and border lands. Kāśī was later absorbed by Kośala. The Buddhist texts contain many stories about men and women of Kośala, and many of them were in some way associated with Pasenadi. In later times North Kośala came to be known as Śrāvastī in order to distinguish it from South Kośala. The Kośalan kings and princes received good education. For details, vide B. C. Law, *Tribes in Ancient India*, Ch. XXVIII.

Kosambī.—Kosambī (Skt.: Kauśāmbī; Chinese: Kiau-Shang-Mi) was the capital of the Vaṃsas or Vatsas (Vatsapattana). It was the birthplace of the sixth Tīrthaṅkara (*Āvassaka Nirjjuti*, 382). A Stone Pillar Inscription was discovered near Kosam, ancient Kauśāmbī, in Allahabad district (*Kosam Inscription of the Mahārāja Vaiśravaṇa* of the year 107; *E.I.*, XXIV, Pt. IV, p. 146). Vaiśravaṇa was one of the rulers of Kauśāmbī, as it is known from this inscription for the first time. The Kosam Inscription of Bhadramagha's reign has been discovered in course of exploration of the ancient site of Kauśāmbī (*E.I.*, XXIV, Pt. VI, April, 1938). Patañjali mentions this city in his *Mahābhāṣya* (2. 1. 1, p. 32; 2. 2. 1, p. 124). According to the Pauranic tradition the royal dynasty of the Vatsa country, to which king Udayana (Pali: Udena) belonged, traced its descent from Puru and once held its royal seat in the Kuru kingdom with Hastināpura as its capital. Kosambī was one of the important stopping places of persons travelling along the great trade-route connecting Sāketa and Sāvatthī on the north with Patiṭṭhāna or Paiṭhāna on the bank of the Godāvarī on the south (Barua and Sinha, *Barhut Inscriptions*, p. 12).

Kosambī is identified by Cunningham with Kosam on the Jumna, about 30 miles south-west from Allahabad. Hiuen Tsang visited this country in the 7th century A.D. According to him, it was more than 6,000 li in circuit, and its capital 30 li in circuit. It was a fertile country with hot climate; it yielded much upland rice and sugarcane. Its people were enterprising, fond of arts and cultivators of religious merit. There were more than ten Buddhist monasteries which were in utter ruin and the monks were Hīnayānists. There were more than fifty Deva-temples, and the non-Buddhists were numerous.[1] An inscription on the gateway of the fort of Kara dated Saṃvat 1093 (A.D. 1036) records the grant of the village of Payalāsa (modern Prās) in the Kauśāmbī-maṇḍala to one Māthura-Vikaṭa of Pabhosā together with its customary duties, royalties, taxes, etc., in perpetuity to his descendants by Mahārājādhirāja Yaśaḥpāla, who was the last Pratihāra king of Kanauj. The Allahabad posthumous stone pillar inscription of Samudragupta refers to Kauśāmbī (*C.I.I.*, Vol. III). The Kosam stone image inscription of Mahārāja Bhīmavarman (the year 139) refers to Kosam, the ancient town of Kauśāmbī (*C.I.I.*, Vol. III). This city was hallowed by the birth of Jina. It contains the temple of Padmaprabhu in which the image of Candanavālā can be seen. Here Candanavālā fasted for about six months in honour of Mahāvīra. The brick-built fort of king Pradyota still exists here.[2] For further details vide B. C. Law, *Tribes in Ancient India*, pp. 136ff.; B. C. Law, *Kauśāmbī in Ancient Literature*, *M.A.S.I.*, No. 60; *Mahāvastu*, Vol. II, p. 2; *Bodhisattvāvadānakalpalatā*, 35th Pallava; *Northern Buddhist Literature* (R. L. Mitra), 269; *Saundarananda-kāvya*, Canto I; B. C. Law, *Geographical Essays*, 26-27; B. C. Law, *Geography of Early Buddhism*, pp. 16-17.

Kosaṃ-Ināṃ } These twin villages stand on the bank of the Jumna
Kosam-Khirāj } at a distance of some 12 miles south from Manjhanpur and nine miles west from Sarai Akil. Kosaṃ-Ināṃ lies to the west and Kosam-Khirāj to the east of the fort.[3]

Kośika.—This mountain does not seem to be far from the Himalaya.[4]

Kośiki.—It is a branch of the Ganges.[5] It is identical with the Kuśī.[6]

Kṛśāṇagrāma.—It is suggested in the *Lalitavistara* to have been situated somewhere near Kapilavastu. Some have identified it with the place where Gautama gave up his crown and sword and cut off locks of his hair.[7]

Kṛṣṇagiri.—It is the Karakorum or the Black mountain.[8] This mountain is continuous with the Hindukush on the west. According to modern geographers it was uplifted earlier and is hence older than the Himalaya proper. It is of Hercynian age, and got considerably folded and faulted subsequent to its uplift.

Krumu.—Below the Kubhā or Kābul this Vedic river forms a western tributary of the Indus. It is identical with modern Kuram, which flows

---

1 Watters, *On Yuan Chwang*, I, 365-66.
2 B. C. Law, *Some Jaina Canonical Sūtras*, pp. 172-173.
3 *Allahabad District Gazetteer*, by Nevill, pp. 262-63.
4 *Apadāna*, p. 381.
5 *Jāt.*, V. 2.
6 Cf. *Kauśiki*, vide *ante*.
7 B. C. Law, *Geographical Essays*, 41; R. L. Mitra, *Northern Buddhist Lit.*, p. 135.
8 *Vāyupurāṇa*, Ch. 36.

into the Indus at a place south of Ishakhed. It pierces through the Sulaiman range.[1]

Kubhā.—Among the western tributaries of the Indus this Vedic river is the most important.[2] According to some classical writers it formed the western boundary of India proper. It is no other than the modern Kābul river, the Kophes of Arrian and the Kophen of Pliny. It is apparently the same river as the Kuhu of the *Purāṇas* and it may be identical with Koa of Ptolemy, which is described to have its source in the Imaos or Himavat.[3] The Kubhā cuts a valley through the Sulaiman range. It flows into the Indus a little above Attock (Skt. Hāṭaka), receives at Prāng a joint flow of its two tributaries called the Svāt (Soastos of Arrian, Skt. Suvāstu) and Gaurī (Garroia of Arrian), identified with the modern Panjkorā, a tributary of the Svāt. The *Vāyu* and *Kūrma Purāṇas* refer to this river (XLV, 95; XLVII, 27).

Kuhu.—Same as *Kubhā.*

Kullu.—It is the Kulūta or Kaulūta of the Epics. The district of Kully in the upper valley of the Beas river exactly corresponds with the kingdom of Kiu-lu-to which is placed by Hiuen Tsang at 700 li or 117 miles to the north-east of Jālandhar (*C.A.G.I.*, 162ff.). Here Aśoka built a stūpa and there were twenty monasteries according to Hiuen Tsang. Traces of Buddhism are still visible there. For further details vide *Annual Report of the A.S.I.*, 1907-8, 261ff.

Kurujāṅgala.—It was probably the wild region of the Kuru-realm that stretched from the Kāmyaka forest on the banks of the Sarasvatī to Khāṇḍava near the Jumna (cf. *Mahābhārata*, III, 5. 3). It was the eastern part of the Kuru land and it is said to have comprised the tract between the Ganges and northern Pañcāla (see *Kurukṣetra*).

Kurukṣetra.—This city, according to the *Mahābhārata* (83. 1–8, 203–208) is considered as holy. Its dust removes the sins of the sinners. Those who live at Kurukṣetra to the south of the Sarasvatī and north of the Dṛṣadvatī, are, as if, living in heaven. It is mentioned by Pāṇini in his *Aṣṭādhyāyī* (4. 1. 172/176; 4. 2. 130). The *Yoginītantra* refers to it (2/1, 2/7, 8). The *Saurapurāṇa* (67. 12) also refers to it as a holy city (cf. *Kūrmapurāṇa*, Pūrvabhāga, 30. 45–48; cf. *Padmapurāṇa*, Uttarakhaṇḍa, vs. 35–38). The ancient Kuru country may be said to have comprised the Kurukṣetra or Thāneśvara. The region included Sonapāt, Āmin, Karnal and Panipat, and was situated between the Sarasvatī on the north and the Dṛṣadvatī on the south. The *Taittirīya Āraṇyaka* (V. 1, 1) points out that Kurukṣetra was bounded on the south by Khāṇḍava, on the north by Tūrghna, and on the west by the Parīṇah (the Parenos of Arrian). The *Mahābhārata* grew up with the Kuru people and their country as its background.[4] In the days of the Buddha it was well known as one of the sixteen *Mahājanapadas*. The territory of the Kurus appears to have been divided into three parts, Kurukṣetra, Kuru's country and the Kurujāṅgala (*Mahābhārata*, Ādiparva, CIX, 4337–40). Kurukṣetra, the cultivated land of the Kurus, comprised the whole tract on the west of the Jumna and included the sacred region between the Sarasvatī and the Dṛṣadvatī (*Mahābhārata*, Vanaparva, LXXXIII, 5071–78, 7073–76; *Rāmāyaṇa*, Ayodhyākāṇḍa, LXX, 12). The Kurujāṅgala, the waste land of the Kurus, was the eastern part of their territory, and appears to have

---

[1] Law, *Rivers of India*, p. 15.

[2] *Ṛgveda*, X, 75, 6.

[3] Ptolemy, VII, 1. 26.

[4] As for the description of Kurukṣetra, vide *Mahābhārata*, III, 83-4; 9. 15; 25, 40; 52, 200; 204–8.

comprised the tract between the Ganges and northern Pañcāla (*Rāmāyaṇa*, Ayodhyākāṇḍa, LXXII; *Mahābhārata*, Sabhāparva, XIX, 793-94). This forest tract of the Kuruland extended as far as the Kāmyaka forest. The middle region between the Ganges and the Jumna seems to have been simply called Kuru's country. In the Brāhmaṇa texts[1] Kurukṣetra is regarded as a particularly sacred country, for within its boundaries flowed the sacred streams, Dṛṣadvatī, Sarasvatī, and the Āpayā.[2] The *Bhāgavatapurāṇa* mentions it (I. 10, 34; III, 3, 12; IX, 14, 33; cf. *Brahmāṇḍapurāṇa*, II, 18. 50). It is called the Dharmakṣetra or the holy land according to the *Bhagavadgītā*. It is a holy place as also mentioned in the *Skandapurāṇa* (Ch. I, 19–23). The field of the Kurus or the region of Delhi was the scene of the war between the Kurus and the Pāṇḍus in which all the nations of India were ranged on one side or the other.[3] The great law-giver Manu speaks of the country of the Kurus and other allied peoples as forming the sacred land of the Brahmarṣis (Brahmanical sages) ranking immediately after Brahmāvarta (*Manusaṃhitā*, II, 17–19).[4] According to Rapson the territories occupied by the Kurus extended to the east far beyond the limits of Kurukṣetra. The Kurus must have occupied the northern portion of the Doab or the region between the Jumna and the Ganges, having as their neighbours on the east, north Pañcālas and on the south, south-Pañcālas, who held the rest of the Doab as far as Vatsabhūmi, the corner where the two rivers meet at Prayāga (Allahabad) (*Ancient India*, p. 165.).

In the time of Hiuen Tsang Thaneswar was the capital of a Vaiśya (Bais) dynasty which ruled parts of the southern Punjab, Hindusthan and eastern Rajputana. In A.D. 648 a Chinese ambassador was sent to Harṣavardhana of Thāneswara. He found that the Senāpati Arjuna had usurped his kingdom and the dynasty then became extinct. Thaneswar continued to be a place of great sanctity but in 1014 A.D. it was sacked by Mahmud of Ghazni, and although recovered by a Hindu rājā of Delhi in 1043 A.D., it remained desolate for centuries.

Kuśapura (*Kuśabhavanapura*).—It is said to have been named after Rāma's son Kuśa. This site was surrounded on the three sides by the river Gumtī (Gomatī) (*C.A.G.I.*, p. 459).

Kuśīvatī.—It is an older name of Kuśīnārā where the Buddha obtained *Mahāparinibbāna* (*Jāt.*, I, 292; V, 278, 285, 293, 294, 297). It was near the modern village of Kāsiā on the smaller Gaṇḍak, 37 miles to the east of Gorakhpur, and to the north-west of Bettia (*C.A.G.I.*, 713, 714; *J.R.A.S.*, 1913, 152). For further details vide Kuśīnārā.

Kuśika.—It is the same as Gādhipura and Kānyakubja (modern Kanauj) and it finds mention in the Kamauli grant of Govindacandra V. S. 1184 (*E.I.*, XXVI, Pt. II, 68ff.).

Kuśīnārā.—Kuśīnārā was one of the cities of the Mallas (*Dīgha*, II, 165). That it was not a city of the first rank like Rājagṛha, Vaiśālī or Śrāvastī in the Buddha's time, is clear from Ānanda's utterance to the Buddha: 'Let not the Exalted One die in this little town, in the midst of the jungle, in this branch township'. This city was known to the Chinese

---

[1] *Aitareya Brāhmaṇa*, VII, 30; *Śatapatha Brāhmaṇa*, IV, 1, 5, 13; XI, 5, 1, 4; XIV, 1, 1, 2; *Maitrāyaṇī Saṃhitā*, ii, 1, 4; iv, 5–9; *Jaiminīya Brāhmaṇa*, iii, 126; *Sāṅkhyāyana Śrautasūtra*, XV, 16, 11.

[2] Apagā or Oghavatī, a branch of Citang.

[3] For an account of the part played by different nations and tribes who were arrayed in the great battle of the Pāṇḍavas against the Kauravas, see *J.R.A.S.*, 1908, 309ff.

[4] *Brahmāvartatīrtha*—*Mahābhārata*, 83. 53.

as Kiu-shi-na-K'ie-lo. It contained a few inhabitants and the avenues of the place were deserted and waste. At the north-east angle of the city-gate there was a stūpa built by Aśoka. The villages were desolate.

It contained the old house of Cunda who invited the Buddha to his house (Beal, *Buddhist Records of the Western World*, II, 31-32). The distance from Kuśīnārā to Pāvā was not great. This is also clear from the fact that the Buddha hastened from Kuśīnārā to Pāvā during his last illness.

According to Cunningham, Kuśīnārā may be identified with the village of Kāsiā in the east of Gorakhpur district (*Ancient Geography of India*, p. 493). This view has been strengthened by the fact that in the stūpa behind the Nirvāṇa temple near this village a copperplate has been discovered bearing the inscription: '*Parinirvāṇa-caitya-tāmra-paṭṭa*' or the copperplate of the *Parinirvāṇa-caitya*. This identification appears to be correct. Different scholars hold different views. V. A. Smith prefers to place Kuśīnārā in Nepal beyond the first range of hills (*Early History of India*, 4th ed., p. 167, f.n. 5; *J.R.A.S.*, 1913, 152). Rhys Davids expresses the opinion that if we rely on the account of the Chinese pilgrims, the territory of the Mallas of Kuśīnārā was on the mountain slopes, to the east of the Śākya land and to the north of the Vajjian confederation. But some would place their territory south of the Sākyas and east of the Vajjians (*Buddhist India*, p. 26).

In the *Divyāvadāna* (pp. 389–94) we read that Aśoka visited this city where the Buddha attained *Mahāparinirvāṇa*. This account is corroborated by what Aśoka says in his lithic records (*R.E.* VIII). The Buddha had to cross the river Kakutthā while going from Kuśīnārā to Rājagṛha. This river is a small stream, known as the Barhi, which falls into the Choṭa-gaṇḍak, eight miles below Kāsiā. Near Kuśīnārā the river Hiraññavatī (Hiraṇyavatī) or the little Gandak,[1] on the bank of which the Śāla-grove of the Mallas of Kuśīnārā stood, flows to the district of Gorakhpur, about eight miles west of the great Gandak and falls into the Gogra (Sarayū).

Kuśāvatī was at first known as the capital city of the Mallas when they had a monarchical constitution (*Jāt.*, V, pp. 278ff.). It was rich, prosperous, populous and in it alms were easily procurable (*Dīgha*, II, 170). But later on in the Buddha's time when the monarchy came to be replaced by a republican constitution, the name of this city was changed to Kuśīnārā. The Buddha himself says that Kuśīnārā was ancient Kuśāvatī. It was a capital city, which was 12 yojanas in length from east to west and 7 yojanas in width from north to south (*ayaṃ Kuśīnārā Kusāvatī nāma rājadhānī ahosi—Dīgha*, II, 146-47, 170). The Buddha narrated the former glory of Kusāvatī which had seven ramparts, four gates and seven avenues of palm-trees (*Dīgha*, II, 170-171). According to the *Divyāvadāna* (p. 227) it was the beautiful city of Mahāsudarśana.

The Mallas of Kuśīnārā had their *santhāgāra* or Council-hall where all matters, political or religious, were discussed. The *Mahāparinibbāna Suttanta* of the *Dīgha Nikāya* mentions a set of officers called *Puriṣas* among the Mallas of Kuśīnārā, who are supposed to be a class of subordinate servants, according to Rhys Davids (*Buddhist India*, p. 21). There was a Mallian shrine called Makuṭabandhana to the east of Kuśīnārā, where the dead body of the Buddha was brought for cremation. When the Buddha felt that his last moment was fast approaching, he sent Ānanda with a message to the Mallas of Kuśīnārā who were then assembled in their Council-hall to discuss some public affairs. On receipt of the news they

[1] *Dīgha N.*, II, 137.

hurried to the Śāla-grove where the Buddha was. As soon as the Buddha passed away, they met together in their Council-hall to devise means for honouring the earthly remains of the Master in a suitable manner. They treated the remains of the *Tathāgata* like those of a *Cakravarttirājā*. They then erected a stūpa over their own share of Buddha's relics and celebrated a feast.

Lachmanjholā.—Not far from Hṛṣikeśa there stands a beautiful spot famous for its mountain scenery. Before proceeding to Kedārnāth and Badrināth pilgrims halt here. The place derives its name from a hanging bridge (Law, *Holy Places of India*, p. 21).

Ladakh.—The Ladakh is a lofty range parallel to the greater Himalaya and lies to the east of the Mānasasarovara lake. It is separated from the Himalayan range by a valley, some 50 miles wide (Law, *Mountains of India*, p. 7).

Lār.—It is a village in the Gorakhpur district, Uttara Pradeśa (United Provinces) where the plates of Govindacandra of Kanauj were discovered (*E.I.*, VII, 98ff.).

Lohāwar.—This city is said to have been founded by Lava, the son of Rāma. It is called Labokla by Ptolemy (*C.A.G.I.*, pp. 226-27).

Lumbinīgrāma.—The Rummindei Inscription of Aśoka mentions Lumminigāma which is now Rummindeī, also called Rupadeī, a small hamlet named after the shrine of Rummindeī. Rummindeī is only ten miles to the east of Kapilavastu and two miles north of Bhagavānpur and about a mile to the north of Paderia. Lumbinīvana was visited by the Chinese pilgrims, Fa-hien and Yuan Chwang. According to the former, it was fifty li (9 or 10 miles) east of Kapilavastu. Yuan Chwang refers to a stone-pillar set up here by Aśoka with the figure of a horse on the top. Afterwards the pillar had been broken in the middle and laid on the ground by a thunderbolt from a malicious dragon. P. C. Mukherji in his 'Antiquities in the Terai' has shown that the extant remains of the Rummindeī pillar of Aśoka agree with the description given by the Chinese pilgrim. There is further evidence of the identification of the Lumbinīvana with the place where the Rummindeī inscription was found. Yuan Chwang mentions that near the Aśokan pillar there was 'a small stream flowing south-east, and called by the people the Oil River'. The tradition survives even today, and this river is now called Tilār-nade, which is a corruption of Telīr-nadī, or the teli's or oilman's river. There is also a temple at Rummindeī comparatively of a later date, which contains a sculptured slab representing the nativity of the Buddha, which is a further proof of the identity of the place with Lumbinīvana. The Rummindeī pillar of Aśoka states that when king Aśoka was anointed twenty years, he himself came and worshipped this spot because the Buddha was born here. He erected a stone-pillar to mark the site of the Buddha's birth. He made the village of Lumbinī free of taxes and paying (only) an eighth share (of the produce) (*C.I.I.*, 264-265).

The inscription on the Niglīva pillar (situated 38 miles north-west of Uskabazar Station on the B.N.W. Rly.) shows that it was erected near the stūpa of Konāgamana but it is not now *in situ*. Lumbinīvana is referred to in the *Buddhacaritakāvya* (I, v. 23; XVII, v. 27) as situated in Kapilavastu which is the birthplace of the Buddha. For different views as to the location of the Lumbinī-grove, vide B. C. Law, *Geography of Early Buddhism*, pp. 29-30; Law, *Geographical Essays*, pp. 185ff.

Madāvar.—It was a large town in Western Rohilkhand near Bijnor. Some have identified it with Madipura or *Mo-ti-pu-lo*. According to Hiuen Tsang it was 1,000 miles in circuit. The people of this place, according to Vivien de St. Martin, may be the Mathae of Megasthenese. (*C.A.G.I.*, pp. 399ff.).

Madhuban.—It is in the Pargana Nathupur in the Azamgaḍh district of the Benaras division (U.P.), where the inscription of Harṣa was discovered (*E.I.*, VII, 155ff.).

Madhuravana.—The name of Madhuravana occurs in the Mathurā Buddhist Image Inscription of Huviṣka. Some have identified it with Madhuvana or Madhurā (modern Muttra), which occurs in Luders' List (Nos. 288, 291). In Luders' List (No. 38) mention is made of a suburb of Mathurā named Mathuravanaka.

Madradeśa.—The country of the Madras, mentioned in the Allahabad Pillar Inscription, roughly corresponds to the modern Sialkot and the surrounding regions between the Rāvī and the Chenāb rivers. Pāṇini refers to Madra in his *Aṣṭādhyāyī* (4. 1. 176, 4. 2. 131, 4. 2. 108). Patañjali also refers to it in his *Mahābhāṣya* (1. 1. 8, p. 345; 1. 3. 2, p. 619; 2. 1. 2, p. 40; 4. 2. 108). The capital was Śākala,[1] identified with Sialkot. Śākala or (Pali) Sāgala[2] was a great centre of trade. It was situated in a delightful country, well-watered and hilly. It contained many hundreds of almshalls of various kinds. The old town of Śākala (*She-ki-lo*), according to Hiuen Tsang, was about 20 li in circuit. There was a monastery here with about 100 priests of the Hīnayāna school, and a stūpa to the north-west of the monastery, about 200 ft. high, was built by Aśoka (Beal, *Records of the Western World*, I, pp. 166ff.). The people of this country were an ancient Kṣatriya tribe of Vedic times. The Madras were a corporation of warriors and enjoyed the status of *rājās*. Śākala came under the sway of Alexander the Great, in 326 B.C. About 78 A.D., Menander (Pali: Milinda), a powerful Greek king, ruled at Sāgala or Śākala. According to the *Milindapañha* this king was converted to Buddhism. Even before Menander's time, Śākala seems to have come under Buddhist influence (see Mrs. Rhys Davids, *Psalms of the Sisters*, p. 48; *Psalms of the Brethren*, p. 359). In the fourth century A.D. the Madras paid taxes to Samudragupta. For further details, vide B. C. Law, *Tribes in Ancient India*, Ch. VII.

Mahāvana.—It was at Kapilavatthu (*Saṃyutta*, I, p. 26). The Buddha once dwelt at Kūṭāgāra hall in the Mahāvana, the great forest stretching up to the Himalayas (*Vinaya Texts*, III, 321ff.).

Mahī.—It is one of the five great rivers mentioned in Pali literature (*Aṅguttara*, IV, 101; *Milindapañha*, p. 114; *Suttanipāta*, p. 3). It is a tributary of the Gaṇḍak.

Mahobā.—It is the ancient Mahotsavapura in the Hammirpur district of the Uttara Pradeśa. Here a stone inscription of Paramardin of the Vikrama year 1240 was discovered by Cunningham in 1843. It contains a *praśasti* of Paramardin and mentions his battles in Aṅga, Vaṅga and Kaliṅga. The *praśasti* was composed by Jayapāla of the Vāstavya family. This inscription has now been edited by V. V. Mirashi (*Bhārata Kaumudī*, Pt. I, pp. 433ff.).

Mainākagiri.—The *Yoginītantra* has a reference to this hill (2. 4, pp. 128-129). It is also mentioned in Bāṇa's *Kādambarī* (p. 86). It is the Siwalik range extending from the Ganges to the Beas. The Siwalik hills proper extend for about 200 miles from the Beas to the Ganges, and are known to the ancient geographers as Mainākaparvata. In the Uttara Pradeśa the Siwaliks are known as the Churia and the Dundwa ranges and

---

[1] *Mahābhārata*, II. 1196; VIII, 2033.

[2] *Milindapañha*, ed. Trenckner, pp. 1-2.

lie between the Ganges and the Jumna. Here the hills rise abruptly from the plains and slope rather gently northwards into the valley of Dehra Dun. (Law, *Mountains of India*, pp. 3, 4, 7).

Manasākaṭa.—It was a Brahmin village in Kośala visited by the Buddha with five hundred monks (*Dīgha*, I, p. 235). To the north of it flowed the Aciravatī. On the banks of this river there was a mango grove.

Mandākinī.—The *Yoginītantra* has a reference to this river (1/15, pp. 87–89). It is the western Kālī (Kālīgaṅgā) which rises in the mountains of Kedāra in Garhwal. It is a tributary of the Alakanandā (*Aṅguttara Nikāya*, IV, 101). Cunningham identifies it with Mandākin, a small tributary of the Paisundi in Bundelkhand which flows by the side of the Citrakūṭaparvata. (Cunningham, *A.S.R.*, XXI, 11.)

Maṇikarṇa.—A place of pilgrimage also known as Maṇikaran on the Pārvatī, a tributary of the Beas in the Kulu valley (*J.A.S.B.*, 1902, p. 36).

Maṇiparvata.—It is in the Himalayan region (*Jāt.*, II, p. 92).

Mankuwar.—This small village mentioned in the Mankuwar stone image inscription of Kumāragupta is situated near the right bank of the Jumna, about nine miles in the south-westerly direction from Arail, the chief town of the Arail pargana in the Karchana tehsil or sub-division of the Allahabad district. (*C.I.I.*, Vol. III.)

Maśakāvatī.—It was the capital town of the Assakenoi according to the Greek writers. It was the kingdom of a ruler called Assakenos. It was stormed by the troops of Alexander. When the town capitulated, a large number of mercenary troops agreed to join the army of Alexander. The mercenaries who were unwilling to help him, secretly planned to escape. At this the Macedonians spared none of them (*Cambridge History of India*, Vol. I, p. 353; Law, *Indological Studies*, I, pp. 2-3).

Mathurā.—In one of the Mathurā Buddhist Rail-pillar inscriptions the name of Vādhapāla (?) Dhanabhūti, son of Dhanabhūti (?) and Vātsī, is recorded as the donor of a railing (*vedikā*) and arches (*toraṇas*) at the Ratnagṛha for the worship of all Buddhas (Luders' List, No. 125). The railing with the arches was dedicated by him together with his parents and the four sections, the monks, nuns, *upāsakas* and *upāsikās* of the Buddhist community. The name of the prince Vādhapāla, the son of king Dhanabhūti, is recorded as the donor of a rail of the Barhut railing (*Ibid.*, No. 869). The name of Vādhapāla's father, king Dhanabhūti, the son of Āgaraju (Aṅgāradyut) and Vātsī, and the grandson of king Viśvadeva, figures prominently as the donor of the ornamental gateways of the stūpa of Barhut (*Ibid.*, Nos. 687-88; cf. also No. 882). It is expressly recorded in the Barhut gateway inscriptions that the gateways were caused to be erected by King Dhanabhūti in the dominion of the Śuṅgas (*Suganaṃ raje*) (Barua and Sinha, *Bārhut Inscriptions*, pp. 1ff.). If prince Vādhapāla the son of king Dhanabhūti of the Bārhut Inscription, be the same person as Vādhapāla (?) Dhanabhūti, the son of Dhanabhūti of the Mathurā Buddhist Rail Inscription, as it seems very likely, one cannot but be led to think that Mathurā was then placed in a territory contiguous to the dominion of the Śuṅgas. From the existing fragment of the inscription it cannot be made out if the epithet of king was affixed to the name of Vādhapāla (?) Dhanabhūti. Vādhapāla introduced as Vādhapāla (?) Dhanabhūti must have been a ruler; otherwise there is no reason why in the dedication he should have been associated with his parents (presumably aged) and a big retinue of all the four sections of the Buddhist community. Prince Vādhapāla's inscription at Bārhut is written in Aśokan Prakrit, while the language of Vādhapāla (?) Dhanabhūti's inscription at Mathurā marks a transition from the Aśokan Prakrit to the typical mixed Sanskrit of the inscription of the Kuṣāṇa age. Its alphabet too stands midway between the Aśokan Brāhmī and that of the Kuṣāṇa period. The interval of time between the two inscriptions was not long enough to account for such a marked change in their languages. The difference can be easily explained on the supposition that Bārhut and Mathurā were situated in two contiguous but slightly different linguistic areas. In the absence of any reference to the dominion of any other ruler or dynasty, it may be legitimate to assume that Vādhapāla (?) Dhanabhūtī and his predecessors were local rulers of Mathurā and that prior to the Kuṣāṇa rule.

Mathurā was the capital of the Śūrasena country. It was built by Rāma's brother Satrughna after killing the Yādava Lavana at the site of the Madhuvana by cutting down the forest there (Pargiter, *Ancient Indian Historical Tradition*, p. 170). Here lived the famous disciple of the Buddha named Mahākaccāyana, Upagupta, the guide of Aśoka, Guṇaprabha,[1] a disciple of Vasubandhu, Dhruva, and Vāsavadattā, the famous courtezan. The city was known to Pāṇini (IV. 2. 82) and the Greek and Chinese pilgrims. Patañjali in his *Mahābhāṣya* mentions it (1. 1. 2, pp. 53, 56; 1. 3. 1, pp. 588-589; 2. 4. 1, p. 223; 1. 1. 8, p. 348). The *Yoginītantra* (2. 2. 120) also refers to it. There is no mention of Mathurā in Vedic literature. The city is on the Jumna, and is included in the Agra division of the United Provinces. It is situated 217 miles in a straight line north-west of Kauśāmbī. There was a bridge of boats between Mathurā and Pāṭaliputra. This city was known as Madhupurī, which is the present Maholi, five miles to the south-west of the modern city of Muttra. The Greeks were acquainted with this city by the name of Methora and Madoura (the city of the gods). The Chinese pilgrim Fa-hien called it *Ma-t'aou-lo* or the peacock city (*Travels of Fahien*, p. 42). Hiuen Tsang named it as Mo(Mei)-t'u-lo (Watters, *On Yuan Chwang*, I. 301). Arrian notices this city in his *Indica* (viii) on the authority of Megasthenes as the capital of the Śūrasenas. Ptolemy also mentions it (VII. I. 50). The Jains knew it as Sauripura or Sūryapura. Mathurā was a rich, flourishing and populous city. Many rich men and big merchants lived here. The ruling family of Mathurā was the Yādava family. Mathurā was the centre of Viṣṇu cult. The Bhāgavata religion, the parent of modern Vaiṣṇavism, also arose here. Buddhism was predominant in Mathurā for several centuries. The Jains seem to have been firmly established in this city from the middle of the second century B.C. onwards.

Pliny (*Natural Hist.*, VI, 19) calls the river Jumna the Jomanes which flowed into the Ganges through the Palibothri between the towns of Methora and Chrysobara.[2] Lassen transcribes Chrysobara as Kṛṣṇapura.[3] He locates it at Agra. Cunningham identifies it with Keśavapura-mahallā of Mathurā.[4] S. N. Majumdar suggests that Gokul on the left bank of the Jumna and five miles S.S.E. of Mathurā may be identified with it.[5] According to the Greeks Methorā (Mathurā) was situated on the banks of the Jumna higher up than Agra from which it ws 35 miles distant. This city was situated to the south of Indraprastha.[6] The way from Śrāvastī

---

[1] *Aṅg.*, I. 67; V. A. Smith, *Early History of India*, p. 199; ***Bodhisattvāvadāna-Kalpalatā***, 72nd Pallava; Beal, *Records of the Western World*, I, p. 191, n.
[2] McCrindle, *Ancient India as described by Ptolemy*, S. N. Majumdar Ed., p. 98.
[3] *Indische Altertumskunde*, I, p. 127, n. 3.
[4] *Archaeological Survey of India Report*, XX, p. 45.
[5] Cunningham, *Ancient Geo. of India*, S. N. Majumdar Ed., p. 707.
[6] *Mahābhārata*, Sabhāparva, XXX, 1105-6.

to Mathurā lay through an important locality called Verañja.[1] Mathurā was situated on the right bank of the Jumna and it stood midway between Indraprastha and Kauśāmbī. Strictly speaking it is the Uttara Madhurā,[2] which is identified with Maholi, five miles to the south-west of the modern town of Mathurā. From Sankissa (Sanskrit Saṃkāśya) on the Ganges the distance of northern Madhurā is said to have been four yojanas only.[3] Modern Mathurā is not on the ancient site. It has moved to the north owing to the encroachment of the river.

Fa-hien saw many monasteries at Mathurā, full of monks.[4] Buddhism was then growing in this city. Hiuen Tsang found it to be above 5,000 li and the capital about 20 li in circuit. The soil was very fertile, and agriculture was the chief industry. The country also produced a fine stripped cotton cloth and gold. The climate was hot. The manners and customs of the people were soft and complacent. There were Buddhist monasteries and deva-temples and the professed adherents of different non-Buddhist sects lived pell-mell.[5] There also existed three topes built by Aśoka.

Mathurā had some disadvantages. The roads were uneven (*visamā*), they were full of dust (*bahurajā*), there were ferocious dogs (*caṇḍasunakhā*), wild animals and demons (*vāḷāyakkhā*)[6] and the alms were not easily procurable (*dullabhapiṇḍā*).[7]

Mathurā which was the home of the Vṛṣṇis and Andhakas, was attacked by demons.[8] The Vṛṣṇis and the Andhakas being afraid of the demons left Mathurā and established their capital at Dvārāvatī.[9] It was also besieged by Jarāsandha, king of Magadha, with a huge army. At the time of his great departure Yudhiṣṭhira installed Vajranābha on the throne of Mathurā.[10] On the eve of the rise of the Gupta power, seven Nāga kings reigned here.[11] Śatrughna reigned in this city with his two sons Suvāhu and Śūrasena.[12] Ugrasena and Kaṃsa were the kings of Mathurā, which was ruled by Andhaka's descendants.[13] Pargiter suggests that the conquest of Śūrasena and Mathurā by Rāma's brother Śatrughna a little earlier than the reign of Sudās, may have led some of the Vaśiṣṭhas into other kingdoms.[14] Bhīma Sātvata expelled Śatrughna's sons from Mathurā and he and his descendants reigned there.[15] After attacking the Sātvata Yādavas on the west of the Jumna and killing Mādhava Lavana, Śatrughna built the capital city of Mathurā in the country thenceforward called Śūrasena. The Andhakas ruled Mathurā which was the chief Yādava capital.[16] Jarāsandha, king of Magadha, rose to the highest power, extended his supremacy around and as far as Mathurā, where Kaṃsa, the Yādava king, who married two of his daughters, acknowledged him as overlord.

---

[1] Malalasekera, *Dictionary of Pali Proper Names*, II, p. 930.

[2] Mathurā of Northern India as distinguished from Dakṣiṇa-Madhurā (modern Madurā), the capital of the Pāṇḍyas in South India.

[3] Kaccāyana, *Pali Grammar*, Book III, Chap. I.

[4] Legge, *Fa-hien*, p. 42.

[5] Watters, *On Yuan Chwang*, I, 301.

[6] Hare translates it as 'festial yakkhas' (*The Book of the Gradual Sayings*, Vol. III, p. 188) but the word Vāḷā means Boa-constrictors and other wild animals.

[7] *Aṅguttara Nikāya*, III, 256.

[8] *Brahmapurāṇa*, Ch. XIV.

[9] *Harivaṃśa*, Ch. 37.

[10] *Skandapurāṇa*, Viṣṇukhaṇḍa.

[11] *Vāyupurāṇa*, Ch. 99.

[12] *Vāyup.*, 88, 185-6; *Brahmāṇḍap.*, III, 63, 186-7; *Rāmāyaṇa*, VII, 62; 6; *Viṣṇup.*, IV, 4, 46; *Bhāgavatap.*, IX, 11. 14.

[13] Pargiter, *Ancient Indian Historical Tradition*, p. 171.

[14] *Ibid.*, p. 211.

[15] *Ibid.*, p. 279.

[16] *Mahābh.*, I, 94, 3725-39.

According to the *Mahābhārata* and the *Purāṇas*, the ruling family of Mathurā was the Yadu or Yādava family. The Yādavas were divided into various septs.[1]

In Buddha's time, a king of Mathurā bore the title of Avantīputra and was, therefore, related on the maternal side to the royal family of Ujjayinī. The *Dīpavaṃsa* tells us that the sons and grandsons of king Sādhīna ruled the great kingdom of Madhurā or Mathurā, the best of towns.[2] According to a Jaina account there was a powerful king named Vāsudeva in the town of Sauryapura (Mathurā).[3]

The Nāgas and the Yaudheyas reigned at Mathurā before they were subjugated by Samudragupta.[4] Menander, king of Kabul and the Punjab, occupied it.[5] The Hindu kings of Mathurā were finally displaced by Hagāna, Hagāmāsa, Rājuvula and other Śaka satraps who probably flourished in or about the first century A.D.[6] In the second century A.D. Mathurā was under the sway of Huviṣka, the Kuṣāṇa king. This is confirmed by the evidence of a splendid Buddhist monastery which bears his name.[7] In the first century B.C. the region of Mathurā passed from native Indian to foreign (Śaka) rule. A Greek king[8] went back to Mathurā with his army in fear of any counter-attack on the part of king Khāravela of Kaliṅga while the latter was engaged in besieging the city of Rājagaha (Rājagṛha) (*J.B.O.R.S.*, XIII, 236). The Yonas as Bactrian Greeks founded principalities in India establishing their suzerainty even over Mathurā.[9] When Megasthenes wrote about the Śūrasenas, their country must have been included in the Maurya empire, and after the Mauryas their capital Madhurā came under the sway of the Bactrian Greeks and the Kuṣāṇas. Whether Mathurā was included in the Śuṅga dominion or not is a matter of dispute.

Mathurā was the centre of Viṣṇu cult. In the Śaka-Kuṣāṇa period the city ceased to be a stronghold of Bhāgavatism.[10] The Mathurā-Nāga Statuette Inscription amply proves the prevalence of serpent-worship in Mathurā which is important in view of the story of Kāliyanāga and his suppression by Kṛṣṇa.[11] It was visited by Śrī Kṛṣṇa with Akrūra after attending the *Dollīlā* ceremony at Vrindāvana. Here he killed a washerman, granted the boon to the garlandmaker named Sudāma, gave the celestial beauty to a hunch-back named Trivakrā, rewarded a weaver for dressing him and his brother Balarāma (*Bhāgavatapurāṇa*, Skandha X, Ch. 41-42), broke the Indra-bow, killed the elephant of Kaṃsa and at last put an end to the life of Kaṃsa, the tyrant king of Mathurā. Mathurā which was the birthplace of Śrī Kṛṣṇa, is considered as the birthplace of Vaiṣṇavism. Buddhism existed also in Mathurā for several centuries. Mahākaccāyana, a disciple of the Buddha, spoke about caste in this city.[12]

---

[1] *Viṣṇup.*, IV, 13. 1; *Vāyup.*, 96, 1-2.

[2] Oldenberg's Ed., p. 27; cf. *Extended Mahāvaṃsa* (Ed. Malalasekera) P.T.S., p. 43.

[3] Ugrasena was placed on the throne of Mathurā by Kṛṣṇa on the death of Kaṃsa according to the *Viṣṇupurāṇa* (V. 21).

[4] Ray Chaudhuri, *Political History of Ancient India*, 4th Ed., 391.

[5] V. A. Smith, *Early History of India*, 4th Ed., p. 210.

[6] *Ibid.*, p. 241 and f.n. 1.

[7] V. A. Smith, *Early History of India*, 4th Ed., pp. 286-87; cf. Cunningham, *Arch. Survey Report*, I, p. 238.

[8] Sten Konow reads the name of the Greek king as Dimita and identifies him with Demetrios but the name of the Greek king cannot be completely made out from Khāravela's Inscription.

[9] Cf. *Hāthigumphā Inscription of Khāravela*: *Madhuraṃ apāyato Yavanarājā.*

[10] Ray Chaudhuri, *Early History of the Vaiṣṇava Sect*, p. 99.

[11] *Ibid.*, p. 100.

[12] *Majjhima*, II, pp. 83ff.

Upagupta who was the teacher of Aśoka, while at Mathurā, was invited at the Naṭavaṭa vihāra. The Upagupta monastery at Mathurā is very important in the history of Buddhism, as he succeeded in converting in this monastery many people.[1] Jainism was firmly established in this city. According to *Vividhatīrthakalpa* (pp. 50ff.) Mathurā came to be known as Siddhakṣetra on account of the perfection duly attained by the two sages. The people of Mathurā and ninety-six neighbouring villages installed Jain idols in their houses and courtyards (*Bṛhat Bhāgavata,* I. 1774ff.). This city was visited by Mahāvīra (*Vivāgasūya,* 6). Numerous inscriptions from Mathurā, which date mostly from the time of the later Kuṣāṇa kings i.e., after 78 A.D., afford sufficient proof that the Jain community was not only established but had become subdivided into small groups at an earlier period.[2]

The artistic traditions of the north-west obtained a strong foothold in the Jain reliefs of Mathurā.[3] Many dated and undated Buddha and Bodhisattva images have been unearthed here. The temples of Mathurā struck Mahmud of Ghazni with such admiration that he resolved to adorn his own capital in a similar style. For explorations at Mathurā, vide *A.S.I.*, Annual Report, pp. 120ff. For further details Vide Law, *Indological Studies*, Pt. III.

Mālava.—According to the Jaina *Bhagavatīsūtra* the Mālava country is included in the list of the sixteen *Mahājanapadas*. The Mālava tribe is mentioned in the *Mahābhāṣya* of Patañjali (IV. 1. 68). The people of this country known as the Mālavas were settled in the Punjab. But it is difficult to locate exactly the territory they occupied. Smith thinks that they occupied the country below the confluence of the Jhelum and the Chenab, i.e., the country comprising the Jhang district and a portion of the Montgomery district (*J.R.A.S.*, 1903, 631). According to McCrindle they occupied a greater extent of territory comprising the modern Doab of the Chenab and the Ravi and extending to the confluence of the Indus and the Akesines identical with the modern Multan district and portions of Montgomery (*Invasion of India,* App. note 357). Some have located them in the valley of the lower Rāvī on both banks of the river (Raychaudhuri, *P.H.A.I.*, 4th Ed., p. 205).

The Mālavas, also called the Malloi, were defeated by Alexander's army. They offered determined opposition from their fortified cities which ultimately fell to the sword of Alexander and his general Perdikas. They then left their city.

The Mālavas seem to have occupied their territory in the Punjab for some time afterwards. The *Mahābhārata* (Droṇaparva, Ch. X, p. 17; Sabhāparva, Ch. 32, p. 7) probably locates them in the same place when it couples them with the Trigarttas, Śivis and Ambaṣṭhas. But before long they seem to have migrated southwards and settled somewhere in Rajputana where they seem to have held their ground at the time of Samudragupta. The Mālava occupation of the Nāgar area near Jaipur in Rajputana is proved by the Nasik Cave Inscription of Uṣavadāta the Śaka, son-in-law of Kṣatrapa Nahapāṇa. The Scythian invasions and conquests could not destroy the tribal organization of the Mālavas, for they are mentioned in the list of tribal states of the western and south-western fringe of Āryāvarta mentioned in the Allahabad Pillar Inscription of Samudragupta. The name of the Mālavas is also associated with the well-

---

[1] Watters, *On Yuan Chwang*, I, pp. 306-7.
[2] *Cambridge History of India*, I, p. 167.
[3] *Cambridge History of India*, I, p. 641.

known Kṛta or Mālava-Vikrama era (cf. Mandasor Inscription of Naravarman, *C.I.I.*, Vol. III). In the Purāṇas we find the Mālavas associated with the Saurāṣṭras, Avantīs, Ābhīras, Śūras and Arbudas, and are described as dwelling along the Pariyātra mountains (*Bhāgavatapurāṇa*, XII, I, 36; *Viṣṇupurāṇa*, Bk. II, Ch. III; *Brahmāṇḍa Purāṇa*, Ch. XIX, v. 17). In later epigraphic records we have mention of Sapta-Mālavas, i.e., seven countries called Mālavas (*E.I.*, V, 229; *A.B.O.R.I.*, Vol. XIII, Pts. 3-4, 1931-32, p. 229). For further details vide B. C. Law, *Indological Studies*, Pt. I, pp. 27ff.; B. C. Law, *Tribes in Ancient India*, Ch. VIII.

Mālyavat Mountain.—It starts from the north-western extremity of the Himalayas, and extends south-westwards, first dividing India including Pakistan from Afghanistan and then through north-eastern Afghanistan. This mountain is known to modern geographers as the Hindukush. A number of spurs run from the main range, such as the Badakhshan spur separating the Oxus from the Kokcha, and the Kokcha spur dividing the Kokcha drainage from that of the Kunduz. The height of the Hindukush varies between 14,000 and 18,000 ft. in the eastern section above which rise several giant peaks to an altitude of 25,000 ft. The range is much dissected and due to steep gradient there is very little soil capping with the result that nothing but grasses can grow there. (Law, *Mountains of India*, p. 7).

Mānapura.—The Khoh copperplate inscription of Mahārāja Sarvanātha (the year 214) mentions this town, which is probably modern Manpur near the river Son, about 47 miles in a south-easterly direction from Ucaharā and 32 miles south-east of Karitalai (*C.I.I.*, Vol. III).

Mānasa-sarovara.—King Vibhrāja repaired to this lake (*Harivaṃśa*, XXIII, 9-10).

Mārkaṇḍeya-āśrama.—It was visited by Bhīṣma who was duly entertained by the dwellers of this hermitage. The *Mahābhārata* (Vanaparva, Ch. 84) places it at the confluence of the Gumti and the Ganges. According to the *Padmapurāṇa* (Ch. 16) the sage Mārkaṇḍeya practised asceticism at the confluence of the Sarayū and the Ganges.

Meharauli.—The Meharauli posthumous Iron Pillar Inscription of Chandra mentions it, which is a corruption of Mihirapurī, a village nine miles almost due south of Delhi. This Vaiṣṇava inscription is to record the erection of a pillar called a *dhvaja* or standard of god Viṣṇu on a hill called Viṣṇupada (the hill containing the footprint of Viṣṇu) (*C.I.I.*, Vol. III).

Meros Mountain.—It is also known as Mar-koh near Jalalabad in the Punjab (P), which was visited by Alexander the Great.

Meru.—This mountain otherwise known as Hemādri and Svarṇācala (Hultzsch, *S.I.I.*, I, 166), is identical with the Rudra Himalaya in Garhwal (*Therīgāthā Commy.*, p. 150) where the Ganges takes its rise (Law, *Geography of Early Buddhism*, p. 42). It is near the Badarikāśrama and is probably the Mount Meros of Arrian. On the western side of this mountain stand Niṣadha and Pāripātra; on the southern side stand Kailāsa and Himavanta, and on the northern side stand Śṛṅgavān and Jarudhi (*Mārkaṇḍeya Purāṇa*, Vaṅgavāsī Ed., p. 240). The great sage Sālaṅkāyana meditated on this mountain (*Kūrmapurāṇa*, 144. 10).

Migasammatā.—This river had its source in the Himalayas (*Jāt.*, VI, 72).

Morā.—It is a small village, seven miles west of Mathurā city and two miles to the north of the road leading from Mathurā to Govardhan (*E.I.*, XXIV, Pt. V, January, 1938, p. 194).

Moriyanagara.—This city was built by some Śākyas when they fled to the Himalayas being oppressed by king Viḍūḍabha, son of king Pasenadi of Kosala (*Mahāvaṃsa-ṭīkā*, Sinhalese Ed., pp. 119–21). It stood around a lake in a forest tract abounding in peepul trees. It is now generally accepted that Candragupta, grandfather of Aśoka the Great, belonged to the Moriyan clan which had its seat of Government at Pipphalivana. The place where this city was founded was always resounded with the cries of peacocks. (*Mahāvaṃsa-ṭīkā*, Sinhalese Ed., pp. 119–21). The Moriyas of Pipphalivana obtained a share of the Buddha's relics and built a stūpa over them. (*Dīgha*, II, 167.)

Mousikanos.—The territory of Mousikanos was well known to Alexander's historians. Alexander took them by surprise and they had to submit to him (*C.H.I.*, I, 377). According to Strabo (H. & F.'s Transl., III, p. 96), they used to eat in public and their food consisted of what was taken in the chase. They made no use of gold or silver. They employed youths in the flower of their age instead of slaves. They studied the science of medicine with due attention. They never liked to go to law-courts by creating constant disputes.

Mūjavant.—Its other equivalent is Muñjavant which occurs in the *Mahābhārata* (X, 785; XIV, 180; see also *Translation of the Ṛgveda* by Ludwig, 3, 198). It is the name of a mountain in the Himalaya. It occurs in the *Ṛgveda*, X. 34, 1, where it is read as Maujavata. In the Siddhānta Kaumudī on Pāṇini (IV, 4, 110) we get another variant Mauñjavata. According to some it was a hill from which the people took their name. Zimmer in his *Altindisches Leben*, 29, says that it was one of the lower hills on the south-west of Kāśmīra.

Mukteśvara.—It is the headquarters of the tahsil of the same name in the Ferozepur district in the Punjab. Here a great Sikh festival takes place every year.

Mūlasthāna (*Mūlasthānapura*).—It was situated on two islands in the Rāvī. The classical writers mention it as Kaspapyros, Kaspeira, etc. Yuan Chwang visited Mou-lo-san-pu-lu (Skt. Mūlasthāna) which he located 900 li to the east of Sindh (Watters, *On Yuan Chwang*, II, 254). Cunningham has identified Mūlasthāna with Multan.

Muruṇḍa country.—The Muruṇḍas are mentioned for the first time by Ptolemy in the 2nd century A.D. under the name of Moroundai. They seem to have occupied an extensive territory, probably the whole of North Bihar on the east of the Ganges as far as the head of the delta. They had six important cities, all to the east of the Ganges: Boraita, Koryagaza, Kondota, Kelydna, Aganagora and Talarga. According to St. Martin Kelydna had some relation with the Kālinadī or Kālindī river, and Aganagora with Aghadīp (Agradvīpa) on the eastern bank of the Ganges a little below Katwā (Ptolemy's *Ancient India*, pp. 215-16). According to Cunningham, the Moroundai of Ptolemy were the same as the Moredes of Pliny. The *Vāyupurāṇa* speaks of the Muruṇḍas as a *mleccha* tribe. Hemacandra's *Abhidhānacintāmaṇi* (IV. 26—*Lampākāstu Maruṇḍāḥ syuḥ*) identifies the Muruṇḍas with the Lampākas, the Lambatai of Ptolemy, who were located near the source of the modern Kabul river in the region around Laghmān and it, therefore, follows that the Muruṇḍas had a settlement in this region as well. For further details, vide B. C. Law, *Tribes in Ancient India*, pp. 93-94.

Nagarahāra.—It is identified with the modern Jalalabad in Afghanistan.[1] Fa-Wei seems to imply that in his time it was a part of the kingdom of Puruṣapura (L. Petech, *Northern India according to the Shui-ching-Chu*,

---

[1] J. Ph. Vogel, *Notes on Ptolemy* (*B.S.O.A.S.*, Vol. XIV., pt. I, p. 80).

p. 60). Nagarahāra was identified by Lassen with Nagara or Dionysopolis of Ptolemy situated midway between Kabura and the Indus. In the beginning of the 5th century A.D. it was simply called Na-kie by Fa-hien, which was then an independent state governed by its own king. In the 7th century A.D. at the time of Hiuen Tsang it was without a king and subject to Kapisene. It was also called Udyānapura (cf. *C.A.S.I.*, 1924, pp. 53-54).

Naimiṣāraṇya (modern Nimsar).—It is situated on the bank of the Gumti in the Sitapur district. The *Vāyupurāṇa* (1. 14.) locates it on the bank of the Dṛṣadvati, which, I think, is erroneous. It is an important place of Hindu pilgrimage being one of 51 Pīṭhasthānas (holy places) and an abode of the ancient Aryan sages who wrote the Purāṇas here. Nārada was honoured by the sages when he visited Naimiṣāraṇya (*Padmapurāṇa*, Uttarakhaṇḍa vs. 77-78). The *Pañcaviṃśa Brāhmaṇa* (XXV. 6, 4) and the *Jaiminīya Brāhmaṇa* (I. 363) mention *Naimiṣiya* which denotes dwellers in the Naimiṣa forest. The *Mahābhārata* (83. 109–111; 84. 59–64) refers to this holy city. According to the *Padmapurāṇa* (VI. 219, 1–12) the twelve-year sacrifice was held in the Naimiṣa forest. The *Kūrma Purāṇa* (Pūrvabhāga, 30. 45–48) makes mention of it among other holy places of India (cf. *Bhāgavatapurāṇa*, 1. 1. 4; III. 20, 7; X. 79, 30; VII. 14. 31; X. 78, 20; *Agnipurāṇa*, Ch. 109; *Padmapurāṇa*, Ch. 16—*Tīrthamāhātmya*). The *Yoginītantra* (2/4) mentions it.

Nauhāi.—This village is situated about 1½ miles north-west of the Kosam Pillar (*E.I.*, XXIV, Pt. VI, April, 1938, p. 253).

Nābhaka.—Nābhaka, which is mentioned in R.E. V and XIII of Aśoka, was somewhere between the North-Western Frontier and the western coast of India. Some think that Nābhaka and Nābhapaṃti were central Himalayan states, north of Kālsi.

Nānyaurā.—The Nānyaurā grant refers to this village in the Panwari-Jaitpur tehsil of the Hamirpur district, U.P.

Nepāla.—The *Yoginītantra* mentions it (1/7, 1/11, 2/2). In the *Nepālamāhātmya* (Ch. I, śl. 30) the former name of Nepāla was Śleṣmātakavana. Paśupatīrtha or Paśupatitīrtha is on the river Bāgmatī. The boundary of Nepāla is as follows: on the east flows the river Kauśikī, on the west the Triśūlagaṅgā, on the north Śivapurī (Kailāśa) and on the south flows a river, the water of which is cold and pure (Ch. 15, śls. 3–5). Nepāla is mentioned in the Allahabad Pillar Inscription as an autonomous frontier state. It was conquered by Samudragupta. Some take it to mean Tippera (*J.A.S.B.*, 1837, p. 973) which seems to be doubtful. The Thankot inscription of the time of Mānadeva Jiṣṇugupta refers to the tax called Mānakara which is collected in the Nepal Valley. This tax is similar to the Taruṣkadaṇḍa in the inscriptions of Gahaḍavāla of Govindachandra; c. 1104–54 A.D. (*E.I.*, II, 361ff.; IV, 11ff.; 98ff.; 104ff.; 116ff.; V, 115ff.; VII, 98ff.; VIII, 153ff.; IX, 321ff.; XI, 20ff.; 155). In the 7th century A.D. Nepal was a buffer state. In the 8th century A.D. she shook off her dependence on Tibet.

According to the Deopara Inscription (*E.I.*, I, 309) Nānyadeva, the ruler of Nepal, about the middle of the 12th century A.D., is said to have been defeated and imprisoned by Vijayasena with many other princes.

In the *Varāhapurāṇa* (Ch. 3), the Nepal Valley originally consisted of a lake called Nāga Bāsa. It was 14 miles in length and 4 miles in breadth (cf. N. L. Dey, *Geographical Dictionary*, p. 140). The temple of Paśupatinātha or Paśupati in Mṛgasthala in Nepal is one of the celebrated Hindu temples situated on the western bank of the Bāgmatī river in the town of Devipatan founded by Aśoka's daughter Cārumatī, about three miles north-west of Katmandu. On the eastern bank of the river fronting the temple there is a hill covered with lofty trees and jungles.

Neruparvata.—It is in the Himalayan region (*Milinda*, p. 129). It is called the golden mountain as mentioned in the *Jātaka* (Jāt., III, 247).

Niglīva.—It lies 38 miles north-west of the Uska Bazar Station of the Bengal and North-Western Railway in the Nepalese tehsil of Taulihvā of the Butaul district (*E.I.*, V, p. 1).

Nirmānd.—The Nirmānd Copperplate Inscription of the Mahāsāmanta and Mahārāja Samudrasena mentions Nirmānd, a village near the right bank of the Sutlej, 21 miles north-east of Plach, the chief town of the Plach tehsil of the Kulla or Kulu division of the Kangra district in the Punjab (*C.I.I.*, Vol. III). This village stands close to an ancient temple dedicated to Paraśurāma. There is another temple here dedicated to the god Tripurantaka or Śiva under the name of Mihireśvara.

Nisabha.—This mountain which was not far off from the Himalaya, was situated to the west of the Gandhamādana and north of the Kābul river, called by the Greeks Paropanisos, now called the Hindukush (cf. *Apadāna*, p. 67).

Oxykanos-territory.—Curtius speaks of the people of this territory as Praesti corresponding perhaps to the Prosṭhas mentioned in the *Mahābhārata* (VI. 9, 61). Cunningham thinks that the territory of Oxykanos lay to the west of the Indus in the level country around Larkhāna (*Invasion of Alexander*, p. 158). Oxykanos tried to oppose Alexander but in vain (*Cambridge History of India*, I, 377; Law, *Indological Studies*, Pt. I, p. 36).

Pabhosā Cave.—The inscriptions record the fact of dedication of the two Pabhosā caves in the neighbourhood of Kauśāmbī to the Kāśyapiya Arhats by king Āṣāḍhasena of Adhicchatrā. In one of them the donor King Āṣāḍhasena is introduced as the maternal uncle of king Bṛhaspatimitra (Lüders' List, No. 904; *E.I.*, X, App.) and in the other we have mention of four generations of kings beginning with Śaunakāyana (B. C. Law, *Pañcālas and their Capital Ahicchatra*, *M.A.S.I.*, No. 67, p. 12).

Paderia.—It lies two miles north of the Nepalese tehsil of Bhagavānpur of the same district. According to Dr. Fuhrer it is situated about 13 miles from Niglīva (*E.I.*, V, p. 1).

Pahlava.—It is a corruption of the word Parthava, the Indian name for the Parthians (Rapson, *Coins of India*, p. 37, f.n. 2). The *Vāyupurāṇa* places the territory of the Pahlavas in the north, while according to the *Mārkaṇḍeyapurāṇa* and the *Bṛhatsaṃhitā* they were located in the south-western region of India (*Vāyupurāṇa*, Ch. 45, V, 115; *Mārkaṇḍeyapurāṇa* Ch. 58; *Bṛhatsaṃhitā*, Ch. 14). According to the *Rāmāyaṇa* the Pahlavas were created during the dissension between the famous sages Vaśiṣṭha and Viśvāmitra regarding the possession of the *Kāmadhenu* (Ādikāṇḍa, LIV, 1018–22). They fought on the side of the Kurus in the Kurukṣetra war. They were the allies of the Haihaya-Tālajaṅghas according to the Epic and Pauranic traditions. They were annihilated by king Sagara along with the Śakas, Yavanas and others. The Junāgaḍh Rock Inscription refers to a Pahlava official named Śivisaka, and Gautamīputra Śātakarṇi is credited in the Nasik Cave Inscription as the uprooter of the Pahlavas, Śakas and Yavanas. For further details, vide B. C. Law, *Tribes in Ancient India*, pp. 6ff.; Law, *Indological Studies*, Pt. I, pp. 39-40.

Pahlādpura.—The Pahlādpura Stone Pillar Inscription mentions this village situated near the right bank of the Ganges, six miles east by south of Dhānāpura in the sub-division of the Gazipur district.

Pahowa.—It is an ancient town and a place of pilgrimage in the Kaithal tehsil of the Karnal district in the Punjab situated on the sacred river Sarasvatī, 16 miles west of Thāneśvar. It lies in Kurukṣetra. (Law, *Holy Places of India*, p. 26).

Paleṭhī.—It is a small hamlet in Paṭṭi Khās situated in deep valley some 12 miles north-west of Devaprayāga standing at the confluence of the Gaṅgā and the Alakanandā. It contains ancient temples in ruins (vide *Siddha-Bhāratī*, Pt. II, pp. 273ff.).

Pali.—It is a village in the Dhuriapar pargana of the Bansgaon tehsil of the Gorakhpur district, where plates of Govindacandra were discovered (*E.I.*, V, 113ff.).

Pañcāladeśa.—It comprised Bareilly, Budaun, Farrukhabad and the adjoining districts of Rohilkhand and the Central Doab in the U.P. It seems to have been bounded on the east by the Gumti and on the south by the Chambal. It extended from the Himalaya mountains to the Chambal river (Cunningham, *Ancient Geography*, p. 360). In the later Vedic *saṃhitās* and the *Brāhmaṇas* the people of Pañcāla are frequently mentioned (*Kāṭhaka-saṃhitā*, XXX, 2; *Vājasaneyī saṃhitā*, XI, 3. 3; *Gopatha-Brāhmaṇa*, I, 2. 9; *Śatapatha-Brāhmaṇa*, XIII, 5. 4. 7; *Taittirīya Brāhmaṇa*, I, 8. 4. 1. 2). In the Upaniṣads and later works we find that the Brahmins of Pañcāla took part in philosophical and philological discussions (*Bṛhadāraṇyaka Upaniṣad*, VI, 1. 1; *Chāndogya*, V, 3. 1; I, 8. 12; *Sāṅkhyāyana Śrauta Sūtra*, XII, 13. 6, etc.). The Vedic literature refers to the kings of this kingdom (*Aitareya Brāhmaṇa*, VIII, 23; *Śatapatha Brāhmaṇa*, S.B.E., Vol. XLIV, p. 400). Pāṇini mentions Pāñcālaka in his *Aṣṭādhyāyī* (7. 3. 13). Patañjali in his *Mahābhāṣya* (1. 2. 2, p. 512; 1. 1. 1, p. 37; 1. 4. 1, p. 634) also mentions it as a *janapada*.

The problem of the origin of the name Pañcāla and its probable connection with the number Five struck the authors of the Purāṇas (*Bhāgavata*, 9-21; *Viṣṇu*, 19th Chapter, 4th Aṅka; *Vāyu*, p. 99; *Agnipurāṇa*, 278). Many are the stories told about the people of this place in the *Mahābhārata* (Ādiparva, Ch. 94, 104; Droṇaparva, Ch. 22, pp. 1012-1013; Udyogaparva, Chs. 156-157; 172-194, 198; Bhīṣmaparva, Ch. 19, p. 830; Karṇaparva, Ch. 6, 1169; Vanaparva, Ch. 253, 513; Virāṭaparva, 4, 570).

Pañcāladeśa continued to be one of the great and powerful countries in northern India down to the time when the Buddha lived (*Aṅguttara*, I, 213; IV, 252, 256 and 260; *Jātaka* (Cowell), VI, 202). *Pañcāla* and its princes figure in Jaina literature (*Uttarādhyayana Sūtra*, *Jaina Sūtras*, II, pp. 60, 61, 87, etc.). In the post-Aśokan period Pañcāla was invaded by the Greeks.

The great kingdom of Pañcāla was divided into northern and southern Pañcāla having Ahicchatra and Kāmpilya as their respective capitals. Northern Pañcāla included districts of the Uttara Pradeśa lying east of the Ganges and north-west of Oudh while the southern Pañcāla included the country between the Jumna and the Ganges on the east and south-east of the Kurus and Śūrasenas (Rapson, *Ancient India*, p. 167).

The kingdom of Pañcāla passed through troublous times after the death of Harṣavardhana but from about the 9th century A.D. under Bhoja and his son it became the principal power in northern India extending from Behar to Sind. In the 12th century A.D. it again became important under the Gaharwar dynasty. For further details vide Law, *Pañcālas and their Capital Ahicchatra* (*M.A.S.I.*, No. 67).

Parauli.—This village is situated two miles to the north of Bhītārgaon in the Kanpur district containing a ruined temple (*A.S.I.*, Annual Report, 1908/9, pp. 17ff.).

Parīṇaḥ.—It is the name of a place in Kurukṣetra mentioned in the *Pañcaviṃśa Brāhmaṇa* (XXV, 13, 1), *Taittirīya Āraṇyaka* (V, 1, 1),

Lāṭyāyana Śrauta Sūtra (X, 19, 1), *Kātyāyana Śrauta Sūtra* (XXIV, 6, 34) and *Sāṅkhyāyana Śrauta Sūtra* (XIII, 29, 32).

Paruṣṇī.—One of the Vedic rivers (*Ṛigv.*, X, 75; VII, 18; VIII, 63. 15). It has been identified with the Rāvī.

Patala.—It is situated in the Indus delta. It was evidently the capital of the province watered by the lower Indus, whence its Greek designation of Patalene. (J. Ph. Vogel, *Notes on Ptolemy*, *B.S.O.A.S.*, XIV, Pt. I, p. 84; vide Prasthala).

Pārireya (Pali: Pārileyyaka, Skt.: Pareraka).—This was the name of a woodland guarded by the elephant Pārileyyaka. Failing to settle the dispute among the monks at Kauśāmbī, the Buddha came to live here and spent one rainy season, being attended by the elephant Pārileyyaka and a monkey. The way to this woodland from Kauśāmbī lay through a village. The Pārileyyakavanasaṇḍa occurs in the Bārhut Jātaka level No. 8 (Barua and Sinha, *Barhut Inscriptions*, p. 62). Its location is unknown. Most probably this forest was not very far from Kauśāmbī (cf. *Saṃyutta*, III, 94-95; *Vinaya-Mahāvagga*, X, 4, 6).

Pārivāta.—It is the same as the Pāripātra mountain. It occurs in Luders' List No. 1123. The earliest mention of the Pāriyātra or Pāripātra is found in the *Baudhāyana-Dharmasūtra* (1, 1, 25) as the southern limit of Āryāvarta. The *Skanda Purāṇa* also refers to it as the farthest limit of the *Kumārīkhaṇḍa* the centre of Bhāratavarṣa. The mountain seems to have lent its name to the country with which it was associated. It is known as *Po-li-ye-ta-lo* to the Chinese pilgrim Hiuen Tsang with a Vaiśya king as its ruler. Pargiter identifies it with that portion of the modern Vindhya range, which is situated to the west of Bhopal together with the Aravalli mountains (Vide Pargiter, *Mārkaṇḍeyapurāṇa*, p. 286). Some of the rivers had their sources in this mountain namely, the Vedasmriti, Vedavatī, Sindhu, Veṇvā, Sadānīrā, Mahī, Carmanvatī, Vetravatī, Vediśā, Siprā and Avarṇī (cf. *Mārkaṇḍeyapurāṇa*, 57, 19-20). The Pāriyātra is the western part of the Vindhya range extending from the sources of the Chambal to the Gulf of Cambay. It is that portion of the Vindhya range from which the rivers Chambal and Betwa take their rise (Bhandarkar, *History of the Dekkan*, Sec. 3).

Pātan.—It is situated three miles south of Khāṭmaṇḍu. It was the capital of a separate principality for a long time before the Gurkha conquest of Nepal.

Pāvā.—Pāvā, Pāpā or Pāvāpurī is the same as Kāsiā, situated on the little Gandak river to the east of the district of Gorakhpur. Cunningham has identified Pāvā with Padrauna, a place of great antiquity (*A.S.R.*, I, 74; XVI, 118). It is considered as one of the sacred places of the Jains. Mahāvīra left his mortal existence when he was dwelling in the palace of king Ṣaṣṭhīpāla of Pāvā. It was at this city that the Buddha ate his last meal in the house of Cunda the smith and was attacked with dysentery. Mahākassapa while coming from Pāvā to Kuśīnārā heard of the decease of the Buddha. According to Fa-hien's version of the *Mahāparinirvāṇa-sūtra* he was at Dakṣiṇagiri, south of Rājagṛha; according to the *Vinaya* of the *Mahāsaṅghika* he was at Gṛdhrakūṭa (*Northern India according to the Shui-Ching-Chu*, by L. Petech, p. 27). The Mallas used to reside in this city, who were devotedly attached to Mahāvīra and Buddha. Four beautiful Jaina temples were built at the spot where Mahāvīra breathed his last.

Pilakkhaguhā.—This cave existed somewhere in the neighbourhood of Ghositārāma and Kauśāmbī. It appeared like a lake or pool because of the accumulation of rain water in it which was really a large hollow.

It became dried up during the summer. It was visited by a wanderer named Sandaka who was converted to Buddhism by Ānanda (*Majjhima*, I, 513ff.).

Piloshana.—Its limits may be defined approximately as extending from Bulandshahar to Firojabad on the Jumna and Kādirgunj on the Ganges. It was 333 miles in circuit (*C.A.G.I.*, p. 423).

Pimprāmā.—It was the stronghold of the Adraistai who lived on the eastern side of the Rāvī (Hydraotes). Some have identified the Adrijas with the Adraistai of the Greeks. The Adraistai or Adhṛṣṭas are said to have bowed down before Alexander's army (*C.H.I.*, I, p. 371 and n. 2).

Pipphalivana.—This was the land of the Moriyas (*Dīgha*, II, 167). One finds an echo of its name in that of Piprāwā, a village in the Birdpur estate in the district of Basti.

Piprāwā.—The oldest northern document was supposed to be the dedication of the Buddha's relics at Piprāwā (*I.A.*, 1907, pp. 117–24). It is situated in the north of the Basti district on the Nepal frontier (*Archaeological Survey*, Vol. XXVI, 1897). The village of Piprāwā (Birdpur Estate), the findspot of the famous Piprāwā Vase, marks, according to Fleet, the site of Kapilavastu (*J.R.A.S.*, 1906, p. 180; *C.A.G.I.*, pp. 711-12). Rhys Davids takes it to be the new city built after the destruction of the old city by Viḍūḍabha (B. C. Law, *Geography of Early Buddhism*, p. 29).

Poṭoḍā.—It may be identified with Poṭal in the Hindol State (*E.I.*, XXVI, pt. II, p. 78).

Prabhāsa.—The modern village of Pabhosā stands on a cliff overlooking the northern bank of the Yamunā, in tehsil Manjhanpur, 32 miles south-west of Allahabad, which represents the ancient site of Prabhāsa. The hill of Prabhāsa, which is the only rock in the Antarvedī or the Doab between the Ganges and the Jumna, is three miles to the north-west of the great fort of Kosam-Khirāj, the ancient Kauśāmbī, where some inscriptions were discovered (*E.I.*, II, 240).

Prasthala (*Patala*).—It is supposed to have stood at or near the site of modern Bāhmanābād which is the most ancient and which includes extensive prehistoric remains (*J.B.B.R.A.S.*, Jan., 1856). The little state of Patalene as called by the Greeks is generally identified with the Indus Delta. It was probably named after its capital city Patala. Long after Alexander's invasion it passed under the rule of the Bactrian Greeks (Hamilton and Falconer, Vol. II, 252-253), and it later on came to the hands of Śaka or Indo-Scythian rulers from the clutches of the Indo-Greek rulers. About the middle of the 2nd century A.D. it was one of the principal Indo-Scythian possessions according to the geographer Ptolemy. For further details vide B. C. Law, *Indological Studies*, Pt. I, 37ff.

Prayāga.—The Rāmāyaṇa (Ayodhyākāṇḍa, sarga 54, vs. 2–5) points out that Rāma, Lakṣmaṇa and Sītā saw smoke coming out of this holy city when they came to the confluence of the Ganges and Jumna after Ayodhyā. According to the *Mahābhārata* (85. 79–83), it is the holiest of all places in the whole world. According to the *Harivaṃśa* (Ch. XXVI. 9) it is highly spoken of by the great sages. The *Yoginītantra* (2. 2. 119) refers to it. The *Kūrmapurāṇa* (Pūrvabhāga, 30, 45–48) and *Padmapurāṇa* (Uttarakhaṇḍa, vs. 35–38) also mention this famous holy place. Some inscriptions discovered at Bhiṭā mention the following kings who were associated with Prayāga: (1) Mahārāja Gautamīputra Śrī-Śivamegha, (2) Rājan Vāśiṣṭhīputra Bhīmasena of the 2nd or 3rd century A.D., and (3) Mahārāja Gautamīputra Vṛṣadhvaja of the 3rd or 4th century A.D. (R. K. Mookerjee, *Gupta Empire*, p. 13). The Aphsad Stone Inscription of Ādityasena (Fleet No. 42) tells us that Kumāragupta who won victory over the Maukhari king Īśānavarman, performed religious suicide at Prayāga (*D. R. Bhandarkar Volume*, pp. 180-81).

Prayāga (Chinese Po-lo-ye-kia) is modern Allahabad. It is a *Kṣetra* according to the *Bhāgavata Purāṇa* (VII. 14, 30; X. 79, 10). In the early Buddhist texts Payāga or Prayāga is mentioned as a *tīrtha* or *ghāṭ* on the Ganges (*Majjhima*, I, 39). Here the palace occupied by Mahāpanāda was submerged. (*Papañcasūdanī*, I, p. 178). There is the confluence (*saṅgama*) of the three rivers: Gaṅgā, Yamunā and Sarasvatī at Prayāga. The *saṅgama* is considered by the Hindus as very holy. The *Saurapurāṇa* (Chap. 67, V. 16). refers to Gaṅgā-Yamunā saṅgama. (cf. *Rāmāyaṇa*, Ayodhyākāṇḍa, 54 sarga, vs. 2–5). Kālidāsa refers to this confluence in his *Raghuvaṃśa* (XIII, 54–57). The Sarasvatī *saṅgama* is, according to the *Mahābhārata* (Chap. 82. 125–128), universally considered as holy. By bathing at this *saṅgama* one accumulates much merit. Rāma, Lakṣmaṇa and Sītā noticed at the confluence of the Gaṅgā-Yamunā two kinds of colour of the water (*Rāmāyaṇa*, Ayodhyākāṇḍa, sarga 54, v. 6).

The Chinese pilgrim Hiuen Tsang found this country to be above 5,000 li in circuit and the capital above 20 li in circuit. He praised the country, the climate, and the people. According to him, there were only two Buddhist establishments and many Deva-temples. The majority of the inhabitants were non-Buddhists (Watters, *On Yuan Chwang*, I, 361). Here green products and fruit trees grew in abundance. The climate was warm and agreeable. The people were gentle and compliant in their disposition. They were fond of learning (Beal, *Buddhist Records of the Western World*, I, 230). According to the *Brahma Purāṇa* (Chs. 10–12), three kings named Kuru, Duṣmanta, and Bharata ruled it. Pururavā, the hero of the *Vikramorvaśī*, is said to have been the ruler of this place. Prayāga was in the possession of Dhaṅga, who is reported to have entered into beatitude by abandoning his body in the waters of the Jāhnavī and the Kālindī (*E.I.*, I, 139, 146). According to the Kamauli grant (A.D. 1172), the Gāhaḍavāla Jaychandra took his bath in the Veṇī at Prayāga (*E.I.*, IV, p. 122), which gave way to Pratiṣṭhānapura towards the latter part of the Hindu rule (Nevill, *Allahabad Dist. Gazetteer*, p. 195).

Pupphavatī.—It was one of the names of Vārāṇasī, the capital of the Kāśī kingdom (Bhandarkar, *Carmichael Lectures*, 1918, pp. 50-51). Canda-Kumāra was the son of Ekarāja of Pupphavatī. He offered charities whole-heartedly and he never ate anything without first giving it to a beggar (*Cariyā-Piṭaka*, Ed. B. C. Law, p. 7).

Pūrvārāma (*Pubbārāma*).—It was a Buddhist monastery situated in the neighbourhood of Śrāvastī to the north-east of Jetavana and erected by Viśākhā, the daughter-in-law of the banker Migāra. The circumstances which led to the erection of this monastery are related in the *Dhammapada Commentary* (Vol. I, 384–420). One day Viśākhā returned home from the Jetavana Vihāra, forgetting all about her valuable necklace which she took off her person and left behind in the monastery. On getting it back she refused to wear it and sold it for a big amount. She utilised the money in purchasing a site whereupon she built a monastery and dedicated it to the Order. Wood and stone were the materials used for the construction of the monastery which stood up as a magnificent two-storied building with innumerable rooms on the ground and first floors (*Dhammapada Commentary*, I, 414). This monastery was known as Pubbārāma-Migāramātupāsāda. The Buddha delivered the *Aggañña Suttanta* while he was dwelling in the palace of Migāramātā (*Dīgha*, III, p. 80). For further details vide B. C. Law, *Śrāvastī in Indian Literature* (*M.A.S.I.*, No. 50).

Puṣkalāvatī (Puṣkarāvatī, Peukelaotis of Arrian and Peukalei of Dionysius Periegetes).—It was an earlier capital of Gandhāra, situated to the west of the river Indus. It is identified with the modern Chārsadda (Chārsada),[1] a little above the junction of the Swat with the Kabul river (V. S. Agrawala, *Geographical Data in Pāṇini's Aṣṭādhyāyī*, *J.U.P.H. Society*, Vol. XVI, Pt. I, p. 18). According to some this city, otherwise known as the lotus city, may be identified with the modern Prang and Chārsadda, 17 miles north-east of Peshwar on the Swat river (Schoff, *The Periplus of the Erythraean Sea*, pp. 183-84; *J.A.S.B.*, 1889, iii; Cunningham, *A.G.I.*, 1924, 57ff.). It is said to have been founded by Puṣkara, son of Bharata and nephew of Rāma (*Viṣṇupurāṇa*, Wilson Ed., Vol. IV, Ch. 4). It was the capital of an Indian prince named Hasti (Greek Astes) at the time of Alexander's expedition (326 B.C.). Ptolemy calls it Proklais which was a very large and populous city. It came under the Śaka rule during the reign of Maues (*cir.* 75 B.C.). (Vide *Cambridge History of India*, Vol. I, 560; Brown, *Coins of India*, p. 24). Kaniṣka's son used to live here according to Tārānāth (vide V. A. Smith, *Early History of India*, 4th Ed., p. 277, f.n. 1). It is mentioned in the *Brihat-saṃhitā* as a city (XIV. 26). For further details vide B. C. Law, *Indological Studies*, Pt. I, p. 14.

Raibhya-āśrama.—It was at Kubjāmra at a short distance to the north of Hardwar (Haridvāra).

Ratnavāhapura.—It was a town in Kośala watered by the river Ghargharā. Here Dharmanātha belonging to the Ikṣvāku family was born of Suvrata, wife of king Bhānu. A caitya was built in honour of Dharmanātha (B. C. Law, *Some Jaina Canonical Sūtras*, p. 175).

Rādhākuṇḍa.—It is also known as Āriṭ because Śrīkṛṣṇa in the guise of an ox killed the demon called Ariṣṭa. As Rādhā, the consort of Kṛṣṇa, refused to touch his body because he killed a cow, he had a pond dug for his bath and for removing the sins accumulated by him. This pond was called the Śyāmakuṇḍa. Rādhā had also a pond dug by the side of the Śyāmakuṇḍa called the Rādhākuṇḍa.

Rājapura (*Ko-lo-she-pu-lo*).—It has been identified with Rajaori to the south of Kāśmīra. The district of Rajaori is bounded on the north by the Pirpañchal, on the west by Punach, on the south by Bhimbar, and on the east by Rihāsi and Aknur (*C.A.G.I.*, 148-149).

Rājghāt.—It is in the city of Benaras where two copperplates of Govindacandradeva were unearthed (*E.I.*, XXVI, Pt. VI, April, 1942, pp. 268ff.).

Rāmadāsapura.—It is Amritsar in the Punjab named after a Sikhguru who built a hut near a natural pool of water which was the favourite resort of Nānak (N. L. Dey, *Geo. Dict.*, p. 165).

Rāmagaṅgā.—Between Farukkabad and Hardai the Ganges receives a tributary called the Rāmagaṅgā having its origin in the Kumaun range above Almora.

Rāmagāma.—It is Rampur Deoriya in the district of Basti in Oudh. The Koliyas had their settlement here. The Koliyas were one of the republican clans in the Buddha's time having two settlements, one at Rāmagāma and the other at Devadaha. The *Sumaṅgalavilāsinī* (pp. 260–62) records an interesting story of their origin. According to the *Mahāvastu* (I, 352–55) the Koliyas were the descendants of the sage Kola. The *Kuṇāla-Jātaka* (*Jāt.*, V, 413) says that the Koliyas used to dwell in the Kola tree. Hence they came to be called the Koliyas. The Buddha brought about a conciliation between the Śākyas and the Koliyas who had

---

[1] *A.S.I.R.*, II (1871), 90ff.; XIX (1885), 96ff.; *A.R.A.S.I.*, 1902-3 (1904), pp. 41ff.

long been in conflict. (*Theragāthā*, V. 529; Jāt., Cowell, V, p. 56). The Śākyas and the Koliyas had the river Rohiṇī confined by a single dam and they cultivated their crops by means of water of this river (*Jātaka*, Cowell, V, 219ff.). Buddha succeeded in restoring peace among his kinsmen when a quarrel broke out between the Śākyas and the Koliyas regarding the possession of this river (*Jātaka*, I, 327; IV, 207). Cunningham identifies it with the modern Rowai or Rohwaini, a small stream which joins the Rāpti at Gorakhpur.

Rohiṇī.—This river formed the boundary between the Śākya and the Koliya countries (*Theragāthā*, V. 529, p. 56).

Sahalāṭavī.—See Vātāṭavī.

Śambhu.—The Greek equivalent of this Indian name is Sambos. According to classical writers Sambos ruled the mountainous country adjoining the territory of Mousikanos. There was no other relation save that of mutual jealousy and animosity between these two neighbours. The capital of this country is called Sindimana. It has been identified with Sehwan, a city on the Indus (McCrindle, *Invasion of Alexander*, p. 404). Sambos submitted to Alexander.

Saṃkāśya (Pali: *Saṃkassa*).—It has been identified with modern Sankisa, a village in the Farrukhabad district of the U.P., situated 36 miles north by west from Kudārkoṭ, 11 miles south-south-east from Aliganj in the Azamnagar Pargana of the Etawah district, and 40 miles north-north-east from Etawah. According to some Saṃkassa is Saṅkissa or Saṅkisa Basantapura situated on the north bank of the river Ikṣumatī, now called Kālīnadī between Atranji and Kanoj and 23 miles west of Fatehgarh in the district of Etawah and 45 miles north-west of Kanoj. According to Patañjali's *Mahābhāṣya* (Vol. I, p. 455), it is four *yojanas* distant from Gavīdhumat (2. 3. 21; vide *A Stone Inscription from Kudārkoṭa*, *E.I.*, I, 179-180). For Archaeological remains, see excavation at Saṅkisa by Hirānanda Shāstrī (*J.U.P.H.S.*, III, 1927, pp. 99–118).

Sapta-sindhu.—It is the Punjab where the early Aryans first settled themselves after their migration to India (*Ṛgveda*, VIII, 24, 27). Patañjali's *Mahābhāṣya* (1. 1. 1, p. 17) refers to it. The seven Sindhus are the following:—Irāvatī, Candrabhāgā, Vitastā, Vipāśā, Śatadru, Sindhu and Sarasvatī.

Sarabhū (*Sarayū*).—The *Rāmāyaṇa* (Ādikāṇḍa, 14 sarga, vs. 1-2) points out that king Daśaratha performed the *Aśvamedha yajña* on the bank of this river. Many foremost Brahmins took part in it headed by Riṣyaśriṅga. Rāma and Lakṣmaṇa visited the confluence of the Sarayū and the Ganges. (*Rāmāyaṇa*, Ādikāṇḍa, 23 sarga, v. 5). The *Mahābhārata* (84. 70) refers to this river as Sarayū. There is a mention of the Sarayū in Pāṇini's *Aṣṭādhyāyī* (VI, 4. 174). The *Yoginītantra* refers to it. (2/5). The *Kālikāpurāṇa* (Ch. 24. 139) mentions Sarayū as a sacred river. It is also mentioned in the *Padmapurāṇa* (Uttarakhaṇḍa, vs. 35–38). Kālidāsa mentions it in his *Raghuvaṃśa* (VIII. 95, IX. 20, XIII. 60–63, XIX. 40). This river issued forth from the Himalayas (*Milindapañha*, p. 114). It is mentioned in the *Ṛgveda* (IV. 30, 18; X. 64, 9; V. 53, 9). Citraratha and Arṇa are said to have been defeated by the Turvaśas and Yadus who crossed this river. It was the Ghagrā or Gogrā, a tributary of the Ganges, on which stood the city of Ayodhyā. It is the Sarabos of Ptolemy and is one of the five great rivers mentioned in early Buddhist texts. This river joins the Ganges in the district of Chapra, Bihar. At the north-west corner of the district of Bahraich it receives a tributary from the north-east which goes by the name of the Sarayū. The ancient city of Ayodhyā stood on this river to which the *Bhāgavata Purāṇa* often refers (V. 19, 18; IX. 8, 17; X. 79, 9). According to the *Rāmayāṇa* (Uttarakāṇḍa, sarga 123, v. 1) the Sarayū river is situated at a distance of half a yojana from the city of Ayodhyā. For further details, vide B. C. Law, *Rivers of India*, p. 22.

Sarasvatī.—The Sarasvatī and the Driṣadvatī are the two historical rivers of northern India that flow down independently without belonging to the Indus group. Manu locates the region of Brahmāvarta between these two sacred streams. The Sarasvatī is described in the *Milindapañha* as a Himalayan river. It flows southwards through the Simla and Sirmur States forming a bulge. Manu applies the name of Vinaśana to the place where it disappears from view.[1] The *Taittirīya Saṃhitā* (VII. 2, 1, 4), *Pañcaviṃśa Brāhmaṇa* (XXV. 10, 1), *Kauśitakī Brāhmaṇa* (XII. 2, 3), *Śatapatha Brāhmaṇa* (I. 4. 1. 14) and the *Aitareya Brāhmaṇa* (II. 19. 1. 2) mention this river. It is also mentioned in the *Ṛgveda* (I, 89. 3; 164, 19; II. 41, 16; 30, 8; 32, 8; III. 54, 13; V. 42, 12; 43, 11; 46, 2; VI. 49, 7; 50, 12; 52, 6; VII. 9, 5; 36, 6; 39, 5; X. 17, 7; 30, 12; 131, 5; 184, 2). The *Padmapurāṇa* (Sriṣṭikhaṇḍa, Ch. 32, v. 105) refers to the Gangodbhedatīrtha which is the meeting place of this river with the Ganges. The *Kātyāyana Śrautasūtra* (XII. 3, 20; XXIV. 6, 22), *Lāṭyāyana Śrautasūtra* (X. 15, 1; 18, 13, 19, 4), *Aśvalāyana Śrautasūtra* (XII. 6, 2, 3) and *Sāṅkhyōyana Śrautasūtra* (XIII. 29) refer to the sacrifices held on the bank of this river as of great importance and sanctity. Kālidāsa mentions it in his *Raghuvaṃśa* (III. 9). The *Yoginītantra* (2/3; 2/5; 2/6) also mentions this river. In the Siddhāntaśiromaṇi the Sarasvatī is correctly described as a river which is visible in one place and invisible in another. The river which still survives flows between the Śatadru and the Yamunā. It was known to the Vedic Aryans as a mighty river which flowed into the sea (Max Müller, *Ṛgvedasaṃhitā*, p. 46). This river issued forth from the Himalayas. It rises in the hills of Sirmur in the Himalayan range, called the Sewalik and emerges into the plains at Ād-Badri in Ambala. It is considered sacred by the Hindus. According to the *Mahābhārata* (83, 151; 84, 66) people offer *piṇḍas* to their ancestors on the bank of this sacred river. There existed on its bank a forest sacred to Ambikā known as the Ambikāvana (*Bhāgavatapurāṇa*, X. 34. 1–18).

Sarda (Sardi).—This holy site is on the right bank of the Kissengaṅgā near its junction with the Madhumatī near Kāmraj in Kāśmīra. The sage Śāṇḍilya performed austerities here. When Lalitāditya, king of Kāśmīra, treacherously killed a king of Gauḍa, the Bengalees entered Kāśmīra on the pretext of visiting this temple and destroyed the image of Viṣṇu mistaking it for that of Parihāsakeśava. Even the celebrated sage Śaṅkarācārya was not allowed to enter this temple till he answered the questions put to him.

Śatadru.—It is modern Sutlej, a tributary of the Ganges. This river is mentioned in the *Ṛgveda* (III. 33, 1; X. 75, 5) as the most easterly river of the Punjab. It is also mentioned in Yāska's *Nirukta* (IX. 26). The *Bhāgavatapurāṇa* refers to it as a river (V. 19, 18). In Arrian's time this river flowed independently into the Gulf of Cutch (*Imperial Gazetteer of India*, 23, 179). Kinnarī Manoharā, wife of Prince Sudhanu, who was the son of Subāhu, king of Hastināpura, while going to the Himalayas, crossed this river and proceeded to Mount Kailāsa (B. C. Law, *A Study of the Mahāvastu*, p. 118). The Śatadru is the Zaradros of Ptolemy and the Hesydrus of Pliny. It is a trans-Himalayan river as its basin lies mainly north of the Himalayas. The source of this river is traceable to the western region

[1] Cf. *Mahābhārata*, 82. 3; *Padmap*, ch. 21.

of the western lake of the Mānasa Sarovara. From this region it has a westerly course until it turns a little towards south-west above Mount Kamet. In ancient times it took an independent course to the confines of Sindhu (Pargiter, *Mārkaṇḍeya Purāṇa*, p. 291, notes). The united streams of the Sutlej and the Beas are known as the Ghaggar. The Śatadru is also mentioned in the *Mahābhārata* (1. 193. 10). For further details vide Law, *Rivers of India*, p. 114.

Śaurīpura.—It was another name of Mathurā mentioned in the Jaina sūtras (*Uttarādhyayana*, S.B.E., XLV, p. 112; *Kalpasūtra*, S.B.E., XXII, p. 276).

Sāgala.—Sāgala or Śākala, also called Euthydemia by Ptolemy, was the capital of the Madras (*Mahābh.*, II, 32, 14). It is still known as Madradeśa. It has been identified by Cunningham with Sanglawala Tiba to the west of the Rāvī river (*Ancient Geography*, p. 180). Some have identified it with Sialkot or the fort of the Madra king Śalya (Fleet's note in the *Proceedings of the Fourteenth Oriental Congress*; vide also Cunningham, *C.A.G.I.*, 686). The old town of Śākala (She-kie-lo), according to Hiuen Tsang, was about 20 li in circuit. Although its wall had been thrown down, the foundation was still firm and strong. There was a monastery here containing 100 priests of the Hīnayāna school. There was a stūpa about 200 ft. high built by Aśoka, situated to the north-west of this monastery. According to the *Milindapañha* (*Questions of Menander*, pp. 1-2), this city was a great centre of trade. It was the famous city of yore in the country of the Yonakas. It was situated in a delightful country, well watered and hilly. Brave was its defence with many strong towers and ramparts. The streets were well laid out. There were many magnificent mansions. The city is frequently mentioned in the *Mahābhārata* (*tataḥ Śākala* (*sāgala*)-*mabhyetya Madrāṇāṃ-puṭabhedanaṃ*). The *Divyāvadāna* also refers to it (p. 434). Śākala came under the sway of Alexander the Great in 326 B.C., who placed it under the satrap of the adjacent territory between the Jhelum and the Chenab (*Cambridge History of India*, I, 549-50). The Macedonians destroyed Sāgala, but it was rebuilt by Demetrios, one of the Graeco-Bactrian kings, who in honour of his father Euthydemos, called it Euthydemia. (*I.A.*, 1884, p. 350.) During the reign of Menander, a powerful Greek king ruling at Śākala about 78 A.D., the people lived happily. Even before Menander's time Śākala seems to have come under the Buddhist influence (cf. Mrs. Rhys Davids, *Psalms of the Sisters*, p. 48; *Psalms of the Brethren*, p. 359). In the early part of the 6th century A.D. Śākala became the capital of the Hūṇa conqueror Mihirakula who established his authority in that city and subdued all the neighbouring provinces (*Cambridge History of India*, I, 549, 550). There were matrimonial alliances between the kings of Madra, Kaliṅga and Benaras (Cowell, *Jāt.*, IV, pp. 144-145; *Jāt.*, V, 22). For further details, vide B. C. Law, *Tribes in Ancient India*, pp. 54ff.; McCrindle, *Ancient India as described by Ptolemy*, ed. by S. N. Majumdar Śāstrī, 1927, pp. 122ff.

Sāketa.—Sāketa was the capital city of northern Kośala. Patañjali mentions it in his *Mahābhāṣya* (3 . 3 . 2, p. 246; 1 . 3 . 2, p. 608). It is the Sogeda of Ptolemy and Shachi of Fa-hien (Legge, *Travels of Fa-hien*, p. 54). It became a highly important city in the kingdom of Kośala wherefrom one might travel to Kosambī across the Yamunā. It could be reached from Sāvatthī by a chariot-drive with seven relays of the best of steeds ('*Sattarathavinitāni*'—*Majjhima*, I, 149). It was a town on the borderland of Kośala towards the south-west. It stood out prominently among the six great cities of India (*Dīgha N.*, II, 146). It was the capital in the period immediately preceding the Buddha's time (*Carmichael Lectures*, 1918, p. 51). It was at this city that the banker Dhanañjaya, the father of Visākhā-migāramātā, lived (*Dhammapada Commentary*, Vol. I, Pt. 2, pp. 386-7). Sāriputta once stayed at Sāketa (*Vinaya*, I, p. 289). Jīvaka came here and cured the ailing wife of a banker (*Ibid.*, I, 270ff.). The road from Sāketa to Śrāvastī was frequented by robbers who were dangerous to passers-by. Even the monks were robbed of their belongings and sometimes killed by the robbers. Royal soldiers used to come to the spot where robbery was committed and used to kill those robbers whom they could arrest (*Vinaya*, I, p. 88). Thirty monks, who were dwellers in the forest, had to stay at Sāketa, being unable to reach Śrāvastī in time, when the Buddha was staying there in the Jetavana of Anāthapiṇḍika (*Vinaya*, I, p. 253). There was a village named Toraṇa-vatthu between Sāvatthī and Sāketa (*Samyutta*, IV, 374ff.). The Jātakas refer to Sāketa as an important city (Vol. III, 217, 272; V, 13; VI, 228). Sāketa is especially said to have belonged to the Guptas.

Śālva.—The *Gopatha-Brāhmaṇa* (1, 2, 9) refers to the country of the Śālvas. In Pāṇini's sūtra (4. 1. 173, 178) it is stated that the Śālvajana-pada consists of Audumvara (Udumvara), Tilakhala, Madrakāra, Yugandhara, Bhūliṅga and Śaradaṇḍa. Pāṇini also refers to a town named Vaidhumāgni built by Vidhumāgni in the Śālva country (4. 2. 76, 4. 2. 133, 4. 1. 169). Patañjali in his *Mahābhāṣya* mentions it (4. 2. 76). The Śālvas probably occupied the territory now occupied by the native state of Alwar (Cunningham, *A.R.A.S.I.*, XX, p. 120; *Matsyapurāṇa*, Ch. 113). The *Viṣṇupurāṇa* (II, Ch. III, śl. 16–18) and the *Brahmapurāṇa* (Ch. 19, 16–18) place the Śālvas in the west. According to the *Mahābhārata* the Śālva country was situated near Kurukṣetra (Virāṭaparva, Chap. I). It was the kingdom of the father of Satyavān, husband of Sāvitrī (Vanaparva, Chap. 282). The capital of the Śālvas was Śālvapura, also called Saubhaga-nagara (*Mahābh.*, Vanaparva, Chap. 14). In the great Bhārata battle, the Śālvas lent their support to Duryodhana against the Pāṇḍavas (Bhīṣmaparva, Chap. 20, 10, 12, 15).

Sāmagāma.—It was situated in the country of the Śākyas, where the Buddha once dwelt (*Aṅg.*, III, 309; *Majjhima*, II, 243).

Sāngala.—This fortified town may be located somewhere in the Gurudaspur district near Fathgarh (*J.R.A.S.*, 1903, 687). It was the main centre of the Cathaeans who were the leading people among the free confederate tribes. For further details vide B. C. Law, *Indological Studies*, Part I, p. 22.

Sārnāth (*Śāraṅganātha*).—The Sārnāth Stone Inscription mentions the ancient site of Sārnāth in the Benaras district, situated at a distance of about seven miles from Benaras city, where there is a large collection of Buddhist ruins (*C.I.I.*, Vol. III). The Sārnāth Stone Inscription was dug out to the north of the Dhamek stūpa, to the south of the raised mound running east and west over the remnants of the old monasteries of the Gupta period (*E.I.*, III, 44; *E.I.*, IX, 319–28). Its ancient name is *Isipatanamigadāya* (*Ṛṣipatana-mrigadāva*) where Buddha first turned the Wheel of Law.[1] Cunningham found it represented by a fine wood, covering an area of about half a mile extending from the great tope of Dhamek on the north to the Chaukundi mound on the south (*Archaeological Report*, I, p. 107). There was a large community of Buddhist monks at Isipatana in the 2nd century B.C. It was a monastic centre in Hiuen Tsang's time,

[1] *Majjhima*, I, 170ff.; *Saṃyutta*, V. 420ff.; *Kathāvatthu*, 97, 559.

for he found 1,500 Buddhist monks studying Hīnayāna Buddhism there. As regards the origin of the Deer Park at Isipatana, readers' attention is drawn to the *Nigrodhamiga Jātaka* (*Jātaka*, I, 145ff.). The Deer Park was a forest given by the king of Benaras for the deer to wander in it unmolested.

Some of the most eminent members of the Buddhist community seem to have resided in this place from time to time. Among the recorded conversions held at Isipatana, those between Sāriputta and Mahākoṭṭhita and between Mahākoṭṭhita and Cittahatthī-Sāriputta are noteworthy (*Saṃyutta*, II, pp. 112–114; III, pp. 167–69; 173–7; IV, pp. 384–6; *Aṅguttara*, III, pp. 392ff.). Isipatana (Ṛṣipatana) Migadāya (Mṛgadāva) was mentioned by the Buddha as one of the four places of pilgrimage which his devout followers should visit (*Buddhavaṃsa Commy.*, p. 3; *Dīgha Nik.*, II, 141). It was so called because sages on their way through the air from the Himalayas, used to alight here or start from here on their aerial flight. In addition to the preaching of his First Sermon several other incidents connected with the life of the Buddha are mentioned in the Buddhist texts as having taken place at Isipatana (*Vinaya*, I, 15ff.; *Aṅguttara Nik.*, I, 110ff.; 279-80; III, 392ff., 399ff.; *Sam. Nik.*, I, 105-6; V, 406–8; *Dīpavaṃsa*, pp. 119-20; *Therīgāthā Commy.*, p. 220; B. C. Law, *Ancient Indian Tribes*, 1926, pp. 22–25). For a brief account of archaeological explorations at Sārnāth see *J.R.A.S.*, 1908, 1088ff.; *A.S.I.R.*, I, 105ff.; *A.R.A.S.I.*, 1904/05, 59ff.; 1906/07, 68ff.; 1907/08, 43ff.; 1914-1915, 97ff.; 1919-1920, 26ff.; 1921-22, 42ff.; 1927-1928, 95ff. B. Majumdar's *Guide to Sarnath*, (1937) may also be consulted.

Sāvatthī (Śrāvastī).—Sāheṭh-Māheṭh[1] is the modern equivalent of the ancient site of Śrāvastī. The entire site lies on the borders of Gonda and Bahraich districts of Oudh in the Uttara Pradeśa, and can be reached from the railway station Balarāmpur. It can also be reached from Bahraich which is at a distance of about 26 miles. It occurs in Luders' List (Nos. 918, 919) as Sāvasti. Some sculptures have been found out at this site, most of them are Buddhistic, very few Jaina, and some Brahmanical. According to the Buddhist commentator Buddhaghosa this city was so called because it was originally the dwelling place of Savattha the sage. It was at first a religious settlement, and the city subsequently grew up around it (*Papañcasūdanī*, I, 59-60; *Paramatthajotikā* (*Suttanipāta Commy.*), p. 300; *Udāna Commy.*, Siamese ed., p. 70). Everything was found there, which was necessary for human beings; hence it was called Sāvatthī (*sabbam-atthi*). This city is said to have been built by king Śrāvasta or Śrāvastaka (*Viṣṇupurāṇa*, Ch. II, aṃśa 4). In the *Matsya* and *Brahma Purāṇas* (XII, 29-30; VII, 53) Śrāvasta is mentioned as the son of Yuvanāśva. The *Mahābhārata* represents Śrāvastaka as the son of Śrāva and the grandson of Yuvanāśva (Vanaparva, 201, 3-4; *Harivaṃśa*, XI, 21, 22). The *Harṣacarita* (Kane's ed., p. 50) refers to Śrutavarma who was once the king of Śrāvastī. The *Kathāsaritsāgara* and the *Daśakumāracarita* (15, 63–79; Ch. V) refer to two kings of Śrāvastī named Devasena and Dharmavardhana respectively. King Dharmavardhana had a beautiful daughter named Navamālikā (*Daśakumāracaritam*, p. 138). Pramati continued his journey to Śrāvastī, where being tired he lay down to rest among vines in a part outside the city (*Ibid.*, p. 136). Sāvatthī figures throughout Buddhist literature as the capital of the kingdom of Kośala,

[1] For brief account of archaeological explorations see *J.R.A.S.*, 1908, 1098ff.; *A.S.I.R.*, I, 330ff.; XI. 78ff.; *A.R.A.S.I.*, 1907-8, 81ff.; 1910-11, pp. 1ff.

and Sāvatthī and Vana-Sāvatthī find mention as two important stopping places on the high road starting from Rājagṛha and extending as far south-west as Aḷaka and Assaka. There must have been another high road by which one could travel from Śrāvastī to Benaras *via* Kiṭāgiri (*Majjhima*, I, 473).

The city of Śrāvastī was situated on the bank of the Aciravatī (*Vinaya-Mahāvagga*, pp. 190-191, 293; *Paramatthajotikā*, p. 511). The Jetavana and the Pubbārāma were the two well-known Buddhist monastic establishments and influential centres of Buddhism, built in the life-time of the Buddha adjoining and to the south of the city of Śrāvastī. Śrāvastī was also an important and powerful seat of Brahmanism and Vedic learning. It had an important Brahmanical institution under the headship of Jānussoṇi (*Dīgha*, I, 235; *Sumaṅgalavilāsinī*, II, 399; *Majjhima*, I, 16). According to the *Bodhisattvāvadānakalpalatā* (61. 2), Svastika, a Brahmin of Śrāvastī, took to cultivation to earn his livelihood. Among the wealthy nobles of Śrāvastī mention may be made of Prince Jeta who laid out, owned and maintained the famous garden bearing his name (*Papañcasūdanī*, I, p. 60). There was another famous garden near the city bearing the name of Mallikā, the queen of Prasenajit of Kośala. Sudatta, noted in the tradition of Buddhism as Anāthapiṇḍika, gained an immortal fame as the donor of the Jetavanavihāra, and Viśākhā immortalised herself by erecting the Pubbārāmavihāra.

The material prosperity of Śrāvastī was due to the fact that it was a meeting place of three main trade routes and a great centre of trade. The Sohgaura copperplate containing an order, either issued by or issued to the *Mahāmātras* of Śrāvastī, stands out as a clear epigraphic record proving that store-houses were built by the State on public roads at reasonable distances and in suitable localities, stocked with loads of ropes and other things useful to the caravans (*Vienna Oriental Journal*, X, 138ff.; *I.A.*, XXV, 216ff.; *J.R.A.S.*, 1907, 510ff., *I.H.Q.*, X, 54–6; *A.B.O.R.I.*, XI, 32ff. *Sāvatiyaṃ mahāmatanaṃ sāsane*). According to the *Lalitavistara*, this city was full of kings, princes, ministers, councillors and their followers, etc. (Ch. I). It accommodated 57,000 families (*Samantapāsādikā*, p. 614). It must have been surrounded by a wall provided with gates on four or more sides. Within the wall the city must have three broad rings or divisions, namely, central, outer and outermost, the royal palace and the court occupying the centre. The road arrangements must have been so planned as to facilitate patrol duty. There must have been proper allocation of sites for quarters of officials, religious and educational institutions, private houses, markets and even prostitutes' quarters.

Śrāvastī was not only a great emporium of Indian trade but also a great centre of religion and culture. Śrāvastī, otherwise called by the Jainas as Candrapurī or Candrikāpurī, was the birthplace of Sambhavanātha and Candraprabhānātha, the two famous Jaina *tīrthaṅkaras* (Jaina *Harivaṃśapurāṇa*, p. 717; Shah, *Jainism of Northern India*, p. 26). According to the *Vividhatīrthakalpa* a *caitya* adorned with the image of Śrīsaṃbhavanātha stood in the city of Śrāvastī. Saint Kapila came here for the purpose of acquiring knowledge. Bhadra, son of king Jitaśatru, became a monk in course of his wanderings and afterwards attained perfection (B. C. Law, *Some Jaina Canonical Sūtras*, 175). It was in this city that Mahāvīra met Gosāla-Maṅkhaliputra for the first time after their separation. Mahāvīra visited it more than once and spent one rainy season here (*Kalpasūtra*, Subodhikāṭīkā, 103, 105, 106; *Āvaśyakasūtra*, 221; Stevenson, *Heart of Jainism*, 42). The Jaṭilas, the Nigaṇṭhas, the

Acelakas, the Eka-sāṭakas and the Paribbājakas were very familiar figures to the people of this city so much so that it was easy for the royal spies to hide their secret mission under the garb of those *religieux* (*Saṁyutta*, I, 78). Many of the Buddha's most edifying discourses were delivered here. This city contributed a fair number of monks and nuns to the Order (*Dhammapada Commentary*, I, 3ff.; *Ibid.*, I, 37ff.; *Ibid.*, II, 260ff.; *Ibid.*, II, 270ff.; *Ibid.*, I, 115ff.; *Ibid.*, III, 281ff.; *Ibid.*, IV, 118; *Psalms of the Brethren*, pp. 7, 13, 14, 19, 20, 25; *Psalms of the Sisters*, 19-20).

This city was visited by the two famous Chinese pilgrims Fā-hien and Hiuen Tsang, in the 5th and 7th centuries A.D. When Fā-hien visited this city, the inhabitants were few. He saw the place where the old Vihāra of Mahāpajāpatī Gotamī was built, the wells and walls of the house of Anāthapiṇḍika and the site where Aṅgulimala attained arahatship (Legge, *Travels of Fā-hien*, 55-56). According to Hiuen Tsang although the city was mostly in ruins, there were some inhabitants. The country used to grow good crops and enjoyed an equable climate, and the people were honest in their ways and given to learning and fond of good works. There were some hundreds of Buddhist monasteries, most of which were in ruins. There were some deva-temples, and the non-Buddhists were numerous. There were several topes, many Buddhist monasteries, and many monks who were adherents of Mahayanism. (Watters, *On Yuan Chwang*, I, 377; II, 200).

Śrāvastī declined in wealth, population and political importance. Anāthapiṇḍika, the famous donor of the Jetavana monastery, died penniless after having spent fifty-four crores on the erection of the Vihāra, lost eighteen crores in business and eighteen crores by the action of the river Aciravatī which swept away his hoarding on its bank (*Dhammapada Commentary*, III, 10). From the days of Buddha to about the middle of the 12th century A.D. this city with its most important establishment the Jetavana, continued to be the centre of Buddhism linking up with it the vicissitudes of a great religion through a passage of about 1,800 years. For further details vide B. C. Law, *Śrāvastī in Indian Literature* (*M.A.S.I.*, No. 50); B. C. Law, *Tribes in Ancient India*, pp. 129ff.; *A.S.I.R.*, I, 330ff.; XI, 78ff.; *A.R.A.S.I.*, 1907/08, 81ff.; 1910/11, pp. 1ff.

Setavya.—It was a city of the Kośala country near Ukkaṭṭha. There was a road from Ukkaṭṭha to Setavya (*Aṅg.*, II, 37). Kumārakassapa once went to Setavya with a large number of monks and converted Pāyāsi, the chief of Setavya, into Buddhism (*Dīgh.*, II, 316ff.).

Set Mahet.—Set or Sāheth is on the borders of the Goṇḍā and the Bahraich districts. It is situated on the river Rāpti in the district of Goṇḍā, 58 miles north of Ayodhyā, and 42 miles north of Goṇḍā. An inscription has been discovered here in a Buddhist monastery, which records that a donor after bathing in the Ganges at Vārāṇasī and worshipping Vāsudeva and other gods, granted some villages to the Buddhist fraternity (*E.I.*, XI, 20–26).

Shorkot.—This place lies at some distance above the junction of the Jhelum and the Chenab. It is described by Hiuen Tsang to be 5,000 li in circuit. It is a huge mound of ruins. The foundation of the city is attributed to a fabulous Rājā Sor. This place was bounded on the east by the Sutlej, on the north by the province of Tāki, on the south by Multan and on the west by the Indus. The antiquity of the place may be ascertained approximately by the coins which are found in its ruins (*C.A.G.I.*, pp. 233ff.).

Siddhāśrama.—According to the *Rāmāyaṇa* (Ādikāṇḍa, 29 sarga, vs. 3-4), this hermitage stood before Vāmana came into existence. It was visited by Rāma and Viśvāmitra. It was an excellent hermitage (*Ibid.*, V. 24). There is a difference of opinion as to the site of this hermitage. According to the *Rāmāyaṇa* (Kiṣkindhyākāṇḍa, Ch. 43), it is said to have been situated in the Himalayas between the Kāñcanjaṅghā and the Dhavalāgiri on the bank of the river Mandākinī. According to others, it is at Buxar in the district of Sahabad. Viṣṇu is said to have been incarnated here as Vāmana. He attained perfection in austerity according to the *Rāmāyaṇa* (Ādikāṇḍa, sarga 29, vs. 3-4).

Sīhappapāta.—It is mentioned in the *Kuṇāla Jātaka* (*Jāt.*, Vol. V, p. 415) as a lake in the Himalaya.

Siṃsapāvana.—It was situated to the north of Setavya, where the Venerable Kumārakassapa dwelt (*Dīgha*, II, 316).

Sindhu (or Indus).—The Sindhu which is the River Indus and the Sintu of the Chinese travellers, is the greatest known river of northern India after which the Indus group is named. The Indus, after passing Attock, flows almost due south, parallel to the Sulaiman Hills. According to the *Ṛgveda* (X. 75), the Sindhu surpassed all the flowing streams. The *Taittirīya-saṃhitā* (VII. 4, 13, 1) uses the term *Saindhava* which may apply to Sindhu or the Indus. Pāṇini mentions it in his *Aṣṭādhyāyī* (4. 3. 32-33; 4. 3. 93). Patañjali refers to it in his *Mahābhāṣya* (1. 3. 1, pp. 588-589). The *Mālavikāgnimitraṃ* (Ed. S. S. Ayyar, p. 148) refers to the fight of Vasumitra, son of Agnimitra, with the Yavanas on the right bank of the river Sindhu.

According to Alberuni the upper course of the Indus above the junction with the Chenab was known as Sindhu; lower that point to Aror it was known by the name of Pañcnād, while its course from Aror down to the sea was called Mihran (*India*, I, p. 260). In the Behistun Inscription of Darius it is referred to as Hindu, and in the ***Vendidad*** as Hendu. The Sindhu lent its name to the country through which it flowed (cf. Beal, *Buddhist Records of the Western World*, I, p. 69; cf. *J.A.S.B.*, 1886, II, p. 323). The *Brihat-saṃhitī* (XIV. 19) mentions it as a river. The Jain *Jambudivapaṇṇati* traces the source of the four rivers called the Gaṅgā, Rohitā (Brahmaputra), Sindhu (Indus) and Harikāntā to the twin lotus lakes, one on the side of the lesser and the other on that of the greater Himalayan range.

The Sindhu is a trans-Himalayan river. It is fed by a number of glaciers. It was also known by the names of Sambheda and Saṅgama. The Sindhu group, as known to Pliny, was constituted of the Sindhu (Indus) and nineteen other rivers. The main tributaries of the Indus are said to be the Hydraotes, the Akesines, the Hypasis, the Hydaspes, the Kophen, the Parenos, the Saparnos and the Saonos. For further details, vide B. C. Law, *Rivers of India*, pp. 6–12.

Ūrṇāvatī.—It is an affluent of the Indus mentioned in the *Ṛgveda* (X. 75. 8).

Sineru.—It is mentioned in the Buddhist texts and commentaries. (*Dham. Commy.*, I, 107; cf. *Jātaka*, 1,202). It is the Mount Meru (*Therīgāthā Commy.*, 150), which was 68,000 leagues high. It is identical with the Rudra Himalaya in Garhwal, near the Badarikāśrama. It is probably the same as the Mt. Meros of Arrian.

Singhapura (*Seng-ho-pu-lo*).—It was situated 117 miles to the south-east of Taxila (*C.A.G.I.*, pp. 142-143).

Sirśa.—It is a town in the Hissar district of the Punjab near which an inscription has been found in a mound (*E.I.*, XXI, Pt. viii).

Śivipura.—According to the Shorkot Inscription the ancient name of Shorkot was Śivipura or Śivapura which was the capital of the Sibis (*E.I.*,

XVI, 1921, p. 16; Law, *Tribes in Ancient India*, p. 83). Śivapura or the town of the Śivas is mentioned by the scholiast on Pāṇini as situated in the northern country (see Patañjali, IV, 2, 2). The Śivas or Sibis were a people inhabiting the Shorkot region in Jhang in the Punjab lying between the Irāvatī and the Candrabhāgā, and therefore, included in the northern region or Uttarāpatha. They seem to have been a very ancient people, probably alluded to for the first time in the *Ṛgveda* (VII, 18, 7). They seem to have maintained their independence for some considerable time, for they are referred to not only by the Greek geographers and the historians of Alexander's time but also by the scholiast on Pāṇini (IV, 2, 109). In later times they seem to have migrated to the extreme south of India (cf. *Daśakumāracaritaṃ*, Ch. VI; *Bṛhat Saṃhitā*, Ch. XIV, v. 12). The *Lalitavistara* (p. 22) and the *Mahāvastu* (Law, *Study of the Mahāvastu*, p. 7) mention the Śivi country as one of the sixteen *janapadas* of Jambudvīpa. Ariṭṭhapura was the capital of the Śivi kingdom (*Jātaka*, IV, p. 401). Ariṭṭhapura (Skt. Ariṣṭapura) is probably identical with Ptolemy's Aristobothra in the north of the Punjab and may perhaps be the same as Dvārāvatī (*Jātaka*, Faüsböll, Vol. VI, p. 421; N. L. Dey, *Geographical Dictionary*, pp. 11, 187). The *Bodhisattvāvadāna-Kalpalatā* of Kṣemendra mentions the city of Śivavatī, which is identical with the capital of the Śivi country, ruled by King Śivi (91st Pallava). Early Greek writers refer to the territory of the Siboi in the Punjab. For further details, vide B. C. Law, *Indological Studies*, Pt. I, pp. 24–26.

Soṇa (*Soṇā*).—It is the greatest known lower tributary of the Ganges. Arrian's Sona, the modern Son, which takes its rise in the Maikāla (Mekala) range in the district of Jabbalpur and flowing north-east through Baghelkhand, Mirzapur and Sahabad districts, joins the Ganges near Patna. According to the *Rāmāyaṇa* (Ādikāṇḍa, 32 sarga, vs. 8-9), this beautiful (*ramyā*) river was flowing through the five hills encircling Girivraja and also through Magadha, hence it was called Māgadhī. The *Padmapurāṇa* (Uttarakhaṇḍa, vs. 35–38) refers to this great river. The *Purāṇas* count it as one of the important rivers that rise from the Ṛkṣa range. Crossing this river Dadhīci reached the site of his father's seclusion (*Harṣacarita*, Ch. I). Kālidāsa refers to this river in his *Raghuvaṃśa* (VII. 36). Its course past Rājagṛha in Magadha was probably known as the Sumāgadhā or Sumāgadhī. It is fed by five tributaries in the district of Baghelkhand, four tributaries in the district of Mirzapur, one in the district of Palamau and one in the district of Sahabad. This river falls into the Ganges above Patna (cf. *Raghuvaṃśa*, VII. 36—*Bhāgīrathīśoṇa ivottaraṅga*). For further details, vide B. C. Law, *Rivers of India*, p. 26.

Soron.—Its ancient name was Sukarakṣetra or the place of the good deed. This large town was situated on the western bank of the Ganges, on the high road between Bareli and Mathurā (*C.A.G.I.*, p. 418). It was in Etawah district, U.P. (*Inscriptions of Northern India*, revised by D. R. Bhandarkar, No. 416, V. 1245).

Śrāvastī.—See Sāvatthī.

Śriṅgaverapura (*Śriṅgiverapura*).—Here Rāma is said to have crossed the Ganges. It is identified by Cunningham with Singror built on a very high bluff, 22 miles to the north-west of Allahabad (*A.S.R.*, XI. 62; *J.R.A.S.B.*, XV, No. 2, 1949, p. 131).

Srughna.—It was situated 38 or 40 miles from Thaneswar. It was known to Hiuen Tsang as *Su-lukin-na*. It was 1,000 miles in circuit. On the east it extended to the Ganges and on the north to a range of lofty mountain, while the Jumna flowed through the midst of it. According to Cunningham, it must have comprised the hilly areas of Sirmor and Garhwal, lying between the rivers Giri and the Ganges with portions of the districts of Ambala and Saharanpur (*C.A.G.I.*, pp. 395ff.).

Sthāneśvara (*Sthāniśvara*).—It was one of the oldest places in ancient India. The name is said to have been derived either from the *sthāna*, i.e., the *abode* of Iśvara or Mahādeva or from the junction of the names of Sthānu and Iśvara. It was known to Hiuen Tsang as *Sa-ta-ni-shi-fa-lo* which was more than 1,100 miles in circuit. According to Bāṇa's *Harṣacarita* (Ch. III), it was the capital of Śrīkaṇṭhajanapada. The famous battlefield of Kurukṣetra is situated on the southern side of Thāneśvara, about 30 miles to the south of Ambala and 40 miles north of Panipat. This town contained an old ruined fort about 1,200 ft., square at the top (*C.A.G.I.*, pp. 376ff., 701). S. N. Majumdar (*C.A.G.I.*, Intro. XLIII) proposes to identify it with Thūna (Sthūna) mentioned in the *Vinaya Mahāvagga* (V. 13, 12) and the *Divyāvadāna* (p. 22). Thūna was a Brahmin village (cf. *Jātaka*, VI, 62) forming the western boundary of the Madhyadeśa (*Vinaya Texts*, S.B.E., XVII, 38-39).

Suktimatī.—The Kosam Inscription of the reign of Mahārāja Vaiśravana of the year 107 refers to this locality, which was probably in the neighbourhood of Kauśāmbī. This city is mentioned in the *Cetiya Jātaka* (No. 422) as Sotthivatinagara (*E.I.*, XXIV, Pt. IV). It was the capital of the Cedi king named Dhṛṣṭaketu (*Mahābhārata*, III, 22). It stood on the river of the same name which is described in the *Mahābhārata* as one of the rivers of Bhāratavarṣa (Bhīṣmaparva, VI, 9).

Sumeru.—The *Padmapurāṇa* (Uttarakhaṇḍa, vs. 35–38) and the *Kālikāpurāṇa* (Ch. 13. 23; Ch. 19. 92) refer to it. Śiva saw the summit of it (*Kālikāpurāṇa*, Ch. 17. 10). The Jambu river flows from this mountain (*Ibid.*, Ch. 19. 32). It is the same as the Sineru or the Mount Meru.

Suṃsumāragiri (*Siśumāra hill*).—It was in the Bharga country (*Saṃyutta*, III, 1). It was situated in a deer park at Bhesakaḷāvana. It was a city and its capital was so called because on the very first day of its construction a crocodile made a noise in a lake near by (*Papañcasūdanī*, II, 65; *Sāratthappakāsinī*, II, 249). Prince Bodhi, the son of Udayana, king of the Vatsas by his queen Vāsavadattā, dwelt on this hill, where he built a palace called Kokanada. According to the Buddhist tradition, it was the capital of the Bharga kingdom and was used as a fort (*Majjhima*, I, 332–8; II, 91–97). Some have identified it with the present Chunar hill (Ghosh, *Early History of Kauśāmbī*, p. 32). A rich householder who used to live on this hill gave his daughter in marriage to the son of Anāthapiṇḍika (R. L. Mitra, *Northern Buddhist Literature*, p. 309).

Sundarikā.—It is one of the seven sacred rivers of ancient India. It was a river in Kośala, which was most probably a tributary of the Aciravatī or Rāptī. It was not far from Śravastī (*Suttanipāta*, p. 79).

Sunet.—It is in ruins in the district of Ludhiana in the Punjab, situated three miles south-west of Ludhiana town (*Journal of the Numismatic Society of India*, Vol. IV, Pt. I, pp. 1-2).

Suvarṇaguhā.—It is on the Citrakūṭaparvata which lies in the Himalayan region (*Jātaka*, III, 208).

Śvetaparvata (*Setapabbata*).—It is in the Himalayas to the east of Tibet (*Saṃyutta*, I, 67).

Takṣaśilā (Chinese *Shi-Shi-Ch'eng*).—It was the capital city of the Gandhāra kingdom. Pāṇini and Patañjali mention it in the *Aṣṭādhyāyī* (4. 3. 93) and in the *Mahābhāṣya* (1. 3. 1; 4. 3. 93; pp. 588-589) respectively. It occurs in the Kaliṅga Rock Edict I. In Aśoka's reign a *Kumāra* was posted as the viceroy at Takṣaśilā, which was always in a state of revolt.

The Edict refers to the early part of Aśoka's reign when there was no such trouble at Taxila. This city as described by Arrian was great, wealthy, and populous. Strabo praises the fertility of its soil.[1] Pliny calls it a famous city and states that it was situated on a level plain at the foot of hills. About the middle of the 1st century A.D. it is said to have been visited by Apollonius of Tyana and his companion, Damis, who described it as being about the size of Nineveh, walled like a Greek city with narrow but well-arranged streets. About 80 years after Takṣaśilā's submission to Alexander, it was taken by Aśoka.

This city was visited by Hiuen Tsang in the 7th century A.D. when it was a dependency of Kāśmīr. According to the Chinese pilgrim, Takṣaśilā was above 2,000 li in circuit, its capital being more than 10 li in circuit. It had a fertile soil and bore good crops with flowing streams and luxuriant vegetation. The climate was genial, and the people were adherents of Buddhism. Although there were many monasteries, some of them were desolate. Monks living in a few of them were Mahayanists (*Watters, On Yuan Chwang*, I, 240).

It figures prominently in Buddhist and Jain stories. It was a great seat of learning in ancient India. Pupils from different parts of India visited this place to learn various arts and sciences. Prasenajit the king of Kośala and Jīvaka the renowned physician at the court of king Bimbisāra of Magadha, were educated here (B. C. Law, *Historical Gleanings*, Ch. I). A very beautiful picture of the student-life of those days has been given in a *Jātaka* (Vol. II, p. 277).

This city has been identified with modern Taxila in the district of Rawalpindi in the Punjab. This city was also known as Bhadraśilā and later on it came to be known as Takṣaśilā, because here the head of king Candraprabha was severed by a beggar-Brahmin (*Divyāvadānamālā*, *Northern Buddhist Literature*, p. 310). The city named Bhadraśilā was rich, prosperous, and populous. It was 12 yojanas in length and breadth, and was well-divided with four gates, and adorned with high vaults and windows. This city was situated to the north of the Himalayas under the rule of a king named Candraprabha (*Bodhisattvāvadāna-Kalpalatā*, 5th Pallava). There was a royal garden in it (*Divyāvadāna*, p. 315). According to the *Bodhisattvāvadāna-Kalpalatā* (59th Pallava), Takṣaśilā belonged to king Kuñjakarṇa when Kuṇāla was sent to conquer it. From the *Divyāvadāna* it appears that this city was included in the empire of Bindusāra of Magadha, father of Aśoka.

Takṣaśilā, which was one of the early capital cities of Gandhāra, was situated to the east of the Indus. Cunningham says that the site of Taxila is found near Shah-Dheri, just a mile to the north-east of Kāla-kā-sarāi in the extensive ruins of a fortified city around which at least fifty-five stūpas, twenty-eight monasteries and nine temples were found out. The distance from Shah-Dheri to Ohind is 36 miles, and from Ohind to Hashtnagar another 38 miles, making 74 miles in all, which is 19 in excess of the distance between Takṣaśilā (Taxila) and Puṣkalāvatī (Peukelaotis) as recorded by Pliny. To reconcile the discrepancy Cunningham suggests that Pliny's 60 miles should be read as 80 miles (LXXX), equivalent to 73½ English miles or within half a mile of the actual distance between the two places (Cunningham, *Ancient Geography*, p. 121). Dr. Bhandarkar holds (*Carmichael Lectures*, 1918, p. 54 f.n.) that in Aśoka's time Takṣaśilā does not appear to be the capital of Gandhāra, for from his Rock Edict XIII it appears that Gandhāra was not in his dominions proper; while

[1] H. & F.'s Trans., III, p. 90.

from Kalinga Edict I, it is clear that Takṣaśilā was directly under him as one of his sons was stationed there. That Takṣaśilā was not the capital of Gandhāra at that time is confirmed by Ptolemy's statement that the Gandarai (Gandhāra) country was situated to the west of the Indus with its city Proklais, i.e., Puṣkarāvatī (cf. Legge, *Travels of Fa-hien*, pp. 31-32; B. C. Law, *Tribes in Ancient India*, pp. 394-95; B. C. Law, *Historical Gleanings*, Chap. I; B. C. Law, *Geography of Early Buddhism*, pp. 52-53; *Journal of the Ganganath Jha Research Institute*, Vol. VI, Pt. 4, August, 1949, pp. 283–288). For an account of the ruins and excavations at Taxila, vide *A.S.I.R.*, II (1871), pp. 112ff.; V (1875), 66ff.; XIV (1882), 8ff.; *A.R.A.S.I.*, 1912-1913 (1916); *A.S.I.*, Annual Report, 1929-30, pp. 55ff.; *A.S.I.*, Annual Report, 1930–34, pp. 149–176; *Annual Report of the Arch. Survey of India*, 1936-37 (1940). For further details, vide J. Marshall, *Guide to Taxila*, 3rd Ed. (1936); B. C. Law, *Indological Studies*, Pt. I, pp. 14–17.

Tamasā.—The Khoh Copperplate Inscription of Mahārāja Sarvanātha mentions this river, which is modern Tamas and Tons. It rises in the Mahiyar State on the south of Nagaudh and running through the northern portion of Rewa, it flows into the Ganges, about 18 miles south-east of Allahabad (*C.I.I.*, Vol. III). *The Mārkaṇḍeya Purāṇa* mentions this river (Canto LVII, 22). According to Pargiter, it flows into the Ganges on the right bank below Allahabad. The *Kūrma Purāṇa* (XLVII, 30) gives a variant Tāmasī. Some hold that the Tamasā or the east Tons has its origin in Fyzabad. It joins the Ganges to the west of Ballia after flowing through Azamgarh. This is considered as the historical river of the *Rāmāyaṇa* fame (*Rāmāyaṇa*, Ādikāṇḍa, 2 sarga, v. 3). Rāma made his first halt on the bank of this river which was not far from the Ganges, and after crossing it undertook a journey on road and afterwards reached the river Śrīmatī. Rāma praised this river and desired to have a bath in it as it was free from mud (*Rāmāyaṇa*, Ādik., 2 sarga, vs. 4–6). According to the *Raghuvaṃśa*, Daśaratha decorated the bank of this river by erecting many sacrificial posts (IX, 20). The bank of this river was crowded with ascetics (*Raghuv.*, IX. 72). The South Tons flows north-east from the Ṛkṣa mountain to fall into the Ganges below Allahabad. It is fed by two tributaries on the left and by two on the right.

Tāmasavana.—Cunningham identifies it with Sultanpur in the Punjab. It is also known as Raghunāthpura (*J.A.S.B.*, XVII, pp. 206, 479).

Thūṇa (Sthūṇa).—See *Sthāneśwara*.

Trigartta.—This country which is mentioned in the *Mahābhārata* (II, 48, 13), was located between the Rāvi and the Sutlej with its centre round Jalandar. It represented Kangra in ancient days (Moti Chandra, *Geographical and Economic Studies in the Mahābhārata*, Upāyanaparva, p. 94). *The Daśakumāracaritam* records an incident in connection with the three rich householders who were brothers living in the country of Trigartta. During their lifetime there was no rain for twelve years, trees bore no fruits, rain-clouds were scarce, many springs and rivers went dry, cities, villages, towns and other settlements decayed (pp. 150-151). For further details, vide Law, *Tribes in Ancient India*, Ch. 12.

Tṛṇavindu-āśrama.—It was visited by Pulastya, son of Prajāpati, who came here to meditate. It was situated by the side of the Mount Meru. While he was engaged in repeating the Vedic hymns, the daughter of the sage Tṛṇavindu appeared before him. Being at first cursed she was eventually married by Pulastya.

Tulamba.—This town is situated on the left bank of the Rāvī at 52 miles to the north-east of Multan (*C.A.G.I.*, 1924, p. 257). It was originally known as Kulamba (*C.A.S.R.*, V, pp. 111ff.).

Tusām.—The Tusām Rock Inscription mentions this village, situated about 14 miles to the north-west of Bhiwani, the chief town of the Hissar district of the Punjab (P), (*C.I.I.*, Vol. III).

Udyāna.—It was situated on the river *Su-p'o-fa-su-tu*, the Śubhavāstu in Skt., the Suastus of Arrian, and the modern Swāt river. Udyāna embraces the four modern districts of Pangkora, Bijāwar, Swāt and Bunir. The capital of Udyāna was called Maṅgala (*C.A.G.I.*, 93ff.; *J.R.A.S.*, 1896, p. 655). According to Fa-hien, who visited India in the 5th century A.D., Udyāna or Woo-Chang was a part of North India. Udyāna, meaning the park, was situated to the north of the Punjab (P) along the Subhavāstu now called the Swāt. The law of the Buddha was flourishing here. There were 500 *saṅghārāmas* or monasteries. The monks inhabiting them were students of Hīnayānism. The Buddha visited this country and left his foot-print. Fa-hien remained in *Woo-Chang* and kept the summer retreat (Legge, *Travels of Fa-hien*, pp. 28-29). The people of Udyāna (*Wu-chang-na*), according to Hiuen Tsang, held Buddhism in high respect. They were believers in Mahāyānism but they followed the Vinaya of the Hīnayānists. There were many monasteries in ruins along the two sides of the Swāt river and the number of monks, who were Mahāyānists, was gradually reduced. There were more than ten deva-temples and various sectarians lived pell-mell (Watters, *On Yuan Chwang*, I, pp. 225ff.).

Ugganagara.—It was not far from Sāvatthī. A certain banker named Ugga came to Sāvatthī for trade from Ugganagara (*Dham. Commy.*, III, 465).

Uhā.—This river is stated to have been located in the Himavanta (*Milinda Pañha*, p. 70).

Upavattanasālavana.—It was in the territory of the Mallas. Here the Buddha attained *mahāparinibbāna* (*Dīgha*, II, 169).

Uśīnara.—Pāṇini refers to this country in his *Aṣṭādhyāyī* (4. 2. 118; 2. 4. 20). Patañjali in his *Mahābhāṣya* (1. 1. 8, p. 354; 1. 3. 2, p. 619; 4. 2. 118) mentions it. This country was situated to the north of the Kuru country (*C.H.I.*, I, p. 84). The *Gopatha Brāhmaṇa* (II. 9) considers the Uśīnaras as northerners. The *Ṛigveda* (X. 59, 10) refers to them. Zimmer thinks that the Uśīnaras earlier lived farther to the north-west. The authors of the *Vedic Index* do not accept his view (Vol. I, p. 103). Pargiter holds that they occupied the Punjab (*A.I.H.T.*, p. 109). The Buddhist Jātakas often mention king Uśīnara (*Nimi Jāt.*, Fausboll, VI, p. 199; *Nāradakassapa Jāt.*, VI, p. 251; *Jāt.*, IV, 181ff.). For further details, vide Law, *Tribes in Ancient India*, pp. 68ff.

Uśīnārā.—See *Uśīradhvaja*.

Uśīradhvaja.—This mountain may be said to be identical with the Uśīragiri, a mountain to the north of Kaṅkhal (*I.A.*, 1905, 179). The Siwalik range through which the Ganges forces her way into the plains, may be identified with the Uśīragiri.

Uśīnārā mentioned in Pali Literature and Uśīnaragiri mentioned in the *Kathāsaritsāgara* are doubtless identical with the Uśīragiri of the *Divyāvadāna* (p. 22) and Uśīradhvaja of the *Vinaya texts* (S.B.E., Pt. II, p. 39).

Uttara-Kośala.—This has been identified with Ayodhyā (cf. *Kamauli Plate of Govindacandra*, V.S. 1184; *E.I.*, XXVI, Pt. II, 68ff.; *I.A.*, XV, p. 8, f.n. 46). In the *Rāmāyaṇa*, Ayodhyā is mentioned as the earlier capital of Kośala, and Śrāvastī as its later capital (cf. also *Jātaka*, Nos. 454 and 385). In later times North Kośala came to be known as Śrāvastī in order to distinguish it from South Kośala. Hiuen Tsang called North Kośala by the name of Śrāvastī, which was about 600 li in circuit. There were many Buddhist monasteries in ruins. The people were honest in their ways and were fond of good work. This city was stocked with good crops and enjoyed an equable climate. For further details, vide B. C. Law, *Tribes in Ancient India*, Ch. XXVIII.

The northern frontier of Kośala must have been in the hills in what is now Nepal; its southern boundary was the Ganges; and its eastern boundary was the eastern limit of the Śākya territory (*Cambridge History of India*, I, 178). The Kośalas were the ruling clan in the kingdom whose capital was Śrāvastī (*Buddhist India*, p. 25).

Uttarakuru.—It is mentioned in the Vedic and later Brahmanical literature as a country situated somewhere north of Kashmir. It is mentioned in the *Bhāgavatapurāṇa* (I. 16, 13) as the country of northern Kurus. Some call it a mythical region. The Kurudīpa mentioned in the *Dīpavaṃsa* (p. 16) may be taken to be identical with Uttarakuru. Tidasapura was the city of Uttarakuru according to the Vinaya Commentary (*Samantapāsādikā*, p. 179). The *Lalitavistara* (p. 19) refers to Uttarakuru as a *pratyanta-dvīpa* (cf. *Bodhisattvāvadāna-Kalpalatā*, pp. 48, 50, 71). For further details, vide Law, *Geographical Essays*, p. 29.

Vaidyūtaparvata.—It is a part of the Kailāsa range at the foot of which the Mānasasarovara is situated.

Vāhlīka.—The *Yoginītantra* (1/14) mentions it. The Meharauli Iron Pillar Inscription of Candra proves beyond doubt that the Vālhīkas were settled beyond the Indus.[1] King Candra, who has been identified by some with Candravarman of the Allahabad Pillar Inscription of Samudragupta, as also with the king of the same name mentioned in the Susunia Rock Inscription, is described to have in battle in the Vaṅga country turned back with his breast the enemies, who uniting together came against him, and by whom having crossed in warfare the seven mouths of the Indus, the Vāhlīkas were conquered. The country of the Vāhlīkas has, therefore, been sought to be identified with the region now known as Balkh. The Vāhlīkas should be identified with the 'Baktrioi' occupying the country near Arachosia in Ptolemy's time.[2] According to the *Rāmāyaṇa* (Kiṣkindhyākāṇḍa, 44, v. 13), the Vāhlīkas are associated with the people of the north. At any rate, the Vāhlīka country should be identified with some region beyond the Punjab.

Vālmīki-āśrama.—Vālmīki, the celebrated author of the *Rāmāyaṇa*, had his hermitage at Bithur, 14 miles from Cawnpore. Here Sītā gave birth to her twin sons, Lava and Kuśa. This hermitage was situated in a lovely corner of the Citrakūṭa mountain. Kālidāsa places this hermitage on the way of Śatrughna proceeding to kill the demon Lavana from Ayodhyā to Madhupagna, five miles to the south-west of modern Muttra.[3] The sage Bharadvāja directed Rāma to go to the confluence of the rivers Gaṅgā and Yamunā. Rāma with Lakṣmaṇa and Sītā crossed the Yamunā and reached its right bank. At a distance of two miles from this place they found a forest region on the bank of the Yamunā. In the evening they reached a plain tract in this forest where they spent the night. At day break they continued their journey and came to the Citrakūṭa mountain. They then found the hermitage of Vālmīki. According to the *Rāmāyaṇa* (I, 2, 3; VII. 57, 3), the hermitage of Vālmīki is said to have been situated near the confluence of the Gaṅgā and the Tamasā (southern

---

[1] B. C. Law, *Tribes in Ancient India*, Ch. XI; *Geographical Essays*, p. 137; *Ancient Indian Tribes*, II, pp. 58–60.

[2] *I.A.*, 1884, p. 408.

[3] *Raghuvaṃśa*, XV, 11, 15.

Tons). It was on the Tamasā (eastern Tons) according to Pargiter.[1] The *Rāmāyaṇa* (VII, Ch. 57) points out that Lakṣmaṇa crossed the Gaṅgā while taking Sītā to Vālmīki's hermitage for banishment.[2] The Tamasā should be the eastern Tons on the bank of which stood Vālmīki's hermitage.[3] This hermitage was also visited by Śatrughna who came here from Madhurā.[4]

Veṇugrāma.—In the Barhut Votive label (No. 22) occurs Veṇugrāma or Veṇuvagrāma (= Bamboo town) which may be identified according to Cunningham with the modern village of Ben-Pūrva to the north-east of Kosam.

Verañja.—Verañja was a place near Madhurā (Mathurā) which was visited by the Buddha at the invitation of some Verañja Brahmins.[5] The Buddha once stopped on the way leading to Verañja from Madhurā and delivered a discourse to a householder.[6] Once Buddha accompanied by monks stayed at Verañja when a famine broke out. The monks could not procure food for them, but they were afterwards helped by some horse-dealers.[7] A Verañja Brahmin questioned the Master why he did not show respects to the aged Brāhmaṇas. The Buddha gave him a suitable reply with the result that the Brahmin was converted to Buddhism.[8] The Master spent the rainy season at Verañja.[9] At the end of the rainy season he left it and reached Benaras (*Vinaya*, III, 11).

Vetravatī.—This river is identified with the modern Betwa, a small tributary of the Ganges. It flows into the Jumna.

Vettavatī.—This city according to the *Jāt.* (Vol. IV, p. 388) was on the bank of the river of the same name.

Vibhraṭa.—It is a big mountain near the Himalaya mountain (*Kālikāpurāṇa*, Ch. 78, 37).

Vindhyācala.—This hill is near Mirzapur on the top of which stands the celebrated temple of Binduvāsinī. The town of Vindhyācala also known as Pampāpura lies five miles to the west of Mirzapur (*Bhaviṣyap.*, Chap. IX). It is mentioned in the *Yoginītantra* (2. 9, pp. 214ff.) and in the *Kālikāpurāṇa* (Ch. 58. 37).

Vindusarovara.—The *Yoginītantra* mentions it (2. 5. 141ff.). It is situated on the Rudra Himalaya, two miles south of Gaṅgotrī where Bhagīratha is said to have performed asceticism for bringing down the Gaṅgā from heaven (*Rāmāyaṇa*, I, 43; *Matsyapurāṇa*, Ch. 121). The *Brahmāṇḍapurāṇa* (Ch. 51) points out that this lake or *sarovara* is situated on the north of the Kailāsa range. (N. L. Dey, *Geographical Dictionary*, 2nd ed., p. 38).

Vipāśā.—The name of this river occurs in Pāṇini's *Aṣṭādhyāyī* (4. 2. 74). It is the Beas, identified with the Vipāsis or Hypasis or the Hyphasis of the Greeks, which is a tributary of the Śatadru or the Sutlej. It was in ancient times most probably an independent river. The *Mahābhārata* refers to the origin of this river. Vaśiṣṭha, broken in heart due to the death of his sons at the hands of Viśvāmitra, wanted to kill himself. He, therefore, tied himself hand and foot and threw himself into the river, but the strong current of the river unfastened him (*vi* = *vigata*+*pāśa*) and saved him by throwing him on the banks. The *Mārkaṇḍeya Purāṇa*

---

[1] *J.R.A.S.*, 1894, 235.

[2] Cf. *Raghuvaṃśa*, XIV, 52.

[3] *J.R.A.S.B.*, XV, 1949, No. 2, Letters, p. 132 f.n. 4.

[4] *Rāmāyana*, Uttarakāṇḍa, Sarga 84, v. 3.

[5] *Dhammapada-aṭṭhakathā*, II, p. 153.

[6] *Aṅguttara Nikāya*, II, 57.

[7] *Vinaya*, III, 6.

[8] *Aṅguttara Nikāya*, IV, 172.

[9] *Jātaka*, III, 494.

refers to this river (Canto LVII, 18). The *Bhāgavatapurāṇa* (X. 79, 11) and the *Padmapurāṇa* (Uttarakhaṇḍa, vs. 35–38) also mention it. This river rises in the Pir Pañjal range at the Rhotang Pass near the source of the Rāvī. It is fed by a number of glaciers. From Chambā it flows in south-westerly direction to meet the Śatadru.

Vitastā.—This river which is mentioned in the *Ṛgveda* (X. 75, 5; *Nirukta*, IX, 26; cf. *Kāśika Vritti* on Pāṇini, 1. 4. 31) is the most westerly of the five rivers of the Punjab. It is the Hydaspes of Alexander's historians and the Bidaspes of Ptolemy. Among the four main eastern tributaries of the Indus, the most western is the Vitastā (Pali: Vitaṃsā) or the Jhelum. It takes its rise in the Pir Pañjal range in the State of Kashmir and flows towards the west in a zigzag course below Punch, and then turns south to flow in a south-westerly direction. It turns west a little to the east of the town of Jhelum and to the west of Mirpur and flows southwards after forming a bulge between Pir Dadan in the north-east and Khosab in the south-west. It meets the Chenab below Jhang and Jhang Maghiana. This river is known in Kashmir under different local names, *Virnag*, *Adpal* and *Sandran*, and flows through Śrīnagar. It was known to the Ṛgvedic Aryans (X, 75) by the name of Vitastā. The *Bhāgavatapurāṇa* (V, 19, 18) mentions it as a river.

Vṛndāvana.—It is a place of Hindu pilgrimage. It is situated six miles to the north of Mathurā. It is described in the *Harivaṃśa* (Ch. LXII, 22-23) as a charming forest on the bank of the Yamunā abounding in grass, fruits and *kadamba* trees. Here Kṛṣṇa sported with the milkmaids.[1] The *Bhāgavatapurāṇa* mentions it (X. 11, 28, 35, 36, 38; X. 22, 29; X. 46, 18).

Vṛṣaparva-āśrama.—It was near the Gandhamādana-parvata which is a part of the Rudra Himalaya, but according to the epic writers it forms a part of the Kailāsa range.

Vyāsa-āśrama.—The hermitage of the sage Vyāsa, the author of the *Mahābhārata* and the *Purāṇas*, is situated at a village called Manal near Badrināth in Garhwal in the Himalayas.

Yamunā.—This river is mentioned in the *Ṛgveda* (X. 75; V. 52, 17; VII. 18, 19; X. 75, 5),[2] *Atharvaveda* (IV. 9, 10) and the *Aitareya Brāhmaṇa* (VIII. 14, 4). It is known as Kalindakanyā because it takes its rise from the Kalindagiri.[3] According to the *Ṛgveda* (VII. 18, 19), the Tritsus and Sudās defeated their enemies on this river. The territory of the Tritsus lay between the Yamunā and the Sarasvatī on the east and the west respectively. According to the *Aitareya Brāhmaṇa* (VIII, 23) and *Śatapatha Brāhmaṇa* (XIII. 5, 4, 11), the Bharatas are famed as victorious on the Yamunā. The *Pañcaviṃśa Brāhmaṇa* (IX. 4, 11; XXV. 10, 24; 13, 4), *Śāṅkhyāyana Śrautasūtra* (XIII. 29, 25, 33), *Kātyāyana Śrautasūtra* (XXIV. 6, 10, 39), *Lāṭyāyana Śrautasūtra* (X. 19, 9, 10) and *Āśvalāyana Śrautasūtra* (XII, 6, 28) mention this river. Patañjali also mentions it in his *Mahābhāṣya* (1. 1. 9, p. 436; 1. 4. 2, p. 670). The *Yoginītantra* (2. 5. 139-140) and the *Kālikāpurāṇa* (Ch. 15, 8) refer to it. This river also known as the Kālindī occurs in the *Bhāgavatapurāṇa* (III. 4, 36; IV. 8, 43; VI. 16, 16; VIII. 4, 23; IX. 4, 30; IX. 4, 37; X. 58, 22) as well as in the *Mahāvastu* (III, 201). Bāṇa in his *Kādambarī* (p. 62) also calls it the Kālindī because its water appears to be dark. It rises on the slopes of Bandarpunch, a peak situated on the watershed between the Yamunā

---

[1] *C.A.G.I.*, pp. 429-30.
[2] *J.R.A.S.*, 1883, p. 361.
[3] *Raghuvaṃśa*, VI, 48.

and the Ganges. The shrine of Yamunotrī stands at the base of the Bandarpuñch. The first and great western tributary of the Ganges is the Yamunā proper, which takes its rise in the Himalayan range below Mount Kamet. It cuts a valley through the Siwalik range and Garhwal before it enters the plains of northern India to flow south parallel to the Ganges; from Mathurā downwards it follows a south-eastern course till it meets the Ganges forming the famous confluence at Prayāga or Allahabad. In the district of Dehra Dun it receives two tributaries on the west side, the upper one of which is known as northern Tons. Between Agra and Allahabad it is joined on the left side by four tributaries, called Carmanvatī (modern Chambal), Kālisindh, Vetravatī (modern Betwa), Ken and Payaṣṇī (modern Paisuni). Many holy places are situated on this river. Śarabhaṅga, a disciple of Kāśyapa, was present at a great sacrifice held at a place between the Ganges and the Yamunā.[1] The Yamunā is known to the Chinese as Yen-mok-na. It served as the boundary between Śūrasena and Kośala, and further down between Kośala and Vaṃśa; Madurā, the capital of Śūrasena, and Kosambī, the capital of Vaṃśa standing on its right bank. The Yamunotrī which is eight miles from Kursoli is considered to be the source of the river Yamunā. It is identical with the Greek *Erannaboas* (Hiraṇyavāha or Hiraṇyavāhu). Yamunā is one of the five great rivers mentioned in early Buddhist texts.[2] It is modern Jumna. The *Skanda Purāṇa* mentions the Vāluvāhinī as a tributary of this river.

Yaugandhara.—It may be identified with the Jhind State of the southern Punjab states lying to the north-west of Delhi. It is mentioned in Pāṇini's *Aṣṭādhyāyī* (4. 2. 130) and in the *Mahābhārata* (III. 129, 9) and is called a gateway to Kurukṣetra.

Yavana Country.—The Yonas or Yavanas were the Greeks on the north-western frontier. They were the most esteemed of the foreigners, but all the Yavanas were regarded as sprung from Śūdra females and Kṣatriya males.[3] The *Rāmāyaṇa* (I, 54, 21) refers to the struggle of the Hindus with mixed hordes of Śakas and Yavanas (cf. *Śakānyavanamiśritān*). In the *Kiṣkindhyākāṇḍa* (IV. 43, 11-12) Sugrīva places the country of the Yavanas and the cities of the Śakas between the countries of the Kurus and the Madras and the Himalayas. Pāṇini mentions it in his *Aṣṭādhyāyī* (4. 1. 175). The *Bṛhatsaṃhitā* of Varāhamihira also mentions it (XIV, 18) as inhabited by the Mleccha people (*Mlecchā hi Yavanā*). The existence of a Yona or Yavana state during the days of Gautama Buddha and Assalāyana is evident from the *Majjhima Nikāya* (II, 149). The *Milindapañha*[4] refers to the land of the Yonas as the place fit for the attainment of *Nirvāṇa*. The *Mahāvastu* (Vol. I, p. 171) speaks of the assembly of the Yonas where anything which was decided was binding on them. Dr. D. R. Bhandarkar (*Carmichael Lectures*, 1921, p. 29) observes that there is nothing strange in Pāṇini flourishing in the 6th century B.C. and in his referring to *Yavanānī*, the writing of the Greeks. Pāṇini does not of course mean by *Yavanānī* any writing but only a feminine form of *Yavana*. Kātyāyana distinguishes between *Yavanānī* and *Yavanī*, restricting the use of the first to some form of Greek writing. It is difficult to determine the exact situation of the Yavana country (Bhandarkar, *Carmichael Lectures*, 1921, p. 26; Ray Chaudhuri, *Political History of Ancient India*, 4th Ed., p. 253). The existence of a pre-Alexandrian Greek (better Ionian) colony may be inferred from the

---

[1] *Mahāvastu*, I, p. 160.
[2] *Aṅguttara*, IV, 101; *Saṃyutta*, II, 135; V, 401, 460, 461.
[3] *Gautama-Dharmaśāstra*, IV, 21.
[4] Trenckner Ed., p. 327.

evidence of the coins similar to those of the earliest type of Athens which are known to have been collected from the North-Western Frontiers of India (*Numismatic Chronicle*, XX, 191; *J.R.A.S.*, 1895, 874). The Yavanas are classed with other peoples of Northern India (*Uttarāpatha*) like the Kāmbojas, Gandhāras, Kirātas and Barbaras (cf. *Mahābhārata*, XII, 207, 43). They are mentioned also in the *Bhāgavatapurāṇa* (II. 4, 18; 7, 34; IV. 72, 23; IX. 8, 5; 20, 30). They are referred to in Aśoka's Rock Edict V, and in the Nāgārjunikoṇḍa Inscriptions of Vīrapuruṣadatta. In R.E. V and XIII, the Yonas are mentioned along with the Kāmbojas (*Inscriptions of Aśoka* by Bhandarkar and Majumdar, 53-54). In the Nasik cave inscription of Vāśiṣṭhiputra Pulumāyi, Gautamīputra Śātakarṇi is extolled as the destroyer of the Śakas, Yavanas and Pahlavas (Parthians) and as the Sātavāhana king, who had exterminated the Kṣaharāta dynasty (B. C. Law, *Ujjayinī in Ancient India*, p. 18). The Yavana country is the same as Ionia of the Naqsh-i-Rustum Inscription of Darius. Not only the Yonas are mentioned in the Inscriptions of Aśoka, but also a Yavana official or a vassal Yavanarājā named Tuṣāspha ruled as governor of Surāṣṭra (Kāthiāwād) with his capital at Girinagara (Girnar) during the reign of Aśoka, as it is evident from the Junāgaḍh Rock Inscription of Mahākṣatrapa Rudradāman (about 150 A.D.). For further details, vide O. Stein, *Yavanas in Early Indian Inscriptions* in *I.C.*, Vol. I, pp. 343ff.; B. C. Law, *Tribes in Ancient India*, Chap. XXXI; B. C. Law, *Indological Studies*, Pt. I, 5ff. Bhandarkar points out that it is impossible to identify the Yonas of R.E. XIII with the Greeks of Bactria, because the same edict was promulgated when Antiochus Theos, king of Syria, was alive. He holds the view that in all likelihood the Yavanas of R.E. XIII must have come and settled in large numbers in some outlying provinces of India long before Alexander (*Carmichael Lectures*, 1921, 27, 28ff.). Such a view is also supported by numismatic evidence.

According to Patañjali's *Mahābhāṣya* (3. 3. 2, p. 246—Kielhorn's Ed.—*Arunad Yavanaḥ Sāketaṃ*; *Arunad Yavano Madhyamikāṃ*), Sāketa or Ayodhyā as well as Madhyamikā (near Chitor) were besieged by a certain Yavana or Greek. There was a conflict between the Śuṅga prince Vasumitra and the Yavana on the southern bank of the Sindhu. The extension of Yavana power to the interior of India was at first thwarted by the Śuṅgas. In western India the last vestiges of Yavana power were swept away by the rising ascendency of the Andhras or Sātavāhanas of the Deccan. In the north-west of India the Yavanas were finally swept away by the onrush of the Parthians.

Yāmadagni-āśrama.—This hermitage is situated in the district of Gazipur in the United Provinces. According to some it is said to have been situated at Khairadi, 36 miles north-west of Balia in the United Provinces.

Yugandhara.—According to the *Mahābhārata* (Virāṭaparva, Ch. I; Vanaparva, Ch. 128) this country which was near Kurukṣetra, appears to have been situated on the west bank of the Yamunā and south of Kurukṣetra.

Zeda.—It is a village near Und (Ohind) in the North-West Frontier Province (*E.I.*, XIX, p. 1).

CHAPTER II

SOUTHERN INDIA

Acyutapuraṃ.—It is near Mukhaliṅgaṃ in the Ganjam district, where plates of Indravarman were discovered. These plates record a gift of land, which was at Kalīṅganagaraṁ, by one of the kings of Kaliṅga of the Gaṅga family (*E.I.*, III, 127).

Adhirājendravaḷanāḍu.—It is the name of a district (*S.I.I.*, I, 134). It is in the Jayaṅkoṇḍa-śora-maṇḍalaṃ.

Agaiyāru.—It is the name of a river which passed through the village of Māndoṭṭam (*Ibid.*, II, 62).

Agastya-malai.—It is a hill in the Travancore State. The river Tāmraparṇi has its source on this hill (W. W. Hunter, *The Imperial Gazetteers of India*, Vol. I, p. 46).

Aimbuṇḍi.—It is the old name of the modern village of Ammuṇḍi (*S.I.I.*, I, pp. 87, 135, 136). A plot of land was given by the inhabitants of this place to their god Śiva.

Airāvaṭṭa.—This has been identified with Raṭāgarh in the Banki Police Station of the Cuttack district (*Bāripādā Museum Plate of Devānandadeva*; vide also *E.I.*, XXVII, Pt. VII, July, 1948, p. 328).

Ajantā.—The two caves of Ajantā are situated 60 miles north-west of Auraṅgabad and about 35 miles south of Bhusaval on the main railway. The caves of Ajantā are approached from Phardapur, a small town at the foot of the Ghāṭ. There is a good motorable road from Auraṅgabad to Phardapur. The 29 caves at Ajantā have been cut, carved and painted at different times. According to V. A. Smith, the bulk of the paintings at Ajantā must be assigned to the 6th century A.D. The resulting political conditions must have been unfavourable to the execution of costly work of art dedicated to the service of Buddhism. *Caitya* and *Vihāra* caves are the two types of caves found at Ajantā. The caves Nos. 9 and 10, which are the earliest, date back to the 1st and 2nd century B.C. The huge images of the Buddha found in the inner cells of the *Vihāras* are almost in the preaching attitude. The frescoes and paintings at Ajantā are the most important features of Buddhist architecture. Decorative painting and ceiling decorations are the earliest specimens of ancient Indian fine arts. The Jātaka scenes are well depicted in these caves. In the cave No. 26 the most notable sculpture on the walls is the large and crowded composition representing the temptation of the Buddha by Māra. The wheel of life, flying *Gandharvas* and *Apsarās* can be found here. The caves present a vivid picture of the feelings and aspirations of the Buddhists during the period to which they belong. Figures of birds, monkeys, wild tribes, etc., are all depicted in these caves. Rivers, seas, rocky shores, fishes, etc., have a very high artistic value. The majestic figure of the Buddha on the wall on the left of the corridor at the back has attracted universal appreciation. Palaces and buildings are represented by a flat roof over the heads of the figures supported by slender pillars. Men of higher rank wear little clothing above the waist, but much jewellery, armlets, necklaces, fillets, etc., and men of lower rank are more covered but they have no jewellery. Monks are clothed in their usual dress. Ladies of distinction wear much jewellery. In the cave No. 10, the paintings between the ribs of the aisles are of much later date. The cave No. 16

is one of the Vihāras of great importance. In the cave No. 20 the flight of steps with a carved balustrade leading to a verandah and the pillars with capitals of elegantly sculptured strut figures of girls, the threshold of the shrines recalling the ancient *toraṇa*, serve as aids to understand the evolution of domestic and socio-religio architecture of India. The portico in front of the shrine is similar to a pavilion (*maṇḍapa*). The group of worshippers in the cave No. 1 is really very artistic. Soldiers are armed with spears, bows, arrows, etc. A high turban with a knob in front is worn by males. A broad heavy neck-chain is prominent. All these remind us of the style of early sculptures of Sāñchī and of the oldest sculpture discovered at Mathurā.

Aḷanāḍu.—It is a sub-division of Arumoridevavaḷanāḍu (*S.I.I.*, Vol. II, pp. 333–456). Here was Rājacuḍāmaṇicaturvedimaṅgalaṃ (vide *Raṅgāchārī's List* 326, Madura District).

Amarakuṇḍa.—It is a town in Āndhra. Nearby there is a mountain on which stands a beautiful temple adorned with the images of Ṛṣabha and Śāntināthа. For further details, vide B. C. Law, *Some Jaina Canonical Sūtras*, p. 185.

Amarāvatī (Pali: Amaravatī).—This is the name of a town which contains the Amareśvara temple (*E.I.*, Vol. VII, p. 17). Its old name is Dhānyaghaṭa or Dhānyaghaṭaka, which is identical with Dhānyakaṭa or Dhānyakaṭaka (corn-town), (Hultzsch, *S.I.I.*, Vol. I, p. 25). It is noted for its stūpa (*E.I.*, VI, 146–157; cf. *C.I.*, VI, 17ff.). It was the capital of Aṃdhāpatiya (N. L. Dey, *Geog. Dic.*, p. 7). Buddha in one of his previous births was born in this city as a Brahmin youth named Sumedha (*Dhammapada-Aṭṭhakathā*, I, p. 83). This city may be identified with the modern city of Amaraoti close to the Dharaṇikoṭṭa river, a mile west of ancient Amarāvatī on the Kṛṣṇā, famous for its ruined stūpa. The Amarāvatī stūpa is found about 18 miles to the west of Bezwada and south of Dharaṇīkoṭa on the right bank of the river Kṛṣṇā, about 60 miles from its mouth in the Kṛṣṇā district of the Madras Presidency. The Amarāvatī tope was built by the Andhrabhṛtya kings who were Buddhists (*J.R.A.S.*, III, 132). The Amarāvatī caitya is the Pūrvaśaila monastery of Hiuen Tsang. For excavations at Amarāvatī, vide *A.S.I.R.*, 1905-6, 116ff.; *A.S.I.*, Annual Report, 1908-9, 88ff.

Ambattūr-nāḍu.—It is the name of a village in the Saidapet taluk of the Chingleput district (*S.I.I.*, Vol. III, p. 287).

Ambāsamudram.—It is situated on the northern bank of the Tāmraparṇī river and is the headquarters of the taluk of the same name in the Tinnevelly district. Iḷaṅgoykuḍḍi was the ancient name of Ambāsamudram. It was a *brahmadeya* in Muḷḷināḍu. (*Ambāsamudram Inscription of Varaguṇapāṇḍya*, *E.I.*, IX, 84; *E.I.*, XXV, Pt. I, pp. 35ff.).

Aṃdhāpatiya.—In the Mayidavolu Copperplate Inscription of the early Pallava king Śivaskandavarman occurs Aṃdhāpatiya (*Andhrāpatha*, *Ep. Indica*, VI, 88). The Sanskrit equivalent of the place-name may as well be Aṃdhāvatī. Aṃdhāpatiya or Andhrāpatha is the Andhra country between the Godāvarī and Kṛṣṇā, which is the eastern Andhra territory as distinguished from the Andhra dominions in western India (Hultzsch, *S.I.I.*, I, p. 113; for details vide Law, *Tribes in Ancient India*, pp. 164ff.). In the Pali texts the Andhakas are mentioned along with the Muṇḍakas, Kolakas and Cīnas (*Apadāna*, Pt. II, p. 359). The five Drāviḍas are the following: Drāviḍa proper (Tamil), Andhra (Telugu), Karṇāṭa (Kanarese country), Mahārāṣṭra and Gurjara. Dhanakaṭaka or Dhānyakaṭaka or Amarāvatī at the mouth of the Kṛṣṇā is its capital (N. L. Dey, *Geographical Dictionary*, p. 7). In the Harāhā Inscription of the Maukhari king Kumāragupta III (554 A.D.) a certain lord of the Andhras (*Andhrādhipati*) is said to have given the Maukhari king a great trouble by his 'thousands of threefold rutting elephants' (*Ep. Indica*, XIV, pp. 110ff.). H. C. Raychaudhuri suggests that the Andhra king referred to was probably Mādhavavarman I (Yanāśraya) of the Polamuru plates belonging to the Viṣṇukuṇḍin family (*P.H.A.I.*, 4th Ed., p. 509). This suggestion seems to have been in agreement with the fact that the Jaunpur Inscription of Īśvaravarman, father of Īśānavarman Maukhari, refers to the victory over the Andhras on behalf of Īśvaravarman (*C.I.I.*, III, p. 230). At the time of the Pallava king Śivaskandavarman, the Andhrāpatha or the Andhra country seems to have come under the sway of the Pallava dynasty whose headquarters were at Dhaṃnakaḍa (Dhānyakaṭaka). In the thirteenth Rock Edict of Aśoka occurs the expression *Bhoja-Patinikeṣu Aṃdhra-Palideṣu.*

The Pulindas of the Andhra region are always associated with the Andhras who probably inhabited the whole land from the Vindhya to the Kṛṣṇā. Vāśiṣṭhīputra Pulumāyi was the first king who extended Sātavāhana power over the Andhra country. Stray references to the Andhra country and people are found in the later epigraphic records. The Indian Museum Inscription of the 9th year of Nārāyaṇapāladeva of the Pāla dynasty refers to the Andhra Vaiṣayika Śākyabhikṣu sthavira Dharmamitra who erected an image of the Buddha.

Ammalapuṇḍi.—This village may probably be identified with Anamarlapūṇḍiagrahāraṃ, 12 miles to the south-east of Tāḍikoṇḍa (*E.I.*, XXIII, Pt. V).

Anadutpālīcala.—This is a hill (*S.I.I.*, II, 373).

Anamalai Hills.—They merge into the Travancore hills (*The Imperial Gazetteers of India*, by W. W. Hunter, Vol. I, pp. 190ff.).

Anantapura.—It is situated in Trivandrum, the capital of Travancore, which contains the celebrated temple of Padmanātha, which was visited by Śrīcaitanya and Nityānanda.

Andhramaṇḍala or Andhraviṣaya.—Telegu country (*S.I.I.*, III, p. 128). The Mayidāvolu plates of the early Pallava ruler Śivaskandavarman prove that the Andhrāpatha or the region of the Andhras embraced the Kriṣṇā district with Dhaññakaḍa or Bezwada as its capital (*E.I.*, VI, p. 88). In the Harāhā Inscription of Maukhari king Kumāragupta III (554 A.D.) a certain lord of the Andhras (Andhrādhipati) is said to have troubled the Maukhari king (*Ep. Ind.* XIV, pp. 110ff.). The Andhra king referred to was probably Mādhavavarman I Yavāśraya of the Polamuru plates belonging to the Viṣṇukuṇḍin family. This is supported by the fact that the Jaunpur Inscription of Īśvaravarman, father of Īśānavarman Maukhari, refers to the victory over the Andhras on behalf of Īśvaravarman (*C.I.I.*, III, p. 230). The Andhras are mentioned in the *Aitareya Brāhmaṇa* (VII, 18) and the *Śatapatha Brāhmaṇa.* V. A. Smith holds that they were a Dravidian people and were the progenitors of the modern Telugu-speaking people occupying the deltas of the Godāvarī and the Kṛṣṇā (*I.A.*, 1913, 276–8). According to some they were originally a Vindhyan tribe that extended its political power from the west gradually to the east down the Godāvarī and the Kṛṣṇā valleys (*Ibid.*, 1918, 71). The *Mahābhārata* (XII, 207, 42) points out that they were settled in the Deccan. The *Rāmāyaṇa* (Kiṣkindhyākāṇḍa, 41, Ch. 11) connects them with the Godāvarī. The epigraphic evidence proves that they occupied the Godāvarī-Kṛṣṇā valley. The *Mārkaṇḍeya Purāṇa* (LVII, 48-49) mentions the Andhras as a southern people. The R.E. XIII of Aśoka mentions the country of the Andhras as a vassal state under Aśoka. There is a reference to the Andhra country in a *Jātaka* (*Jāt.*, I, 356ff.) where a Brahmin youth came after completing his education at Taxila to profit by practical experience. According to Pliny the Andhras possessed a large number of villages, 30 towns defended by walls and towers, and supplied their king with a huge army consisting of infantry, cavalry and elephants (*I.A.*, 1877, 339).

The Sātavāhanas are claimed by the *Purāṇas* to have been Andhras or Andhrabhṛtyas. They ruled even the whole of Andhradeśa and the adjoining regions (B. C. Law, *Tribes in Ancient India*, 164-5).

This country as known to the Chinese as An-ta-lo was about 3,000 li in circuit. The soil was rich and fertile. It was regularly cultivated. The temperature was hot. The people were fierce and impulsive. There were some *Saṅghārāmas* and *Deva temples* (Beal, *Buddhist Records of the Western World*, II, 217-18).

The capital of the Andhradeśa seems to have been Dhanakaṭaka which was visited by Yuan Chwang. The earliest Andhra capital (Andhapura) was situated on the Telavāha river, probably identical with Tel or Telingiri, both flowing near the confines of the Madras State and the Madhya Pradeśa (*P.H.A.I.*, p. 196, f.n. 4). For further details, vide B. C. Law, *Indological Studies*, Pt. I, pp. 47ff.; Law, *Tribes in Ancient India*, p. 166; *Imperial Gazetteers of India* (W. W. Hunter), Vol. I, p. 198; *Buddhist remains in Andhra and Andhra History*, 225–610 A.D. by K. R. Subramanian.

Aṅgarāyankuppam.—This is the modern village of Aṅgaraṅkuppam, six miles north of Viriñcipuram (*S.I.I.*, I, p. 133).

Aṅgāra.—A southern country mentioned in the *Brahmāṇḍap.*, II, 16. 59.

Annadevavaram.—This village founded for the habitation of the Brahmins is said to have been situated at Visari-nāṇḍu at the junction of the Pinnasāni and the Gaṅgā (another name of the Godāvarī) (*E.I.*, XXVI, Pt. I, January, 1941).

Annavaram.—It is near Tuni in the east Godāvarī district, where the Rajahmundry Museum plates of the Telugu Coḍa Annadeva were discovered (*E.I.*, XXVI, Pt. I, January, 1941).

Antaravedī.—It forms the last of the seven sacred places on the Godāvarī (*Imperial Gazetteers of India*, by W. W. Hunter, Vol. I, p. 204).

Aragiyasorapuram.—It is a sub-division of Rājarājavaḷanāḍu. It is a village in Poyirkūrram (*S.I.I.*, II, pp. 449, 492).

Araiśūr.—It is the name of a village on the banks of the Pennar (*Ibid.*, III, 448).

Arakatapura.—It may be the same as modern Arcot. It was conquered by King Khāravela as we learn from the Hāthigumphā Inscription (B. C. Law, *Geography of Early Buddhism*, pp. 61-62).

Araśil.—It is the name of a river. It is also known as Ariśil of Araśileiyāru (*S.I.I.*, II, p. 52).

Arikamedu.—It is on the east coast of India, two miles south of Pondicherry. Some places at the site were excavated by the *A.S.I.*, in 1945.

Arugūr.—This is modern Ariyūr (*Ibid.*, I, p. 71) near Velūr.

Arumadal.—It is a village. Its modern name is Arumadal. It was in Kirśengilināḍu, a sub-division of Pāṇḍyakulāśanivaḷanāḍu (*Ibid.*, Vol. II, p. 479).

Asaka.—It is generally supposed to be identical with Aśmaka on the Godāvarī (Shāma Śāstrī's Tr. of the *Arthaśāstra*, p. 143).

Assaka or Aśmaka Country.—The Assaka or Aśmaka country is mentioned in the *Suttanipāta* (P.T.S., p. 190) as situated on the bank of the river Godāvarī immediately to the south of Patiṭṭhāna (v. 977). Dr. Bhandarkar points out that according to the *Suttanipāta* a Brahmin guru called Bāvarī having left the Kośala country settled near a village on the Godāvarī in the Assaka territory in the Dakṣiṇāpatha (*Carmichael Lectures*, 1918, pp. 4, 53, f.n. 5). Rhys Davids points out that Aśmaka was situated immediately north-west of Avantī. The settlement on the Godāvarī, according to him, was a later colony (*Buddhist India*, pp. 27-28). Asaṅga in his *Sūtrālaṅkāra* mentions an Aśmaka country in the basin of the Indus.

According to Kauṭilya's *Arthaśāstra* Assaka (Asaka) is generally supposed to be identical with Aśmaka on the Godāvarī, i.e., Mahārāṣṭra (Shama Śāstrī's transl., p. 143, n. 2). The Aśmakas fought on the side of the Pāṇḍavas in the Kurukṣetra war (*Mahābhārata*, VII, 85, 3049). Pāṇini mentions Aśmaka in one of his *sūtras* (IV, 1, 173). There was a connection between the Ikṣvākus and the Aśmakas (*Bṛhannāradīya Purāṇa*, Ch. 9).

The capital city of the Aśmakas or Assakas was Potana or Potali, the Paudanya of the *Mahābhārata* (I, 77, 47). At one time the city of Potali was included in the kingdom of Kāśī. According to the *Assaka-Jātaka* (*Jāt.*, II, 155) there was a king named Assaka who reigned in Potali which is stated therein to be a city in the kingdom of Kāśī.

The people called Aspasians by the Greeks may be regarded as denoting some western branch of the well-known Aśvaka or Aśmaka-tribe. The Iranian name Aspa corresponds to Sanskrit Aśva or Aśvaka (*C.H.I.*, Vol.I, p. 352, n. 3; B. C. Law, *Indological Studies*, Part I, pp. 1-2; Law, *Tribes in Ancient India*, pp. 180ff.).

Atri-āśrama.—This hermitage was visited by Rāma with Lakṣmaṇa and Sītā, while the sage was living there with Anusūyā. Many hermits were engaged in spiritual practices there.

Attili.—This town is at present situated in the south-west of the Tanuku taluk of the west Godāvarī district. The Coḍa king Annadeva defeated on the borders of Attili all the southern kings, who were hostile to him, and offered protection to 10,000 of the enemy's forces who took refuge within the walls of that town (*E.I.*, XXVI, Pt. I).

Ayodhyā.—This is the name of a country (*S.I.I.*, I, p. 58). Fifty-nine emperors sat on the throne of Ayodhyā. Vijayāditya, a king of this family, went to the Deccan to conquer it.

Ayyampalayam.—This village is in the Palladam taluk of the Coimbatore district, about 4½ miles to the north-east of the Somanur railway station, containing a small shrine (*Journal of the Indian Society of Oriental Art*, Vol. XV).

Adhirājamaṅgalliyapuram.—It is Tiruvādi in the Cuddalore taluk. It is 14 miles west by north of Cuddalore and one mile south of Panruti railway station. It is also called Adigaimānagar. It is situated on the north bank of the Geḍilam (*E.I.*, XXVII, Pt. III, p. 98).

Adipur.—It is a village in the Pāñcapir sub-division of Mayurbhanj State (*E.I.*, XXV, Pt. IV, p. 147).

Ālampuṇḍi.—It is a village in the Señji division of the Tiṇḍivanam taluk of the South Arcot district (*E.I.*, III, 224).

Ālappakkam.—It is a village in the Cuddalore taluk of the South Arcot district (*E.I.*, XXVII, Pt. III, p. 97).

Ālūr.—This village is in Padināḍu and may be identical with Ālūr in the Cāmarājanagar taluk in the Mysore district (*S.I.I.*, Vol. II, pp. 425–7).

Āmūr (*Āmbūr*).—This is a town in the Velūr taluk of the North Arcot district (*Ibid.*, Vol. III, p. 165). It is in the Tirukkoyilur taluk of South Arcot district. Two Tamil inscriptions were discovered here (*E.I.*, IV, 180ff.).

Āmurkoṭṭam.—It is a district (*Ibid.*, Vol. II, Intro. p. 28) in Jayakoṇḍacoḷamaṇḍalam.

Ānaimalai.—This is a sacred hill in the Madurā district (*Ibid.*, III, p. 239). It is known as the 'elephant hill'. It runs from north-east to south-west nearly parallel to the Madura-Melur road from the 5th mile-stone from Madura (*Madras Dist. Gazetteers, Madura*, by W. Francis, pp. 254ff.).

Ānandūru.—It is the headquarters of the Ānandūru Three Hundred (district) mentioned in the Akkalkot Inscription of Śilāhara Indarasa (*E.I.* XXVII, Pt. II, April, 1947, p. 71). It may be identified with modern Ānadūru, chief town of the taluk of that name in the Usmanabad district in the Hyderabad State. It is about 20 miles to the north of Akkalkoṭ.

Anāṅgur.—It is two miles south-east of Villupuram (*E.I.*, XXVII, Pt. III, p. 98). It must have been the principal place in Ānāṅgur-nāḍu.

Āndhra.—This is present Telugu country (*Ibid.*, Vol. II, Intro., p. 4).

Ānnadevavaraṃ.—It was a village on the bank of the Gaṅgā to the west of Pallūri-Śailavaraṃ. King Annadeva granted this village to the Brāhmaṇas (*E.I.*, XXVI, Pt. I—*Rajahmundry Museum plates of Telugu Coḍa Annadeva*).

Ārāma.—It was not far from Sonepur where the royal camp was often pitched. It is described to be a prosperous city with palatial buildings, temples, gardens, tanks, etc., (*E.I.*, XXIII, Pt. VII).

Āsuvulaparru.—This village stood on the Kṛṣṇā river in Bezwada taluk (*E.I.*, XXIII, Pt. V).

Āvūrkuṟṟaṃ.—It is a district, a sub-division of Nittavinodavaḷanāḍu (*S.I.I.*, Vol. II, p. 95).

Badakhimedi.—It is in the Ganjam district. In a village of this estate a set of copperplates of Gaṅga Indravarman were found (*E.I.*, XXVI, Pt. V, October, 1941, p. 165).

Baṅgavāḍi.—It is in the Kolar district of the Mysore State (*E.I.*, VI, 22ff.; vide also *E.I.*, VII, 22).

Basinikoṇḍa.—It is a village near Madanapalle (*E.I.*, XXIV, Pt. IV, 183ff.—*Three Inscriptions of Vaidumba-Mahārāja Gaṇḍatrinetra*).

Bavāji Hill—It is situated near Velapādi, a suburb of Vellore in the North Arcot district (*S.I.I.*, Vol. I, p. 76). A rock inscription of Kannaradeva has been found below the summit of this hill (*E.I.*, IV, 81ff.).

Bādāmi.—It is a village. It is also called Vātāpi (*S.I.I.*, Vol. II, p. 399, n. 504). Siruttoṇḍar invaded it in 650 B.C.

Bāhūr.—It is the modern name of the village called Aragiyaśora-caturvedimaṅgalaṃ, same as Bāhugrāma. It is near Pondicherry. It is included in the district of Aruvā-nāḍu. The village of Bāhūr is the headquarters of a commune in the French territory and was the site of a battle between the English and the French in 1752 A.D. (*Ibid.*, Vol. II, pp. 27 (Intro), 505, 513, 514, 519). It is in the French territory (Vide *Raṅgāchāri's List*, pp. 1693-94, 1-18).

Beḷuguḷa.—The Kap Copperplate of Keladi Sadāśiva-Nāyaka refers to Beḷuguḷa which is Śravaṇa Belgola in the Mysore State.

Bharaṇipāḍu.—Kāmarāja, a Coḍa king, subdued king Simga near this town in a battle (*E.I.*, XXVI, Pt. I).

Bhāgīrathī.—This is the same as the river Gaṅgā (Hultzsch, *S.I.I.*, Vol. I, p. 28).

Bhāskarakṣetra.—It is Hampi in the Bellary district, which was the capital of the Vijayanagar kings (*E.I.*, XXV, Pt. IV, October, 1939, p. 190).

Bheṭhiśṛṅga.—It is mentioned in the Indian Museum plates of Gaṅga Indravarman, which may possibly be identified with Barsinga on the Brāhmaṇī river (*E.I.*, XXVI, Pt. V, October, 1941, p. 168).

Bhīmarathī (or Bhīmaratha).—The river Bhīmarathī, mentioned in the Daulatabad plates of the Western Cālukya king Jayasiṃha II, may be identified with the modern Bhīmā, the main tributary of the Kṛṣṇā (*I.C.*, VIII, p. 113). On the north bank of this river a battle was fought between Pulakeśin and Appāyika and Govinda (*E.I.*, VI, 9). The *Vāyu* (XLV, 104) and *Varāha Purāṇas* mention this river. It figures prominently as a Sahya river in the Purāṇas, which appears to flow in the north-western portion of the district of Poona, from which place it takes a south-easterly course and flows into the Kṛṣṇā north of the district of Raichur, Hyderabad. It is fed by many streams (vide B. C. Law, *Rivers of India*, p. 49).

Bhogavaḍhana (Skt. Bhogavardhana, the wealth-increaser; Barua and Sinha, *Barhut Inscriptions*, p. 15).—According to the Purāṇas, it is one of the countries in the Deccan. It seems that Bhogavardhana was situated in the Godāvarī region but the location of the place is unknown. The Bhogavardhanas (Bhogavaḍam) are placed in the southern region along with the Maulikas, Aśmakas, Kuntalas, etc. (cf. *Mārkaṇḍeya Purāṇa*, LVII, 48-49).

Bhojakaṭa and Bhojakaṭapura (Skt.: Bhojakaṭa or Bhojya; Bhojya; Barua and Sinha, *Barhut Inscriptions*, p. 7).—The Arulala-Perumal Inscription and the Raṅganātha Inscription of Ravivarman refer to a Bhoja king belonging to the Yadu family of the Kerala country in South India (*E.I.*, Vol. IV, Pt. III, 146). The Khalimpur grant of Dharmapāladeva of Gauḍa (*c.* 800 A.D.) speaks of the king of Bhoja along with the kings of Matsya, Kuru, Yadu and Yavana as having uttered benedictions at the coronation ceremony of the king of Kānyakubja. The next important mention of the Bhojas is made in the Hāthigumphā Inscription of the Ceṭa King Khāravela (1st century B.C.), which informs us that Khāravela, the Mahārājā of Kaliṅga, defeated the Rāṭhikas and Bhojakas and compelled them to do homage to him. The Rāṭhikas and Bhojakas are evidently the Rāṣṭrikas and Bhojas of Aśoka's Rock Edicts V and XIII (vide B. C. Law, *Tribes in Ancient India*, p. 372). The R.E. XIII refers to the Bhojas and Pitinikas who held the present Thānā and Kolābā districts of the Bombay Presidency. The Sabhāparva of the *Mahābhārata* (Ch. 30) mentions Bhojakaṭa and Bhojakaṭapura as two places in the south conquered by Sahadeva. If Bhojakaṭa be the same as Bhoja and Bhojya of the *Purāṇas*, then it must be a country of the Vindhya region. The expression Daṇḍakyabhoja in the *Brāhmaṇas* may indicate that this Bhojakaṭa was either included in or within the reach of Daṇḍaka. It is clear from the *Mahābhārata* list that Bhojakaṭa (= Elichpur) was distinct from Bhojakaṭapura or Bhojapura, the second capital of Vidarbha (modern Berar). Bhoja coincides with Berar or ancient Vidarbha and Chammaka, four miles south-east of Elichpur in the Amaraoti district. In the *Khila-Harivaṃśa*, Bhojakaṭa is expressly identified with Vidarbha (cf. *Viṣṇupurāṇa*, LX, 32). In the Barhut Votive label No. 45 occurs Bhojakaṭa (Barua and Sinha, *Barhut Inscriptions*, p. 131). Aśoka's R.E. XIII refers to the Bhojas, Pārimdas or Pāladas. Bhoja is mentioned in the *Ṛgveda*

(II, 53, 7) as well as in the *Aitareya Brāhmaṇa* (VIII, 14). The *Śatapatha Brāhmaṇa* (XIII, 5, 4, 11) seems to imply that the Sātvatas were located near the Gaṅgā and the Yamunā, which locality was the realm of the Bharatas. The Bhojas spread over central and southern India in very early times. According to the *Purāṇas* the Bhojas and the Sātvatas were allied tribes both belonging to the Yadu family (*Matsya Purāṇa*, Ch. 43, p. 48; Ch. 44, pp. 46–8, *Vāyu Purāṇa*, Ch. 94, p. 52; Ch. 95, p. 18; Ch. 96 pp. 1-2; *Viṣṇu Purāṇa*, IV, 13, 1–6). The descendants of Sātvata, son of Mahābhoja, were known as Bhojas (*Bhāgavata Purāṇa*, Ch. IX, p. 24; *Kūrma Purāṇa*, Ch. 24, śl. 40; *Harivaṃśa*, Ch. 37). The Bhojas were related to the Haihayas who were a branch of the Yādavas (*Agni Purāṇa*, Ch. 275, śl. 10; *Vāyu Purāṇa*, Ch. 94, pp. 3–54; *Matsya Purāṇa* Ch. 43, pp. 7–49). The Jain sacred books refer to the Bhojas as Kṣatriyas (*Jaina Sūtras*, *S.B.E.*, II, p. 71, f.n. 2). The Bhojas along with the Andhakas and Kukuras helped the Kurus in the Kurukṣetra war (*Mahābhārata*, Udyogaparva, Ch. 19). They were associated with the Śriñjayas and the Cedis (*Mahābhārata*, V. 28). The Jaina *Uttarādhyayana-Cūrṇī* (2, p. 53) mentions that a ruler of Ujjenī came to Bhogakaḍa after becoming an ascetic. For further details, vide B. C. Law, *Indological Studies*, Pt. I, pp. 43ff.; Law, *Tribes in Ancient India*, pp. 366ff.

Bhuvaneśvara.—It is a village in the Khurda sub-division, 18 miles south of Cuttack and 30 miles north of Puri town. It is mostly inhabited by the Hindus. It is built on rocky soils composed of laterites overlying small mounds of sandstone. On account of the exposed rocks in the neighbourhood of the place, it becomes hot in summer. This place is not only holy but very healthy, situated on the Balianti river. It enjoys a mild but bracing winter and is not unpleasant during the rains. It is full of nux vomica trees. There are many tanks, some of which may be mentioned, namely, Kedārgaurī near Kedāreśvara, Brahmagaurī near Brahmeśvara, Kapilahrada outside the Kapileśvara temple. The biggest of the tanks is Vindusāgara. The water of the Kedārgaurī tank is quite good for dyspepsia. The Liṅgarāja temple which is the main temple, is unique from the architectural standpoint. Liṅgarāja is otherwise called Bhuvaneśvara or Tribhuvaneśvar. The probable date of its construction is Śaka 588 (A.D. 666-7). Yayāti Keśarī began the construction of the temple, which was completed by Lalāṭa Keśarī. It covers an area of 4½ acres and is surrounded by a high thick wall of laterite and oblong in shape. A courtyard inside is flagged with stone and is crowded with 60 or 70 side temples. The temple of Bhagavatī, wife of Śiva, in the north-west corner is important. The main temple consists of four structures, namely, the dancing hall, the refectory hall, the porch and the tower.

At Bhuvaneśvara there stands the Paraśurāmeśvara temple, which according to some, has been dated the 5th or 6th century A.D. (M. M. Ganguli, *Orissa and her Remains*, 270ff.). Scholars differ as to the date of this temple (vide *J.R.A.S.B.*, XV, No. 2, 1949, Letters, 109ff.). The Udyotakeśarin of the Bhuvaneśvara Inscription has been identified with the prince of the same name whose inscriptions have been discovered in Orissa in the Lalatendu Keśarī and Navamuni caves (*E.I.*, XIII, 165-66). The Bhuvaneśvara Stone Inscription of Narasiṃha I of the 12th century A.D. refers to the building of a Viṣṇu temple by Candrikā, sister of Narasiṃha, at Ekāmra or modern Bhuvaneśvara in the Utkalaviṣaya (*Brahmapurāṇa*, Ch. 40). The Bhuvaneśvara Stone Inscription incised on a slab of stone is on the western wall of the courtyard of the temple of Ānanda Vāsudeva at Bhuvaneśvara in the Puri district (*E.I.*, XIII, 198–203).

For further details, vide Law, *Geographical Essays*, p. 218; *B. and O. Dist. Gazetteers*, Puri, by O'Malley, revised by Mansfield, 1929, pp. 265ff.; *Bengal Dist. Gazetteers*, 1908, Puri, by L. S. S. O'Malley, pp. 234ff.; K. C. Panigrahi, *New light on the early History of Bhubaneśvara* (*Journal of the Asiatic Society, Letters*, Vol. XVII, No. 2, 1951, pp. 95ff.).

Birajākṣetra.—According to the *Brahmapurāṇa* (42. 1–4), it contains the deity named Birajā. It is on the sacred river Vaitaraṇī. The temple of Birajā is situated at Jājpur. There are eight holy places in this kṣetra, e.g., Kapila, Gograha, Soma, Mṛtyuñjaya, Siddheśvara, etc. (*Brahma-purāṇa*, 42. 6-7). The *Yoginītantra* mentions it (2. 2, p. 120).

Bobbili.—It is in the Vizagapatam district of the newly founded Andhra State (*E.I.*, XXVII, Pt. I, p. 33).

Bommehāḷu.—It may be identified with Bommeparti, situated at a distance of seven miles from Anantapura (*E.I.*, XXV, Pt. IV, p. 190).

Brahmagiri.—For details, vide *Half Yearly Journal of the Mysore University*, Sec. A, I, 1940. In it a survey of the site is given before the excavation has been made. A set of Minor Rock Edicts of Aśoka has been discovered here.

Buguḍa.—It is in the Gumsūr taluk of the Ganjam district (*E.I.*, III, p. 41).

Candaka.—It is a mountain near the Mahiṃsaka kingdom, where the Bodhisatta built a leaf-hut at the bend of the river Kannapeṇṇā. It is the Malaya-giri or the Malabar ghats.

Candanapurī.—It is the modern Candanpurī, a small town on the Girṇā river, three miles to the south-west of Malegaum, about 45 miles to the north-west of Ellora (*E.I.*, XXV, Pt. I, January, 1939, p. 29).

Candāura.—This capital city may be identified with modern Candāvar, situated in the Honavar taluk and about five miles south-east of Kumta, north Kanara district (*North Kanara Gazetteer*, Pt. II, p. 277; *E.I.*, XXVII, Pt. IV, p. 160).

Candragiri.—It is a hill at Śravaṇa-Belgola, the well-known Jaina town in the Hassan district of the Mysore State (*E.I.*, III, 184). It was known to the ancients as *Deya Durgā*.

Candravalli.—It was situated at a distance of 45 miles to the south-west of Brahmagiri. For details of the excavations at the site, vide M. H. Krishna, *Excavations at Chandravalli* (*Supplement to the Annual Report of the Archaeological Dept. of the Mysore State*, 1929).

Cape Comorin (Skt. Kanyākumārī).—Its Tamil name is Kanni Kumārī or Kanniya Kumārī (*E.I.*, II, p. 236 f.n. 3), famous in early Tamil classics.

Cauduar.—The extensive ruins of Cauduar spread on the northern bank of the Birupa, a branch of the Mahānadī about four miles to the north of Cuttack. Jayakeśarin, the 25th King of the Keśarin dynasty, made Cauduar or the city with four gates his capital. It was once a śaiva centre. Buddhism flourished side by side with Śaivism at Cauduar. A seated image of Prajñāpāramitā with a smiling face has been discovered here. A seated image of two-armed Avalokiteśvara has been acquired from this place for the Indian Museum. Most of the sculptures found here seem to mark the initial stage of the later mediaeval sculptures of Orissa. For further details, vide R. P. Chanda, *Exploration in Orissa*, *M.A.S.I.*, No. 44, pp. 20ff.

Cārāla.—It is in the Punganur taluk of the Chittoor district (*E.I.*, XXV, Pt. VI, p. 241).

Cebrolu.—It is in the Bāpatlā taluk of the Kistna district (*E. I.*, V, 142ff.).

Cellūr.—It is the name of a village in the Coconada taluk of the Godāvarī district (*S.I.I.*, I, pp. 50, 51). A copperplate grant of Viṣṇuvardhanavīra-coḍa, now in the Madras Museum, throws light on the connection between the eastern Cālukyas and the Coḷas.

Cellūru.—This is a modern village of Cellūr (*Ibid.*, I, p. 52, f.n. 3).

Cendalur.—It is in the Ongole taluk of the Nellore district, where some copperplates of Sarvalokāśraya, dated 673 A.D., were discovered (*E.I.*, VIII, 236ff.).

Cera.—This country comprised present Malabar, Cochin and Travancore (*S.I.I.*, Vol. II, p. 21). Cera is a corruption of Kerala. The people of Kerala are known as the Kairalaka (*Bṛhat-Saṃhitā*, XIV, 12). Originally its capital was Vañji, now Tiru-Karūr on the Periyār river near Cochin, and its later capital was Tiruvañjikkalaṃ near the mouth of the Periyār. It had important trading centres on the western coast at Toṇḍi on the Agalappulai about five miles north of Quilandi, Muchiri, Palaiyur (near Chowghāṭ) and Vaikkarai. After the Coḷas the Ceras became the leading power in the south. Keralaputra finds mention in Aśoka's R.E. II. The Tamil kingdom of Chera is mentioned in the Sanskrit Epics and *Purāṇas*. (*Mahābhārata*, IX. 352, 365; Sabhāparva, XXX, pp. 1174-75; *Rāmāyaṇa*, IV, Ch. 41 (Bombay Edition); *Mārkaṇḍeya Purāṇa*, Ch. 57, 45; *Vāyu Purāṇa*, XLV, 124; *Matsya Purāṇa*, CXIII, 46). For further details, vide B. C. Law, *Tribes in Ancient India*, 193ff.

Cerāṃ.—This village in Pulināḍu may be identified with Cārāla in the Puṅgānur taluk of the Chittoor district (*E.I.*, XXV, Pt. VI, April, 1940, p. 254).

Cerupūru.—This village may be identified with the modern Chipurupalle in the Vizagapatam district. Some think it to be identical with Cerupūru of the Chipurupalle copperplate of Viṣṇuvardhana I, situated in the Plakiviṣaya.

Cevūru.—This village lies in the Kaikalūr taluk of the Kistna district, where a set of copperplates was discovered (*E.I.*, XXVII, Pt. I, p. 41).

Cidambaram.—It is situated between the Velar on the north, the Bay of Bengal on the east, the Coleroon on the sŏuth, and the Vīraṇam tank on the west. This is a town in the South Arcot district (*S.I.I.*, Vol. I, pp. 64, 86, 92, 97, 98, 168), noted for its temples.[1] Śirrambalam is the Tamil name of Cidambaram. It is also known as Tillai (*Ibid.*, II, pp. 258, 279, etc.) and as Cidambalam according to the *Devī-Bhāgavata* (VIII, 38). It was a subsidiary capital of the Coḷas, many of whom had their coronations performed in the sacred hall of the temple. It played an important part in the Carnatic and Mysore wars. South India has five elementary images of Mahādeva, one of which is the sky image (*vyoma*) at Cidambaram. The idol of Naṭarāja (the dancing attitude of Śiva) is the most important. According to the *Liṅgapurāṇa* (Uttara, Ch. 12), Śiva has eight images of which five are elementary.

Cidivalasa.—It is near Narasannapeta in the Ganjam district, near which three plates were found (*E.I.*, XXVII, Pt. III, p. 108).

Cikmagalur.—It is the headquarters town of the Kaḍur district and the Cikmagalur taluk of that district in Mysore (*E.I.*, VIII, 50ff.).

Cingleput.—This is the name of a district (*S.I.I.*, Vol. II, p. 340) of which Cingleput is the headquarters.

Cirāpalli.—It is the ancient name of Trichinopoly (*Annual Report for* 1937-38 *of South Indian Epigraphy*, p. 78).

---

[1] Chidambaram, by L. N. Gubil, *Modern Review*, LXXI, 1942.

Cittāmūr.—It is in the Gingee taluk of the South Arcot district, containing two Jain temples (*Annual Report for* 1937-38 *of south Indian Epigraphy*, 109).

Coḷa.—The Coḷa country (Śoramaṇḍalam) includes the Tanjore, and Trichinopoly districts (*S.I.I.*, I, pp. 32, 51, 59, 60, 79, 92, 96, 97, 100, 111, 112, 118, 134, 135, 139, etc.). It was watered by the river Kāverī (*Ibid.*, Vol. II, pp. 21, Introduction, and 503). The Coḷa kingdom stretched along the eastern coast from the river Penner to the Vellar and on the west reaching to about the borders of Coorg. It included the modern districts of Trichinopoly and Tanjore and part of Pudukkottah State (K. A. Nilkanta Śāstrī, *The Coḷas*, Ch. II, p. 22). Its capital was Uraiyūr (Old Trichinopoly) which corresponds to Sanskrit Uragapura. Daṇḍin in his *Kāvyādarśa* (III, 166—Rāmacandra Tarkavāgīśa's Ed.) mentions Coḷa country but the commentator includes it in Karṇāṭa. The country of Coḷa known to the Chinese as Chūlli-ye was about 2,400 li in circuit. The population was very small. It was deserted and wild. The climate was hot, and the people were dissolute and cruel. They were fierce by nature. There were some *saṅghārāmas* in ruins and deva temples (Beal, *Buddhist Records of the Western World*, II, 227). Rājarāja desirous of the Coḷa kingdom conferred the Veṅgī country on his paternal uncle Vijayāditya. The origin of the name Coḷa is uncertain. The name Coḷa indicated from the earliest times the people as well as the country subject to the Coḷa dynasty of rulers. The Coḷa kings were alleged to belong to the tribe of Tiraiyar or 'men of the sea'. Ptolemy refers to the kingdom of Sora (Coḷa) ruled by Arkatos, and the kingdom of Malanga ruled by Bassaronagas. Ptolemy calls the Coḷas by the name of Soringae whose capital was Orthoura (McCrindle, *Ancient India as described by Ptolemy*, Majumdar Ed., pp. 64-65, 185-186). Pāṇini mentions Coḷa in his *Aṣṭādhyāyī* (4. 1. 175). Aśoka's Rock Edicts II and XIII mention the Coḷas along with others as forming outlying provinces (*Pracaṃta*) outside his empire. The *Rāmāyaṇa* (IV, Ch. 41, Bom. Ed.), the *Mārkaṇḍeya* (Ch. 57, v. 45), the *Vāyu* (Ch. 45, v. 124) and *Matsya* (Ch. 112, v. 46) refer to Coḷas. The *Bṛhatsaṃhitā* (XIV. 13) mentions it as a country. The early history of the Coḷa country is obscure.

According to the *Mahāvaṃsa* (166, 197ff.) the Damiḷas who once invaded Laṅkā came from the Coḷa country. The Coḷas are mentioned in the *Vārttikas* of Kātyāyana. Coḷa is Tamil Sora, and is probably identical with Sora of Ptolemy (cf. *Sora Regia Arcati*). The Coḷa capital was Uraiyur (Uragapura), and their principal port was at Kāviripaṭṭanaṃ or Pugār on the north bank of the Kāverī. For further details, vide B. C. Law, *Tribes in Ancient India*, pp. 186ff.

Coleroon (Koḷḷidaṃ).—It is the name of a river (*S.I.I.*, Vol. II, pp. 60 and 282 f.n.) which passes the village of Settimaṅgalaṃ. It issues from Trichinopoly and falls into the Bay below Porto Novo.

Conjeevaraṃ.—It is the modern name of the village Kaccī or Kāñcī or Kāñcīpura (*Ibid.*, II, p. 259 f.n.). Patañjali in his *Mahābhāṣya* (IV. 1. 4; IV. 2. 2) mentions Kāñcīpura. It was one of the notable centres of Buddhist learning in South India (B. C. Law, *Geographical Essays*, I, pp. 79-80). This ancient place in South India is divided into two parts: Śivakāñcī and Viṣṇukāñcī. Some have divided it into three parts: Large Kāñcī, Small Kāñcī and Pilayar Koliyam. The temple at Śivakāñcī is the most ancient, and the temple at Viṣṇukāñcī was built later. The city of Kāñcī was influenced by Śaivism, Buddhism and Jainism. The Kāmākṣī temple at Conjeevaram is the most important. In the temple of Kailāsanāth there is a figure of Ardhanārīśvara. In the temple of Kacchapeśvara, Viṣṇu in the form of Kūrma is shown worshipping Śiva. There are many Viṣṇu temples. In the western part of the town which is called Viṣṇu-Conjeevaram various forms of Viṣṇu are depicted in sculptures in the temple of Baikuṇṭha-perumāl.

Cranganore.—It is the modern name of the village called Koḍuṅgolūr (*S.I.I.*, Vol. II, p. 4, Intro.). It is known as the capital of the ancient Ceras.

Daḍigamaṇḍala.—Fleet thinks that Taḍigaipāḍi may probably be identical with Daḍigamaṇḍala (*Ibid.*, Vol. II, p. 3, Intro.; cf. *Indian Antiquary*, Vol. XXX, pp. 109ff.).

Daḍigavāḍi.—It is an ancient district identical with Taḍigaipāḍi located in the Mysore district (*S.I.I.*, Vol. II, p. 3, Intro.).

Dakṣiṇa Jhārakhaṇḍa.—The Kendupatna copperplate grant of Narasiṃhadeva II refers to Dakṣiṇa Jhārakhaṇḍa, the northern portion of which covers the Ganjam Agency. It is also known as the Mahākāntāra in the Allahabad Praśasti of Samudragupta who came into conflict with its chief Mahākāntāraka Vyāghrarāja.

Damiḷa.—It is mentioned in the *Sāsanavaṃsa* (p. 33) that it was a kingdom where Thera Kassapa lived. The Damiḷas or the inhabitants of Damiḷa were a powerful south Indian tribe. They were disrespectful to the Buddhist stūpas (*Mahāvaṃsa Commy.*, p. 447). They came into conflict with the Ceylonese kings. For further details, vide Law, *Geographical Essays*, pp. 76–80.

Daṇḍapalle.—It is a village in the Palamner taluk of the Chittoor district where the plates of Vijayabhūpati were discovered (*E.I.*, XIV, 68ff.).

Dantapura.—It was the capital of Kaliṅga (*Jāt.*, II, 367, 371, 381; III, 376; IV, 230–32, 236). The Jirjingi plates of Gaṅga Indravarman refer to Dantapura (*E.I.*, XXV, Pt. VI, April, 1940, p. 285) which is a beautiful city, more beautiful than Amarāvatī, the city of gods. It is the Dantapur or Dantakura of the Great Epic (Udyogaparva, XLVII, 1883) and Pālura of the Nāgārjunikoṇḍa Inscriptions, which is near Chicacole. It is also mentioned in the Pali *Mahāgovinda Suttanta* (*Dīgha*, II, p. 235) as the ancient capital of Kaliṅga. Dantapura really means 'Tooth City' which is believed to have been an important city even before the days of the Buddha (*Mahāvastu*, III, 361 and *Jātaka*, II, 367). The sacred tooth of the Buddha is said to have been taken to Ceylon from this place (cf. *Dāṭhāvaṃsa*, B. C. Law, Ed.). The Jaina *Āvaśyaka Niryukti* (1275) refers to Dantavakka as the ruler of Dantapura. This town has been identified with Rājmahendrī (Rajahmundry) on the Godāvarī. Some have identified it with Puri in Orissa (Dey, *Geographical Dictionary*, p. 53). S. Levi identified it with Paloura of Ptolemy. According to Subba Rai it is in the ruins of the fort of Dantapura, situated on the southern bank of the river Vaṃśadharā, three miles from Chicacole Road Station.

Darsi.—It is in the Nellur district of the Madras State where a Pallava copperplate grant was discovered (*E.I.*, I, 397).

Deuli.—This village is situated at Jājpur sub-division, two miles west of police station of Dharmshala. It contains a temple situated on the bend of river Brāhmaṇī. The roof of the pillared hall has fallen. In front of the temple there is a banyan tree, at the foot of which stands a life-size monolithic image of Viṣṇu (*B. and O. Dist. Gazetteers*, Cuttack, by O'Malley, 1933).

Devapura.—It may be identified with one of the two villages, Devāḍa in the Sruṅgavarapukoṭa taluk or Devāḍi in the Chicacole taluk (*E.I.*, XXIV, Pt. II, p. 50).

Devarāṣṭra.—It is the Yellamañcili taluk of the Vizagapatam district (*A.S.R.*, 1908-09, 123; 1934-35, 43, 65).

Dharaṇīkoṭa (Dhannakaḍa).—The Jaina *Āvaśyaka Niryukti* (324) mentions it. It is in the Guntur district, where the Dharmacakra Pillar Inscription has been discovered (*E.I.*, XXIV, Pt. VI, April, 1938, p. 256). This was known as Pityundrā by Ptolemy as the capital of Maisolia. It was situated about 20 miles above Bezwada on the Kṛṣṇā (McCrindle, *Ptolemy's Ancient India*, Majumdar Ed., p. 187). The Bāhmaṇi invasion was checked by the Reddis at the Dharaṇīkoṭa and turned back (*E.I.*, XXVI).

Dhauli.—This village is situated four miles south-west of Bhubaneśwara on the south bank of the Dayā river. Close to this village two short ranges of low hills exist running parallel to each other. On the north face of the southern range the rock has been hewn and polished. Here some rock edicts of Aśoka are inscribed. The inscription is deeply cut into the rock and is divided into four tablets. Above the inscription there is a terrace, on the right side of which is the forepart of an elephant hewn out of the solid rock. There are some caves, natural and artificial, and temples. The edicts of Aśoka are the most interesting remains of Dhauli, which show a broad catholic view and inculcate a lofty ethical doctrine (*B. and O. District Gazetteers*, Puri, by O'Malley, 1929, pp. 278ff.).

Dhavalapeṭa.—This village is situated about 12 miles from Chicacole in the Vizagapatam district of Madras where copperplates of Mahārāja Umāvarman were discovered (*E.I.*, XXVI, Pt. III, p. 132).

Dibbida Agrahāraṃ.—It is a village in the Vīravilli taluk of the Vizagapatam district (*E.I.*, V, 107).

Dinakāḍu.—It is a village mentioned in the Dinakāḍu Inscriptions. Some lands of this village were given by Vijayāditya to Mādhava (*Journal of the Andhra Historical Research Society*, Vol. V, Pt. I, p. 56).

Dīrghāsi.—It is a village four miles north of Kaliṅgapatam in the Ganjam district, where an inscription of Vanapati (Śaka Samvat 997) was discovered (*E.I.*, IV, 314ff.).

Dommara-Nandyāla.—It may be identified with the two villages of Nandigāma and Pasiṃḍikuru (*E.I.*, XXVII, Pt. VI, p. 274).

Drākṣārāma.—It is the name of a village. It is described as 'the crest-jewel of the Andhra country'. It stands on the northern bank of the Iñjaram canal in the Rāmacandrapuram taluk of the east Godāvarī district. It is one of the most sacred places in the Godāvarī district with a big temple dedicated to Bhimeśvara (*S.I.I.*, I, pp. 53, 61; *E.I.*, XXVI, Pt. I). The Coḍa king Annadeva caused the pinnacle of the temple of Bhīmeśvara to be overlaid with gold. Two *sattras* for Brahmins were founded here (cf. Sewell, *Lists of Antiquities*, I, p. 25).

Drāviḍa.—It is the name of a country (*S.I.I.*, I, p. 113). It is the Sanskrit name of the Tamil country. It is mentioned in the *Mahābhārata* (Ch. 118. 4), the *Bhāgavata-Purāṇa* (IV. 28, 30; VIII. 4, 7; VIII. 24, 13; IX. 1, 2; X. 79, 13; XI. 5, 39) and in the *Bṛhat-saṃhitā* (XIV. 19). The Jaina *Brihatkalpa-bhāṣya* also mentions it (Vr. I, 1231).

Duṇṇiviṭṭha.—It was a Brahmin village in the kingdom of Kaliṅga (*Jāt.*, VI, 514).

Eḍeru.—It is the name of a village (*E.I.*, V, 118; *Ibid.*, I, p. 36) near Akiripalle in the Kistna district, 15 miles north-east of Bezwada. It is also known as Iḍāra Nuzvid taluk, Kistna district.

Ekadhīra-Caturvedimaṅgalam.—It is the name of a village somewhere near Tirunāma-nallūr in the South Arcot district. The name Ekadhīra-maṅgalam corresponds to Ekadhīra-Caturvedimaṅgalam (*S.I.I.*, Vol. II, p. 529; vide *Raṅgāchārī's List*, p. 1695, F.T. 21, for another version).

Elāpura.—The Ellora plates of Dantidurga mention it. It is Ellorā, where Dantidurga built the Daśāvatāra cave temple and where his successor Kṛṣṇa built the Kailāśa temple (*E.I.*, XXV, Pt. I, p. 29, January, 1939).

Ellore.—It is also known as Ellūra or Ilvalapura. It is probably the modern name of Kamalākarapura or Kolanu in Telugu. It is on the bank of the Kolleru lake in the Godāvarī district (*S.I.I.*, Vol. II, p. 308). It is famous for its Kailāśanātha temple. The caves at Ellore or Ellora in the north-west of the Nizam's territory, about 16 miles from Aurangabad, are some of the most important Buddhist caves of India. *Bhikṣugrihas*, known as *Dumaleṇas* are the first excavations made at the site. There are Brahmin and Jaina caves in addition to the Buddhist caves. The Buddhist caves contain distinct signs of later Mahayana sect. The cave No. 2 contains galleries full of images of the Buddha, seated on a lotus in a preaching attitude. In the north-east corner there is a figure of the Buddha very rough and almost unfinished. There is also a colossal Buddha seated on a *Sīhāsana*. In these caves the Buddha is seen in the attitude of preaching or in the *Dharmacakra-mudrā*. The walls are covered profusely with images of Buddha and Buddhist sages. The cave No. 3 is a Vihāra cave containing twelve cells for monks. The walls have also many carvings of Buddhist sages. The cave No. 4 is in ruins. At the north end of this cave there is a prominent figure of Padmapāṇi attended by two females. The cave No. 6 contains an ante-chamber in front of a shrine full of sculptures. In the cave No. 9 there is an image of the Buddha with various attendants. The cave No. 10 is a beautiful Caitya-cave, where there is a large open court in front. The carvings are very beautiful and the façade is highly ornamental. The inner side of the gallery within the chapel is divided into three compartments, full of figures. A gigantic figure of the Buddha is carved in front of the dagoba. The cave No. 11 is two-storied, and this cave is similar to the cave No. 13 in outer appearance. The caves Nos. 11 and 13 contain an open court, cells in the walls, and show signs of Mahāyānism.

The copperplates of the earliest Rāṣṭrakūṭa Emperor Dantidurga were discovered at Ellora (ancient Elāpura) (*E.I.*, XXV, Pt. I, pp. 25ff.).

Eḷumbur.—It is the same as Egmore, a part of Madras (*S.I.I.*, Vol. III, 133).

Elūr.—It is the name of a village (*S.I.I.*, I, p. 108). It contains some temples.

Eluru.—A village in the west Godāvarī district in the Veṅgīviṣaya.

Enādapāḍi.—It is the name of a village (*S.I.I.*, I, p. 83).

Eraṇḍapalla.—It has been identified by Fleet with Eraṇḍol in east Khandesh and by Dubreuil with Eraṇḍapali, a town near Chicacole in the Ganjam district. Some have identified it with Yeṇḍipalli in Vizagapatam (Raichaudhuri, *P.H.A.I.*, 5th ed., p. 540; *Journal of Indian History*, Vol. VI, Pt. III, pp. 402-403).

Eyil.—It is the name of a village, in the Tiṇḍivanam taluk of the South Arcot district (*S.I.I.*, I, pp. 123, 147). This village seems to have given its name to Eyirkoṭṭam.

Eyirkoṭṭam.—This district was probably called after Eyil (fort), a village in the Tiṇḍivanam taluk of the South Arcot district (*Ibid.*, I, p. 123). It is a district of Jayaṅkoṇḍaśoḷamaṇḍalam. Conjeevaram is said to be situated in it.

Gaḍaviṣaya.—It is identical with Khiñjalīyagaḍaviṣaya of the Antirigam plates of Jayabhañjadeva (*E.I.*, XXIV, Pt. I, January, 1937, p. 18).

Gaṅgā.—This is the name of a river (*S.I.I.*, I, pp. 57, 58, etc.). This river is also called Mandākinī which descends from the sky with all the fury of its rushing waters and which is borne by the God Śiva on one of his matted locks (*S.I.I.*, II, p. 514). The Puruṣottamapura plates of Rāmcandra mention this river which is the Godāvarī (*E.I.*, XXV, Pt. V, p. 208).

Gaṅgāpāḍi.—It is included in the modern Mysore State (*S.I.I.*, Vol. II, pp. 8, 17).

Gaṅgāpura.—This village is identified with the modern Saṅgūr situated at a distance of about eight miles south-west of Hāverī on the road to Sirsi in the North Kanara district. This was included in the Candraguttināḍu belonging to Goveyarājya (*E.I.*, XXIII, Pt. V, pp. 182ff.).

Gautamī.—It is another name of the Godāvarī river (*E.I.*, XXVI, Pt. I, January, 1941). It may be identified with the Akhaṇḍa-Gautamī, i.e., the Gautamī before it divides itself into the seven branches collectively known by the name of the Saptagodāvarī (*E.I.*, XXVI, Pt. I, p. 40).

There is a village by the name of Gautamī, which is in the Badakhimedi Estate of the Ganjam district, where three copperplates were discovered (*E.I.*, XXIV, Pt. IV, 180ff., *Gautamī Plates of Gaṅga Indravarman*, year 4).

Gāṅganur.—It is the name of a village near Velūr (*Ibid.*, I, pp. 77, 128). It is the same as Gāṅgeya-nallūr in Karaivari-Āndināḍu in Vellore taluk of North Arcot district.

Gāṅgeya-nallūr.—This is modern Gāṅganūr (*Ibid.*, I, p. 77), a village in Karaivari-Āndināḍu, a division of Paḍuvurkoṭṭam.

Geḍilaṃ.—The Sendamaṅgalaṃ Inscription of Manavaḷapperumal refers to this river, which rises in the Kallakurci taluk of the South Arcot district and flows into the Bay of Bengal under the ruined bastions of Fort St. David near Cuddalore in the same district (*E.I.*, XXIV, Pt. I, January, 1937, p. 27). On the bank of this river the two villages of Tiruvaḍi and Tirumāṇikuli are situated (*E.I.*, XXVII, Pt. III, p. 97).

Ghanasela mountain.—It is in the kingdom of Avantī in South India (*Avantīdakkhiṇāpathe*: *Jātaka*, V, 133).

Ghaṇṭasāla.—It is a small village in the Kistna district, 13 miles west of Masulipatam. Ikhasirivadhamāna appears to be its ancient name (*E.I.*, XXVII, Pt. I, 1947-48, 1ff.). Five Prakrit Inscriptions have been discovered here.

Ghaṭikācala.—It is the name of a hill. It is at Sholinghur in the North Arcot district (*Ibid.*, II, p. 502).

Gingu.—It is in the South Arcot district containing some ancient monuments (*A.S.I.*, *Annual Report*, 1917-18, Pt. I, p. 13).

Godāvarī.—It is the name of a river (*Mahābh.*, 85, 33; 88, 2; *Bhāgavata Purāṇa*, V. 19, 18; *Brahmāṇḍap*, 1. 12. 15; *Matsya*, 22. 46; *Padmapurāṇa*, Uttarakhaṇḍa, vs. 35–38). According to the *Rāmāyaṇa* (Āraṇyakāṇḍa, Sarga 15, vs. 11–18, 24), it was full of lotuses and not far from it antelopes freely moved about. Swans, *kāraṇḍavas* and *cakravākas* sported themselves in this river. This beautiful river had trees on both sides. Lakṣmaṇa took his bath in this river and returned to the leaf-hut taking with him many lotuses and fruits. Kālidāsa refers to it in his *Raghuvaṃśa* (XIII, 33). The Pañcavaṭī forest was situated on it. According to the *Brahmapurāṇa* (Ch. 77, vs. 9-10; *Saura*, Ch. 69, v. 26) it has its source in the Trayamvaka-tīrtha. Many holy places are situated on the bank of this river: Kuśāvartatīrtha, (*Brahmap.* Ch. 80), Daśāśvamedhikatīrtha (*Mahābh.*, Ch. 83, 64), Govardhanatīrtha (*Ibid.*, Ch. 91), Sāvitrītīrtha (*Ibid.*, Ch. 102), Vidarbha (*Ibid.*, 121), Mārkaṇḍeya-tīrtha (*Ibid.*, Ch. 145) and Kiṣkindhyātīrtha (*Ibid.*, 157). It is mentioned in the *Suttanipāta* (p. 190). It is the largest and the longest river in South India, the source of which can be traced to the Western Ghats. It flows in a south-easterly direction below the Vindhya range cutting a valley through the Eastern Ghat. It falls in three distributaries into the Bay of Bengal in the district of Godāvarī forming a large delta at its mouth. In its course through Hyderabad and Madras State it is joined by many tributaries. It issued from the Sahya mountains along with the Tuṅgabhadrā, Kāverī, Bhīmaratha (or Bhīmarathī), Kṛṣṇaveṇhā, etc. This river which is considered to be one of the holiest in South India had really its source in Brahmagiri situated on the side of a village called Trayamvaka which is 20 miles from Nasik. It is near the Kaviṭṭha forest (*Jātaka*, V, 132). This river is known in the Jain Literature as Goyāvarī (*Brihatkalpa-Bhāṣya*, 6. 6244ff.). The *Mahābhārata* has a reference to Sapta-Godāvarī (Ch. 85. 44).

Gokarṇa.—The Kap copperplate of Keladi Sadāśiva-nāyaka refers to Gokarṇa which is a village of that name in North Kanara. It is not far from the river Revā (*Saurapurāṇa*, Ch. 69, śl. 29). The Gokarṇa copperplates of Kadamba Kāmadeva, Śaka, 1177, were discovered at Gokarṇa (cf. *E.I.*, XXVII, Pt. IV, pp. 157ff.). The *Rāmāyaṇa* (Ādik. 42 sarga v. 12) points out that the sage Bhagīratha came to this place and engaged himself in asceticism because he was childless for a long time. The *Mahābhārata* (85. 24–27) and the *Padmapurāṇa* (Ch. 21) refer to it as a holy place. The *Kūrmapurāṇa* (30. 45–48; cf. *Agnipurāṇa*, 109) and the *Padmapurāṇa* (Ch. 133) also mention it as such. The *Saurapurāṇa* (Ch. 69, śl. 33) mentions southern Gokarṇa which, according to it, is situated on the river Sindhu (Indus).

Gokarṇeśvara.—It is a village at Deuli in the Jajpura sub-division of the Cuttack district situated two miles west of the police station of Dharamśālā. It contains a small temple of Gokarṇeśvara which is picturesquely situated on a bend of the river Brāhmaṇī. It is one of the ancient temples of Orissa. A life-size monolithic image of the four-handed Viṣṇu can be found here at the foot of a Banyan tree.

Gollapuṇḍi.—It may be identified with the village of Gollapūḍi on the northern bank of the Kṛṣṇā river near Bezwada in the Kistna district, about 12 miles to the north of Tāḍikoṇḍa (*E.I.*, XXIII, Pt. V—*Tāṇḍikoṇḍa Grant of Ammarāja*, II).

Gomukhagiri.—It is the name of a hill with a temple dedicated to the Gomukhagiriśvara by king Annadeva (*E.I.*, XXVI, Pt. I).

Goṇṭūru.—It is the name of a village (*S.I.I.*, Vol. I, 38). It is doubtful to identify Goṇṭūra with the modern town of Guṇtur in the Kistna district. This village is bounded on the east by Goṅguva, on the south by Goṇayūru, on the west by Kaluceruvulu and on the north by Maḍapalli (*Ibid.*, I, p. 43).

Gottaikelā.—This village also known as Gotarkela is about three miles from the town of Sonepur (*E.I.*, XXIII, Pt. VII, July, 1936, p. 250).

Govindavāḍi and Dāmal.—Two villages in the Conjeevaram taluk of the Chingleput district. Govindavāḍi is close to Tirumalpuram in the Arkonam taluk of the North Arcot district and is identical with Govindapāḍi of the inscription at Tirumalpuram (*S.I.I.*, Vol. III, p. 254). Govindapāḍi is in Vellanāḍu which is a district of Damarkoṭṭam.

Guddavāṭiviṣaya.—This is the same as Goddavāḍi-viṣaya (*Ind. Ant.*, Vol. XIV, p. 53). Guddavāṭi-viṣaya or Guddavāḍi-viṣaya is perhaps identical with Gudravāra, Gudrāvāra or Gudra-hāraviṣaya and connected with the modern Guḍivāḍa, the headquarters of a taluk of the Kistna district (Hultzsch, *S.I.I.*, Vol. I, p. 52 and f.n.)

Guḍla-Kaṇḍeruvāṭi.—It was the ancient name of a tract of country lying on the southern bank of the Kṛṣṇā river round Amarāvatī, which was noted for its beautiful temples and caityas of Amaravateśvara and the Buddha. The term 'Guḍla' means 'of the temples', and the district Kaṇḍeravāḍi or Kaṇḍeruvāṭi seems to acquire its name from the Gaṇṭur taluk of the ancient township Kaṇḍeru or the modern Kaṇṭeru, a village in Guntur district, which must have been a very important place in former times. Guḍla-Kaṇḍeruvāṭiviṣaya was the name for the northern portion of Guṇṭur and eastern portion of Sattenapalli taluk. The central portion of Guṇṭur together with the south-eastern part of Sattenapalli taluk was called the Uttara-Kaṇḍeruvāṭiviṣaya. (*E.I.*, XXIII, Pt. V, p. 166.)

Gudravāraviṣaya.—It has been identified with Gūḍūru near Masulipatam as well as with Guḍivāḍa, the headquarters of the taluk of the same name in the Kistna district (*E.I.*, XVII, No. 10, p. 45).

Gūdrū.—It is a town near Masulipatam. It is Koddoura of Ptolemy (McCrindle, *Ancient India as described by Ptolemy*, Majumdar Ed., p. 68).

Guṇḍugolanu.—It is a village in the Veṅgināṇḍuviṣaya granted to a Brahmin inhabitant of Kalluru, where a number of plates was found (*I.A.*, XII, 248).

Gutti.—It is the headquarters of a taluk in the Anantapura district, known as Gooty (*E.I.*, XXV, Pt. IV, p. 190).

Haduvaka.—It is a village, which is evidently the same as Sudava, situated in the eastern division of the Parlakimedi State in the Ganjam district of the Madras Presidency (*E.I.*, XXVI, Pt. 2, April, 1941, p. 63).

Hagarī.—This river formed the common boundary of the Kadamba country and the Naḷavāḍi in the north and the Kadamba country and Sire 300 in the south (*Q.J.M.S.*, January and April, 1950, p. 88).

Halampura.—The Gurzala Brāhmī Inscription refers to this place. According to some it may be identified with Allūru in the Nandigama taluk of the Kistna district. According to others it seems to be identical with Ālampūr in the Nizam's dominions. The latter place is situated at the apex of the Raichur Doab on the western bank of the Tuṅgabhadrā, a little distance before its junction with the Kṛṣṇā. It abounds in antiquities, temples and other structures (*E.I.*, XXVI, 124ff.; *Annual Report of the Archaeological Department of Nizam's Dominions*, 1926-27).

Haṃsaprapatana.—It is a holy place situated to the left of the Bhāgīrathī and north of Pratiṣṭhāna (*Kūrmap.*, Pūrvabhāga, Ch. 36, Śl. 22).

Hanumkoṇḍa (Anmakoṇḍa).—It is near Warangal in the Nizam's State, wherein the inscription of Prola was discovered. To the south of this place stands a billock on the top of which a small temple of Padmākṣī was built (*E.I.*, IX, 256ff.).

Hemāvatī.—It is the name of a village. It was the ancient capital o Nuḷambbapāḍi also called Nigarili-Śorapāḍi which appears to have extended into the Anantapur district (*S.I.I.*, Vol. II, p. 425).

Iḍaiturainīḍu.—This is the country of Edatore, the headquarters of a taluk in the Maisūr district (*Ibid.*, I, p. 96).

Ilangoykkuḍi.—It is the ancient name of Ambā-samudraṃ. It was a *brahmadeya* in Muḷḷināḍu (*E.I.*, XXV, Pt. I, January, 1939).

Iramaṇḍalaṃ.—Ira was called Mummuḍiśoramaṇḍalam after the well-known surname Mummuḍicoḷa of Rājarāja (*S.I.I.*, Vol. II, pp. 108, etc.).

Iraṭṭa-pāḍi.—It is the western Calukyan empire. Its revenue amounts to 7½ lakhs (*Ibid.*, I, p. 65). It was invaded by the Coḷa king mentioned in 1365 of Tanjore inscriptions (vide *Raṅgāchārī's List*).

Isila.—It was a seat of government in the Deccan ruled over by a *mahāmātra*. It may have been the ancient name of Siddāpura in the Chitaldroog district of the Mysore State (Aśoka's *M.R.E.*, I; *E.I.*, II, No. 4, p. 111).

Jagannāthanagarī.—This may be identified with Jagannāthapuraṃ which is the portion of the town of Cocanada lying south of the river (*S.I.I.*, I, pp. 51–60; Sewell, *List of Antiquities*, Vol. I, p. 24).

Jaggavāga.—This city was captured by the Coḍa King Annadeva (*E.I.*, XXVI, Pt. I).

Jambugrāma.—The Kālibhanā copperplate inscriptions of king Mahābhavagupta I Janamejaya mention it, which may be the same as the modern Jāmgāon near Kālibhanā (*I.H.Q.*, XX, No. 3).

Jambukeśvara.—It is Śrīraṅgaṃ according to some (cf. *Devīpurāṇa* Ch. 102). It is two miles away to the north of Trichinopoly. It contains a temple having the water-liṅga. The deity is so called because it remains in water. Śiva stands in the middle with Brahmā and Viṣṇu to the right and left respectively.

Jaṭinga-Rāmeśvara.—It is a hill near Siddāpura in the Moḷakālmuru taluk of the Chitaldroog district in Mysore State (*E.I.*, IV, 212).

Jayaṅkoṇḍacoḷamaṇḍalaṃ.—It is the Coḷa country (*S.I.I.*, I, pp. 79-80, 102, 123).

Jayapuraviṣaya.—The Cuttack Museum plates of Mādhavavarman refer to it, which is the same as Jayakaṭakaviṣaya of Koṅgodamaṇḍala mentioned in the Dharakota plate of Śubhākaradeva. It may be identified with the present Jeypore contiguous to the Ganjam district in Orissa (*E.I.*, XXIV, Pt. IV, October, 1937, p. 151).

Jājpur.—It is an old site in the Jajpur district of Orissa. This place is called Birajākṣetra in the *Mahābhārata*. It was a sacred spot as early as the 2nd or 3rd century A.D. It contains a temple having the image of Satī under the name of Birajā or the passionless one. This temple cannot be of an earlier date than the 14th century A.D. Jājpur, also known as Birajākṣetra on the Vaitaraṇī in the Cuttack district, is a place of historical importance. Four colossal images which are the notable objects of antiquarian interest have been discovered here. One of them is an image of the Bodhisattva Padmapāṇi of decomposed Khondalite of the later Gupta period, 16 ft. in height. The other three are the images of Vārāhī, Cāmuṇḍā and Indrāṇī. Of these images, those of Cāmuṇḍā and Indrāṇī are very badly mutilated. The colossal image of Vārāhī at Jājpur has lost both the right fore-arms, and both of her left arms are mutilated. She is seated in easy posture on a throne. Her vehicle, buffalo, is carved on the base. As pointed out by R. P. Chanda the makers of the images of the mothers and of the allied gods and goddesses found at Jājpur followed the *Devī-māhātmya*, which knows only seven mother-goddesses. All the old temples of Jājpur are said to have been destroyed by Mahommedan invaders. Jājpur was the capital of Orissa at the time of Hiuen Tsang, as rightly pointed out by Waddell and R. P. Chanda. It may be recognized as an old centre of the cult of Birajā or Durgā. The magnificent images of the mothers and the allied deities, e.g., Śivadūti and Ganeśa, found at Jājpur, are the best specimens of the early mediaeval Buddhist sculptures. The early mediaeval stone-temples of Jājpur are not of much architectural importance. For further details, vide R. P. Chanda, *Exploration in Orissa*, *M.A.S.I.*, No. 44.

Jeypore.—It is in the Vizagapatam district of the newly formed Andhra State (*E.I.*, XXV, Pt. V, January, 1940).

Jijjika.—This village is the same as the modern village of Jirjiṅgi in the Tekkali Zamindari of the Ganjaṃ district where some plates of Gaṅga Indravarman were found out (*E.I.*, XXV, Pt. VI, April, 1940, pp. 281 and 286).

Jurāḍā.—It may be identical with Jaraḍā, a village in the Kodola taluk of the Ganjam district. Surada the headquarters of a taluk of the same name in the Ganjam district, represents Jurāḍā (*E.I.*, XXIV, Pt. I, January, 1937, p. 18).

Kacci.—This is modern Conjeevaram (*S.I.I.*, Vol. III, p. 206).

Kaccipeḍu.—It is Kāñcīpuram, modern Conjeevaram (*S.I.I.*, I, pp. 113, 114, 117, 139, 141, etc.; Vol. III, p. 267).

Kaḍaba.—It is in the Tumkur district of the Mysore State, where copperplates of Prabhūtavarṣa (Śaka saṃvat 735) were discovered (*E.I.*, IV, 332ff.).

Kaḍabhra.—It is the name of a country (*S.I.I.*, Vol. II, pp. 343, 356).

Kaḍaikkoṭṭūr.—It is the name of a village (*Ibid.*, I, p. 105). Ariṣṭanemi ācārya belonged to it.

Kaḍalāḍi.—It is in the North Arcot district (*E.I.*, XIV, 310).

Kaḍapā.—Ptolemy calls it Karige. It is situated five miles from the right bank of the North Pennar on a small tributary of that river (*Ptolemy's Ancient India*, Majumdar Ed., p. 186).

Kaḍāraṃ (or Kiḍāraṃ).—It is now the headquarters of the taluk of Ramnad Zemindary in the Madura district (*S.I.I.*, II, p. 106). Kaḍāraṃ, being the first port of call for ships from India to Further India and China, was the place best known to the people of the Tamil country and, therefore, Tamil inscriptions refer to the conquest of Kaḍāraṃ. The smaller Leyden copperplates dated 1090 A.D. record an embassy from Kaḍāraṃ to the Coḷa court at Āyiraṭṭali (*E.I.*, XXII, 267–71).

Kaḷanjiyam.—It is the name of a village (*S.I.I.*, I, p. 83).

Kaḷavalināḍu.—The Tiruppūvanaṃ plates of Jaṭāvarman Kulaśekhara I refer to it. It was divided into two parts, north and south (*E.I.*, XXV, Pt. III, p. 98).

Kaḷavapūṃdī.—The Koduru grant of Ana-vota-reddi (Śaka 1280) refers to it, which may be identified with modern Kaluvapūḍi in the Guḍivāḍa taluk of the Kistna district (*E.I.*, XXV, Pt. III, p. 140).

Kaliṅga.—This is the name of a country (*E.I.*, Vol. II, pp. 8, 17, 35, 123, etc.).

Kaliṅganagara.—In the Narasiṅgapalli plates of Hastivarman and the Sāntabommāli plates of Indravarman, Kaliṅganagara has been identified with modern Kaliṅgapatam at the mouth of the Vaṃśadharā river or Mukhaliṅgaṃ near Chicacole (*E.I.*, IV, 187). According to some, Mukhaliṅgaṃ is a place of pilgrimage, 20 miles from Parlakimedi in the Ganjam district (*E.I.*, XXIII, Pt. II, April, 1935, p. 76). Fleet has identified it with Kaliṅgapataṃ (*Ind. Antiquary*, XVI, p. 132) as a kingdom. Kaliṅga occurs in Pāṇini's *Aṣṭādhyāyī* (IV. I. 170). Patañjali mentions it in his *Mahābhāṣya* (3. 2. 2, p. 191). It was a well-known country on the eastern coast of India lying between the Mahānadī and the Godāvarī (*J.U.P.H.S.*, XV, Pt. II, p. 34). It is also mentioned in the Triliṅga Inscription of Devendravarman, son of Gunārṇava (Gaṅga year 192). The India Office plate of Lakṣmaṇasena refers to Kaliṅga (*E.I.*, XXVI, Pt. I; XXV, Pt. V, January, 1940) which also occurs in the Tekkali plates of Anantavarman of the Gaṅga year 358 (*E.I.*, XXVI, 174ff.) and the Indian Museum plates of Gaṅga Devendravarman, year 308 (*E.I.*, XXIII, Pt. II). Randle is right in pointing out that the tribute on the *pratipad* days in the shape of a gift of woman was paid by the ruler of Kaliṅga to Lakṣmaṇasena while he was young (*E.I.*, XXVI, Pt. I, p. 11., F.N. 4). The kingdom of Kaliṅga included Pithuḍaka, Pithuḍaga or Pithuṇḍa on the sea-coast, which existed near the river Lāṅguliyā. The Kaliṅga Edict I tells us that a Kumāra was in charge of Kaliṅga with his headquarters at Tosalī (Tosala) or Samāpa (Law, *Geography of Early Buddhism*, p. 64 f.n.). According to the Hāthigumphā Inscription king Khāravela brought back to his realm the throne of Jina from Aṅga-Magadha.[1] He stormed a stronghold of the Magadhan army in the Barabar hills, known as the Gorathagiri, and caused a heavy pressure to be brought to bear upon the citizens of Rājagṛha, the earlier capital of Magadha. He also compelled king Bahasatimita of Magadha to acknowledge his suzerainty. Khāravela repaired the buildings, walls, and gates in the city of Kaliṅga, which were badly damaged by the stormy wind, raised the embankments of the Isitāla tank, and restored all the damaged gardens. According to the Hāthigumphā Inscription King Khāravela is said to have defeated the Bhojakas and Rāṭhikas (i.e., the Bhojas and Rāṣṭrikas of Aśoka's inscriptions) in the 4th year of his reign and to have compelled them to do him homage. King Khāravela has been described in his own Inscription as *Kaliṅgādhipati*, and as *Kaliṅgacakkavatti* in the Inscription of his chief queen. The Hāthigumphā Inscription clearly shows that Kaliṅganagara was the capital of Kaliṅga during Khāravela's reign. It has been satisfactorily identified with Mukhaliṅgaṃ on the Vaṃśadharā and the adjacent ruins in the Ganjam district. Khibīra was really the capital of Kaliṅga in Khāravela's time. It had its connection with a river near it by a canal opened up three hundred years back by a king named Nanda. It was brought into the heart of this capital by its further extension from the Tanasuliya road. It appears from the location of the new royal palace that the capital was situated on the bank of a stream known by the name of Prācī, which flows on the northern part of the Puri district showing many temples in ruins on its both banks. The river Prācī flows southwards within five or six miles east from the Liṅgarāja temple (B. M. Barua, *Khāravela as King and Builder* published in the *Journal of the Indian Society of Oriental Art*, Vol. XV, p. 52).

The ancient Kaliṅga country seems to have comprised modern Orissa to the south of the Vaitaraṇī and the sea-coast southwards as far as Vizagapatam (cf. *Mahābhārata*, III, 114. 4). It also included the Amarakaṇṭaka range which is said to be in its western part (*Mahābhārata*, Vanaparva, CXIV, 10096–10107; *Kūrma-Purāṇa*, II, XXXIX, 19; Cunningham, *A.G.I.*, pp. 734-35; for further details, vide Law, *Geography of Early Buddhism*, pp. 63-64). The *Matsyap.* refers to Jaleśvara which is a *tīrtha* in the Amarakaṇṭaka hill of Kaliṅga (186. 15–38; 187. 3–52). The *Bhāgavata Purāṇa* refers to it and to its people (IX, 23. 5; X, 61, 29, 37) and the *Bṛhat-saṃhitā* also mentions it (XIV, 8). The Kaliṅga country lies between the Godāvarī and Mahānadī rivers (Hultzsch, *S.I.I.*, I, pp. 63, 65, 95, etc.). The capital of Kaliṅga was Dantapuranagara (*E.I.*, XIV). Many other Kaliṅga capitals existed in the Ganjam district (*E.I.*, IV, 187). The Sonepur grant of Mahāśivaguptayayāti refers to Kaliṅga, Koṅgoda, Utkala and Kośala ruled by Lakṣmaṇasena of Gauḍa. Kaliṅga formed a geographical unit by itself, and had its own rulers from the earliest times. Two eastern Gaṅgā copperplate grants from Sudava (*E.I.*, XXVI, Pt. II, p. 63) also refer to Kaliṅganagara which has been variously located at modern Kaliṅgāpatam or at Mukhaliṅgaṃ. According to this copperplate Kāmarūpa is located in ancient Kaliṅga.

---

[1] Barua, *Old Brāhmī Inscriptions*, pp. 272-273.

In the Aihole Inscriptions of the seventh century A.D., Pulakesin II claims to have subdued the Kaliṅgas and took the fortress of Piṣṭapura (*E.I.*, VI, pp. 4ff.). Harṣadeva or Śrīharṣa is described in a Nepalese inscription to have been the king of Kaliṅga, Oḍra, Gauḍa and other countries (*J.R.A.S.*, 1898, pp. 384-5; *I.H.Q.*, 1927, p. 841). Another reference to Kaliṅga is found in the Bheraghat Inscription of Alhaṇadevī, the queen of Gayā-karṇa of the Kalacuri dynasty, the grandson of the famous Lakṣmīkarṇa. It informs us that when Lakṣmīkarṇa gave full play to his heroism, Vaṅga trembled with Kaliṅga (*E.I.*, II, p. 11).

Most of the early Gaṅgās of Kaliṅga like Hastivarman (*E.I.*, XXIII, 65), Indravarman (*E.I.*, XXV, 195), Devendravarman (*E.I.*, XXVI, 63), who described themselves as lords of Kaliṅga issued their grants from the victorious camp at Kaliṅganagara. (*E.I.*, XXVI, 67). The plates of the early Gaṅgā kings of Kaliṅga, like Jayavarmadeva and Indravarman, refer to the victorious residence of Śvetaka (*E.I.*, XXIII, 261; XXIV, 181; XXVI, 167), which has been identified with Cikaṭi, in the Ganjam district. For a list of ancient districts of Kaliṅga country as mentioned in the different Kaliṅga inscriptions of various dates, vide *Indian Culture*, XIV, p. 137.

In the fifth century A.D. the well-known Komarti grant introduces us to a Śrī Mahārāja named Candravarman, who is described as Kaliṅgādhipati or the lord of Kaliṅga (Sewell, *Historical Inscriptions of Southern India*, p. 18). To this dynasty Umāvarman and Viśākhavarman, who were the lords of Kaliṅga, probably belonged. To about the same date as that of the Komarti grant may be ascribed the inscription of a certain Kaliṅgādhipati Vaśiṣṭhīputra Śaktivarman of the Māṭhara family who granted from Piṣṭapura (Pithapuram) the village of Rākaluva in Kaliṅgaviṣaya (*E.I.*, XII, pp. 1ff.). A copperplate grant of eastern Calukya king Bhīma I mentions a village in Elamañci-Kaliṅgadeśa, which formed part of a province called Devarāṣṭra. According to the Kharod Inscription of Ratnadeva III, the lord of Kaliṅga was the youngest son of Kokalla (*E.I.*, XXI, p. 159). According to some Kaliṅgarāja came to be regarded as the son and not merely a descendant of Kokalla. The Kharod Inscription further says that Kaliṅgarāja became the Lord of Tummāṇa, which has been identified by some with Tumana in the Bilaspur district (*I.A.*, LIII, pp. 267ff.). According to the Amoda plates, Kaliṅgarāja churned the king of Utkala and contributed prosperity to the treasury of Gāṅgeyadeva (*E.I.*, XIX, p. 75). According to a South Indian Inscription dated 1135 A.D., a Gaṅga king of Kaliṅga was defeated by Durjaya Maṇḍa II (*E.I.*, VI, 276). The ruler of Kaliṅga along with those of Kāñcī, Kośala, Mālava, Lāṭa, Taṅka, etc., was defeated by Dantidurga, according to the Ellora Inscription, V. 23, and the Begumra plates of Indra III (*E.I.*, IX, 24ff.).

Govinda III came to the bank of the Narmadā and conquered Kaliṅga and other countries including Mālava, Kośala, Veṅgī, Ḍāhala and Oḍraka (*E.I.*, XXIII, Pt. VIII, p. 297—*Manna Plates of Stambha*). Kaliṅga was visited by Hiuen Tsang in the 7th century A.D. According to him, it was 5,000 li in circuit. It was regularly cultivated and it produced abundant flowers and fruits. It contained extensive forests. It was thickly populated. The climate was hot. The people were vehement and impetuous, mostly rough and uncivilized. There were some *saṅghārāmas* and *deva temples* (Beal, *Buddhist Records of the Western World*, II, 209-10).

According to the *Mahāvastu* (Vol. III, p. 361), Dantapura was the capital of the Kaliṅga kingdom, and it existed ages before the Buddha

(*Jāt.*, II, p. 367). Probably it was the Dantapura where the Kaliṅgas were destroyed by Kṛṣṇa (*Mahābhārata*, Udyogaparva, XLVII, 1883). Dandagula or Dandaguḍa, the capital of Calingoe, mentioned by Pliny, shows that the original form was Dantakura and not Dantapura (*C.A.G.I.*, p. 735). According to the *Kauṭilīya Arthaśāstra* (p. 50), the elephants of Kaliṅga and Aṅga were excellent. According to the *Daśakumāracaritaṃ*, Mantragupta came to Kaliṅga. At a little distance from this city he sat on the slope of a hill in a wild forest adjoining a cemetery. The daughter of the king of Kaliṅga named Kanakalekhā was sent for (pp. 167-168). A Brahmin came from the Andhra capital, who told a story about Kardana, the king of Kaliṅga and the father of Kanakalekhā (*Ibid.*, p. 172). Kālidāsa styles the king of Kaliṅga as the 'Lord of the Mahendra' (*Raghuvaṃśa*, IV, 43; VI, 54). According to him Kaliṅga was extended up to the Godāvarī. For further details, vide S. K. Aiyangar's *Ancient India and South Indian History and Culture*, Vol. I (1941), Ch. XIII, pp. 396ff.

Kaliṅgapaṭṭanaṃ.—It was a flourishing seaport at the mouth of the Godāvarī.

Kaliṅgāraṇya.—This forest which finds mention in the *Milindapañha* (p. 130) lay between the Godāvarī river on the south-west and the Gaoliya branch of the Indrāvatī river on the north-west (*C.A.G.I.*, p. 591). According to Rapson, it was between the Mahānadī and the Godāvarī (*Ancient India*, p. 116).

Kalluru.—This ancient village is situated in the Repalle taluk of the Guntur district (*I.A.*, XII, 248).

Kalpatti.—It is in Pālghāṭ, where a stone inscription was discovered (*E.I.*, XV, 145ff.).

Kalubarigā.—It is the modern Gulbargā in the Hyderabad State (*E.I.*, XIII, 157).

Kaluceruvulu.—It is the name of a village (*S.I.I.*, I, p. 43).

Kalyāṇa.—This city was founded by the Coḍa king Kāmarāja, which became famous as Kāmapurī, 'the crest-Jewel of the Āndhra country' (*E.I.*, XXVI, Pt. I).

Kamakapalli.—It is situated in the Girigaḍa village of the Karvannāḍga district (*E.I.*, XVI, 270).

Kamalapādaṣa.—It is the name of a village (*S.I.I.*, I, p. 83).

Kamalāpuram.—It is in the Cuddappah district where an inscription of Indra III was discovered.

Kampili.—This is modern Kampli, a town on the southern bank of the Tuṅgabhadrā in the Hospet taluk of the Bellary district (*S.I.I.*, Vol. III, p. 194; *Madras District Gazetteers*, Bellary, by W. Francis, pp. 282ff.). Dantivarman's grant records the donation of a village to a Buddhist monastery at Kāmpailya (*E.I.*, VI, 287). It will not be safe to identify this Kāmpailya with Kāmpilya, the capital of Southern Pañcāla, for lack of proper evidence.

Kanaḍa (or *Kannaḍa*).—This is Karṇāṭa country (*S.I.I.*, Vol. II, pp. 117, 311), a portion of the Carnatic between Rāmnād and Seriṅgapatam. It is also called Kuntaladeśa. The Mysore State was also called Karṇāṭaka (*J.R.A.S.*, 1912, p. 482). The kingdom of Vijayanagara was also called Karṇāṭa (*Imperial Gazetteers of India*, Vol. IV).

Kanakavalli.—A village (*S.I.I.*, I, pp. 78, 79) belonging to Paṅgalanāḍu, a division of Paḍuvur-Koṭṭam in Jayaṅkoṇḍa-Colamaṇḍalam.

Kaṇḍarādityam.—It is the name of a village (*Ibid.*, I, p. 112) on the northern bank of the Kāverī in the Trichinopoly district. A chieftain of this name occurs in the inscriptions.

Kaṇḍeruvāḍi.—It is Kaṇḍeruvāṭiviṣaya district (*Ibid.*, I, pp. 38, 44). An order was issued to its inhabitants by the Cālukya Bhīma II (vide 98 of Kistna district in *Raṅgāchārī's List*). Kaṇḍeruvāṭiviṣaya seems to have been subdivided into three or four small districts. It comprised apparently the whole of Guntur taluk, the eastern portion of Sattenapalli and the northern parts of Tenāli taluk. The central portion of Guntur together with the south-eastern part of Sattenapalli taluk was called Uttara Kaṇḍeruvāṭiviṣaya (*E.I.*, XXIII, Pt. V).

Kaṇṇamaṅgalam.—It is the name of a village which is situated in the Ārṇī Jāgīr about half way between Ārṇī and Vellore (*S.I.I.*, I, p. 83).

Kaṇṇi.—It is the name of a river which flowed in ancient times near Cape Comorin (Vailūr Inscription of Kopperunjiṅgadeva, *E.I.*, XXIII, Pt. V, p. 180).

Kanteru.—The Kanteru plates of Sālankāyana Vijayaskandavarman refer to this village in the Gaṇṭur taluk, Gaṇṭur district (*E.I.*, XXV, Pt. I, January, 1939, p. 42). According to some it is situated a few miles north-east of Guṇṭur near the main road leading to Bezwada (*E.I.*, XVIII, p. 56).

Kanyā.—It is the same as Kanyākumārī, the Tamil name of Cape Comorin (*S.I.I.*, Vol. III, p. 22 f.n.). It is also called Gaṅgaikoṇḍacoḷapuram. Here an inscription of Kulottuṅgacoḷa I has been discovered (*E.I.*, XXVI, Pt. VI, April, 1942, pp. 274ff.). It is a very ancient place of great reputation. It was known to the Greek writers as Komaria Akron or Cape Komaria. The temple of the Goddess Kanyākumārī is situated on the very brink of the Indian Ocean. Here the inscription of Vīra Rājendradeva was discovered (*E.I.*, XVIII, p. 21).

Karaivari-āṇḍi-nāḍu.—It is the name of a district (*S.I.I.*, I, pp. 77, 78, 129).

Karamadai.—This town is on the railway line between Coimbatore and Mettupalayam, about 17 miles from Coimbatore containing the Śrī-raṅganātha Perumal Temple.

Karaṇipākkam.—It is also spelt as Kaḷanipākam. It is a village situated in Vellore taluk in North Arcot district, near Viriñcipuram (*S.I.I.*, I, 136).

Karañjāḍu.—This village may be identical with Komaṇḍa or with Karaḍā situated about 16 miles north of Komaṇḍa (*E.I.*, XXIV, Pt. IV, p. 173).

Karavaṇḍapuram.—This is the same as the village now known as Ukkirankoṭṭai in Kaḷakkuḍi-nāḍu in the Tinnevelly taluk. It was of great strategic importance in the time of the early Pāṇḍyas. Vestiges of a fort and a moat are even now visible, which give evidence to its former greatness. There are two Śiva temples called Arikeśarīśvaram and Rājasiṅgiśvaram, in the vicinity of the village named after the Pāṇḍya kings, Arikeśari and Rājasiṃha (*E.I.*, XXIII, Pt. VII, p. 284).

Karkāṭṭūr.—It may be identified with Kaḷakattūr near Palamaner in the Chittoor district (*E.I.*, XXII, p. 113).

Karkuḍi.—This is the ancient name of Uyyakkoṇḍan Tirumalai in the Nandipanmamaṅgalam on the southern bank of the Kāverī (*S.I.I.*, III, p. 231). It is in Rājāśrayacaturvedimaṅgalam in Pāndikulasaṃvaḷanāḍu (vide *Raṅgāchārī's List*, 1952).

Karṇāṭa country.—This country (*S.I.I.*, I, pp. 69-70, 82, 130, 160, 164) figures prominently in Tamil classics. It is also mentioned in the *Bhāgavata Purāṇa* (V. 6, 7). It has been described as a vast country (*dharāmaṇḍala*). It is occupied by the Kanarese speaking people. The kings of Karṇāṭa were nominally dependent on the kings of Vijayanagara.

Karṇika.—A branch of the Kāverī. It is the Coleroon surrounding Śrīraṅgam (*Padmapurāṇa*, Ch. 62).

Karur or Karuvūr.—It is a village of the Coimbatore district (*S.I.I.*, p. 126, f.n. 1). It is also called Vañji which was the old capital of the Chera kingdom. Ptolemy calls it Karur the capital of the prince of Kerala (Burnell, *South Indian Paleography*, 2nd ed., p. 33, note 2; *Z.D.M.G.*, Vol. XXXVII, p. 99; Hultzsch, *S.I.I.*, I, p. 106 f.n. 2). It is a town in the present Trichy district prominently mentioned in Tamil classics. According to Ptolemy, Karoura was the capital of Kerobothros, i.e., Keralaputra. Karūra means the black town (McCrindle, *Ancient India as described by Ptolemy*, S. N. Majumdar Ed., p. 182).

Karuvūr.—It is the name of a village in the Coimbatore district. It is also the name of a town in the same district (*S.I.I.*, II, pp. 250, 260, 288, 305; Vol. III, p. 31).

Kaurāla.—It has been identified by some with Colair lake and according to others with Sonpur district of C.P., and Korāḍa in South India.

Kālahasti.—It is in the North Arcot district, a place of pilgrimage on the river Suvarṇamukharī (*E.I.*, I, 368).

Kālibhanā.—The Kālibhanā Copperplate Inscriptions of king Mahābharagupta I Janamejaya (*I.H.Q.*, XX, No. 3) mention this village, lying about nine miles to the north-east of Bolangir, the chief town of the Patna State in the Sambalpur district.

Kāḷidurga.—This is modern Calicut, a town (*S.I.I.*, Vol. II, pp. 364–72). The Tamil form of this name is Kaḷḷikoṭṭai.

Kāliyūrkoṭṭam.—It is the name of a district (*S.I.I.*, I, pp. 116, 117, etc.). Its subdivision was Erikalnāḍu (vide 236 of *Raṅgāchārī's List*).

Kāmapurī.—It is also known as Kalyāṇa, the crest-jewel of the Āndhra country (*E.I.*, XXVI, Pt. I, January, 1941). This city was founded by the Coḍa king Annadeva in the Āndhra country, which perhaps became the capital of his principality (*Ibid.*, XXVI, Pt. I).

Kāṃkaraparti (Kāṃkarapartti).—It stands on the bank of the Gautamī (another name of the Godāvarī). It may be identified with the modern village of Kākaraparṛu on the west bank of the Godāvarī. It is at present included in the Tanuku taluk of the West Godāvarī district (*E.I.*, XXVI, Pt. I, January, 1941).

Kāṇa-nāḍu.—It is stated to be a division of Pāṇḍimaṇḍalam. The western part of Tiṛumeyyam taluk, which is the southernmost part of the Pudukoṭṭai State, had in it the ancient district of Kāṇanāḍu. It was contiguous to Keraḷasiṅgavaḷanāḍu (*E.I.*, XXV, Pt. II, April, 1939).

Kānapper.—It is the name of a village in the Pāṇḍya country (*S.I.I.*, Vol. II, p. 149). It is famous for its temple.

Kāñcīpura (Kāñcī or Kāñcīpura) :—Vide *Conjeevaram.*—It was an important place of pilgrimage from very early times. The *Bhāgavatapurāṇa* (X. 79, 14) refers to it as a city. Patañjali mentions it in his *Mahābhāṣya*, II, p. 298. The *Skandapurāṇa* (Ch. I, 19–23) mentions it among other places as holy. The *Yoginītantra* (1. 17) also mentions it. In the Drāviḍa country there existed a city called Kāñcī where lived a rich merchant's son named Śaktikumāra who was anxious to find out a virtuous wife. For this purpose he went to the Siri country on the right bank of the river Kāverī (*Daśakumāracaritam*, p. 153). Kāñcīpura finds mention in the Mayidavolu Copperplate Inscription of Śivaskandavarman (cf. *E.I.*, XXV, Pt. VII, p. 318). Kāñcīpura mentioned in the Aihole Inscription was conquered by Pulakeśin. The Tālaguṇḍa Inscription of Śāntivarman also refers to Kāñcī. It is known as Kāñcīpeḍu. It is Conjeevaram, the capital of Drāviḍa or Coḷa on the river Palār, 43 miles south-west of Madras (cf. *Mahābhārata*, Bhīṣmaparva, Ch. IX). Śiva Kāñcī and Viṣṇu Kāñcī form the western and eastern parts of the city. There is also Jaina Kāñcī, called Tirupparutti-kunram. Of all the temples at Conjeevaram the Kāmākṣī temple is the most important. In this temple the only peculiarity is the Cakra placed in front of the deity. This city is said to have been founded by Kulottunga Coḷa on the site of a forest, called Kurumbhar-bhūmi, afterwards called Toṇḍamaṇḍala. It was one of the capitals of the ancient Coḷas and the capital of the later Pallavas (vide S. K. Aiyangar, *Ancient India and South Indian History and Culture*, Vol. I, 1941, pp. 520ff.). It was one of the notable centres of Buddhist learning. The geographer Ptolemy (McCrindle, *Ancient India as described by Ptolemy*, pp. 185-86) refers to the kingdom of Malanga, ruled by Bassaronaga, which, according to some, was Kāñcī. According to Ptolemy, Malanga was the capital of Arouarnoi (Arvarnoi) (McCrindle, *Ancient India as described by Ptolemy*, p. 185). Kāñcīpura contains the temple of Kailāśanāthasvāmin built in the Pallava style of the 6th century architecture. There is another temple by the name of Rājasiṃhavarmeśvara temple. Besides there are numerous small temples both Śaiva and Viṣṇu (Hultzsch, *S.I. Inscriptions*, I, pp. 1, 2, 3, 19, 29, 77, 113, 116, 118, 120, 123, 125, 139, 140, 141, 145, 146, 147).

Kāñcī was attacked by the Rāṣṭrakūṭa king Govinda and his father. As soon as it was invaded by Govinda, the then ruler of Kāñcī was defeated some time before 803 A.D. as far as we can learn from the British Museum plates of Govinda III (*I.A.*, XI, 126). The Siddhaliṅgamādaṃ Inscription from South Arcot district, as old as the fifth year of Kṛṣṇa's reign, refers to the conquest of Kāñcī and Tanjai or Tanjore (*Madras Epigraphical Collection for* 1909, No. 375). An inscription from the Ukkala Viṣṇu temple in the North Arcot district mentions the king Kannaradevavallabha as the Conqueror of Kāñcī and Tanjore (*E.I.*, IV, 82).

Kāṇḍalur.—It is the name of a village. It may be identified with Cidambaram (*S.I.I.*, I, pp. 63–65, 95, 140). Rājarāja I is said to have destroyed the ships here.

Kāp.—This village is in the South Kanara district of the Madras State where a copperplate was discovered (*Ep. Ind.*, XX, p. 80).

Kāraikkāl (Karikal).—This is a sea-port town. It is the French settlement in the Tanjore district (Hultzsch, *S.I.I.*, Vol. II, p. 295).

Kāruvagrāma.—It is either Koregaon or Karva about six and four miles respectively from Karāḍ on the right bank of the Kṛṣṇā (*E.I.*, XXVI, Pt. VII, p. 323).

Kāṭṭuppāḍi.—It is a village close to the Vellore station of the Madras State (*E.I.*, I, p. 129, f.n. 3).

Kāṭṭuttumbūr.—It is the name of a village. It was in Paṅgalanāḍu, a division of Paḍuvūrkoṭṭam (*E.I.*, I, pp. 78-79). It is really in the Vellore taluk of the North Arcot district.

Kāvanūr (Kāvannūr).—It is the name of a village in the Guḍiyāttaṃ taluk of the North Arcot district (*E.I.*, I, p. 133; *E.I.*, XXIII, Pt. IV, October, 1935, p. 147). It is in the Saidpet taluk, Chingleput district.

Kāverī (or Kāvirī).—It is the name of a river which starting from Coorg passes through the districts of Coimbatore, Trichinopoly, and falls into the Bay of Bengal. It is called 'the beloved of the Pallavas'. This means that a Pallava king ruled over the country along the banks of the Kāverī river (*S.I.I.*, I, p. 29). This river is mentioned in the *Rāmāyaṇa* (Kiṣkindhyākāṇḍa, XLI, 21, 25; cf. *Harivaṃśa*, XXVII, 1416–22; cf.

Mahābhārata, Bhīṣmaparva, IX, 328; Vanaparva, LXXXV, 8164, 5 etc.) and in the *Yoginītantra* (2/6, pp. 178ff,). According to the *Kālikāpurāṇa* (Ch. 24, 130–135) this river has its origin in the Mahākāla lake. The *Kāvyādarśa* of Daṇḍin refers to the lands on the bank of the Kāverī (III, 166). The Tīrthayātrā sections of the Purāṇas and Epics mention this river as very holy. It is the Khaberos of Ptolemy, which is said to have its source in the Adeisathron range which may be identified with the southern portion of the Sahya. The *Bhāgavatapurāṇa* refers to this river (V. 19, 18; VII. 13, 12; X, 79, 14; XI, 5, 40; cf. *Padmapurāṇa*, Uttarakhaṇḍa, vs. 35–38). It is also mentioned in the *Bṛhatsaṃhitā* (XIV. 13) as well as in Kālidāsa's *Raghuvaṃśa* (IV. 45). In the South Indian inscriptions the river Kāverī is associated with the name of the Coḷas. Hara asked Guṇabhara: 'How could I standing in a temple on earth view the great power of the Coḷas or the river Kāverī?' (Hultzsch, *S.I.I.*, I, 34). The Cālukya King Pulakesin II crossed this river with his victorious army to enter the Coḷa country when this river had her current obstructed by the causeway formed by his elephants. The glory of the Kāverī forms an inexhaustible theme of early Tamil poetry. According to the *Maṇimekhalai* (I. 9–12; 23-4) this noble stream was released by the sage Agastya from his waterpot at the request of the king Kānta and for the exaltation of the 'children of the sun'. She was the special banner of the race of the Coḷas and she never failed them in the most protracted drought. The yearly freshes in the Kāverī formed the occasion of a carnival in which the whole nation took part from the king down to the meanest peasant. It is a famous river in South India, which rises in the Western Ghats and flows south-east through Mysore, and falls into the Bay of Bengal in the district of Tanjore in the Madras State. In ancient times, this river, noted for pearl-fishery, flowed down into the sea through the southern portion of the ancient kingdom of Coḷa. The principal Coḷa port was at Kāverī-paṭṭanam or Pugār on the northern bank of the Kāverī, while Uragapura, the ancient capital of Coḷa, was situated on the southern bank of this river. For further details, vide B. C. Law, *Rivers of India*, p. 51.

Kāvirippūmbaṭṭanam.—It is the full Tamil name of Kāverīpaṭṭanam at the mouth of the Kāverī river (*S.I.I.*, II, p. 287). It must be Kāverīppumpaṭṭinam, ancient sea-port capital of the Coḷas, washed away by the deluge according to Tamil classics (vide also V. R. R. Dikshitar, *Pre-Historic South India*, p. 31).

Kendrāpārā.—It is the headquarters of the Kendrāpārā subdivision of the Cuttack district.

Kerakera.—The Ādipur copperplate of Narendrabhañjadeva refers to this village in Ghoshdapir in Ādipur pargana, situated about 12 miles to the south-south-east of Khicing. (*E.I.*, XXV, Pt. IV, p. 158.)

Kerala country.—Kerala is the Kanarese form of the Tamil Ceraḷa. Pāṇini mentions it in his *Aṣṭādhyāyī* (4. 1. 175). The *Bhāgavata Purāṇa* refers to it (X. 79, 19; X. 82, 13). The country was anciently called Ceraḷam or Ceraḷa-nāḍu. Ceraḷam means mountain range. The Kerala country (*S.I.I.*, I, pp. 51, 59, 86, 90, 92, 94) is the same as Cera. According to V. A. Smith, Kerala generally means the rugged region of the Western Ghats south of the Candragiri river (*E.H.I.*, p. 466). It was conquered by Rājendra-Coḍa. It is present Malabar, Cochin and Travancore.

Keralaputra (variant *Ketalaputo*).—It is the Kerala country in South India. Patañjali in his *Mahābhāṣya* (IV, I, 4th āhnika) mentions Kerala (or Malabar). Keralaputra was situated at the south of Kupāka (or Satya), extending down to Kannati in Central Travancore (Karunagapalli taluk). South of it lay the political division of Mūṣika (*J.R.A.S.*, 1923, 413). It was watered by the river Periyār on the bank of which stood its capital Vañji near Cochin and at its mouth there was the seaport of Muchiri (*C.H.I.*, I, 595). The Chera or Kerala country comprised Travancore, Cochin and the Malabar district. The Koṅgudeśa (corresponding to the Coimbatore district and the southern part of Salem district) was annexed to it. Its original capital was Vañji, now Tiru-Karur on the Periyār river near Cochin; but its later capital was Tiru-Vañjikkalam near the mouth of the Periyār. It had important trading centres on the western coast at Toṇḍi on the Agalappulai about five miles north of Quilāndi, Muchiri near the mouth of the Periyār, Palaiyūr Chowghāṭ and Vaikkari close to Koṭṭayaṃ.

In his second and thirteenth Rock Edicts Aśoka mentions Ketalaputas or Keralas as a people living on the border though outside his own realm. Later on, during the age of the *Periplus* Cerobothra (i.e. Keralaputra) was included within Damirica. Subsequently during the time of Ptolemy the kingdom of Karoura was ruled by Cerobothros (Keralaputra).

The Kerala country finds mention in the Epics and *Purāṇas*. According to the *Mahābhārata* (Sabhāparva, XXX, 1174-5; Ch. XXXI; cf. Bhīṣmaparva IX, 352, 365; *Rāmāyaṇa*, Bombay ed., IV, Ch. 41) the Keralas were a forest tribe. The *Vāyupurāṇa* (XLV, 124), *Matsyapurāṇa* (Ch. CXIII, 46) and *Mārkaṇḍeya-purāṇa* (Ch. 57, 45, *Bibliotheca Indica Series*) mention the Coḷas, Pāṇḍyas and Keralas among the peoples of the Dakṣiṇāpatha.

Senguttavan Cera was the first notable Cera monarch. From the Coḷas the hegemony of the south was wrested for a time by the Ceras, but it soon went to the Pāṇḍyas and ultimately to the Pallavas. For further details, vide B. C. Law, *Tribes in Ancient India*, pp. 193-94; *Cambridge History of India*, I, 595; B. C. Law, *Indological Studies*, Pt. I, pp. 58-59.

Keralasiṅga-vaḷanāḍu.—The Tiruppuvanam plates of Jaṭāvarman Kulaśekhara I refer to it, which covered a very large portion of the Tiruppattūr tāluk of the Ramnad district, a part of the Pudukkottai State and it seems to have extended into the Śivagaṅgā Zamindari (*E.I.*, XXV, Pt. II, April, 1939, p. 96).

Keśavapurī.—It may be identified with the modern Keśapurī (*E.I.*, XXV, Pt. V, January, 1940).

Khaḍipadā.—It is a small village, about 24 miles to the south-east of Bhadrak, a sub-divisional town in the Balasore district and about eight miles to the north-west of Jaipur, an important town in the Cuttack district, where an image inscription of the time of Śubhākara was discovered (*E.I.*, XXVI, Pt. VI, April, 1942, p. 247).

Khaṇḍa-dīpa.—*The Bodhisattvāvadāna-Kalpalatā* mentions this country which was burnt by the king of Kaliṅga (8th Pallava, p. 27).

Khaṇḍagiri and Udayagiri.—The twin hills of Khaṇḍagiri and Udayagiri were known to the authors of the Hāthigumphā Cave Inscriptions as the Kumāra and the Kumārī hills. The two hills form part of a belt of sandstone rock, which, skirting the base of the granite hills of Orissa, extends from Autgar and Dekkunāl in a southerly direction past Khurdah and towards the Chilka lake (*J.A.S.B.*, Old Series, Vol. VI, p. 1079). In the north-west of the Khurdah subdivision stands the Khaṇḍagiri hill at a distance of three miles north-west of Bhuvaneswar in the Puri district. The Khaṇḍagiri (broken hill) is the name applicable to three peaks, Udayagiri, Nīlagiri and the Khaṇḍagiri. The crest of the Khaṇḍagiri is the highest point, being 123 ft. high, while the crest of the Udayagiri is 110 ft. high. The Udayagiri has a small Vaiṣṇava hermitage at its foot. It has forty-four caves, the Khaṇḍagiri has nineteen and the Nīlagiri has three. In the Udayagiri the caves are divided into two groups, one higher and the other lower. In the Khaṇḍagiri all the caves except two lie along the foot track. Among the Udayagiri caves the Rāṇīgumphā or the Queen's Palace is the biggest. The other important caves are the Ganeshgumphā, the Jaya-Vijaya cave, the Mañcapurī, the Bāghgumphā (the Tiger cave) and the Sarpagumphā (the Snake cave). In addition to these the Hāthigumphā or the elephant cave and the Anantagumphā are noteworthy.

The crest of the Khaṇḍagiri has been levelled so as to form a terrace with stone edges. In the middle of this terrace stands a Jain temple. The main temple consists of a sanctuary and a porch. Sir John Marshall points out that the Hāthigumphā cave which is the earliest of all these caves is a natural cavern enlarged by artificial cutting. The next in point of time was the Mañcapurī cave which seems to have been the prototype of all the more important caves excavated on this site. Next again was the Anantagumphā. All these caves may be dated not much earlier than the middle of the first century B.C. (*Cambridge History of India*, Vol. I, pp. 639-640). Next in chronological sequence comes the Rāṇīgumphā. (For details vide *Asiatic Researches*, Vol. XV (1824); Fergusson, *Illustrations of the Rock Cut Temples of India* (1845); R. L. Mittra, *Orissa*, Vol. I, Ch. I; *A.S.I.*, Vol. XIII; Fergusson, *History of Indian and Eastern Architecture* (1876) and *Cave Temples* (1880); *Cambridge History of India*, Vol. I, Ch. XXVI; B. M. Barua, *Old Brāhmī Inscriptions in the Udayagiri and Khaṇḍagiri Caves*, 1929; B. C. Law, *Geographical Essays*, Ch. X).

Khedrapur.—It is situated south-west of Mirāj containing an ancient temple. Two sculptures decorate the pedestal of the Koppeśvara temple which was repaired by the Yādava king Singhanadeva (*J.R.A.S.*, Pts. 3 and 4, 1950, pp. 105ff.).

Kīḷ-muṭṭugūr.—It is a village in the Guḍiyāttaṃ taluk of the North Arcot district where three Tamil inscriptions were discovered (*E.I.*, IV, 177ff.).

Kīḷ-vemba-nāḍu.—It is a subdivision of the Pāṇḍya country in which Tinnevelley is situated (*S.I.I.*, III, p. 450).

Kiṇḍeppa.—This village was situated in the Tellavallivisaya (*E.I.*, XXIII, Pt. II, April, 1935, p. 59).

Kisanpura.—It is a village in the Padmapur pargana of the district of Cuttack. An inscription on a stone slab has been discovered in the temple of Śiva Cāteśvara. This temple is about 12 miles north-east from Cuttack. The stone inscription discovered here traces the genealogy of the Gaṅga-rulers from Coḷagaṅga to Anaṅgabhīma (*J.A.S.B.*, LXVII, 1898, pp. 317–27).

Kisarakellā.—It may be identified with the village of Kesarakelā about six miles to the east of Bolangir in the Patna State of the Sambalpur district (*E.I.*, XXII, p. 136).

Koḍūru.—It is in the Guḍivāḍa taluk of the Kistna district where a set of plates (five in number) were discovered (*E.I.*, XXV, Pt. III, p. 137).

Kolāru.—It is the name of a village. Elliot reads it as Kaleru. The name of the village may have something to do with the Kolar or Kolleru lake in the Guḍivāḍa taluk (*S.I.I.*, I, pp. 52, 62; cf. *I.A.*, XIV, p. 204).

Kolāulapura.—It has been identified by Rice with the modern Kolār in the east of Mysore (*E.I.*, XXVI, Pt. V, October, 1941, 167; Rice, *Mysore and Coorg from the Inscriptions*, p. 32).

Kolleru.—It is the name of a lake in the Godāvarī district (*E.I.*, II, p. 308; VI, 3). It is a great lake in the Veṅgimaṇḍala.

Koḷḷippākkai.—This is a village, same as Killippāka. Its walls are surrounded by *Śuḷḷi* trees (*S.I.I.*, I, p. 99). There is a Killippāga in Guntur district (vide 92 of ***Raṅgāchārī's List***).

Komaṇḍa.—It is a village in the Nayāgarh State of Orissa where three copperplates were unearthed (*E.I.*, XXIV, Pt. IV, p. 172—*Komaṇḍa Copperplates of Nettabhañja*).

Komarti.—This village is situated two miles south-west of Narasannapeta, the headquarters of a taluk in the Ganjam district, where three copperplates of Candavarman of Kaliṅga were discovered (*E.I.*, IV, 142).

Komāramaṅgala.—This village is to be identified with Komāramaṅgalaṃ in the Tirucengode taluk of the Salem district. It lies at a distance of about 30 miles from Salem (*Salem Plates of Gaṅga Śrīpuruṣa*: Śaka 693—*E.I.*, XXVII, Pt. IV, p. 148).

Konamaṇḍala.—It is a country in the Godāvarī delta with which the Haihayas were closely connected (*E.I.*, IV, 84, 320). The chiefs of Konamaṇḍala trace their descent from Haihaya, Kṛtavīrya and Kārtavīrya, who belonged to the race of the Yadus.

Konāḍu.—This is one of the ancient provinces of the Tamil country, a part of Pudukkottah State. Koḍumbāḷur in the Pudukkottai State was its chief town (*S.I.I.*, II, p. 458).

Konāraka.—This sandy tract also known as Konārka is situated on the beautiful and holy sea-shore. It is situated near the northernmost end of the sandy strip stretching from the Chilka lake to the Prāchi river. One can come near this site by motor-car in cold weather from Pipli. It contains a deity named Konāditya (*Brahma Purāṇa*, 28, 18). It is famous for the Hindu temple which is one of the best specimens of Indian architecture. This temple which has been dedicated to the Sun-god is commonly known as the Black Pagoda, which is situated at a distance of 21 miles north-east of Puri town. The sea is about a mile and a half to the south-east of the temple. The erection of the temple has been ascribed to the king Narasinhadeva of Khurda of the 13th century A.D. (*J.A.S.B.*, LXXII, 1903, Pt. I, p. 120). The compound of the Black Pagoda (Konārak Temple) is enclosed by a wall and the principal gateway is to the east. A fine hall has been excavated with elaborate carvings in front of the porch. The magnificent temple has sunk down considerably and much has been done to protect it from mischief. The porch is a massive building on a high basement. The stone slab representing 9 planets known as the *Navagraha slab* is an important discovery. (For details vide Burnier, *Konarak* (*Marg*, Vol. II, Nos. 2 and 4); *B. and O. Dist. Gazetteers*, 1929, Puri, by O'Malley, 308ff.; Jarrett's Tr. of Abul Fazle's *Ain-i-Akbari*; Fergusson, *History of Indian and Eastern Architecture*, Book VI, Ch. 2; *A.S.I.R.*, 1902-03, pp. 48-49; 1903-04, p. 9; Hunter, *Orissa*, I; R. L. Mittra, *Antiquities of Orissa*, II, 145).

Koṅgoda.—This has been identified by Kielhorn with Kung-yü-t'o of Yuan Chwang. Cunningham identifies it with Ganjam. Fergusson places it somewhere between Cuttack and Aska in the Ganjam district. Koṅgodamaṇḍala mentioned in the inscriptions (*E.I.*, VI, 136) was under Śaśāṅka and its inhabitants defied Harṣavardhana of Kanauj.

Koṅgu.—It comprises the modern districts of Salem and Coimbatore (*S.I.I.*, III, p. 450).

Koṅkān.—According to the ***Mārkaṇḍeya Purāṇa*** (25) it lies on the river Veṇvā. Southern Koṅkān was conquered by the Vijayanagar General Mādhava. Mādhava gained celebrity as a Śaiva through the favour of his master Kāśīvilāsa (*E.I.*, VI and VIII; *I.A.*, XLV, 17). His zeal for his religion is attested by the Mañcalapura plates. For further epigraphic references regarding southern Koṅkān, vide *E.C.*, VII, 313, 375; *E.C.*, VII, No. 34; *E.C.*, VIII, 152, 166, 382.

Koṅkuduru.—It is a village five miles north of Rāmacandrapuram in the Godāvarī district (*E.I.*, V, 53ff.).

Kopaṇa.—The Kap copperplate of Keladi Sadāśiva-Nāyaka refers to Kopaṇa which is Kopal, a famous place of pilgrimage of the Jainas in the Nizam's Dominions.

Koppaṃ (*Kuppaṃ*).—This is a village on the bank of the river Perāru (Palāru) (*S.I.I.*, I, p. 134). Here Rājendra is said to have a victory over Āhavamalla.

Kopparaṃ.—It is in the Narasaraopet taluk of the Guntur district, where the copperplate of Pulakesin II was discovered (*E.I.*, XVIII, 257).

Korakai.—Its Sanskritised form is Korgāra in the Tinnevelly district, the ancient capital of the Pāṇḍyas (*S.I.I.*, I, p. 168). It is generally spelt in Tamil classics as Korkai. It was a flourishing seaport (V. R. R. Dikshitar, *Pre-Historic South India*, p. 31).

Kori or *Koli.*—It is the same as Uraiyūr, a suburb of Trichinopoly, supposed to be the ancient capital of the Coḷas (*S.I.I.*, II, pp. 252, 459).

Korosaṇḍa.—This village also named as Korosaṇḍā lies six miles to the south of Parlakimedi in the Ganjam district of the Madras State (*E.I.*, XXI, p. 23).

Korukoṇḍa.—It is a hill fort in the Godāvarī valley situated at a distance of about nine miles to the north of Rajahmundry (*E.I.*, XXVI, Pt. I, January, 1941).

Kośala-nāḍu (*Kośalai-nāḍu*).—This is southern Kośala which, according to Cunningham, corresponds to the upper valley of the Mahānadī and its tributaries (*S.I.I.*, I, p. 97; *Archaeological Survey of India*, Vol. XVII, p. 68). According to the Kuruspal Stone Inscription of Someśvaradeva, Mahākośala or Dakṣiṇa Kośala extended from Berar to Orissa and from Amarakaṇṭaka to Bastar (*E.I.*, X, No. 4). In the Ratanpur Inscription of Jājalladeva we find that Kāliṅgarāja acquired the land of Dakṣiṇa Kośala and fixed his capital at Tummāṇa. According to the Bilhari Inscription, Lakṣmaṇarāja is stated to have defeated the lord of Dakṣiṇa-Kośala (*E.I.*, II, p. 305; I, p. 254). Dakṣiṇa-Kośala is generally taken to represent the modern division of Chattisgarh, while Tummāṇa has been identified with the modern village of Tumana in the Bilaspur district (*E.I.*, I, 39ff.; 45ff.).

According to the Jaina *Jambuddīvapaṇṇatti* Kuśāvatī was the capital of Dakṣiṇa-Kośala. It may have been precisely the city which is associated with the Vaitāḍhya range along which there were sixty Vidyādhar towns (*sattiṃ vijjāharaṇa-garāvāsā*, I, 12).

Koṭṭāru.—It is a well-known town near Cape Comorin. This ancient town belongs to the Travancore State and is about 10 miles north of Cape Comorin (*S.I.I.*, III, p. 147).

Koṭṭura.—It is identified with Kothoor, 12 miles south-east of Mahendragiri in Ganjam. There is another Koṭṭura in the Vizagapatam district (*Vizagapatam District Gazetteer*, I, 137).

Koṭyāśrama.—It is the hermitage of Vaśiṣṭha, which has been identified with Kuting, 32 miles from Baripada (*E.I.*, XXV, Pt. IV, p. 154).

Kroṣṭukavarttanī-Viṣaya.—It is the name of a district mentioned in some of the early and later Gaṅga records. This has been identified by Hultzsch with modern Chicacole (*E.I.*, XXVI, Pt. II, pp. 66ff.; *E.I.*, XXV, Pt. V, January, 1940, p. 196). This district (*viṣaya*) also occurs in the

Chicacole plates of Devendravarman. It has been identified by some with the country to the north of the river Vaṃśadharā in the Ganjam district (*Journal of the Mythic Society*, XIV, p. 263).

Kṛṣṇagiri.—It is the Karakorum or the Black mountain (*Vāyup.*, Ch. 36). The Karakorum was known to the ancient geographers as the Kṛṣṇagiri. This mountain is continuous with the Hindukush on the west. According to modern geographers, it is older than the Himalayan proper. It is of Hercynian age (Law, *Rivers of India*, pp. 4 and 7; Rapson, *Andhra Coins*, XXXIII; *Bombay Gazetteer*, I. ii. 9; cf. *Rāmāyaṇa*, VI. 26–30).

Kṛṣṇaverṇā.—This is modern Kṛṣṇā river (*S.I.I.*, I, p. 28). The Kṛṣṇavenvā in the *Purāṇas*, Kaṇhapeṇṇā in the *Jātakas* and Kaṇhapemṇā in the Hāthigumphā Inscription of Khāravela, is a famous river in South India. It occurs in the *Rāmāyaṇa* (Kiṣkindhyākāṇḍa, XLI, 9) as Kṛṣṇaveṇī or Kṛṣṇaveṇā (cf. *Indische Alterthumskunde*, Vol. I, p. 576). It has its source in the Western Ghats. It flows east through the Deccan plateau and breaking through the Eastern Ghats in a gorge, it falls into the Bay of Bengal. (For further details, vide B. C. Law, *Rivers of India*, p. 48). Its variant readings are Veṇa (*Varāha-Purāṇa*, LXXXV), Veṇā or Varṇā (*Kūrma Purāṇa*, XLVII, 34), Vaiṇi (*Vāyu Purāṇa*, XLV, 104), Vīṇā (*Mahābhārata*, Bhiṣmaparva, IX, 328), and Veṇṇā (*Bhāgavata Purāṇa*, XIX, 17). Pargiter suggests its identification with the river Penner between the Kṛṣṇā and the Kāverī (*Mārkaṇḍeya Purāṇa*, p. 303, notes).

Kṛṣṇā.—It is a river which is the same as Kṛṣṇaveṇā as in the Purāṇas or Kṛṣṇaveṇī as in the *Yoginītantra* (2. 5, pp. 139-140; Hultzsch, *S.I.I.*, II, 232). It is also mentioned in the *Bhāgavatapurāṇa* (V. 19, 18) and in the *Bṛhat-saṃhitā* (XIV. 14). It survives in its modern name Kṛṣṇā. It issues from the Sahya mountains according to the *Mārkaṇḍeyapurāṇa* (57, 26, 27). It is also known as Kaṇhapeṇṇā as in the *Jātakas* and Kaṇhapemṇā as in the Hāthigumphā Inscription of Khāravela. It has its source in the Western Ghats; flowing east through the Deccan plateau and breaking through the Eastern Ghats in a gorge, it falls into the Bay of Bengal. Its course lies through the Bombay State, the State of Hyderabad and the Madras State. From the north-east of Alampur to a place below Jaggayyapeta the Krishṇā flows forming the southern natural boundary of Hyderabad. Near about Athni the river is joined by the combined waters of several streams of which the Yerla, the Koind and the Varṇā are well-known. Before it enters Hyderabad it receives the Mālprabhā on its right bank below Muddebihal. In its course through Hyderabad and Madras it is joined by many tributaries including the Dhon, the Bhīmā, the Dindi, the Peddavagu, the Musi-Aler, the Paler, the Muner and the Tuṅgabhadrā. (For details, vide Law, *Rivers of India*, p. 48.)

Kṛṣṇāpura.—It is a deserted village at the western extremity of the ruins of Vijayanagara, where an inscription of Kṛṣṇaraya engraved on a rough stone-tablet dated śaka 1451 was discovered (*E.I.*, I, 398). There is a village by this name situated six miles south-east of Tinnevelly, where copperplates of Sadāśivaraya were discovered (*E.I.*, IX, 328ff.).

Kṛtamālā.—This river is identified with the Vaigai which flows past the town of Madhurā, the capital of the kingdom of Pāṇḍya.

Kuḍamalaināḍu.—It is the same as Coorg (*S.I.I.*, I, p. 63; II, p. 8, 17, 35; III, p. 144). According to Hultzsch it is Malabar.

Kuḍamukkil.—It is Kumbhakonam (*S.I.I.*, III, p. 450).

Kuḍiyāntaṇḍal.—This village is in the Chingleput district (*E.I.*, XIV, 232).

Kudrāhāra.—It is probably the same as Kudūrahāra of the Koṇḍamuḍi with its plates of Jayavarmaṇ. It is the name of a district headquarters at Kudūra, which is the same as the modern Kūḍuru in the Bandar taluk of the Kistna district (*E.I.*, XXV, Pt. I, January, 1939, p. 46).

Kūḷambandal.—It is a village which lies on the road from Conjeeveram to Wandiwash at a distance of five miles south of Māmaṇḍur (*S.I.I.*, III, p. 1). It is in Cheyyar taluk, North Arcot district.

Kumāramaṅgalaṃ.—It is the name of a village, situated east of Korramaṅgalaṃ, north-west of Aimbuṇḍi which lay to the north of Poygai (Rājendra-Coḷanallūr) and south of the river Pālāru (*S.I.I.*, I, pp. 87-88).

Kumārapura.—In the Juraḍa grant of Nettabhañjadeva Kumārapura is identified with the village of the same name in the Berhampur taluk of the Ganjam district (*E.I.*, XXIV, Pt. I, January, 1937, p. 18).

Kumāravalli.—This is the modern name of Kumāravallicaturvedimaṅgalaṃ (*S.I.I.*, II, Intro., p. 23).

Kumārī.—It is the Tamil name of a sacred river near Cape Comorin, and it corresponds to the Sanskrit Kumārī (*S.I.I.*, I, p. 77).

Kumbhakonaṃ.—It is situated on the river Kāverī, a great educational centre and one of the oldest cities of South India. The Śāraṅgapāṇi temple, Kumbheśvara temple, Nāgeśvara temple, and Rāmaswāmī temple deserve mention. The city derived its name from the deity Kumbheśvara. The Nāgeśvara temple contains a separate shrine for Sūrya. Śāraṅgapāṇi is a Vaiṣṇava deity and an incarnation of Viṣṇu. The Rāmasvāmī temple is said to have been built by a king of Tanjore in the 16th century A.D.

Kummaṭa.—It is situated in the Doravadināḍu. It may be identified with Kumāra-Rāmana Kummaṭa, situated at a distance of about eight miles from Ānegoṇḍi (*E.I.*, XXIII, Pt. V).

Kūniyūr.—This village is in the Ambāsamudraṃ taluk of the Tinnevelly district, where copperplates of the time of Venkaṭa II were discovered (*E.I.*, III, 236).

Kuntala.—This is a district of the Karṇāṭa country (*S.I.I.*, I, 156, 160). According to some Mysore Inscriptions (Rice, *Mysore and Coorg from Inscriptions*, p. 3; Fleet, *Dynasties of the Kanarese Districts*, p. 284, f.n. 2), the Kuntala region included the southern part of the Bombay Presidency and the northern portion of Mysore. The identity of the Gondaloi with Kuntala proposed by Yule may be accepted. It is so called because it resembles the hair (*kuntala*) of the goddess of the earth. It was ruled at one time by the kings of the Nanda dynasty. The Kuntalas of the Deccan appear to have risen to a considerable importance in historical times. The Kuntala country is frequently referred to in the inscriptions of the 11th and 12th centuries, when it consisted of the southern Mārāṭhā country and the adjoining Kanarese districts (*E.I.*, XXIV, pp. 104ff.). Literary and epigraphic references prove beyond doubt that there were several families of the Sātakarṇis of the Deccan, and one or more of these families ruled over Kuntala of the Kanarese districts before the Kadambas. An Ajanta Inscription mentions a Vākāṭaka king Pṛthvīsena I, who conquered a Kuntaleśvara (lord of Kuntala). Pṛthvīsena extended his sovereignty over Nachne-Kitalai and Ganj in Bundelkhand as well as over the borders of Kuntala (*E.I.*, XVII, 12; *I.A.*, 1876, p. 318). A Vākāṭaka king Harisena claimed victory over Kuntala. (For further details, vide B. C. Law, *Tribes in Ancient India*, pp. 176ff.). The Rewah Stone Inscription of Karṇa refers to Kuntala, which was the country of the later Cālukyas (*E.I.*, XXIV, Pt. 3, July, 1937, p. 110). According to some, Kuntala is situated between the Bhīmā and Vedavatī, comprising the Kanarese districts of Bombay and Madras States and of Mysore State, and also perhaps a part of Mahārāṣṭra with Vidarbha having its capital at Pratiṣṭhāna on the Godāvarī (Vide V. V. Mirashi, *Hyderabad Archaeological*

Memoir, No. 14, p. 9 f.n.). The Tālaguṇḍa Pillar Inscription informs us that a Kadamba king of Vaijayantī in Kuntala gave his daughters in marriage to Gupta and other kings. Some mediaeval kings of Kuntala traced their lineage to Candragupta (R. K. Mookerjee, *Gupta Empire*, p. 48).

Kūra.—It is a village which possessed 108 families that studied the four *Vedas* (*S.I.I.*, Vol. I, p. 154).

Kūraṃ.—This is a village near Kāñcīpuraṃ. The village of Kūraṃ belonged to the *nāḍu* (country) or in Sanskrit Manyavāntararāṣṭra of Nīrveḷur, a division of Ūrrukkāṭṭukkoṭṭam (*S.I.I.*, I, 144, 147, 154, 155). An inscription records the sale of land by the *sabhā* of Kūraṃ alias Śolamāṭṭaṇḍu Caturvedimaṅgalam in Nīrvelūrnāḍu, a district of Ūrrukkūṭṭukoṭṭam.

Kuvalayasiṅganallūr.—It was situated in the Aṇḍanāḍu subdivision which is represented by Periyakoṭṭai and its vicinity in the Madura district (*E.I.*, XXV, Pt. I, January, 1939, p. 40).

Kuvaḷālapura.—It is a town. Its modern name is Kolār (*S.I.I.*, Vol. II, p. 380).

Lālguḍi.—It is in the Trichinopoly district where the three Tamil inscriptions were found (*E.I.*, XX, p. 46).

Lāmu.—It is situated two miles to the south of Tāḍikoṇḍa in the Guntur district (*E.I.*, XXIII, Pt. V, p. 166).

Lāṅguliya.—This river, also known as the Nāgāvatī, lies between the delta of the Godāvarī and the Mahānadī. It rises in the hills at Kalahandi and flows south through the district of Ganjam to empty itself into the Bay below Chicacole in Madras. It is called the Lāṅgulinī in the *Mārkaṇḍeyapurāṇa* (LVII, 29). It is the river Lāṅgalī mentioned in the *Mahābhārata* (Sabhāparva, IX. 374).

Lekumārī.—It may be identified with Lokamudi in the Kaikalur taluk of the same district (*E.I.*, XXV, Pt. I, p. 46).

Lohitagiri.—This is a hill (*S.I.I.*, II, p. 372).

Lokāloka mountain.—It is the name of a mountain which is supposed to be beyond the ocean of fresh water and beyond which again is the cell of the mundane egg. (*S.I.I.*, III, p. 414; cf. *Viṣṇu Purāṇa* (Wilson), p. 202 note 6).

Luputurā.—Lupaturā or Luputurā is probably the same as Lipatuṅga of the Patna plates of the 6th year (*E.I.*, III, 344). Some have identified it with Lepta, six miles south-east of Bolangir in the Patna State while others are inclined to think that either Nuptara or Nuparsinga within the Sonepur State should be identical with Lupaturā. (*Ep. Ind.*, XXIII, Pt. VII, July, 1936, p. 250).

Madhyama-Kaliṅga.—It was the name of the territory which roughly corresponds to the modern district of Vizagapatam (*E.I.*, VI, 227, 358; *Annual Report of the South Indian Epigraphy*, 1909, p. 106; *Ibid.*, 1918, p. 132). According to some it seems to be identical with Modocalingae of Megasthenes (*I.A.*, VI, 338).

Madurai.—This is Madura (*S.I.I.*, Vol. III, p. 206), capital of the Pāṇḍyas.

Maduramaṇḍalaṃ.—It is the name of a country (*S.I.I.*, I, pp. 97, 99, 112). It is the ancient Pāṇḍya country, the capital of which was Madura. This is known as Modoura by Ptolemy. It is situated on the bank of the river Vaigāi.

Madurā.—According to the *Rāmāyaṇa* (Uttarakāṇḍa, Sarga 83, v. 5) this beautiful city was full of Rākṣasas (demons) for a long time. This city is situated on the right bank of the river Vaigāi. It stands on the main line of the Southern Railway, 345 miles from Madras. (*Madras Dist. Gazetteers, Madura*, by W. Francis, pp. 257ff.). It is full of temples, and is undoubtedly a religious city. The temple of Viṣṇu is within a mile from the railway station, and the inside of it is made up of black marble with a pathway for circumambulation. The biggest of all temples at Madurā is that of Mīnākṣī, who is Lakṣmī. This temple covers a very large area, a portion of which is dedicated to Mīnākṣī and the other to Śiva. Madurā was the capital of the Pāṇḍya kings. It was the capital of Jaṭāvarman who ascended the throne in the 13th century A.D. and conquered the Hoysala king Someśvara of Karnāṭaka (*E.I.*, III, 8). Prof. Dikshitar in his *Studies in the Tamil Literature and History* (p. 13) distinguishes Dakṣiṇa Madurā from the modern city of Madurā.

Madurodaya-vaḷanāḍu.—It is one of the districts of the Pāṇḍya country (*E.I.*, XXV, Pt. II, April, 1939, p. 96).

Mahābalipuram.—This place is situated on the sea at a distance of about 35 miles to the south of Madras and 20 miles on the south-east of Chingleput. According to a Vaiṣṇava saint Śiva lived here with Viṣṇu and hence we find shrines of both these deities situated close to each other. It is a place of seven pagodas. Besides there are several caves, natural and artificial. In some of them we find very attractive cultural representations of Pauranic scenes. Mention may be made of the sculptures representing Mahiṣa-mardinī destroying the Rākṣasas, Arjuna's penance, Śrīkṛṣṇa supporting the hill to protect the cattle from the anger of the rain-god, etc. The *Varāha* or the boar incarnation of Viṣṇu is of great importance. This deity is seen standing with his right foot, resting on the god of snakes, and the goddess of the earth resting on his right thigh (Law, *Holy Places of India*, p. 39).

Mahā-Gaurī.—The *Mārkaṇḍeya Purāṇa* (LVII, 25) refers to it which is a synonym of Brāhmaṇī. It is the modern river Brāhmaṇī in Orissa (cf. *Mahābhārata*, Bhīṣmaparva, IX, 341).

Mahākāntāra.—According to some Sambalpur on the Mahānadī was probably its capital. It is identified with the eastern Gaṇḍavana or with the southern Jhārakhaṇḍa.

Mahārāṣṭra.—The Mahārāṣṭra country or Mo-ho-la-cha is the Deccan in the narrowest sense (*S.I.I.*, I, p. 113, f.n. 3). Mahārāṣṭra is really the country watered by the upper Godāvarī and that lying between this river and the Kṛṣṇā. According to the Aihole Inscription there are three divisions in it, each called Mahārāṣṭraka in the 7th century A.D. (*I.A.*, XXII, 1893, p. 184).

According to Hiuen Tsang this country was about 5,000 li in circuit. The soil was rich and fertile and it was regularly cultivated. The climate was hot and the people were honest and simple. They were of tall stature and vindictive in nature. There were some *Saṅghārāmas* and *Deva temples* (Beal, *Buddhist Records of the Western World*, II, 255ff.). It is said to be the Ariake of Ptolemy (p. 39). It was 6,000 li in circuit, and the capital was on the west of a great river. The ancient capitals of Mahārāṣṭra were (1) Pratiṣṭhān or Paiṭhāna on the Godāvarī, (2) Kalyāṇa on the eastern shore of the Bombay harbour, (3) Vātāpi of the early Cālukyas, (4) Bādāmi which was the real capital in Yuan Chwang's time. According to Saupārā and Māski inscriptions the Mahārāṣṭra country formed a part of the empire of Aśoka. One of the missionaries sent by Aśoka to spread the gospel of the Buddha in the Mahārāṣṭra country was Dhammarakkhita (*Mahāvaṃsa*, Ch. XII, p. 97, Geiger's Ed.). For further details, vide *C.A.G.I.*, notes, pp. 745ff.; N. L. De, *Geographical Dictionary*, p. 118; S. R. Shende, *How, whence and when Mahārāṣṭra came into being* published in the *Siddha-Bhāratī*, Pt. II, pp. 285ff; H. D. Sankalia, *Ancient and Pre-historic Mahārāṣṭra*, *J.B.B.R.A.S.*, Vol. 27, Pt. I, 1951, New Series.

Mahāvināyaka hill.—It is in the Jajpur subdivision. It is worshipped by the followers of Śiva as the union of Śiva, Ganeśa and Gaurī. (*B. and O. Dist. Gazetteers*, Cuttack, by O'Malley, 1933).

Mahendravāḍi.—It is a village three miles east-south-east of the Sholinghur railway station on the line from Arkonam junction to Arcot, where an inscription of Guṇabhara written in Archaic Pallava alphabet was discovered (*E.I.*, IV, 152).

Mahendrācala.—The *Yoginītantra* (2. 4. 128ff.) has a reference to the Mahendra mountain. The Gautamī plates of Gaṅga Indravarman mention it. It probably refers to the hills of this name in the Ganjam district (*E.I.*, XXIV, Pt. IV, October, 1937, p. 181). The Mahendra range of mountains extended from Ganjam as far south as the Pāṇḍya country to the whole of the Eastern Ghat range. The Mahendrādri or the Mahendra mountain was situated between the Gaṅgāsāgarasaṅgama and the Sapta-Godāvarī. A portion of the Eastern Ghats near Ganjam is still called the Mahendra hill. Pargiter thinks that the name should be limited to the hills between the Mahānadī, Godāvarī and Wen Gaṅgā, and may perhaps comprise the portion of the Eastern Ghats north of the Godāvarī. (*Mārkaṇḍeyapurāṇa*, p. 305 note). According to Bāṇa's *Harṣacarita* (Ch. VII) the Mahendra mountain joins the Malayaparvata. The *Raghuvaṃśa* (IV. 39, 43; VI. 54) places it in Kaliṅga. The name is principally applied to the range of hills separating Ganjam from the valley of the Mahānadī. Kālidāsa styles the king of Kaliṅga as the Lord of the Mahendra (*Raghuvaṃśa*, IV. 43; VI. 54).

The minor hills associated with the Mahendra mountain were the Śrīparvata, Puṣpagiri, Venkaṭādri, Aruṇācala and Ṛṣabha.

The whole range of hills extending from Orissa to the district of Madura was known as the Mahendraparvata. It included the Eastern Ghats. It joined the Malaya mountain. Paraśurāma retired to this mountain after being defeated by Rāmacandra.

The Eastern Ghats must have been known to the geographers of ancient India as the Mahendragiri, as the highest peak of the Eastern Ghats is still called by that name. They run as detached hills more or less parallel to the eastern coast of India, which are known by different names in different parts of the country. For details vide B. C. Law, *Mountains of India*, Calcutta Geographical Society Publication No. 5, p. 22.

Mahiṣa.—Rice has identified it with Mysore (*Mysore and Coorg from Inscriptions*, p. 14). Some have identified it with Māhiṣmatī and others with Mahāśvara on the northern bank of the Narmadā in the Nimar district of the old Indore State.

Mainākaparvata.—The *Rāmāyaṇa* locates it in South India. According to Aśvaghoṣa it entered the river to check the course of the ocean (*Saundaranandakāvya*, Ch. VII, verse 40). This legendary account is also found in the Rāmāyaṇa, which locates the Mainākaparvata in the Dakṣiṇāpatha. This mountain also known as the Malayagiri had three cavities crowded with serpents (*Daśakumāracarita*, p. 36).

Malabar.—It is the Kerala country (*S.I.I.*, II, pp. 4, 241).

Malaikkuṟṟam.—This is a district which may be identified with the Malakūṭa (Mo-lo-Kū-t'a) (Watters, *On Yuan Chwang*, II, pp. 228ff.), of Hiuen Tsang which he located in the delta of the Kāverī (*S.I.I.*, III, p. 197).

Malaināḍu.—It is confined to Malayalam or Malabar. It comprises the territory of the Pāṇḍyas besides those of the Cera king. It is mentioned in the inscription of Rājendra Coḷa (*S.I.I.*, II, pp. 236, 242, etc.).

Malaiyūr.—It is situated on a fine hill with a fort (*Ibid.*, Vol. III, p. 469).

Malayagiri.—It is the name of a hill (*Ibid.*, III, p. 422). It is mentioned in the *Brihat-saṃhitā* (XIV. 11). A Pāṇḍya king leaving his own country sought refuge in this hill. Pargiter correctly identifies this range of hills with the portion of Western Ghats from the Nilgiris to the Cape Comorin. The hermitage of Agastya was situated on the Malayakūṭa which was also known as Śrīkhaṇḍādri or even as Candanādri (cf. Dhoyi's *Pavanadūtam*). The southern extension of the Western Ghats below the Kāverī, now known as the Travancore hills, really forms the western side of the Malayagiri. According to some the mount Candaka mentioned in the *Jātaka* (V. 162) is the Malayagiri or the Malabar State.

Malayācala.—The Epic tradition locates it in South India. Jīmūtavāhana took shelter on this mountain after renouncing his sovereignty (*Bodhisattvāvadāna-Kalpalatā*, 108 Pallava, p. 12). The *Padmapurāṇa* (Ch. 133) mentions Kalyāṇatīrtha in Malayācala. Dakṣiṇādri mentioned in the *Kāvyādarśa* (III, 150) by Daṇḍin is the same as the Malayācala according to the commentator.

Malkhed.—The Salotgi Inscription of Kṛṣṇa III describes this imperial capital of the Rāṣṭrakūṭas as 'Sthirībhūta-Kaṭake', i.e., the place where the military forces were located (*E.I.*, IV, 66; XIII, 176ff.).

Mallai.—This is modern Mahābalipuraṃ in the Chingleput district (*Vailūr Inscription of Kopperunjingadeva, E.I.*, XXIII, Pt. V, 180).

Managoḷi.—This village is situated about 11 miles to the north-west of Bagewāḍi, the chief town of the Bagewāḍi taluk of the Bijapur district (*E.I.*, V, p. 9).

Maṇalūr.—It is a village on the Tuṅgabhadrā (*S.I.I.*, Vol. II, p. 230). There is a village named Maṇalūr in Pāṇḍyan territory (vide *Raṅgāchārī's List*, Tinnevelly, 515).

Manayirkoṭṭam.—It is the name of a district (*S.I.I.*, I, p. 147).

Mandārthi.—This village is situated in the Udipi taluk of the South Canara district containing a temple of Śrī Durgāparameśvarī (*J.I.S.O.A.*, Vol. XV).

Maneikallu.—An ancient site in the Guntur district of the Madras Presidency where an early Brāhmī inscription was discovered.

Maṇimaṅgalaṃ.—It is a village at the eastern extremity of the Conjeeveram taluk of the Chingleput district, about six miles west of Vaṇḍalur, a station on the Southern Railway. In Sanskrit verses the name of the village is Ratnāgrahāra (*S.I.I.*, Vol. III, pp. 48, 49, 50). In the inscriptions Narasimhapuraṃ (Chingleput) came to be known as Kiḍāraṃgoṇḍaśoḷapuraṃ (*Madras Epigraphical Reports*, 244 and 245 of 1910). A battle was fought here by Narasimhavarman, the Pallava king, in which Pulakeśin was defeated (*S.I.I.*, Vol. I, 144, 145; Vol. II, 363).

Inscriptions of the reign of Rājarāja I refer to Maṇimaṅgalaṃ as Lokamahādevī-Caturvedimaṅgalaṃ called after his queen Lokamahādevī, but the inscriptions recorded after his fifteenth year and in the reigns of his successors down to the reign of Kulottuṅga I, call the village by the name of Rājacūḍāmaṇicaturvedimaṅgalaṃ (*M.E.R.*, 289 and 292 of 1897 and of 1892; cf. *S.I.I.*, Vol. III, Nos. 28–30).

Mañjirā.—It is a tributary of the Godāvarī, which rises from the Bālāghāt ranges and flows south-east and north to join the Godāvarī. It is fed by three streams on the left and by five on the right. Its another variant is Vañjulā (*Vāyu-Purāṇa*, XLV, 104).

Manneru.—It is a river in the Nellore district (*S.I.I.*, II, p. 4).

Marudur.—It is a village in the Kovilpatti taluk of the Tinnevelly district (*E.I.*, XXIV, Pt. IV).

Maṭṭepād.—It is a village in the Ongole taluk of the Guṇṭur district, where the inscription engraved on five copperplates of Dāmodaravarman was discovered (*E.I.*, XVIII, 327ff.).

Māḍakkuḷam.—It lies to the west of Madurā (*E.I.*, XXIV, Pt. IV, p. 170).

Māhiṣaka (***Māhiṣika***).—It is in the south and the people inhabiting it are referred to in the *Purāṇas* (*Mārkaṇḍeya*, LVII, 46; *Matsya*, CXIII, 47; cf. *Mahābhārata*, Sabhāparva, IX, 366) as a South Indian people.

Māhiṣmatī (Pali: Māhissati).—It is mentioned in the Sabhāparva of the *Mahābhārata* (XXX, 1025–63). Some say that it was situated about 40 miles to the south of Indore. It seems to have been situated on the right bank of the river Narmadā between the Vindhya and the Ṛkṣa and it can be safely identified with the modern Mandhātā region, where there was a river called the Māhiṣiki mentioned in the *Rāmāyaṇa* (Kiṣkindhyākāṇḍa, XLI, 16). According to the *Harivaṃśa* (XLV, 5218ff.), the founder of Māhiṣmatī seems to have been Mucukunda. Some consider Māhiṣmat to be its founder. According to the *Purāṇas* (*Matsya P.*, XLIII, 10–29; XLIV, 36; *Vāyu*, 94, 26; 95, 35), Māhiṣmatī was founded by a prince of the Yadu lineage. The *Bhāgavata Purāṇa* refers to it as a city of the Haihayas (IX. 15, 26; IX. 16, 17; X. 79, 21). The *Padma Purāṇa* (183. 2) points out that Māhiṣmatī was situated on the river Narmadā. The *Daśakumāracarita* (p. 194) tells us that Queen Vasundharā and the royal children were conducted to this city and presented to Mitravarma. Bhandarkar says that Avantī-Dakṣiṇāpatha had Māhiṣmatī or Māhissati as its capital. The *Purāṇas* style the first dynasty of Māhiṣmatī as Haihaya (*Matsya P.*, 43, 8–29; *Vāyu P.*, 94, 5–26). The *Mahābhārata* distinguishes between Avantī and Māhiṣmatī (II, 31, 10). Patañjali's *Mahābhāṣya* mentions Māhiṣmatī along with Vaidarbha and Kāñcīpura (IV. 1, 4th Āhnika).

Māmallapuram.—This is a village which is generally called the seven pagodas situated on the sea coast, 32 miles south of Madras, famous for the Pallava remains (*S.I.I.*, I, p. 1; Fergusson and Burgess, *Cave Temples*, pp. 105–159). It also served as the sea port of the Pallavas.

Māramaṅgalaṃ.—It is in the Tinnevelly district. Māraneri and Māramaṅgalaṃ were called in ancient times Māramaṅgalaṃ (*E.I.*, XXI, Pt. III).

Māvinūru.—It is the name of a village which is perhaps identical with Māvinūru of the Konnūr Inscription (*E.I.*, VI, 28). Kielhorn has identified it with the modern Mannoor, eight miles east by south of Konnūr. The Venkaṭāpur Inscription of Amoghavarṣa (Śaka 828) records the gift of a garden with one thousand creepers at Māvinūru to one Candrateja-Bhaṭṭāra (*E.I.*, XXVI, Pt. II, p. 60).

Māyiruḍiṅgaṃ.—This is an island surrounded by the deep sea as a moat (*S.I.I.*, II, p. 109).

Melpaṭṭi.—It is in the Guḍiyāttaṃ taluk of the North Arcot district, where the inscription of Vijaya-kampa-Vikrama-Varman has been found (*E.I.*, XXIII, Pt. IV, October, 1935, p. 143).

Melpāḍi.—It is a village in North Arcot district, six miles north of Tiruvallam (*S.I.I.*, II, pp. 222, 249, etc.). It is situated on the western bank of the river Nīvā (*Ibid.*, III, p. 23). According to the Ambāsamudram

Inscription of Solanralaikoṇḍa Vīrapāṇḍya, it is in the Chittoor district (*E.I.*, XXV, Pt. I, January, 1939). The Karhad plates of Kṛṣṇa III were issued when the Rāṣṭrakūṭa king Govinda III was encamped here, engaged in taking possession of all the properties of the defeated feudatories (*E.I.*, IV, p. 278).

Melur.—It is a village, about 16 miles north-west of Madurā (*E.I.*, XXI, Pt. III, July, 1931). According to Francis it is situated at a distance of 18 miles north-east of Madura on the road to Trichinopoly. (*Madras District Gazetteers*, Madura, p. 288).

Meru.—This is a mountain which contains gold deposits, and is supposed to be situated to the north of the Jambudvīpa. The temple at Cidāmbaram seems to have been looked upon as the southern Meru, as it contained a large amount of gold on the roof of its golden hall (*S.I.I.*, I, p. 166; II, p. 235).

Miṇḍigal.—It is a village about 11 miles north-west of Cintāmaṇi, the headquarters of the Cintāmaṇi taluk of the Kolar district in Mysore State (*E.I.*, V, 205ff.).

Miyāru-nāḍu.—It included the present Tiruvallam in the North Arcot district and the surrounding region (*E.I.*, XXIII, Pts. II, IV, October, 1935).

Morounda.—Ptolemy speaks of this city as an inland town of the Aioi (*Ptolemy's Ancient India*, by McCrindle, pp. 215-216). The country of the Aioi was probably some region south of the Kerala country, but this city has not yet been identified. It was probably a city of the Muruṇḍas, and the Moroundai had another settlement in the farthest south (Law, *Tribes in Ancient India*, 93).

Mṛṣika (Mūṣika or Mūṣaka) Country.—The *Mārkaṇḍeya Purāṇa* (LVIII, 16) mentions the country of the Mṛṣikas in the south-east. Pargiter suggests that the Mṛṣikas were probably settled on the bank of the river Musi on which stands modern Hyderabad (*Mārkaṇḍeya Purāṇa*, p. 366). Both in the *Mahābhārata* (Bhīṣmaparva, IX, 366) and the *Mārkaṇḍeya Purāṇa* the Mṛṣikas are mentioned as a people living in the south.

Mudumaḍuvu.—The Inscriptions of Vaidumba Mahārāja Gaṇḍatrinetra mention it, which may be identified with Mudimaḍugu in the Anantapur district (*E.I.*, XXIV, Pt. IV, October, 1937, p. 191).

Mugaināḍu.—This is a district, a division in the middle of Paṅgalanāḍu (*S.I.I.*, I, pp. 97, 99, 101), forming part of Jayaṅkoṇḍa-Coḷamaṇḍalam.

Mūlaka.—The country of the Mūlakas seems to have been mentioned as Maulika in Varāhamihira's *Bṛhat-saṃhitā* (XIX, 4). The Mūlakas were a small tribe very closely related with the Aśmakas of the south. According to Bhaṭṭasvāmī, the commentator of Kauṭilya's *Arthaśāstra*, their country was identical with Mahārāṣṭra. In the *Vāyu Purāṇa* (Ch. 88, 177-8) the Mūlakas and the Aśmakas are said to be scions of the same Ikṣvāku family. Mūlaka, the originator of the Mūlaka tribe, is described in the *Garuḍa Purāṇa* (Ch. 142, 34) as the son of king Aśmaka, a descendant of Bhagīratha. The Godāvarī formed the border line between the territories of the Assaka and Aḷaka or Mūḷaka (B. C. Law, *Geography of Early Buddhism*, p. 21; *Paramatthajotikā on the Suttanipāta*, p. 581). Opinions differ as to the peoples of these two countries. The Pauranic tradition as recorded in the *Viṣṇudharmottara* (Pt. I, Ch. 9) proves that they were different. According to the Sona-Nanda-Jātaka (*Jātaka*, V, 317) the Assaka country is associated with Avantī. According to D. R. Bhandarkar (*Carmichael Lectures*, 1918, pp. 53-54) the contiguity mentioned in the *Sonananda-Jātaka* can only be explained, if it is assumed that in later times Mūlaka was included in Assaka, and that the latter country was thus contiguous with Avantī. As late as the second quarter of the 2nd century A.D. we find the Mūlakas distinguished from the Aśmakas in the Nasik Inscription of Gautamī. For further details vide B. C. Law, *Indological Studies*, I, 49ff.

Muṇḍa-rāṣṭra.—It is mentioned in the Uruvupalli and Pikira grants of Simhavarman. It is identical with the later Muṇḍa-nāḍu or Muṇḍai-nāḍu of the Nellore Inscriptions (*E.I.*, XXIV, Pt. VII, p. 301).

Muralā.—It is a river flowing in Kerala (*Raghuv.*, IV, 54-55).

Murappu-nāḍu.—It is a village in the Śrīvaikuṇṭam taluk of the Tinnevelly district, six miles east of Palamcottah and is situated on the right bank of the river Tāmraparṇī (*E.I.*, XXIV, Pt. IV, p. 166; Sewell, *List of Antiquities*, I, p. 312).

Murasīman.—The Kālibhanā copperplate inscriptions of King Mahābhavagupta I Janamejaya mention it, identified with Mursing in the Jarasinghā Zemindari in the Patna State, Orissa (*I.H.Q.*, XX, No. 3).

Mūrūr.—This village may be identified with the modern Mūrūr, about 10 miles north of Kumta in the Kumta taluk of the North Canara district (*E.I.*, XXVII, Pt. IV, p. 160).

Mūṣaka (Mūṣika).—See *Mriṣika.*

Mūṣikanagara.—It is referred to in the Hāthigumpā Inscription of king Khāravela of Kaliṅga, who, in the second year of his reign, is said to have struck terror into the heart of the people of that place (*E.I.*, XX, 79, 87; Barua, *Old Brāhmī Inscriptions*, p. 176; *J.R.A.S.*, 1922, p. 83). Dr. Thomas finds no reference in the passage to any Mūṣika city (*J.R.A.S.*, 1922, p. 83; B. C. Law, *Tribes in Ancient India*, p. 384).

Mutgi.—It is a village in the Bāgewāḍi taluk of the Bijapur district. It is situated some 6½ miles to the south-west of the Bāgewāḍi town. Its ancient name is Muritage, where two inscriptions were found (*E.I.*, XV, 25ff.).

Mūtiba.—It is located in the south (*Mahābhārata*, XII, 207, 42; cf. *Vāyu Purāṇa*, 45, 126; *Matsya Purāṇa*, 114, 46–8). The people inhabiting it were known as the Mūtibas who were probably the same as the Modubae of Pliny. For details vide Law, *Tribes in Ancient India*, p. 173.

Naḍagām.—It is a village in the Narasannapeta taluk of the Ganjam district (*E.I.*, IV, 183).

Nakkavāram.—This is the Tamil name of the Nicobar Islands (*S.I.I.*, III, p. 195).

Nalatigiri or Naltigiri or Lalitagiri.—It lies about six miles to the south-east of Balicandrapura on the Birūpa river. It is near Dhanmandal railway station. It is a big village within which there are three hills. A standing image of the Bodhisattva Vajrapāṇi, two armed Padmapāṇi Avalokīteśvara and four armed Tārā have been discovered here. For a detailed study, vide R. P. Chanda, *Exploration in Orissa*, *M.A.S.I.*, No. 44, pp. 8-9.

Nandagiri.—The Indian Museum plates of Gaṅga Indravarman refer to Nandagiri, which is identified with Nandidrug, the well-known fortified hill to the west of the Kolar district, Mysore State (*E.I.*, XXVI, Pt. V, October, 1941, 167).

Nandipuram.—It is the name of a village identical with Nāthankovil near Kumbakonam (*S.I.I.*, III, p. 233).

Nandivelugu.—It is in the Guntur district where an inscription has been found engraved on the roof of a Śiva temple (*Annual Report of South Indian Epigraphy*, 1921, p. 47).

Narasapatam.—It is a taluk of the Vizagapatam district (*E.I.*, XI, 147–58).

Narasiṅgapalli.—This village is in the Chicacole taluk of the Ganjam district, where the plates of Hastivarman of Kaliṅga of the year 79 were discovered (*E.I.*, XXIII, Pt. II, April, 1935, p. 62).

Naravana.—This village was given to some Brahmins by a Cālukya king at the request of Rāṣṭrakūṭa Govindarāja, according to the Naravana plates of Vikramāditya II dated Śaka 664. According to the Narwan plates of Cālukya Vikramāditya II it is a village on the seashore in the Guhāgarpeta of the Ratnagiri district (*E.I.*, XXVII, Pt. III, p. 127).

Navagrāma.—The Ganjam copperplates of Vajrahasta III mention it which may be identified with modern Naogam in the Tekkali taluk of the Ganjam district (*E.I.*, XXIII, Pt. II, April, 1935, p. 69).

Navakhaṇḍavāḍa.—According to the Pithāpuram Inscription of 1186 A.D. this village, situated about a mile and a half from Pithāpuram, was dedicated to the god Kuntimahādeva (*E.I.*, IV, p. 53).

Navatula or Navatulā.—The Triliṅga Inscription of Devendravarman, son of Guṇārṇava, refers to this village situated in the Korasoḍaka-pañcālī-viṣaya, which has been identified with the hamlet of Nantala, situated about six miles to the south-west of Parlakimeḍi. The Korashaṇḍā plates of Viśākhavarman and the Chicacole plates of Indravarman (*I.A.*, XIII, pp. 122ff.) mention Korasoḍaka-pañcālī, which may be identified with the modern Korashaṇḍa, a village six miles to the south of Parlakimeḍi in the Ganjam district (*I.H.Q.*, XX, No. 3).

Nayanapalle.—This village is situated about three miles from Moṭupalle in the Bapatla taluk of the Guntur district where a stone inscription of Gaṇapatideva has been discovered (*E.I.*, XXVII, Pt. V, p. 193).

Nāgārjunikoṇḍa.—This hill belongs to the Palnad taluk of the Guntur district of the Madras State. It overhangs the right bank of the river Kṛṣṇā. Nāgārjuna's hill which is a large rocky hill, lies 16 miles west of Macherla railway station. This remarkable site was discovered in 1926. Several brick-mounds and marble-pillars have been discovered. Some of the pillars bear inscriptions in Prakrit and in Brāhmī characters of the 2nd and 3rd centuries A.D. A number of ruined monasteries, apsidal temples, stūpas, inscriptions, coins, relics, pottery, statues, and more than 400 magnificent bas-reliefs of the Amarāvatī type are the discoveries made here. The inscriptions recovered from Nāgārjunikoṇḍa go to show that in the 2nd and 3rd centuries A.D. the ancient city of Vijayapurī must have been one of the largest and most important Buddhist settlements in South India. The stūpas, monasteries and temples were built of large bricks, the bricks being laid in mud-mortar and the walls covered with plaster. The mouldings and other ornamentation of these brick-structures were usually executed in *stucco* and the buildings were whitewashed from top to bottom. At Nāgārjunikoṇḍa each monastic establishment was complete in itself. For a detailed study vide A. H. Longhurt, *The Buddhist Antiquities of Nāgārjunikoṇḍa*, Madras Presidency (*M.A.S.I.*, No. 54).

Nāndīkaḍa.—It is mentioned in the Basim plates of Vākāṭaka Vindhyaśakti II (*E.I.*, XXVI, Pt. III, July, 1941). It may be identified with Nanded, the chief town of a district of the same name in the Nizam's dominions.

Nagapatam taluk.—It is a seaport in the present Tanjore district, once famous for the Buddhist images (*S.I.I.*, Vol. II, p. 48). It is situated about 10 miles south of Kārnikkāl known to Ptolemy as an important town. It became a centre of trade and of many religions including Buddhism long before it attracted the attention of European merchants and missionaries (Law, *Tribes in Ancient India*, p. 186).

Nellur.—It is modern Nellore, the headquarters of the district of the same name in the Madras Presidency. The eastern Cālukyas ruled the northern portion of this district (*S.I.I.*, II, 372).

Neṭṭur.—A village of this name is situated in the Śivagaṅgā Zamindari, five miles west of Iḷaiyanguḍi (*Ibid.*, III, p. 206).

Niḍūr.—This village is situated on the north bank of the Kāverī in the Māyāvaram taluk of the Tanjore district (*E.I.*, XVIII, p. 64).

Nīla-Gaṅgavaraṃ.—It is in the Vinukoṇḍa taluk of the Guntur district, where an inscription has been found (*E.I.*, XXV, Pt. VI, April, 1940, p. 270).

Nīlakaṇṭha-caturvedi-maṅgalaṃ.—This is also known as Gāṅgeyanallūr, Nellore talu , North Arcot district. It is a village in Karaivari-āndināḍu (*S.I.I.*, I, pp. 77-78).

Nīlācala.—This hill stands in the centre of Utkala (*Skandap.*, Ch. I, 12-13).

Nīlguṇḍa.—This village is in the Bellary district, Madras State, where the plates of Vikramāditya VI were discovered (*E.I.*, XII, 142ff.).

Nīvā.—It is the name of a river, a tributary of the Pālāru (*S.I.I.*, III, p. 88).

Nutimaḍugu.—This village is in the Anantapur district where some copperplates were discovered (*E.I.*, XXV, Pt. IV, p. 186).

Oḍḍaviṣaya.—The country of the Uḍras or Oḍḍas or Oḍras (Telegu Oḍhrulu; Kanarese Oḍḍaru and the U-Cha of Hiuen Tsang) is the modern Orissa (*S.I.I.*, I, p. 97). It is mentioned in the *Bṛhat-saṃhitā* (XIV. 6) as Uḍra. The *Yoginītantra* (2. 9. 214ff.) mentions it as Oḍra. In the *Mahābhārata* the Uḍras are associated with the Utkalas, Mekalas, Kaliṅgas, Puṇḍras and Andhras (Vanaparva, LI, 1988; Bhīṣmaparva, IX, 365; Droṇaparva, IV, 122). The Pali *Apadāna* (II, 358) mentions Oḍḍakas who were the same as Oḍrā or Uḍrā. According to the *Brahmapurāṇa* (28, 29, 42) the country of the Oḍras extended northwards to Birajāmaṇḍala (Jājpur), and consisted of three kṣetras called Puruṣottama or Śrīkṣetra, Savitu or Arkakṣetra, and Birajākṣetra through which flew the river Vaitaraṇī. Hiuen Tsang who visited this country travelled from Karṇasuvarṇa south-west for about 722 li and then reached the Wu-t'u or U-Cha country. The Tirumalai Rock Inscription of the 13th year of king Rājendracoḷa refers to the conquest of Oḍḍaviṣaya by king Rājendracoḷa. According to the Ādipur copperplate of Narendrabhañjadeva (*E.I.*, XXV, Pt. IV, p. 159) Oḍraviṣaya originally denoted only a small district but it was afterwards applied to the whole province. This country was above 7,000 li in circuit. It was rich and fertile, though the climate was hot. The people were fond of learning and most of them believed in the law of the Buddha. There were many *Saṅghārāmas* and some *Deva* temples (Beal, *Buddhist Records of the Western World*, II, 204; cf. Watters, *On Yuan Chwang*, II, pp. 193-194).

Olliṅga.—This village may be identified with Delang situated in the Ānandpur sub-division of the Keonjhar State (*E.I.*, XXV, Pt. IV, p. 173).

Oymā-nāḍu.—It is otherwise known as Vijayarājendravaḷanāḍu, the district of Jayaṅkoṇḍacoḷamaṇḍalaṃ. It is the tract of the country in which the modern town of Tiṇḍivanaṃ in the South Arcot district is situated (*S.I.I.*, II, 425).

Paḍuvūr-koṭṭam.—The Melpaṭṭi Inscription of Vijaya-Kampavikramavarman refers to it which existed in Toṇḍaimaṇḍalam. It roughly comprised the modern Vellore and Guḍiyāttaṃ taluks in the North Arcot district (*E.I.*, XXIII, Pts. II and IV, October, 1935, p. 147).

Paiṭhān.—It is the modern name of ancient Pratiṣṭhāna which was a flourishing city during the rule of the Sātavāhana kings. It is on the north bank of the Godāvarī in the Aurangabad district of Hyderabad. In the *Suttanipāta* (P.T.S., p. 190) this city is mentioned as the capital of the Assaka or Aśmaka country. It is the same as Potana which is described as the (capital) city of the Assakas in the Pali *Nikāyas* (*Dīgha Nik.*, II, 235). It was also the capital of king Śātakarṇi (Sātavāhana or Śālivāhana) and his son Śaktikumāra who are generally identified with the king Śātakarṇi and the prince Śakti-śrī of the Nānāghāṭ Inscriptions (*Cambridge History of India*, Vol. I, p. 531). According to the Jaina tradition Sātavāhana defeated Vikramāditya of Ujjayinī and made himself the king of Pratiṣṭhānapura. He conquered many territories between the Deccan and the river Tāptī. He embraced Jainism and established the image of Mahālakṣmī on the bank of the Godāvarī. (Law, *Some Jaina Canonical Sūtras*, p. 185.) For further details vide B. C. Law, *Indological Studies*, Pt. I, 46. See Pratiṣṭhāna.

Palakkaḍa-sthāna.—It was the place of issue of the Uruvupalli plates of Simhavaran. Some have tried to identify it with Palātkaṭa. But this identification is doubtful. Palakkaḍa may be identified with the modern village of Palakalūru in the Guntur taluk. Some suggest that Palukuru in the Kandukūr taluk of the Nellore district might be the ancient Palakkaḍa or Palātkaṭa (*E.I.*, XXIV, Pt. III, July, 1937).

Palni.—It is the sacred hill of Muruga, Madras. For details vide J. M. Somasundaram, *Palni*, 1941.

Pampāpati.—It is known to the modern geographers as Hampe, situated on the southern bank of the Tuṅgabhadrā river and at the north-western extremity of the ruins of Vijayanagara, where an inscription of Kṛṣṇarāya was discovered (*E.I.*, I, 351).

Panamalāi.—This is a village which is situated in the Villupuram taluk, South Arcot district (*S.I.I.*, I, p. 24). The Panamalāi cave was founded by Rājasiṃha. The Pallavas ruled as far south as Panamalāi at the time of Rājasiṃha.

Pañcadhāra.—Here Kāmarāja, a Coḍa king, fought a battle with Gajapati and won victory over the latter (*E.I.*, XXVI, Pt. I, *Rājahmundry Museum Plates of Telugu Coḍa* (Annadeva).

Pañcadhārala.—It is in the Yellamancili taluk of the Vizagapatam district (*E.I.*, XXV, Pt. VII, p. 335).

Pañcapāṇḍavamalai—(or the hill of the five Pāṇḍavas).—About four miles to the south-west of the town of Arcot stands a rocky hill called the Pañcapāṇḍavamalai, which, according to the popular belief, is connected with the five Pāṇḍavas (*E.I.*, IV, 136ff.).

Panmānāḍu.—It is a division of a Manavirkoṭṭam or Manayirkoṭṭam in South Arcot district (*S.I.I.*, I, pp. 120, 147, 155).

Parivainīḍu.—It owes its name to the Bāṇa capital Parival of Parivipurī which may be identified with Parigi in the Anantapur district (*Ibid.*, II, p. 425).

Paruviṣaya.—It is the same as Paruvi-viṣaya of the Penukoṇḍa plates. It may be identified with Parigi, seven miles north of Hindupur in the Anantapur district (*E.I.*, XXIV, Pt. V, p. 238).

Paṭṭesam.—This village stands on a picturesque island in the Godāvarī and is at present included in the Rajahmundry taluk (*E.I.*, XXVI, Pt. I, 40). It is famous for the shrine of Vīrabhadra (*Ibid.*, XXVI, Pt. I, p. 40).

Payalipaṭṭana.—This village is situated in the western boundary of Mānyakheṭa or Malkhed, the Rāṣṭrakūṭa capital (*E.I.*, XXIII, Pt. IV, October, 1935).

Pāguṇāraviṣaya.—It is the same as Pāvunavāraviṣaya of the Vandaram plates of Ammarāja II. The village named Tāṇḍivāḍa is situated in Pāguṇāraviṣaya, which appears to have comprised the modern Tanuku taluk of the Kṛṣṇā district (*E.I.*, XXIII, Pt. III, July, 1935, p. 97).

Pālakka.—This kingdom, mentioned in the Allahabad Pillar Inscription, has been identified by V. A. Smith with Pālghāṭ or Pālakkāḍu in the south of the Malabar district.

Pālāru.—It is the chief river of the North Arcot district named Pālār (*S.I.I.*, I, pp. 87, 88, 134 and 155) which flows to the south of little Kāñchī.

Pālār (*Pāler*).—It is also known as the Milk river (Kṣīranadī). This river has its origin in the hills of north of Nalgondā. It flows into the Kṛṣṇā just at the point where the latter enters the Madras State. It runs through the North Arcot district and falls into the Bay of Bengal near Sadras in the Chingleput district. Vellore, Arcot and Chingleput are situated on its bank.

Pālura.—This is the same as Dantapura, a town in Kaliṅga.

Pāñcapālī.—It may be identified with Pañcupālī situated in the Ānandpur sub-division of the Keonjhar State (*E.I.*, XXV, Pt. IV, p. 173).

Pāṇḍya.—The Pāṇḍya country to which Pāṇini refers in his *Aṣṭādhyāyī* (4. 1. 171) comprised Madura and Tinnevelly districts (*S.I.I.*, I, pp. 51, 59, 63, etc.). According to Ptolemy it was known as Pandion with Modoura as its royal city (McCrindle, *Ancient India as described by Ptolemy*, Majumdar Ed., p. 183). It was conquered by Rājendra Coḍa. The Pāṇḍya kingdom also comprised Travancore in the 1st century of the Christian era. Originally it had its capital at Kolkai on the Tāmraparṇī river in Tinnevelly, and its later capital was Madurā (Dakṣiṇa Mathurā). In the *Mahābhārata* and in many *Jātakas* the Pāṇḍus are spoken of as the ruling race of Indraprastha. Kātyāyana in his *Vārttika* derives Pāṇḍya from Pāṇḍu. The country of the Pāṇḍyas is also mentioned in the *Rāmāyaṇa* (IV, Ch. 41), where Sugrīva is said to have sent his monkey-soldiers in quest of Sītā. In the *Mahābhārata* (Sabhāparva, Ch. 31, V. 17) it is stated that Sahadeva, the youngest of the Pāṇḍu princes, went to the Dakṣiṇāpatha after having conquered the king of the Pāṇḍyas. The *Purāṇas* also refer to the Pāṇḍyas (*Mārkaṇḍeya*, Ch. 57, V. 45; *Vāyu*, 45, 124; *Matsya*, 112, 46). Aśoka's Rock Edicts II and XIII mention the Pāṇḍyas whose territory lay outside his empire. Aśoka was in friendly terms with the Pāṇḍyas who probably had two kingdoms, one including Tinnevelly on the south and extending as far north as the highlands in the neighbourhood of the Coimbatore Gap, the other including the Mysore State. Strabo (XV, 4, 73) mentions an embassy sent to Augustus Caesar by a king 'Pandion', possibly a Pāṇḍya of the Tamil country. (For further details, vide B. C. Law, *Tribes in Ancient India*, pp. 190ff.)

The Jaina legends connect the sons of Pāṇḍu with the Pāṇḍya country of the south with Mathurā or Madhurā (modern Madoura) as its capital. Dr. Barnett rightly observes 'The Pāṇḍiyans, however, were not Pāṇḍavas, and the Jaina identification of the two dynasties is probably based on popular etymology. A like attempt to connect the two families occurs in the Tamil chronicle given in Taylor's *Oriental Historical MSS.* (Vol. I, pp. 195ff.) which states that Madura at the time of the Bhārata war was ruled by Babhruvāhana, the son of Arjuna by the daughter of the Pāṇḍiyan king of Madurā. The *Mahābhārata* on the other hand makes Babhruvāhana, the son of Arjuna by Citrāṅgadā, the daughter of Citravāhana, the king of Manipura'.

The association of the Pāṇḍiyas of the south with the Śūrasenas of Mathurā and the Pāṇḍus of northern India is probably alluded to in the confused statement of Megasthenes regarding Heracles and Pandaia (B. C. Law, *Tribes in Ancient India*, p. 190; Raychaudhuri, *Political History of Ancient India*, 4th ed., p. 272; McCrindle, *Ancient India* (Megasthenes and Arrian), pp. 163-164). In the Pali Chronicles of Ceylon the Pāṇḍiyas are invariably represented as Pāṇḍus or Paṇḍus (*Mahāvaṃsa*, Ch. VII, v. 50; *Dipavaṃsa*, Ch. IV, v. 41).

The distinction between the Pāṇḍya and the Coḷa divisions of the Tamil country is well known. Damiḷa, mentioned in the Nāgārjunikoṇḍa Inscriptions of Vīrapuruṣadatta, is the Tamil country. According to the *Mahāvaṃsa*, Vijaya married a daughter of the Pāṇḍu king whose capital was Madhurā in South India. Madhurā is Madurā in the south of the Madras Presidency. Another capital was probably at Kolkai. The rivers Tāmraparṇī and Kritamālā or Vaigāi flowed through it.

Pārada.—The country of the Pāradas, according to some, may be located in the Deccan but Pargiter places it in the north-west (*A.I.H.T.*, pp. 206, 268 and f.n.). The Pāradas seem to have been a barbarous tribe (*Mahābhārata*, Sabhāparva, L. 1832; LI, 1869; Droṇaparva, CXXI, 4819). According to the *Harivaṃśa* (XIII, 763-4) king Sagara degraded them. For further details, vide B. C. Law, *Tribes in Ancient India*, pp. 364-65; B. C. Law, *Indological Studies*, Pt. I, p. 48.

Pārikuḍ.—It is in the Puri district, where the plates of Madhyamarājadeva were discovered (*E.I.*, XI, 281ff.).

Peḍakomḍapurī.—Kāmarāja, a Coḍa king, vanquished Daburukhānu and others with their Rākṣasa forces near this place (*E.I.*, XXVI, Pt. I).

Pedda-maddali.—It is a village in the Nuzvid taluk of the Kistna district, where inscriptions were found (*I.A.*, XIII, 137).

Pedda-Vegi.—This village may be identified with the ancient Veṅgīpura in the vicinity of Ellore, where a number of plates were discovered (*E.I.*, XIX, 258).

Penner.—The North Penner flows north-north-east up to Pamidi in the district of Anantapur, Madras, from which place it turns south-east and reaches the Bay of Bengal. The South Penner, otherwise known as the Ponnaiyar, flows into the Bay of Bengal.

Perambair.—This village is situated in the Chingleput district containing many prehistoric remains (*A.S.I.*, Annual Report, 1908-9, pp. 92ff.).

Peravali.—It is identical with the village of Peravali where an inscription was found (*Annual Report of South Indian Epigraphy*, 1915, p. 90).

Perumugai.—It is the modern Perumai near Velūr (*S.I.I.*, I, p. 75). It is in the present Vellore taluk, North Arcot district.

Perunagar.—It is a village about 13 miles from Conjeeveram on the road to Wandiwash (*E.I.*, XXIII, Pt. IV, October, 1935, p. 146).

Perungari.—It is known as Peringkarei by Ptolemy. It is situated on the river Vaigāi, about 40 miles lower down its course than Madurā (McCrindle, *Ptolemy's Ancient India*, Ed. S. N. Majumdar, p. 183).

Pherava.—This village according to some is the modern Barna in the Sompeṭa taluk but this is doubtful (*E.I.*, XXVII, Pt. III, p. 113).

Phulsara.—It is a village in the Aṭhagaḍa taluk of the Ganjam district, where an inscription has been discovered (*E.I.*, XXIV, Pt. I, January, 1937, p. 15).

Piṇṇi.—It is the name of a river, also called the Peṇṇai, which flows through the South Arcot district (*E.I.*, XXIII, Pt. V).

Pippalāla.—It is the modern Pimpral, 12 miles south-east of Candanpurī and about 33 miles from Ellora (*E.I.*, XXV, Pt. I, January, 1939, p. 29).

Pirānmalai.—It is in the Ramnad district. It contains the Maṅgaināthésvara temple. (*E.I.*, XXI, Pt. III, July, 1931.)

Piśājipadaka (*Piśācipadraka*).—It occurs in the Lüders' list No. 1123. It is on the west side of the mount Tiraṇhu (Triraśmī).

Piṭhapurī.—It is the same as Piṭṭāpuram, a sacred place containing the residence of a *rājā* in the east Godāvarī district (*S.I.I.*, I, pp. 53, 61; cf. *E.I.*, XII, p. 2). The Tāṇḍivāda grant of Pṛthivī Mahārāja refers to Piṣṭapura which is the ancient name of Piṭhāpuram (*E.I.*, XXIII, Pt. III, July, 1935, p. 97). Piṣṭapura formed part of the kingdom of Devarāṣṭra during the reign of its king Guṇavarman (*E.I.*, XXIII, 57). Piṭhāpuram is a provincial town in the Godāvarī district. It contains a Vaiṣṇava temple named Kuntimādhava. At the eastern entrance of this temple, in front of the shrine itself, stands a quadrangular stone-pillar bearing four inscriptions of different dates. The kings belonged to a dynasty which Hultzsch calls 'chiefs of Velanāṇḍu'. The chiefs of Velanāṇḍu trace their descent from the fourth Śūdra caste. A distant ancestor of Pṛthviśvara named Malla I subdued the kings of the Gaṅgas, Kaliṅgas, Vaṅgas, Magadhas, Andhras, Pulindas, etc. (*E.I.*, IV, 32ff.).

Pithuṇḍa.—In the Hāthigumphā Inscription of Khāravela there is a mention of a place known as Pithuḍaga or Pithuḍa, founded by the former kings of Kaliṅga. Pithuḍa is the shortened form of Pithuḍaga which is the same as Sanskrit Pṛthudaka, which is a holy place according to the *Padmapurāṇa* (Ch. 13—*Tīrthamāhātmya*). The Gaṇḍavyūha refers to Pṛthurāṣṭra which is not different from Pitundra mentioned by Ptolemy in his *Geography*. Sylvain Levi points out that in the Jaina *Uttarādhyayana Sūtra* (Sec. XXI) there is a mention of Pithuṇḍa (Pihuṇḍa) as a sea-coast town, reminding us of Khāravela's Pithuḍa (Pithuḍaga) and Ptolemy's Pitundra. Ptolemy locates Pitundra in the interior of Maisolia between the mouths of the two rivers, Maisolos and Mānadas, i.e., between the delta of the Godāvarī and the Mahānadī, nearly at an equal distance from both. (McCrindle, *Ancient India as described by Ptolemy*, pp. 68, 185 and 386-387). It may be located in the interior of Chicacole in Kaliṅgapatam towards the course of the river Nāgāvatī, also known as the Lāṅguliya. Khāravela is said to have rehabilitated Pithuḍa or Pithuḍaga. Pithuṇḍa was caused to be ploughed with an ass plough, i.e., reclaimed according to some.

Podiyil.—It is a hill in the Tinnevelly district. It is also called the southern mountain. It is said to have been the seat of Agastya (*S.I.I.*, III, 144, 464).

Poliyūr-nāḍu.—It may be identified with the present Polur village, three miles north-north-west of Arkonam Junction (*E.I.*, VII, p. 25).

Ponni.—This is the same as Kāverī (*S.I.I.*, I, 94-95).

Ponnuṭuru.—This village is situated on the northern bank of the river Vaṃśadharā about a mile from Somarājapuram in the Parlakimedi State in the Pātapaṭnam taluk of the Vizagapatam district, where a set of plates of Gaṅga Samantavarman, year 64, was discovered (*E.I.*, XXVII, Pt. V, 216).

Pottapi.—It is on the western bank of the Ceyyeru river and north of Taṅgaṭṭuru in the Rājampet taluk of the Cuddapah district. (*E.I.*, Vol. VII, p. 121, n. 5.)

Praśravanagiri.—The hills of Aurangabad were situated on the bank of the Godāvarī, graphically described by Bhavabhūti in his *Uttararāmacarita* (Act III, 8). This hill has numerous streams and caves (*Uttararāmacarita,* Act III, 8). According to the *Hemakoṣa*, Mālyavanagiri is the same as Praśravanagiri which extends up to Janasthāna (*Uttararāmacaritam,* Act I, 26). But according to Bhavabhūti (*Uttararāmacarita,* I) they are two different hills.

Pratiṣṭhāna.—Pratiṣṭhāna (modern Paiṭhān), on the north bank of the Godāvarī in the Aurangabad district of Hyderabad, is famous in literature as the capital of king Śātakarṇi (Sātavāhana or Śālivāhana) and his son Śaktikumāra, who are generally identified with the king Śātakarṇi and the prince Śaktiśrī of the Nānāghāt inscriptions. Paiṭhān, or ancient Pratiṣṭhāna or Supratiṣṭhāhāra or Supratiṣṭhita on the Godāvarī[1] in the Nizam's dominions, is the place where three plates of Govinda III (Śaka saṃvat 716) were discovered (*E.I.*, III, 103). Pratiṣṭhāna also occurs in the Poona plates of the Vākāṭaka Queen Prabhāvatīguptā (*E.I.*, XV, 39). The Petenikas of Asokan inscriptions, as mentioned in *R.E.*, V and XIII, have been identified with the Paiṭhānikas or inhabitants of Paiṭhāna on the Godāvarī. Paiṭhān is the present name of ancient Pratiṣṭhāna, a flourishing city during the rule of the Sātavāhana kings. Some suggest that they were the ancestors of Sātavāhana rulers of Paiṭhān (*J.R.A.S.*, 1923, 92; Woolner, *Asoka*, p. 113). According to the author of the *Periplus* Paiṭhān is situated at a distance of 20 days' journey to the south of Barygaza (identified with Bharukaccha, modern Broach). It is spoken of as the greatest city in Dakṣiṇāpatha. Sātavāhana defeated Vikramāditya of Ujjayinī and made himself the king of Pratiṣṭhānapura. He conquered many territories between the Deccan and the river Tāptī. He embraced Jainism, built many *caityas* and established the image of Mahālakṣmī on the bank of the Godāvarī (B. C. Law, *Some Jaina Canonical Sūtras*, p. 185). According to the Jaina *Vividhatīrthakalpa* (pp. 59-60) this town which was in Mahārāṣṭra became in course of time an insignificant village.

Puduppākkam.—It is in the Walajapet taluk of the North Arcot district. (*Vailur Inscription of Kopperunjingadeva*—*E.I.*, XXIII, Pt. V).

Pugar.—It is the modern Kāviripaṭṭinam in the Tanjore district (*E.I.*, XXIII, Pt. V, p. 180).

Pulikkunram.—It is a village on the west of the river Nugā, on the north of Kukkānur and on the south of Pālainellur (*S.I.I.*, Vol. III, p. 25). A hamlet is given as gift to Perunjigai Īśvara shrine.

Pulināḍu.—It is said to be in Tyagabharaṇavaḷanāḍu in a 36th year record of Rājarāja, I. It is included according to some in Paduvurkoṭṭam of Jayaṅgoṇḍaśoḷa-maṇḍalam in a 4th year record of the later Choḷa king named Vīrarājendra. It was the western-most part of Paduvur-koṭṭam lying adjacent to the Mysore country. It comprised the whole of the modern Punganur taluk and that part of the adjoining Palamner taluk in the south which lay north of the Devarakoṇḍa and the Karaveri hill ranges.

Pulināḍu was surrounded by the divisions of Toṇḍaimaṇḍalam in the east and south-east, by the Mahārājavāḍi country and Rattapadikoṇḍaśoḷamaṇḍalam in the north, by the Gaṅga country in the west known as Gaṅgarusasira, and by the Nigariśoḷamaṇḍalam in the south and south-west (*Indian Geographical Journal*, Vol. XXV, No. 2, pp. 14–18).

---

[1] Cf. *Padmapurāṇa*, Ch. 176, śl. 20. There was a king named Vikrama in this town of Pratiṣṭhāna.

Pulindarājarāṣṭra.—The Navagrām grant of Mahārāja Hastin refers to it, wherefrom it is clear that the dominion of the chief of the Pulindas may be located within the territory of the Nṛpatiparivrājaka family (*E.I.*, XXI, Pt. III). The Pulindas are referred to in *R.E.*, XIII of Asoka as a vassal tribe. The *Aitareya Brāhmaṇa* (VII, 18) tells us that the Pulindas are mentioned along with the Andhras. In the *Purāṇas* (*Matsya*, 114, 46–48; *Vāyu*, 45, 126) they are mentioned with the Śavaras and are referred to as *Dakṣiṇāpathavāsinaḥ* together with the Vaidarbhas and Daṇḍakas. The *Mahābhārata* (XII, 207, 42) refers to them as the people of the Dakṣiṇāpatha. Pulindanagara, the capital of the Pulindas, was situated near Bhilsa in the Jubbalpore district in the Central Provinces. The Pulindas must have certainly included Rūpnāth, the findspot of a version of Aśoka's Minor Edicts.

Puḷḷamaṅgalaṃ.—It is the same as Puḷḷamaṅgai, a village near Paśupatikoyil, about nine miles south of Tanjore (The *Udaiyarguḍi Inscription of Rājakeśarivarman*, *S.I.I.*, Vol. III, p. 450).

Pūnaka (*Puṇya*).—According to two copperplate grants of the Rāṣṭrakūṭa king Kriṣṇa I, Pūnaka or Puṇya was the ancient name of modern Poona. In the second half of the 8th century A.D. Pūnaka was the headquarters of a district (*viṣaya*) and as such it corresponded to the Haveli taluk. Early in the 16th century A.D. the city of Poona was known as Pūrṇā-nagara which was visited by Śrīcaitanya and his party as mentioned in Govindadāsa's *Kaḍcā* (*J.B.B.R.A.S.*, N.S., Vol. VI, 1930, pp. 231ff.).

Purandara.—This town is in the south according to the *Padmapurāṇa* (Ch. 176, śl. 2).

Puri—(*Puruṣottamakṣetra*).—It is in the Puri district of Orissa. According to the *Brahmapurāṇa* (42. 13-14) this holy city stands on the sea. The *Yoginītantra* mentions it as Puruṣottama (2. 9. 214ff.). The *Kālikāpurāṇa* (Ch. 58. 35) also calls it by the same name (Puruṣottama). It is sandy and ten yojanas in extent containing the famous deity, Puruṣottama. It includes two distinct portions, the Bālukhaṇḍa lies between two sacred *tīrthas*: *Svargadvāra* and *Cakratīrtha*. It is famous for the Hindu temple of Jagarnātha and it lies exactly on the shore of the Bay of Bengal. It is otherwise called Śrīkṣetra which is one of the most sacred places of the Hindus. It is also known as Puruṣottamakṣetra. It extends from the Lokanātha temple on the west to the Baleśvara temple on the east and from Svargadvāra or the Gate of Heaven on the south to the Matia stream on the north-east. It is said to resemble in shape a conch-shell in the centre of which lies the Jagarnatha temple. From the architectural standpoint the temple is not as important as that of Bhuvaneśvara. Besides the main temple there are many other minor temples, such as Mārkaṇḍeśvara, Lokanātha, Nīlakaṇṭheśvara and some tanks. About two miles from the great temple lies the Guṇḍicābārī. (For details vide *B. and O. Dist. Gazetteers*, Puri by O'Malley, 1929, pp. 326ff.; Jarrett's tr. of the *Ain-i-Akbari*, II, 127; Stirling, *Orissa*, 1824.)

Purikā.—It is the name of a city (Barua and Sinha, *Barhut Inscriptions*, pp. 17, 21), and is the same as Pulika of the *Mahābhārata*, Purikā of the *Khila-Harivaṃśa*, and Paulika Paurika and Saulika of the *Purāṇas*. In the *Purāṇas* it is included in the list of countries of the Deccan. In the *Khila-Harivaṃśa* (XCV, 5220–28) the city of Purikā is placed between two Vindhya ranges, near Māhiṣmatī and on the bank of a river flowing from the Ṛkṣavanta mountain (cf. *Viṣṇupurāṇa*, XXXVIII, 20–22).

Puruṣottamapurī.—In the Puruṣottamapurī plates of Rāmacandra (*E.I.*, XXV, Pt. V, p. 208) Puruṣottamapurī is mentioned as lying on the southern bank of the Godāvarī in the Bhir district.

Puśkarī.—It is situated in the Poḍāgaḍh region of the Jeypur State now in the Koraput district of Orissa (*E.I.*, XXVIII, Pt. I, January, 1949).

Puṣpagiri.—It lay eight miles to the north of Cuddapah (*E.I.*, III, 24).

Puṣpajāti (or Puṣpajā or Puṣpavatī).—This river is mentioned in the *Vāyupurāṇa* (XLV, 105; cf. *Kūrmapurāṇa*, XLVII, 25) which rises from the Malaya mountains.

Raṇḍuvalli.—It is a village in the Gudrahāraviṣaya granted to a Brahmin, where an inscription has been found (*Annual Report of South Indian Epigraphy*, 1914, p. 85).

Ratnagiri.—It is an isolated hill of the Asia range, four miles to the north-east of Gopalpur, and stands on a small stream called Kelua, a branch of the Birupa. This hill really stands on the eastern bank of the Kelua and has a flat top. It contains the ruins of a big stūpa. For details, vide R. P. Chanda, *Exploration in Orissa*, *M.A.S.I.*, No. 44, pp. 12-13.

Raṭṭapāḍikoṇḍa—Śoḷamaṇḍalam.—It is represented by the tract of country round about Puṅganur in the Cittoor district and the adjoining Cintāmaṇi taluk of the Mysore State (*E.I.*, XXV, Pt. VI, April, 1940, p. 254).

Rāgolu.—It is near Chicacole in the Ganjam district (*E.I.*, XII, p. 1).

Rājagambhīra hill.—It is also called Rājagambhīran-malai. This hill was probably called after Rājagambhīrasaṃbuvarāyan (*S.I.I.*, I, p. 111). It is in the North Arcot district.

Rākaluva.—This village may be identified with Ragolu near Chicacole in the Ganjam district where the plates of Śaktivarman were discovered (*E.I.*, XII, 1ff.).

Rāmaparkaṭi.—It may be identified with the village called Rāmasahi in Kiapir in Joshipur Pargana (*E.I.*, XXV, Pt. IV, p. 158).

Rāmatīrtha.—It is a village in the Vizagapatam district where an inscription has been found on the wall of a cave in a hill, belonging to Viṣṇuvardhana Mahārāja (*Annual Report of South Indian Epigraphy*, 1918, p. 133).

Rāmeśvaram.—It is a sacred island in the Bay of Bengal. The temple of Rāmanāthasvāmī is the famous temple here. According to tradition it was built by Rāmacandra when he crossed over to Ceylon to save his captivated wife Sītā from the clutches of Rāvaṇa, the tyrant king of Laṅkā. It is a fine specimen of Dravidian architecture with big towers, carved walls and extensive corridors. The temple is surrounded by a high wall on all sides covering an area of about 900 square feet. It contains many *gopurams* built of hewn stones. There are tanks inside the temple. A *śivaliṅga* and images of Annapūrṇā, Pārvatī and Hanumāna are found in the temple. (B. C. Law, *Holy Places in South India, Calcutta Geographical Review*, September, 1942).

Rānī-Jhariāl.—This village is situated at a distance of 21 miles west of Tiṭilagarh in the Patna State of Orissa (*E.I.*, XXIV, Pt. V, p. 239).

Rāṣṭrakūṭa territory.—It included at least the Aurangabad district and parts of Nasik and Khandesh districts as early as the 8th century A.D. (*E.I.*, XXV, Pt. I, January, 1939).

Renāṇḍu.—This country roughly lies between the two tributaries of the river Pennār, namely the Citrāvatī in the north-west and the Ceyyeru in the south-west comprising a major portion of the Cuddapah and parts of Kolar and Cittoor districts (*E.I.*, XXVII, Pt. V, p. 225).

Rohaṇa.—It is the Adam's peak in Ceylon (*S.I.I.*, I, p. 164).

Rohaṇaki.—The Narasingapalli plates of Hastivarman mention it, which may be identified with modern Roṇaṅkī (*E.I.*, XXIII, Pt. II).

Ṛṣyamukha.—This mountain is situated eight miles from Anagandi on the bank of the river Tuṅgabhadrā. The river Pampā rises in this mountain and falls into the Tuṅgabhadrā after flowing westward. It was at this mountain that Hanumāna and Sugrīva were met for the first time by Rāmacandra (*Rāmāyana*, Ch. IV, Kiṣkindhyākāṇḍa). The *Mārkaṇḍeya Purāṇa* (translated by Pargiter, Canto LVII, 13) refers to Ṛṣymukha which has been identified by Pargiter with the range of hills stretching from Ahmadnagar to beyond Naldrug and Kalyāṇi dividing the Mañjira and the Bhīma rivers (*J.R.A.S.*, April, 1894, p. 253). The *Bṛhat-Saṃhitā* mentions it as a mountain in the south (XIV, 13).

Rudragayā.—According to the *Padma Purāṇa* (186. 1) it is Kolapur in Dakṣiṇāpatha.

Sagara.—Here the Coḍa king Annadeva overcame the Karṇāṭa army (*E.I.*, XXVI, Pt. I).

Sahyādri.—This is a mountain lying on the Western Ghats (*S.I.I.*, I, pp. 168-69). The Western Ghats were known to the ancients as the Sahyādri, which form the western boundary of the Deccan and run continuously for a distance of about 1,000 miles from the Kundaibari Pass in the Khandesh district of the Bombay State down to Cape Comorin, the southernmost point of India. The Western Ghats are known by different local names. There are important passes too. (For details, vide B. C. Law, *Mountains of India*, *Calcutta Geographical Society Publication*, No. 5, pp. 22-23.

Śaiyam.—This is the Tamil name of the Sahya mountain and the Sanskrit name of the Western Ghats (*S.I.I.*, III, p. 147).

Salem.—It is a well known district in South India, where an inscription was found in the 26th year of Rājarāja (*Inscriptions of the Madras Presidency*, 73).

Samalipada (Luders' List, 1134).—It was a village on the eastern road in the Govardhana district in the Godāvarī region (Govardhana, Luder's list, 1124–1126, 1133, etc.).

Saṅgukoṭṭam.—It is the name of a country (?) on the sea (*S.I.I.*, Vol. I, p. 99).

Saṅgūr.—Saṅgūr, which is variously called as Saṅgavūru, Caṅgūra and Caṅgāpura, is a village situated at a distance of eight miles south-west of Haveri taluk on the road to Sirsi in the north Kanara district, where an inscription has been found engraved on the Nandipillar standing near the temple of Vīrabhadra (*E.I.*, XXIII, Pt. V, 189).

Sankanipalli.—It is the modern Sankaraṣaṇapura in the Gūḍivāḍa taluk of the Kistna district (*E.I.*, XXV, Pt. III, p. 140).

Saṅkaram.—It is near Anakapalli in the Vizagapatam district. For archaeological exploration at the site during the period 1907-8, see *J.R.A.S.* 1908, pp. 1112ff.

Śarapadraka.—The village of Saradaha in Karanjia Pargana may be the modern representative of Śarapadraka (*E.I.*, XXV, Pt. IV, p. 158).

Sarasvatī.—This is the name of a river (*S.I.I.*, Vol. I, p. 57).

Sarephā.—The Balasore plate of Bhānudatta refers to it, which may be identified with Soro in the Balasore district of Orissa (*E.I.*, XXVI, Pt. V, January, 1942).

Satiyaputra.—The Rock Edicts II and XIII of Aśoka refer to it. It lay to the west of the territories of Coḷas and Pāṇḍyas and extended along the western sea-coast of south India (Barua, *Asoka and his Inscriptions*, p. 111). Some have identified it with Satyavratakṣetra or Kāñcīpura (*J.R.A.S.*, 1918, 541-42). Aiyangar agrees with R. G. Bhandarkar in identifying Satiyaputra with Satpute. According to him Satiyaputra is a collective name denoting the various matriarchal communities like the Tulus and the Nayars of Malabar (*J.R.A.S.*, 1919, 581–84). Vincent Smith identifies it with the Satyamangalam taluk or sub-division of Coimbatore district lying along the Western Ghats and bordering on Mysore, Malabar, Coimbatore, and Coorg (*Aśoka*, 3rd ed., p. 161). According to some Satiyaputra is the same as Satyabhūmi of the Keralolpatti, i.e., a territory roughly equal to North Malabar including a portion of Kasergode taluk, South Canara (*J.R.A.S.*, 1923, 412). According to Barnett and Jayaswal the names Sātavāhana and Śātakarṇi are derived from that of Sātiyaputra (cf. Raychaudhuri, *P.H.A.I.*, 4th ed., p. 343, n. 2.) All the identifications based upon the equation of satiya of Satiyaputra with *satya* meaning truth are questionable. For further details vide B. C. Law, *Indological Studies*, I, p. 58).

Sattenapalli.—It is in the Guntur district where a set of four copper-plates was discovered (*E.I.*, XXIII, Pt. V, p. 161).

Satyamaṅgalaṃ.—This village is the Vellore taluk where the plates of Devaraya II were discovered (*E.I.*, III, p. 35).

Śavaradeśa.—It is somewhere in the Dakṣiṇāpatha (*Matsya Purāṇa*, 144, 46–8; *Vāyu Purāṇa*, 45, 126). The *Mahābhārata* (XII, 207, 42) places it in the Deccan. Ptolemy (McCrindle, *Ptolemy's Ancient India*, ed. S. N. Majumdar, p. 173) mentions a country called Sabarai which is generally held to be identical with the region inhabited by the Śavaras. Cunningham identifies the Sabarai of Ptolemy with Pliny's Suari. According to him Savaradeśa extended as far southward as the Pennar river. For further details vide Law, *Tribes in Ancient India*, p. 172.

Śavarī-āśrama.—It was formerly owned by the sage Mātaṅga and his disciples. Rāma and Lakṣmaṇa visited it and were greeted with respect by Śavarī. With her matted lock, meagre garment and skin of black deer as wrapper, she maintained the tradition of this hermitage (*Rāmāya a*, I, 1. 55ff.; cf. *S.I.I.*, III, 77, 6ff.)

Sādule—It is Sādolā about three miles south by east (*E.I.*, XXV, Pt. V, p. 208).

Sīkṣīgopāla.—It is a village situated within 10 miles of Puri. There is a tradition that here Kṛṣṇa stopped and turned himself to stone. This village contains a temple which is frequently visited by pilgrims (Law, *Holy Places of India*, p. 17).

Śālaigrāma.—It is a village in the Paramagudi taluk of the Ramnad district where two Pāṇḍya records of the 10th century A.D. have been discovered (*Ancient India*, Bulletin of the *A.S.I.*, No. 5, January, 1949). This village contains an old temple of Śiva (*E.I.*, XXVIII, Pt. II, April, 1949, pp. 85ff.).

Sānta-Bommāli.—This village is in the Ganjam district, where copper-plates were discovered (*E.I.*, XXV, Pt. V, January, 1940, p. 194).

Sāraḍḍī.—It may be conveniently identified with Āraḍā about 10 miles east of Komaṇḍa (*E.I.*, XXIV, Pt. IV, p. 173).

Sāsanakoṭa.—This village is in the Hindupur taluk of the Anantapur district, where plates of Gaṅga Mādhavavarman were discovered (*E.I.*, XXIV, Pt. V, January, 1938, p. 234). Specimens of old pottery, beads and other relics were collected from a big mound here.

Śeṇbaga-Perumāl-nallūr.—It is modern Śumaṅginellūr (*S.I.I.*, Vol. I, p. 74).

Śendamaṅgalaṃ.—It is identical with the village of the same name, where the Śendamaṅgalaṃ Inscription of Manavalapperumal has been discovered (*E.I.*, XXIV, Pt. I, January, 1937). It is in the Tindivanam taluk of the South Arcot district.

Śeṅgama.—It is in the South Arcot district (*S.I.I.*, Vol. II, p. 497).

Setapadu.—It is in the Gaṇṭur taluk (*Setapadu Inscription*, *Annual Report of South Indian Epigraphy*, 1917, 116).

Sīmācalam.—About nine miles from Waltair stands this place where there is a celebrated Hindu temple on the top of a hill, dedicated to god Varāha-narasiṃhasvāmī.

Siṃhapura.—The Komarti plate of Candravarman and the Bṛhatproṣṭhā grant of Umavarman mention it, which may be identified with Siṅgupuram between Chicacole and Narasannapeta (*E.I.*, IV, p. 143; *E.I.*, XXVII, p. 35).

Siripuram.—It is a village near Chicacole, where the plates of Anantavarman, lord of Kalinga, were discovered (*E.I.*, Pt. I, XXIV, 47ff.).

Siritana.—It appears to be the Prakrit for Śrīstana or Śrīsthāna. It is the well-known Śrīśaila in Telingana on the bank of the Kṛṣṇā.

Sirriyāṛṛur.—It may be identified with Śittāttūr of the Walajapet taluk of the North Arcot district (*S.I.I.*, Vol. III, p. 289).

Śirukaḍambūr.—It is the name of a village (*Ibid.*, I, pp. 80, 82).

Śiśupālgaḍh.—It is in Orissa where excavations are being carried out by the Archaeological department. The historical site of Śiśupālagarh is situated near Bhuvaneśvar in Orissa. It is famous for its mediaeval temples and a square fort having an elaborate system of gateways. The ruins of Śiśupālagaṛh are located about 1½ miles to the east-south-east of the town of Bhuvaneśwar in the Puri district of Orissa. The traces of ancient habitation in the form of pottery and other objects are noticeable outside the fort. The fort is circumscribed by the waters of a streamlet called the Gandhavatī. The main current which flows past the western side of the fort has its source in the hilly tracts to the west of Manceśvar, some six miles north of Śiśupālagarh and joins the Dayā river, seven miles further south. To the south-south-east of the fort at a distance of about three miles the Dhauli hills lie containing the Edicts of Aśoka. About six miles to the west-north-west of Śiśupālagaṛh stand the Khaṇḍagiri and Udayagiri hills. The excavations at the site have brought to light some objects among which may be mentioned several beads, a terracotta *bulla*, terracotta ear-ornaments and plain pottery. The Śiśupālagarh had no defences in the early period of its history. At the beginning of the early middle period the most significant event was the construction of the defences. (*Ancient India, Bulletin of the A.S.I.*, No. 5, January, 1949, pp. 62ff.). A rare gold coin of Kuṣāṇa-Roman type belonging to king Dharmadamadhara has been discovered. As to the date of the coin it is later than 200 A.D. (*J. Numismatic Society of India*, Vol. XII, Pt. I, June, 1950, pp. 1–4).

Śivanvāyal.—It is a village situated about nine miles north-east of Tiruvallūr, the headquarters of the taluk of the same name in the Chingleput district, Madras State (*E.I.*, XXVII, Pt. 2, p. 59).

Śivīndiram.—The ancient name of the present Śucīndram near Cape Comorin (*S.I.I.*, Vol. III, p. 159).

Śolāpuram.—It is a village about eight miles south of Vellore, where four inscriptions were discovered (*E.I.*, VII, 192ff.).

Somalāpura.—It is in the Bellary taluk of the Bellary district where three copperplates were discovered (*E.I.*, XVII, 193ff.).

Śorai.—This is a village near Ūrtti (*E.I.*, XXV, Pt. IV).

Śoraikkāvūr.—It is near Kuttālaṃ in the Tanjore district, where the three copperplates of Virupākṣa of the Śaka Samvat 1308 were discovered (*E.I.*, VIII, 298ff.).

Śorapuraṃ.—It is the name of a village near Velūr (*S.I.I.*, Vol. I, pp. 78, 128).

Soremaṭi.—It may be located in the Noḷamba territory adjoining Madanpalle (*E.I.*, XXIV, Pt. IV, p. 191).

Śrāvaṇa-Belgolā.—It is situated between two hills named Candrabetta and Indrabetta in the Channarāyapaṭṇa taluk of the Hassan district, Mysore, where the inscription of Prabhācandra was discovered (*E.I.*, IV, 22ff.; cf. *E.I.*, III, 184). It was an ancient seat of Jaina learning which was visited by Bhadrabāhu, the Jaina teacher, who died there (Law, *Holy Places of India*, p. 54). Chandragupta Maurya who embraced Jainism is said to have died here (Rice, *Mysore Gazetteer*, I, 287).

Śrīkṣetra.—It is Puri in Orissa, famous for the temple of Jagannātha built in the 12th century A.D. Śricaitanya visited this place (*Devī Bhāgavata*, Book VII, Ch. 30; Hunter, *Orissa*, *A.S.R.*, 1907-8).

Śrī-madhurāntaka-caturvedi-maṅgalaṃ.—This is an independent village in Kaḷatturkoṭṭaṃ, a district of Jayaṅgoṇḍasoḷamaṇḍalaṃ (*S.I.I.*, III, p. 204).

Śrī-Mallinātha-caturvedī-maṅgalaṃ.—It is the name of a village in North Arcot district (*Ibid.*, I, pp. 77, 78 and 129), the people of which have been described as great.

Śrīparvata.—The ***Mārkaṇḍeya Purāṇa*** (LVII, 15), the *Kūrma Purāṇa* (30. 45–48; cf. *Agni Purāṇa* 109), and the *Saura Purāṇa* (69. 22) refer to this mountain. It is also called Śrīśaila. According to the ***Padma Purāṇa*** (Ch. 21, śl. 11-12) the summit of this holy mountain is beautiful where the deity called Mallikārjuna resides. This lofty rock overhangs the river Kṛṣṇā in the Kurnool district. It is usually identified with Siriṭana of the Nasik Praśasti. It is the site of a famous temple called Mallikārjuna, one of the twelve liṅga-shrines (*A.S.S.I.*, Vol. I, p. 90; *A.S.W.I.*, p. 223). The *Agni Purāṇa* (CXIII, 3, 4) places it on the river Kāverī. According to it, it was dedicated to the goddess Śrī by Viṣṇu because she had once performed some austerities (*Arch. Sur. of South India*, by Sewell, Vol. I, p. 90; Pargiter, *Mārkaṇḍeya Purāṇa*, p. 290). The introductory verses of Bāṇa's *Harṣacarita* mention Śrīparvata which is the name of a range of mountains in Teliṅgana. (*Harṣacarita*, Tr. by Cowell and Thomas, p. 3 f.n.).

As to its location it may be said that on the southern bank of the river Kṛṣṇā stands this ancient religious shrine on the Ṛṣabhagiri hill (vide B. C. Law, *Holy Places of India*, Calcutta Geographical Society Publication, No. 3, p. 41).

Śrīpura.—This is modern Sirpur which lies north-west of Mukhaliṅgam on the left bank of the Vaṃśadharā river, 18 miles from Parlakimedi in the Ganjam district (*E.I.*, XXIII, Pt. IV, p. 119). The Pāṇḍyas ruled over Kośala from Śrīpura in the 8th and 9th centuries. It may also be Siripuraṃ which now forms part of the Zemindari of Vāvilavalasa in the Vizagapatam district. It is only three miles south of the Nāgāvalī river on whose northern bank Varāhavardinī, the well-known district of Kaliṅga, was situated (*Korasaṇḍa Copperplates of Viśākhavarman*, *E.I.*, Vol. XXI, pp. 23-24).

Śrīraṅgam.—It is the name of an island near Tirucirapalli or Trichinopoly (*S.I.I.*, III, p. 168; cf. *E.I.*, III, 7ff.; ***Raṅganātha Inscription of***

Sundara-Pāṇḍya; *Śrīraṅgaṃ Plates of Mādhava Nāyaka* (*E.I.*, XIII, 211ff.; cf. *The Śrīraṅgaṃ Inscription of Kākātiya Pratāparudra*: Śaka 1239; *E.I.*, Vol. XXVII, Pt. VII, July, 1948). Here stands the Raṅganātha temple. It was the place where Rāmānuja and Maṇavāḷa-mahāmuni dwelt for some time. The Śrīraṅgaṃ Inscription of Acyutaraya refers to the well-known place of pilgrimage in South India, especially sacred to the Vaiṣṇavas (*E.I.*, XXIV, Pt. VI, April, 1938, p. 285). The Śrīraṅgaṃ Inscription of Garuḍa-vāhana Bhaṭṭa dated the Śaka 1415 has the object of registering a gift of land made by Śrīnivāsa (*E.I.*, XXIV, Pt. II, April, 1937). This island contains the Śaiva temple of Jambukeśvara where an inscription of Valakakāmaya (Śaka saṃvat 1403) was discovered (*E.I.*, III, p. 72). This island is situated three miles to the north of the town of Trichinopoly between the two branches of the river Kāverī. The great temple stands in the centre of this island, which was built by the Nāyaka rulers of Pāṇḍya. It is a great place of pilgrimage as mentioned in the *Matsyapurāṇa*, *Padmapurāṇa* and *Śrīraṅgamāhātmya*, forming a part of the *Brahmāṇḍa-Purāṇa*. The celebrated Vaiṣṇava reformer Rāmanuja lived and died here in the middle of the 11th century A.D. Rāmachandra is said to have lived here on his way to Laṅkā. The great temple which is a very old one, was renovated and improved by the Coḷa, Pāṇḍya and other kings of South India. The Śrīraṅgam copperplates of Harihara-Raya belong to the Śrīraṅganātha temple at Śrīraṅgaṃ (*E.I.*, XVI, 222ff.). This place contains an inscription of Coḷa Kulottuṅga (*Ancient India, Bulletin of the A.S.I.*, No. 5, January, 1949). For further details vide Law, *Holy Places of India*, p. 40.

Srungavarapukoṭa.—This village is in the district of Vizagapatam where a set of three copperplates of Andutavarman, king of Kaliṅga, was found (*E.I.*, XXIII, Pt. II, April, 1935, p. 56).

Sudasuṇa (or *Sudisaṇa*).—This was the name of a village on the southern road in the Govardhana district in the Godāvarī region (Luders' List, 1134).

Sudava.—This village is also known as Sudava situated in the eastern division of the Parlakimedi State in the Ganjam district where two sets of copperplates were discovered in course of excavations near the temple of Dharmaliṅgeśvara (*E.I.*, XXVI, Pt. II, p. 62).

Śūdīḍupīrai-malai.—This is the name of a mountain (*S.I.I.*, I, pp. 76, 77). It must have been the old name of the Bavāji hill. It was situated in the north of Paṅgalanāḍu, a division of Poḍuvurkoṭṭam.

Suprayogī.—This river is mentioned in the *Mahābhārata* (Bhīṣmaparva, IX, 28; Vanaparva, CCXXI). It was one of the western tributaries of the Kṛṣṇā.

Śurankuḍi.—It is a village in the Kovilapatti taluk of the Tinnevelly district (*E.I.*, XXIV, Pt. IV).

Śūravaraṃ.—Here Annadeva, a Coḍa king, won victory over a certain king named Annavota (*E.I.*, XXVI, Pt. I).

Śuruḷimalai.—It is the name of a hill (*S.I.I.*, III, p. 450) wherefrom the Śuruḷiyāru takes its rise.

Śuruḷiyīru.—This river takes its rise from the Śuruḷimalai, seven miles from Cumbum in the Periyakulam taluk of the Madura district and flows past Cumbum and Siṇṇamanūr and joins the Vaigāi (*Ibid.*, III, p. 450).

Suvarṇagiri.—As to the location of Suvarṇagiri mentioned in the Minor Rock Edict I of Aśoka (Brahmagiri text) we may have some hint from the inscriptions of the later Mauryas of Koṅkan and Khāndesh (*E.I.*, Vol. III, p. 136). Hultzsch identifies it with Kanakagiri in the Hyderabad State, south of Māski, and north of the ruins of Vijayanagara (*C.I.I.*, Vol. XXXVIII). Bühler is inclined to look for it somewhere in the Western Ghats. Krishṇa Śāstrī has identified it with Māski, situated to the west of Siddāpur in Mysore. It was most probably situated in the neighbourhood of Vāda in the north of the Thānā district and at Waghli in Khandesh, as the later Maurya inscriptions of Koṅkān and Khāndesh have been found at Vāda. An *Āryaputra* was stationed at Suvarṇagiri as a viceroy. He was either the son or brother of Aśoka. (Barua, *Aśoka and His Inscriptions*, p. 62; V. A. Smith, *Aśoka*, 44).

Suvarṇamukharī.—It is a famous river according to the *Skandapurāṇa* (Ch. I, śl. 36–48), 5 yojanas in extent, situated to the north of the Hastiśaila mountain.

Suvarṇapura (Svarṇapura).—It is the modern town of Sonepur situated at the confluence of the rivers Tel and Mahānadī (*Tel-Mahānadī-saṅgama-vimalajalapavitrikṛta*); cf. *Sonepur Plates of Mahābhavagupta* II, Janamejaya; *E.I.*, XXIII, Pt. VII, July, 1936, p. 250; *Kharod Inscription of Ratnadeva III*, *J.B.O.R.S.*, II, 52; *E.I.*, XIX, p. 98).

Śvetaka.—Śvetaka is mentioned in the Indian Museum Plates of Gaṅga Indravarman (*E.I.*, XXVI, Pt. V, October, 1941, pp. 165ff.; XXIV, Pt. IV, October, 1927; XXIII, Pt. I, January, 1935, pp. 29-30). The Ganjam Grant of Jayavarmadeva was issued from Śvetaka (*E.I.*, IV, pp. 199–201). It may be identified with modern Cikaṭi Zamindari in the Sompeṭa taluk of the Ganjam district. It seems to have been situated in the northern part of the Ganjam district (vide also *E.I.*, XXVII, Pt. III, p. 112). According to some Śvetaka was perhaps the country adjoining Kaliṅga to the west (*E.I.*, XXIV, Pt. IV, p. 181).

Tadpatri.—This town is in the Anantapur district on the edge of the river Pennar, containing an ancient temple called Śrī Baggu Rāmaliṅga Īśvara temple (*J.I.S.O.A.*, XV).

Tagara.—This city has been identified with Ter, 12 miles to the north of modern Osmanabad in Hyderabad State (*E.I.*, XXIII, Pt. II—*Kolhapur Copperplates of Gaṇḍarādityadeva*, Śaka 1048). Fleet has identified it with Ter, 95 miles south-east of Paiṭhān (*J.R.A.S.*, 1901, pp. 537ff.; *Bombay Gazetteer*, Vol. I, Pt. II, p. 3, n.6; *Ibid.*, p. 16, n. 4). It has been identified by some with Devagiri, by others with Junnar, and by R. G. Bhandarkar with Dharur in Hyderabad. Ptolemy places it to the north-east of Baiṭhāna and Paiṭhāna and the author of the *Periplus*, to the east of it at a distance of ten days' journey. Yule places it at Kulburga lying to the south-east of Paiṭhāna at a distance of about 150 miles. Duff identifies it with a place near Bhir on the Godāvarī. The *Periplus* mentions it as a very great city. For further details, vide *J.R.A.S.*, 1902, p. 230; *A.S.R.*, 1902-3; *Important Inscriptions from Baroda State*, Vol. I, pp. 43-44. It may be noted here that the original home of the Śilāhāras was Tagara (*E.I.*, III, p. 269).

Takkaṇalāḍam.—It is southern Lāṭa (Gujarat), Dakṣiṇa Lāṭa (*S.I.I.*, I, p. 97). It is southern Lāṭa in Gaṇḍadeśa. Umāpatideva *alias* Jñānaśivadeva of Dakṣiṇa Lāṭa was granted the village of Ārpakkam in the Chingleput district by one Edirilisoḷa Sambuverāyan.

Takkoḷaṃ.—Two records of Parantaka I from Takkoḷaṃ refer to this village in the Arkonam taluk of the North Arcot district (*E.I.*, XXVI, Pt. V, January, 1942, p. 230). It is stated to have been situated in the

Toṇḍaināḍu (*E.I.*, XIX, p. 81). It contains an old temple of the Coḷa type. The god of this temple was, in ancient times, called Tiruvūral-Mahādeva.

Taḷḷapākkam.—It is on the west of Attirāla and south of the Cheyyeru (*S.I.I.*, V, No. 284).

Taḷḷāru.—The Vailūr Inscription of Kopperunjiṅgadeva (*E.I.*, XXIII, Pt. V, p. 180) refers to Taḷḷāru, which may be identified with the village of the same name in the North Arcot district.

Tambapaṃni (Tāmraparṇī).—It is Taṇporunda-āru according to the Tinnevelly Inscription of Māravarman Sundara II Pāṇḍya (*E.I.*, XXXIV, Pt. IV, p. 166). It is generally identified with Tāmraparṇī which name was generally applied to Ceylon. In the *Kauṭilīya Arthaśāstra* (II, XI) it has been referred to as Pārasamudra. It is called Taprobane by Greek writers. It is mentioned in Aśoka's Rock Edicts II and XIII. Vincent Smith thinks that the name Tāmraparṇī does not denote Ceylon but merely indicates the river Tāmpraparṇī in Tinnevelly. He refers to the Girnar text *ā Taṃbapaṃni* which, according to him, indicates the river and not Ceylon (*Aśoka*, 3rd Ed., 162). The *Bhāgavatapurāṇa* refers to it as a river (IV, 28, 35; V, 19, 18; X, 79, 16; XI, 5, 39). Opinions differ as to this point. This river must have flowed below the southern boundary of the kingdom of Pāṇḍya, and may be identified with the modern Tāmravarī. The port of Korkai was situated, according to Ptolemy, at the mouth of this river, which was well-known for its pearl-fishery. According to Kālidāsa's *Raghuvaṃśa* (IV, 49-50) the Tāmraparṇī locally called Tambaravari is celebrated for its pearl-fishery. According to the *Bṛhat-saṃhitā* pearls are obtained at Tāmraparṇī (XIV, 16; LXXXI, 2, 3). It may justify us in identifying this river with the Gundur, the name under which the combined waters of the three streams flow into the sea in two streams. This river is also called Tāmravarṇā (*Brahmāṇḍapurāṇa*, 49). It was a sacred river according to the *Mahābhārata* (Vanaparva, LXXXVIII, 8340). In the Rock Edict XIII the people of Tāmraparṇī are expressly mentioned as Tambapaṃniyā, i.e., Tāmraparṇyas. In this edict Tāmraparṇī or the country of the Tāmraparṇyas is placed below Pāṇḍya. In the great Epic also Tāmraparṇī is placed below Pāṇḍya or Drāviḍa and the mount Vaidūryaka is mentioned as its rocky land-mark. The *āśramas* of Agastya and his disciple and the Gokarṇatīrtha are located in it. All these facts enable us to identify Tāmraparṇī with Hiuen Tsang's Malayakūṭa also placed below Drāviḍa with Mount Potalaka (Vaidūryaka) as its land-mark. By Tāmraparṇī or Taprobane Ceylon is meant, the word *dvīpa* or island is associated with it. In one of the Nāgārjunikoṇḍa Inscriptions Taṃbapaṃna is clearly distinguished from the island of Tambapaṇṇi (Barua, *Aśoka and His Inscriptions*, Ch. III). For further details vide Law, *Indological Studies*, Pt. I, pp. 59-60.

Tanasuli.—Tanasuli or Tanasuliya was situated not far from the kingdom of Kaliṅga. It was from this place that a canal opened by king Nanda was led by extension into the city of Kaliṅga (vide *Hāthigumphā Inscription of Khāravela*, Barua, *Old Brāhmī Inscriptions*, p. 14).

Taṇḍantoṭṭam.—It is a village near Kumbhakonam (*E.I.*, XV, 254).

Tangaṭuru.—This village is situated in the Proddutur taluk of the Cuddapah district (*E.I.*, XIX, p. 92).

Tanjore (Tañjai).—It is the name of a village (*S.I.I.*, I, p. 92; *E.I.*, XXVII, Pt. VII, July, 1948—*Tiruvorriyur Inscription of Caturanana Pa dita*). The Tanjore temples contain a small shrine of Caṇḍeśvara. It was the capital of the Coḷa kings, Nayak rulers, and the Mahrāṭhā *rājās*. It is noted for its great Brahadiśvara (Bṛhadeśvara) temple which is the highest temple in India. Inscriptions of the Hoysala kings, Someśvara and Rāmanātha, are found as far south as Tanjore (*Madras Archaeological Report*, 1896-97). Puñjai (Tanjore district) came to be known as Kiḍā-ramgoṇḍān (*M.E.R.*, 188, 191 and 196 of 1925). The ancient town of Tanjore is situated on the Kāverī river, about 218 miles south-west of Madras. The Bṛhadeśvara temple contains a very big Śivaliṅgam. It is 217 ft. high and is a wonderful specimen of Indian architecture. It is surrounded by a big moat on all sides. The massive stone-built Nandi bull is found seated in front of the big temple. The temple contains massive *toraṇa* (gate) and *maṇḍapa* (pavilion), all built of stone. This temple was built at the time of king Rājendra Coḷa. (Law, *Holy Places of India*, p. 41.)

Taṅkaṇa (Taṅgana).—It is mentioned in the *Brihat-saṃhitā* as a country (XIV, 12).

Taṇporunda-āru.—It is the name of the river Tāmraparṇī mentioned in the Tinnevelly Inscription of Maravarman Sundara-Pāṇḍya II (*E.I.*, XXIV, Pt. IV, p. 166).

Taraḍaṃsakabhoga.—The Mellār Plates of Mahāśivagupta mention it, which may be identified with Talahārimaṇḍala (*E.I.*, XXIII, Pt. II).

Tālaguṇḍa.—It is in the Shikarpur taluk of the Shimoga district of the Mysore State, where a pillar inscription of Kakustha-varman was discovered (*E.I.*, VIII, 24ff.).

Tālapuraṃsaka.—It is a village situated in the district of Nāgapura-Nandivardhana, granted to a Brahmin. The grant was made by Kṛṣṇa III (*alias* Akālavarṣa) of the Rāṣṭrakūṭa family of the Deccan in the name of his brother Jagattuṅga Kṛṣṇa II. Akālavarṣa frightened the Gurjaras, destroyed the pride of Lāṭa, taught humility to the Gauḍas, and his command was obeyed by the Aṅgas, Kaliṅgas, Gaṅgas and Magadha (*E.I.*, V, 192ff.).

Tālatthera.—It is the name of a village situated in the district of Kroṣṭukavarttanī. An eastern Gaṅga Copperplate Grant from Suḍava records the gift of this village to a learned Brahmin Viṣṇusomācārya by Mahārāja Anantavarman, son of Mahārājādhirāja Devendravarman of the Gaṅga dynasty (*E.I.*, XXVI, Pt. II, 65ff.).

Tāmar.—It is a village identified with the modern Dāmal (*S.I.I.*, II, 390). It is also known as Nittavinodanallūr, Chingleput district.

Tāmaraceru.—This village is in Varāhavarttanī mentioned in an early Gaṅga Grant (*I.A.*, XIII, 275).

Tāṇḍikoṇḍa.—It is the modern village at Tāḍigoṇḍa or Tāḍikoṇḍa in the Guntur taluk of the Guntur district and is situated at a distance of about eight miles to the north of the headquarters of the district. Among the boundaries of Tāṇḍikoṇḍa the two tanks known as Cayitataṭāka and Bhīmasamudra are still existing. Bhīmasamudra is a big tank on the bank of which there is a large mound where there are extensive ruins of a Śiva temple. Cayitataṭāka seems to be the ancient name of a big tank, which occupies an area of about three or four square miles adjoining the village. It is the source of irrigation for an extensive area in the vicinity. (*Tāṇḍi-koṇḍa Grant of Ammarāja II—E.I.*, XXIII, Pt. V, p. 166).

Tāṇḍivāḍa.—It is a village in the Konurūnāṇḍuviṣaya granted to a Brahmin of Vangiparu where an inscription was found (*Annual Report of South Indian Epigraphy*, 1917). It may be identical with Tāḍiparru in Tanuku taluk of the Kṛṣṇā district (*E.I.*, XXIII, Pt. III, July, 1935, p. 97).

Tekkali.—It is in the Ganjam district. Three plates have been discovered here belonging to the Śailodbhavas of Koṅgoda (*J.B.O.R.S.*, IV,

162–167; *E.I.*, IX, 41–47). Some plates of Rājendravarman's son Devendravarman were discovered here (*E.I.*, XVIII, 311).

Telavāha.—This river is mentioned in the *Jātaka* (I, p. 111; vide also *S.I.I.*, Vol. I, p. 111) on which stood Andhapura which was visited by the traders who came from the Seriva Kingdom after crossing this river. Some have identified it with the modern Tel or Teliṅgiri (*I.A.*, 1918, 71; Bhandarkar, *Aśoka*, p. 34).

Tiruccendūr.—It is in the Tinnevelly district where an inscription has been found belonging to Varaguṇamahārāja II (*E.I.*, XXI, Pt. III).

Tirukkalukkunram.—It is a large village in the Chingleput district where four ancient Tamil Inscriptions were discovered. It is well known as Pakṣitīrthaṃ (*E.I.*, III, 276).

Tirukkoḍunkunram.—The Piranmalai Inscription of Kṛṣṇadevarāya refers to it, which is said to have been in Tirumalainādu, named after the modern village of Tirumalai in the Śivagupta taluk (*E.I.*, XXI, Pt. III, July, 1931).

Tirukkuḍamūkkil.—The Tamil name for Kumbhakonam (*S.I.I.*, III, p. 283), which is in the Tanjore district. It was one of the capitals of the Coḷa kingdom and a great seat of learning. The temple of Kumbhakonam containing the image of Śiva is famous in Southern India.

Tirumalai hill.—This is the name of a hill, also called Arhasugiri and Enguṇavirai-Tirumalai (*S.I.I.*, I, p. 106). It is in the North Arcot district, about 96 miles south-west of Madras (*E.I.*, XXVII, 24).

Tirumalai village.—It is the name of a village (*S.I.I.*, I, pp. 94, 97, 100, 101, 105, 106, 108). It is much closer to the Pallava country than to the modern Chalukya country. It is noted for its temples. It is a Vaiṣṇava centre sacred to God Veṅkaṭeśa. The temple on the top of the hill was patronized by successive dynasties of rulers in South India.

Tirumale.—The Kap Copperplates of Keladi Sadāśiva-Nāyaka refer to Tirumale which is Tirupati in the Chitoor district (vide *E.I.*, XIV, p. 83).

Tirumāṇikulī.—This village is situated on the bank of the river Gedilam. It is also known as Udavi Tirumāṇikulī which is situated not far from Cuddalore. Here the ancient Coḷa king Seṅgannāṇ is said to have worshipped the god Śiva. A part of Tirumāṇikulī was constituted as Perambalamponmeyaṇḍaperumalnallūr (*E.I.*, XXVII, Pt. III, p. 97).

Tirumuḍukunram (ancient holy mountain).—Its Sanskrit equivalent is probably Vṛddhācalaṃ, the headquarters of a *taluk* in the South Arcot district (*S.I.I.*, Vol. I, p. 123).

Tirunāmanallūr.—It is situated in the Tirukkovalūr taluk of the South Arcot district (*Ibid.*, Vol. III, pp. 197-98; cf. *E.I.*, VII, 132ff.). It was formerly known as Tirunāvalūr. It is 19½ miles south-east of Tirukoilūr taluk (*E.I.*, XXVII, Pt. III, p. 98).

Tirupati.—Tirupati or Tripati or Tripadī is in the North Arcot district, 72 miles north-west of Madras. On the top of a cluster of seven hills stands the Tirupati temple. The seven hills are said to represent the seven heads of a serpent on which Venkaṭācalapati stands; the centre of the serpent's body is that of Narasiṃha and the tail-end is the abode of Mallikārjuna. The beginning, middle and end presided over by Brahmā, Viṣṇu and Śiva, form a wonderful specimen of south Indian architecture (Law, *Holy Places of India*, 41-42).

Tiruppūvanaṃ.—The Tiruppūvaṇaṃ Plates of Jaṭāvarman Kulaśekhara I refer to this village in the Śivagaṅgā Zamindarī of the Ramnād district. It is situated on the south bank of the river Vaigai (Skt. Vegavati). It is 12 miles south-east of Madurā and 16 miles west of Śivagaṅgā (*E.I.*, XXV, Pt. II, April, 1939, p. 64).

Tiruvadi.—It is in the Cuddalore taluk of the South Arcot district near Paurutt where an inscription of Ravivarman was discovered (*E.I.*, VIII, 8ff.). This village is situated on the river Geḍilam (*E.I.*, XXVII, Pt. III, p. 97).

Tiruvadikundram.—This village may be identified with the village of the same name in the Gingutaluk of the South Arcot district (*E.I.*, XXVII, Pt. VII, July, 1948, p. 311).

Tiruvallam.—This is a village in the North Arcot district (*S.I.I.*, I, p. 169). It contains a number of Coḷa Inscriptions. It contains Bilvanātheśvara shrine (*E.I.*, III, 70).

Tiruvayindirapuram.—It is the modern Tiruvendipuram in the Cuddalore taluk (*E.I.*, XXVII, Pt. III, p. 98).

Tiruvendipuram.—It is a village 4½ miles west-north-west of Cuddalore, the headquarters of the South Arcot district (*E.I.*, VII, 160ff.).

Tiruvoṟṟiyūr.—An inscription found here dated in the 3rd year of Vijayagaṇḍagopāla, a contemporary of Rājarāja III, records a gift of land to a Śaiva monastery by a certain Kiḍārattaraiyan (*Madras Epigraphical Reports*, 239 of 1912; *B. C. Law Volume*, Pt. II, p. 423).

Toṇḍi.—This is a sea-port in the Madura district (*S.I.I.*, III, 197).

Toṇṭāpara.—This village has its representative in the modern village named Toṭāḍa in the Chicacole taluk (*E.I.*, XXIV, Pt. II, p. 50).

Tosali.—Tosalī is mentioned in Aśoka's Kaliṅga Rock Edict I and the Nāgārjunikoṇḍa Inscriptions of Vīrapuruṣadatta. It is the Tosalei of Ptolemy. According to some it was ancient Kośala. Tosali is the same as Dhauli in the Puri district in Orissa. Hultzsch refers to two copperplate inscriptions found in the Cuttack district, where occur northern and southern Tosalī (*E.I.*, IX, 286). A viceroy was stationed there in Aśoka's time. As regards Uttara Tosala and Dakṣiṇa Tosala (*E.I.*, XV, 1–3, v. 5; IX, 286-7, v. 4), Dakṣiṇa Tosala is perhaps the same as the country of Amita Tosala of Dakṣiṇāpatha, which, according to the *Gaṇḍavyūha*, had a city named Tosala. It was, therefore, the name of a wide territorial division. Some inscriptions point out that it consisted of a *viṣaya* called Anarudra and a *maṇḍala* of the name of Koṅgoḍa (*E.I.*, VI, 141, 21). Uttara Tosala appears to have been smaller in extent than Dakṣiṇa Tosala, and its *viṣayas* were Pañcāla, Vubhyudaya and Sarephāhāra (*E.I.*, V, 3, 6; *E.I.*, XXIII, 202). The Neulpur Grant mentions some villages of Uttara Tosala which have been located in the Balasore district (*E.I.*, XV, 2-3). The copperplates of Soro (Balasore district) record the grant of land in a village adjoining Sarephā in Uttara Tosala (*E.I.*, XXIII, 199). It seems that the Balasore region was the centre of the Uttara Tosala country. Uttara Tosala formed only a part of Oḍraviṣaya (*Indian Culture*, Vol. XIV, pp. 130-131).

Tribhuvanam.—It is near the Tiruviḍaimarudūr railway station in the Tanjore district, where a Sanskrit inscription of Kulottuṅga III has been found engraved in two copies at two places in the Kampahareśvara temple. This inscription mentions Cidāmbaram and records the construction of a *mukhamaṇḍapa* before Naṭarāja's shrine. It also mentions the Ekāmreśvara of Kāñcīpuram, the Sundareśvara temple of Madura, the temple of Madhyārjuna and the Rājarājeśvara. It also records the extension of the Valmīkeśvara temple by the addition of a *maṇḍapa* and a *gopura* (*D. R. Bhandarkar Volume*, pp. 3-4).

Trikaliṅga.—The Jirjingi Plates of Gaṅga Indravarman refer to it (*E.I.*, XXV, Pt. VI, April, 1940, p. 286). It comprised within it the tracts of country anciently known as Kaliṅga, Tosala and Utkala, while some believe that it included Uḍra (Orissa proper), Kongoḍa, and Kaliṅga (*J.B.O.R.S.*, Vol. XIV, p. 145). Ramdas holds that Trikaliṅga denoted the highlands intervening between Kaliṅga and Dakṣiṇa Kośala or the modern Chattisgarh (*Journal of the Andhra Historical Research Society*, Vol. I). Trikaliṅga mentioned in the Kumbhi Copperplate Inscription (*J.A.S.B.*, 1839) comprised, according to Pliny, the regions inhabited by the Kaliṅgas, Macco-Kaliṅga and Gangarides-Kalingae (Cunningham, *A.G.I.*, p. 519). The kings of South Kośala were called the Trikaliṅga kings. According to Cunningham (*Ancient Geography*, 1924, p. 591) the three Kaliṅgas were the three kingdoms of Dhanakaṭaka or Amarāvatī on the Kṛṣṇā, Andhra or Warangal and Kaliṅga or Rājamahendrī (McCrindle, *Ptolemy*, p. 233). Trikaliṅga country in the Godāvarī district (*S.I.I.*, Vol. I, p. 46) was ruled by Vikramāditya for one year. According to some Trikaliṅga means high or hilly Kaliṅga, i.e., the highland intervening between Kaliṅga proper and Dakṣiṇa Kośala. Trikaliṅga country extended from the river Ganges in the north to the river Godāvarī in the south (*J.A.H.R.S.*, Vol. VI, p. 203).

Tripurī.—The Ratnapur Stone Inscription of Jājalladeva of the Cedi year 866 refers to Tripurī, which was ruled by one of the eighteen sons of the Cedi ruler named Kokalla (*E.I.*, I, 33). For literary references vide Law, *Tribes in Ancient India*, pp. 50, 399.

Trisāmā.—The Trisāmā, otherwise called Tribhāgā or Pitṛsomā, and the Ṛṣikulyā are mentioned in the *Purāṇas* as two separate rivers. But it seems that they were one and the same river, the Ṛṣikulyā bearing the descriptive name of Trisāmā-Ṛṣikulyā. The Ṛṣikulyā and the Pitṛsomā issued from the Mahendra ranges according to the *Mārkaṇḍeyapurāṇa* (Tr. by Pargiter, pp. 57, 28-29). The *Kūrmapurāṇa* (XLVII, 36) speaks of the Trisāmā, Ṛṣikulyā and Vamśadhāriṇī as the rivers that issued from the Śuktimat range.

Triśirāpalli.—This is modern Trichinopoly (*S.I.I.*, I, 28) situated on the bank of the Kāverī. Two cave inscriptions engraved on two pillars in a rock-cut cave not far from the summit of the Triśirāpalli rock, were discovered (*E.I.*, I, 58). Originally Uruiyūr, a suburb of the place, was the capital of the early Coḷas. Later Trichinopoly was for some time the capital of the Nāyaka rulers of Madurā. It played a great part in the Carnatic wars.

Tuṇḍākaviṣaya (or *Tuṇḍakaviṣaya*).—This is the same as Toṇḍaimaṇḍalam (*S.I.I.*, I, pp. 106, 146).

Tuṅgabhadrā.—This river is mentioned in the *Padma Purāṇa* (187. 3) as flowing in the south with the tower called Hariharpura standing on it. The *Bhāgavatapurāṇa* mentions it as a river (V. 19, 19). This is the most important among the lower tributaries of the Kṛṣṇā. The two streams, called the Tuṅga and the Bhadrā, have their origin in the Western Ghats on the western border of Mysore. The Tuṅgabhadrā meets the Kṛṣṇā north of Nandikotkur in the district of Kurnool. Within the belt of the Kṛṣṇā and the Tuṅgabhadrā are to be found the four sets of Aśoka's edicts.

Udagāi.—This has been taken to be a Pāṇḍya city. The king Rājarāja I is stated to have burnt it during his Malaināḍu campaign (cf. *Carala Plates of Vīrarājendradeva*, *E.I.*, Vol. XXV).

Udayagiri.—See under Khaṇḍagiri.

Udayagiri.—It is the most easterly peak of the Asia range, situated in the Jajpur sub-division, three miles north of Gopalpur on the Patamundai canal. There is a two-armed image of the Bodhisattva Avalokiteśvara bearing an inscription written in characters of the 7th or 8th century (*B. and O. District Gazetteers, Cuttack*, by O'Malley, 1933).

Udayagiri.—It is in the Nellore district containing the temple of Kriṣṇā (*A.S.I.*, *Annual Report*, 1919/1920, p. 15).

Udayendiram.—It is in the Guḍiyātaṃ taluk of the North Arcot district, where the copperplates of the Bāṇa king Vikramāditya II were discovered (*E.I.*, III, 74).

Udumbaravatī.—It is a river in Southern India mentioned in the *Harivaṃśa* (CLXVIII, 9511).

Ulagīi.—It seems to have been a city of the Pāṇḍyas. The Takkolaṃ Inscription reads Udagāi (*S.I.I.*, Vol. III, p. 69).

Upàlada.—It is otherwise known as Upalabaḍā. It is a village in the Parlakimedi taluk of the Ganjam district, where a set of copperplates of Rāṇaka Rāmadeva have been discovered (*E.I.*, XXIII, Pt. IV, October, 1935, p. 141).

Uragapura.—It was situated on the southern bank of the Kāverī. Some have identified it with Uraiyūr which is near Trichinopoly and on the southern bank of the Kāverī. Hultzsch has identified it with Negapatam which is a coastal town about 40 miles to the south of the mouth of the Kāverī (*E.I.*, XXVII, Pt. III, p. 116). It is mentioned in *Raghuvaṃśa* (VI, vv. 59-60).

Urlām.—It is in the Chicacole taluk of the Ganjam district (*E.I.*, XV, p. 331).

Ūrttiviṣaya.—It may be identified with the village named Ūrtti in the Keonjhar State about 12 miles to the north-west of Khicing on the right bank of the river Vaitaraṇī (*E.I.*, XXV, Pt. IV, p. 154).

Utkalaviṣaya.—According to the *Skandapurāṇa*, Utkala is situated on the southern sea, containing *tīrthas* or holy places (Ch. VI, 2-3; *Brahmāṇḍapurāṇa*, II, 16. 42; III, 7. 358). A twelfth century epigraph of Gāhaḍavāla Govindacandra refers to Utkaladeśa where lived a Buddhist scholar named Śākyarakṣita. The Bhuvaneśvara Stone Inscription of Narasiṃha I. refers to the building of a Viṣṇu temple by Candrikā, sister of Narasiṃha, at Ekāmra, modern Bhuvaneśvara in the Utkalaviṣaya. It is clear from this inscription that Utkalaviṣaya comprised the Puri and Bhuvaneśvara regions. In the Bhāgalpur Grant of Nārāyaṇapāla, a king of the Utkalas (*Utkalānāmadhīśa*) fled from his capital at the approach of Jayapāla of the Pāla dynasty. The Bādal Pillar Inscription of the time of Guḍavamiśra credits king Devapāla with having destroyed the race of the Utkalas along with the pride of the Hūṇas and the conceit of the rulers of Drāviḍa and Gurjara. A Sonpur Grant of Mahāśivagupta Yayāti distinguished Utkaladeśa from Kaliṅga and Koṅgoḍa. The *Brihatsaṃhitā* (XIV, 7) mentions it as denoting modern Orissa. According to the *Skandapurāṇa* (Ch. VI, 27) Utkala comprises the territory from the river Ṛṣikulyā to the rivers Suvarṇarekhā and Mahānadī. The eastern boundary of Utkala seems to have extended up to the river Kapiśā and to the realm of the Mekalas in the west (*Raghuvaṃśa*, IV, 38). For further details, vide B. C. Law, *Tribes in Ancient India*, pp. 333ff.; *Exploration in Orissa* (*M.A.S.I.*, No. 44).

Utpalāvatī (Sutpalāvatī).—This river is mentioned in the *Mahābhārata* (Bhīṣmaparva, IX, 342). The *Harivaṃśa* (CLXVIII, 9510–12) gives another variant which is Utpala. It rises from the Malaya mountains (vide B. C. Law, *Geographical Essays*, p. 102).

Uttama-Gaṇḍa-Coḍānnadevaraṃ.—This is a village called after the name of the Coḍa king Annadeva in the district of Visari and situated at the confluence of the rivers Gaṅgā and Pimasānī (*E.I.*, XXVI, Pt. I).

Uttama-Kākula.—This is northern Kākula. This appears to refer to Chicacole in the Ganjam district as distinguished from the more southern Śrikākulaṃ in the Kistna district (*S.I.I.*, II, p. 373).

Uttiralāḍam.—This is northern Lāṭa (*S.I.I.*, I, pp. 97–99).

Vaigavūr.—This is a village at the foot of the Tirumalai hill. It belonged to the Mugai-nāḍu, a division of Paṅgala-nāḍu (*Ibid.*, I, p. 97).

Vaigāi.—It is a mountain which is the same as Tirumalai (*S.I.I.*, I, pp. 94-95). It is also the name of a river which flows past Madhurā (cf. *Caitanyacaritāmṛta*, Ch. 9, p. 141). It has been identified with the Kṛtamālā (cf. *Kūrmapurāṇa*, XLVII, 35; *Varāhapurāṇa*, LXXXV, etc.).

Vaikaṇṭha.—It is a place of pilgrimage, about 22 miles to the east of Tinnevelly on the river Tāmraparṇī, visited by Śrīcaitanya according to the *Śrīcaitanya-caritāmṛta*.

Vailūr.—This village is situated in the Wandiwash taluk of the North Arcot district, where an inscription has been found engraved on a rock. It is different from Vāyalūr in the Chingleput district (*E.I.*, XXIII, Pt. V, p. 174—*The Vailūr Inscription of Kopperunjingadeva*).

Vaitaraṇī.—This river rising among the hills in the north-west of the Keonjhar State, flows first in a south-westerly and then in an easterly direction, forming successively the boundaries between the Keonjhar and Mayurbhanj States and between Keonjhar and Cuttack. It enters the district of Cuttack near the village of Balipur and after flowing in a winding easterly course across the delta, where it marks the boundary line between Cuttack and Balasore, it joins its waters with the Brāhmaṇī and passing by Cāndbālī finds its way into the sea under the name of the Dharma river. The principal branches thrown off from the right bank of the Vaitaraṇī are cross-streams connecting it with the Kharsua. According to Hindu tradition Rāma when marching to Ceylon to rescue his wife Sītā from the clutches of the ten-headed demon Rāvaṇa, halted on its bank on the borders of Keonjhar. In commemoration of this event large number of people visit this river every January. (Law, *Holy Places of India*, p. 15.) This river which is mentioned in the *Mahābhārata* (Vanaparva, Ch. 113; cf. *Mahābh.*, 85, 6-7) is situated in Kaliṅga. According to the *Padma* and *Matsya Purāṇas*, this sacred river is brought down to the world by Paraśurāma. The *Padmapurāṇa* (Ch. 21) refers to it as a holy river. It is referred to in the *Saṃyutta Nikāya* (I, 21), where it is stated to be the river Yama (*Yamassa Vetaraṇiṃ*). The Buddhist tradition therefore seems to support the Brahmanical tradition of the Vaitaraṇī being the Yama's river.

Vallavāḍa.—It is to be identified with Vaḷayavāda, also called Vaḷavāḍa, the site of the present Rādhānagarī, about 27 miles to the south-west of Kolhapur (*E.I.*, XXIII, Pt. I, January, 1935).

Vallāḷa.—It may probably be identified with Tiruvallaṃ in the Guḍiyāttaṃ taluk of the North Arcot district (*E.I.*, XXVI, Pt. III, July, 1941) which was an important place in the old Bāṇa territory.

Vallimalai.—This is a hill situated about a mile west of Melpāḍi in the Chittur taluk of the North Arcot district. It was an ancient site of the Jain worship (*S.I.I.*, III, p. 22). Here Jaina rock inscriptions have been found out mentioning the names of two Jaina preceptors and the founder of the two images (*E.I.*, IV, 140).

Vallūru.—It is a village in the modern Cuddapah district (*S.I.I.*, III, p. 106). It was the capital of Trailokyamalla Mallideva Mahārāja.

Vaṃśadharā.—It is an internal river of Ganjam, which flows through the district from north to south and receives a tributary on the left. It falls into the Bay at Kaliṅgapataṃ (Law, *Rivers of India*, p. 44).

Vanapalli.—This village is in the Amalapuram taluk of the Godāvarī district (*E.I.*, III, 59ff.).

Vanavāsī country.—The *Brihat-saṃhitā* (XIV, 12) refers to it as the country included in the southern division. Vanavāsī is in the North Kanara district of the Bombay Presidency (*S.I.I.*, I, p. 96). It is the name of a village in the Shimoga district of Mysore State (*E.I.*, XX). Formerly it was a seat of splendid royalty. It is a decayed village in the Sirsi taluk of the North Kanara district where the two inscriptions of the Kadamba Kīrttivarma were discovered (*E.I.*, XVI, 353ff.). It contains the temple of Madhukeśvara, the ancient tutelary deity of the Kadamba princes. It is identical with Vanavāsī mentioned in the Nāgārjunikoṇḍa Inscriptions of Vīrapuruṣadatta. The elder Rakkhita was sent as a missionary to this country for the spread of Buddhism (*Mahāvaṃsa*, Ch. XII, v. 4). During the Buddhist period and later North Kanara was known as Vanavāsī. According to Bühler, it was situated between the Ghats, Tuṅgabhadrā and Baroda. This country was known to the author of the *Harivaṃśa* (XCV, 5213, 5231–33). The *Vāyupurāṇa* (XLV, 125) refers to the Vanavāsikas, and the Bhīṣmaparva of the *Mahābhārata* (IX, 366) mentions Vanavāsakas. According to the *Daśakumāracaritam* (pp. 192-193) Vasantabhānu instigated Bhānuvarmā, the lord of Vanavāsī, to make war on Anantavarmā who mobilized his forces as soon as his boundary was violated. Of all his vassals the first to help him was the lord of Aśmaka. When the others gathered they made a short march encamping on the bank of the Narmadā. The kingdom of Vanavāsī is ancient Vaijayantīpura, also known as Jayantīpura, capital of the Kadambas, and Vejayantī of the epigraphic records, situated on the river Varadā on the western frontier of the Sorale taluk (Rice, *Mysore and Coorg*, I, pp. 289 and 295). It is held to be the same as the Busantion of the *Periplus*. It is known as Banaouasei by Ptolemy. According to Saint Martin, this city was visited by Hiuen Tsang, which was called by him as Kon-Kin-na-pu-lo, i.e., Koṅkanapura. (McCrindle, *Ancient India as described by Ptolemy*, Ed. S. N. Majumdar, p. 179).

Vañji.—It is also known as Karūr in Tamil classics. It is a town on the northern bank of the Kāverī or the Ponni river (*S.I.I.*, Vol. III, p. 444). According to some it was originally the capital of the Keralas or Ceras now known as Tiru-Karūr on the Periyār river near Cochin (*C.H.I.*, I, p. 595).

Varadā.—This river which retains its Puranic name, rises from the Western Ghats, north of Anantapur, and meets the Tuṅgabhadrā, east of Karajgi. The Varadā, also known as Vedavatī, is a southern tributary of the Kṛṣṇā. The Vāhyā of the *Mārkaṇḍeya Purāṇa* is the Varadā of the *Agnipurāṇa* (Law, *Rivers of India*, pp. 46, 50).

Varaguṇamaṅgalam.—It is also called Rājasiṅgakuḷakki. It may be identified with Rājasiṅgamaṅgalaṃ in the Śivagaṅgā Zemindarī (*S.I.I.*, Vol. III, p. 450). It is one of the 18 sacred places of the Vaiṣṇavas in the Pāṇḍya country. It is 18 miles north-east of Tinnevelly (*E.I.*, XXI, Pt. III).

Varāhavarttanī.—It probably lies near Chicacole. The Narasiṃhapalli Plates of Hastivarman refer to it (*E.I.*, XXIII, Pt. II, April, 1935, p. 65). The village of Rohaṇaki, situated in the district of Varāhavarttanī may be identified with modern Ronaṅkī, a hamlet of Siṅgupura of Chicacole taluk. The Varāhavarttanī district roughly corresponds to the coastal region between Chicacole and Tekkali. (*E.I.*, XXIII, Pt. II, April, 1935, p. 65.)

Vatsagulma.—The Bāsim Plates of Vākāṭaka Vindhyaśakti II refer to this place which was probably the capital of Vindhyaśakti (*E.I.*, XXVI, Pt. III, July, 1941). Rājaśekhara in his *Karpūramañjarī* (p. 27) mentions Vacchomī which corresponds to the Sanskrit Vātsagulmī. Vacchomī is derived from the name of its capital Vacchoma (Vatsagulma) and is identical with Vaidarbhī. Rājaśekhara tells us that Vacchoma was situated in Dakṣiṇāpatha. It was a centre of learning in Rājaśekhara's time. This place is identical with Bāsim, the headquarters of the Bāsim taluk of the Akola district in Berar (vide *Akola District Gazetteer*, pp. 325ff. for the derivation of this place-name).

Vāghaura.—It is Wāghur, four miles south by west (*E.I.*, XXV, Pt. V, p. 208).

Vātāpi.—It is the name of a village (*S.I.I.*, I, pp. 144, 152). The battle of Vātāpi was fought in 642 A.D. Siruttoṇḍa was present in the battle.

Veḥkā.—This is the Tamil name of the river Vegavatī which passes Conjeeveram and joins the Pālāru river near Villivalaṃ (*Ibid.*, III, 186).

Velanāṇḍu.—The Sakarambu Inscription refers to it (*Annual Report of South Indian Epigraphy*, 1917, p. 116; *E.I.*, XXIV, Pt. VI, p. 273). Velanāṇḍuviṣaya corresponds to the modern Repalle taluk of the Guntur district (*I.A.*, XII, 91). Some later Velanāṇḍu chiefs claimed Kīrtipura in Madhyadeśa as their original home.

Veḷapāḍi.—This is a suburb of Vellore in the North Arcot district (*S.I.I.*, I, p. 76; cf. *E.I.*, IV, p. 81).

Vellūra.—It is a town in the south mentioned in the *Brihat-saṃhitā* (XIV, 14). It is the same as Verūḷ, Yeruḷā, Elūrā or Ellora in the Nizam's dominions well-known for the cave temples.

Velukaṇṭaka.—This forest was in the Dakṣiṇāpatha (*Ang.*, IV, 64).

Velungaguṇṭa.—It is modern Veligallu in the Chittoor district (*E.I.*, XXIV, Pt. IV, p. 191).

Velura.—There are two villages of this name, one small and the other large, according to the Svalpa-velura Grant of Gaṅga Anantavarman (*E.I.*, XXIV, Pt. III, July, 1937, p. 133).

Veṇā.—It is a river in the south mentioned in the *Brihat-saṃhitā* (XIV, 12).

Veṇāḍ.—It is taken to include the present Travancore State with its capital at Kollaṃ (Quilon). It is sometimes used to include the territories ruled by all the branches of the Vañchi dynasty (*E.I.*, XXVII, Pt. VII, July, 1948, p. 305 f.n.).

Vengai-nāḍu.—It is the well-known country of Veṅgī (*S.I.I.*, Vol. I, p. 63). It is an eastern Chalukya territory. Kulottuṅgadeva or Rājanārāyaṇa at first ascended the throne of Veṅgī, conquered Kerala, Pāṇḍya, Kuntala, and other countries and was anointed to the Coḍa kingdom (*Ibid.*, Vol. I, p. 51).

Veṅgī (Veṅgīpura).—It is identified with Pedda-Vegī, a village near Ellore in the Godāvarī district (*E.I.*, XXV, Pt. I, January, 1939, p. 45; *E.I.*, IX, p. 58). It stands between the Godāvarī and Kṛṣṇā. According to the Kuruspal stone inscription of Someśvaradeva, Vīracoḍa was the viceroy of this country appointed by his father. The Carala Plates of Vīra-Rājendradeva (Śaka 991) refer to Veṅgī country which was reconquered by King Vallabha-Vallabha (*E.I.*, XXV, Pt. VI, April, 1940). Hastivarman, king of Veṅgī, is supposed to have belonged to Śālaṅkāyana dynasty according to the Peḍḍa-vegi Plates of Nandivarman II. The Teki Plates dated c. 1087 A.D. of Kulottuṅga I show that his son Vīra-coḍa was the governor of Veṅgī. The sons of Kulottuṅga ruled Veṅgī as viceroys by turn. The boundary of Veṅgī is given as the Mahendra mountain in the north and Manneru in the Nellore district in the south (*E.I.*, VI, 346; vide also S. K. Aiyangar, *Ancient India*, p. 145).

Veṅkaṭagiri.—It is the Tirumalai mountain near Tirupati in the North Arcot district, about 72 miles to the north-west of Madras, where Rāmānuja, the celebrated Vaiṣṇava reformer, performed the worship of Viṣṇu in the 12th century A.D. (Law, *Mountains of India*, p. 21). It is known as the Venkaṭācala according to the *Skandapurāṇa*, (Ch. I, śl. 36–48), which is seven yojanas in extent and one yojana in height.

Veppambaṭṭu.—It belonged to Āndi-nāḍu, a division of Agārapaṟṟa (*S.I.I.*, Vol. I, pp. 80–82, 131), North Arcot district.

Vijayanagara.—Vijayanagara is the same as Bījānagar, situated in the midst of the Karṇāṭadeśa. In its glorious days this kingdom included the whole of the present Madras State, Mysore and the districts of Dharwar and North Canara in the Bombay Presidency excepting the districts north of the Kṛṣṇā river, the district of Malabar in the West Coast, Travancore and Cochin. Its lovely palaces were as high as mountains (*S.I.I.*, Vol. I, pp. 69-70, 161, 164). There were in it many populous and flourishing towns besides villages. Many of the towns were old and only some sprang up in the Vijayanagara period. The vast population of the empire may be divided into different classes. Broadly speaking they may be brought under two classes: the consumers and the producers. Certain classes of people took a great part in the social activities of the age, such as games and amusements, and were patronized both by the state and by the people. There was a village *Sabha*. There were professional associations and guilds. It was the capital of the Vijayanagar kings, noted for temples, palaces, etc. partially destroyed in 1565 by the Muslims. The Vijayanagara Inscriptions in Mysore are nearly as numerous as those of the Hoysalas. From some inscriptions in the famous Kṛṣṇa temple at Vijayanagar it is known that when in 1514 A.D. Kṛṣṇa Deva Rāya, the greatest of all the Vijayanagar rulers, captured the fortress of Udayagiri from Pratāprudra, the Gajapati king of Orissa, he took with him from that place an image of Bālakriṣṇa and enshrined it in a Kriṣṇa temple in his own capital (*A.S.I.*, *Annual Report*, 1916/17, Pt. I, p. 14; *The Second Vijayanagar Dynasty* by Krishṇa Shāstrī, *A.S.I.*, *Annual Report*, 1908/9, Pt. II; *Economic Life in the Vijayanagar Empire*, by T. V. Mahalingam, published by the University of Madras, 1951). The ancient Pampā, now known as Hampe, was the name of the site of Vijayanagara.

Vijayavāṭi.—It is modern Bezwada on the river Kṛṣṇā (*E.I.*, XXXII, Pt. V, 163).

Vikramapura.—It is the ancient name of Kaṇṇanūr in Musuri taluk, Trichy district (*E.I.*, III, pp. 8-9).

Vilavaṭṭi.—It is possibly the village Vavveru. According to some it may be the village Viḍavalūru about 12 miles east of it (*E.I.*, XXIV, Pt. VII, p. 301).

Viḻiñam.—This is a port in the Travancore State (*S.I.I.*, III, p. 450).

Vinnakoṭa.—It may be identified with modern Vinnakoṭa in the Gūḍivāḍa taluk of the Kistna district (*E.I.*, XXV, Pt. III, p. 140).

Viṣamagiri.—This village is situated in the Aska taluk of the Ganjam district (*E.I.*, XIX, p. 134—*Viṣamagiri Plates of Indravarmadeva*).

Visari-nāṇḍu.—It figures in an epigraph belonging to the middle of the 13th century among the countries conquered by Eruva-Bhīma, one of Annadeva's ancestors (*E.I.*, XXVI, Pt. I, p. 40; No. 308 of 1935-36 of the *Madras Epigraphical Collection*; *Bhārati*, XV, p. 158).

Vyāghrāgrahāra.—It is the Sanskrit equivalent of Puliyūr (Tiger Village), one of the names of Cidāmbaram (*S.I.I.*, Vol. I, 112 f.n.).

Vyāsa-sarovara.—It is a tank which is now silted up, situated at a distance of two miles from Jajpur Road station. (*B. and O. District Gazetteer, Cuttack*, by O'Malley, 1933).

Yaugaḍha.—It lies 18 miles to the north-west of Ganjam containing an edict of Aśoka (*C.I.I.*, Vol. I; *A.S.R.*, Vol. XIII).

Yayātinagara.—It is the ancient name of Kaṭaka in Orissa (*E.I.*, III, 323ff.). Some have identified it with Jājpur in Orissa but it seems to be unacceptable on the ground that Yayātinagara was on the Mahānadī while Jājpur is on the Vaitaraṇī. Moreover the charter contained in the Inscription was issued from the city of Kaṭaka which is evidently the modern town of Cuttack (*E.I.*, III, p. 341).

Yeḍatore (*Iḍaliturainādu*).—This is a small village in the Mysore district. Fleet identifies it with the territorial division of Eḍedore (*S.I.I.*, Vol. III, 465).

Yewur.—It is a village in the Sorapur taluk of the Gulbarga district of the Nizam's territory, where inscriptions of the time of Jayasimha II and of the time of Vikramāditya VI were discovered (*E.I.*, XII, 268ff.).

Chapter III

EASTERN INDIA

Agradvīpa.—It is an island in the Bhāgīrathī in the Nadia district (*Imperial Gazetteers of India*, by W. W. Hunter, Vol. I, p. 59).

Ahiāri.—This village is situated a little to the south-east of Kamtaul about 15 miles north-west of Darbhanga. As traditionally known this place was the shrine of the sage Gautama whose wife Ahalyā was remarkable for her beauty (*Darbhanga*, by O'Malley, p. 141, *Bengal District Gazetteers*).

Airāvāṭṭamaṇḍala.—This was included in the Paṭodāviṣaya. It has been identified with Raṭāgarh in the Banki Police Station of the Cuttack district (*E.I.*, XXVI, Pt. 2, p. 78; *J.B.O.R.S.*, XVII, 4).

Ajaya.—This river joins the Bhāgīrathī at Katwā in the district of Burdwan and forms a natural boundary between the districts of Burdwan and Birbhum (Law, *Rivers of India*, p. 27). It is also known as Ajamatī. It is Amyastis flowing past the city of Kāṭadvīpa according to the *Indika* of Arrian (*Ancient India as described by Megasthenes and Arrian*, p. 191). Jayadeva the great Bengalee poet was born on the bank of this river near Kenduli (*Kenduvilva*).

Allakappa.—Allakappa lay not very far from Veṭhadīpa which is stated to be situated on the way from Masar in the Shahabad district to Vaiśālī. It was ten leagues in extent and its king was intimately related to king Veṭhadīpaka of Veṭhadīpa (*Dhammapada Commentary*, English Transl., Harvard Oriental Series, No. 28, p. 247). The Bulis who were a republican people belonged to Allakappa. They obtained possession of a portion of the Buddha's relics and built a *stupa* over them (*Dīgha Nikāya*, II, p. 167). According to some the Bulis dwelt in the modern Muzaffarpur and Sahabad districts on both banks of the Ganges (L. Petech, *Northern India according to the Shui-Ching-Chu*, p. 52).

Ambalaṭṭhikā.—It was a Buddhist site in and about Rājagṛha, mentioned in the *Dīgha Nikāya* (I, 1). The Rājāgāraka at Ambalaṭṭhikā was a garden-house of king Bimbisāra (*Sumaṅgalavilāsinī*, I, 41). According to Buddhaghosa it was an appropriate name for the royal park with a young mango-grove at its door (*Sumaṅgalavilāsinī*, I, 41). This royal garden-house stood mid-way between Rājagaṛha and Nālandā (*Vinaya*, II, p. 287). It was the first halting place on the high road extending in the Buddha's time from Rājagṛha to Nālandā and further east and north-east (*Dīgha Nikāya*, I, 1; *Ibid.*, II, 72ff.).

Ambapālivana.—This mango-orchard was in Vaiśālī where Buddha dwelt for some time. It was a gift from the courtezan named Ambapālī (*Dīgha*, II, 94).

Ambasaṇḍā—(= Āmrakhaṇḍa).—It was a Brahmin village situated to the east of Rājagṛha to the north of the Vediyaka mountain and the Indasālaguhā (*Dīgha Nikāya*, II, 263). It was so called because there were mango-orchards not far from it (*Sumaṅgalavilāsinī*, III, 697).

Ambavana.—It was a thicket of mango trees (*Sumaṅgalavilāsinī*, II, 399). It was a mango-orchard at Rājagṛha, belonging to Jīvaka, the royal physician. Here Buddha dwelt for some time (*Dīgha*, I, 47, 49). King Ajātasattu of Magadha came here to see the Buddha.

Andhakavinda.—It was in Magadha, where Buddha once dwelt. Brahmā Sahampati met the Master here and uttered some verses in his presence. (*Sam. Nik.*, I, 154). It was connected with Rājagaha by a cart-road (*Vinaya-Mahāvagga*, I, 109).

Andhapura.—The inhabitants of the kingdom of Seri, who were dealers in pots and pans, crossed the river Telavāha and entered this city.

Aṅga.—Aṅga was one of the sixteen *Mahājanapadas* of ancient India and was very rich and prosperous (*Aṅg.*, I, 213; B. C. Law, *India as described in early texts of Buddhism and Jainism*, p. 19; cf. *Mahābhārata*, 822, 46; *Mahāvastu*, II, 2; *Vinaya Texts*, S.B.E., II, 146 note). It is mentioned in the *Yoginītantra* (2. 2. 119). The *Atharvaveda* refers to the Aṅgas as a distinct people along with the Magadhas, Mūjavants and Gandhāris without specifying their territories (V. 22. 14). They were despised as *Vrātyas* or peoples who lived outside the pale of orthodox Brahmanism (*J.R.A.S.*, 1913, 155ff.; *J.A.S.B.*, 1914, 317ff.). In the *Gopatha-Brāhmaṇa* they are mentioned as Aṅga-Magadha (11. 9). Pāṇini groups together Aṅga, Vaṅga, Kaliṅga, Puṇḍra, etc., all placed in the Midland (VI, 1. 170; II, 4, 62). The *Mahābhārata* makes the races of Aṅga, Vaṅga, Kaliṅga, etc. to be the descendants of the saint Dīrghatamas by Sudeṣṇā, wife of Bāli (I. 104). According to Zimmer and Bloomfield the Aṅgas were settled on the rivers Son and Ganges in later times but their early seat was presumably there also (*Altindisches Leben*, 35; *Hymns of the Atharvaveda*, 446, 449). Pargiter regards them as a non-Aryan people that came over-sea to eastern India (*J.R.A.S.*, 1908, p. 852). Ethnographically they were connected with the Kaliṅgas and other peoples of the plains of Bengal (*Cambridge History of India*, I, p. 534). According to the Belāva Copperplate of Bhojavarman, the Varman kings extended their power over this country (N. G. Majumdar, *Inscriptions of Bengal*, Vol. III, pp. 15ff.). The Rewal Stone Inscription of Karṇa refers to Aṅga along with Kīra in the Kangra valley, Lāṭa Kuntala and Kulāñca. Aṅga comprised the country round the modern Bhagalpur (*E.I.*, XXIV, Pt. 3, July, 1937). According to the Sarnath Inscription of Kumāradevī, Queen of Kanauj, Aṅga was governed by a viceroy named Mohana under king Rāmapāla who was the maternal grandfather of Kumāradevī (*E.I.*, IX, p. 311). The Nilgund Stone Inscription of Amoghavarṣa of the 9th century A.D. states that the rulers of Aṅga, Vaṅga and Magadha worshipped him (*E.I.*, VI, 103). In the Deoli Grant of Kṛṣṇa III, Kṛṣṇa II is said to have been worshipped by the Aṅgas, Magadhas and others (*E.I.*, V, 193).

The Aṅgas were named after an eponymous king Aṅga.[1] According to the *Rāmāyaṇa*, Aṅga was so named because the cupid God, Madana, fled to this country to save himself from the wrath of Rudra and became *anaṅga* or bodiless by giving up his *aṅga* here—an amusing philological explanation of the origin of the name.[2] The Ānava kingdom, the nucleus of which was Aṅga, became divided into five kingdoms said to have been named after five sons of king Bali. Pargiter points out that the Ānavas held all East Bihar, Bengal proper and Orissa comprising the kingdoms of Aṅga, Vaṅga, Puṇḍra, Suhma and Kaliṅga.[3] This statement of Pargiter is not corroborated by any other reliable evidence. The princes of Aṅga were very beautiful and their dwelling place was known as Aṅga.[4] The

---

[1] Aṅga Vairocana is included in the list of anointed kings in the *Aitareya Brāhmaṇa* (VIII, 22).

[2] *Rāmāyaṇa*, 47, 14.

[3] *A.I.H.T.*, p. 293.

[4] *Sumaṅgalavilāsinī*, Pt. I, p. 279.

Aṅgas occupied the territory corresponding to the district of Bhagalpur and probably including Monghyr.[1]

The capital of the Aṅgas was first called Mālinī which name was changed to Campā or Campāvatī[2] in honour of a king named Campa, Lomapāda's great grandson.[3] The city of Campā was built by Mahāgovinda.[4] It was here that the Buddha was compelled to prescribe the use of slippers by the monks.[5] At the time of the Buddha Campā was a big town and not a village.[6] It was once ruled by Aśoka's son Mahinda and his sons and grandsons of the Ikṣvāku race.[7] The *Uvāsagadasāo*, a Jain work,[8] points out that a temple called Caitya Puṇṇabhadda existed at Campā at the time of Sudharman, a disciple of Mahāvīra. This city was hallowed by the visits of the Buddha and Mahāvīra. Mahāvīra spent three rainy seasons here.[9] It was the birthplace and the place of death of Vāsupūjya, the twelfth Tīrthaṅkara of the Jains.[10] It is said to have been the headquarters of Candanā and her father.[11] It was a great centre of Jainism. It was visited by Prabhava and Sayambhava. It was here that Sayambhava composed the *Daśavaikālika Sūtra*.[12] A Brahmin of Campāpurī presented to Bindusāra, king of Pāṭaliputra, a daughter named Subhadrāṅgī.[13]

Campāpurī or Campānagara or Campāmālinī is described as a place of pilgrimage in the *Mahābhārata*.[14] Yuan Chwang calls this city as Chanp'o. It is a sacred place of the Jains. The city of Campā is situated at a short distance from modern Bhagalpur. The river named Campā formed the boundary between Aṅga and Magadha.[15] It was surrounded by groves of Campaka trees even at the time of the *Mahābhārata*.[16] Buddhaghosa, a Buddhist commentator, refers to a garden near the tank called Gaggarā which was full of five kinds of Campaka flowers.[17] According to the Jaina *Campakaśreṣṭhikathā* Campā was in a very flourishing condition. There were perfumers, spice-sellers, sugar-candy-sellers, jewellers, leather-tanners garland-makers, carpenters, goldsmiths, weavers, etc.[18] It was a seat of Magadhan viceroyalty from the time of Bhattiya, father of Bimbisāra. Near Campā there was a tank dug by queen Gaggarā of Campā known as Gaggarāpokkharaṇī which was famous as a halting place of the wandering ascetics and recluses, resounding with the din of philosophical discussions (*Samayapavādakā*). In the *Daśakumāracarita* we find that Campā[19] has been described as abounding in rogues. Campā was besieged by Candravarman whose king Sinhavarman was indomitable as a lion (*Daśakumāracaritam*, p. 52). There lived a great sage named Marīci in the Aṅga country on the bank of the river Ganges outside the capital city of Campā (*Ibid.*, p. 59). In this city there was a prosperous merchant named Nidhipālita

---

[1] B. C. Law, *India as described in early texts of Buddhism and Jainism*, p. 50.

[2] *Mahābhārata*, XII, 5, 134; XIII, 42, 2359; *Vāyu Purāṇa*, 19, 1056; *Matsya*, 48, 97; *Brahmāṇḍa*, 13, 43; *Viṣṇu*, IV, 18, 4.

[3] *Harivaṃśa*, XXXI, 1699-1700; *Mahābhārata*, Śāntiparva, 34, 35.

[4] *Dīgha*, II, p. 235.

[5] *Vinayapiṭaka*, I, pp. 179ff.

[6] *Dīgha*, II, p. 146.

[7] *Dīpavamsa*, p. 28; cf. *Vamsatthappakāsinī* (P.T.S.), pp. 128-129.

[8] Hoernle's Ed., p. 2 notes.

[9] S. Stevenson, *Heart of Jainism*, p. 41.

[10] C. J. Shah, *Jainism in North India*, p. 26, f.n. 5.

[11] *Indian Culture*, Vol. III.

[12] Hemchandra's Pariśiṣṭaparvan, Cantos IV and V.

[13] R. L. Mitra, *Nepalese Buddhist Literature*, p. 8.

[14] Vanaparva, Ch. 85.

[15] *Jātaka*, IV, 454.

[16] Anuśāsanaparva, Ch. 42.

[17] *Sumaṅgalavilāsinī*, I, 279-80.

[18] Shah, *Jainism in North India*, p. 95.

[19] (Madanmohan Tarkālaṃkāra Ed.), Ch. I, pp. 3, 6; Ch. II, pp. 7, 11, 12.

who had a quarrel with Vasupālita on the subject of good looks and of cash (*Ibid.*, p. 67).

Fa-hien, a Chinese pilgrim, who visited India in the fifth century A.D., followed the course of the Ganges, and descending eastwards for 18 yojanas, he found on the southern bank the kingdom of Campā, where he saw some topes.[1]

Yuan Chwang who came to India in the seventh century A.D., visited Campā which was situated on the south side of the Ganges and more than 4,000 li in circuit. He saw the monasteries mostly in ruins and there were more than 200 Hīnayāna monks in the city of Campā, which was visited by the Buddha.

Aṅga included Īraṇaparvata which along with Campā supplied war elephants.[2] According to the *Rāmāyaṇa* Sugrīva sent his monkey followers in quest of Sītā to the countries lying on the east among which Aṅga was one.[3]

There were 80,000 villages in Aṅga, which is an exaggerated traditional figure.[4] Aṅga was the country of the well-known author (Aurava) of the *Rig Veda*.[5] There was a distinct local alphabet of Aṅga according to the *Lalitavistara*.[6] A Brāhmaṇa youth named Kapila referred to the riches owned by the king of Aṅga.[7]

Ancient Aṅga is said to have included the hermitage of the sage Ṛṣyaśriṅga, Karṇagaḍ or the fort of Karṇa, Jahnu-āśrama or the hermitage of the sage Jahnu and Modāgiri or Monghyr. The *Mahābhārata* mentions Aṅga and Vaṅga as forming one *viṣaya* or kingdom (44. 9). The kingdom of Aṅga was in the Buddha's time a centre of activities of some well-known heretical teachers.[8]

In the kingdom of Aṅga there were many towns, such as Āpana[9] and Bhaddiyanagara where Viśākhā, the daughter of Sumanādevī, lived.[10] The way from Bhaddiya to Āpana lay through Aṅguttarāpa, obviously a lowland.[11] There was another town of the Aṅgas named Assapura which was visited by the Buddha.[12]

In the Buddha's time there were in Aṅga-Magadha several Mahāśālās or Snātaka institutions maintained on royal fiefs granted by the kings Pasenadi and Bimbisāra. According to the Mahāgovinda Suttanta seven such colleges were founded by Mahāgovinda in seven main kingdoms of his time including Aṅga with Campā as its capital. These were all theological colleges granting admission only to the Brahmin youths (*māṇavakā*). The numerical strength of each of them was no less than three hundred students. The high reputation of the head of the institution attracted students from various quarters and various localities.[13]

The sale of wives and children and the abandonment of the afflicted were prevalent among the Aṅgas.[14] There was a custom-house between Campā and Rājagṛha for the realization of taxes from the public.[15]

---

1 Legge, *The Travels of Fa-hien*, p. 100.
2 Watters, *On Yuan Chwang*, II, pp. 181-182.
3 *Rāmāyaṇa*, 652, 22-23.
4 *Vinayapiṭaka*, I, p. 179.
5 X, 138; Pargiter, *A.I.H.T.*, p. 132.
6 *Lalitavistara*, 125-26.
7 Rockhill, *Life of the Buddha*, p. 129.
8 *Majjhima Nikāya*, II, p. 2.
9 *Saṃyutta Nikāya*, V, pp. 225-26.
10 *Dhammapada Commentary*, I, 384ff.
11 *Vinaya*, I, 243ff.; *Dhammapada-aṭṭhakathā*, III, 363.
12 *Majjhima Nikāya*, I, 281ff.
13 *Nānādisā nānājanapadā māṇavakā āgacchanti—Dīgha*, I, 114.
14 *Mahābhārata*, VIII, 45, 14–16; 28, 34.
15 *Divyāvadāna*, p. 275.

The king of the Aṅga country was invited at the horse-sacrifice of king Daśaratha.[1] The sage Ṛṣyaśriṅga, son of Bibhāṇḍaka, came to Aṅga at the invitation of Romapāda, who was then the powerful king of the Aṅga country. King Romapāda received him cordially and gave his daughter Śāntā in marriage to him because the sage succeeded in removing drought from his kingdom.[2] At the request of king Romapāda of Aṅga, Ṛṣyaśriṅga with his wife Śāntā came to Ayodhyā to perform the sacrifice of king Daśaratha who was a great friend of Romapāda.[3]

Karṇa was placed on the throne of Aṅga at the instance of his ally, Duryodhana and other Kaurava chieftains.[4] The Pāṇḍavas, especially Bhīmasena, banned him as lowborn (*sūtaputra*), whom Bhīmasena declared as no match for his brother Arjuna with the result that Karṇa became an inveterate enemy of the Pāṇḍavas.[5] At the Svayamvara ceremony of Draupadī, daughter of king Drupada of the Pañcāla-country, Karṇa was present with other Kṣatriya princes, such as Śalya of Madra and Duryodhana of Hastināpura. It was here that Arjuna won the hand of Draupadī by a wonderful feat of archery. Bhīma and Arjuna were then disguised as Brāhmaṇas. A quarrel ensued over the acquisition of Draupadī and a duel took place between Arjuna and Karṇa with the result that the latter was defeated.[6] Arjuna on his way to Maṇipura (in Assam) visited Aṅga as a pilgrim and distributed riches there.[7] Bhīmasena fought with Karṇa, king of Aṅga, and convinced him of his prowess prior to the *Rājasūya* sacrifice of Yudhiṣṭhira. He killed the king of Modāgiri (Monghyr).[8] Karṇa is said to have attended the *Rājasūya* sacrifice of Yudhiṣṭhira at Indraprastha.[9] On the eve of the Pauṇḍarika sacrifice of Duryodhana, the Aṅga country is referred to in connection with the *digvijaya* or military campaign of Karṇa.[10] Bhīṣma, while lying on a bed of arrows in the battle-field of Kurukṣetra, asked Karṇa to refrain from this fratricidal war, as he was not the son of a charioteer. His mother was Kuntī. But Karṇa said that he had already promised to fight for Duryodhana against the Pāṇḍavas.[11] He was made the commander-in-chief of the Kaurava army by Duryodhana.[12] Arjuna went to the Aṅga country in quest of the sacrificial horse. The kings of Aṅga, Kāśī and Kośala and Kirātas and Taṅganas were compelled to pay him homage.[13] King Jarāsandha is said to have extended his supremacy over the Aṅgas, Vaṅgas, Kaliṅgas and Puṇḍras.[14] The Aṅgas were also defeated in a battle by Vāsudeva as we learn from the Droṇaparva of the *Mahābhārata*. In the Śāntiparva of the *Mahābhārata*,[15] we find Vasūpama, king of Aṅga, visiting a golden mountain called Yuñjavat on the ridge of the Himalayas.

Seṇiya Bimbisāra was the king of Aṅga-Magadha when the Buddha renounced the world and Mahāvīra became a *Jina*. During the reign of king Bhātiya of Magadha, his son Bimbisāra ruled Aṅga as his viceroy.

Throughout Jaina literature Kūṇika Ajātaśatru is represented as a king of Aṅga, but the fact is that he was only the viceroy of Aṅga, which

---

[1] *Rāmāyaṇa*, 27, 25.
[2] *Ibid.*, 9th and 10th sargas, pp. 20–22; cf. Pargiter, *Mārkaṇḍeya Purāṇa*, p. 464 and notes.
[3] *Ibid.*, 24, 10–31.
[4] *Mahābhārata*, Vaṅgavāsī ed., p. 140.
[5] *Ibid.*, I, 25, pp. 140-141.
[6] *Ibid.*, I, 4, 178-179.
[7] *Ibid.*, 9, 195; 195, 10.
[8] *Ibid.*, V, 2, p. 242.
[9] *Ibid.*, 7, 245.
[10] *Ibid.*, 8-9, 513.
[11] *Ibid.*, 1–39, 993-4.
[12] *Ibid.*, 43–56, p. 1174.
[13] *Ibid.*, 4-5, p. 2093.
[14] *Ibid.*, XII, Ch. 6607.
[15] CXXII, 4469–75.

formed a part of the kingdom of Magadha.[1] The annexation of Aṅga to Magadha was a turning point in the history of Magadha. It marked the first step taken by the king of Magadha in his advance to greatness and the position of supremacy which it attained in the following centuries. The *Campeyya Jātaka* records a fight between the two neighbouring countries of Aṅga and Magadha. From time to time Aṅga and Magadha were engaged in battles. Once the Magadhan king was defeated and pursued by the army of Aṅga but he escaped by jumping into the river named Campā flowing between Aṅga and Magadha. Again he defeated the king of Aṅga, recovered his lost kingdom and conquered Aṅga as well. He became intimately associated with the Aṅga king and used to make offerings on the bank of the Campā every year with great pomp.[2] The *Vinaya Mahāvagga* goes to prove that Aṅga came under Bimbisāra's sway.[3] Immediately prior to the rise of Buddhism there were four powerful monarchies in northern India, each of which was enlarged by the annexation of neighbouring territories. Thus Aṅga was annexed to Magadha, Kāśī to Kośala, Bhagga to Vatsa and probably Śūrasena to Avantī.

The *Sonadaṇḍa Suttanta* of the *Dīgha Nikāya* refers to the bestowal of Campā, the capital of Aṅga, as a royal fief on the Brāhmin Sonadaṇḍa.[4] Magadha was brought under the sway of Aṅgarāja.[5] Dhataraṭṭha, king of Kāśī and Aṅga, was a contemporary of Sattabhū, king of Kaliṅga, and Reṇu, king of Mithilā.[6] It is interesting to note that Aṅga and Magadha were conquered by the king of Benaras.[7] Bindusāra married the daughter of a Brāhmin of Campā, who gave birth to a son named Aśoka.[8] Srī Harṣa mentions a king of Aṅga named Dṛḍhavarman being restored to his kingdom by Udayana, king of Kauśāmbī.[9] According to the *Harivaṃśa* and the *Purāṇas* Dadhivāhana was the son and successor of Aṅga. This Dadhivāhana could not have been the same king Dadhivāhana who is represented by the Jainas as a contemporary of Mahāvīra and a weak rival of king Śatānika of Kauśāmbī.[10] From the Hāthigumphā inscription we learn that after the defeat of king Bahasatimita, king Khāravela of Kaliṅga carried back to his capital the riches collected from Aṅga-Magadha.[11]

Pali Buddhist literature gives us some information about the religion of the Aṅgas.[12] The monks of Campā, the capital of the Aṅgas, were in the habit of performing some acts contrary to the rules of *Vinaya*.[13] The Buddha, while he was dwelling at Campā, heard Vaṅgīsa, a famous disciple of the Buddha, uttering a stanza in praise of him.[14] Many sons of the householders of Aṅga and Magadha followed the Buddha in course of his journey from Rājagriha to Kapilavastu.[15] The chaplain of king Mahākosala, father of Pasenadi, became his disciple with many others.[16] An Ājīvika declared himself to be a disciple of the Buddha.[17] Bimbisāra was converted to Buddhism with many Brāhmin householders of Aṅga and

---

[1] Cf. *Nirayāvalī sūtra*, *Sthavirāvalicarita*, etc.
[2] *Jātaka*, Fausboll, IV, 454-55.
[3] *S.B.E.*, XVII, p. 1.
[4] *Dīgha*, I, pp. 111ff.
[5] *Jātaka*, VI, p. 272.
[6] *Dīgha*, II, 220ff.
[7] *Jātaka*, Fausboll, V. 316.
[8] *Divyāvadāna*, pp. 369-70.
[9] *Priyadarśikā*, Act IV.
[10] *J.A.S.B.*, 1914, 320ff.
[11] Barua, *Old Brāhmī Inscriptions*, pp. 272-73.
[12] *Vinaya*, I, 312-15, 179ff.; *Dīgha*, I, 111-26; *Ibid.*, III, 272; *Majjhima*, I, 271ff., 281ff.
[13] *Vinayapiṭaka*, I, 315ff.
[14] *Saṃyutta*, I, 195-96.
[15] *Jātaka*, I, *Nidānakathā*, p. 87.
[16] *Dhammapada Commentary*, III, 241ff.
[17] *Ibid.*, II, 61-62.

Magadha.[1] Viśākhā was converted by the Buddha, while dwelling in Aṅga.[2] All the available evidence points to the fact that within the first decade of the Buddha's enlightenment, Buddhist headquarters were established in various localities adjoining many important towns including Campā. At everyone of these places sprang up a community of monks under the leadership and guidance of a famous disciple of the Buddha.[3]

The inhabitants of Aṅga and Magadha evinced a keen interest in the annual sacrifice performed by the Jaṭilas of the Gaya region under the leadership of Uruvela Kassapa.[4]

Aṅgāra.—This village has been identified either with Mangraon or its neighbour Sangraon (*E.I.*, XXVI, Pt. VI, April, 1942, p. 245).

Añjanavana.—It was at Sāketa where the Buddha once dwelt (*Sam.*, I, 54; V. 73, 219). It was a grove in which the trees were planted (*Samantapāsādikā*, I, p. 11).

Antaragiri.—It is in the Rajamahal hills in the district of Santal Parganas (*Matsya Purāṇa*, Ch. 113, v. 44; Pargiter's *Mārkaṇḍeya Purāṇa*, p. 325 note).

Apara-Gayā.—It was near Gayā. Buddha came here at the invitation of Sudarśana (*Mahāvastu*, III, pp. 324-325; B. C. Law, *A study of the Mahāvastu*, pp. 156-157).

Apāpapurī.—See *Pāvāpurī*.

Aphsaḍ.—The Aphsad or Aphsaṇḍ Inscription of Ādityasena refers to Aphsad or Aphsaṇḍ, also called Jafarpur, a village near the right bank of Sakarī river about 15 miles towards the north-east of Nawādā in the Gayā district (*C.I.I.*, Vol. III).

Aśokārāma.—It was a Buddhist establishment at Pāṭaliputra built by Aśoka (*Mahāvaṃsa*, V, v. 80). The building of the establishment was looked after by an elder (*thera*) named Indagutta (*Samantapāsādikā* I, pp. 48-49). Here the third Buddhist council was held in Aśoka's time (*Ibid.*, p. 48). According to the *Milindapañho* (pp. 17-18), a merchant of Pāṭaliputra said to the revered Nāgasena standing at the cross-road not far from Pāṭaliputra, 'This is the road leading to the Aśokārāma. Please accept my valuable blanket.' Nāgasena accepted it and the merchant departed therefrom being very much pleased. Nāgasena then went to the Aśokārāma to meet the revered elder Dhammarakkhita. He learnt from him the valuable words of the Buddha occurring in the three Piṭakas and also their deep meanings. At this time many elders, who assembled at the Rakkhitatala on the Himalayan mountain, sent for Nāgasena who left the Aśokārāma and came to them.

The *Mahāvaṃsa* refers to a tank in the Aśokārāma (V. 163). Aśoka sent a minister to this *ārāma* asking the community of monks to hold here the *Uposatha* ceremony (*Ibid.*, V, 236). A compilation of the true *Dhamma* was made in this *ārāma* (*Ibid.*, V, 276). From this *ārāma* the elder named Mittiṇṇa came to Pāṭaliputra with many monks (*Ibid.*, XXIX, v. 36).

Audamvarika.—The Vappaghosavāṭa Inscription of Jayanāga (*E.I.*, XVIII, pp. 60ff.) mentions this *viṣaya*. Some have established the geographical connection between Udumvara of Sarkar Audambar (cf. *E.I.*, XIX, pp. 286-287) and the south of the village of Mallasārul, Burdwan Division, Bengal (*E.I.*, XXIII, Pt. V—*Mallasārul Copperplate of Vijayasena*).

---

1 *Petavatthu Commentary*, p. 22.
2 *Dhammapada Commentary*, I, 384ff.
3 Law, *Historical Gleanings*, p. 45.
4 *Vinaya*, I, 27ff.

Ādipur.—This village is in the Pānchpir sub-division of Mayurbhanj in Orissa (*E.I.*, XXV, Pt. IV, October, 1939).

Āḷavi.—As a principality it was included in the Kośalan empire. This town was 30 yojanas from Śrāvastī and 12 from Benaras (Watters, *On Yuan Chwang*, II, 61). It lay between Śrāvastī and Rājagṛha. The way from Śrāvastī to Aḷavi lay through Kiṭāgiri (*Vinaya*, II, 170ff.). Some think that Āḷavi was on the Ganges. According to some, it is identical with Newal or Nawal in Unao district in U.P., while according to others, it is Aviwa, 27 miles north-east of Etwah. There was a shrine called the Aggāḷava Cetiya near the town of Āḷavi where the Buddha once dwelt (*Jātaka*, I, 160).

Āmgāci.—It is a village in the Dinajpur district of Bengal, where the copperplate inscription of Vigrahapāla III was discovered (*E.I.*, XV, 293ff.).

Āmragarttikā.—It may be the modern Ambahulā also called Sīmāsimī to the south of Mallasārul (*E.I.*, XXIII, Pt. V, p. 158).

Āraṇaghāṭā.—It is a village situated about six miles north of Rānāghāt in the district of Nadia. The river Cūrṇī flows by the village and on its bank stands the Hindu temple of Jugalkishore. It is a holy place of the Hindus. (For further details, vide B. C. Law, *Holy Places of India*, p. 2).

Ārāma.—It is described to be a prosperous city in Orissa with palatial buildings, temples, gardens, tanks, etc. It seems to have been situated not far from the town of Sonpur. Really speaking, it was a pleasure-garden where the king occasionally lived (*E.I.*, XXIII, Pt. VII).

Āriyālkhāl.—From the right side of the Padmā, which in its lower course becomes known as the Kīrtināśā or the destroyer of memorable works amongst the monuments and buildings of Rājā Rājvallabh at Rājnagar in the district of Faridpur, issues the Āriyālkhāl river below the town of Faridpur. It flows down into the Bay of Bengal through the Madaripur sub-division of Faridpur and the district of Backerganj. This *khāl* and the Madhumatī are connected by a small river which flows from the former a little above the town of Madaripur and joins the latter a little above Gopālganj in Madaripur sub-division (Law, *Rivers of India*, p. 28).

Ātreyī.—The river Ātreyī and the lesser Yamunā meet together in the district of Rajshahi, and then the united stream receives two small tributaries, one on the right and the other on the left. Then it bifurcates east of Nator. The main stream flows into the Ganges south-east of Boalia in the district of Rajshahi and the lesser stream into the Karatoyā (Law, *Rivers of India*, p. 29).

Baḍagaṅgā.—It is a small rivulet about 14 miles north-west of Dabokā (*E.I.*, XXVII, 18).

Badāl.—It is in the Dinajpur district of North Bengal. A pillar inscription of the time of Nārāyaṇapāla has been discovered at a distance of three miles from this place. A pillar containing the figure of a mythical bird Garuḍa was found here (*E.I.*, II, 160–167). The Badāl Pillar Inscription of the time of Guḍavamiśra credits king Devapāla with having eradicated the race of the Utkalas along with the pride of the Hūṇas.

Baḍkāmtā.—It is situated near the northern bank of the river Meghnā. It was known as Karmānta near Comilla town in East Bengal. The modern village of Baḍkāṃtā (*Jaya-Karmāntavāsakāt*, *E.I.*, XVIII, p. 35), is situated 12 miles west of the town of Comilla.

Bahuputta.—It was a *caitya* (shrine) in Vaiśālī (*Dīgha*, II, p. 118).

Baidyanātha.—It is also known as Hārddapīṭha and Deoghar. It is a small town four miles to the south of Jasidih Junction Station of the East Indian Railway and about 200 miles due west of Calcutta. During the later Moslem rule, it formed a part of the Birbhum district. It is now included in the Santal Parganas in Bihar. It is a place of Hindu pilgrimage. It is situated on a rocky plain, having a small forest on the north, a low hill on the north-west, a large hill called the Trikūṭaparvata about five miles to the east and other hills to the south-east, south and south-west at varying distances. Immediately to the west of the town there is a small rivulet called Yamunājor. Its area is about two miles. The soil is fertile and the crops are rich. It is a sub-division of Dumka. The temple of Baidyanātha is one of the famous temples in Bihar. It is visited by pilgrims throughout the year. Its antiquity is carried back in some of the *Purāṇas* [1] to the second age of the world according to Dr. Rajendralala Mitra. The temple of Baidyanātha stands in the middle of the town and is surrounded by a courtyard of an irregular quadrilateral figure. The principal temple is a plain stone structure. Its surface is cut into a check pattern by plain perpendicular and horizontal mouldings. The presiding deity of the temple is the *Jyotirliṅga* or *Baidyanātha*. The ritual of worship is simple enough. The mantras are few and the offerings limited. This temple has now (Sept. 25, 1953) been thrown open to all Hindus irrespective of caste. There are many small temples at Deoghar (now called *Baidyanāthadhām*), e.g., that of Pārvatī, the consort of the presiding deity in the main temple; that of Kāla Bhairava; that of Sandhyādevī, the goddess of Vesper or the Sāvitrīdevī, the wife of the Sun.[2]

Balabalabhi.—*The Bhuvaneśvara Praśasti* refers to Balabalabhi. H. P. Śāstrī has identified it with Bāgḍi.

Bansi.—It is a village in the district of Bhagalpur situated near the base of the Mandar hill. The numerous buildings, tanks, large wells and stone-figures found round the base of this sacred hill show that a great city must have once been in existence there. How the city fell into ruin is unknown, though the local tradition ascribes its destruction to Kālāpāhār. After the destruction of the temple of Madhusudana on the Mandar hill, the image of the deity was brought to Bansi where it now remains. On the last day of the Bengali month of *Pauṣ* the image is carried every year from Bansi to the foot of the hill. There is a sacred tank at the foot where the pilgrims bathe, as they consider the water of the tank to be sacred (vide *Bhagalpur*, by Byrne, *B. D. Gazetteers*, 1911, pp. 162-163).

Barabar hill (vide *Khalatika*).—There are some caves in these hills situated about 16 miles north of Gayā. The caves known as *Sātgharā* (seven houses) are divided into two groups, the four southernmost in the Barabar group being more ancient. The Nyagrodha cave is hewn in the granite ridge and faces south. There is an inscription recording the gift of the cave to the Ājīvikas by Aśoka. The Lomasrishi cave is similar to this cave, but is unfinished. The side walls of the outer chamber are dressed and polished but the inside of the inner chamber is very rough. The entrance is finished and is, no doubt, the earliest example of the rock-cut *caitya* hall. The fourth cave of the Barabar group is the Viśvajhopri. It consists of chambers, but it is unfinished. There is an inscription on the

---

1 *Baidyanātha-māhātmya of the Śiva Purāṇa*, Ch. 4; *Baidyanātha-māhātmya of the Padma Purāṇa*, Ch. 2.

2 For details vide *On the Temples of Deoghar* by Dr. Rajendralala Mitra published in *J.A.S.B.*, 1883, pp. 164ff.

wall of the outer chamber recording the gift of the cave by Aśoka (Law, *Geographical Essays*, pp. 17, 341).

Baranārk.—The Deo-Baranārk Inscription of Jivītagupta II refers to it. It is ancient Vāruṇika, a village about 25 miles south-west of Arrah in the Shahabad district (*C.I.I.*, Vol. III).

Barantapura (Barantpur).—It is situated about 15 miles from Madhipura in the district of Bhagalpur, containing the ruins of a fort which is said to have been the residence of king Virāṭa mentioned in the *Mahābhārata*. The Pāṇḍavas, as told in the *Mahābhārata*, accepted service in disguise under him. Kīcaka, the brother-in-law of king Virāṭa, wanted to take Draupadī, the wife of the Pāṇḍava brothers, and was killed by Bhīmasena at this village. It is said that a party of king Duryodhana took away many heads of cattle belonging to king Virāṭa. Arjuna fought with them and recovered the cattle. The *Uttaragogṛha* or the northern grazing field was situated in the vicinity of this village (*Bhagalpur* by Byrne, *Bengal District Gazetteers*, 1911, p. 162).

Barākar.—It is in the Burdwan district containing some late mediaeval temples (*A.S.I.*, Annual Report, 1917/18, Pt. I, p. 9). Its ancient name is unknown.

Basārh.—This village, situated 20 miles north-west of Hajipur, has been identified with Vaiśālī (*Muzaffarpur*, by O'Malley, *Bihar District Gazetteers*, pp. 138-139).

Bāṅgarh.—It is in the Dinajpur district of Bengal, where the grant of Mahīpāla I was discovered (*E.I.*, XIV, 324ff.). The ruins of Bāṅgarh or Bānnagara are found on the eastern bank of the river Punarbhavā, one and a half mile to the north of Gaṅgārāmpur which is 18 miles south of Dinajpur. For further details vide *Introducing India*, Pt. I, 79-80; *Proceedings of the Indian History Congress*, III, 1939–40; K. G. Goswami, *Excavations at Bāṅgarh* (Calcutta, 1948). See *Koṭivarṣaviṣaya*.

Bāripādā.—It is in the Mayurbhanj district of Orissa (*E.I.*, XXVI, Pt. II, p. 74).

Beluvagāma.—It was a village in Vaiśālī (*Saṃyutta Nikāya*, V, 152).

Belwā.—It is situated at a distance of about 15 miles east of Hili Station. It is within the Ghoraghat P.S. in the Dinajpur district (*J.A.S.*, *Letters*, Vol. XVII, No. 2, 1951).

Bhaddiyanagara.—This city lay in the kingdom of Aṅga, where Visākhā was born (*Dhamma. Commy.*, Vol. I, p. 384).

Bhagavānganj.—This village is situated in the south-east of the Dinajpur sub-division, a few miles south-east of Bharatpur. It contains the remains of a *stūpa* which has been identified with Droṇa-stūpa referred to by Hiuen Tsang. This Droṇa was a Brāhmin who distributed Buddha's relics after his death (cf. *Mahāparinibbāna Suttanta*, *Dīgha*, II). This *stūpa* is a low circle mound about 20 feet high. Not far from it flows the Punpun river (*A.S.I.*, *Reports*, Vol. VIII).

Bhaṇḍagāma.—It was situated in the country of the Vajjīs (*Aṅg. Nik.*, II, 1).

Bhāgīrathī.—This river is mentioned in the *Harivaṃśa* (I, 15) and in the *Yoginītantra* (2. 4, pp. 128-129). It is so called because Bhagīratha brought this sacred river (*Brahmāṇḍa*, II, 18. 42). It flows through Suhma in Bengal (Dhoyī's *Pavanadūta*, V. 36). According to the Sena and Candra Copperplates, the Bhāgīrathī is the Ganges (*Inscriptions of Bengal*, Vol. III, p. 97). The Naihati copperplate of Ballālasena points out that the Bhāgīrathī was regarded as the Ganges, and the queen mother performed a great religious ceremony on its banks on the occasion of the solar eclipse (*Ibid.*, p. 74). The Govindapur copperplate of Lakṣmaṇasena states that the Hooghly river was called Jāhṇavī, which flowed by the side of Betaḍ in the Howrah district (*Ibid.*, pp. 94, 97).

Bhānī.—The Kamauli plate of Govindacandra (V.S. 1184) records the gift of the village of Bhānī, situated in the *paṭṭala* called Maḍavattala. Both these places are not yet identified (*E.I.*, XXXVI, Pt. 2, April, 1941).

Bhāṭerā.—This village lies about 20 miles from Sylhet (*E.I.*, XIX, p. 277—*The Bhāṭerā copperplate inscription of Govinda-Keśavadeva* (1049 A.D.).

Bhāṭśāla.—A village in Ghoraghat P.S. within the district of Dinajpur (*J.A.S.*, *Letters*, Vol. XVII, No. 2, 1951, p. 117).

Bhojpur.—This village lies two miles north of Dumraon in the Buxar sub-division. It contains remains of ancient places of the Bhojrājās (*B. and O. Dist. Gazetteers*, Shahabad, by O'Malley, 1924, p. 158).

Bodh-Gayā (Buddha-Gayā).—Its ancient name was Uruvilva or Uruvelā which stood for a great sand bank, according to Buddhaghosa (*mahāvelā*). According to the *Samantapāsādikā* (V. 952), whenever any evil thought arose in any one person, he was instructed to carry a handful of sand to a place nearby. The sand thus carried gradually formed a great bank. It is situated six miles to the south of Gayā. The distance from Buddha-Gayā to Gayā was three *gāvutas*, i.e., a little more than six miles (*Papañcasūdanī*, II, p. 188). It was called Buddha-Gayā because here Gautama Buddha attained the perfect enlightenment under the famous Bo-tree. The Bodh-Gayā Inscription of Mahānāman (the year 169) mentions the famous Buddhist site at Bodh-Gayā (*C.I.I.*, Vol. III, No. 71, pp. 274ff.). In this inscription the enclosure round the Bo-tree is mentioned as the *Bodhimaṇḍa*. In a postscript of a Bodh-Gayā inscription we find that a gold embroidered *Kāṣāya* (yellow garment) was brought by a Chinese pilgrim to be hung in the Mahābodhi-vihāra.

According to the Ghosrawan Inscription of the time of Devapāladeva,[1] Vīradeva, son of Indragupta, was born at Nagarahāra (modern Jelalabad). After studying the Vedas he decided to adopt Buddhism, and with this object in view he went to Kaniṣkavihāra. After receiving instructions from Sarvajñaśānti, he embraced Buddhism and came to eastern India, intending to visit the Vajrāsana at Mahābodhi. He stayed there for a long time at Yaśovarmapuramahāvihāra and received respectful attention from Devapāla. The Vīradeva arrived at Mahābodhi to worship the Vajrāsana. He then proceeded to Yaśovarmapuramahāvihāra in order to meet some monks of his own province.[2]

Brahmaputra.—The Brahmaputra is the principal river of Assam. The *Yoginītantra* mentions it (Jīvānanda Vidyāsāgar ed., 1/11, p. 60; 2. 4, pp. 128-29). It is also known as the Lauhitya (*Brahma Purāṇa*, Ch. 64; *Raghuvaṃśa*, IV, 81; *Yoginītantra*, 2. 2. 119), which according to Kālidāsa, formed the western boundary of Prāgjyotiṣa. According to the *Jambudīvapaṇṇatti*, the source of this river is traced to the stream which channels out through the eastern outlet of the eastern Lotus lake. Modern geographical exploration goes to show that its origin can be traced to the eastern region of the Mānasa-sarovara. There are three important head-waters of the Brahmaputra—the Kupi, the Chema-Yungdung and the Angsi Chu. All these headwaters rise from glacial tongues. The discharge of the Kupi river being the highest, Sven Hedin fixed the source of the Brahmaputra in the Kupi glacier. But according to Swami Prana-

---

[1] *J.A.S.B.*, XVII, Pt. I, pp. 492–501; *I.A.*, XVII, 307–12; *Gauḍalekhamālā.*

[2] For literary references, vide Law, *Geography of Early Buddhism*, pp. 45ff.; Law, *Geographical Essays*, I, pp. 35ff.; Barua, *Gayā and Buddha-Gayā*, 162ff.

vānanda of the Holy Kailāsa and Mānasa-sarovara, the Brahmaputra rises from the Chema-Yungdung glacier (for further details, vide S. P. Chatterjee, *Presidential Address to the Geographical Society of India, Geographical Review of India*, September, 1953). The *Kālikā Purāṇa* (Ch. 82) contains a legendary account of the origin of the Brahmaputra. It is stated therein that the Brahmaputra is situated between the four mountains of which the Kailāsa and Gandhamādana stand to the north and south respectively (Ch. 82, 36). It flows in a south-westerly direction from Sadiyā down to the place above the Garo hills. It flows south again to meet the Ganges at a little above the Goalanda Ghat. The course of the Brahmaputra through the tableland of southern Tibet is known as the Sunpa. For further details, vide B. C. Law, *Rivers of India*, pp. 29-30.

There is a deep pool in the Brahmaputra known by the name of Brahmakuṇḍa on the eastern border of the Lakhimpur district of Assam. Paraśurāma, one of the ten incarnations of Viṣṇu, is said to have surrendered his axe at this pool, with which he destroyed the Kṣatriyas. The pool is situated at the place where the river emerges from the mountains and is surrounded on every side by hills. It is frequently visited by Hindu pilgrims from every part of India.

Brāhmaṇī.—It is a sacred river which flows from north-west to south-east through the district of Balasore in Orissa (*Mbh.*, Bhīṣmap., Ch. 9; *Padma P.*, Ch. 3).

Burbalang.—This river represents the lower course of Karkai, which takes its rise in the hills of Dhalbhum and flows through the district of Balasore (Law, *Rivers of India*, p. 45).

Buridihing.—This river which is an important tributary of the Brahmaputra meets the Brahmaputra south of Lakhimpur in Assam. For details, Law, *Rivers of India*, p. 30.

Campā.—This river forms the boundary between Aṅga in the east and Magadha in the west.[1] It is probably the same river as the one to the west of Campānagar and Nāthnagar in the suburb of the town of Bhāgalpur. It was formerly known by the name of Mālinī.[2] Kālidāsa refers to the ripples of the Mālinī river on the banks of which Śakuntalā came with her friends (*Abhijñānaśakuntalaṃ*, Act III). According to the *Padma Purāṇa* (Ch. 11) it was a place of pilgrimage.

Campāpurī (Campā).—It was the capital of Aṅga and was formerly known as Mālinī (*Matsya Purāṇa*, Ch. 48). The Jaina *Aupapātika Sūtra* refers to it, as a city adorned with gates, ramparts, palaces, parks and gardens. According to it the city was a veritable paradise on earth full of wealth and prosperity, internal joy and happiness (B. C. Law, *Some Jaina Canonical Sūtras*, p. 73). Here the twelfth Jina named Vāsupujya was born, who attained Kevalajñāna (perfect knowledge) and *nirvāṇa*. Karakaṇḍu installed the image of Pārśvanātha in the tank of Kuṇḍa. He afterwards attained perfection. Kuṇika, son of king Śreṇika, left Rājagṛha on the death of his father and made Campā his capital.[3] We get a beautiful description of sea-faring merchants of Campā from *Jaina Nāyādhammakahā*.[4] It was variously known as Campānagara, Campāmālinī, Campāvatī, Campāpurī and Campā. It was frequented by Gośāla, the founder of Ājīvikism and Jamāli (*Bhagavatī*, 15; *Āvaśyaka Cūrṇī*, p. 418).

---

[1] *Jātaka*, IV, 454.

[2] *Mahābhārata*, XII, 5. 6-7; *Viṣṇu*, IV, 18. 20; *Matsya*, 48. 97; *Vāyu*, 99. 105; *Harivaṃśa*, 31-49.

[3] B. C. Law, *Some Jaina Canonical Sūtras*, p. 176.

[4] 97ff. For details, vide *Aṅga*, ante.

This city was situated at a distance of about four miles to the west of Bhāgalpur. According to the *Mahābhārata* (Vanaparva, Ch. 85) it was a place of pilgrimage visited by Hiuen Tsang who described it as such. It was about 4,000 li in circuit and known to the Chinese as *Chenpo*. The land was level and fertile, which was regularly cultivated. The people were simple and honest. There were *Saṅghārāmas* mostly in ruins. There were also some Deva temples.[1]

Candradvīpa.—The Rāmpāl grant of Śrīcandra refers to Candradvīpa which was ruled by king Trailokyacandra of the 10th or 11th century A.D.[2] This country included some portions of Backerganj. Some scholars hold that Baklā Candradvīpa was the only Candradvīpa meant in early literature,[3] while others hold different views.[4] It corresponded to Baklā Candradvīpa.[5] The Madhyapāḍā Inscription of Viśvarūpasena mentions '-ndradvīpa', which has been restored by some scholars as Kandradvīpa, Indradvīpa and Candradvīpa. It is supported by the fact that the territory in question included Ghāgharakāṭṭipāṭṭaka. Ghāghara is the name of a stream flowing past Phullaśrī in the north-west of Backerganj in the 15th century A.D. (*History of Bengal*, Vol. I, 18).

Candranātha.—This peak is regarded as a place beloved of Śiva, for here, tradition relates, the right arm of Satī fell when severed by the disk of Viṣṇu. It is in the Chittagong district and is visited by pilgrims from all parts of Bengal. In the vicinity of Sītākuṇḍa stands the temple of Candranātha and Śambhunātha. The shrine on the top of the hill contains a *liṅgaṃ* or symbolical representation of Śiva and the ascent to it is said to redeem the pilgrim from the miseries of future births. (*Introducing India*, Pt. I, pp. 83-84.)

Chandimau.—This village is situated on the old road from Silao to Giriyek in the Bihar sub-division of the Patna district at a distance of about three miles from the Giriyek police station. A number of very fine Buddhist images were found here (*A.S.I.*, Annual Report, 1911/12, pp. 161ff.).

Chattivaṇṇā (Brihat).—It is a village mentioned in the Irdā copperplate grant of King Nayapāladeva. Some have identified it with modern Chatna in the thana Dāspur in the Midnapur district, Bengal (*E.I.*, XXIV, Pt. I, 1937, January, pp. 43–47).

Chinnamastā.—This village is in the Golā sub-division of the Hazaribagh district where formerly human beings were killed and offered to the deity. It is situated in the midst of a jungle and the deity is worshipped by pilgrims from all parts of India. It can be reached by a bus from Ramgarh which is situated at a distance of 30 miles from Hazaribagh town. (Law, *Holy Places of India*, p. 14).

Corapapāta.—It seems to have been a hill near Rājagṛiha (*Dīgha.*, II, p. 116).

Daṇḍabhukti.—The Irdā copperplate grant of king Nayapāladeva refers to Daṇḍabhukti. It seems that originally this village was known as Daṇḍa which was the headquarters of a *bhukti*. The origin of the name is unknown. Daṇḍa though originally a *bhukti* is found to be a *maṇḍala* under the Varddhamānabhukti (*Uttara Rāḍha*) (*E.I.*, Vol. XXIV, Pt. I, 1937, January, pp. 46-47). Daṇḍabhutti, otherwise known as Daṇḍabhukti,

---

[1] Beal, *Buddhist Records of the Western World*, II, 191-192.
[2] N. G. Majumdar, *Inscriptions of Bengal*, Vol. III, 2ff.
[3] *Indian Culture*, II, p. 151.
[4] *History of Bengal*, Dacca University, p. 18; *Bhārata Kaumudi*, Pt. I, pp. 53-54.
[5] *J.R.A.S.*, 1874.

is the name of a country, the gardens of which are full of bees (Hultzsch, *S.I.I.*, I, p. 99).

Ḍavāka.—Ḍavāka which occurs in the Allahabad Pillar Inscription along with Samataṭa, Kāmarūpa and Katrīpura, has been identified with modern Daboka in Naogong district, Assam. K. L. Barua identifies it with Kopili valley in Assam (*History of Kāmarūpa*, p. 42). According to Fleet, it was the ancient name of Dacca.[1] V. A. Smith takes it as corresponding to Bogra, Dinajpur and Rajshahi districts.

Dāmodara.—The Dāmodara which is the tributary of the Bhāgīrathī takes its rise in the hills near Bagodar in the district of Hazaribagh, and flows south-east through Hazaribagh and between the districts of Manbhum and Santal Parganas, and then through the districts of Burdwan and Hooghly. The Damodar flows into the Hooghly in several channels through the district of Hooghly (Law, *Rivers of India*, p. 27).

Dāmodarpur.—This village lies about eight miles west of Phulbari P.S. in the district of Dinajpur, where five copperplates bearing inscriptions of the Gupta period were discovered (*E.I.*, XV, p. 113).

Dāpaṇiyā-pāṭaka.—It was a village referred to by the Mādhāinagar copperplate of Lakṣmaṇasena as situated near Kāntāpura in Varendrī within the Pauṇḍravardhanabhukti.

Dehār.—It is near Viṣṇupura in the Bankura district containing a small temple of Sareśvara (*A.S.I.*, Annual Report, 1913/14, Pt. I, p. 5).

Deo Barunārak.—It lies six miles north-east of Mahadeopur and 27 miles south-west of Arrah. It contains a shrine dedicated to the sun, having an image of Viṣṇu (*B. and O. Dist. Gazetteers*, *Shahabad*, by O'Malley p. 167).

Deokāli.—This village is situated 11 miles west of Sītāmarhī containing the fort of King Drupada of the *Mahābhārata* fame (*A.S.I.*, *Reports*, Vol. XVI, 29-30; *Muzaffarpur*, by O'Malley, *B. D. Gazetteers*, p. 144).

Deopani.—It is a river in the Shibsagar district in Assam. Close to it in a jungle an inscription on a Viṣṇu image was discovered (*E.I.*, XVIII, 329).

Deulbāḍi.—It is a village situated about 14 miles south of Comilla, on the Trunk road from Comilla to Chittagong (*E.I.*, XVII, 357).

Devagrāma.—The Bhuvaneśvara Praśasti refers to Devagrāma which may be located in the Nadia district of East Bengal (cf. *Stone Inscription of Bādāla-Maitra*, *Gauḍalekhamālā*, I, pp. 70ff.).

Dhaleśvarī.—It is a river of great importance in the district of Dacca. It receives the waters of the Lakshyā below Habiganj before it flows into the Meghnā as a river of great breadth. (For details, vide B. C. Law, *Rivers of India*, p. 33.)

Ḍhekkarī.—The Rāmganj copperplate of Īśvaraghoṣa refers to Ḍhekkarī. Some have located Ḍhekkarī and the river Jatodā on which Ḍhekkarī was situated, near Katwa in the Burdwan Division (see, for instance, *Introduction to the Rāmacarita* by H. P. Śāstrī, p. 14). According to others, both are located in the Goalpārā and Kāmarūpa districts of Assam (see, for instance, N. N. Vasu, *Vaṅger Jātiya Itihāsa*, pp. 250-51).

Dhruvilati.—It is mentioned in the copperplates belonging to Dharmāditya and Gopacandra. Pargiter identifies it with modern Dhulat in the Faridpur district of East Bengal.

Disarā.—The Disarā takes its rise in the Patkai hills. It flows north-west and west to join the Brahmaputra to the north-west of the town of

---

[1] Cf. Raychaudhury, *P.H.A.I.*, 4th ed., p. 456. Note 4.

Shibsagar in Assam. It is included in the **Brahmaputra-Meghnā** river system (Law, *Rivers of India*, p. 30).

Duārbāsinī.—It is in the Malda district, noted for its shrine which is much frequented by Hindu pilgrims (Law, *Holy Places of India*, p. 1).

Durvāsā-āśrama.—It is said to have been situated on the highest peak of a hill called Khallipāhāḍ. It is two miles to the north of Colgong in the district of Bhagalpur and two miles to the south of Pāthārghāṭā (Martin, *Eastern India*, II, p. 167; *J.A.S.B.*, 1909, p. 10).

Ekanālā.—It was a Brahmin village in Dakṣiṇagiri, an important locality, which lay to the south of the hills of Rājagṛha. A Buddhist establishment was founded there (*Sāratthappakāsinī*, I, p. 242). The *Saṃyutta Nikāya* (I, p. 172) distinctly places it in Magadha outside the area of Rājagṛha.

Gaggarā.—It was a tank not far from the city of Campā. It was dug by the queen Gaggarā. On the bank of this tank the Master taught the people of Campā his doctrine (*Sumaṅgalavilāsinī*, I, 279). This tank may be identified with the large silted-up lake now called Sarovar situated on the skirts of Campānagara, from the depth of which Buddhist and Jaina statues were recovered (*J.A.S.B.*, 1914, p. 335).

Garāi-Madhumatī.—The Garāi issuing from the Gaṅgā above Pānsā in the district of Faridpur, flows down under the name of Madhumatī, forming the boundary between Faridpur and Jessore districts, and reaches the Bay of Bengal, a little above Pirojpur in the district of Backerganj under the name of Haringhāṭā (Law, *Rivers of India*, p. 28).

Gargaon.—It is near Nazira in the Shibsagar district (*A.S.I.*, Annual Report, 1918/19, Pt. I, p. 7).

Gāro.—The Gāro hills are the eastern continuation of the Meghalaya plateau.[1] These hills rise abruptly from the Brahmaputra Valley in the north and west and present an abrupt scarp towards the plains of Assam and Bengal (Law, *Mountains of India*, p. 9).

Gauḍa.—It was the capital of Bengal during the Hindu and Muslim periods. According to the commentary on the Jaina *Ācārāṅgasūtra* (II 361*a*), Gauḍadeśa was noted for silk garments (*dukūla*). According to some, the name of Gauḍa is derived from Guḍa, i.e., molasses, as Gauḍa was formerly a trading centre of molasses. The ruins of Gauḍa lie at a distance of 10 miles to the south-west of the modern town of Malda. It was an ancient town situated at the junction of the Ganges and Mahānandā. It occurs in the Epics and the Purāṇas. The *Padma Purāṇa* (189. 2) refers to Gauḍadeśa which was ruled by the king named Narasiṃha. It was the capital of Devapāla, Mahendrapāla, Ādisūra, Ballālasena and Mahommedan rulers up to about the close of the 16th century A.D. It formed a part of the kingdom of the Imperial Guptas during the 4th, 5th and 6th centuries A.D. There is no trace, at present, of Rāmāvatī, the capital of ancient Gauḍa under Pāla rulers. It lay several miles to the north of the present site of the ruins of Gauḍa near the river Kālindī. Lakṣmaṇāvatī, built by king Lakṣmaṇasena was the later capital of Gauḍa under the Sena and Muslim rulers. Near the present site of Gauḍa stands the ancient site of Rāmakeli, which was visited by Caitanyadeva. King Ballālasena built a castle at Gauḍa known as the Ballālabāḍi or Ballālabhiṭā. The ruins of this fort are found at Shahdullāpura. One of the biggest tanks in Bengal, known as Sāgardīghi, is attributed to him. The abodes of Rūpa and Sanātana, the Rūpasāgara tank, the Kadamba tree,

---

[1] *Le Plateau de Meghalaya*, S. P. Chatterjee, Paris, 1937.

some wells and the ancient temple of Madanamohana are still found there. There are some relics of the Muslim age, worthy of notice, e.g. *Jān Jān Mea mosque*, ruins of Haveli khas, Soṇā mosque, Lotan mosque, Kadam Rasul mosque and Feroze Minar. Besides, there are the temples of Gauḍeśvarī, Jaharavāsinī, Śiva, etc. There is another village called Khalimpur near the ancient site of Gauḍa where a copperplate inscription of king Dharmapāla of the Pāla dynasty of Bengal has been discovered (*E.I.*, IV, 243ff.). The first epigraphic mention of Gauḍa is made in the Harāhā Inscription of A.D. 554 (*E.I.*, XIV, pp. 110ff.), which tells us that king Īśāṇavarman of the Maukhari dynasty claims victories over the Gauḍas and the Gauḍa country. The Gauḍa country is also referred to in the Aphsaḍ Inscription of Ādityasena (*c.* 655 A.D.), which mentions Sukṣmaśiva, the engraver of the inscription, to be an inhabitant of the Gauḍa country. Gauḍa is also mentioned in the India Office plate of Lakṣmaṇasena (*E.I.*, XXVI, Pt. I). Devapāla is described in the Gauḍa Pillar Inscription of Bāḍal as the Lord of the Gauḍa country (*E.I.*, II, 160ff.). In the Deoli plates the Rāṣṭrakūṭa king Kṛṣṇa II is credited to have taught humility to the Gauḍas (*Ibid.*, V, p. 190). The people of the Gauḍa country are represented to have been humiliated by the Rāṣṭrakūṭa king Kṛṣṇa III (*Ibid.*, IV, p. 287). The Sirur and Nilgund Inscriptions of Amoghavarṣa I (866 A.D.) refer to the peoples of Gauḍa. The Kāmarūpa copperplate of Vaidyadeva refers to the lord of Gauḍa (*E.I.*, II, p. 348). The Mādhāinagar copperplate of Lakṣmaṇasena describes Lakṣmaṇasena as having suddenly seized the kingdom of Gauḍa. This grant also informs us that Lakṣmaṇasena in his youth took pleasures with the females of Kaliṅga. In the Nagpur Stone Inscription of the Mālava rulers (1104-05 A.D.) the Paramāra king Lakṣmadeva is said to have defeated the lord of Gauḍa (cf. *E.I.*, II, p. 193). The haughty foes are described in the Harāhā Inscription of A.D. 554 (*E.I.*, XIV, pp. 110ff.) as living on the seashore (*samudrāśraya*). Some consider the haughty foes to be the Gauḍas who indulged themselves in frequent conquests in the 6th century A.D. The Sanjan grant of Amoghavarṣa states that Dhruva took away the royal parasols of the king of Gauḍa, as he was fleeing between the Ganges and the Jumna (*E.I.*, XVIII, p. 244). Harṣa, the successor of Rājyavardhana, concluded an alliance with Bhāṣkaravarman, king of Kāmarūpa, whose father Susthitavarman Mṛgāṅka fought against Mahāsenagupta. According to the Nidhanpur plates of Bhāṣkara this alliance was not beneficial to the Gauḍas. When these plates were issued, Bhāṣkaravarman was in possession of Karṇasuvarṇa, which was the capital of the Gauḍa king Śaśāṅka. The king who was overthrown by Bhāṣkara might have been Jayanāga, whose name occurs in the Vappaghoṣavāṭa Inscription (*E.I.*, XVIII, pp. 60ff.). The Gauḍas did not acquiesce in the loss of their independence.

Gautama-āśrama.—According to the *Rāmāyaṇa* (Ādik. 48 sarga, vv. 15-16), this hermitage was well-honoured by the gods. Here the great sage Gautama performed austerity with Ahalyā for many years. The *Yoginītantra* mentions it (2. 7. 8). It was situated near Janakapura. According to some it was situated at Gonda. Gautama was the author of *Nyīyadarśana*. Viśvāmitra visited this hermitage with Rāma and Lakṣmaṇa on his way to the royal palace of Janaka. There he narrated the incident as to how Ahalyā, the wife of Gautama, was doomed as a result of her husband's curse. But after this unhappy incident the sage left the hermitage and remained absorbed in spiritual practices in the Himalayas. Rāma found this hermitage deserted.

Gayā.—The *Mahābhārata* mentions this holy city (Ch. 84, 82–97; cf. *Brahma Purāṇa*, 67. 19; *Kūrma Purāṇa*, 30. 45–48; cf. *Agni Purāṇa*, 109). The *Yoginītantra* also mentions it (1. 11. 62-63; 2. 5. 141ff.; 2. 5. 166). Gayā comprises the modern town of Sahebganj on the northern side and the ancient town of Gayā on the southern side. The *Vāyu Purāṇa* (II, 105ff.) contains a description of the sacred places in Gayā which also contains Akṣayavaṭa or the undying banyan tree (*Vāyu Purāṇa*, 105. 45; 109. 16). According to the same *Purāṇa* (Ch. 105, ślś. 7-8), Gayā is named after Gaya who performed a *Yajña* (religious sacrifice) here. Gayātīrtha is a holy place[1] where Gayāsūra performed asceticism. Brahmā performed a religious sacrifice on a slab of stone placed on the head of Gayāsūra (*Vāyu Purāṇa*, Ch. 105, 4-5). The Buddha once stayed at Gayā and was met by the Yakkha Suciloma (*Suttanipāta*, p. 47). Gayā is mentioned in the Buddhist literature as a village (*gāma*) and a sacred place (*tittha*).[2] It corresponds to Gayāpurī of the *Gayāmāhātmya* in the *Vāyu Purāṇa*.

According to Fa-hien who visited the city of Gayā in the 5th century A.D., all was emptiness and desolation inside the city (Legge, *Travels of Fa-hien*, p. 87). According to Hiuen Tsang, the city of Gayā was strongly situated. It had few inhabitants and more than one thousand Brahmin families. Above 30 li to the north of the city there was a clear spring, the water of which was held sacred. Five or six li to the south-west of the city was the Gayā mountain (Gayāśiras) with dark gorges and inaccessible cliffs. On the top of this mountain there was a stone tope more than 100 feet high built by Aśoka. There was also a tope at the native city of Kāśyapa on the south-east from the Gayā mountain (Watters, *On Yuan Chwang*, II, pp. 110ff.).

Gayāsīsa.—Gayāsīsa which is the principal hill of Gayā (*Vinaya Piṭaka*, I, 34ff.; II, 199; Law, *A Study of the Mahāvastu*, p. 81) is the modern Brahmayoni and identical with what is called Gayāśira in the *Mahābhārata* (III, 95, 9) and Gayaśira in the Purāṇas (vide Barua, *Gayā and Buddha-Gayā*, I, p. 68). Gayāśira or Gayāśīrṣa is the rugged hill to the south of Gayā town which rises some 400 feet above this town (B. M. Barua, *Gayā and Buddha-Gayā*, I, 11). The *Agni Purāṇa* (Ch. 219, V. 64) mentions it as a place of pilgrimage. The *Yoginītantra* (2. 1. 112-113) refers to Gayāśira. The Wai-Kuo-Shih has wrongly applied the name of Dharmāraṇya hermitage to this hill. On the Gayāsīsa Devadatta lived with five hundred monks after making a dissension in the Buddhist Church (*Jātaka*, I, 142; *Vinaya Piṭaka*, II, 199; *Jātaka*, II, 196). While he was on this hill, he proclaimed that what the Buddha preached was not the right doctrine and that his was the right one (*Jātaka*, I, 425). Here he also tried to imitate the Buddha in his deeds but he was unsuccessful (*Jātaka*, I, 490ff.; *Jātaka*, II, 38). The fire sermon was delivered here by the Master and after listening to it one thousand Jaṭilas attained saintship (*Jātaka*, IV, 180; *Saṃyutta*, IV, 19; *Vinaya Piṭaka*, I, 34-35). Here the Master also gave a discourse on the intuitive knowledge before the monks (*Aṅguttara*, IV, 302ff.). A monastery was built by prince Ajātaśatru on this hill for Devadatta and his followers who were daily provided with food by him (*Jātaka*, I, 185ff., 508). The early Buddhist commentators account for the origin of its name by the striking resemblance of its shape with that of the head of an elephant (*Sāratthappakāsinī*, Sinhalese ed., 4).

---

[1] Cf. *Kūrma Purāṇa, Pūrvabhāga*, Ch. 30, ślś. 45–48; *Agni Purāṇa*, Ch. 109.

[2] *Sāratthappakāsinī*, I, 302; *Paramatthajotikā*, II, p. 301; cf. *Udāna Commentary* (Siamese ed.), p. 94.

Ghosravān.—This village lies seven miles south-west of Bihar. It was the site of an old Buddhist settlement, the remains of which are marked by several mounds. A temple was built here by Vīradeva who was patronized by Devapāla. A vihāra was also built here (*A.S.I.*, Reports, Vol. I; *J.A.S.B.*, Vol. XLI, 1872).

Giñjakāvasatha.—It was at Nādikā near Pāṭaliputra (*Aṅguttara*, III, 303, 306; *Ibid.*, IV, 316; V, 322).

Girivraja.—This city was also called Vasumatī because it was built by Vasu (*Rāmāyaṇa*, Ādikāṇḍa, Sarga 32, v. 7). It was also known as Rājagṛha which was the earlier capital of Magadha. For further details, vide *Rājagṛha*.

Godhagrāma.—It may be identical with Gohagrām on the Damodar, to the south-east of Mallasārul, which is a village within the jurisdiction of Galsi police station of the Burdwan district, Bengal (*E.I.*, XXIII, Pt. V, p. 158).

Gokula.—This village lies near Mahāsthān in Bogra district. (For details, *A.S.I.*, Annual Report, 1935/36, p. 67).

Gondrama.—The Baripada Museum plate of Devānandadeva and four other copperplate inscriptions of Orissa mention the name Gondrama (*E.I.*, XXVI, Pt. II, 74ff.), which seems to be the same as *Aṣṭādaśāṭavirājya* (eighteen forest chiefdoms) of the Betul plates of Samkṣobha (*E.I.*, VIII, pp. 286-87).

Gopikā.—It is the name of the largest cave in the Nagarjuni hills. It is more than 40 feet long and more than 17 feet wide, both ends being semi-circular. The vaulted roof has a rise of four feet. Immediately over the door-way there is a small panel containing an inscription recording the dedication of the cave to the Ājīvikas by Daśaratha on his accession to the throne. (Law, *Geographical Essays*, p. 196; R. K. Mookerjee, *Aśoka*, p. 89).

Gorathagiri (*Goradhagiri*).—It is the modern Barabar hills (*J.B.O.R.S.*, Vol. I, Pt. II, p. 162; Barua, *Old Brāhmī Inscriptions on the Udayagiri and Khaṇḍagiri Caves*, p. 224). It is mentioned in the *Mahābhārata* (Sabhāparva, Ch. XX, v. 30—*Gorathaṃgiriṃ āsādya dadriśur Māgadhaṃ puraṃ*). The city of Magadha could be seen from the Gorathagiri. According to some, Pāsāṇakacetiya was either identical with Gorathagiri or some hill near it (Barua, *Gayā and Buddha-Gayā*, Vol. I, p. 84). Gorathagiri was stormed by king Khāravela of Kaliṅga who then marched towards Magadha. The hill is known as the Goragiri in the Jaina *Nisīthacūrṇi*, p. 18.

Gosiṅgaśālavana.—It was a forest tract near Nādikā. According to Buddhaghosa, the forest was so called because the branches grew up like the horns of a cow from the trunk of a big śāla tree which stood in this forest (*Papañcasūdanī*, II, p. 235).

Gotamaka.—It was a *caitya* or shrine in Vaiśālī (*Dīgha.*, III, pp. 9-10).

Govindapur.—It is in the Nawada sub-division of the Gayā district, Bihar, where a stone inscription of the poet Gaṅgādhara was discovered (*E.I.*, II, pp. 330ff.).

Gṛdhrakūṭaparvata (Pali *Gijjhakūṭa*).—It was one of the five hills that surrounded Girivraja which was the inner area of Rājagṛha. It was so called either because it had a vulture-like peak or because the vultures used to dwell on its peak. According to Fa-hien, about three *li* before reaching the top of the Gṛdhrakūṭa hill there is a cavern in the rock facing the south where the Buddha meditated. Thirty paces to the north-west stands another cavern where Ānanda sat in meditation. While he was meditating, Māra assuming the form of a large vulture took his seat in front of the cavern and frightened Ānanda. The Buddha by his supernatural power made a cleft in the rock, introduced his hand and struck Ānanda's shoulder so that his fear might pass away at once. The footprints of the bird and cleft for the Buddha's hand are still there, and hence the name of 'the Hill of Vulture Cavern' has come into vogue (Legge, *Travels of Fa-hien*, p. 83). It stood to the south of Vepulla. According to the *Vimānavatthu Commentary* (p. 82), it was a mountain in Magadha. It could be approached from the eastern gate of the city. This mountain is also known as the Giriyek hill or the Indasilāguhā of Hiuen Tsang, situated on the southern border of the district of Patna across the river Pañcānā which is the ancient Sappinī, having its source in the Gijjhakūṭa mountain. According to Cunningham, the Gijjhakūṭa hill is a part of the Śailagiri, the Vulture Peak of Fa-hien, and lies six miles to the south-west of Rājgir. Relying on the evidence of the Chinese sources Gṛdhrakūṭa may be sought for somewhere on Ratnagiri. (For a discussion on this point, vide L. Petech, *Northern India according to the Shui-Ching-Chu*, *Serie Orientale Roma*, II, pp. 45-46). From the top of this hill Devadatta tried to kill the Buddha by hurling a block of stone. The Kālaśilā on a side of Isigili (Ṛṣigiri, or 'Hermit hill') was situated in front of it. The Deer Park at Maddakucchī lay near about it. The Gṛdhrakūṭa hill was so called because the great sages attained the final beatitude by meditating on it. A Śiva-liṅga was installed on it. This hill bears also the footprints of Śiva. It contains a cave where the pilgrims offer oblations to the manes and a banyan tree. The *Vāyu Purāṇa* (108, 61-64) refers to a sanctified boundary for offering *piṇḍas* to enable the spirits of the departed fore-fathers to go to heaven. This Gṛdhrakūṭa stood near the old city of Gayā. Dr. Barua says that it is a mistake to think that the Gṛdhrakūṭa of the *Gayāmāhātmya* was one of the five hills encircling Girivraja or old Rājagṛha, the ancient capital of Magadha. (B. M. Barua, *Gayā and Buddha-Gayā*, p. 13).

Gupteswar.—It contains caves situated in a narrow precipitous glen in the Kaimur plateau, about eight miles from Shergarh (*B. and O. District Gazetteers, Shahabad*, by O'Malley, p. 170).

Haduvaka.—An eastern Gaṅga copperplate grant records the gift of this village, situated in the district of Puṣyagiri-Pañcālī, to a learned Brahmin teacher named Pataṅgaśivācārya by one Mahārāja Devendravarman, son of Guṇārṇava (*E.I.*, XXVI, Pt. II, April, 1941, pp. 62ff.).

Hajo.—It is a village in the Kamrup district of Assam, situated on the north bank of the Brahmaputra, 15 miles by road from Gauhati. It is famous for a temple of Śiva, which is said to have been originally built by a sage and to have been restored after it was damaged by the Mahommedan general Kālāpāhār. It is an object of veneration not only to the Hindus but also to the Buddhists (Law, *Holy Places of India*, p. 13; *Assam District Gazetteers*, Vol. IV, pp. 93-94).

Harikela.—Harikela was an eastern country. Some have identified it with Vaṅga (*I.H.Q.*, II, 322; *Ibid.*, XIX, 220). Some hold that it was the coast land between Samatata and Orissa (*History of Bengal*, Dacca University, Vol. I, 134-35). Some are of opinion that it may be identified with some portions of Backerganj and Noakhali districts (P. L. Paul, *Early History of Bengal*, I, pp. iii-iv). Some go so far as to identify it with Chittagong and with a tract roughly covering the southern part of the district of Tipperah (*I.H.Q.*, XX, 5).[1] Harikela[2] (*O-li-ki-lo* or *A-li-ki-lo*) was visited by two Chinese priests according to I-tsing. Both these priests came to Harikela by the southern sea-route. It seems that Harikela was an inland country. It was situated some forty yojanas to the north of Tāmralipti. It lay wholly on the west of the river Meghnā. According to the *Karpūramañjarī* (Nirṇayasāgar ed., p. 13), it was situated in eastern India (cf. *I.C.*, XII, 88ff.).

Hatthigāma.—It was in the Vajjī country. Buddha, in course of his journey from Rājagṛha to Kuśinārā, passed through it (*Dīgha Nikāya*, II, p. 123; *Saṃyutta Nikāya*, IV, 109).

Hiraṇyaparvata (Golden Mountain).—According to Cunningham, this hill was situated on the bank of the Ganges (*A.S.R.*, XV, pp. 15-16). It was known to the ancients as Modāgiri as mentioned in the *Mahābhārata*. It was also called the Mudgalagiri, modern Monghyr in Bihar. In the 11th century, it was known as Mun-giri (Alberuni's *India*, I, 200). Its limits may be fixed as extending from Lakṣmīsarai to Sultanganj on the Ganges in the north and from the western end of the Pārśvanāth hill to the junction of the rivers Barakar and Dāmudā in the south (*C.A.G.I.*, pp. 545ff.).

Ichāmatī.—The Ichāmatī is one of the oldest rivers in the district of Dacca. It flows between the Dhaleśvarī and the Padmā. For details, vide Law, *Rivers of India*, p. 33.

Indakūṭa.—It was a hill near Rājagṛha (*Saṃyutta*, I, 206). On this hill there was the dwelling of the Yakkha Indaka, presumably a prehistorical sanctuary (*Saṃyutta*, I, 206). Either the hill derived its name from the Yakkha or the Yakkha derived his name from the hill (*Sāratthappakāsinī*, I, 300). The abode of the Yakkha was a stone-structure like a hall marked by the presence of a sacred tree. This hill seems to have stood either opposite to the Gijjhakūṭa or by its side (*Saṃyutta*, I, 206).

Indasāla-guhā.—The Indasāla-guhā cave finds mention in the Barhut Jātaka label No. 6. It is named after an Indasāla tree standing at its door (Barua and Sinha, *Barhut Inscriptions*, p. 61). The village called Ambasaṇḍa which exists outside the area of Rājagṛha but within Magadha, indicates the location of this cave on the Vediyaka mountain standing to the north of it. It was in this cave the Buddha delivered the *Sakkapañha-Suttanta* to Indra, the lord of gods (*Dīgha*, II, pp. 263-4, 269), Fa-hien and Hiuen Tsang suggest a name for the cave in Chinese which corresponds to Skt. Indraśailaguhā-mountain (*In-t'o-lo-shi-io-kia-ho-shan*). According to Fa-hien, the cave and the mountain were situated nine yojanas to the south-east of Pāṭaliputra and according to Hiuen Tsang, it was situated 30 li (about five miles) to the east of the town of Kālapināka. Cunningham, however, identifies the mountain with Giriyek six miles from Rājgir (Cunningham, *A.G.I.*, ed. Majumdar, 539ff.; Barua and Sinha, *Barhut Inscriptions*, p. 126; Law, *Geography of Early Buddhism*, p. 42).

Isigilipassa.—It was one of the five hills encircling Rājagṛha (*Majjhima*, III, 68ff.; *Paramatthajotikā*, II, 382; *Vimānavatthu-aṭṭhakathā*, p. 82). All the five hills except the Isigili had different names in different ages (*Majjhima*, III, 68ff.). The *Mahābhārata* (II, 21. 2) refers to this mountain as Ṛṣigiri. As this mountain swallowed up the hermit teachers (*Isigilatīti Isigili-Majjhima*, III, 68; *Papañcasūdanī*, II, P.T.S., p. 63), it got the name of the 'mount swallow-sage' (Chalmers, *Further Dialogues of the*

---

[1] On the identification of Harikela—*Proceedings of the Indian History Congress*, VII, 1944.

[2] *A Record of the Buddhist Religion* by I-tsing (Tr. by Takakusu, 1896), p. xlvi.

Buddha, II, p. 192). By the side of this mountain, there was a black rock (*Kālaśilā*) on which Godhika and Vakkali committed suicide (*Saṃyutta*, I, 120ff.; III, 123-124). Monks desired to have a lodging place at the black rock on the Isigilipassa (*Vinaya*, II, p. 76). The Buddha lived on this mountain at Rājagṛha and addressed the monks (*Majjhima*, III, p. 68). His happy reminiscences of the sites at Rājagṛha are vividly recorded in the *Mahāparinibbāna suttanta*. He told Ānanda that he would dwell at Kālaśilā at Isigilipassa (*Dīgha.*, II, 116ff.). Once the Master lived here with many monks including Mahāmoggallāna who was very much praised by the revered Vaṅgīsa in the presence of the Master (*Saṃyutta*, I, 194-195). The Buddha came to Rājagṛha and took up his abode in the bamboo-grove as soon as he received the death-news of Sāriputta. Then an elder who attained perfection in supernatural power dwelt on the slopes of the Mount Isigili. Several attempts were made on his life by the heretics but all in vain (*Jātaka*, No. 522, Vol. V). According to the Pali *Isigilisutta*, five hundred *paccekabuddhas* (individual Buddhas) lived on this hill for ever (*ciranivāsino*). They were seen entering the mountain but not coming out. This *sutta* mentions many of them by name (*Majjhima*, III, 68–71). Dr. Barua thinks that the Mount Isigili was hallowed by the death of these hermits or holy personages (*Calcutta Review*, 1924, p. 61).

The name Isigili was evidently a Māgadhī or local form of the Sanskrit Ṛṣigiri, meaning a hermit-hill. The name in its Prakrit spelling acquired even in the Buddha's time a popular etymology, which though fantastic, has some importance of its own.

Itkhori.—It is about 10 miles south of Champaran which is at the head of the Danua Pass from Gayā on the G.T. Road. It is a most neglected place in the district of Hazaribagh, where several stone images of Hindu, Buddhist and Jain deities have been found scattered. Nearby there is an extensive forest. An inscription of king Mahendrapāla on an image of Tārā has been discovered here (*A.S.I.R.*, 1920-21, p. 35; *Hazaribagh*, by Lister, *B. and O. District Gazetteers*, 1917, p. 201).

Jahnu-āśrama.—This hermitage of the sage Jahnu was situated at Sultanganj on the west of Bhāgalpur. The temple of Gaivināth Mahādeva, which was on the site of this hermitage, was situated on a rock which came out from the bed of the Ganges in front of Sultanganj. The Ganges on her way to the ocean was quaffed down in a draught by the sage when interrupted in his meditation by the rush of water and was let out by an incision on his thigh (or knee) at the intercession by Bhagīratha. Hence the Ganges is called the Jāhnavī or the daughter of the sage Jahnu (Law, *Holy Places of India*, p. 14; *J.A.S.B.*, X, 1914; XXXIII, p. 360; Cunningham, *A.S.R.*, XV, 21).

Jaintia.—This hill lies to the east of the Barail range. It rises gradually from the Brahmaputra Valley in the north and presents an abrupt scarp southwards to the Surma Valley (Law, *Mountains of India*, p. 9).

Japla.—It is the ancient name of Husainabad, a small pargana lying along the bank of the Son. It was formerly in the Gayā district (*B. and O. District Gazetteers*, *Palamau*, by O'Malley, p. 183).

Jayapura.—The Baripada Museum plate of Devānandadeva seems to refer to this place. It was presumably the capital of the Nanda family of Orissa and has been identified with Jaipur, a village situated in the Dhenkanal State (*E.I.*, XXVI, Pt. II, pp. 74ff.; *J.B.O.R.S.*, XV, 89; XVI, 457ff.; XVII, 17; *Bhandarkar's List*, No. 2076).

Jīvaka-ambavana.—It was nearer Jīvaka's dwelling house than Venuvana (*Sumaṅgalavilāsinī*, I, 133). Jīvaka converted the mango-grove into a *vihāra*, and made a gift of it to the Buddha and his Order. It was visited by king Ajātaśatru of Magadha. (For further details, vide B. C. Law, *Rājagṛha in Ancient Literature*, *M.A.S.I.*, No. 58).

Jhāmatpura.—It is a village four miles to the north of Katwa (Kāṭadvīpa) which was the dwelling place of Kṛṣṇadāsa Kavirāja, the famous author of the *Śrīcaitanyacaritāmrita* (Law, *Geographical Essays*, p. 220).

Kailān.—The new Kailān plate of Śrīdharana Rāta of Samataṭa mentions this village which is under the Cāndinā police station of the Sadar sub-division of the Tippera district, East Bengal, and about 10 miles south of Cāndinā (*I.H.Q.*, XXII and XXIII).

Kajaṅgala (Kayaṅgala).—This extensive hill tract lay to the east of Aṅga and extended from the Ganges in the north-east to the Suvarṇarekhā in the south-east. It was a Brahmin village, which was the birth-place of Nāgasena (*Milindapañha*, p. 10). The Buddha once dwelt at Veluvana in Kajaṅgala (*Aṅguttara Nikāya*, V. 54). The Master delivered the *Indriyabhāvanāsutta* during his sojourn at Mukheluvana in Kajaṅgala (*Majjhima Nikāya*, III, 298). In the Buddha's time, food could be easily obtained here (*dabbasambhārā sulabhā*—*Jātaka*, IV, 310). In the *Mahāvagga* (*Vinaya texts*, S.B.E., II, 38) as well as in the *Sumaṅgalavilāsinī* (II, 429), it is stated to have been the eastern limit of Madhyadeśa beyond the Brahmin village of Mahāsāla. It is the *Ka-chu-wen-ki-lo* of Yuan Chwang. It was 2,000 li in circuit and was bounded on the north by the Ganges. It is to be located somewhere in the Rajmahal district. It formed the western boundary of the Pūrvadeśa. There was a river called the Salalavatī in the south-east.

Kalandakanivāpa.—This woodland existed at Veluvana in Rājagṛha where the Buddha once lived (*Aṅguttara*, II, pp. 35, 172, 179; III, 35; IV, 402; *Majjhima*, III, p. 128). King Bimbisāra made a gift of this Bamboo-grove to the Buddha. This grove was situated in the outer area of Rājagṛha neither very far nor very near and yet, at the same time, a peaceful retreat most favourably situated (*Vinaya-Mahāvagga*, I, 39; Fausboll, *Jātaka*, I, 85). It came to be so named as food was regularly given here to squirrels (*Samantapāsādikā*, III, 575). A party of six nuns went to attend the *Giraggasamajjā*, a kind of festival, at Kalandakanivāpa, while the Buddha was dwelling there (*Vinaya*, IV, 267). A highly popular music of the day known as the *Giraggasamajjā* was played here in the presence of a party of six monks, while the Master was there (*Vinaya*, II, 107).

Kalavāḷagāma.—This village was in Magadha. While residing near this village Moggallāna fell into sloth on the seventh day after the day of his reception into the Order. Aroused by the Master, Moggallāna shook off sloth and completed meditation. He then attained arhatship (*Dhammapada Commentary*, I, 96).

Kapilāśrama.—The *Yoginītantra* (2. 9, pp. 214ff.) mentions it. The *Bṛhat Dharmapurāṇa* (Ch. 22) also refers to it. This hermitage is situated in the Sagar island near the mouth of the Ganges.

Karaṇgarh (*Karaṇāgarh*).—It is a hill near Bhagalpur town in the Bhagalpur district and is said to have derived its name from the pious Hindu king Karṇa. The only objects of interest are the Śaiva temples of some celebrity, one of which is very ancient (Byrne, *Bhagalpur*, *B. D. Gazetteers*, 1911, p. 166).

Karatoyā.—This is a branch of the Brahmaputra. It formed the western boundary of Kāmarūpa (cf. *Mahābhārata*, Vanaparva, Ch. 85).

The *Padma Purāṇa* (Ch. 21) mentions it as a holy river. It is also mentioned in the *Mārkaṇḍeya Purāṇa*, (57, 21–25) as well as in the *Yoginītantra* (1. 11. 60; 1. 12. 69; 2. 1. 114). This river was, according to the *Kālikā Purāṇa* (Ch. 51, 65ff.; Ch. 58, 37), 30 yojanas long and 100 yojanas wide. This river has its origin above Domār in the district of Rungpur and is joined on the left by a tributary in the same district and by another on the left in the district of Bogra. It has been identified by some with the Sadānīrā (cf. *Amarakoṣa*, I, 2, 3, 32; *Haimakoṣa*, IV, 151; Law, *Rivers of India*, p. 24). For further details, Law, *Rivers of India*, pp. 32-33.

Karṇaphulī.—The Karṇaphulī popularly known as the Kaincā is the largest of the three main rivers of Chittagong and Chittagong Hill Tracts. It rises from the Lushai Hills that connect the Chittagong Hill Tracts with the south-western part of Assam, and flows south-west down to Rāṅgāmāṭī, the headquarters of the Chittagong Hill Tracts. Between Rāṅgāmāṭī and Chittagong town this river is fed by a few small tributaries. It is navigable up to Rāṅgāmāṭī. For further details, vide B. C. Law, *Rivers of India*, p. 36.

Karṇasuvarṇa.—At the time of issuing Nidhanpur plates of Bhāṣkaravarman, Karṇasuvarṇa, which was once the capital of the Gauḍa king Śaśāṅka, was in the possession of Bhāṣkara (*E.I.*, XII, pp. 65–79). Jayanāga was an inhabitant of Karṇasuvarṇaka and while he was here, he issued a grant which is supposed to date from the latter half of the 6th century A.D. (*E.I.*, XVIII, p. 63). The Rohtāsgaḍh stone seal-matrix of Mahāsāmanta Śaśāṅkadeva mentions it (*C.I.I.*, Vol. III). Rāṅgāmāṭī in the district of Murshidabad lying on the western coast of the Ganges, is believed to have been the site of Karṇasuvarṇa. It is situated at a distance of 94 miles from Bandel and a mile and a half to the south-east of Chirati railway station. The soil of this place is red and hard, and offers a clue to the name of this place. According to some, the name is derived from Raktamṛtti or Raktabhitti (*lo-to-wei-chi*), the name of an old Buddhist monastery, which the Chinese traveller Hiuen Tsang found in Karṇasuvarṇa in the 7th century A.D. This kingdom, which was known to the Chinese as *Kie-lo-na-su-fa-la-na*, was about 14 or 15 hundred *li* in circuit. It was thickly populated, and the householders were rich. The land was regularly cultivated, and produced abundance of flowers. The climate was agreeable. The people were honest and amiable in manners. They were fond of learning. Among the people there were believers and heretics. There were some *Saṅghārāmas* and *Deva temples* (Beal, *Buddhist Records of the Western World*, II, 201). Many coins of the Kuṣāṇa and Gupta ages, a few mounds of brick and clay called Thākura-vāḍidāṅgā, Rājavāḍidāṅga, Sannyāsī-dāṅga, etc., and a few tanks are found there. A Hindu deity made up of stone with eight hands called Mahīṣamardinī has been discovered here.

Karūṣa.—According to the *Rāmāyaṇa* (Bālakāṇḍa, XXVII, 18–23), the country of the Karūṣas or Karūṣadeśa seems to have been situated in the Sahabad district (Bihar). The southern district of Sahabad between the rivers Son and Karmanāśā was called Karūṣadeśa (Martin, *Eastern India*, I, p. 405). This is supported by a modern local inscription discovered at Masār in the Sahabad district designating the territory as Karūṣadeśa (Cunningham, *A.S.R.*, III, 67–71). Vedagarbhapurī or modern Buxar is referred to in the *Brahmāṇḍa Purāṇa* (Pūrvakhaṇḍa, Ch. 5) as being situated in Karūṣadeśa. The people of this country known as the Karūṣas fought with the Pāṇḍavas in the Kurukṣetra war. (Vide Udyoga, Bhīṣma and Droṇaparvans of the *Mahābhārata*). They may be identified with the Chrysei (M. V. St. Martin, *Etude sur la Geog: Grecque*, p. 199).

A king of the Karūṣas named Dadhra met his death at the hand of his son (*Harṣacarita*, 6th Ucchāsa). According to the *Kauṭilya-arthaśāstra* (p. 50), the elephants of Karūṣadeśa were inferior to those of Aṅga and Kaliṅga. For further details, vide Law, *Tribes in Ancient India*, pp. 87–89.

Kassapakārāma.—This monastery was at Rājagṛha (*Saṃyutta*, III, p. 124).

Kauśikī.—It is a river mentioned in the Nidhanpur charter of Bhāṣkaravarman, king of Kāmarūpa. The *Rāmāyaṇa* (Ādiparva, Ch. 34), the *Mahābhārata* (Ch. 110, 20–22), the *Varāha Purāṇa* (Ch. 140) and the *Padma Purāṇa* (Ch. 21) also refer to this river. It is also mentioned in the *Kālikā Purāṇa* as the Mahākauśikī issuing out of the Himalaya mountain (Ch. 14. 14, Ch. 14. 31). It is to be identified with Kusiara of Sylhet flowing through the area known as Pañca-Khaṇḍa. But there is a difference of opinion as to its identification (*I.C.*, I, pp. 421ff.). Hunter points out that the Kuśi or the Kauśikī formerly joined the Karatoyā river (*Statistical Account of Bengal*, Purnea). There have been changes in the course of this river (*J.A.S.B.*, LXIV, pp. 1–24).

Kādambarī.—It was a forest near Campā. There was a mountain called Kālī near it. Here Pārśvanātha wandered about for four months in front of Kālikuṇḍa which was a large tank (B. C. Law, *Some Jaina Canonical Sūtras*, p. 177).

Kālaśilā.—It was a black rock on a slope of Ṛṣigiri (Isigili) (*Dīgha*, II, 116; *Papañcasūdanī*, II, 63). The rock stood so close to Gijjhakūṭa that it was possible for the Buddha to watch from the latter hill, when the Jaina ascetics were practising there the difficult penance of remaining in a standing posture, rejecting seats (*Majjhima Nikāya*, I, 92). On this rock Godhika and Vakkali committed suicide (*Saṃyutta Nikāya*, I, 120ff.; III, 124). The Kālaśilā was, perhaps, no other than what is called the site of Guṇaśilacaitya in the Jaina *Uvāsagadasāo*.

Kālnā.—It is in the district of Burdwan, and is considered to be a very sacred place of the Hindus. It was the abode of the famous Vaiṣṇava saints, Sūryadāsa, Gaurīdāsa, Jagannāthadāsa and Bhagavāndāsa. It is also famous as Ambikā-Kalnā (*Introducing India*, Pt. I, p. 76).

Kāmarūpa.—It is bounded on the north by Bhutan, on the east by the districts of Darrang and Nowgong, on the south by the Khasi hills and on the west by Goalpara. The greater part of Kāmarūpa consists of a wide plain, through the lower portion of which the Brahmaputra makes its way, flowing a steady course from east to west. South of the river this plain is much broken up by hills (B. C. Allen, *Kāmrup*, *Assam District Gazetteers*, Vol. IV, Ch. I). It is mentioned in the Allahabad Pillar Inscription as one of the frontier states outside the limits of the Gupta empire of which the capital was Prāgjyotiṣapura (*Kālikā Purāṇa*, Ch. 38), identified with modern Gauhati (*J.R.A.S.*, 1900, p. 25). The ancient kingdom of Kāmarūpa generally occupied an area larger than that of the modern province and extended westwards to the Karatoyā river. According to the *Yoginītantra* (1. 11. 60-61; 1. 12. 68; 2. 2. 119) the kingdom of Kāmarūpa comprised the whole of the Brahmaputra (Lauhitya) valleys, together with Rangpur and Cooch Behar (*Imperial Gazetteer of India*, XIV, p. 331). The kingdom included Manipur, Jaintia, Cachar, West Assam, and parts of Mymensingh and Sylhet. The modern districts extended from Goalpara to Gauhati (Lassen, *I.A.*, I, 87; II, 973). The country of Kāmarūpa was about 10,000 li in circuit, and the capital town was about 30 li. The land, though low, was regularly cultivated. Vaidyadeva was the ruler of the kingdom of Kāmarūpa (*E.I.*, II, p. 355). In the Kamauli grant of Vaidyadeva, the village granted is said to have been situated in Kāmarūpamaṇḍala and Prāgjyotiṣabhukti (*E.I.*, II, 348). The king of Kāmarūpa used to pay taxes to Samudragupta (Fleet, *C.I.I.*, III, pp. 6–8). According to the Silimpur inscription dated the 11th century A.D., a Brahmin belonging to Varendrī was given gold coins by Jayapāla, a king of Kāmarūpa (*E.I.*, XIII, 292, 295). Kāmarūpa was conquered by Vijayasena and Lakṣmaṇasena according to the copperplate inscription discovered at Deopārā and Mādhāinagar. The Belāva copperplate of Bhojavarman informs us that king Vajravarman crippled the power of the king of Kāmarūpa (N. G. Majumdar, *Inscriptions of Bengal*, Vol. III, pp. 15ff.). The India Office Plate of Lakṣmaṇasena refers to Kāmarūpa along with Kaliṅga, Kāśī, etc. (*E.I.*, XXVI, Pt. I). Kāmarūpa is also called Prāgjyotiṣa; but in the *Raghuvaṃśa* (IV, 83-84), the people of Kāmarūpa and Prāgjyotiṣa are described as two different nations. The lord of Prāgjyotiṣa performed magic rites with the dust from his feet. (For details, see B. C. Law, *Prāgjyotiṣa*, *J.U.P.H.S.*, XVIII, Pts. I and II, pp. 43ff.)

In 1912 three copperplates were discovered at the village of Nidhanapura [1] in Pañcakhaṇḍa-parganā in the district of Sylhet. These plates form parts of a grant of land to some Brāhmaṇas by Bhāṣkaravarman, king of Kāmarūpa, issued from the camp at Karṇasuvarṇa. Subsequently, two more plates were found. The copperplates inscribed under the orders of Vaidyadeva, king of Kāmarūpa, were found in Kamauli near Benaras city (*E.I.*, II, 347ff.). For further details, vide *I.H.Q.*, Vol. VI, No. 1, pp. 60ff.

According to the Chinese pilgrim Hiuen Tsang, the country of Kāmarūpa, known in Chinese as *Kia-mo-leu-po*, was situated above 900 li (or 150 miles) east from Puṇḍravardhana and was 10,000 li in circuit. It was low and moist, and the crops regular. The climate was genial and the people were honest. They were persevering students, and were of small stature and black-looking. The pilgrim did not see any Aśokan monument there. The people did not believe in Buddhism. But some hold that a very debased form of later Buddhism was prevalent in Kāmarūpa for some centuries (K. L. Barua, *Early History of Kāmarūpa*, p. 304). *Deva* temples were many in number, and the various systems had professed adherents. The king was a lover of learning and his subjects followed his example. Though the king was not a Buddhist, he treated the accomplished monks with due respect.

Kāmarūpa in the north-east seems to have been independent, and it remained outside the sphere of Aśoka's religious propaganda. The enumeration of the frontier kingdoms and republics whose rulers did homage and paid tribute to Samudragupta, enables us to define the boundaries of his dominions with accuracy and to realize the nature of the political divisions of India in the 4th century A.D. Kāmarūpa was one of the tributary kingdoms on the eastern side of India (V. A. Smith, *Aśoka*, 3rd ed., p. 81; *Early History of India*, 1924, p. 302). It retained the Brahmanical supremacy for a long time. Although it paid taxes to the great Gupta kings, yet it retained its autonomy in internal administration. Harṣa, the successor of Rājyavardhana, concluded an alliance with Bhāṣkaravarman, king of Kāmarūpa, whose father Susthitavarman Mṛgāṅka fought against Mahāsenagupta. That Susthitavarman was associated with the river Lohitya (Lauhitya) or Brahmaputra clearly shows that he was a king of

---

[1] The Nidhanpura grant of Bhāṣkaravarman is also known as the Nadhanpur grant. (Vide *A Volume of Eastern and Indian Studies presented to F. W. Thomas*, edited by Katre and Gode, pp. 85ff.).

Kāmarūpa. Kāmarūpa was conquered by Devapāla, the son and successor of Dharmapāla of the Pāla dynasty. According to the *Rāmacarita* Rāmapāla also conquered it. It was also conquered repeatedly by the kings of Gauḍa. The kingdom of Kāmarūpa was included in the dominion of some of the Pāla kings of Bengal. The Candra king Balacandra's son Vimalacandra ruled Kāmarūpa. Early in the 13th century A.D. the Ahom chiefs made themselves masters of this country.

Kāmākhyā.—It is a place of pilgrimage in Assam (*Bṛhat-Dharma Purāṇa*, I, 14; *Kālikā Purāṇa*, Ch. 62). The temple of Śakti, Śiva's wife, at Kāmākhyā near Gauhati was famous in ancient times. It was a great centre of the sensual form of worship inculcated in the Tantras. There was a deity named Mahāmāyā who was ever ready to fulfil human desires. The *Kālikā Purāṇa* and the *Yoginītantra* (Pūrva Khaṇḍa, Ch. 12) preserve the names of several kings whose titles betray their aboriginal descent, and who were followed by Naraka the founder of the ancient and famous city of Prāgjyotiṣapura. According to tradition Naraka ruled from the Karatoyā river to the extreme east of the Brahmaputra Valley. Bhagadatta, son of Naraka, was an ally of Duryodhana (*Mahābhārata*, Udyogaparva, Ch. 4). The temple of Kāmākhyā in Kāmarūpa is a special object of veneration to the devotees of this creed, as it is said to cover the place where the genitals of Śakti fell when her body was cut into pieces by Viṣṇu. But Śaktism is not popular with the inhabitants of Assam. The devotees of Śiva who is the male counterpart of Śakti are mostly found in the Surma Valley. Another small sect remarkable for the peculiarity of its tenets is the *Sahajbhajan*. Each worshipper endeavours to secure salvation by taking a woman as a spiritual guide. The temple of Kāmākhyā on the Nīlācala hill near Gauhati and the temple of Hayagrīva Mādhava at Hajo, about 15 miles by road north-west of Gauhati, are the important temples. For further details, vide Banikanta Kakati's *The Mother Goddess Kāmākhyā*, 1948.

Kāmtāpur.—It is situated at a distance of about 19 miles to the south-west of the town of Cooch Behar. It is now in ruins. Dr. Buchanan Hamilton has left an interesting account of it in his *Eastern India*. According to him, Kāmtāpur was protected on three sides by an earthen rampart, about 20 to 40 ft. in height. The Kāmteśvarī temple which was very important was destroyed by the Pathans.

Kedārpur.—It is a village in the district of Faridpur within the jurisdiction of the police station Pālang. A copperplate inscription of Śrīcandradeva has been discovered here, containing the emblem of Buddhist *dharmacakra* and two couchant deer on two sides (*I.H.Q.*, Vol. II, pp. 313ff.).

Kenduli—(*Kendvavilla*).—It is a village in the Bolpur Thana of the Suri sub-division, situated on the north bank of the river Ajaya, a few miles west of Ilambazar and about 22 miles south of Suri in the district of Birbhum. It is famous as the birthplace of the great Sanskrit poet Jayadeva who flourished in the 12th century A.D. and composed the well-known *Gītagovinda*, a Sanskrit lyrical poem in praise of Rādhikā and Kṛṣṇa. The body of Jayadeva was buried and not burnt after his death, and his tomb is still to be seen here surrounded by beautiful groves and trees. This place is visited by pilgrims, mostly Vaiṣṇavas (*Introducing India*, Pt. I, *R.A.S.B.*, Pub. 1947, p. 72).

Kerakera.—It is the name of a village in Ādipur pargana, situated about 12 miles to the south-south-east of Khiching (*E.I.*, XXV, Pt. IV, October, 1939).

Keśipura.—The *Yoginītantra* (I. 14. 84-85) mentions it.

Khaḍ-daha.—It is a village in the Barrackpore sub-division, situated on the bank of the river Hooghly, 12 miles north of Calcutta. It is a place of pilgrimage for the Vaiṣṇavas. Nityānanda, one of the greatest disciples of Caitanya, lived here for some time. He came here to practise asceticism. For further details, vide B. C. Law, *Geographical Essays*, p. 219.

Khalatika hills.—These are the modern Barabar hills in the district of Gaya. The Barabar hill cave Inscriptions of Aśoka inform us that four cave-dwellings were dedicated to the Ājīvikas by Aśoka in the Khalatika hills (cf. Patañjali's *Mahābhāṣya*, 1, 2, 2; B. C. Law, *India as described in the early texts of Buddhism and Jainism*, p. 27). The Khalatika (Bald-headed) hills became known in the later inscriptions by the name of Gorathagiri (Goradhagiri), and still later by the name of Pravaragiri (see B. C. Law, *Rājagriha in Ancient Literature, M.A.S.I.*, No. 58).

The Barābar hill in the Jahanabad sub-division in the district of Gayā contains the Sātgharā and the Nāgārjunī caves of the time of Aśoka and his grandson Daśaratha. It is about seven miles to the east of Belā station of the Patna-Gaya railway. To the south and near the foot of the hill are the seven rock-cut caves called Sātgharā. Out of these seven caves three are on the Nāgārjunī hills.

A shrine on a large stone was converted in the Buddha's time into a Buddhist retreat known as the Pāsāṇaka-cetiya, which was situated in the religious area of Magadha. Some have identified it with Gorathagiri or some other hill near it.

Khaṇḍajotika.—It is possibly Khāṇḍajulī between Mallasārul and Gohagrām in the Burdwan division, Bengal (*E.I.*, XXIII, V, p. 158).

Kharagpur hills.—A range of hills is situated immediately to the south of Monghyr town. These hills which are an off-shoot from the northern face of the Vindhya hills, measure 30 miles in length (*J.A.S.B.*, Vol. XXI).

Khasia.—See Garo.

Khāḍi.—The Sena copperplates of the 12th century A.D. mention Khāḍiviṣaya and Khāḍi-maṇḍala. Khāḍi is to be identified with Khāḍi-pargana in the Sunderbans (Diamond Harbour sub-division) (*Inscriptions of Bengal*, III, 60, 170).

Khālimpur.—It is near Gaur in the Maldah district (*E.I.*, IV, 243), where the plate of Dharmapāladeva was discovered.

Khānumata.—It was a prosperous Brahmin village in Magadha where a Vedic institution was maintained on a land granted by king Bimbisāra (*Sumaṅgalavilāsinī*, I, 41; *Dīgha*, I, 127). It was a gift to the Brahmin Kūṭadanta by the Magadhan king Bimbisāra. It was the place where the Brahmin Kūṭadanta lived with all the powers over life and property, as if he were the king himself. Annually a great sacrifice was made involving the slaughter of many bulls, calves, goats and rams (*Dīgha*, I, 127).

Khetur.—It is a village in the Rajshahi district visited by Śrīcaitanya, the great Hindu religious reformer of the 16th century A.D., in whose honour a temple was built there. (*Introducing India*, Pt. II, p. 78.)

Kolhuā.—It is situated at a distance of three miles to the north-west of Basārh containing a stone pillar surmounted by a lion, a ruined stūpa, an old tank and some small eminences marking the site of ancient buildings. All these remains clearly correspond with the account of the remains to the north-west of Vaiśālī as given by Hiuen Tsang (*Muzaffarpur*, by O'Malley, *B. D. Gazetteers*, pp. 141-42).

Kolikagāma.—This village was located eight or nine li (1½ miles) south-west of the Nālandā monastery. It is associated with Sāriputta (Watters, *On Yuan Chwang*, II, 171). In this village Moggallāna was born and died (*Dhammapada Commentary*, *P.T.S.*, Vol. I, p. 89).

Kollāga.—This suburb (*sannivesa*) lay beyond Kuṇḍapura in a further north-easterly direction. It appears to have been principally inhabited by the Kṣatriyas of the Nāya or Jñātrī clan to which Mahāvīra himself belonged (Hoernle, *Uvāsagadasāo*, Vol. II, Transl., p. 4, note 8).

Koṭigāma.—It was a village of the Vijjians (*Saṃyutta Nikāya*, V, 431). Buddha in course of the journey from Rājagṛha to Kuśinārā passed through it (*Dīgha Nikāya*, II, 90-91).

Koṭiśilā.—It was a *tīrtha* (sacred place) in Magadha. Many saints practised penances here and attained perfection (Law, *Some Jaina Canonical Sūtras*, p. 178).

Koṭivarṣaviṣaya—(Jain Koḍivarisa or Koḍivarisiyā).—It is recorded as a sub-division of the Puṇḍravardhanabhukti. It is in the epigraphic records of the Pālas and Senas of Bengal that the name frequently occurs. It must have included the whole or a part of Dinajpur. Bāṇagrām, modern Bāngarh, was the chief town of Koṭivarṣa. According to the Jaina *Āvaśyaka Niryukti* (1305) King Cāliya of Koḍivarisa became a Jain ascetic. The ruins of Bāngarh are found on the eastern bank of the river Punarbhavā, one and a half mile to the north of Gaṅgārāmpur, which is 18 miles south of Dinajpur. The region round Gaṅgārāmpur may be identified with Koṭikapura or ancient Devakoṭa, the capital of Koṭivarṣa in Northern Bengal. According to tradition Bāngarh was the site of the fortified town of the demon king Bāṇa whose wife Kālārāṇī is said to have a tank dug called Kāladīghi at Gaṅgārāmpur. According to the copper-plate inscription of Mahīpāla I, discovered at Bāngarh, Mahīpāla regained his lost paternal kingdom. Some of the old relics of Bāngarh are now kept in the Dinajpur palace. Here we find a richly carved stone-pillar made of touch-stone, a Śiva temple and a Buddhist *caitya* of about the 11th century A.D. According to the Dāmodarpur grant of the time of Budhagupta and Jayadatta (*E.I.*, XV, 138ff.), Doṅgā, a village, existed in the sub-division of Himavacchikhara (lit. on the summit of the Himalayas) in the *Koṭivarṣaviṣaya* of the Puṇḍravardhanabhukti (*I.C.*, V, p. 433).

Koṭyāśrama.—This hermitage of Vaśiṣṭha has been identified with Kuting, 32 miles from Bāripādā (*E.I.*, XXV, Pt. IV, October, 1939).

Krauñcaśvabhra.—It is the name of a donated village mentioned in the Khalimpur copperplate grant of Dharmapāladeva (*Gauḍalekhamālā*, I, pp. 9ff.). It was situated in the district of Mahantāprakāśa within the jurisdiction of the Vyāghrataṭi-maṇḍala in the Pauṇḍravardhanabhukti (*E.I.*, IV, pp. 243ff.).

Krinila.—The Nālandā Plate of Samudragupta refers to this *viṣaya* also mentioned in the Monghyr grant of Devapāla, which according to it, is stated to have been situated in the *bhukti* of Śrīnagara or Patna (*E.I.*, XXV, Pt. II, April, 1939).

Kripā (or Kūpā).—This river may be identified with the modern Kopā, a tributary of the Bāblā in Eastern India. (Law, *Rivers of India*, p. 45).

Kukkuṭapādagiri (also called *Gurupādagiri*).—Stein has located it on the Sobhnāth hill, the highest peak in a range of hills further south-west from Kurkihār and about four miles distant from the village of Wazirganj (*I.A.*, March, 1901, p. 88). Some have identified it with Gurpā hill about 100 li east of Bodh-Gayā (*J.A.S.B.*, 1906, p. 77). Cunningham has identified it with the three peaks situated about a mile to the north of Kurkihār and 16 miles north-east of Gayā (*C.A.G.I.*, ed. Majumdar, p. 721). The three peaks are said to have been the scene of some of the miracles of the Buddhist saint Mahākāśyapa. According to Hiuen Tsang, the lofty peaks of the Kukkuṭapāda or the Gurupāda mountain are the endless cliffs and its deep valleys are boundless ravines. Its lower slopes have their gullies covered with tall trees, and rank vegetation clothes the steep heights. A threefold cliff projects in isolated loftiness reaching the sky and blending with the clouds. Mahākāśyapa took up his abode on this mountain (Watters, *On Yuan Chwang*, II, p. 143).

Kukkuṭārāma.—This monastery was at Pāṭaliputra (*Saṃyutta*, V, 15, 17, 171, 173). A king of Magadha named Muṇḍa came here to see the sage Nārada and listen to his doctrine. The sage instructed him and brought him solace as he was overwhelmed with grief at the death of his queen Bhaddā. Thereafter he attended to his duties as usual (*Aṅg.*, III, 53ff.). A monk named Bhadda dwelt at this *ārāma* and he had conversations with Buddha's famous disciple Ānanda (*Saṃ.*, V, 15-16, 171-2). According to Buddhaghosa this *ārāma* was built by Kukkuṭaseṭṭhī (*Majjhima Commentary*, II, 571). Hiuen Tsang says that it existed to the south-east of the old city of Pāṭaliputta and was built by Aśoka when he was converted to Buddhism (Beal, *Records of the Western World*, II, 95). The *Divyāvadāna* often refers to it (pp. 381ff., 430ff.). This *ārāma* was different from that which existed at Kauśāmbī bearing the same name (*Vinaya*, I, 300).

Kulāñca.—It is a town founded by the sage Kācara, which is identical with Kolāñca, Kroḍāñci or Kroḍānja. This place seems to have been a stronghold of the Brāhmaṇas of the Śāṇḍilyagotra. Five ancestors of these Brāhmaṇas came to Vaṅga from Kolāñca at the invitation of king Ādisūra for the performance of a Vedic sacrifice. This place seems to have been situated on the Ganges (*E.I.*, XXIV, Pt. III, July, 1937). Some hold that it is situated in eastern or northern India.

Kuluha hill.—It lies six miles south-west of Hunterganj. It contains some ruined temples. It is a place of pilgrimage of the Hindus (*B. and O. District Gazetteers, Hazaribagh*, 1917, p. 202).

Kumārī.—This river may be identified with the modern Kumārī which waters the Dalma hills in Manbhum (Law, *Rivers of India*, p. 45).

Kumbhīnagara.—Kumbhīnagara may be identified with Kumhira in Rampurhat of the Birbhum district of Bengal (vide, *Śaktipur Copperplate of Lakṣmaṇasena*, *E.I.*, XXI, p. 214).

Kuṇḍapura.—Also called Khattiyakuṇḍaggāma identified with Basukuṇḍ, a suburb of Vaiśālī, was the birthplace of Mahāvīra (*Āvaśyaka Cūrṇi*, p. 243).

Lakṣyā.—It is mentioned in the *Yoginītantra* (1/11, pp. 60-61) as the confluence of Lakṣyā. The Lakṣyā is the prettiest river in the district of Dacca. It is found to have been formed from the three streams that took off from the old Brahmaputra. It flows into the Dhaleśvarī at Madanganj. (Law, *Rivers of India*, p. 34).

Lambeva.—It may be identified with Limbu in the Narasinghapur State of Orissa (*E.I.*, XXVI, Pt. II, p. 78).

Laṭṭhivana (= Skt. Yaṣṭhivana).—It is about two miles north of Tapovana in the district of Gayā. It was a palm-grove (*tālujjāna*) according to the Pali commentator Buddhaghosa (*Samantapāsādikā*, Sinhalese ed., p. 158; P.T.S. ed., V. 972). Here Bimbisāra was converted by the Buddha (*Manorathapūraṇī*, p. 100). This grove which was situated in the outskirts of the city of Rājagṛha (*Rājagahanagarupacāre*) was considered far away as compared with Veṇuvana (*Jāt.*, I, 85; cf. *Vinaya-Mahāvagga*, I, 35). It was the name of the royal park of Bimbisāra where the Buddha arrived from Gayāsīsa and halted with the Jaṭila converts on his way to Rājagṛha (*Vinaya-Mahāvagga*, I, 35). Hiuen Tsang describes it as a dense forest of bamboos which covered a mountain, and points out that above 10 li to the south-west of it were two hot springs (Watters, *On Yuan Chwang*, II, 146).

Lauhitya.—See Brahmaputra. It is mentioned in the *Yoginītantra* (2. 5. 139ff.). It is considered as very sacred (*Kālikā Purāṇa*, Ch. 58, 39).

Lauriya-Nandangarh.—This village well-known for its Aśokan pillar is situated in the Gandak valley some 16 miles to the north-west of Bettiah in the Champaran district, at the meeting point of two of the principal routes leading to Nepal border. It must have enjoyed a position of considerable importance from very early times. For an account of explorations at this site vide, *A.S.I.*, Annual Report, 1906-1907, pp. 119ff.; 1935-36, pp. 55ff. For earlier explorations vide, *A.S.I.R.*, I, pp. 68ff.; XVI, 104ff.; XXII, 47ff.

Lohit.—The great tributary, which meets the Brahmaputra in the district of Sadiyā, is the Lohit or Lauhitya (*Mahābhārata*, Bhīṣmaparva, Ch. 9; Anuśāsanaparva, 7647; cf. *Rāmāyaṇa*, Kiṣkindhyākāṇḍa, XL, 26; *Asiatic Researches*, Vol. XIV, p. 425). It flows from north-east above the Namkiu mountains as the united flow of four streams (Law, *Rivers of India*, p. 30). This river formed the boundary of Prāgjyotiṣa or Gauhati in Assam (*Raghuvaṃśa*, IV, 81).

Lupaturā.—It is probably the same as Lipatuṅgā of the Patna State (Orissa). Some have identified it with Lepta, six miles south-east of Bolangir in the Patna State (*E.I.*, XXIII, Pt. VII).

Lushāi.—The Lushāi Hills stretch southwards from the Manipur State. They are bounded on the east by the Chin Hills and on the west by the Chittagong hills. The Arakan Yoma lies to the south of the Lushāi Hills. (For details, vide B. C. Law, *Mountains of India*, p. 9).

Macalagāma.—It was a well laid village in Magadha where the Sun-god and the Moon-god were worshipped by the people. It was bedecked with roads, resthouses, tanks and big buildings long before the advent of the Buddha (*Jāt.*, I, 199, 206; *Dhammapada Commy.*, I, 265–80; *Sumaṅgalavilāsinī*, III, 710ff.).

Maddakucchi-migadāya (*migadāva*).—This deer park at Maddakucchi was an important site in or about Rājagṛha (*Vinaya*, I, 105; *Samyutta*, I, p. 27). Buddhaghosa takes Maddakucchi to be the actual name of the park where the antelopes were allowed to live freely (*Sāratthappakāsinī*, I, 77). The site was apparently on the plains and it occupied a space near a curve in one of the hills of Rājagṛha.

Magadha.—Pāṇini in his *Aṣṭādhyāyī* (4. 1. 170) and Patañjali in his *Mahābhāṣya* (1. 1. 2, p. 56) refer to it. Pāṇini uses the form Māgadha and Patañjali also uses Sumagadhā (2. 1. 2, p. 48). According to the *Daśakumāracaritam* (ed. H. H. Wilson), the lord of Magadha went to wage war with the monarch of Mālava, with the result that the king of Mālava was defeated and captured alive. But the Magadhan king mercifully reinstated him in his kingdom (pp. 3ff.). The royal ladies of Magadha were kept in security in a spot in the Vindhya forest inaccessible to enemies (p. 6). The *Raghuvaṃśa* (Sarga I, v. 31) points out that king Dilīpa had a lawfully wedded queen named Sudakṣiṇā belonging to the Magadhan royal family.

Magadha is also mentioned in the Bhabru Edict of Aśoka as well as in the *Bhāgavata Purāṇa* (IX. 22, 45; X. 2, 2; X. 52, 14; X. 73, 33; X. 83,

23). In the Tibetan Buddhist Geography Magadha is not within *Prācī* but within *Madhyadeśa*. It comprises the districts of Gayā and Patna. Some place it to the west of Aṅga being separated from the latter kingdom by the river Campā. King Aśoka in his Bhabru Edict after saluting the *Saṃgha* (Buddhist Church) wished them good health and comfortable movement. It seems probable that in the Sarnath Pillar Inscription of Aśoka we have just the first two syllables (Pāṭa) of the name of Pāṭaliputra. But it is definite from the Barhut inscriptions that three persons went there from Pāṭaliputra. The Hāthigumphā inscription shows that when Bṛhaspatimitra was the king of Aṅga-Magadha (2nd century B.C.), king Khāravela of Kaliṅga marched towards Magadha after having stormed Gorathagiri and brought pressure to bear upon Rājagṛha, the ancient capital of Magadha (*Rājagahaṃ upapīḍāpayati—E.I.*, X, App. No. 1345; cf. *Acta Orientalia*, I, 265; Barua, *Old Brāhmī Inscriptions in the Udayagiri and Khaṇḍagiri Caves*, p. 17).[1] The Magadhan empire did not wholly perish on the death of Skandagupta. It was ruled by Puragupta, Narasinhagupta, Kumāragupta II and Buddhagupta. Then the imperial line passed on to a dynasty of eleven Gupta princes. The Dāmodarpur plates, Sarnath Inscriptions, the Eran epigraph of Buddhagupta and the Betul plates of Parivrājaka Mahārāja Saṃkṣobha, dated in the year A.D. 518, testify to the fact that the Gupta empire continued to exert sovereign rights in the latter half of the 5th as well as the 6th and 7th centuries A.D. In the first half of the 7th century the Gupta power, though overshadowed, was ruined by Ādityasena who assumed the titles of *Paramabhaṭṭāraka* and *Mahārājādhirāja*. As proved by the Aphṣad and Deo-Baranārk inscriptions, Ādityasena and his successors were the only North Indian sovereigns who appear actually to have dominated Magadha and Madhyadeśa. About the early part of the 8th century A.D. the throne of Magadha was occupied by Gopāla, a Gauḍa king as the Pāla inscriptions seem to indicate. According to the Rāgholi plates of Śaktivarman, Śaktivarman, king of Kaliṅga, is said to belong to the Magadha family. It is distinctly stated in the plates that the glorious Mahārāja Śaktivarman adorns the Magadha family (*Māgadha-kulālaṅka*) (*E.I.*, XII, 2ff.). The Sirpur Stone Inscription of the time of Mahāśivagupta (*E.I.*, XI, 184ff.) states that Vāsalā, the mother of Mahāśivagupta, was the daughter of the king of Magadha (Magadhādhipatya) named Sūryavarman. The Mahākūṭa Inscription of Mangaleśa (*I.A.*, XIX, 14ff.) states that Kīrtivarman I alias Puru-raṇaparākramāṅka obtained victories over the kings of many cities including Magadha. The inscription of Jayadeva at Katmandu refers to the grand-daughter of the great Ādityasena, king of Magadha (*Magadha-dauhitrī Magadhādhipasya mahataḥ Ādityasenasya*).

The Aihole Inscription of Mahāmaṇḍaleśvara Cāmuṇḍa II (*I.A.*, IX, 96ff.) states that the brave king Cāmuṇḍarāja (*prabala-balayutaṃ vīra-Cāmuṇḍa-bhūpālāṃ*) deserves praise from Magadha, Gurjara, Āndhra, Drāviḍa and Nepāla. The Sirur Inscription of the time of Amoghavarṣa I (*E.I.*, VII, 202ff.) points out that Atiśayadhavala (Amoghavarṣa I) is worshipped by the lords of Vaṅga, Aṅga, Magadha, Mālava and Veṅgi (*Vaṅga-Aṅga-Magadha-Mālava-Veṅgiśair arccito'tiśayadhavalaḥ*). Similarly

---

[1] Difference of opinions exists about the reading and interpretation of the various terms in the following passage: *Aṭhame ca vase mahatā sen* (*ā*) . . . . *Goradhagiriṃ ghāṭāpayitā Rājagahaṃ upapiḍāpayati*. The term Goradhagiri is taken by Jayaswal and R. D. Banerji to mean a rocky fortress on the outskirts of Rājagṛha, but Dr. Barua takes it to be the name of a person. (See *Old Brāhmī Inscriptions in the Caves of Udayagiri and Khaṇḍagiri*, pp. 223–27; cf. *J.B.O.R.S.*, I, 162.)

in the Nilgund Inscription of the time of Amoghavarṣa I, we find mention of this fact in detail. It is stated there that the feet of Atiśayadhavala are rubbed by the diadems of hostile kings. It is further pointed out that his heroism is praised throughout this world and that he is worshipped by the lords of the above-mentioned places. The Govindapur Stone Inscription of the poet Gaṅgādhara (*E.I.*, II, 330ff.) informs us that the illustrious ruler of Magadha (*Śrī-Magadheśvara*) gave him the name of Vyāsa. According to the Ablur inscription (*E.I.*, V, 237ff.) Bijjana (Bijjala), the Kalacuri king, defeated the Magadhas along with the Andhras, Gurjaras, Vaṅgas, Kaliṅgas, Coḷas, Lāṭas, etc. For a full account of Magadha vide B. C. Law, *The Magadhas in Ancient India* (*R.A.S.*, Monograph No. 24).

Mahādeva.—This hill as described by Hiuen Tsang was a small solitary double-peaked one. Here the Buddha overcame the Yakkha Vakula. According to some it was situated on the western frontier of Hiraṇyaparvata. To the west of it were some hot springs (*J.A.S.B.*, Vol. LXI, Pt. I, 1892).

Mahānadī.—The *Yoginītantra* mentions it (2. 5, pp. 139-140). The Mahānadī is the largest river in Orissa, which rises from the hills at the south-east corner of Berar. It flows past Sihoa and passes through Bastar in the Central Provinces. It reaches the southern border of the district of Bilaspur. It is fed by five tributaries. It follows a south-easterly course and flows past the town of Cuttack. For further details vide Law, *Rivers of India*, p. 44.

Mahāsthān.—See *Pauṇḍravardhanabhukti*. A burnt clay figure of a female deity belonging to the Śunga period was found at Mahāsthān-garh[1] in the Bogra district in course of digging an outlet. This helps us to confirm the fact that Mahāsthān represents one of the earliest city-sites of Bengal and was in occupation from the 2nd century B.C. to the 12th century A.D. (*A.S.I.*, Annual Reports, 1930–34, p. 128).

The most important epigraphical discovery is that of a small tablet of buff sandstone at Mahāsthān. It is engraved with six-lines of writing in ancient Brāhmī characters of about the 3rd century B.C., and is the first record of its kind ever found in Bengal. The distinct mention of Puḍanagara (Skt. Puṇḍranagara) in this inscription[2] confirms the identification of Mahāsthān with the city of Puṇḍranagara or Puṇḍravardhana which was first proposed by General Cunningham (*A.S.R.*, XV, 104ff.). For an account of exploration, see *A.S.I.*, Annual Reports 1934-1935, pp. 40ff.; *Excavations at Mahāsthān* by T. N. Ramachandran, *A.R.A.S.I.*, 1936/37 (1940).

Mahāvana.—It was a natural forest outside the town of Vaiśālī lying in one stretch up to the Himalayas. It was so called because it covered a large area (*Sumaṅgalavilāsinī*, I, 309; *Saṃyutta*, I, 29-30).

Mahāvana-vihāra.—This monastery was in the Vriji country according to the *Mahāvaṃsa* (IV. 32). Fa-hien refers to it in his travels.

Maināmāti.—The Maināmāti copperplate of Ranavaṅkamalla Harikāladeva of the Śaka Era 1141 refers to the Maināmāti hills, about five miles to the west of the town of Comilla in the district of Tipperah. The copperplate only mentions the Maināmāti hills instead of the Lalmai (*Haraprasād Memorial Volume*, pp. 282ff.). The name Maināmāti is probably associated with Mayanāmatī, the queen of Mānikchandra, a king of the Candras, who ruled Bengal in the 10th and 11th centuries A.D. This queen and her son Gopicandra played an important part in Bengali folk-songs. Queen

[1] *Introducing India*, Pt. I, p. 79.
[2] *E.I.*, XXI, 83–91.

Mayanāmatī seems to have been a disciple of a great Śaiva Yogī, Gorakṣanātha, while her son was a disciple of a low caste *siddha*. An Officer of the royal groom is mentioned as embracing Sahajayāna Buddhism at Paṭṭikeraka. A village of the Tipperah district, which extends up to the Maināmāṭi hills, even now retains the name of Pāṭikārā or Paitkārā. The existence of the kingdom of Paṭṭikera may be traced back as far as the 8th century A.D. Coins similar to those of the Candra dynasty and terracotta plaques with figures of Arakanese and Burmese men and women have been found at Maināmāṭi. In these coins the name of Paṭikera occurs. It appears that there was an intimate relation between Burma and the kingdom of Paṭṭikera. Ranavaṅkamalla Harikāladeva was a chieftain of this place, while the Devas were then the independent rulers. The Paṭṭikeraka Vihāra of the Pāla period was an important monastery. A mound at Maināmāṭi, known as the ruins of Ānandarājā's palace, seems to be a monastery. Some rulers of the Candra dynasty mentioned in the inscriptions, e.g., Śrīcandra, Govindacandra, Suvarṇacandra, Pūrṇacandra, ruled eastern and southern Bengal between 900 and 1050 A.D. with Rohitāgiri as their capital. The naked stone image of a Jaina *tīrthaṅkara* found at Maināmāṭi shows the influence of Jainism in this region. The discovery of such deities as Ganeśa, Hara-Gaurī, Vāsudeva, shows the influence of Hinduism there. Ānandarājā's palace, Bhojarājā's palace, Caṇḍimurā, Rūpabānmurā, Śālbanrājā's palace are some of the mounds situated here, worthy of notice. In one of these mounds we find temples of Śiva and Caṇḍī. A square monastery like that of Pāhāḍpura existed there. The central temple contains on its walls projecting mouldings, lotus petals, etc. Many carved terra-cotta plaques containing the figures of *Yakṣas*, *Kimpuruṣas*, *Gandharvas*, *Vidyādharas*, *Kinnaras*, *Buddha*, *Padmapāṇi*, warriors, animals, lotus flowers, etc. have been discovered. The potteries found there are mostly in ruins. Some small bronze images of the Buddha have also been found.[1]

Makulaparvata.—Some have identified it with Kaluhā hill which is about 26 miles to the south of Buddha Gayā and about 16 miles to the north of Chātrā in the district of Hazaribagh. The place abounds in Buddhist architectural remains and figures of the Buddha. The Buddha is said to have spent his sixth rainy season on this mountain.

Mallaparvata.—It is the Pareśnāth hill in the district of Hazaribagh, two miles from the Isri railway station. It is a sacred hill for the Jains. It is the Mount Maleus of the Greeks (McCrindle, *Megasthenes and Arrian*, pp. 63, 139). It is also known as the Sametśikhara, Samidagiri and Samādhigiri.

Mallasārul.—It is a village situated about a mile and a half from the north bank of the Damodar river within the jurisdiction of the Galsi police station of the Burdwan district, Bengal, where a copperplate of Vijayasena was discovered (*E.I.*, XXIII, Pt. V, p. 155).

Mandāra hills.—The *Kālikā Purāṇa* mentions this *parvata* (Ch. 13. 23). It is situated in the Baṅkā sub-division of the district of Bhāgalpur, 30 miles to the south of Bhāgalpur, and three miles to the north of Bansi. This hill is about 700 feet high. The oldest buildings are the two temples, now in ruins. The Sītākuṇḍ tank is the largest, 100 feet long by 500 feet wide. According to Fleet it is situated about 35 miles south of Bhāgalpur

[1] For details, vide T. N. Ramachandran, *Recent Archaeological discoveries along the Maināmāṭi and Lalmai Ranges*, published in the *B. C. Law Volume*, Pt. II, pp. 213ff.; *Introducing India*, Pt. I, pp. 82-83; *Harikela and the ruins at Maināmāṭi*—*I.H.Q.*, XX, 1944, pp. 1–8.

(*C.I.I.*, 211; *A.S.R.*, VIII, 130). It is known to Megasthenes and Arrian as Mallus. It is an isolated hill on the top of which stands a Hindu temple. There are also ruins of Buddhist temples and images (*Bhāgalpur* by Byrne, *B. D. Gazetteers*, pp. 162, 163, 169). A detailed description of this hill is given in Ch. II (pp. 31ff.) of *Bhāgalpur* by Byrne.

Mangraon.—It is a village in the Buxar sub-division of the Sahabad district, Bihar, situated about 14 miles south-west of Buxar where an inscription of Viṣṇugupta's time (the year 17) has been discovered. (*E.I.*, XXVI, Pt. VI, April, 1942, pp. 241ff.)

Markaṭahrada.—While the Buddha was at Vaiśālī, he dwelt in the pinnacled hall (*Kūṭāgāraśālā*) on the bank of the lake Markaṭa (*Divyāvadāna*, p. 200). The *Mahāvastu* refers to the Markaṭahrada Caitya where the Buddha also stayed (Law, *A Study of the Mahāvastu*, p. 44).

Masār.—This village situated about six miles west of Arrah has been identified with *Mo-ho-so-lo* visited by Hiuen Tsang in the 7th century A.D. Mahāsāra was its ancient name (*A.S.I. Reports*, Vol. III).

Meghnā.—The lower course of the Surmā river flowing through the district of Dacca is generally known as the Meghnā. This river represents the combined waters of Surmā, the Barāka and the Puini. The Meghnā flows a tortuous course between the districts of Dacca and Tipperah till it joins the Dhaleśvarī, a little below Munshiganj. The united waters of the Padmā and the Meghnā flow together into the Bay of Bengal (Law, *Rivers of India*, p. 25).

Mehār.—This village is situated in the Chandpur sub-division in the district of Tipperah where a copperplate of Dāmodaradeva was discovered. It is also known as Mehāragrāma. The Mehār plate of Dāmodaradeva places the village of Mehār in the sub-division called Vāyisagrāma which was included in the Paralāyi-viṣaya of the Samataṭamaṇḍala lying within the Pauṇḍravardhanabhukti (*E.I.*, XXVII, Pt. IV, pp. 182 and 185).

Mesikā.—It is a donated village mentioned in the Monghyr copperplate grant of Devapāladeva (*Gauḍalekhamālā*, I, pp. 33ff.). It was situated in the district of Krimila within the jurisdiction of the Śrīnagarabhukti, which, according to some, included the districts of south Bihar (*I.H.Q.*, XXVI, II, p. 138).

Mishmi.—This mountain forms part of the northern frontier of Assam, overlooking the eastern bend of the Brahmaputra. This has been much dissected by agents of erosion, giving rise to a tangled mass of ridges capped by peaks of 15,000 ft. in height (B. C. Law, *Mountains of India*, p. 9).

Mithilā.—Mithilā was the capital of Videha (*Mahābhārata*, Vanaparva, 254; cf. *Mahāvastu*, III, p. 172; *Divyāvadāna*, p. 424), which was also called Tīrabhukti (modern Tirhut). According to the *Rāmāyaṇa* (Ādikāṇḍa, XLIX, 9–16; cf. Śāntiparva of the *Mahābhārata*, CCCXXVII, 12233–8), it was the name of the capital as well as of the country itself. It has been identified with the modern Janakapura, a small town within the Nepal border. The districts of Muzaffarpur and Darbhanga meet to the north of it (Law, *Geography of Early Buddhism*, p. 31; Cunningham, *Ancient Geography of India*, S. N. Mazumder ed., p. 718; Cunningham, *A.S.R.*, XVI, 34). Beal quotes Vivian De St. Martin who connects the name of Chen-su-na with Janakapura (Beal, *Buddhist Records of the Western World*, II, p. 78 n.). During the reign of Janaka, king of Videha, the royal sage Viśvāmitra took four days to reach Mithilā from Ayodhyā, resting at Viśālā on the way for one night only (*Rāmāyaṇa*, Vaṅgavāsī ed., 1–3; *Ibid.*, Griffith's Tr., pp. 90-91). Mithilā, according to Rhys Davids, was situated about 35 miles north-west of Vaiśālī (*Buddhist India*, p. 26). It was seven leagues and the kingdom of Videha 300 leagues in extent (*Jātaka*, III,

365; *Ibid.*, IV, p. 316). It was situated at a distance of 60 yojanas from Campā, the capital of Aṅga (*Jātaka*, VI, p. 32). Tīrabhukti (modern Tirhut) was bounded by the river Kauśikī (Kośī) in the east, the Ganges in the south, the Sadānīrā (Gaṇḍak or the Rapti) in the west and the Himalayas in the north (Law, *Geography of Early Buddhism*, 30-31). Tīrabhukti is derived from *Tīra* meaning bank and *bhukti*, limit. Cunningham is right in pointing out that the name seems rather to refer to lands lying along the banks of rivers than to the boundaries of a district and these lands may be identified with the valleys of the Būr Gaṇḍak and the Bāgmatī rivers (Cunningham and Garrick, *Reports of Tours in North and South Bihar in* 1880-81, *A.S.I.*, p. 1-2). Videha was so named after Māthava, the Videgha, who colonized it according to the *Śatapatha Brāhmaṇa* (I. IV. 1). Videha took its name from the early immigrants from Pubbavideha, the eastern sub-continent of Asia, placed to the east of Mount Sineru (*Papañcasūdanī*, Sinhalese ed., I, p. 484; *Dhammapada-Aṭṭhakathā*, Sinhalese ed., II, 482). This very region is called Bhadrāśvavarṣa in the great Epic (*Mahābhārata*, Bhīṣmaparva, 6, 12, 13; 7, 13; 6, 31).

According to the *Bhaviṣya Purāṇa*, Nimi's son Mithi founded the beautiful city of Mithilā. He came to be known as Janaka, because he was the founder of this city (cf. *Bhāgavata Purāṇa*, IX, 13, 13). According to the *Mahāgovinda Suttanta* of the *Dīgha Nikāya* (II, p. 235), Videha was demarcated as a principality with Mithilā built by Govinda as its capital. The *Viṣṇu Purāṇa* (388ff.) gives a fanciful account of the origin of the name of Mithilā. Vaśiṣṭha, having performed the sacrifice of Indra, went to Mithilā to commence the sacrifice of king Nimi. On reaching there he found Gautama engaged by the king to perform the sacrificial rites. Seeing the king asleep he cursed him thus, 'King Nimi will be bodiless.' The king on awakening cursed Vaśiṣṭha saying that he would also perish as he had cursed a sleeping king. The sages churned the dead body of Nimi and as a result of the churning a child was born afterwards known as Mithi (cf. *Bhāgavata Purāṇa*, IX, 24, 64). Mithilā was named after Mithi and the kings were called the Maithilas (*Vāyu Purāṇa*, 89, 6; *Brahmāṇḍa Purāṇa*, III, 64, 6, 24; *Vāyu*, 89, 23; *Viṣṇu*, IV, 5, 14).

Mithilā had at each of its four gates a market-town (*Jātaka*, VI, p. 330). It had plenty of elephants, horses, chariots, oxen, sheep and all kinds of wealth of this nature together with gold, silver, gems, pearls and other precious things (Beal, *Romantic Legend of Śākya Buddha*, p. 30). This city was splendid, spacious, and well-designed by architects with walls, gates and battlements, traversed by streets on every side and adorned with beautiful tanks and gardens. It was a gay city. The Brahmins inhabiting the city dressed themselves in Kāśī cloths, perfumed with sandal and decorated with gems. Its palaces and all their queens were decorated with stately robes and diadems (*Jātaka*, VI, 46ff.; cf. *Mahābhārata*, III, 206, 6–9). It was a fertile city on the northern bank of the Ganges (*Rāmāyaṇa*, Griffith's Tr., XXXIII, p. 51). It was a peaceful city surrounded by long walls (*Ibid.*, Canto LXVI, p. 89). According to the *Rāmāyaṇa*, Mithilā was a lovely and fair city; nearby there was a wood which was old and deserted (*Ibid.*, Canto XLVIII, p. 68). The city was well-guarded and had well-laid roads. Its inhabitants were healthy who used to take part in frequent festivities (*Mahābhārata*, Vanaparva, 206, 6–9). It was one of the nineteen cities ruled severally in succession by the various dynasties of princes of the Solar race (*Vamsatthapakāsinī*, I, p. 130). There was a shrine at Mithilā where the Mahāgiri teachers lived (Law, *Pañcālas and their Capital Ahichchhatra*, *M.A.S.I.*, No. 67, p. 11).

Polygamy appears to have been in vogue among the Videhan kings (*Jātaka*, IV, 316ff.). Videha was a centre of trade in the Buddha's time. The great prosperity of the Videhans was due to trade with other countries, e.g., Benaras. People came from Śrāvastī to Videha to sell their wares. A disciple of the Buddha took cart-loads of articles and went to Videha for trade (*Paramatthadīpanī on the Theragāthā*, Sinhalese ed., III, 277-78).

Among the kings of Mithilā, the most important was Janaka who performed his sacrifice at Mithilā (*Mahābhārata*, Vanaparva, Chs. 132, 134, etc.). Janaka's imperial sway was obeyed by the people of Mithilā. He was an ally of Daśaratha, king of Ayodhyā. He was highly cultured and firm in his determination (*Rāmāyaṇa*, Griffith's Tr., Canto XII, pp. 23, 95). There is a saying attributed to Janaka. Seeing his city burning in a fire, he sang thus: 'In this nothing of mine is burning' (*Mahābhārata*, XII, 17, 18-19; 219, 50; cf. *Uttarādhyayana sūtra*, *Jaina sūtras*, II, 37). Some suitors came to win Sītā, the daughter of Janaka (*Rāmāyaṇa*, XXXIII, p. 89). Paraśurāma to take revenge for breaking Śiva's bow, arrived at Mithilā, insulted Rāma and demanded a conflict in which he was defeated (Keith, *Sanskrit Drama*, p. 245). Nimi was the Ādipuruṣa of the Royal family of Mithilā (*Rāmāyaṇa*, I, 71. 3). King Aṅgati of Mithilā had three ministers to help him in his administration. According to the *Sūryaprajñapti*, Jiyasattu was a king of Mithilā. He was no other than king Prasenajita of Kośala (cf. *Bhagavatī sūtra*, p. 244; Hoernle, *Uvāsagadasāo*, Tr., p. 6). According to the Jaina *Nirayāvaliya sutta* Videha claimed Ceṭaka as its king (*Jaina sūtras*, I, p. xiii). He was an influential leader of the Licchavi confederacy. His daughter Cellanā was married to Śreṇika Bimbisāra of Magadha and became the mother of Ajātaśatru. King Puṣpadeva was the ruler of Mithilā who had two pious sons named Candra and Sūrya (*Bodhisattvāvadānakalpalatā*, Pallava 83, p. 9). The munificent king Vijitāvī of Mithilā was banished from his kingdom (*Mahāvastu*, III, p. 41). Karṇa conquered Mithilā during his *digvijaya* (*Mahābhārata*, Vanaparva, 254). King Sādhina of Mithilā lived in happiness for many years. He ruled this city righteously (*Jātaka*, Vol. IV, 355ff.). Mahājanaka was the reigning king of Mithilā. After his death he was succeeded by his elder son and his younger son was made the viceroy. The law of primogeniture seems to have been in vogue in the city of Mithilā (*Jātaka*, Vol. VI, 30ff.). After defeating the Kaivarta usurper, Rāmapāla of the Pāla dynasty conquered Mithilā. After the Senas of Bengal had taken possession of Varendra and Magadha, a dynasty seems to have sprung up in Tirhut under the leadership of Nānadeva (Cunningham and Garrick, *Report of Tours in North and South Bihar in* 1880-81, *A.S.I.*, pp. 1-2).

Mithilā was hallowed by the dust of the feet of Vardhamāna Mahāvīra, the founder of Jainism, and Gautama Buddha, the founder of Buddhism. King Makhādeva of Mithilā seeing a grey hair plucked from his head, realized the impermanence of worldly things. He afterwards became a recluse and developed very high spiritual insight (*Jātaka*, I, 137-38). Sādhina, a righteous king of Mithilā, kept the five precepts and observed the fast-day vows (*Jātaka*, Vol. IV, 355ff.).

In the history of the Indian hermits the kingdom of Videha played an important part (*Majjhima*, II, 74ff.). The Buddha stayed at Mithilā and preached there the Makhādeva and Brahmāyusuttas (*Majjhima*, II, 74 133). A female elder named Vāsiṭṭhī first met the Buddha at Mithilā and entered the order after listening to his religious instructions (*Theratherīgāthā*, P.T.S., 136-37). The Buddha Koṇāgamana also preached at Mithilā and the Buddha Padumuttara preached his sermons to his cousins in the park of Mithilā (*Buddhavaṃsa Commentary*, Sinhalese ed., p. 159).

The *Bhāgavata Purāṇa* (IX, 13, 27) points out that the Maithilas were generally skilled in the knowledge of *ātman*. Brahminism was prevalent in Videha in the Buddha's time (*Majjhima*, II, 74ff., 133ff.). The Buddhist *Nikāyas* are silent as to the Buddha's missionary work in Videha and Mithilā. Only in the *Majjhima Nikāya* we find that the Master stayed at the mango-grove of Makhādeva at Mithilā and converted a distinguished Brahmin teacher named Brahmāyu.

The kings of Mithilā were men of high culture. Janaka was the great seer of the Brahmanic period. He was not only a great king and a great sacrificer, but also a great patron of culture and philosophy (*Āśvalāyana Śrautasūtra*, X, 3. 14). His court was adorned with learned Brahmins from Kośala and Kuru-Pañcāla countries.

In the Buddhist age king Sumitra of Mithilā devoted himself to the practice and study of the true Law (Beal, *Romantic Legend of Śākya Buddha*, p. 30). King Vedeha of Mithilā had four sages to instruct him in Law (*Jātaka*, VI, 333). His son was educated at Taxila (*J.A.S.B.*, XII, 1916). A young man of Mithilā named Piṅguttara came to Taxila and studied under a famous teacher. He soon completed his education (*Jātaka*, VI, 347ff.). A Brahmin of Mithilā named Brahmāyu was well versed in history, grammar and casuistry and was endowed with all the marks of a great man (*Majjhima*, II, pp. 133-34).

Mithilā was one of the five Indies. The civilization of Bengal—the new learning, especially that of logic which made the schools of Nadia famous throughout India, came from Mithilā, when Magadha had ceased to give light to eastern India (V. A. Smith, *Early History of India*, 4th ed., p. 353, f.n. 2).

After the Muslim conquest of India the new school of Indian logic was founded at Mithilā by Gaṅgeśa and it was from Mithilā that this school found its place at Navadvīpa in Bengal. Vidyāpati, the celebrated Vaiṣṇava poet and singer, flourished as the precursor of the Vaiṣṇava poets and preachers in Bengal, Assam and Orissa. For further details, vide Law, *Indological Studies*, Pt. III; Law, *Tribes in Ancient India*, Ch. XLVII.

Mora.—The river Mora is the modern Mor (also known as Mayūrākṣī). It is mentioned in the Śaktipur copperplate of Lakṣmaṇasena (*E.I.*, XXI, p. 124). Some have identified it with Morakhi. This river used to flow in the territory of Uttararāḍha. It enters the Birbhum district from the Santal Parganas on the west and follows a course towards the east. The Mayūrākṣī river project is the first of its kind in West Bengal.

Moranivāpa.—It was on the bank of Sumāgadhā visited by the Buddha. It was at Rājagṛha (*Dīgha*, III, p. 39; *Aṅguttara*, I, p. 291).

Mudgagiri.—The Monghyr copperplate inscription of Devapāladeva, son of Dharmapāla, mentions it, which has been identified by Sir Charles Wilkinson with the modern Monghyr (*Gauḍalekhamālā*, I, pp. 33ff.). It indicates that Monghyr (Modāgiri or Mudgagiri) was included in the kingdom of Devapāla. Mudgagiri or Modāgiri is generally identified with the hills of Monghyr in Bihar. Monghyr was also known as Mudgalapurī, Mudgalāśrama, etc. The Mudgalas or the people of Monghyr are referred to in the *Mahābhārata* (Droṇaparva, XI, 397). It is interesting to learn that after defeating Karṇa, king of Aṅga, Bhīmasena fought a battle at Modāgiri and killed its chief. The place is known to have been the site of the royal camp of the Pāla kings in the 10th century A.D. For further details, vide *A.S.I.*, *Reports*, Vol. XV; *B. and O. District Gazetteers, Monghyr*, by O'Malley, pp. 232–248.

Mukshudābād or Mukshusābād (Murshidabad).—It is situated at a distance of 122 miles from Calcutta on the bank of the river Bhāgīrathī. It was the capital of the last independent ruler of Bengal, well built by Nawab Murshidkuli Khan, who was then the Subedar (Viceroy) of Bengal. This city contained many magnificent buildings and palaces. It was extensive, populous and prosperous. The Imambara, Motijhil, Hazarduari, Tomb of Nawab Sharfaraj Khan, who became the Nawab of Murshidabad for one year after the death of Suja Khan, Tripolia Gate, Topkhana, Nizamat-Adalat, and Sadar Diwani Adalat are noteworthy. The tomb of Nawab Siraj-ud-daula stands on the other side of the Ganges flowing through the town of Berhampur (*Introducing India*, Pt. I, pp. 76-77).

Nagarabhukti—The Nālandā plate of Dharmapāladeva refers to it which has been identified with modern Patna, which as a division, included the districts of Gaya, Patna and Sahabad (*E.I.*, XXIII, Pt. VII, p. 291). We learn from the Nālandā Inscription of Devapāla that Nagarabhukti included the *viṣayas* of Rājagṛha and Gayā.

Nandapura.—The Nandapura copperplate inscription (dated the Gupta year 169) of Budhagupta refers to Nandapura, which is a village in the district of Monghyr. It lies on the southern bank of the Ganges at a distance of about two miles to the north-east of Surajgarhā in the district of Monghyr (*E.I.*, XXIII, Pt. II, April, 1935, p. 53).

Navadvīpa.—It is a sacred place of the Vaiṣṇavas. It is so called because it is a combination of nine islands. It stands to the west of the present railway station of Navadvīpaghāṭ, which is eight miles from the town of Krishnagar in the district of Nadia.

Śrīcaitanya, the great founder of new Vaiṣṇavism in Bengal, left this place which was his birthplace at the age of 24 and lived the life of a hermit. The ruins of the palace built by Ballālasena are still found on the eastern coast of the Ganges, half a mile to the north of the present Māyāpura. A court of justice was established here by Aśokasena, grandson of Lakṣmaṇasena and great-grandson of Ballālasena. At one time, it was a great centre of Sanskrit learning (*Introducing India*, Pt. I, 73-74).

Navagrāma.—Navagrāma in Dakṣiṇa-Rāḍha has been identified with the village of the same name in the Bhurshut Pargana of the Hooghly district in Bengal. The *Halāyudha-stotra* in the Amareśvara temple refers to it (*Indian Culture*, I, 702; II, 360; *E.I.*, XXV, Pt. IV, October, 1939, p. 184).

Nāgavana.—It was in the countries of the Vrijians (*Aṅg.*, IV, 213).

Nāgā hills.—The Nāgā hills form part of the eastern frontiers of Assam. The district of the Nāgā hills is bounded on the north by Śibsāgar; on the west by Śibsāgar, Nowgong, and the North Cachar hills; on the south by Manipur, and on the east by mountain ranges inhabited by independent Nāgā tribes. The district consists of a narrow strip of hilly country and has a maximum length of 138 miles and an average breadth of about 25 miles. The hills are covered with dense evergreen forests. North of Kohima the main range gradually declines in height. The Nāgā hills are generally composed of pretertiary rocks overlain by tertiary strata. The most important coal-fields in the Nāgā hills lie outside the borders of the district.

During winter the climate of the high hills is cold and bracing. The days are generally bright and sunny but frost at night is by no means uncommon. The low ranges of hills adjoining the plains are unhealthy, and the Nāgās who settle there suffer much from fever and generally deteriorate in physique.

The great mass of the Nāgās are still faithful to the religion of their forefathers. They believe in the existence of a supreme creator. Sickness and other misfortunes which befall them they ascribe to the malignant action of the evil spirits. They try to appease them with sacrifices. Most of them believe that there is something in a man which survives the death of the body, but they cannot say what it is and where it goes (B. C. Allen, *Nāgā Hills and Manipur, Assam District Gazetteers*, Vol. IX, 1905, pp. 1-39).

Nāgārjuni hill.—The Nāgārjuni hill cave inscription of Anantavarman mentions the Nāgārjuni hill which is a part of the Vindhya range. It is situated about a mile away on the northern side of the village of Japhra which is about 15 miles to the north by east of Gayā (*C.I.I.*, Vol. III; vide also *Khalatika hills*).

Nālakagāma.—It was a village in Magadha where Sāriputta died (*Saṃyutta*, V, 161). Some have located it in the eastern part of Magadha (*Vimānavatthu Commentary*, P.T.S., p. 163). This village may be identified with Nalagāmaka which was not far from Rājagṛha (*Saṃyutta*, V, 161). The name of the village, where the Elder Sāriputta was born, is mentioned in the *Jātaka* (I, 391) as Nāla. It is stated in this *Jātaka* that he died at Varaka.

Nālandā.—Nālandā is a suburb of Rājagṛha in Magadha. The name Nālandā is derived from the name of a dragon called Nālandā which used to live in a tank to the south of the Nālandā monastery in a mango wood. Ju-lai as a *P'usa* had once been a king with his capital at Nālandā. As the king had been honoured by the epithet 'Nālandā' or 'Insatiable in giving' on account of his kindness and liberality, this epithet was given as its name to the monastery. The grounds of the establishment were originally a Mango Park bought by 500 merchants for ten koṭis of gold coins and presented by them to the Buddha. Soon after the Buddha's death, Śakrāditya, a former king of this country, esteeming the one Vehicle and reverencing the Three Precious Ones, built the monastery (Watters, *On Yuan Chwang*, II, p. 164). Yuan Chwang does not accept the explanation of the word, 'Nālandā' which derived its name from that of the dragon of the tank in the Mango Park. He prefers the Jātaka story which refers the name to the epithet 'Insatiable in giving' (*na-alaṃ-dā*) given to the Buddha in a former existence as the king of this country (Watters, *On Yuan Chwang*, II, 166).

The distance of Rājagṛha (modern Rājgīr) to Nālandā is one *yojana* (*Sumaṅgalavilāsinī*, I, 35). But according to the *Mahāvastu*, it is situated at a distance of half a *yojana* from Rājagṛha (Vol. III, 56) and it is described therein as a rich village. It is identified with modern Baragaon, seven miles to the north-west of Rājgīr in the district of Patna (Cunningham, *Ancient Geography*, S. N. Majumdar's ed., p. 537). There was a road from Rājagṛha to Nālandā and the Buddha took this road in course of his journey. Gautama was seen seated on this road (*Saṃyutta Nikāya*, II, p. 220).

Nālandā was influential, prosperous, full of folk, crowded with people devoted to the Exalted Buddha. It contained many hundreds of buildings. A rich and prosperous householder of Nālandā had a beautiful bathing hall containing many hundreds of pillars. There was a park called Hastiyāma (*Jaina Sūtras*, II, 419ff.). The village of Baragaon or Nālandā surrounded by ancient tanks and ruined mounds possessed very fine specimens of sculpture. The remains there consist of numerous masses of brick ruins, among which the most conspicuous is the row of lofty conical mounds running north to south. These high mounds are the remains of gigantic temples attached to the famous University of Nālandā. There are many monasteries and several inscribed domes scattered over the ruins of Baragaon. There are many objects worthy of notice at Baragaon, as for example, the colossal figure of the ascetic Buddha, a life-size ascetic Buddha and a number of smaller figures in a Hindu temple; two low mounds to the north of the village of Baragaon, one having a four-armed image of Viṣṇu on Garuḍa and the other having two figures of Buddha seated on chairs; a Jain temple having the same style of architecture as the Great Temple at Buddha Gayā. There are several Jain figures. There are tanks which surround the ruins on all sides (vide Cunningham, *Archaeological Survey of India Reports*, 1862–1865, Vol. I, pp. 28ff.; *Annual Report, Archaeological Survey of India*, 1915-16, Pt. I, pp. 12-13). Besides there are many statuettes and seals discovered at the site of Nālandā. The ruins of many monasteries have been discovered and the official seal of the Nālandā establishment is an important discovery made by the Archaeological Department (*Annual Report of the Archaeological Survey of India*, Pt. I, 1916-17, p. 15). All available evidences point to the fact that within a few years of Buddha's enlightenment Buddhist headquarters were established in many important places among which the name of Nālandā occurs (vide B. C. Law, *Life and Work of Buddhaghosa*, p. 49). T. W. Rhys Davids points out that Nālandā was one of the stopping places for those who took up the trade route between Sāvatthī and Rājagṛha (*Buddhist India*, p. 103). In the 5th century A. D. Narasiṃha Gupta of the Gupta Dynasty built a brick temple more than 300 ft. high at Nālandā in Magadha, which was remarkable for the delicacy of its decoration and the lavishness of its furniture (V. A. Smith, *Early History of India*, 4th ed., p. 329).

Buddha spent much of his time at Nālandā in the mango grove of Pāvārika. It was at this place that Sāriputta came to see him and there was a discussion held between them on the subject of the lineage of the faith (*D.N.*, II, 81–83). The Buddha held a comprehensive talk with the monks about right conduct, earnest interpretation and intelligent discourse (*D.N.*, II, 83-84). While the Master was here, a rich burgess presented him with a *vihāra* and a park. Sāriputta came to him and said, 'There is nobody whether a monk or a Brahmin who is greater than the Exalted One as regards the higher wisdom and this is the faith which I cherish in my mind.' In reply the Buddha delivered a discourse on the faith that satisfied him (cf. *D.N.*, III, 99). Here the Master was met by a Jaina named Dīghatapassī. He asked the Jain as to the number of acts (*karmas*) mentioned by Nigaṇṭha Nāthaputta in order to destroy sinful deeds (*Majjhima*, Vol. I, 371ff.). Upāli, a householder, came to see the Buddha at Nālandā and asked him about the cause of his passing away from this life (*Saṃyutta*, IV, 110). A village headman named Asibandhakaputta went to the Buddha who told him that one should sow seeds according to the fertility of the soil (*Saṃyutta*, IV, pp. 311ff.). While the Buddha was staying at Nālandā, he spoke about the three wonders of the gods to Kevaḍḍha, a young householder (*Dīgha*, I,—*Kevaḍḍha Sutta*). While the Buddha was staying in a mango grove at Nālandā, he held a discussion with the Jain Dīghatapassī, about three kinds of penalty, etc. The Buddha declared the mental action as the most sinful (Law, *Historical Gleanings*, pp. 91-92). Here at Nālandā Mahāvīra met Makkhali Gosāla. The consequence of this meeting seems to be disastrous. For six years Mahāvīra and Makkhali Gosāla lived together practising austere asceticism, but afterwards Gosāla separated himself from Mahāvīra and set up a religious system of his own (*Uvāsagadasāo*, pp. 109ff.; cf. *Cambridge History of India*, Vol. I, pp. 158-59). Mahāvīra spent fourteen rainy seasons in the suburb of Nālandā and he spent the greater part of his missionary life in this place which contains a beautiful Jain temple of Mahāvīra (N. L. Dey, *Geographical Dictionary*, 137).

The stone inscription of Bālāditya was found on the door of a temple belonging to Nālandā (*Gauḍalekhamālā*, I, p. 102). This temple was built by Bālāditya for the Buddha at Nālandā (*E.I.*, XX, 37ff.). The terra-cotta seal of Viṣṇugupta was excavated from the monastery site No. 1 at Nālandā (*E.I.*, XXVI, Pt. V, January, 1942). Two Maukhari seals were discovered at Nālandā at the monastery site No. 1 (*E.I.*, XXIV, Pt. V, April, 1938). The Shahpur Stone Image Inscription of Ādityasena refers to it in the neighbourhood of Shahpur, being identified by Cunningham with the modern Baragaon, seven miles north of Rajgir. A stone image inscription, known as the Nālandā Vāgīśvarī Stone Image Inscription, has been discovered in the ruins of Nālandā. This inscription records the erection of a statue of Vāgīśvarī at Nālandā, in the first year of the reign of Gopāladeva (*J.A.S.B.*, 1908, VI, new series, pp. 105-6). According to the Ghosrawan inscription of the time of Devapāladeva (*I.A.*, XVII, 307ff.), Vīradeva, son of Indragupta of Nagarahāra, was entrusted with the administration of Nālandā (*Nālandāparipālanāya niyataḥ Saṅghashite yaḥ sthitaḥ*). Among the seals connected with the Buddhist Saṅghas, the majority belongs to the Mahāvihāra at Nālandā (*E.I.*, XXI, 72ff.; *Ibid.*, 307ff.). Nālandā had scholars well-known for their knowledge of the sacred texts and arts (*E.I.*, XX, 43).

After Buddha's passing away, five kings named Śakrāditya, Buddhagupta, Tathāgatagupta, Bālāditya and Vajra built five monasteries at Nālandā (Watters, *On Yuan Chwang*, II, pp. 164-5). The University of Nālandā received royal recognition in the year 450 A.D. (S. C. Vidyābhūṣaṇa, *History of Indian Logic*, p. 515). According to the Tibetan account the quarter in which the University with its grand library was located was called Dharmagañja or Piety Mart. It consisted of three grand buildings called *Ratnasāgara*, *Ratnodadhi*, and *Ratnarañjaka* respectively. In the *Ratnodadhi* which was a nine-storeyed building, the sacred scripts called *Prajñāpāramitā* and the Tantric work *Samājaguhya* were kept (*Ibid.*, 516). Dharmapāla, a native of Kāñcīpura, modern Conjeeveram in Madras, studied in this University and acquired great distinction. In course of time he became the head of this University (*Ibid.*, p. 302; cf. Beal, *Buddhist Records of the Western World*, II, p. 110). Śilabhadra, a Brahmin, who came from the family of the king of Samataṭa (lower Bengal), was a pupil of Dharmapāla. He, too, became the head of this University (Beal, *Buddhist Records of the Western World*, II, p. 110). I-tsing who started for India in 671 A.D. arrived at Tāmralipti at the mouth of the Hooghly river in 672 A.D. He studied at Nālandā, the centre of Buddhist learning, at the east end of the Rājagaha Valley (I-tsing, *A Record of the Buddhist Religion*, Intro., p. XVII). He said that venerable and learned priests of the Nālandā University used to ride in sedan chairs and never on horseback (*Ibid.*, p. 30). According to him the number of priests exceeds 3,000 in the Nālandā monastery. There are eight halls and three hundred apartments in this monastery. The worship can only take place separately (*Ibid.*, p. 154). I-tsing spent a number of years in studying Buddhist literature at this University. The Chinese traveller Hiuen Tsang also was a student of this University for several years. According to him there were thousands of similar institutions in India but none comparable to Nālandā in grandeur. There were 10,000 students who studied various subjects including literature both Buddhist and Brahmanical and discourses were given from 100 pulpits every day. There were lecture halls and all necessary materials for the vast concourse of the teachers and the taught were supplied. The revenues of about 100 villages were remitted for this purpose and two hundred of these villages supplied in turn the daily needs of the inmates. Hence the students here were so abundantly supplied that they did not require to ask for the four requisites, viz., food, clothes, bedding and medicine. From morning till night the students and the teachers engaged themselves in discussions. Learned men from different cities used to come there in large numbers to settle their doubts, and the students of Nālandā were regarded as the best students wherever they went. Nālandā was meant for advanced students and the students had to pass a severe preliminary test. The University of Nālandā was surely the embodiment of the highest ideal of education. For further details, see B. C. Law, *The Magadhas in Ancient India*, *R.A.S.*, Monograph No. 24, pp. 41–43; Hirānanda Śāstrī, *Nālandā and its Epigraphic material* (*M.A.S.I.*, No. 66); Nilakanta Śāstrī, *Nālandā*, published in the *Journal of the Madras University*, Vol. XIII, No. 2; A. Ghosh, *A Guide to Nālandā*, Delhi, 2nd ed., 1946; *Nālandā in Ancient Lit.*, 5th Indian Oriental Conference, 1930; R. K. Mookerjee, *The University of Nālandā*, *J.B.O.R.S.*, XXX, Pt. II, 1944; *A.S.I.*, *Reports*, Eastern Circle, 1901-2, 1915-16, 1919-1920, 1920-21; *J.B.O.R.S.*, March, 1923; *B. and O. District Gazetteers*, *Patna*, by O'Malley, pp. 217–223. For an account of excavations at Nālandā vide *A.S.I.*, *Annual Reports*, 1930–34, pp. 130–140; 1936-37 (1940).

Nānyamaṇḍala.—It occurs in the Rāmpāl copperplate of Śrīcandra and it belonged to Pauṇḍravardhanabhukti (N. G. Majumdar, *Inscriptions of Bengal*, III, p. 2).

Nehakāṣṭhi.—The Rāmpāl copperplate of Śrīcandra mentions it as a village situated in Nānyamaṇḍala of the Pauṇḍravardhanabhukti (N. G. Majumdar, *Inscriptions of Bengal*, III, p. 2).

Nerañjarā (Nairañjanā, Chinese *Ni-lien-Ch'an*).—It is the river Phalgu. Its two branches are the Nīlājanā and the Mohanā, and their united stream is called the Phalgu. This river has its source near Simeria in the district of Hazaribagh. At a short distance to the west of this river lies Buddha-Gayā (Bodhgayā). Dr. Barua relying on the evidence of the Pali canonical texts holds that the river Nairañjanā should not be confounded with the river Phalgu or Gayā. According to him both are distinct (*Gayā and Buddha Gayā*, p. 101).

The river Nerañjarā which was closely connected with Uruvelā, had clear water, pure, blue and cold with bathing places having gradual descents of steps (*Papañcasūdanī*, P.T.S., II, 173; cf. *Lalitavistara, Biblio. Indica Series*, p. 311; *Mahāvastu*, II, 123, 124). The Suppatitthita was a bathing place on its bank where Bodhisattas took their bath on the day of enlightenment (*Jāt.*, I, 70). There was a big *śāla* grove on its bank (*Mahābodhivaṃsa*, p. 28). Here antelopes were found (Jāt., IV, 392, 397). This river was occasionally graced by the presence of the Nāga maidens who found delight in sporting in it (*Lalitavistara*, p. 386; *Mahāvastu*, II, 264). The Jaṭila brothers also practised diving in it in winter at night (*Vinaya*, I, 31).

This river was visited by Siddhārtha when he was a Bodhisatta. The golden plate on which the rice-gruel was offered by Sujātā was kept by the Bodhisatta on its bank. He then bathed and partook of the rice-gruel. The plate was then thrown into this river by him saying, 'Let it go against current, if I be the Buddha today.' (*Jāt.*, I, 70; *Ibid.*, I, 15-16; *Thūpa V.*, P.T.S., p. 5; *Buddha V.*, Ch. II, v. 64; *Ibid.*, Ch. XX, v. 16; *Mahābodhi V.*, p. 8; *Jinacarita*, V. 207; *Lalitavistara*, Ch. 18, p. 267; *Dhammapada Commy.* I, 86; *Papañcasūdanī*, II, 183).

There was a great thicket close to this river where the Bodhisatta once spent the daytime (*Dh. Commy.*, I, 86; cf. *Mahābodhi V.*, p. 29). The Bodhisatta was met by five monks who became his disciples, while he was staying on its bank (*Majjhima*, I, 170; *Ibid.*, II, 94; *Saṃ.*, III, 66; *Vinaya Texts*, S.B.E., I, p. 90). Māra was bold enough to tempt him on its bank, but all his attempts were baffled (*Saṃyutta*, I, 103ff.; *Ibid.*, I, 122ff.; *Suttanipāta*, P.T.S., p. 74, V. 425; *Niddesa*, I, p. 455; *Jinacarita*, vs. 239–245; *Lalitavistara*, Ch. 21; *Mahāvastu*, II, 315; *Divyāvadāna*, p. 202; Rockhill, *The Life of the Buddha*, p. 31).

No less important were the activities of the Buddha on the bank of this river. Here at the foot of the Bo-tree the Buddha spent some time after attaining enlightenment (*Vinaya*, I, i; cf. *Buddhacarita*, Bk. XII, vv. 87-88). The famous Jaṭila brothers were converted here by the Master to his faith (*Vinaya*, I, 25ff.). On its bank the Buddha lived at Uruvelā at the foot of the Ajapāla banyan tree. Here he was met by Brahmā who discussed with him many topics. The Master got confirmation from him as to his thought that he should live honouring the *Dhamma* (doctrine) and preaching it (*Aṅguttara*, II, 20-21; *Saṃyutta*, I, 136ff.). The Master was told by Brahmā that he had carefully thought of the five sense-faculties (*Saṃyutta*, V, 232ff.). He had also the occasion to make it clear to some Brahmins that he had respect for the old and aged Brahmins (*Aṅguttara* II, 22-23). He fully realized the fourfold mindfulness leading to the attainment of *Nirvāṇa* (*Saṃyutta*, V, 167ff.; *Ibid.*, 185ff.). On the day of his enlightenment the Buddha gave the pot which he used to the serpent Mahākāla on the bank of this river (*Mahābodhivaṃsa*, p. 157). Here the Master after his enlightenment systematically set forth the doctrine of dependent origination (*Udāna*, pp. 1–3). He gave a discourse to the serpent king Mucalinda on its bank at the foot of the Mucalinda tree (*Ibid.*, p. 10) and spoke about existences which are impermanent and full of suffering (*Ibid.*, pp. 32-33).

Nigrodhārāma.—This monastery was at Rājagṛha (*Dīgha*, II, 116).

Ollāṅga.—This village may be identified with Delāng situated in the Ānandapur sub-division of the Keonjhar State (*E.I.*, XXV, Pt. XXV, Pt. IV, October, 1939).

Palāśī.—It is in the Nadia district, 93 miles from Calcutta. The name of this place is derived from the *Palāśa* trees (*Butea Frondosa*) which were plenty there. The battlefield, where the British under Lord Clive defeated the army of Siraj-ud-daula, the last independent ruler of Bengal, on the 23rd June, 1757, is situated about two miles to the west of the railway station. The historic battle in the mango-grove has been ably described in verses in Nabincandra's *Palāśir Yuddha.* About four or five miles from Palāśī stands the tomb of Mir Madan, the general of Siraj-ud-daula (*Introducing India*, Pt. I, p. 74).

Palāśinī.—This river has been identified by some with the modern Parās, a tributary of the Koel in Chotanagpur. It is one of the streams that is said to have issued, according to the *Mārkaṇḍeya Purāṇa*, from the Śaktimat range, which has been identified with the chain of hills extending from Śakti in Raigṛh, C.P., to the Dalma hills in Manbhum and perhaps even to the hills in the Santal Parganas (B. C. Law, *Rivers of India*, p. 45).

Pañcapālī (Pāñcapālī).—This village may be identified with Pañcupālī in the Ānandapur sub-division of the Keonjhar State (*E.I.*, XXV, Pt. IV, October, 1939).

Pandua.—It is in the Hooghly district also known as Pradyumnanagara. It is commonly known as Peḍo. For details, vide *Introducing India*, Pt. I, p. 76.

Paribbājakārāma.—It was a notable retreat built for the wanderers in the landed estate of Udumbaradevī in the neighbourhood of Rājagṛha and Gṛdhrakūṭa (*Dīgha*, III, 36; *Sumaṅgalavilāsinī*, III, 832). It existed a few paces from the Moranivāpa on the bank of the Sumāgadha tank (*Dīgha*. III, 39).

Paścima-Khāṭikā.—It occurs in the Govindapur plate of Lakṣmaṇasena. It is included in the Vardhamāna-bhukti. The present river Hooghly formed the natural boundary between the two Khāṭikās, Pūrva and Paścima (*E.I.*, XXVII, Pt. III, 121).

Paṭibhāṇakūṭa.—It was a peak with a fearful precipice in the neighbourhood of the Gijjhakūṭa (*Saṃyutta*, V. 448). According to the Pali commentator Buddhaghosa it was a boundary rock which looked like a large mountain (*Sāratthappakāsinī*, III, 301).

Patkai hills.—To the south of the Lakhimpur district of Assam run these hills with an average elevation of about 4,000 ft. The main range contains peaks about 7,000 ft. in height. The passes across the hills afford the only means of land communication between Burma and Assam (Law, *Mountains of India*, p. 9).

Paṭṭikerā.—The Maināmāṭi copperplate inscription records a grant of land in a village called Bejakhaṇḍa in favour of a Buddhist vihāra built in the city of Paṭṭikerā. The inscription preserves the name of a monarch, who came to the throne of Paṭṭikerā in the year 1203-4 A.D. (*Haraprasād Memorial Volume*, pp. 283ff.; *B. C. Law Vol.*, Pt. I, pp. 215-216).

Pauṇḍravardhanabhukti (*Puṇḍravardhana-bhukti*).—The Pauṇḍras or Pauṇḍrakas mentioned several times in the Great Epic are once linked with the Vaṅgas and Kirātas (Sabhāp., XIII, 584), while on another occasion they are mentioned in connection with the Udras, Utkalas, Mekalas, Kaliṅgas and Andhras (Vanap., LI, 1988; Bhīṣmap., IX, 365, Droṇap, IV, 122). They are also mentioned in the *Aitareya Brāhmaṇa* (VII, 18). According to the *Daśakumāracaritaṃ*, the Puṇḍra country was attacked by the army of Viśālavarmā (p. 111). The major portion of North Bengal, then known as Puṇḍravardhana-bhukti, formed an intregal part of the Gupta empire from A.D. 443 to 543 and was governed by a line of *uparika mahārājas* as vassals of the Gupta emperor.[1] According to the Dāmodarpur copperplate inscription of the time of Bhānugupta (A.D. 533-34), a noble man (*kulaputra*) belonging to Ayodhyā approached the local government of Koṭivarṣa of which Svyambhudeva was the governor, under the provincial government of Puṇḍravardhana-bhukti, during the reign of Bhānugupta, and prayed that he might be granted, by means of a copperplate document in accordance with the prevailing custom, to transfer some rent-free waste lands. His prayer was granted. Pauṇḍravardhana is identical with the *Pun-na-fa-tan-na* of Yuan Chwang. Pargiter thinks that the Pauṇḍras once occupied the countries that are at present represented by the modern districts of Santal Parganas, Birbhum and northern portion of Hazaribagh. In order to include Puṇḍravardhana the eastern boundary of the Madhyadeśa has been extended still further to the east (cf. *Divyāvadāna*, pp. 21-22). In ancient times Puṇḍravardhana-bhukti included Varendra, roughly identical with North Bengal. The *bhukti* of Puṇḍravardhana seems to have included the whole of Bengal. A village called Vyāghrataṭi (Bāgḍi) mentioned in the Khalimpur grant of Dharma-

[1] Raychaudhuri, *Political History of Ancient India*, 4th ed., pp. 456-457.

pāla, the Nālandā inscription of Devapāla and the Anulia copperplate of Lakṣmaṇasena, was one of the divisions of Bengal, according to the interpretation put upon Kālidāsa's account of Raghu's exploits. H. P. Shāstrī has identified Balavalabhi with Bāgḍi. The Anulia copperplate refers to the land granted within the jurisdiction of Vyāghrataṭi which belonged to the Pauṇḍravardhanabhukti. S. N. Majumdar has identified Vyāghrataṭi with Bāgḍi (*Sir Ashutosh Commemoration Volume*, Orientalia, Pt. II, p. 424). The city of Puṇḍravardhana is also referred to in the following Pāla records: The Khalimpur grant of Dharmapāla, the Nālandā grant of Devapāla, the Bāngarh grant of Mahīpāla I, the Āmagachia grant of Vigrahapāla III and the Manhali grant of Madanapāla. Among the Sena records, it is referred to in the Barrackpur grant of Vijayasena, the Anulia, the Tarpaṇdīghi, the Mādhāinagar and the Sunderban copperplates of Lakṣmaṇasena, the Edilpur copperplate of Keśavasena, the Madanapāḍā and the Sāhitya Parishat copperplates of Viśvarūpasena. Pauṇḍrabhukti, a shortened form of Puṇḍravardhana-bhukti, is referred to in the Rāmpāl copperplate of Śrīcandradeva, Belāva copperplate of Bhojavarman and Dhulla plate of Śrīcandra (vide N. G. Majumdar, *Inscriptions of Bengal*, Vol. III, pp. 2, 15).[1] The Sangli plate of the Rāṣṭrakūṭa king Govinda IV refers to Pauṇḍravardhana. Varendrī is assigned to Pauṇḍravardhana in the Tarpaṇdīghi grant of Lakṣmaṇasena. The Deoparah inscription of Vijayasena refers to a guild of artists belonging to Varendra which occupies a considerable portion of Puṇḍravardhana. The Kamauli plate of Vaidyadeva, the Viṣṇu image inscription and Deoparah inscription also refer to Varendra.

In the time of the Pālas (*circa* 730–1060 A.D.) Puṇḍravardhana-bhukti must have comprised a larger area, while the Senas must have ruled over a still larger division. The records of these two dynasties refer to the following sub-divisions as included in the larger division of Puṇḍravardhana-bhukti: the Koṭivarṣaviṣaya (Dinajpur), the Vyāghrataṭimaṇḍala (Malda), the Khāḍiviṣaya (identical with the Sunderbans and the 24 Pergs.), Varendrī (roughly identical with Rajshahi, Bogra, Rungpur and Dinajpur) and Vaṅga (East Bengal, more particularly the Dacca division). That Puṇḍravardhana included Varendrī as well as Gauḍa (Malda and Dinajpur) is also proved by a reference in Puruṣottama's lexicon (11th century A.D.), where we have '*Puṇḍrāh syur Varendrī-Gauḍa-nirvṛti*', i.e., the Puṇḍras include the Varendrī and Gauḍa countries. According to the *Rāmacaritam* of Sandhyākaranandi (11th century A.D.) Śrī Puṇḍravardhanapura seems to have been situated in Varendrī, for it is stated there that Varendrī was the foremost place of the east and Puṇḍravardhanapura was its crest-jewel or the most beautiful ornament (*Kavipraśasti*, V. 1). It was the biggest province of the Gauḍa empire. According to a Damodarpur plate it extended from the Himalayas in the north to Khāḍi in the Sunderban region in the south. The Madhyapāḍā plate of Viśvarūpasena extends its eastern boundary to the sea. According to the Meher copperplate of the 13th century A.D., it comprised a portion of the Tippera district (*History of Bengal*, Vol. I, p. 24; for further details see *Samataṭa*). The Tippera copperplate grant of Sāmanta Lokanātha (*E.I.*, XV, 301–15) refers to some feudatory chiefs ruling in the region round Tippera. A new copperplate was found while taking out mud from a tank by a villager at Gunaighar, a village about 18 miles to the north-west of the town of Comilla and a mile and a half to the south-west of the police station of

[1] For details, see B. C. Law, *Geographical Essays*, p. 37; Law, *Geography of Early Buddhism*, pp. 33 and 68.

Devidvāra in the district of Tippera. This is also known as the Gunaighar grant of Vainyagupta (*I.H.Q.*, VI, 45ff.). In the *Epigraphia Indica* (XXI, p. 85) we find that the city of Puṇḍravardhana was the seat of a Mahāmātra in the Maurya age, but this is doubtful. According to Dr. D. R. Bhandarkar the capital of the Saṃvaṃgīyas at the time of the Mahāsthān inscription was Puṇḍranagara, which was the headquarters not of the Vaṅgīyas but of the Puṇḍras after whom it was undoubtedly called Puṇḍranagara (*E.I.*, XXI, p. 91).

The present ruins of Mahāsthān or Mahāsthāngarh lie seven miles north of the modern town of Bogra. Cunningham identifies this site with the ancient city of Puṇḍravardhana. The river Karatoyā, which still washes the base of the mounds of Mahāsthān, separated Puṇḍravardhanabhukti from the more easterly kingdom of Prāgjyotiṣa or Kāmarūpa in Assam. Puṇḍravardhana was visited by Hiuen Tsang in the 7th century A.D. According to the Chinese pilgrim it was more than 4,000 li in circuit and its capital was more than 30 li. The city lost its importance from the third quarter of the 12th century A.D., for the later Sena kings of Bengal shifted their capital first to Deopārā in the Rajshahi district and later to Gauḍa in the Malda district. Towards the end of the 13th or the beginning of the 14th century A.D. Puṇḍravardhana was occupied by the Mahommedans.

Pāhāḍpur.—Somapura has been identified with Pāhārpur in the Dinajpur district of Bengal (*Nalanda Inscription of Vipulaśrīmitra, E.I.*, XXI, Pt. III, July, 1931). The huge mound of bricks, 80 ft. in height, that stands at Pāhāḍpur, probably gave rise to the name of this place as it looked like a rock. There was a monastery named after Dharmapāla at Somapura, identified with Pāhāḍpur by Dikshit. The monastery at Pādāḍpur is the biggest one that was ever erected in India for the Buddhist monks. It was built in the 8th century A.D. under the Pāla kings of Bengal. The most numerous specimens of antiquity from Pāhāḍpur are the terra-cotta plaques. The Brahmanical and Buddhist gods are equally found here. The Brahmanical gods represented in them are Brahmā, Viṣṇu, Ganeśa, and possibly Sūrya. The place must have gained considerable importance as a seat of Buddhism in Northern India during the Pāla period.

The ruins of Pāhāḍpur are situated at a distance of three miles to the west of the Jamalgunge railway station in the district of Rajshahi. The Pāhāḍpur monastery resembles such great monasteries as Borobudur and Prambanam monasteries at Java and Ankarbhat monastery in Cambodia. In the Buddhist vihāra at Pāhāḍpur we find a square sanctuary with many chambers each having a courtyard in front and a small portico. A high altar is found probably for religious worship. To the east of this sanctuary there stands a little stūpa, called *Satyapirerbhitā*, where we have a temple of Tārā. The terra-cotta plaques on the walls of the monastery contain the tales of the *Pañcatantra* and the *Hitopadeśa*. The stone images of Rādhā and Kṛṣṇa, some lovely figures telling the story of the life of Kṛṣṇa, slaying of Dhenukāsūra, holding of Mt. Govardhana by Śrīkriṣṇa are found here. The Epic and Pauranic scenes like the fight of Bāli and Sugrīva, the death of Bāli, the abduction of Subhadrā, etc. are all found here. There was a Jaina temple at Pāhāḍpur in the 5th century A.D. The famous Tibetan Buddhist scholar, Dīpankara Śrījñāna is said to have spent many years under his teacher Ratnākara Śānti in the Somapuramahāvihāra. For an account of the excavations at Pāhāḍpur vide *A.S.I.*, *Annual Report*, 1929-30, pp. 138ff.; *A.S.I.*, *Annual Reports*, 1930–34, pp. 113–128; K. N. Dikshit, *Excavations at Pāhārpur*, *M.A.S.I.*, No. 55; *Introducing India*, Pt. I, p. 78; *I.C.*, VII, 1940-41, pp. 35–40 regarding the date of the Pāhārpur temple by S. K. Sarasvati.

Pālāmaka.—The Nālandā Grant of Devapāla mentions this village in the Gayāviṣaya (*E.I.*, XVII, pp. 318ff.).

Pāṇḍavaparvata.—It may be identified with the modern Vipulagiri, north-north-east of Rājagṛha. (B. C. Law, *Rājagṛha in Ancient Literature*, *M.A.S.I.*, No. 58, pp. 3–6, 28–30).

Pāṇḍuyā.—(i) This place commonly known as Peḍo is situated at a distance of 38 miles from Calcutta. It is in the Hooghly district and is quite distinct from Pāṇḍuyā of the Malda district. In the 15th century A.D. Samsuddin Isuf Shah, king of Gauḍa, conquered this Hindu kingdom of Pāṇḍuyā, which contained many Hindu temples. An ancient Hindu temple dedicated to Sun God was converted into a mosque. There is a minar 127 ft. high and there are two tanks, known as the Jorāpukur and the Pīrpukur.

(ii) The ruins of Pāṇḍuyā in the district of Malda lie to the east of the river Mahānandā. A clear trace of Hindu relics is found here in a dilapidated culvert with images of Hindu deities beneath it. Many remains of the Muslim age are found at this site, e.g., *Ādinā mosque*, *Soṇā mosque*, *Āsānsāhī Dargā*, *Selāmi Dargā*, *Bāisk-Hāzāri Dargā*, *Eklākhī mosque*, etc. (*Introducing India*, Pt. I, p. 76).

Pāpahāriṇī.—Name of a hill in Bihar. There is a beautiful tank at the foot of the Pāpahārinī hill, which is frequented by the people on the last day of the month of Pauṣ, when the image of Madhusudana is brought to a temple at the foot of the hill from Baṃśī. This tank was caused to be excavated by Koṇadevī, the wife of Ādityasena, who became the independent sovereign of Magadha in the 7th century, after the kingdom of Kanauj was broken up on the death of Harṣavardhana (*C.I.I.*, III, 211).

Pārśvanātha.—It is in the district of Hazaribagh, which is very frequently visited by the Jains. The height of this hill is about 5,000 ft. It is the highest mountain south of the Himalayas. It is a remarkably handsome mountain, sufficiently lofty to be imposing, rising out of an elevated country. (For details—*B. and O. District Gazetteers, Hazaribagh*, pp. 202ff.) There is a Dīgambara Jaina temple on its top and some Śvetāmbara temples are found at its foot. This hill also known as Sametśikhara stands in a dense forest infested with wild animals. Parśvanāth before his passing away came to the foot of this hill and attained salvation (B. C. Law, *Geographical Essays*, p. 213).

Pāṭaliputra.—The later capital of Magadha was Pāṭaliputra (Modern Patna). Its ancient Sanskrit names were Kusumapura and Puṣpapura from the numerous flowers which grew in the royal enclosure. The Greek historians call it Palibothra and the Chinese pilgrims, Pa-lin-tou.

Hiuen Tsang the great Chinese traveller gives an account of the legendary origin of the name of the city (Watters, *On Yuan Chwang*, Vol. II, p. 87). According to Jaina tradition Udaya, the son of Darśaka, built this city. The first beginnings were made by the Magadhan monarch, Ajātaśatru. The Buddha, while on his way to Vaiśālī from Magadha, saw Ajātaśatru's ministers measuring out a town (vide, *Modern Review*, March, 1918).

Pāṭaliputra was originally a Magadhan village, known as Pāṭaligrāma, which lay opposite to Koṭigrāma on the other side of the Ganges. The Magadhan village was one of the halting stations on the high road extending from Rājagṛha to Vaiśālī and other places. The fortification of

Pāṭaligrāma which was undertaken in the Buddha's life-time by two Magadhan ministers, Sunīdha and Varṣakāra, led to the foundation of the city of Pāṭaliputra (*Dīgha*, II, 86ff.; *Sumaṅgalavilāsinī*, II, p. 540). Thus it may be held that Ajātaśatru was the real founder of Pāṭaliputra.

Pāṭaliputra was built near the confluence of the great rivers of Mid-India, the Ganges, Son, and Gandak, but now the Son has receded some distance away from it. This city was protected by a moat 600 ft. broad and 30 cubits in depth. According to Megasthenes it was 80 stadia in length and fifteen in breadth (McCrindle, *Ancient India as described by Megasthenes and Arrian*, p. 65).

At a distance of 24 feet from the inner ditch there stood a rampart with 570 towers and 64 gates (cf. McCrindle, *Ancient India as described by Megasthenes and Arrian*, p. 67). This city had four gates, Aśoka's daily income from them being 4,00,000 *kahāpaṇas*. In the Council (*Sabhā*) he used to get 1,00,000 *kahāpaṇas* daily (*Samantapāsādikā*, I, p. 52).

Fa-hien, who came to the city in the 5th century A.D., was much impressed by its glory and splendour. He says that the royal palace and halls in the midst of the city were magnificent. There was in this city a Brahmin professor of Mahayanism named Rādhasāmi. There was a Hīnayāna monastery by the side of Aśokan tope. Its inhabitants were rich, prosperous and righteous (Legge, *Fa-hien*, pp. 77-78). Fa-hien further gives an interesting description of a grand Buddhist procession at Pāṭaliputra (*Ibid.*, p. 79). According to Hiuen Tsang, who visited it in the 7th century A.D., an old city lay to the south of the Ganges above 70 li in circuit, the foundations of which were still visible, although the city had long been a wilderness. This old city, according to him, was Pāṭaliputra (Watters, *On Yuan Chwang*, Vol. II, p. 87). The poet Daṇḍin speaks of Pāṭaliputra as the foremost of all the cities and full of gems (*Daśakumāracaritaṃ*, 1st Ucchvāsa, śl. 2, *pūrva-pīṭhikā*).

Pāṭaliputra was the capital of later Śiśunāgas, the Nandas and also the great Maurya emperors, Candragupta and Aśoka, but it ceased to be the ordinary residence of the Gupta sovereigns after the completion of the conquests made by Samudragupta (V. A. Smith, *Early History of India*, 4th ed., p. 309). During the reign of Candragupta Vikramāditya it was a magnificent and populous city and was apparently not ruined until the time of the Hūṇa invasion in the 6th century. Harṣavardhana, who was the paramount sovereign of Northern India in the 7th century A.D., made no attempt to restore it (V. A. Smith, *Early History of India*, 4th ed., p. 310). Śaśāṅka Narendragupta, king of Gauḍa and Karṇasuvarṇa destroyed the Buddha's footprints at Pāṭaliputra and demolished many Buddhist temples and monasteries (S. C. Vidyābhūṣaṇa, *History of Indian Logic*, p. 349). Dharmapāla, the most powerful of the Pāla kings of Bengal and Bihar took steps to renew the glory of Pāṭaliputra (V. A. Smith, *Early History of India*, 4th ed., pp. 310-11).

The Buddha was invited by the lay worshippers of Pāṭaligāma on the occasion of the opening ceremony of a living house (*āvasathāgāra*) (*Vinaya-piṭaka*, I, pp. 226–8). A monastery was built at Pāṭaliputra by an influential Brahmin householder of Benares for a Buddhist monk named Udena (*Majjhima*, II, 157ff.). A monk named Bhadda dwelt at Kukkuṭārāma near Pāṭaligāma and had conversations with the Buddha's famous disciple named Ānanda (*Saṃyutta*, V. 15-16, 171-2). King Paṇḍu of Pāṭaliputra was converted to Buddhism (Law, *Dāṭhāvaṃsa*, Intro., xii-xiv). Sthulabhadra, who was the leader of some of the Jaina monks, summoned a council at Pāṭaliputra, about 200 years after the death of

Mahāvīra, to collect sacred Jaina literature. Bhadrabāhu refused to accept the work of this Council (Stevenson, *Heart of Jainism*, p. 72).

Interesting discoveries have been made by the Archaeological Department of the Government of India on the site of Pāṭaliputra. Some may be mentioned here: (1) remains of wooden palisades at Lohanipura, Bulandibagh, Mahārājganja and Mangle's Tank; (2) punch-marked coins found at Golakpur; (3) Didarganj Statue; (4) Dārukhiā Devī and Perso-Ionic capital; (5) the railing pillar probably belonging to the time of Śuṅgas; (6) coins of Kuṣāṇa and Gupta kings; (7) votive clay tablet found near Purabdarwāzā; (8) remains of Hīnayāna and Mahāyāna monasteries at the time of Fa-hien; the temples of Sthūlabhadra and other Jaina temples, and the temples of Choṭi and Bari Patan Devī (*Pāṭaliputra* by Monoranjan Ghose, pp. 14-15). For further details, vide Law, *Indological Studies*, Pl. III; Law, *The Magadhas in Ancient India* (*J.R.A.S. Publication*, No. 24); Law, *Tribes in Ancient India*, Ch. XLVI.

Pātharghāṭā.—This hill is in the Bhagalpur district situated on the bank of the Ganges. On the north side of this hill there are some ancient rock sculptures. This hill also contains some caves. Some have identified it with Vikramaśilā (*Bhagalpur*, by Byrne, *B. D. Gazetteers*, p. 171).

Pāvāpurī.—Pāvāpurī is the modern name of the ancient Pāpā or Apāpapurī. It is a village in the Bihar sub-division situated three miles north of Giriyek. 'It was at this place that Mahāvīra, the founder of Jainism, died while he was dwelling in the palace of Ṣastipāla of Pāvā.

Four beautiful Jain temples were built at the spot where Mahāvīra left his mortal existence. Here the Buddha ate his last meal at the house of Cunda the smith and was attacked with dysentery. The Mallas used to reside here. The nine Malla chiefs, to mark the passing away of the great Jina, were among those that instituted an illumination on the day of the new moon saying: 'Since the light of intelligence is gone, let us make an illumination of material matter'.

There is a difference of opinion as to the location of Pāvā, Pāpā or Pāvāpurī. According to some it is the same as Kāsiā situated on the little Gandak river to the east of the district of Gorakhpur. It seems that the city was situated near Rājgīr in Bihar. For further details vide B. C. Law, *Geographical Essays*, p. 210; P. C. Nahar, *Tīrthapāvāpurī*, 1925; *A.S.I.*, Reports, Vols. VIII and XI; *B. and O. District Gazetteers*, *Patna*, by O'Malley, pp. 223-24.

Pāvārika-ambavana.—It was a mango orchard belonging to a banker named Pāvārika of Nālandā, which was used as a pleasure-grove. Pāvārika built a monastery here being pleased with the Master after listening to his discourse. He dedicated it to the congregation of monks headed by the Buddha (*Papañcasūdanī*, III, p. 52). The Buddha once lived here and spoke on the subject of miracles to Kevaḍḍha, the son of a householder (*Dīgha Nikāya*, I, 211).

Phalgu.—This river joins the Ganges in the district of Monghyr, north-east of Lakhisarai. It is but a united flow of the two hill-streams called the Nairañjanā (modern Nīlājāna) and Mahānada (modern Mohanā), which meet together above Bodh-Gayā. It receives two tributaries, one in the district of Patna and the other in the district of Monghyr. Nīlājāna or Nirañjanā has its source near Sameria in the district of Hazaribagh. Buddhagayā is situated at a short distance to the west of this river. According to the commentary on the *Majjhima Nikāya* (Siamese edition, Pt. II, p. 233) this river flows on in a glassy stream showing the bathing places with gradual descents of steps. It has cool and crystal water, mudless and pure (*Papañcasūdanī*, Pt. II, p. 233; cf. *Lalitavistara*, p. 311;

Mahāvastu, Vol. II, p. 123). The *Lalitavistara* describes it as a river with the banks adorned with trees and shrubs. According to Pali scholiasts the name Nerañjarā signifies a stream of faultless water (*Nelā-jalā*) or one of bluish water (*nīlā-jalā*). For further details vide B. M. Barua, *Gayā and Buddha-Gayā*, pp. 5, 103-4, etc.

Phalgugrāma.—The Madanapāḍā grant of Viśvarūpasena and the Edilpur grant of Keśavasena were issued from Phalgugrāma. Some have identified it with a place situated on the bank of the river Phalgu in the Gayā district, but this is doubtful.

Phuliā.—It is a village, which is situated about four miles from Śāntipura in the district of Nadia. It is nine miles from Ranaghat and 54 miles from Calcutta. It is the birthplace of the great Bengali poet Kīrttivāsa, the author of the Bengali *Rāmāyaṇa*. Here Yavana Haridāsa, the well-known Muslim follower of Śrīcaitanya, spent his days in religious practices. A new township has been recently started by the Government at Phuliā (*Introducing India*, Pt. I, p. 74).

Piñjokāṣṭi.—This village is mentioned in the Madanapāḍā grant of Viśvarūpasena situated in the Vikramapura division of Vaṅga within the Pauṇḍravardhanabhukti.

Pippalaguhā or Pippaliguhā or Pipphaliguhā.—It was situated on the north face of the Vaibhāragiri. The cave stood some 300 paces south-west from the Charnelfield (Legge, *Fa-hien*, pp. 84, 85). It was a favourite resort of Mahākassapa (*Saṃyutta*, V. 79; *Udāna*, p. 4). Fa-hien knew it to be a dwelling among the rocks in which the Buddha regularly sat in meditation after taking his midday meal (Legge, *Fa-hien*, p. 85). According to Hiuen Tsang, this cave was visited by the Buddha where he often lodged (Watters, *On Yuan Chwang*, II, 154). Buddha came to this cave when Mahākassapa fell seriously ill (*Saṃyutta*, V. 79). The cave was called Pippali or Pipphali because it was marked by a Pippali or Pipphali tree which stood beside it (*Udānavaṇṇanā*, p. 77). The *Mañjuśrīmūlakalpa* (p. 588) places it in the Varāha mountain. In some of the Chinese accounts it is placed in the Gijjhakūṭa mountain (cf. Watters, *On Yuan Chwang*, II, 155).

Pipphalivana.—It was the Moriyan capital which was identical with Nyagrodhavana or Banyan Grove mentioned by Hiuen Tsang where stood the famous Embers Tope (Watters, *On Yuan Chwang*, II, pp. 23-24). This is in agreement with the Tibetan account given in the *Dulva* (Rockhill, *Life of the Buddha*, p. 147). Some hold that Pipphalivana probably lay between Rummindei in the Nepalese Tarai and Kasia in the Gorakhpur district. (H. C. Raychaudhury, *Political History of Ancient India*, 4th ed., p. 217). The Moriyas of Pipphalivana were a republican clan that existed in the Buddha's time (*Dīgha*, II, 167). They got a portion of the Buddha's relics and erected a stūpa over the same (*Buddhist Suttas*, S.B.E., p. 135). According to the *Mahāvaṃsa* (v. 16) Candragupta, the grandfather of Aśoka, was born in the family of the Moriya Khattiyas.

Prabhāsavana.—It is situated on the Gridhrakūṭa hill in Rājagriha (R. L. Mitra, *Northern Buddhist Literature*, p. 166).

Pravaragiri.—The Barābar hill cave inscription of Anantavarman refers to ancient Pravaragiri, situated on the northern side of the village of Panāri, about 14 miles to the north by east of Gayā, the chief town of the Gayā district (*C.I.I.*, Vol. III).

Prāgjyotiṣa.—Pragjyotiṣa[1] was a famous country according to both

[1] For literary and other sources vide B. C. Law, *Prāgjyotiṣa*, *J.U.P.H.S.*, Vol. XVIII, Pts. I and II.

the epics. It is also mentioned in the *Yoginītantra* (1. 12, p. 65). According to the *Kālikāpurāṇa* (Ch. 40. 73) it was a beautiful city under the sovereignty of Naraka. It was looked upon as Indra's mansion by the king of Videha (Ch. 38. 152). It seems to have included not only the Kāmarūpa country but also a considerable portion of North Bengal and probably also of North Bihar. The Kamauli grant of Vaidyadeva refers to the *maṇḍala* of Kāmarūpa and the *viṣaya* of Prāgjyotiṣa, which implies that the latter was the larger administrative division including Kāmarūpa. It is taken to mean the city of eastern astrology. According to Sir Edward Gait Prāgjyotiṣa is represented by the modern town of Gauhati. It was ruled by Indrapāla who was styled as the Mahārājādhirāja (*Gauhati Copperplate Grant of Indrapāla of Prāgjyotiṣa*). Here the realization of taxes from the tenants and the infliction of punishments were rare (vide *Nowgong Copperplate*). According to the India Office plate of Lakṣmaṇasena (*E.I.*, XXVI) the lord of Prāgjyotiṣa performed magic rites with the dust from the feet of king Lakṣmaṇasena. In the Bargaon grant of Ratanapāla the city of Prāgjyotiṣa is referred to as impregnable and rendered beautiful by the Lohitya or Brahmaputra river (*E.I.*, XII, pp. 37ff.). Prāgjyotiṣa is well known in both the Epics. The *Mahābhārata* refers to it as a *mleccha* kingdom, which was ruled by king Bhagadatta (Karṇaparva, V. 104-5; Sabhāparva, XXV, 1,000ff.). In the same Epic it is also referred to as an *asura* kingdom (Vanaparva, XII, 488). This country seems to have bordered on the realms of the Kirātas and Cīnas (*Mahābhārata*, Udyogaparva, XVIII, 584ff.). According to the *Raghuvaṃśa* it lay evidently to the north of the Brahmaputra river.

In Hemacandra's *Abhidhānacintāmaṇi* (IV. 22) there is a mention of *Prāgjyotiṣāḥ Kāmarūpāḥ*. According to Puruṣottama (Trikāṇḍa, p. 93) Prāgjyotiṣa is Kāmarūpa. The *Bṛhat-saṃhitā* (XIV. 6) mentions it. According to the *Kālikā Purāṇa* (Ch. XXXVIII) the capital town of Prāgjyotiṣa has been identified with Kāmākhyā or Gauhati (*J.R.A.S.*, 1900, p. 25). The *Kāvyamīmāṃsā* of Rājaśekhara (Ch. XVII) places Prāgjyotiṣa in the east. According to the *Harṣacarita* a messenger named Bhāṣkaradyuti was sent to Śrī Harṣa by the prince of Prāgjyotiṣa. This prince was named Kumāra according to Kielhorn. For further details vide *Prāgjyotiṣa* by B. C. Law in *J.U.P.H.S.*, Vol. XVIII, Pts. 1 and 2; S. C. Roy, *Prāgjyotiṣapura* in *Modern Review*, March, 1946; B. K. Barua, *A Cultural History of Assam*, Vol. I, pp. 9ff.

Pretakūṭa (*Pretaśilā*).—It is a peak mentioned in the *Gayā-māhātmya*. This hill stands 540 ft. in height, situated five miles north-west of Gayā. It is a sacred spot for the pilgrims. On the top of this hill a granite boulder is to be seen appearing like a sitting elephant (B. M. Barua, *Gaya and Buddha-Gaya*, p. 14). At the foot of the Pretakūṭa there was a bathing place called the Pretakuṇḍa also known as the Brahmakuṇḍa (*Vāyu Purāṇa*, 108. 67).

Punappuna.—It is the modern Punpun which meets the Ganges just below Patna. It takes its rise in the district of Daltonganj and receives two tributaries. (Law, *Rivers of India*, p. 26.)

Puṇḍravardhanabhukti.—See *Pauṇḍravardhanabhukti*.

Pūrvakhāṭikā.—It seems to have covered a large part of the western Sunderban area (*E.I.*, XXVII, Pt. III, p. 121).

Puṣkaraṇa.—The Susunia Rock Inscription of Candravarman refers to Puṣkaraṇa which is modern Pokhrana on the Damodar river in the Bankura district, about 25 miles east of the Susunia hill, which was the seat of administration of king Candravarman (*A.S.I.*, *Annual Report*, 1927-1928, p. 188; *Introducing India*, Pt. I, 72).

Puṣkarāmbudhi.—It is mentioned in Luders' List as a country (No. 961).

Rāḍha.—The Bhuvaneśvara Inscription of Bhaṭṭa-Bhavadeva refers to this province. The Tirumalai Rock Inscription of Rājendra Coḷa mentions Uttara Rāḍha and Dakṣiṇa Rāḍha as two distinct *janapadas*. Uttara Rāḍha is also mentioned in the Belāva copperplate of Bhojavarman as well as in the Naihati copperplate of Ballālasena as belonging to the Vardhamānabhukti. According to some Uttara-Rāḍha which also occurs in the Kolhapur copperplates of Gaṇḍarādityadeva (Śaka 1048—*E.I.*, XXIII, Pt. II), and in the Indian Museum Plates of Gaṅga Devendravarman of the year 398 (*E.I.*, XXIII, Pt. II, April, 1935, p. 76) is that part of Bengal which includes a portion of the Murshidabad district. The province of Rāḍha seems to have comprised the modern districts of Hooghly, Howrah, Burdwan, Bankura and major portions of Midnapur. The *Ācārāṅga Sūtra* (*Āyārāṃga Sutta*) speaks of Lāḍha (Rāḍha) as a pathless country with its two sub-divisions: Subbhabhūmi (probably the same as Skt. Suhma) and Vajjabhūmi, which may be taken to correspond to the modern district of Midnapur. It also speaks of the inhabitants of the Rāḍha country as rude and generally hostile to the ascetics. The dogs were set upon them by the Rāḍha people as soon as the ascetics appeared near their villages (1, 8, 3-4). The mischief-makers whom the lonely ascetics had to reckon with were the cowherds (gopālakā) who made practical jokes on them (*Ācārāṅga Sūtra*, 18, 3–10; cf. *Majjhima*, I, 79).

Rājagaha (*Rājagṛha*).—A town occurs in the *Mahābhārata* (84, 104) and in Luders' List No. 1345. It was the ancient capital of Magadha also known as Girivraja. It was so called because it was built by a king and every house in it resembled a palace. It was also called Kuśāgrapura (city of the superior reed grass). As it was surrounded by five hills,[1] it acquired the name of Girivraja which occurs in the Epics as the capital of king Jarāsandha of Magadha. According to the *Sāsanavaṃsa* it was built by Mandhāta (p. 152). It had 32 gates and 64 posterns (Spence Hardy, *Manual of Buddhism*, p. 323). According to the *Vinaya Piṭaka* (Vol IV, pp. 116-17) this city had a gate which was closed in the evening, and nobody, not even the king, was allowed to enter the city after the gate was closed. Rājagṛha was extensive from east to west and narrow from north to south (Watters, *On Yuan Chwang*, II, p. 148). It was a gay city where festivities were held in which people indulged themselves in drinking wine, eating meat, singing and dancing (*Jāt.*, I, 489). There was a festival known as the Nakkhattakīḷā held here, which lasted for a week in which the rich took part (*Vimānavatthu Commy.*, pp. 62–74). Another festival known as the *Giraggasamajjā* was held in this city, and a party of six monks attended it (*Vinaya Piṭaka*, II, 107; cf. also *Ibid.*, IV, 267). This city was an abode of many wealthy bankers (*Petavatthu Commy.*, pp. 1–9). Meetings were held in the Mote Hall at Rājagṛha where the people met and discussed means of welfare (*Jātaka*, IV, pp. 72ff.). Here the inhabitants were always willing to satisfy the needs of the monks under the belief that such pious acts would bring about re-birth in a higher region (*Vimānavatthu Commy.*, pp. 250-51). Many prominent disciples of the Buddha including Sāriputta and Moggallāna visited this city and they were converted by the Buddha here (*Kathāvatthu*, I, p. 97). It was here that Upāli was also ordained as a monk. The Buddha's activity in the city was

---

[1] For a full account of these hills see B. C. Law, *Rājagriha in Ancient Literature*, *M.A.S.I.*, No. 58; B. C. Law, *The Magadhas in Ancient India*, pp. 33ff.

remarkable.[1] Mahāvīra spent 14 rainy seasons here. (*Nāyādhammakahāo*, II, 10). It was the birthplace of the twentieth Tīrthaṅkara (*Āvaśyaka Niryukti*, 325, 383). Here the Buddha summoned all the monks and prescribed several sets of seven conditions of welfare for the Buddhist Fraternity. Ajātaśatru, king of Magadha, built *dhātu-caityas* all round Rājagṛha (*Mahāvaṃsa*, ed. Geiger, p. 247) and repaired 18 great *vihāras*, (*Samantapāsādikā*, I, pp. 9-10).

Jīvaka, the court-physician of king Bimbisāra of Magadha, was an inhabitant of Rājagṛha (*Vin. Pit.*, II, 119ff.). There was another physician named Ākāsagotta belonging to this city (*Vin. Pit.*, I, 215).

Rājagṛha is famous in the history of Buddhism as the place where 500 distinguished elders met under the leadership of Mahākassapa to recite the doctrine and discipline of the Buddha and fix the Buddhist canon (*Vinaya*, Cullavagga, XI). The main reason for selecting Rājagṛha for the purpose was that it could sufficiently make room for 500 elders. The city of Rājagṛha was much frequented by the Buddha and his disciples (*Vimānavatthu Commy.*, pp. 250-1; *Dhammapada Commy.*, I, pp. 77ff.; *Samantapāsādikā*, I, pp. 8-9). The *Vinaya-Cullavagga* speaks of a banker of Rājagṛha who acquired a block of sandalwood and made a bowl out of it for the monks (*Vin. Texts*, III, 78). Another banker of Rājagṛha built a *vihāra* for the monks. He had to take the consent of the Buddha as to the dwelling of the monks in it (*Vin. Pit.*, II, 146). It was in this city that the two famous disciples of the Buddha, Sāriputta and Moggallāna, were converted by him (*Vin. Pit.*, I, 40ff.). When the Buddha was in this city, Devadatta's gain and fame were completely lost (*Vin. Pit.*, IV, 71). It was in this city that the great banker of Śrāvastī named Anāthapiṇḍika was converted by the Buddha (*Sam.*, I, pp. 55-56). Merchants used to visit it to buy or sell merchandise. (*Vimānav. Commy.*, p. 301). Many people of Rājagṛha were engaged in trade and commerce (*Jāt.*, I, pp. 466-7; *Petavatthu Commy.*, pp. 2–9). This city had many names in the course of its long history (*Sumaṅgalav*, I, 132; *Udānavaṇṇanā*, p. 32, etc.).

During the reigns of Bimbisāra and Ajātaśatru Rājagṛha was at the height of its prosperity. It must have lost its glory with the removal of the capital to Pāṭaliputra by Udāyibhadra some 28 years after the Buddha's death.

It was intimately associated not only with the development of Buddhism but also with Jainism and earlier creeds such as *Nāga* and *Yakkha* worship. It was the earliest known stronghold of heresy and heterodoxy of the age (cf. *Majjhima*, I, pp. 1–22). For further details vide B. C. Law, *Rājagṛha in Ancient Literature*, *M.A.S.I.*, No. 58; *Geographical Essays*, Vol. I, 208ff.; *Geography of Early Buddhism*, pp. 6, 8, 9, 15, 16, 28, 31, 33 etc.; *The Magadhas in Ancient India*, pp. 24–33; *A Guide to Rajgir* by Kuraishi and revised by A. Ghosh, 1939; *A.R.A.S.*, 1936/1937 (1940) regarding excavations at Rajgir; *A.S.I.R.*, I (1871), pp. 21ff.; *A.R.A.S.I.*, 1905-06 (1909), 86ff.; 1913-1914 (1917), p. 265; 1925/26 (1928), 121ff.; 1930/1934, Pt. I (1936), 30ff.; 1935-1936 (1938), pp. 52ff.

Rājmahal ranges.—These ranges belong to the Santal Parganas in Bihar, inhabited by the Antargiryas, mentioned in the Bhīṣmaparva list of the *Mahābhārata*. The Antargiryas were the people dwelling on the outskirts of the hills of the Bhagalpur and Monghyr regions. It is also

---

[1] *Vinaya Piṭaka*, IV, p. 287; II, p. 146; *Dīgha*, II, pp. 76–81; III, pp. 36ff.; *Saṃyutta*, I, pp. 8ff.; pp. 27-28, 52, 160-61, 161–63, 163-64; *Aṅguttara*, II, pp. 181-82; III, 366ff., 374ff., 383ff.; *Therīgāthā*, pp. 16, 27, 41, 142; *Jātaka*, I, pp. 65–84, 156.

known as Kālakavana according to Patañjali (*Mahābhāṣya*, II, 4, 10; cf. Baudhāyana, I, 1, 2).

Rākṣasakhāli.—This island is situated about 12 miles east of the sacred Sāgar island at the mouth of the river Hooghly (*E.I.*, XXVII, Pt. III, p. 119).

Rāmakeli.—This village stands about 18 miles to the south-east of Maldah in the district of Rajshahi, visited by Śrīcaityana (*Caitanya-Bhāgavata*, Ch. IV).

Rāmpūrva.—This village is in the Champaran district of Bihar, well known for the Aśoka pillar discovered by Carlleyle in 1877 (*J.R.A.S.*, 1908, 1085ff.).

Rāṇīpur-Jharial.—It is a village about 21 miles west of Titilāgarh in the Patna State of Orissa, where some inscriptions were found. It is famous for its many old temples (*E.I.*, XXIV, Pt. V, January, 1938).

Revatikā.—The spurious Gayā copperplate grant of Samudragupta records the grant of this village in the *Gayā-viṣaya* to a Brahmin by Samudragupta (*C.I.I.*, Vol. III).

Rohitāgiri.—The Rohtāsgaḍh stone seal matrix of Mahāsāmanta Śaśāṅkadeva mentions the hill fort of Rohtāsgaḍh, 24 miles south by west of Sahasrām, the chief town of the Sahasrām sub-division of the Shahabad district (*C.I.I.*, Vol. III). According to Rampal copperplate of Śrīcandra, the Candras were the rulers of Rohitāgiri, which may be identified with Rohtāsgaḍh in the Sahabad district of Bihar (N. G. Majumdar, *Inscriptions of Bengal*, Vol. III, pp. 2ff.). Rohtāsgaḍh the ancient hill fort of Rohtas is named after Prince Rohitāsva the son of Hariścandra of the solar dynasty (*Harivaṃśa*, Ch. 13). It is also mentioned in the copperplates discovered from Orissa relating to a Tunga family. Both the Tuṅgas of Orissa and the Candras of East Bengal came from Rohitāgiri (*I.H.Q.*, II, 655-656). According to some Rhotas hill is a spur of the Kymore range, a branch of the Vindhya mountain (N. L. Dey, *Geographical Dictionary*, p. 170). For further details vide *B. and O. District Gazetteers, Shahabad*, by O'Malley, pp. 174ff.

Ṛṣigiri (Pali Isigili).—It is near Rājagṛha. It is one of the five hills encircling Girivraja, the ancient name of Rājagṛha (*Vimānavatthu Commy.*, P.T.S., p. 82).

Ṛṣyaśṛṅga-āśrama.—The sage Ṛṣyaśṛṅga had his hermitage at Riṣikuṇḍa, 28 miles to the west of Bhagalpur and four miles to the south-west of Bariarpur. It was situated in a circular valley formed by the Maira hill (Maruk hill). The Riṣikuṇḍa was a tank which was the collection of the combined water of springs, hot and cold, near this hermitage. On the north side of this tank the sage Ṛṣyaśṛṅga and his father Bibhāṇḍaka used to meditate. The Ṛṣyaśṛṅga-parvata, situated at a distance of eight miles to the south of the Kajra station, claims the honour of being the hermitage of the sage (*Rāmāyaṇa*, Ādikāṇḍa, Ch. 9). From the proximity of the Riṣikuṇḍa to the Ganges, which afforded facility to the public women sent by Lomapāda, king of Aṅga, to entice away the young sage from this seclusion, preference should be given to it as the likely place where the sage and his father performed austerities. According to the *Mahābhārata* (Vanaparva, Chs. 110 and 111) this hermitage is said to have been situated not far from the river Kuśī (ancient Kauśikī) and 24 miles from Campā.

Rūpanārāyaṇa.—This river forms the boundary between the districts of Howrah and Midnapur. It rises in the hills of Manbhum, and flows through the districts of Bankura, Hooghly and Midnapur to join the Hooghly river near Tamluk. (For details, Law, *Rivers of India*, p. 27.)

Salandi.—This river issuing from the hills in the Keonjhar State flows through the district of Balasore above the Vaitaraṇī. (Law, *Rivers of India*, p. 45).

Samataṭa.—Samataṭa is mentioned in the Allahabad Pillar Inscription of Samudragupta (*C.I.I.*, Vol. III, No. 1) as one of the most important among the north-east Indian frontier kingdoms which submitted to the mighty Gupta emperor. It was so called because the rivers in it had 'flat and level banks of equal height on both sides' (*C.A.G.I.*, ed. S. N. Majumdar, p. 729). It was included in the larger divisions of Vaṅga. Some scholars hold that it was distinct from Vaṅga which lay between the Meghnā on the east, the sea on the south and the old Buḍigaṅgā course of the Ganges on the north. Samataṭa finds mention in the *Bṛhatsaṃhitā* (Ch. XIV) and it seems to have been identical with the delta of the Ganges and Brahmaputra and must have comprised, according to the epigraphic evidence, the modern districts of Tipperah, Noakhali, Sylhet (*J.A.S.B.*, 1515, pp. 17-18), and portions probably of Barisal. The Karmānta identified with Baḍ-Kāmtā, 12 miles west of Comilla, has often been identified as the capital of Samataṭa (Dey, *Geographical Dictionary*, p. 175; *J.A.S.B.*, 1914, p. 87; Bhaṭṭasāli, *Sculptures in the Dacca Museum*, p. 6). The Bhagalpur grant of Nārāyaṇapāla, the Baghaura inscription of Mahīpāla I, Barrackpur grant of Vijayasena, a Bodhgayā inscription of Vīryendrabhadra, and Asrafpur copperplate refer to Samataṭa (N. G. Majumdar, *Inscriptions of Bengal*, Vol. III). The Mehergrām copperplate of Dāmodaradeva (edited by Barua and Chakravarty) offers us a definite location of the Samataṭamaṇḍala within the Puṇḍravardhanabhukti. It speaks of the district of Paraṇayi (viṣaya), the sub-division called Vaisagrāma (Khaṇḍala), which included the village of Meher in the present Chandpur sub-division of the district of Tipperah. The Deva kings ruled over the district of Tipperah and Chittagong in the beginning of the 13th century A.D., before Daśarathadeva succeeded in supplanting the Senas of Puṇḍravardhanabhukti. A new copperplate has been discovered at Gunaighar, a village about 18 miles to the north-west of the town of Comilla. This plate is the earliest record found in East Bengal. It is earlier than the four Faridpur plates with which it bears fruitful comparison. The plate records a gift of land from the camp of victory at Krīpura by Mahārāja Vaiṇyagupta made at the instance of his vassal Mahārāja Rudradatta, in favour of a Buddhist congregation of monks belonging to the Vaivartika sect of the Mahayana, which was established by a Buddhist monk, Ācārya Śāntideva, in a *vihāra* dedicated to Avalokiteśvara. For further details vide *I.H.Q.*, Vol. VI, No. 1, pp. 45ff. The Gunaighar grant records the grant of land in the Gunaikāgrahāra, which may be identified with Gunaighar, the findspot of the grant in the Tippera district dated 508 A.D. The Dūtaka was Mahāsāmanta Mahārāja Vijayasena, who seems to be a man of some importance of his time.

When Hiuen Tsang visited the country (*cir.* 640 A.D.), Samataṭa was an important kingdom. He described it as the country having rivers with flat and level banks of equal height on both sides. This country, known to the Chinese as *San-mo-ta-cha*, was about 3,000 li in circuit. It was rich in crops, fruits and flowers. The climate was soft and the habits of the people agreeable. The men were hardy by nature, of short stature and of black complexion. They were fond of learning (Beal, *Buddhist Records of the Western World*, II, 199). There were many Buddhist *saṅghārāmas* as well as Hindu temples. This country had also many Jain ascetics. During the visits of Hiuen Tsang and Sengchi Samataṭa seems to have been under the rule of the Khaḍga dynasty (*M.A.S.B.*, Vol. I,

No. 6). The Candra dynasty appears to have mastered the whole of Vaṅga including Samataṭa. In the beginning of the 11th century A.D. the Candras were ousted from their possession of Samataṭa by the Varmans, who, in their turn, gave place to the Senas towards the end of the same century.

Sappasoṇḍika-pabbhāra.—It was a snakehood-like declivity of the neighbouring rock (*Sāratthappakāsinī*, III, 17). It was near the cemetery grove or the Sītavana in Rājagṛha.

Sappinī.—It was a river or rivulet in the neighbourhood of Rājagṛha. It was a stream with a winding course. Buddha used to sojourn occasionally on its bank (*Samyutta*, I, 153). It seems that it flowed in the Buddha's time on the south side of Rājagṛha. The Master went from the Gijjhakūṭa mountain to the bank of this river to meet some wanderers (*paribbājakas*) (*Aṅg.*, II, 29, 176). The Pañcāna river is probably the ancient Sappinī.

Saptagrāma.—It formerly implied seven villages: Bansberia, Kṛṣṭapura, Bāsudevapura, Nityānandapura, Śivapura, Samvacorā and Baladghāṭī. The remains of ancient Saptagrāma are found near the present railway station Ādisaptagrāma, about 27 miles from Calcutta. It was an important city and a port of Rāḍha, situated on the Ganges. It is so called because the seven sons of king Priyavrata became sages after practising penances here. It lost its importance as a port owing to the silting of the river bed of the Sarasvatī. In the 9th century A.D. Saptagrāma was ruled by a powerful Buddhist king named Śrī-Śrī Rūpanārāyaṇa Simha. It was visited by the Egyptian traveller Ibn Batuta in the 13th century A.D. It was later conquered by Jafar Khan whose tomb is still found at Triveṇī. Many coins of Muslim rulers have been found here. During the reign of Alauddin Husen Shah of Gauḍa it was the seat of an imperial mint. In the 16th century A.D., a Hindu king named Rājīvalocana conquered it from Sulaiman, the then Sultan of Gauḍa. It is the birthplace of the author of the *Caṇḍī*. From Bankimcandra's *Kapālkuṇḍala* and Haraprasād Śāstrī's *Bener Meye* we get a glimpse of its prosperity. It is a sacred place of the Vaiṣṇavas being the home of Uddhāraṇa Datta, a follower of Śrīcaitanya. Nityānanda, the right-hand man of Śrīcaitanya, spent many years in this place. For further particulars see Law, *Holy Places of India*; *J.A.S.B.*, 1810; *Periplus*, 26; *Introducing India*, Pt. I, p. 75.

Satata-padmāvatī.—The Edilpur copperplate of Śrīcandra of the 11th century A.D. refers to this district (*E.I.*, XVII, 190).

Sattapaṇṇi Cave.—It was on a side of the Vebhāra mountain where the First Buddhist Council was held under the presidency of Mahākassapa and under the patronage of king Ajātaśatru (*Samantapāsādikā*, I, p. 10). It derived its name from the Saptaparṇa creeper which stood beside it marking it out. According to the *Mahāvastu* (Vol. I, p. 70), it stood on the north side on an excellent slope of the Vaihāra mountain. It agrees with the account of Fa-hien which places the cave on the north of the hill (Legge, *Fa-hien*, pp. 84-85). Hiuen Tsang in agreement with Fa-hien locates the cave about 5 or 6 li south-west from the Bamboo Park, on the north side of the south mountain in a great bamboo wood (Watters, *On Yuan Chwang*, II, 159).

Sālindiya.—It was a Brahmin village on the east side of Rājagṛha (*Jātaka*, III, 293).

Śālmalī.—It may be identical with Mallasārul, a village about a mile and a half from the north bank of the Damodar river, within the jurisdiction of Galsi police station of the Burdwan district, Bengal (*E.I.*, XXIII, Pt. V, p. 158).

Śānavatya.—The country which is mentioned in the *Mahābhārata* (II, 48, 15) is in the Gaya district. Some have identified the people of this country with the Santals, which I think is doubtful (Moti Candra, *Geographical and Economic Studies in the Mahābhārata*, p. 110).

Śāntipur.—In the district of Nadia stands this place on the Ganges. It contains many Hindu temples. Here lived the great Vaiṣṇava reformer Advaitācārya, a contemporary and admirer of Śrīcaitanya, who used to practise asceticism. (*Introducing India*, Pt. I, p. 74).

Sāvathideśa (or *Sāvathikā*).—It roughly corresponds to north Bogra and south Dinajpur in Bengal (*E.I.*, XXIII, Pt. IV, Oct., 1935, p. 103—*Three Copperplate Inscriptions from Gaonri*).

Senānigāma (*Senāni-nigama* according to Buddhaghosa).[1]—It was one of the Magadhan villages containing a beautiful forest and a river. It was a prosperous village where alms were easily obtainable (*Vinaya Mahāvagga*, I, pp. 166-167).

Senāpatigāma.—It was in Uruvilva, where the Buddha was engaged in deep meditation for six years. A public woman named Gavā kept a coarse cloth on a tree for the Buddha's use after meditation (B. C. Law, *A Study of the Mahāvastu*, p. 154).

It should be noted that Senānigāma which was really the principal locality in Uruvelā in the Buddha's time, corresponds to Senāpatigrāma of the Sanskrit Buddhist works (*Lalitavistara*, ed. Mitra, p. 311; *Mahāvastu*, II, 123). It served as a military station in a remote period according to Buddhaghosa (B. M. Barua, *Gayā and Buddha-Gayā*, p. 103).

Shāhpur.—The Shāhpur stone Image Inscription of Ādityasena refers to it. This village stands on the right bank of the Sakarī river, about nine miles to the south-east of Bihar (*C.I.I.*, Vol. III).

Śibsāgar.—It possibly formed part of the old kingdom of Kāmarūpa. The district of Śibsāgar in Assam is bounded on the north by the districts of Darrang and Lakhimpur, on the east by Lakhimpur and hills occupied by the tribes of the independent Nāgās, on the south by these hills and by the Naga Hills district and on the west by Nowgong district. Śibsāgar falls into three natural divisions. The most populous and important portion is a wide and healthy plain lying between the Naga Hills and the Brahmaputra. The Brahmaputra and the Dhansiri are the famous rivers in this district.

The plain is of alluvial origin and consists of a mixture of clay and sand in varying proportions ranging from pure sand near the Brahmaputra to clay so stiff as to be quite unfit for cultivation.

Śibsāgar like the rest of Upper Assam enjoys a cold winter and a cool and pleasant spring. The average rainfall varies from 90 to 95 inches in the year. This town is seldom visited by destructive hurricanes but it is liable to earthquakes like the rest of Assam.

Rice is the staple food of the people and agriculture is the staple occupation. Other important crops are tea, and orchard and garden crops. The rearing of the lac insect and of silk worms, the manufacture of rough earthenware and metal vessels and jewellery, mat-making and weaving are the industries of Śibsāgar. Three different kinds of silk are also produced

---

[1] *Sāratthappakāsinī*, I, 172.

in this district (*Assam District Gazetteers*, Vol. VII, *Śibsāgar*, by B. C. Allen, 1906).

Śibsāgar contains numerous temples built by the Ahom kings, which are made of thin bricks of excellent quality and are generally ornamented with bas-reliefs. The fact that the figures of camels which frequently appear suggests that they were made under the direction of foreign artisans, as camels must always have been very scarce in a marshy country like Assam. There temples were generally built by the side of large tanks. There was a small temple in ruins where a human being was annually offered to the deity by the Chutiya priests.

Siddhala.—This is the name of a village in Uttara-Rāḍha and is mentioned in the Belāva copperplate of Bhojavarman and the Bhuvaneśvara Inscription of Bhaṭṭa Bhavadeva (N. G. Majumdar, *Inscriptions of Bengal*, Vol. III, pp. 16ff.). Some identify Siddhala with the present village of Sidhala near Ahmadpur in Birbhum district (vide *Birbhum-Vivaraṇa* by H. K. Mukherjee, Pt. II, 234).

Śilā-saṅgama (or *Vikramaśilā-saṅghārāma*).—This hill contains seven rock-cut caves of a very ancient date with niches for the images of the deities mentioned by Hiuen Tsang, when he visited Campā in the 7th century A.D. Some have identified it with the Pātharghāṭā hill (vide Vikramaśilā).

Silimpur.—It is in the Bogra district of the Rajshahi division, where the stone slab inscription of the time of Jayapāladeva was discovered (*E.I.*, XIII, 283ff.).

Silua.—It is in the Noakhali district of East Bengal. The ancient remains at this site consist of a low mound with fragments of a colossal image upon it, the pedestal of which had an inscription of the 2nd century B.C. (*A.S.I.*, *Annual Reports*, 1930–34, p. 38).

Siṃhapura.—The identification of Siṃhapura is not certain. Some identify this place with Sīhapura which is mentioned in the *Mahāvaṃsa* (VI, 35ff.) as situated in the Lāḷa country, i.e. Rāḍha. It was probably a part of Kaliṅga which might have included a portion of Rāḍha. According to others, it may be the same as the modern Singupuram between Chicacole and Narasannapeta (*E.I.*, IV, p. 143). The Belāva copperplate of Bhojavarman proves that the Varmans ruled over Siṃhapura (N. G. Majumdar, *Inscriptions of Bengal*, Vol. III, p. 16).

Singaṭia.—This is the name of a river mentioned in the Naihati copperplate of Ballālasena. It flowed in the north of the village of Khāṇḍayillā, identified with modern Khāruliā, and to the west of the village of Ambayillā (Ambagrāma) in the Murshidabad district, Bengal (N. G. Majumdar, *Inscriptions of Bengal*, Vol. III, pp. 71ff.).

Sitahāṭi.—It is in the Katwa sub-division of the Burdwan district. Between this village and the village of Naihati the plate bearing the grant of Ballālasena was discovered (*E.I.*, XIV, p. 156).

Sītavana.—It was the name of a cemetery grove (*Sāratthappakāsinī*, III, p. 17, Siamese edition). The site was used for a charnelfield where the dead bodies were thrown or left to undergo a natural process of decay (*Saṃyutta*, I, pp. 210-11), or to be eaten by carnivorous beasts, birds and worms (*Dīgha Nikāya*, II, pp. 295, 296). This grove was enclosed by a wall and fitted with doors that remained closed during the night (*Saṃyutta*, I, p. 211). It was situated near the north face of the Vaibhāra hill beyond Veṇuvana. Its location must be beyond Jarāsandha-Kā-Baiṭhak (B. C. Law, *Rājagṛha in Ancient India*, pp. 10-11).

Sītākuṇḍa.—It is a village in the Chittagong district, 24 miles north of Chittagong town. It gives its name to a range of hills running north from Chittagong town, which reaches its highest elevation at Sītākuṇḍa. It is the holiest place of the Hindus in the Chittagong district, for tradition states that Rāma and Sītā, while in exile, roamed about on the hills in the vicinity and that Sītā bathed in the hot spring which is associated with her name.

There exists a village by this name in the Monghyr sub-division, situated four miles east of the town of Monghyr, containing a hot spring known as the Sītākuṇḍ spring which is so called after the well-known episode of the *Rāmāyaṇa*. For further details vide *J.A.S.B.*, 1890; *B. and O. District Gazetteers, Monghyr*, by O'Malley, pp. 259–262.

Somapura.—See Pāhārpur.

Srīhaṭṭa.—The *Yoginītantra* (2. 1. 112-113; 2. 2. 119) mentions it. Sylhet occupies the lower valley of the Surma river. It is bounded on the north by the Khasi and Jaintia hills, on the east by Cachar, on the south by the State of Hill Tipperah and on the west by the districts of Tipperah and Mymensingh. It is a broad and level valley bounded on either side by hills of great height. The Barak is the principal river, which flows through Manipur, Cachar, and Sylhet and finally empties itself into the old bed of the Brahmaputra near Bhairab Bazar. The climate of Sylhet is warmer and not less humid than that of the Assam valley (B. C. Allen, *Sylhet, Assam District Gazetteers*, Vol. II).

Śrīnagarabhukti.—The Monghyr copperplate grant of Devapāladeva mentions it which has been identified by Sir Charles Wilkinson with the modern Patna.

Śṛṅgavera.—It is identified with Singra police station in the Natore sub-division of Rajshahi district (*I.H.Q.*, XIX).

Suhma.—The Suhma country was a portion of the more comprehensive region which was later known as Rāḍha. It was on the Ganges (Dhoyi's *Pavanadūta*, V. 27). Subbhabhūmi seems to be identical with the country of Suhmas. According to the Epic and Pauranic accounts the Suhma country is distinguished from Vaṅga and Puṇḍra. The account of Bhīma's eastern conquests as given in the *Mahābhārata* makes the country of the Suhmas distinct from Vaṅga and Tāmralipta. Nīlakaṇṭha's Commentary on the *Mahābhārata* informs us that the Suhmas and Rāḍhas were one and the same people. The Jaina *Āyārāṅga-Sutta* tells us that the Suhma country formed a part of the Rāḍha country. From the *Mahābhārata* (Sabhāp., Ch. 30, 16) we learn that the Pāṇḍavas led their victorious army to Suhma. Suhma was conquered by Pāṇḍu (*Mbh.*, Ādiparva 113) and by Karṇa respectively (*Mbh.*, Karṇaparva, 8, 19). Buddha delivered the *Janapada-kalyāṇi Sutta* while he was at Suhma (*Jāt.*, I. 393). The inhabitants of Suhma saved themselves by submitting to Raghu (*Raghuvaṃśa*, 49, 35). Raghu crossed the river Kāpisā and proceeded towards Kaliṅga. The king of Utkala showed him the way (*Ibid.*, 49, 38). In the account of Mitragupta's journey there is a reference to the Suhma country which was then ruled by king Tuṅgadhanvā (*Daśakumāracarita* 6th Ucchvāsa, p. 102). This king went out to starve himself to death in the pure water of the Ganges (*Daśakumāracarita*, p. 119). The *Kāvyamīmāṃsā* (Ch. 17) by Rājaśekhara refers to many countries including Suhma. According to the *Harṣacarita* (6th Ucchvāsa) Devasena, king of the Suhmas, was killed by Devakī.

Dāmalipti is described in the *Daśakumāracarita* as having been a city of the Suhmas (Ch. VI, *J.A.S.B.*, 1908, 290 n.). A great festival took place outside the city of Dāmalipti in the Suhma country, which had a childless king named Tuṅgadhanvā who prayed for two children at the feet of Pārvatī (*Daśakumāracaritam*, ed. Wilson, pp. 141-142).

Śuktimat range.—It is identified by Cunningham with the hills south of Sehoa and Kanker separating Chattisgarh from Baster (*A.S.R.*, XVII, pp. 24, 26). Beglar places this range in the north of the Hazaribagh district (*Ibid.*, VIII, pp. 124-5). Pargiter identifies it with Garo, Khasi and Tippera hills (*Mārkaṇḍeya Purāṇa*, 285, 306, notes). C. V. Vaidya locates it in Western India and identifies it with Kāthiawāḍ range (*Epic India*, p. 276). Others have identified the Śuktimat with the Sulaiman range (*Z.D.M.G.*, 1922, p. 281, note). Some have applied the name to the chain of hills extending from Śakti in Raigarh, C.P., to the Dalma hills in Manbhum drained by the Kumārī river and perhaps even to the hills in the Santal Parganas washed by the affluents of the Bāblā (H. C. Raychaudhuri, *Studies in Indian Antiquities*, pp. 113–120).

Sultanganj.—This village is situated close to the Ganges in the district of Bhagalpur containing extensive remains of Buddhist monasteries. An old stūpa stands near the railway station. It contains two great rocks of granite, one of which is occupied by the famous temple of Gaivināth (Ghāivināth) Mahādeva, which is a place of great sanctity in the eyes of the Hindus. (*Bhāgalpur*, by Byrne, *B.D. Gazetteers*, p. 175.)

Sumāgadhā.—It was a tank near Rājagṛha (*Saṃyutta Nikāya*, V, p. 447).

Sumbha.—It was the country of the Sumbhas with Setaka as its capital. Some have identified it with Sumha (modern Midnapur district) but the location is uncertain. This country was visited by the Buddha who dwelt in a forest in this country near the town of Desaka where he told a tale concerning the *Janapadakalyāṇi Sutta* (Cowell, *Jātaka*, I, p. 232).

Sunderban.—A grant is said to have been discovered in the Sunderban (Bengal), which is now lost. The forest region of Sunderban was formerly included in the kingdom of Samataṭa or Bāgḍī (Vyāghrataṭī). The Chinese pilgrim Hiuen Tsang saw many Hindu, Buddhist and Jain temples at Samataṭa in the 7th century A.D. but no trace of them has yet been found. Some decorated bricks, fragments of stone sculptures, coins of Huviṣka and Skandagupta, an image of Sūrya and a *Navagraha* slab have been discovered there (*Introducing India*, Pt. I, p. 84).

Surmā.—It is the second important river of Assam. It represents the upper course of the Meghnā. It is joined on the right by five tributaries before forming a confluence with the Barāka at Habiganj. For further details vide B. C. Law, *Rivers of India*, p. 34.

Susunia Hill (See Puṣkaraṇa).—It is the name of a hill in the Bankura district of Bengal, situated about 12 miles north-west of Bankura (*E.I.*, XIII, p. 133).

Suvarṇapura.—It is the same as the modern town of Sonepur situated at the confluence of the Tel and the Mahānadī (*C.I.I.*, XXIII, Pt. VII; *J.B.O.R.S.*, II, 52; Bhandarkar's List No. 1556).

Suvarṇarekhā.—This river rises in the district of Manbhum and flows past Jamshedpur, and farther down through the districts of Dhalbhum and Midnapur to fall into the Bay of Bengal (Law, *Rivers of India*, p. 43).

Tarpandīghi.—This village is situated in the district of Dinajpur where a copperplate grant of Lakṣmaṇasena has been discovered (*E.I.*, XII, p. 6).

Tarpaṇghāṭ.—It is in the Nawabgunj Thana of the district of Dinajpur. It is the place where the sage Vālmīki, the author of the *Rāmāyaṇa*, bathed and performed religious rites (*Introducing India*, Pt. I, p. 80).

Tāmralipti.—Tāmralipti is the same as Tamluk in the Midnapur district of Bengal, about twelve miles from the junction of the Rūpnārāyaṇa with the Hooghly. It is now situated on the western bank of the Rūpnārāyaṇa formed by the united stream of the Silai (Silāvatī) and Dalkisor (Dvārikeśvarī) in the district of Midnapur. According to the *Raghuvaṃśa* (IV. 38) Tamluk is situated on the bank of the river Kapiśā identified by Pargiter with the Kasai flowing through the district of Midnapur. This ancient city is mentioned in the *Mahābhārata* (Bhīṣmaparva, Ch. 9; Sabhāparva, Ch. 29, 1094–1100), according to which Tāmralipta and Suhma were two distinct countries. It is called Tamalites by Ptolemy. According to the Dudhapani Rock Inscription (*E.I.*, II, pp. 343–45), three brothers went to Tāmralipti from Ayodhyā to trade and they made plenty of money. It was the capital of the ancient kingdom of Sumha in the 6th century of the Christian era, and it formed a part of the Magadhan kingdom under the Mauryas (Smith, *Aśoka*, p. 79). According to Daṇḍin, the author of the *Daśakumāracarita*, who flourished in the 6th century A.D., the temple of Binduvāsinī was situated at Tāmralipti which was visited by the Chinese pilgrims Fa-hien in the 5th century and Hiuen Tsang in the 7th century A.D. This ancient temple was destroyed by the action of the river Rūpnārāyaṇa.

Fa-hien describes Tāmralipti as being situated on the seaside, 50 yojanas east from Campā (Cunningham, *A.G.I.*, ed. S. N. Majumdar, p. 732). In the 7th century A.D. I-tsing resided at Tāmralipti in a celebrated monastery called the Barāha. Traditionally Tāmralipti or Damalipti was the capital of Mayūradhvaja and his son Tāmradhvaja, who fought with Arjuna and Kṛṣṇa. According to the *Kathāsaritsāgara* (Ch. 14), Tāmralipti was a maritime port and an emporium of commerce from the 4th to the 12th century A.D. According to the *Vāyu Purāṇa* the Ganges passes through it. The temple of Bargabhīmā, mentioned in the *Brahma Purāṇa*, which was an ancient Vihāra, still exists at Tāmralipti (Tamluk). The Jaina canonical text *Prajñāpaṇā* refers to Tāmralipti. It is known from the *Mahāvaṃsa* (XI, 38; XIX, 6) that the mission of Aśoka started from this port for Ceylon. Tāmralipti, as known to the Chinese as *Tan-mo-li-ti*, was 14 or 15 hundred li in circuit. The ground was low and rich, which was regularly cultivated. The temperature was hot. The inhabitants were hardy and brave. There were some *saṅghārāmas* and *deva* temples (Beal, *Buddhist Records of the Western World*, II, 200). For further details, vide *Introducing India*, Pt. I, p. 73.

In 1940 excavations were carried out at the ancient site of Tamluk by the Archaeological Department. Among the finds were earthenware vessels of a curious shape and some of them were in good condition. It is difficult to assign a definite date to the specimens discovered at Tamluk but they no doubt bear testimony to the commercial relations between Egypt and the Indian port of Tāmalitti. (J. Ph. Vogel, *Notes on Ptolemy*, *B.S.O.A.S.*, XIV, Pt. I, p. 82).

Tārācaṇḍī.—It is in the vicinity of Sahasrām (Sasaram) in the Shahabad district in South Bihar. An inscription has been discovered on a rock (*E.I.*, V, Appendix, p. 22).

Tetrāvān.—This village lies in the south of Bihar sub-division, 10 miles north-east of Giriyek and six miles south-east of Bihar, containing several mounds, marking the sites of old Buddhist buildings. The monastery here was an important one (*A.S.I. Reports*, Vol. XI ; *J.A.S.B.*, Vol. XLI, 1872).

Tezpur.—It is the chief town of the Darrang district of Assam where the five copperplates of Vallabhadeva were discovered (*E.I.*, V, 181).

Tīrabhukti (Tirhut).—It was bounded on the north by the Himalayas, on the south by the Ganges, on the west by the river Gaṇḍak and on the east by the river Kosi. It comprised the modern districts of Champaran, Muzaffarpur and Darbhanga as well as the strip of Nepal Terai. According to tradition Tīrabhukti means the land in which the three great sacrificial fires were performed (*Devī Purāṇa*, Ch. 64). Cunningham (*A.S.I.*, *Reports*, Vol. XVI) holds that the lands lying in the valleys of the little Gaṇḍak and Bāghmatī rivers were included in the Tīrabhukti (*Darbhanga*, by O'Malley, *Bengal District Gazetteers*, pp. 157-158; *Muzaffarpur*, by O'Malley, *Bengal District Gazetteers*, pp. 159-60).

Tosaḍḍa.—It may be identified with the Tosarā village in the Patna State, E.S.A. Some identify it with Tusdā near Dumarpalli, about 30 miles to the south-east of Arang (*E.I.*, XXIII, Pt. I, 20).

Triśrotā.—The *Kālikā Purāṇa* (Ch. 78, 43; cf. 78, 60) mentions this river, which fulfils the desire of one who bathes in it.

Triveṇī.—It is also known as the Muktaveṇī (*Bṛhat Dharma Purāṇa*, Pūrvakhaṇḍa, Ch. 6). It is 5 miles from the present Bandel Junction station. It is a sacred place of the Hindus, situated at the confluence of the Sarasvatī and the Bhāgīrathī. The site is ancient as it is mentioned in Dhoyī's *Pavanadūta* (v. 33). Kālidāsa refers to this river in his *Raghuvaṃśa* (XIII. 54ff.). The Muslim historians call it Tirpāṇi or Firozabad. During the Muslim period it was an important city and a port. It was once a centre of Sanskrit learning. Mukundarāma, the mediaeval Bengali poet, mentions it as a sacred place. It contains the tomb of Jafar Khan, the conqueror of Saptagrāma, which was built over a Hindu shrine containing some inscribed scenes from the Epics. (*Introducing India*, Pt. I, 75-76).

Udena.—It was a *caitya* or shrine situated to the east of Vaiśālī (*Dīgha*, II, 102-103, 118).

Udumbarapura.—It was a city in the Magadha-Janapada, mentioned in the *Mañjuśrīmūlakalpa* (Gaṇapati Śāstrī's ed., p. 633—*Māgadhaṃ janapadaṃ prāpya pure Udumbarāhvaye*).

Ukkācelā.—It was on the bank of the river Ganges in the Vajji country (*Majjhima Nikāya*, I, pp. 225–27). Not long after the passing away of Buddha's two chief disciples Sāriputta and Moggallāna, the Master dwelt here with a large number of monks (*Saṃyutta Nikāya*, V, p. 163).

Upatissagāma.—This village was not far off from Rājagṛha (*Dhammapada Commentary*, I, 88).

Upyalikā.—This village belonged to Kauśāmbī—Aṣṭagacchakhaṇḍala in the Adhaḥpaṭṭana-maṇḍala of the Paundravardhanabhukti (N. G. Majumdar, *Inscriptions of Bengal*, Vol. III, pp. 15ff.).

Uren.—This village is situated in the Monghyr sub-division, three miles west of Kajra railway station, containing several Buddhistic remains which were first discovered by Col. Waddell. For further details vide Waddell's article, *Discovery of Buddhist remains at Mount Uren in Mungir (Monghyr) district*, *J.A.S.B.*, Pt. I, 1892; *B. and O. Dist. Gazetteers*, *Monghyr*, by O'Malley, pp. 263–67.

Ūrttiviṣaya.—It may be identified with a village called Ūrti in the Keonjhar State, about 12 miles to the north-west of Khiching on the north bank of the river Vaitaraṇī (*E.I.*, XXV, Pt. IV, October, 1939).

Uruvelā (*Uruvilva*).—It was in Magadha. The Bodhisattva after his adoption of ascetic life selected this place as the most fitting for meditation and attainment of enlightenment (*Jāt.*, I, 56). The Buddha, just after his attainment of enlightenment, lived at Uruvelā at the foot of the Ajapāla banyan tree on the bank of the river Nerañjanā (*Saṃ.*, I, 103ff. 122; V.

167, 185). Here he was met by some aged Brahmins and had a discussion with them on the subject of respecting the elders (*Aṅg.*, II. 20ff.). After spending the first lent at Isipatana the Buddha again visited Uruvelā (*Jāt.*, I. 86). On his way to Uruvelā he converted thirty Bhaddavaggiya princes at a grove called Kappāsiya. On reaching Uruvelā he also converted the three Jaṭila brothers together with their followers at Gayāsīsa (*Jāt.*, I, 82; IV. 180). Between this place and Rājagṛha lived two teachers named Ārāḍa Kālāma and Udra Rāmaputra who founded schools for the training of pupils in Yoga (*Majjhima*, I, 163ff.; *Jāt.*, I, 66ff.; *Lalitavistara*, 243ff.; *Mahāvastu*, II. 118; III. 322; *Buddhacarita*, VI, 54; Watters, *On Yuan Chwang*, II. 141). This place was visited by the Buddha where he saw nice trees, pleasing lakes, plain grounds and the clear water of the Nairañjanā river (*Mahāvastu*, II, 123). Uruvela or Uruvelā may be identified with the modern village of Urel near Bodh-Gayā (vide *A.S.I. Annual Report*, 1908-9, pp. 139ff.).

Vadathika.—It is one of the caves in the Nāgārjuni hills, containing inscriptions of Daśaratha.

Vahiyakā.—It is a cave in the Nāgārjuni hills near Gayā (Luders' List No. 954). It contains inscriptions of Daśaratha.

Vaibhāragiri—(Pali Vebhāra; Sans. Vyavahāra).—It is in Magadha. It is one of the five hills encircling the ancient city of Girivraja, 'a hill-girt city' (cf. *Vimānavatthu Commentary*, p. 82). It extends southwards and westwards ultimately to form the western entrance of Rājgir with the Soṇagiri. In the Jaina *Vividhatīrthakalpa* the Vaibhāragiri is described as a sacred hill affording possibility of the formation of kuṇḍas of tepid and cold water (*taptaśitāmbukuṇḍam*). Buddhaghosa associates the hot springs giving rise to the Tapodā river with Mount Vebhāra. It is the same mountain as Vaihāra described in the *Mahābhārata* as a *Vipulaśaila* or massive rock. The city of Rājagṛha shone forth in the valley of Vaibhāragiri with Trikūṭa, Khaṇḍika and the rest as its bright peaks. Some dark caves existed in this hill. Close to this hill were the Sarasvatī and many other streams flowing with pleasant waters with properties to heal diseases. The Buddhists built *Vihāras* on this hill, and the Jainas installed the images of the elect in the shrines built upon it. The Vebhāra and the Pāṇḍava appear to have been the two hills that stood on the north side of Girivraja and were noted for their rocky caves (*Theragāthā*, XLI, v. 1). The Vaibhrāj is undoubtedly the Vaibhāragiri of Rajagṛha.

The Jains relying on a much later tradition thus locate the seven hills encircling Rājagṛha: If one enters Rājgir from the north, the hill lying to the right is the Vaibhāragiri; that lying to the left is the Vipulagiri; the one standing at right angles to the Vipula and running southwards parallel to the Vaibhāra is the Ratnagiri; the one forming the eastern extension of Ratnagiri is the Chaṭhāgiri and the hill standing next to the Chaṭhāgiri is the Śailagiri. The one opposite to the Chaṭhāgiri is the Udayagiri; that lying to the south of Ratnagiri and the west of the Udayagiri is the Soṇagiri. (Law, *Rājagṛha in Ancient Lit.*, *M.A.S.I.*, No. 68, p. 3.)

Vaiśālī.—Vaiśālī the large city, was the capital of the Licchavis who were a great and powerful people in Eastern India in the 6th century B.C. It is renowned in Indian history as the capital of the Licchavi rājās and the headquarters of the great and powerful Vajjian confederacy. This great city has been identified by Cunningham with the present village of Basarh in the Muzaffarpur district, in Tirhut, as marking the spot where stood Vaiśālī in ancient days (*Arch. Surv. Report*, Vol. I, pp. 55-56 and Vol. XVI, p. 6). Vivien de Saint Martin has agreed with him. The evidence adduced by Cunningham to arrive at this conclusion was not put forward with much fulness and clearness. Rhys Davids says that the site of Vaiśālī is still to be looked for somewhere in Tirhut (*Buddhist India*, p. 41). Dr. W. Hoey seeks to establish the identity of Vaiśālī with Cherand in the Chapra or Saran district (*J.A.S.B.*, 1900, Vol. LXIX, Pt. I, pp. 78–80, 83). This identification has been proved to be entirely untenable by V. A. Smith in his paper on Vaiśālī (*J.R.A.S.*, 1902, p. 267, n. 3). He has succeeded in establishing that the identification by Cunningham of the village of Basarh with Vaiśālī admits of no doubt. This identity has been proved still more decisively by the Archaeological excavations carried out at the site by Dr. T. Bloch in 1903-4. Bloch excavated a mound called Rājā Viśāl kā gaṛh and only eight trial pits were sunk. Three distinct strata have been found out, the uppermost belonging to the period of Mahomedan occupation of the place, the second at a depth of about 5 ft. from the surface relating to the epoch of the Imperial Guptas, and the third at a still greater depth belonging to an ancient period of no definite date (*A.S.I. Annual Report*, 1903-4, p. 74). The finds in the second stratum are valuable, especially the find in one of the small chambers of a hoard of seven hundred clay seals, evidently used as attachment to letters or other literary documents. They belonged partly to officials, partly to private persons, generally merchants or bankers, but one specimen bearing the figure of *liṅga* with a *triśūla* on either side and the legend Āmrātakeśvara evidently belonged to a temple (*A.S.I. Annual Report*, 1903-4, p. 74).

The names of some Gupta kings, queens and princes on some of these seals coupled with palaeographic evidence clearly demonstrate that they belonged to the 4th and 5th centuries A.D., when the Imperial Guptas were on the throne (*Ibid.*, p. 110). Some of the impressions show that the name Tīrabhukti was applied to the province even in those early times and some show the name of the town itself, Vaiśālī. One of the clay seals of a circular area shows a female standing in a flower group with two attendants and two horizontal lines below reading '(Seal) of the householders of . . . . at Vaiśālī' (*Ibid.*, p. 110). All these go to prove the identity of the site with Vaiśālī and there seems to be no ground to question this conclusion any longer. It is a great pity that further excavations at this site have been given up by the Archaeological Department for want of funds.

Vaiśālī owes its name to its being Viśāla or very large and wide in area. According to the *Rāmāyaṇa* (Ch. 47, vv. 11, 12) it was founded by a son of Ikṣvāku and a heavenly nymph Alambuṣā; after his name Viśāla, the city itself came to be called Viśālā. The *Viṣṇu Purāṇa* (Wilson, Vol. III, p. 246) states that Triṇabindu had by Alambuṣā a son named Viśāla who founded this city.

Vaiśālī was visited by the Chinese pilgrim Fa-hien in the 5th century A.D. According to him there was a large forest to its north, having in it the double-galleried Vihāra where the Buddha dwelt and the tope over half the body of Ānanda (Legge, *Fa-hien*, p. 72). Another Chinese pilgrim Hiuen Tsang who visited it in the 7th century A.D., relates that the foundations of the old city Vaiśālī were 60 or 70 li in circuit and the 'palace city' was 4 or 5 li in circuit (Watters, *On Yuan Chwang*, Vol. II, p. 63). This city was above 5,000 li in circuit, a very fertile region abounding in mangoes, plantains and other fruits. The people were honest, fond of good works, and esteemers of learning. They were orthodox and heterodox in faith (*Ibid.*, II, p. 63). According to the Tibetan account (*Dulva*, III, f. 80) there were three districts in Vaiśālī. In the first district there were 7,000 houses with golden towers; in the middle district there were 14,000 houses with silver towers; and in the last district there were 21,000 houses with copper towers; in these lived the upper, the middle and the lower classes according to their positions (Rockhill, *Life of the Buddha*, p. 62). In the Buddha's time this city was encompassed by three walls at a distance of a *gāvuta* from one another and that at three places there were gates with watch-towers and buildings (*Jātaka*, I, p. 504).

Vaiśālī was an opulent, prosperous town, populous, abundant with food; there were many high buildings, pinnacled buildings, pleasure-gardens and lotus ponds (*Vinaya Texts, S.B.E.*, Pt. II, p. 171; cf. *Lalitavistara*, ed. Lefmann, Ch. III, p. 21). This great city is intimately associated with the early history of both Jainism and Buddhism. It carries with itself the sacred memories of the founders of the two great faiths that evolved in north-eastern India five-hundred years before Christ.

Vaiśālī claims Mahāvīra, the founder of Jainism, as its own citizen. He was therefore called Vesālie or Vaiśālika, i.e., an inhabitant of Vaiśālī (*Jaina Sūtras, S.B.E.*, Pt. I, Intro. xi). Kuṇḍagrāma, a suburb of Vaiśālī, was really his birthplace (*Ibid.*, XXII, pp. x-xi). During his ascetic life he did not neglect his place of birth and spent no less than twelve rainy seasons at Vaiśālī (Jacobi, *Jaina Sūtras*, Pt. I, *Kalpasūtra*, sec. 122).

The connection of the Buddha with Vaiśālī is no less close and intimate. This city was hallowed by the dust of his feet early in his career and many of his immortal discourses were delivered here (*Aṅguttara*, P.T.S., II, 190–94; 200–02; *Saṃyutta*, V, 389-90; *Aṅguttara*, III, 75–78; 167-68; V. 133; *Therīgāthā*, V. 270; *Majjhima*, I, 227–37).

After the Buddha entered into *Nirvāṇa*, Vaiśālī drew to itself the care and attention of the whole Buddhist Church. The representatives of the entire congregation met here and condemned the conduct of its pleasure-seeking monks. This was the second general council of the Buddhist Church (Kern, *Manual of Indian Buddhism*, pp. 103–09). For further details concerning *Vaiśālī* vide Law, *Some Kṣatriya Tribes of Ancient India*, Ch. 1; Law, *Ancient Indian Tribes*, pp. 294ff.; Law, *Indological Studies*, Pt. III.

Vaitaraṇī.—It is one of the sacred rivers of India which rises in the hills in the southern part of the district of Singhbhum, and a little below the point where it enters Orissa (for details, Law, *Rivers of India*, p. 43).

Vakkataka.—It seems to be the modern Baktā, a place immediately to the east of Gohagrām on the Damodar river, Burdwan division, Bengal. The Vakkatakavithī representing a part of Vardhamānabhukti included a strip of the country along the north bank of the Damodar river (*E.I.*, XXIII, Pt. V, p. 158).

Vaṃka.—It was a mountain near Rājagṛha. Its older name was Vepulla (see *Annals of the Bhandarkar Oriental Research Institute*, VIII, 164; cf. *Saṃyutta*, II, 191-92). It is mentioned in the *Jātaka* (VI, 491, 513, 520, 524-25, 580, 592).

Vaṃśavāṭī.—It is in the district of Hooghly where there is an ancient temple of Haṃseśvarī. The Vāsudeva temple with Pauranic scenes on its walls is also ancient (Law, *Rivers of India*, p. 44).

Vaṅga.—It is the ancient name of Bengal (vide *Prakrit Inscriptions from a Buddhist site at Nāgārjunikoṇḍa*). Vaṅga which is the designation of Bengal proper is mentioned in the *Aitareya Āraṇyaka* (II, 1, 1, 1; cf. Keith, *Aitareya Āraṇyaka*, 200) as well as in the *Baudhāyana Dharmasūtra* (I, 1, 14). Pāṇini refers to it as Vaṅga in his *Aṣṭādhyāyī* (4, 1, 170). The *Bhāgavata Purāṇa* (IX. 23, 5) and the *Kāvyamīmāṃsā* (Ch. 3) mention it as a country. The *Yoginītantra* mentions Vaṅga (2. 2. 119). In the Tirumalai Rock Inscription of Rājendra Coḷa of the 11th century A.D. and in the Goharwa Plate of Cedi Karṇadeva, Vaṅga country is referred to as *Vaṅgāladeśaṃ*, which in the thirteenth century came to be called Baṅgāla and in Mahommedan times, Bāṅglā. The Tirumalai Inscription distinguishes Vaṅga not only from South Rāḍhā (Takkana Lāḍhaṃ) but also from North Rāḍhā (Uttila Lāḍham). This is the very location of the kingdom of Vaṅga indicated in the Ceylon Chronicle that places Lāḷha between Vaṅga and Kaliṅga. The first epigraphic mention of the Vaṅga countries is probably made in the Meharauli Iron Pillar Inscription (*C.I.I.*, Vol. III, pp. 141ff.), where the mighty king Candra is said to have 'in battle in the Vaṅga country turned back with his breast the enemies who uniting together came against him and by whom having crossed in warfare the seven mouths of the Indus the Vālhīkas were conquered'. H. P. Śāstrī identifies the mighty king Candra with king Candravarman of the Allahabad Pillar Inscription and the king of the same name of Pokhrāṇā which he locates in Marwar in Rajputana. The Vaṅga countries are also referred to in the Mahākūṭa Pillar Inscription (*E.I.*, Vol. V) which tells us that in the sixth century A.D. Kīrtivarman of the Cālukya dynasty gained victories over the kings of Vaṅga, Aṅga and Magadha, that is, three Kaliṅgas (*Trikaliṅga*). In the Pithapuram plates of Prithvīsena (A.D. 1108) the king of the Vaṅgadeśa was subdued by king Malla. Vaṅgadeśa is also referred to in the Copperplate grant of Vaidyadeva of Kāmarūpa, who was victorious in southern Vaṅga (*E.I.*, Vol. II, p. 335), and also in the Edilpur Plate of Keśavasena, the Madanapāḍā Plate of Viśvarūpasena and the Sāhitya Parisat Plate of the same king (*Inscriptions of Bengal*, Vol. III, pp. 119, 133, 141). The Rāmpāl Plate of Śrīcandradeva (*E.I.*, Vol. XII, p. 136) informs us that a Candra dynasty appears to have mastered the whole of Vaṅga including Samataṭa. The kings of Vaṅga, Pāṇḍya, Lāṭa, Gurjara, and Kāśmīra were conquered by Lakṣmaṇarāja, according to the Goharwa grant of Lakṣmīkarṇa (*E.I.*, XI, 142). For literary references vide B. C. Law, *Tribes in Ancient India*, Ch. LI.

From the Bheraghat Inscription of Alhaṇadevī we learn that the victory of the Cālukya king Karṇa, son and successor of Gāṅgeyadeva, seems to have been obtained over the king of Vaṅga or East Bengal (*E.I.*, XXIV, Pt. III, July, 1937).

An attempt has recently been made on the evidence of the Belāva copperplate of king Bhojavarman of the Vaiṣṇava Varman dynasty of East Bengal that Tilokasundarī, the second queen of Vijayabāhu I, mentioned in the *Cūḷavaṃsa*, is no other than Trailokyasundarī, praised in the Belāva Plate as the daughter of king Sāmalavarman, the father and immediate predecessor of Bhojavarman.

It is rightly pointed out that in the Belāva copperplate the Varmans of East Bengal claim to have their descent from the royal family of Siṃhapura, and Bhojavarman expresses in pathetic terms his solicitude for the contemporary Ceylon King in his difficulties arising from an inimical action on the part of the *rākṣasas*. Once the personal relationship between Bhojavarman and Vijayabāhu I is assumed as a historical fact, it becomes easy to understand why the former should express this solicitude for the lord of Laṅkā. The possibility of matrimonial connection of the Ceylon king Vijayabāhu I with the Varmans of East Bengal lies in the fact that Vijayabāhu and his successors themselves felt proud in claiming their descent from the royal family of Siṃhapura which was most probably a place in Kaliṅga (*J.R.A.S.*, 1913, p. 518; *D. R. Bhandarkar Volume*, p. 375).

According to a copperplate grant of Viśvarūpasena Nāvya was a part of Vaṅga (*Vaṅga Nāvye*).

Northern Bengal was invaded by an army of a Vaṅgāla king in course of which the Buddhist teacher Karuṇāśrīmitra's house at Somapura Vihāra (modern Pāhāḍpura) was set on fire and he was burnt to death (*E.I.*, XXI, 97-131). According to the Nālandā Inscription of Vipulaśrīmitra (dated about the middle of the 12th century A.D.) Karuṇāśrīmitra was removed by two generations of teachers from Vipulaśrīmitra.

Vaṅgāla.—It is probably East Bengal mentioned in Tirumalai Inscription of Rājendra Coḷa I as well as in the Buddhist Sanskrit text entitled the *Ḍākārṇava* (*E.I.*, XXI, Pt. III). (Vide also *Vaṅga*).

Vardhamānabhukti.—The Mallasārul copperplate inscription refers to Vardhamānabhukti, and it also records a gift of land to a Brahmin for performing five great sacrifices. This inscription was found in a village near Galsi in the Burdwan district, Bengal. Vardhamānabhukti as mentioned in the Naihati copperplate seems to have extended at least as far as the western bank of the Ganges near Calcutta. The Chittagong plates of Kāntideva of the 9th century A.D. mention Vardhamānapura. The Irda Copperplate Grant of king Nayapāladeva, which records the grant to a Brahmin of some land in the Daṇḍabhūtimaṇḍala of the Vardhamānabhukti, was issued from the capital of Priyaṅgu, founded by king Rājyapāla. The bhukti of Vardhamāna is in Uttara-Rāḍha, and the capital of Priyaṅgu is in Dakṣiṇa-Rāḍha in Bengal (*E.I.*, XXIV, Pt. I, January, 1937). Vardhamāna or Vardhamānabhukti is identical with modern Burdwan.

Vaṭumbī.—It forms part of the āvritti Vāścaśa situated in the Pauṇḍravardhanabhukti (*E.I.*, XXVI, Pt. I).

Vāllahiṭṭha.—Name of a donated village which was situated in the Svalapadakṣiṇavithī belonging to the Uttara-Rāḍhāmaṇḍala of the Vardhamānabhukti. This is identified with the present Bāluṭiyā, about six miles to the west of Naihati on the northern boundary of the Burdwan district (N. G. Majumdar, *Inscriptions of Bengal*, Vol. III—*Naihāti Copperplate of Ballālasena*, pp. 69ff.).

Vālukārāma.—The Second Buddhist Council was held in the Vālukārāma at Vesālī during the reign of Kālāsoka (*Samantapāsādikā*, pp. 33-34).

Vāṇiyagāma.—It is identified with Baniya, a village near Basarh in Muzaffarpur. It was frequently visited by Mahāvīra (*Āvaśyaka Niryukti*, 496).

Vārahakonā.—Vārahakonā is the modern Barkund in Suri about half a mile north of the Mor and 1¼ miles from Sainthia railway station (*Śaktipur Copperplate of Lakṣmaṇasena*, *E.I.*, XXI, p. 124).

Vārakamaṇḍalaviṣaya.—The Faridpur Copperplate Inscription of King Dharmāditya refers to Vārakamaṇḍalaviṣaya, which is the modern Goalando and Gopalganj sub-division of the Faridpur district, Bengal.

Vātasvana.—It is a hill which has been identified with Bathan in South Bihar (*A.S.R.*, VIII, 46).

Vebhāra.—This hill is in the Magadha country. It is one of the five hills encircling Girivraja (*Vimānavatthu Commentary*, p. 82). Vide *Vaibhāragiri*.

Vedathikā.—It is a cave in the Nagarjuni hills near Gayā (Luders' List No. 956).

Vediyaka.—This hill is identified by Cunningham with the Giriyek. It contains the famous cave called Indasālaguhā (*Dīgha*, II, 263; *Sumaṅgala*-

vilāsinī, III, 697; B. C. Law, *India as described in the Early Texts of Buddhism and Jainism*, p. 29).

Veluvana (= Veṇuvana).—It was a charming grove at Rājagṛha, which was surrounded by bamboos (*Samyutta*, I. 52; *Suttanipāta Commy.*, p. 419; *Divyāvadāna*, pp. 143, 554). It was protected by a wall 18 cubits high and adorned with beautiful gates and towers decorated with *lapis lazuli* (*Samantapāsādikā*, III, 575). The fuller name of the site was Veluvana-Kalandakanivāpa, the second part of the name indicating that here the squirrels freely roamed about and found a nice feeding ground.[1] The site was outside the inner city of Rājagṛha and neither very near nor far from it. The Chinese pilgrims have given different locations of the grove. But combining the two accounts given by Fa-hien and Hiuen Tsang it may be located at a distance of 1 li from the north gate of the inner city, ½ mile south of the cemetery (*śmaśāna*), 300 paces north-east of the Pippala cave in Mount Vaibhāra and 200 paces to the south of the Kalanda tank.

Vepulla.—It is a mountain in Magadha. It was known in a very remote age by the name of Pācīnavaṃsa, which was later changed to Vaṅkaka. It then received the name of Supassa, and afterwards it became known as Vepulla (*Sam.*, II, 190ff.) and the people of the locality by the name of Magadhas. (Cf. B. C. Law, *India as described in the Early Texts of Buddhism and Jainism*, pp. 29-30). It was one of the five hills encircling Rājagṛha. King Vessantara was banished to this hill. It took him three days to reach its summit (*Vinaya Piṭaka*, II, 191-92). The Vipula mountain runs for some length towards the south-east leading to the northern range of hills extending up to the village called Giriyek on the Behar-sharif-Nawadah road. Hiuen Tsang has definitely represented the mountain as *Pi-pu-lo*, which verbally equates with Vipula. He tells us that to the west of the north gate of the mountain-city was the Vipula mountain. He further points out that on the north side of the south-west declivity there had once been five hundred hot springs of which there remained at his time several, some cold and some tepid. The source of the streams was the Anavatapta Lake. The water was clear and the people used to come from various lands to bathe in the water which was beneficial to the people suffering from old maladies. On the Vipula mountain there was a tope where the Buddha once preached. This mountain is frequently visited by Digambara Jains (Watters, *On Yuan Chwang*, II, pp. 153-154). The Vipula mountain is described as the best among the mountains of Rājagṛha (*Saṃyutta*, I, 67). It lay to the north of the Gijjhakūṭa and stood in the midst of the girdle of the Magadhan hills.

Veṭhadīpa.—Hiuen Tsang locates the site of Droṇastūpa, that is Veṭhadīpa, 100 li south-east of Mahāsāra identified with Masār a village six miles to the west of Arrah. Some have identified it with Kasia (*A.G.I.*, 1924, 714) and with Bettiah in the Champaran district of Behar (*J.R.A.S.*, 1906, 900). Veṭhadīpa which was the home of the Brahmin Droṇa, lay not far from Allakappa (B. C. Law, *Geography of Early Buddhism*, p. 25).

Vettragarttā.—It appears to have been situated within Vakkatto-kavithi representing a part of the Vardhamānabhukti (modern Burdwan division, Bengal; *E.I.*, XXIII, Pt. V).

Viḍḍāraśāsana.—It was a village having the Ganges as its eastern boundary. It may be identified with modern Betaḍ in the Howrah district.

Vikramapura.—It lies in the Munshiganj sub-division of Dacca. A portion of it is included in the Faridpur district. The name Vikramapura

1 *Samantapāsādikā*, III, 575; *Papañcasūdanī*, II, p. 134.

is generally applied to the tract of country bounded by the Dhaleśvarī on the north, the Idilpur Pargana on the south, the Meghnā on the east and the Padmā on the west. The name of this place is derived from a king named Vikrama who ruled it for some time. Rāmapāla, the ancient capital of Vikramapura, lay three miles west of Munshiganj. The name Śrīvikramapura occurs in the Sītāhāṭi copperplate inscription of Ballālasena. A copperplate inscription of Śrī Candradeva of the Candra dynasty has been discovered here. Rāmapāla, the birthplace of Śilabhadra, the principal of the famous Buddhist University of Nālandā, was the eastern headquarters of the Hindu kings of Bengal for some time. The ruins of Ballālabāḍi, many ancient ponds, and many Hindu and Buddhist deities of the Pala period have been found here. The village of Vajrayoginī lying on the south-west corner of Rāmapāla, was the birthplace of the famous Buddhist savant of the 10th century A.D. named Dīpaṅkara Śrījñāna. The Kedārpur copperplate of Śrīcandra, the Edilpur copperplate of Keśavasena, the Barrackpur copperplate of Vijayasena, the Anuliā copperplate of Lakṣmaṇasena, and the Belāva copperplate of Bhojavarman refer to Vikramapura which is still known by the same name. The Varmans ruled over it only for a short period. From the Barrackpur copperplate of Vijayasena it appears that Vikramapura was probably one of the capitals of Vijayasena who had something like a permanent residence here. Almost all the grants of the Sena kings were issued from Vikramapura (N. G. Majumdar, *Inscriptions of Bengal*, Vol. III, pp. 10ff., 60ff.; *Introducing India*, Pt. I, pp. 81-82.

Vikramaśilā.—This village lies in the Bihar sub-division, 10 miles south of Bihar. It was famous for its Buddhist monastery which was a great seat of learning in the 11th century A.D. This monastery appears to have flourished till the Mahommedan conquest when it was burnt by the invaders. The modern name of the village is Śilao which is a contraction of Vikramaśilā (*A.S.I. Reports*, Vol. VIII; *J.A.S.B.*, Vol. LX, Pt. I, 1891). The Vikramaśilā Vihāra was a Buddhist monastery situated on a bluff on the right bank of the Ganges. It had ample space for a congregation of 8,000 men with many temples and buildings. On the top of the projecting steep hill of Pātharghāṭā there are the remains of a Buddhist monastery. This Pātharghāṭā was the ancient Vikramaśilā (*J.A.S.B.* new series, Vol. V, No. 1, pp. 1–13). In this University many commentaries were composed. It was a centre of Tantrik learning. At the head of the University there was always a most learned and pious sage. Grammar, metaphysics (including logic) and ritualistic books were especially studied here. On the walls of the University were painted images of learned men, eminent for their learning and character. The most learned sages were appointed to guard the gates of the University which were six in number (B. C. Law, *The Magadhas in Ancient India*, pp. 43-44).

Vinjhāṭavi.—It was a forest without any human habitation. It represented the forest through which lay the way from Pāṭaliputra to Tāmralipti (*Mahāv.*, XIX, 6; *Dīp.*, XVI, 2; *Samantapāsādikā*, III, 655).

Viṣṇupura.—It is in the Bankura district of West Bengal. It is named after Viṣṇu, the deity of the royal family. For a long time it had been the capital of the Mallarājās, who gave the name of Mallabhūmi (the land of wrestlers) to the country ruled by them. The Mallabhūmi comprised the whole of the modern district of Bankura and parts of the adjoining districts of Burdwan, Midnapur, Manbhum and Singhbhum. Ādimalla, who was the first Malla king, was noted for his great skill in wrestling and archery. Raghunātha was the founder of the Malla dynasty of

Viṣṇupura. He defeated the neighbouring chiefs of Pradyumnapura in the Joypore police station which he made his seat of government. The royal ensign of the rulers of Mallabhūmi bore the device of a serpent's hood. The Hindu *rājās* of Viṣṇupura were the rulers of a great portion of Western Bengal long before the Mahommedan conquest by Bakhtiyar Khilji. Jagatamalla, a ruler of Viṣṇupura, shifted the capital from Pradyumnapura to Viṣṇupura. The *rājās* of Viṣṇupura were Śiva worshippers. The temple of Malleśvara-mahādeva is the oldest of the shrines found here. The *rājās* afterwards became ardent worshippers of Mṛṇmayī, an aspect of Śakti, whose temple still stands there. The worship of *Dharma* introduced by Ramāi Paṇḍita became very popular here. The celebrated Bengali mathematician Subhaṅkara Rāya lived under the Malla kings of Viṣṇupura. The temples of Viṣṇupura are mostly square buildings with a curved roof, having a small tower in the centre. Some of them have towers in four corners of the roof. Some temples contain scenes from the *Rāmāyaṇa* and the *Mahābhārata* on their walls. The Śyāma Rāi temple is one of the oldest temples of Pañcaratna (five-towered) type in Bengal. In the 16th century A.D., the magnificent temple of *Rāsamañca* was built by Bīr Hamir to whom may be attributed the big stone gateway of the Viṣṇupura fort and the great cannon called Dalmardan (*Introducing India*, Pt. I, pp. 71-72).

The Dalmardan cannon was lying half-buried by the side of the Lalbundh lake and was mounted and preserved under the *Ancient Monuments Preservation Act*. It is made of sixty-three hoops or short cylinders of wrought iron welded together and overlying another cylinder also of wrought iron. Though exposed to all weathers, it is still free from rust, and it has a black polished surface. Its length is twelve feet and five and a half inches, the diameter of the bore being eleven and a half inches at the muzzle. It is the same cannon which was fired by Madanmohana when Bhāskar Paṇḍita attacked Viṣṇupura at the head of the Mahrattas. It bears a Persian inscription. A couple of cannons still lie on the high rampart just outside the front gate.

The fort of Viṣṇupura is surrounded by a high earthen wall and has a broad moat round it. The approach is through a fine large gateway built of laterite with arrowslits on either side of the entrance for archers and musketmen.

In the vicinity of the town and within the old fortifications there are seven beautiful lakes which were made by the ancient rulers who, taking advantage of the natural hollows, built embankments across them. They served the city and the fort with a constant supply of fresh water. These lakes have now silted up and a considerable portion of them has been turned into paddy fields.

The rampart to the north of the stone gate, better known as the *Murchapāhār*, the silent spectator of many historic events, has always been a favourite haunting place of thoughtful minds. Standing there one has his mind filled with sadness looking at the panorama of historic scenes on all sides, when the sun slowly fades behind the Mahārāṣṭradāṅga to the west. A pall of darkness has now fallen over this historic city and its ruins (J. N. Mitra, *The Ruins of Viṣṇupura*, pp. 13–16).

Viśvāmitra-āśrama.—It was situated at Buxar in the district of Sahabad in Bihar. Rāmacandra is said to have killed here the female demon named Tāḍakā. (Cf. *Rāmāyaṇa*, Bālakāṇḍa, Ch. 26).

Vyāghrataṭi.—This is identified with Bāgḍī, one of the four traditional divisions of Bengal. Bāgḍī comprises the delta of the Ganges and the

Brahmaputra (Cunningham, *A.S.R.*, XV, pp. 145-46). For further details, vide *Paundravardhana*.

Yaṣṭivana (Stick or staff wood).—Grierson has identified it with Jethian, about two miles north of Tapovana near Supa-tīrtha in the district of Gayā (*Notes on the District of Gayā*, p. 49). It was situated some 12 miles from Rājagṛha. It was a palm grove according to Buddhaghosa (*Samantapāsādikā*, Sinhalese ed., p. 158). It was the name of the royal park of Bimbisāra where the Buddha arrived from Gayāsīsa and halted with the Jaṭila converts on his way to the city of Rājagṛha (*Vinaya-Mahāvagga*, I, p. 35; Fausböll, *Jātaka*, I, 83). This palm grove which was situated in the outskirts of the city of Rājagṛha was considered far away as compared with Veṇuvana (*Jātaka*, I, 85). It was famous in the Buddha's time for a Banyan shrine called Supatiṭṭha Cetiya (*Samantapāsādikā*, Sinhalese ed., p. 158). The site undoubtedly lay to the west of Rājagṛha. The *Mahāvastu* locates it in the interior of a hill (*antagirismin*—III, 441). Hiuen Tsang describes Yaṣṭivana as a dense forest of bamboos which covered a mountain, and points out that above 10 li (nearly two miles) to the south-west of it there were two hot springs (Watters, *On Yuan Chwang*, II, 146). For further details, vide B. C. Law, *Rājagṛha in Ancient Literature*, *M.A.S.I.*, No. 58, pp. 16–18, 25, 39, 40.

Yatodbhava.—This river is also known as Yatodā, which is a tributary of the Brahmaputra, flowing through the districts of Jalpaiguri and Cooch Behar (cf. *Kālikā Purāṇa*, Ch. 77).

Chapter IV

WESTERN INDIA

Ablūr.—It is a village about two miles west of Koḍ, the chief town of the Koḍ taluk in the Dharwar district of the Bombay State. Its name occurs in ancient records in a fuller form as Abbalūr (*E.I.*, V, 213ff.).

Adrijā.—This river is mentioned in the *Mahābhārata* (Anuśāsanaparva, CLXV, 7648). It issues from the Ṛkṣa and the Vindhya mountains.

Agastya-āśrama.—This hermitage was situated at Akolha to the east of Nasik (*Rāmāyaṇa*, Āraṇyakāṇḍa, Ch. 11; *Mahābhārata*, Ch. 96. 1-3; cf. *Padma Purāṇa*, Ch. 6, śl. 5). It is stated in the *Rāmāyaṇa* (Āraṇyakāṇḍa, 11 sarga, verses 40-41) that this hermitage was situated on the south side of his brother's hermitage, at a distance of one mile from the latter. The *Yoginītantra* (2. 7. 8) has a reference to this hermitage. Some hold that at a distance of twenty-four miles to the south-east of Nasik at Agastipurī there existed the hermitage of the sage Agastya. Some think that this hermitage was situated on the summit of the Malaya range or Malayakūṭa which was also known as Śrikhaṇḍādri or even as Candanādri (Ch. Dhoyī's *Pavanadūtam*). It was visited by Balarāma. Manu performed austerities here (*Bhāgavata*, VI. 3. 35; X. 79. 16; *Matsya*, I. 12). Agastya, who was the famous author of the *Agastyasaṃhitā*, introduced Aryan civilization into South India. This hermitage was rendered impregnable to all kinds of trouble, as the mighty sage killed the demons by his spiritual prowess. He was met by Rāma, Lakṣmaṇa and Sītā while he was engaged in offering oblations. The sage welcomed them and gave Rāma his divine bow, arrow and other weapons. At a distance of about seven miles from this hermitage lay the Pañcavaṭī forest.

Alandatīrtha.—This may be identified with the modern Ālundah, five miles north-east of Bhor, the chief town of the Bhor State, and about thirty-five miles north of Satara (*I.A.*, XX, 304).

Alinā.—The Alinā Copperplate Inscription of Śilāditya VII (the year 447) refers to this village situated about fourteen miles north-east of Nadiād, the chief town of the Nadiād taluk in Gujarat (*C.I.I.*, III).

Amalakaṭaka.—It is Amod, 12 miles to the south-west of Āmti (*Important Inscriptions from the Baroda State*, Vol. I, p. 20).

Ambarnāth.—This place contains a beautiful temple which is a fine specimen of genuine Hindu architecture dated the 9th century A.D. It is near Kalyan (Law, *Holy Places of India*, p. 42).

Ambāpāṭaka.—It is the same as Āmaḍpur, situated on the Pūravī or Pūrṇā and about five miles from Nausāri. This village was some centuries ago called Āmrapura (*E.I.*, XXI, July, 1931).

Amreli.—It is the headquarters of a district of this name belonging to the Baroda State in the south of Kathiawar. Its antiquity is proved by the Amreli plates of Kharagraha I (*Important Inscriptions from the Baroda State*, Vol. I, p. 7).

Aṇastu.—This village stands about two and half miles to the north-west of Karjan, the headquarters of the taluk of this name in the Baroda district where two copperplate grants were discovered (*Important Inscriptions from the Baroda State*, Vol. I, p. 16).

Añjaneri.—It is a village in the headquarters taluk of the Nasik district, where grants of Pṛthivīcandra Bhogaśakti were discovered (*E.I.* XXV, Pt. V, January, 1940, p. 225).

Antikā.—It may be identified with the modern Āmti in the Pādrā taluk of the Baroda district (*Important Inscriptions from the Baroda State*, Vol. I, p. 20).

Anūpanivrit.—Anūpa country (Luders' List, No. 965). The country of the Anūpas lay near Surāṣṭra and Ānarta. Epigraphic evidence lends support to the view that the Anūpas occupied the tract of country south of Surāṣṭra around Māhiṣmatī on the Narmadā. The Nasik Cave Inscription of queen Gautamī Balaśrī records that Anūpa was conquered by her son along with other countries. The Junāgaḍh Rock Inscription of Rudradāman refers to his sway extended over this country. For details, vide B. C. Law, *Tribes in Ancient India*, p. 389; B. C. Law, *Indological Studies*, Pt. I, pp. 53-54.

Asika.—It appears to correspond with Arsak or the Arsacidae the name of the well-known Parthian ruler of Persia. It is mentioned in the Nasik Inscription that Gautamīputra is said to have ruled over it (*Nasik, the Gazetteer of the Bombay Presidency*, 1883, Vol. XVI).

Asitamasā.—It is referred to in the Barhut Inscriptions (Barua and Sinha, p. 32). Cunningham locates it somewhere on the bank of the Tamasā or Ton river. The *Vāmana Purāṇa* mentions Asinīla and Tāmasa among the countries of western India.

Ayyapolil.—It is the Tamil name of Ayyavoḷe, which is identical with Aihole in the Hungund taluk of the Bijapur district, Bombay Presidency. It was famous as the headquarters of a very prosperous trading corporation (*E.I.*, XXIII, Pt. VII).

Ābhīra-deśa.—The Abiria or Ābhīra country was ruled over by the western Kṣatrapas or Śaka rulers of western India, who seem to have held sway over the entire realm of Indo-Scythia of Greek geographer Ptolemy (cf. *E.I.*, VIII, pp. 36ff.). According to the Guṇḍa Inscription of the Śaka king Rudrasiṃha (A.D. 181) a tank was excavated by Rudrabhūti, an Ābhīra general, in his realm. Shortly afterwards (188–90 A.D. according to Bhandarkar; after 236 A.D. according to Rapson) a native of Ābhīra named Īśvaradatta held the office of Mahākṣatrapa. He was probably identical with the Ābhīra king named Īśvarasena, who became Mahākṣatrapa of western India and captured portions of Mahārāṣṭra in the 3rd century A.D. from the Sātavāhana rulers. It is suggested that the dynasty of Īśvarasena was identical with the Traikūṭaka line of Aparānta, and the establishment of the Traikūṭaka era commencing from 248 A.D., marks the time when the Ābhīras succeeded the Sātavāhanas in the government of northern Mahārāṣṭra and the adjoining region (cf. Raychaudhuri, *Political History of Northern India*, 4th ed., p. 418, f.n. 2). The Ābhīra country is also mentioned in the Allahabad Iron Pillar Inscription of Samudragupta as one of the tribal states of western and south-western India, who paid homage to the great Gupta Emperor and who were a semi-independent people living outside the borders of his empire (For a complete history, vide Law, *Tribes in Ancient India*, p. 81; *E.I.*, X, pp. 99 and 127). Some have located them in the province of Ahirwādā between the Pārvatī and the Betwa in Central India. The Ābhīras, who were associated with Śūdras, most likely identified with the Sodrai or Sogdoi of the Greek historians of Alexander's time, are placed, according to the *Viṣṇu Purāṇa* (Wilson, II, Ch. III, pp. 132–5), in the extreme west along with the Surāṣṭras, Śūdras, Arbudas, Kārūṣas and Mālavas dwelling along the Pāripātra mountains. The *Mārkaṇḍeya Purāṇa* (Ch. 57, vv. 35-36) groups them with the Vāhlīkas, Vāṭadhānas, Śūdras, Madrakas, Surāṣṭras and Sindhu-Sauvīras, all of whom occupied the countries included in the Aparāntaka (Western India). Pargiter points out that the Ābhīras had something to do with the events following the great Bhārata war. The Yādavas of Gujarat were attacked and broken up by the rude Ābhīras (*A.I.H.T.*, p. 284). According to the *Mahābhārata* (Sabhāparva, Ch. 51), they were located in the western division of India. This evidence of the *Mahābhārata* is supported by the author of the *Periplus of the Erythraean Sea* as well as by Ptolemy. The *Mahābhārata* (IX, 37, 1) definitely locates the Ābhīras in western Rajputana where the river Sarasvatī disappears. Patañjali in his *Mahābhāṣya* (1. 2. 3) is perhaps the first to introduce them into Indian history. By the middle of the second century B.C. the Ābhīras and their country must have been overpowered by the Bactrian Greeks, who seem to have occupied the whole of the country, which Ptolemy designates as Indo-Scythia and which included Aberia or Abiria. The *Mārkaṇḍeya Purāṇa* (Chs. 57-58, vv. 45-8 and v. 22) places them with those dwelling in the southern country. The *Vāyu Purāṇa* (Ch. 45, 126) supports it and describes the Ābhīras as *Dakṣiṇāpatha-vāsinaḥ*. For further details, vide B. C. Law, *Indological Studies*, Pt. I, pp. 54ff.

Ālūr.—It is a village in the Gadag taluk of Dharwar district of the Bombay State (*E.I.*, XVI, p. 27).

Ānandapura.—The Maliya Copperplate Inscription of Dharasena II refers to it. Its modern name is Ānand, the chief town of the Ānand taluk (*C.I.I.*, Vol. III).

Ānandapura or Vaḍnagar.—This is also called Nagar, the original home of the Nagar Brāhmans of Gujarat, which was surrounded by Kumārapāla with a rampart (*E.I.*, I, p. 295).

Ānartta.—It is the name of a country in North Kathiawar (Luders' List No. 965). According to some this tract lies round Dvārakā, while according to others, it is situated round Vaḍanagar (cf. *Bombay Gazetteer*, I, 1. 6). This country seems to have been reconquered from Gautamīputra by Śaka Mahākṣatrapa Rudradāman (vide B. C. Law, *Indological Studies*, Pt. I, pp. 52-53). According to the *Skanda Purāṇa* (Ch. 1, 5-6) there was a hermitage (*āśrama*) in this country full of ascetics chanting vedic verses.

Āsaṭṭigrāma.—This village has been identified by Bühler with Astgām, seven miles south-east of Navsārī (*E.I.*, VIII, 229ff.; *I.A.*, XVII, p. 198). Some hold that Aṣṭagrāma is the proper name and not Āsaṭṭigrāma (*E.I.*, VIII, p. 231).

Āṭavikarājyas.—Fleet (*C.I.I.*, III, 114) says that the Āṭavikarājyas or forest kingdoms were closely connected with Ḍabhālā, i.e. the Jabbalpur region (*E.I.*, VIII, 284–87; B. C. Law, *The Magadhas in Ancient India*, Royal Asiatic Society Monograph, Vol. XXIV, p. 19). It was Samudragupta who made the rulers of the Āṭavikarājyas his servants (cf. *Allahabad Stone Pillar Inscription of Samudragupta .... paricārakīkrita sarvāṭavikarājasya*). The Āṭavyas[1] or Āṭavikas were probably the aboriginal tribes dwelling in the jungle tracts of Central India.

Badarikā.—The Ellora plates of Dantidurga mention it which lies in southern Gujarat (*E.I.*, XXV, Pt. I, January, 1939, p. 29).

---

[1] *Vāyup.*, XLV, 126; *Matsyap.*, CXIII, 48; Law, *Tribes in Ancient India*, p. 383.

Bahāl.—This village is in the Chalisgaon sub-division of the Khandesh district of the Bombay State, where an Inscription of the Yādava king Singhana (Śaka saṃvat 1144) was discovered (*E.I.*, III, 110).

Balegrāma.—It is a village which may be identified with modern Belgaum Taralha in the Igatpuri taluk of the Nasik district (*E.I.*, XXV, Pt. V, January, 1940, p. 230—*Two Grants of Pṛthivīcandra Bhogaśakti*).

Balisa.—A grant of Allaśakti (acquired by the *Bhārata Itihāsa Saṃśodhakamaṇḍala*, Poona) mentions this village, which was given by the Sendraka Prince Allaśakti. This village has been identified with Wanesa in the Bardoli taluk of the Surat district (*D. R. Bhandarkar Volume*, p. 53).

Balsāṇe.—It is in the Pimpalner taluk of the West Khandesh district of the Bombay State, well-known for its several temples of the Chalukyan style (*E.I.*, XXVI, Pt. VII, July, 1942, pp. 309ff.).

Baṅkāpur.—It was also known as Baṅkāpur taluk in the Dharwar district of the Bombay Presidency. The ancient town known as Male Baṅkāpur lies nearly two miles south by south-west from the modern town (*E.I.*, XIII, p. 168).

Bargaon.—It is a village situated at a distance of 27 miles north by west of Murwārā, the chief town of the Murwārā tahsil of the Jubbulpore district, where an inscription has been found incised on a broken stone slab (*E.I.*, XXV, Pt. VI, April, 1940).

Bāmaṇī.—This village is situated five miles south-west of Kāgal, the chief town of the Kāgal State in Kolhapur territory, where a Stone Inscription of Vijayāditya of the Śilāhāra family was discovered (*E.I.*, III, 211).

Bāsuraviṣaya.—It comprised 140 villages and included the southern part of the Haveli taluk of the Dharwar district (*E.I.*, XXIII, Pt. V, p. 194).

Beḷvola.—The Veṅkaṭapur Inscription of Amoghavarṣa (Śaka 828) refers to this place which comprised portions of the modern Gadag, Ron and Navalgand taluks of the Dharwar district (*E.I.*, XXVI, Pt. II, April, 1941, pp. 59ff.).

Bhadrakasat.—It was in Kānyakubja or Kanauj. There was a matrimonial alliance between the royal house of Benaras and king Mahendraka who was the tribal king of Bhadrakasat (R. L. Mitter, *Northern Buddhist Lit.*, 143ff.).

Bhadrāraka.—It may be identified with Bhadara which is about two miles to the south-west of Āmtī (*Important Inscriptions from the Baroda State*, Vol. I, p. 20).

Bhairaṇmaṭṭi.—It is a village ten miles east of Bāgalkot, the chief town of the Bāgalkot taluk of the Bijapur district in the Bombay State, where a stone inscription was found (*E.I.*, III, 230).

Bharaṇa.—It is a small village near Khambhalia, a seaport in the Gulf of Cutch in the Jamnagar State, Kathiawar. A stone inscription has been found here.

Bharukaccha (Bhṛgukaccha).—Bharukaccha (sea-marsh), Bhṛgukaccha, Bhirukaccha,[1] are all identical with modern Broach or Bharoch which is the Barygaza of Ptolemy[2] and the *Periplus of the Erythraean Sea.*[3] Modern Broach is Kathiāwāḍ. In the name Barygaza given to it by Ptolemy we have a Greek corruption of Bhṛgukṣetra or Bhṛgukaccha (*Ancient India as described by Ptolemy*, pp. 153-4). Bharukaccha was a seaport town. Julien restored the name as 'Barou-gatcheva' which Saint

---

[1] *Matsya Purāṇa*, CXIII, 50; *Mārk. Purāṇa*, LVII, 51.

[2] *Ancient India as described by Ptolemy*, pp. 38, 153.

[3] *Ibid.*, pp. 40, 287.

Martin made as 'Bāroukatcheva'. It was known as *Po-lu-ka-che-p'o* at the time of the Chinese pilgrim, Hiuen Tsang. Bhṛgukaccha is the Skt. form of Bharukaccha which means high coast-land. This town was exactly situated on a high coast-land. The *Bṛhatsaṃhitā* (XIV. 11) and the *Yoginītantra* (2. 4) refer to it. It is also mentioned in the Mathurā Buddhist image Inscription of Huviṣka. A grant of the Gurjara king Jayabhaṭṭa III, (Kalacuri year 486; *E.I.*, XXIII, Pt. IV, Oct., 1935; cf. Luder's List, No. 1131) also makes mention of this town. The *Bhāgavata Purāṇa* (VIII, 18, 12) places it on the northern bank of the Narmadā. According to the Greek geographer Ptolemy, Barygaza was a large city situated about 30 miles from the sea on the north side of the river Narmadā (*Ancient India as described by Ptolemy*, p. 153). The *Mārkaṇḍeya Purāṇa* (Vaṅgavāsī ed., Ch. 58, v. 21) locates it on the river Veṇvā.

According to the *Divyāvadāna* (pp. 545–576) Bharukaccha was a rich and prosperous city, thickly populated. Hiuen Tsang, who visited this place in the 7th century A.D., described it to be 2,400 or 2,500 li in circuit. The soil was impregnated with salt. It was brackish and its vegetation sparse. Salt was made by boiling sea-water, and the people were supported by the sea. Trees and shrubs were scarce and scattered. The climate was hot. The people were mean and deceitful, ignorant, and believers in both orthodoxy and heterodoxy. There were more than ten Buddhist monasteries with 300 brethren who were the adherents of the Mahāyāna Sthavira school. There were about ten deva-temples in which there were sectaries of various kinds.[1]

The *Divyāvadāna* (pp. 544–586) records a very interesting story accounting for the name of Bharukaccha or Bhṛgukaccha. It is said that Rudrāyana, king of Roruka (identified by some with Alor, an old city of Sind) in Sovīra, was killed by his son, Śikhaṇḍin. As a punishment for this crime, the realm of Śikhaṇḍin, the parricide king, was destroyed by a heavy shower of sand. Three pious men only survived: two ministers and a Buddhist monk, who went out in search for a new land. Bhiru, one of the two ministers, established a new city, which came to be named after him—Bhiruka or Bhirukaccha, whence came the name Bharukaccha. The legend concerning the foundation of the Bhiru kingdom with its capital in the Buddha's time cannot be believed for the simple reason that the kingdom and its seaport had existed long before.

The Aryans seem to have sailed from Kāthiāwāḍ to Bharukaccha and from Bharukaccha to Śūrpāraka.[2] In early Buddhist literature as well as in the early centuries of the Christian era, Bharukaccha was an important seat of sea-going trade and commerce. From Ujjayinī every commodity for local consumption was brought down to Barygaza (Bhṛgukaccha, *Periplus of the Erythraean Sea*, section 48). The *Periplus* (section 49) notices that the Onyx-stones were imported into Barygaza. According to Ptolemy, it was the greatest seat of commerce in western India.[3] The *Sussondi Jātaka* refers to the journey of the minstrel Sagga from Benaras to Bharukaccha, which was a seaport town (*Paṭṭana-gāma*) from which ships sailed for different countries. Some merchants of this port were sailing for Suvarṇabhūmi (identified with Lower Burma). A minstrel who came to Bharukaccha approached them and promised to play music, if he was taken by them on their ship. They took him on the ship and his

---

[1] Watters, *On Yuan Chwang*, II, p. 241; Beal, *Records of the Western World*, pp. 259, 260.

[2] Bhandarkar, *Carmichael Lectures*, 1918, p. 23.

[3] *Ancient India as described by Ptolemy*, p. 153.

music excited the fish in the water so much that the ship was badly wrecked.[1] At Bharukaccha a master mariner lost both his eyes being injured by salt-water. He was then appointed by the king as the valuer. He gave up this post and came back to Bharukaccha where he lived. Some merchants asked him to sail their ship, although he was blind. Being pressed much by them he consented. He at last saved the ship from destruction and brought it back safely to its place of destination, which was the seaport town of Bharukaccha.[2]

The *Bodhisattvāvadāna Kalpalatā* of Kṣemendra points out that Surpāraga in his old age undertook a voyage with some merchants to trade with the inhabitants of Bharukaccha.[3] The *Gaṇḍavyūha*, a Northern Buddhist text, refers to a goldsmith of Bharukaccha named Muktasāra.[4]

The *Milinda-pañho*[5] refers to the people of Bharukaccha (*Bharukacchaka*) among the peoples of many countries in connection with the building of a city by an able architect. At Bharukaccha Vaḍḍha belonged to the family of a commoner. He renounced his household life and entered the Order.[6] Vaḍḍha's mother was reborn in a clansman's family at this town. She later entered the Order after handing her child over to her kin.[7]

Vijaya of the country of Lāḷha, son of Sīhavāhu, stopped for three months at Bharukaccha and then went again on board the ship.[8]

There was a forest in this seaport town called Koriṇṭa. It was on the bank of the Narmadā. Jina Suvrata visited it for instructing Jitaśatru who was then engaged in horse sacrifice.

Bharukaccha has many popular shrines. Vāhaḍadeva, son of Udaya, restored Sittujja, and his younger brother, Ambaḍa, restored the Śakuṇikā Vihāra.[9]

Bhāja.—It is situated about 2½ miles south of the Bombay-Poona road and about a mile from the Malavli railway station. The cave No. 1 is a natural cavern. The next caves are plain *vihāras*. The cave No. 6 is a *Vihāra*, very much dilapidated. There is an irregular hall with three cells. There is a beautiful *Caitya*. The caves are earlier than 2000 B.C. There are vaults and ornamental cornices. Buddhist emblems are traceable in four of the pillars. The roof is arched, and there are ornamental arches in front and a double railing. There are many small *vihāras* near about.

Bhāṇḍup.—It is a village in the Salsette taluk of the Thana district of the Bombay Presidency, where the plates of Chittarājadeva were discovered (*E.I.*, XII, 250ff.).

Bheṭālikā.—This village is situated in the district of Pacchatrī (*E.I.*, XXVI, Pt. V, January, 1942, p. 209).

Bilviśvara.—Bilviśvara mentioned in the Surat plate of Kīrtirāja, may be identified with Balesara or Baleśwara, a small town, two miles to the north of Palasenā (*I.A.*, XXI, p. 256).

Brahmagiri.—It is a mountain in the Nasik district near the Trayambaka in which the Godavari has its source.

Brahmapurī.—It is the local name of a part of Kolhapur adjoining the bank of the river Pañcagaṅgā (*E.I.*, XXIII, Pt. I, January, 1935; *E.I.*, XXIII, Pt. II).

---

1 *Jātaka*, III, pp. 188ff.
2 *Ibid.*, IV, pp. 137ff.
3 Cf. R. L. Mitra, *Northern Buddhist Literature*, p. 51.
4 *Ibid.*, p. 92.
5 Trenckner ed., p. 331.
6 Mrs. Rhys Davids, *Psalms of the Brethren*, p. 194.
7 *Therīgāthā commentary*, p. 171.
8 *Dīpavaṃsa*, IX, V. 26.
9 *Vividhatīrthakalpa*, ed. Jinavijaya Sūri, pp. 20–22.

Brāhmaṇābād.—The little state of Patalene as the Greeks called it was probably named after its capital city Pattala. Patalene is generally identified with the Indus delta and its capital town Patala (Skt. Prasthala) is supposed to have stood at or near the site of modern Brāhmaṇābād. According to Diodoros the constitution of Patala (Tauala) was similar to that of Sparta. There was a council of elders vested with the supreme authority in the management and conduct of usual administration. According to Strabo (H. and F., II, 252-253) Patalene long after Alexander's invasion passed under the Bactrian Greeks. Later on it came to the hands of the Śakas or Indo-Scythian rulers from the clutches of the Indo-Greek rulers. For further details, vide B. C. Law, *Indological Studies*, Pt. I, p. 37; *C.H.I.*, 1, 378-79; *I.A.*, 1884, 354.

Caḍija.—It may be identified with Ganje near Uran, about two miles west of Uran in the Panvel taluk of the Bombay State (*E.I.*, XXIII, Pt. VII).

Cambay.—It is in the Khaira collectorate in Gujarat. A stone inscription has been found in a Jaina temple. Stambha-tīrtha is modern Cambay.

Campaka.—It is modern Cāmpāner (*E.I.*, XXIV, Pt. V, p. 217). It is also known as Campakapura (*Ibid.*, p. 219).

Campānaka.—The Saindhava copperplate grants from Ghumli mention this village which may be identified with Cāvaṇḍ, situated about 15 miles north of Junāgaḍ (*E.I.*, XXVI, Pt. V, January, 1942, p. 223).

Candrapurī.—It is probably identical with Candraci Met, 12 miles south-west of Añjaneri (*E.I.*, XXV, Pt. V, p. 230).

Cikula.—It is mentioned in the Barhut Inscriptions (Barua and Sinha, p. 14). Cikula is Cekula or Ceula which is probably Caul near Bombay (*E.I.*, II, 42).

Ciplūn.—It is the chief town of the Ciplūn taluk of the Ratnagiri district, where two plates of Pulakesin II were discovered (*E.I.*, III, 50ff; *Important Inscriptions from the Baroda State*, I, p. 44).

Dadhipadra.—It is identified with Dohad founded by Kumārapāla. It is mentioned in the Inscriptions of Jayasiṃha (*E.I.*, XXIV, Pt. V, p. 220).

Dadhipadraka.—This village is situated in the district of Pacchatrī, which is the same as Pāctardī, six miles west of Ghumli (*E.I.*, XXVI, Pt. V, January, 1942, p. 204).

Daṇḍaka forest.—The Daṇḍaka forest (Daṇḍakāraṇya) which is celebrated in the *Rāmāyaṇa* (Ādik. Sarga i, v. 46) in connection with the story of Rāma's exile, seems to have covered almost the whole of Central India from the Bundelkhand region to the river Kṛṣṇā (*J.R.A.S.*, 1894, 241; cf. *Jātaka*, v. 29), but the *Mahābhārata* seems to limit the Daṇḍaka forest to the source of the Godāvarī (Sabhāparva, XXX, 1169; Vanaparva, LXXXV, 8183-4). According to the *Bhāgavata Purāṇa* (IX. 11. 19; X. 79. 20) this forest in the Deccan was traversed by Rāma and visited by Balarāma. The *Padma Purāṇa* (Ch. 21) mentions it among other holy places. In the heart of this forest there was a stream. There also existed a cave (*Daśakumāracaritaṃ*, p. 20). This forest was also known as the Citrakuñjavat to the west of Janasthāna (*Uttaracaritaṃ*, Act I. 30). The tracts of the Daṇḍaka forest had a jumble of watering places, hermitages, hills, streams, lakes, etc. (*Ibid.*, Act II. 14). Bāṇa refers to this forest in his *Harṣacarita* (Ch. 1). This forest is also mentioned in the *Milindapañha* (p. 130). The Jaina *Nisīthacūrṇī* has a peculiar story of the burning of this forest to ashes (16. 1113). The Daṇḍakāraṇya along the Vindhyas practically separated the Majjhimadesa from the Dakkhiṇāpatha.

Daśapura.—The *Bṛhatsaṃhitā* (Ch. XIV. 20) mentions it as a city. It is a well-known place on the Rajputana-Malwa branch of the Western

Railway. It is identified with Mandasor in Western Malwa in the Gwalior State (vide Fleet's note in *C.I.I.*, III, 79). According to Bāṇa's *Kādambarī* (Bombay ed., p. 19) it was in Malwa, not far from Ujjayinī. Most likely it was in Western Malwa (*Gazetteer of the Bombay Presidency*, 1883, *Nasik*, p. 636). The ancient Daśapura stood on the north or left bank of the Siwana, a tributary of the river Śiprā. The Mandasor Stone Pillar Inscription of Yaśodharman mentions Mandasor, or more properly Dasor, which is the chief town of the Mandasor district of the Scindhia's dominions in Western Malwa (*Gwalior State Gazetteer*, I, 265ff.). The Mandasor Inscription of Bandhuvarman mentions Lāṭa and Daśapura. Daśapura, which is referred to in the Inscriptions of Kumāragupta I, was presumably the main city of the Mālavagaṇa or Western Mālavas. It was ruled by Naravarman and his son Viśvavarman, who were independent kings. It was an important Viceregal seat of the early Gupta Empire. It was evidently from the hands of the Kṣaharāta Kṣatrapa Nahapāṇa that such places as Daśapura, Nāsika, Śūrpāraka, Bhṛgukaccha and Prabhāsa, were wrested by the earlier Sātavāhanas. During the reign of Kṣaharāta Kṣatrapa Nahapāṇa his son-in-law Uṣavadāta emulated the fame of Aśoka by carrying out many works of public utility at Daśapura. Daśapura and Vidiśā were the two neighbouring cities that vied with Ujjayinī in its glory during the Gupta period. During the reign of the imperial Guptas the use of the Mālava or the Kṛta era was restricted to Daśapura. The Mālavas seem to have migrated to the Mandasor region, where most of the records connected with the successors of Samudragupta, have been found. This region is to be identified with the ancient mahājanapada of Avantī mentioned in the *Aṅguttara Nikāya*, as well as Avantī of the Junāgaḍh Rock Inscription of Rudradāman and Malaya (Mālava) of the Jaina Bhagavatī Sūtra. The Jaina *Āvaśyaka Cūrṇi* (pp. 400ff.) points out that Daśapura was inhabited by some merchants and since then this place was known as such. The princes of Mandasor used the Kṛta era commencing from 58 B.C. traditionally handed down by the Mālavagaṇa. The inscriptions associating the Mālavas with this era have not only been found in the Mandasor region but also in other places at Kāṃsuvāṃ in the Kotah State and Nāgarī in the Udaipur State. The Mandasor Stone Pillar Inscription of Yaśodharman records the defeat of the Hūṇa adventurer Mihirakula by king Yaśodharman of Malwa (*C.I.I.*, iii; cf. *E.I.*, XII, 315ff.; cf. Mandasor Inscription of the time of Naravarman, Mālava year 461). In the middle of the 5th century A.D., it fell to the Hūṇas who were driven from Malwa. Mandasor contains an ancient temple of the Sun built during the reign of Kumāragupta I. The village of Sondni, three miles south-west of Mandasor, contains two magnificent monolithic sandstone pillars with lion and bell capitals.

The Mandasor Stone Inscription of Kumāragupta and Bandhuvarman contains a description of Daśapura as a city. The court panegyrist of Yaśodharman of Daśapura gives a vivid poetic description of the royal territory extending from the river Revā to the Pāripātra mountain and the region of the lower Indus (for further details, Law, *Ujjayinī in Ancient India*).

Dābhigrāma—(*E.I.*, I, 317).—It may be identified with Ḍābhi in north Gujarat.

Debal.—It was a port, the emporium of the Indus, during the middle ages. Some place it at Karachi. According to others it occupied a site between Karachi and Thatha. It may be fixed on the Baghār river. According to Hamilton it was near Lāribandar. V. A. Smith thinks that it was near the existing shrine of Pir Patho (*Early History of India*, 3rd ed., p. 104). For further details, vide *C.A.G.I.*, pp. 340ff.

Deothan.—It is a small village in the Yeola taluk of the Nasik district, some 16 miles east of Yeola, whence it may be approached by car for 14 miles on the metalled road to Aurangabad (*A.S.I.*, *Annual Reports*, 1930–34, p. 318).

Dhambhika.—It is a village situated in Nasik district (Luders' List No. 1142).

Dhaṅkatīrtha.—It is a village situated in the district of Pacchatrī. It is obviously the same as Dhānk in the Gondal State situated about 25 miles east of Ghumli. Dhānk is situated on the outskirts of a hill of the same name and figures as a holy place of the Jains (*E.I.*, XXVI, Pt. V, January, 1942, p. 199).

Dhulia.—It is in the Khandesh district of the Bombay State where plates of Karkarāja were discovered (*E.I.*, VIII, 182ff.).

Dohad.—It is the chief town of the Dohad sub-division of the Pāñchmahals, Bombay Presidency, 77 miles north-east of Baroda (*E.I.*, XXIV, Pt. V, January, 1938, p. 212).

Dvāravatī (= Dvārakā = Jaina Bāravai).—It is also called Kuśasthalī. It is a holy place according to the *Skanda Purāṇa* (Ch. 1, 19–23). The *Yoginītantra* (2. 4, pp. 128-129) also refers to it. It is a holy spot according to the *Kālikā Purāṇa* (Ch. 58. 35). It was originally situated near the mountain Girnar, but in later times it has been recognized as Dvārakā on the sea-shore on the extreme west coast of Kāthiāwāḍ. It is the 'Barake' of the *Periplus* (p. 389). The Jain *Nāyādhammakahāo* (V, p. 68) points out that Bāravai or Dvāravatī was the home of Kriṣṇa Vāsudeva (Kaṇha Vāsudeva). It was built by Revata. Kriṣṇa performed the Aśvamedha sacrifice here (*Bhāgavata*, I. 8. 10–27; X. 89. 22). The *Antagaḍadasāo* (p. 5) also refers to it as the home of Andhaka-Vṛṣṇis (Andhagavaṇhi). According to the *Harivaṃśa* (Ch. CXV, 45–49) this city was properly protected by doors, adorned with the most excellent walls, girt by ditches, filled with palaces, decorated with pools, streamlets of pure water and with gardens. Ten brothers who were the sons of Andhaka-Veṇhu desired to conquer the whole of India. After conquering Ayodhyā they proceeded to Dvāravatī which had sea on one side and mountains on the other. This city had four gates. At first they failed to take it, but afterwards they succeeded. They lived in the city after dividing it into ten parts (*Jātaka*, IV, pp. 82–84). Vāsudeva, the eldest of the ten brothers, had a beloved wife named Jambāvatī, who was a Caṇḍāla by caste. One day he went out of Dvāravatī and while going to a park he saw a very beautiful girl on the way. He fell in love with her and made her his chief queen. She gave birth to a son named Śivi who became the ruler of Dvāravatī after his father's death (*Jātaka*, VI, p. 421). This city contains a very beautiful Hindu temple. The Kukuras seem to have occupied the Dvārakā region which is described as *Kukurāndha Vṛṣṇibhiḥ Yuptāḥ*. The *Bhāgavata* [1] and the *Vāyu Purāṇas* refer to this tribe when it represents Ugrasena, the king of the Yādavas, as originated from the Kukuras (*Kukurodbhava*). The Kāmbojas had their country on a trade route connecting it with Dvārakā (*Petavatthu*, p. 23). Vāsudeva's son by a Caṇḍāla woman reigned here (*Jātaka*, VI, p. 421). Vijaya, king of Dvāravatī, was among a few ancient kings who reached perfection as hermits (*Uttarādhyayana-*

[1] See the topographical list of the *Bhāgavata Purāṇa*, *I.A.*, Vol. XXVIII, (1899), p. 2.

sūtra, XVIII). The Andhakaveṇhu youths of Dvāravatī roughly handled Kaṇha-Dīpāyana and ultimately put him to death. For further details, vide B. C. Law, *Indological Studies*, I, p. 52.

Eraṇḍapalla (mentioned in the Allahabad Pillar Inscription).—It may be identified with Eraṇḍol, the chief town of a sub-division of the same name in the Khandesh district, Bombay State (*J.R.A.S.*, 1898, pp. 369-70). According to some it is identified with Eraṇḍapali, probably near Chicacole on the coast of Orissa, mentioned in the Siddhantam plates of Devendravarman (*E.I.*, XII, p. 212).

Eraṇḍi.—It is the river Uri, a tributary of the Narmadā (*Padma Purāṇa*, Ch. IX).

Eruthana.—It is mentioned in the Surat plate of Kīrtirāja. It is modern Erathan, two miles north-west from Balesara.

Gadag.—It is the chief town of the Gadag taluk in the Dharwar district of the Bombay State. Here stands the temple of Trikūleśvara. An inscription was found engraved on a stone standing up against the back wall of this temple. This inscription records a grant of land by the Hoysala king Vīravallāla II (*E.I.*, VI, 89ff.; *E.I.*, XV, 348ff.). A Stone Inscription of the Yādava Bhillama was found out in the temple of Trikuleśvara at Gadag (*E.I.*, III, 217).

Gaṃdhārikābhūmi.—It is a locality in the Kalyāṇa (Luders' List, No. 998).

Gābhalāgrāma (*E.I.*, II, 26).—It is in North Gujarat, possibly near Dilmal.

Gādhipura.—Kanauj (vide Kanauj).

Gharapurī.—It is the well-known island of Elephanta in the harbour of Bombay about six miles north-east of the Apollo Bundar. Elephanta was the name given by the Portuguese owing to the fact that they found a large stone elephant standing at the entrance to the great cave. The caves of Elephanta are influenced by Brahmanism and Buddhism. Three of these caves are in ruins. A cave contains a Buddhist *Caitya*. *Trimūrti* or Brahmanical Trinity is found on the wall of the main hall.

Ghumli.—It is in the Nawanagar State of Kāthiāwaḍ where six copper-plate grants were discovered. It is known to the ancients as Bhūtāmbilikā. According to tradition Bhūtāmbilikā was the old capital of Jeṭhvā Rajputs whose present representatives are the Rāṇās of Porbandar (*E.I.*, XXVI, Pt. V, October, 1941, pp. 185ff.).

Girinagara (Girnar).—It is mentioned in Luders' List (Nos. 965, 966) as a town. According to the Jaina *Anuyogadvāra* (*Sūya*, 130, p. 137) Girinayara or Girinagara was located near the Ūrjayantaparvata. The Junāgaḍh Inscription of Skandagupta mentions Junāgaḍh as the chief town of the native state of Junāgaḍh in the Kāthiāwāḍ peninsula of the Bombay State. It is also known as Girinagara or Girnar, which is also called Ūrjayat in the inscriptions (*C.I.I.*, III). A vassal Yavanarāja named Tuṣāspha ruled Surāṣṭra as its governor with Girinagara as its capital during the reign of King Aśoka, as we learn from the Junāgaḍh Rock Inscription of Mahākṣatrapa Rudradāman. Close to Junāgaḍh in Gujarat stands the Girnār or Raivataka hill, which is considered to be the birthplace of Neminātha, the Jaina Tīrthaṅkara. This hill contains a footprint called *Gurudattacaraṇa*. It is sacred to the Jainas, as it contains the temples of Neminātha and Pārśvanātha. It also contains the hermitage of Ṛṣi Dattātreya. The river Suvarṇarekhā (= Palāśinī) flows at the foot of this hill. According to the Jaina *Uttarādhyayana Sūtra* (Ch. XLV), Ariṣṭanemi died here in his old age. Śrīcaitanya, the celebrated Vaiṣṇava reformer, visited Girinagara as we learn from Govindadāsa's *Karcā*. For further details, vide Law, *Some Jaina Canonical Sūtras*, p. 180. See also *Ūrjayat*.

Girṇā.—This river issues from the Sahya or Western Ghats and flows north-east to join the Tāptī below Chopdā in Khandesh. It is included in the Tāptī group and is fed by one stream on the right and two on the left (Law, *Rivers of India*, p. 42).

Gopālpur.—This village is situated some three miles south-east of Bheraghāṭ in the Jubbulpur district. It lies on the right bank of the river Narmadā (*E.I.*, XVIII, 73).

Govardhana.—According to the *Yoginītantra* (I. 14, p. 83), this hill was made by collecting the bodily ashes of the demon Keśī. It was so called because the cows were fed and reared up by the grass grown on it. According to the *Harivaṃśa* (Ch. LXII, 25-26) it is huge with a high summit like the Mount Mandāra. In its centre a big fig tree stands having high branches and extending over a yojana. It is a sacred spot and one becomes free from sins by visiting it. It is near modern Nasik in the Bombay State (*Mathurā Buddhist Image Inscription of Huviṣka*). It is also known as Govardhanapura (vide *Mārkaṇḍeya Purāṇa*, Ch. 57; Bhandarkar, *Early History of the Dekkan*, p. 3). It appears to have been of some importance during the reigns of Nahapāṇa and Puḷumāvi. Uṣabhadāta made a rest house in Govardhana. It appears from the inscriptions that Govardhana was the political headquarters in Nahapāṇa's time as it was afterwards under Puḷumāvi. It may be identified with a large modern village of Govardhan-Gaṅgāpur on the right bank of the Godāvarī, six miles west of Nasik (*Gazetteer of the Bombay Presidency*, Vol. XVI, 1883, *Nasik*, pp. 636-637).

Gurjara.—It was known to Hiuen Tsang as Kiu-che-lo. It was situated 300 miles to the north of Valabhi or 467 miles to the north-west of Ujjain. The people of this place once dwelt in the Punjab and migrated to the peninsula of Kāthiāwaḍ which is now called Gujarat after them (*C.A.G.I.*, pp. 357ff.; 696). In ancient times, in the country of Gurjara, Jayasiṃhadeva constructed the new temple of Nemi. Vastupāla and Tejapāla were the distinguished ministers of the king of Gurjara. Mahanadevī, the daughter of the king of Kānyakubja, inherited Gurjara from her father. Tejapāla constructed a beautiful town in Girnar and built the temple of Pārśvanātha. He also excavated a beautiful lake called Kumārasara. The temple of Daśadaśā stands on the bank of the Suvarṇarekhā. He built three *caityas*. Vastupāla built Marudevī's temple (Law, *Some Jaina Canonical Sūtras*, pp. 181-182).

Hariścandragarh.—It is a fort in the Akola taluk of Ahmednagar district, Bombay, 19 miles south-west of Akola and one of the most interesting points on the Western Ghats. It stands on an elevation of more than 4,000 ft. above sea-level. The fort and the temples on the summit are annually visited by numerous pilgrims (Law, *Holy Places of India*, p. 43).

Hariseṇāṇaka.—This village is situated in the district of Svarṇamañjarī. It is probably the same as the modern village of Hariāsana situated in the Nawanagar State (*E.I.*, XXVI, V, January, 1942, p. 218).

Hastavapra (*Hastakavapra*).—It is modern Hāthab, a village six miles south of Goghā in the Bhavnagar State of Kathiawar, which is known to have been under Śilāditya III. It is just opposite to the Broach district (*Important Inscriptions from the Baroda State*, Vol. I, p. 18). Severa Valabhi copperplate charters of the 6th century mention it as the headquarters of a district (J. Ph. Vogel, *Notes on Ptolemy*, *B.S.O.A.S.*, Vol. XIV, Pt. 1).

Hullumgūr (Hulgūr).—This village lies in the Baṅkāpur division of Dharwar district of the Bombay State, some eight miles to the north-east from Shiggaon where the inscription of the reign of Vikramāditya VI was discovered (*E.I.*, XVI, p. 329).

Inṭwā.—The ancient site of Inṭwā is situated on a hill in the midst of a thick jungle about three miles from the famous rock at Junāgaḍh in Saurāṣṭra containing the inscriptions of Aśoka, Rudradāman and Skandagupta (*E.I.*, XXVIII, Pt. IV, October, 1949, p. 174).

Jarak.—This little town is situated about midway between Haiderabad and Thatha overhanging the western bank of the Indus. It is the present boundary between the middle Sind and the lower Sind (*C.A.G.I.*, pp. 329-30).

Jayapura.—This village is the same as modern Jitpur, six miles east of Nandod and about eight miles south-east of Toran (*E.I.*, XXV, Pt. VII, July, 1940).

Jīrṇadurga.—It is not to be identified with modern Junāgaḍh, but it may be identified with one of the forts. The fort within the city on the outskirts of the Damodar Ghat and on the rising slope of Girnar was known as the Jīrṇadurga (*E.I.*, XXIV, Pt. V, p. 221).

Junāgaḍh.—See Girinagar (Girnar).

Junninagara.—It is probably identical with Junnar, a well-known place about 55 miles north of Poona (*E.I.*, XXV, Pt. IV, p. 168).

Kaccha.—It is a country in Western India (Luders' List, No. 965). It may be identified with Cutch or Marukaccha (cf. *Bṛhatsaṃhitā*, Ch. XIV). Pāṇini mentions it in his *Aṣṭādhyāyī* (4. 2. 133).

Kaliyāṇagrāma (*I.A.*, VI, 205ff.).—It is in North Gujarat, and may be identified with Kālianā.

Kallivan.—It is Kalvan in the north-western part of the Nasik district (*E.I.*, XXV, Pt. V, p. 230—*Two Grants of Pṛthivīcandra Bhogaśakti*).

Kanheri.—About 20 miles north of Bombay a big group of caves known as Kanheri is situated. For a considerable number of years these caves were occupied by the Buddhist monks. They are situated near Thānā. They have been excavated in a large bubble of a hill situated in the midst of a dense forest. The majority of these caves contain a small single room with a small verandah in front. The architecture may be dated as late as the 8th or 9th century A.D. To the north of these caves, there is a large excavation containing three *dagobas* and some sculptures. According to Fergusson, this cave temple is 86 ft. long and 39 ft. wide. It contains 34 pillars and a plain *dagoba*. There are two colossal figures of the Buddha and standing figures of the Bodhisattva Avalokiteśvara. There are many dwarf cells built one over the other. The cave No. 10 is the Durbar hall which is situated on the south side of the ravine. On the south side of the ravine there are several ranges of cells, excavated in the slope of the hill. There are some stone seats outside the caves. There is also a *dagoba* with an umbrella carved on the roof. It is difficult to fix the date of these caves, but it must be admitted that there has been much degradation of style between these caves and those at Karli. Some of the sculptures are surely of a much later date.

Karahakaṭa (Karahāṭanagara or Karahāṭa).—It is mentioned in the Barhut Inscriptions (ed. Barua and Sinha, pp. 11, 12, 17, 33). It is a town identified by Hultzsch with modern Karhad in the Satara district of the Bombay Presidency, where the copperplates of Kṛṣṇa III were discovered (*E.I.*, IV, 278ff.). According to the *E.I.* (XXVI, p. 323), it is the modern Karāḍ.

Kardama-āśrama.—The sage Kardama had his hermitage at Siddāpura in Gujarat (*Bhāgavata Purāṇa*, III, 24. 9).

Kālayāna (Kāliana, Kaliyaṇa, Kāliyana).—Name of a town (Luders' List, Nos. 1024, 986, 1032 and 998).

Kāllaṇa (Kalyāṇa or Kālayana).—Name of a town (Luders' List, No. 988).

Kānhairī.—It may be identified with Kaṇhera, eight miles south-west of Cālisgaon in Khandesh (*E.I.*, XXV, Pt. V, January, 1940, p. 208).

Kārli.—In the Borghāṭā hills between Bombay and Poona there are two well-known Buddhist cave temples at Kārli and Bhāja. They are all dated about the beginning of the Christian era. The caves at Kārli are situated about two miles to the north of the Bombay-Poona road. The nearest railway station is Malavli. The names of Nahapāṇa and Uṣabhadāta occur in the inscriptions on the caves. In the two inscriptions mention is made of the great king Dhutapāla, supposed to be Devabhūti of the Śuṅga dynasty. The pillars of these caves are quite perpendicular. The original screen is superseded by a stone one ornamented with sculpture. At the entrance of these caves stands a pillar surmounted by four lions with gaping mouths and facing four quarters. On the right hand side stands a Śiva temple and close to it there is a second pillar surmounted by a *cakra* or wheel. The outer porch is wider than the body of the building. There are many miniature temple-fronts crowned with a Caitya-window. The pairs of large figures on each side of the doors appear like those at Kanheri. Buddha is here attended by Padmapāṇi, and most probably Mañjuśrī is seated on the Sīhāsana with his feet on the lotus. The entrance consists of three doorways under a gallery. There are fifteen pillars, and their bases consist of the water-pot of Lakṣmī; the shaft is octagonal representing the *Saṃgha*. From architectural stand-point all these caves are of high order. The net-work (jāli-work) is almost perfect. The *Caitya* in caves Nos. 1 and 2 is a three-storied *Vihāra*. The top storey has a verandah with four pillars. On the left side in the top storey there is a raised platform in front of five cells. The doors are well fitted. The cave No. 3 is a two-storied *Vihāra*. The cave No. 4 is situated to the south of the *Caitya*, and it appears from inscriptions that it was given by Haraphana in the reign of the Andhra king Gautamīputra Pulamāyī (For the inscriptions in the caves at Kārli, vide *E.I.*, VI, 47ff.).

Keḷoḍi (*Keḷawaḍi*).—It is a village situated about 10 miles north of Bādāmi, the chief town of the Bijapur district, where an inscription of the time of Someśvara I (dated 1053 A.D.) was discovered (*E.I.*, IV, 259ff.).

Kharjūrikā.—This village may be found in the neighbourhood or within the province of Malwa. The Khajuriya is very common around Ujjain (*E.I.*, XXIII, Pt. IV, October, 1935).

Khānāpur.—It is the chief town of the Khānāpur taluk of the Satara district of the Bombay State (*E.I.*, XXVII, Pt. VII, July, 1948, p. 312).

Kheda.—According to Hiuen Tsang it was situated fifty miles to the north-west of Malwa. Some have placed it in Gujarat. According to the Chinese pilgrim it was five hundred miles in circuit (*C.A.G.I.*, pp. 563ff.).

Kheṭaka.—It is modern Kherā in Gujarat (*E.I.*, XXIII, Pt. IV, October, 1935, p. 103). Some identify it with Kaira (*Important Inscriptions from the Baroda State*, Vol. I, p. 29).

Koḍavalli.—It may be identified with Kodoli, about seven miles to the east of Kolhapur (*E.I.*, XXIII, Pts. I and II, 1925).

Kollagiri.—It is mentioned in the *Bṛhatsaṃhitā* (XIV, 13). Some have identified it with Kolhapur.

Kollāpura.—This is the ancient name of modern Kolhapur (*E.I.*, III, 207; XXIII, Pt. II; XXIII, Pt. I, January, 1935, p. 30).

Kolūr.—This village lies in the Karajgi taluk of the Dharwar district, about three miles nearly west from Karajgi town (*E.I.*, XIX, p. 179).

Koṭinārā.—It is an important town in Surāṣṭra where lived a Brahmin named Soma who was well posted in *Vedas* and *Āgamas*. He duly performed the six prescribed rites (Law, *Some Jaina Canonical Sūtras*, p. 181).

Kukura.—It is a country near Ānarta in north Kathiawar (Luders' List No. 965). The Kukuras mentioned in the *Bhāgavata Purāṇa*, seem to have occupied the Dvārakā region. The *Bṛhatsaṃhitā* (XIV, 4) locates them in Western India. According to the Nasik Cave Inscription of Gautamī Balaśrī, her son conquered them along with the Suraṭhas, Mūlakas, Aparāntas, Anūpas, Vidarbhas and others. Most of these peoples along with the Kukuras were again conquered by him, as we learn from the Junāgaḍh Rock Inscription of Rudradāman. These were probably wrested from the hands of the contemporary Sātavāhana ruler of the Deccan. For further details, vide B. C. Law, *Tribes in Ancient India*, p. 390.

Kulenur.—It is a village in the Dharwar district of the Bombay State where the inscription of the reign of Jayasiṃha II was discovered (*E.I.*, XV, 329ff.).

Kumbhāroṭakagrāma (*E.I.*, XIX, 236).—It is in North and Central Gujarat, and may be identified with Kāmrod, 13 miles east of Modasa.

Kuśasthalapura.—It is mentioned in the Allahabad Pillar Inscription as Kuśthalapura. Kuśasthalapura is the name of a holy city of Dvārakā.[1] It was the capital of Ānarta (i.e., Kāthiāwār).

Kuśāvartta.—It is mentioned in the *Yoginītantra* (2. 4, pp. 128-129). It is a sacred tank near the source of the Godāvarī, 21 miles from Nasik.

Lakṣmeśvara.—It is the headquarters of the Lakṣmeśvara taluk within the limits of the Dharwar district of the Bombay State, where the Pillar Inscription of Yuvarāja Vikramāditya was discovered (*E.I.*, XIV, 188ff.).

Lāṭa.—In the Mandasor Inscription of Bandhuvarman we find mention of Lāṭa. According to the Ghāṭiyālā Inscription of the Pratihāra king Kakkuka, the king obtained great renown in the Lāṭadeśa (*E.I.*, IX, pp. 278–80). According to some, Lāṭa was southern Gujarat including Khandesh situated between the rivers Mahī and lower Tāpti. Some hold it as lying between the rivers Mahī and Kim (*Important Inscriptions from the Baroda State*, Vol. I, p. 29). It comprised the collectorates of Surat, Broach, Kheda and parts of Baroda (N. L. Dey, *Geographical Dictionary*, p. 114). It was the ancient name of Gujarat and northern Konkan. According to Bühler, Lāṭa is central Gujarat, the district between the Mahī and Kim rivers, and its chief city was Broach. The Rewah Stone Inscription of Karṇa refers to Lāṭa generally identified with central and southern Gujarat (*E.I.*, XXIV, Pt. III, July, 1937, p. 110). Lāṭarāṣṭra (Pāli Lāḷaraṭṭha—*Dīpavaṃsa*, p. 54; *Mahāvaṃsa*, p. 60) is identical with the old Lāṭa kingdom of Gujarat, the capital city of which is stated in the *Dīpavaṃsa* (p. 54) to have been Siṃhapura (Sīhapura).

The earliest mention of the country seems to have been made by Ptolemy. According to him Lārike lay to the east of Indo-Scythia along the sea-coast (McCrindle, *Ptolemy's Ancient India*, pp. 38, 152-53). The Pāli Chronicles of Ceylon refer to the country of Lāḷa in connection with the first Aryan migration to Ceylon led by Prince Vijaya. It has been

---

[1] Cf. *Bhāgavata Purāṇa*, I, 10. 27; VII, 14. 31; IX, 3. 28; X, 61. 40; X, 75, 29; X, 83, 36; XII, 12, 36.

attempted to identify Lāḷa both with Lāṭa or Lāḍa in Gujarat and Rāḍha in Bengal, and both countries claim the honour of first Aryanization of Ceylon. In the days of the early Imperial Guptas the Lāṭa country came to be formed into an administrative province in the Lāṭaviṣaya. The Lāṭa country was probably the same as the Lāṭeśvara country mentioned in the early Gurjara and Rāṣṭrakūṭa records. In the Baroda copperplate inscription (v. 11) the capital of Lāṭeśvara is said to have been at Elapur. Under the Cālukyas of Aṇahilavāḍapāṭana (A.C. 961) the name Lāṭa was gradually displaced by the name Gurjarabhūmi. Lassen identifies Lārike with Sanskrit Rāṣṭrika, in its Prākrita form Lāṭika, which is easily equated with Lāṭa, though the equation of Rāṣṭrika and Lāṭika is not convincing. For further details, vide B. C. Law, *Indological Studies*, Pt. I, p. 27; Law, *Tribes in Ancient India*, pp. 351–53.

Lona.—It may be identified with Lonad, a village six miles east of Bhiwandi in the Bhiwandi taluk (*E.I.*, XXIII, Pt. VII, p. 257).

Mahalla-Lāṭa.—It means larger Lāṭa, which may be represented by Laḍki in the Morsi taluk of the Amraoti district, about 18 miles north by west of Belorā (*E.I.*, XXIV, Pt. VI, April, 1938).

Mahenjo-daro.—It is in the Larkāna district of Sindh. The ruins at the site present to us a well-developed urban civilization in the second half of the third millennium B.C. It is generally admitted that in Mahenjo-daro we have abundant remnants of the civilization of the chalcolithic age. The prehistoric monuments of the Indus Valley, so far as they are unearthed, have been carefully studied from different points of view, but the most baffling part of the researches so far made, still remains to be played and this is the decipherment of the Indus inscriptions. The underground drainage system was good. The great Bath at this site which was 39 ft. long, 29 ft. wide, and 8 ft. deep, had steps leading to the floor. Some houses were one-storeyed and some two-storeyed. For details, vide J. Marshall, *Mohenjo-daro and the Indus Civilisation*, I–III; Mackay, *Further Excavations at Mahenjo-daro*, III; Presidential Address of the *R.A.S.B.*, 1948.

Mahī.—The variants are Mahatī (*Vāyu*, XLV, 97), Mahita (*Mahābhārata*, Bhīṣmaparva, IX, 328) and Rohi (*Varāha Purāṇa*, lxxxv). This river issues from the Pāripātra mountains and empties itself into the Gulf of Cambay. It has a south-westerly course up to Banswara, from which it turns south to pass through Gujarat.

Mamjaravāṭaka.—It is the modern village of Maṃjarḍe, nine miles to the north-east of Tasgaon, the headquarters of the taluk of the same name in the Satara district (*E.I.*, XXVII, Pt. V, p. 210).

Managoḷi.—It is a village about 11 miles to the north-west of Bāgewāḍi, the chief town of the Bāgewāḍi taluk of the Bijapur district (*E.I.*, V, 9ff.).

Mandasor.—See *Daśapura.*

Mankaṇikā.—It is modern Māmkaṇī in the Sankheḍā taluk of the Baroda district (*Important Inscriptions from the Baroda State*, Vol. I, p. 4).

Maureyapallikā.—It is Morwadi, three miles south-west of Nasik (*E.I.*, XXV, Pt. V, January, 1940, p. 230—*Two Grants of Pṛthivīcandra Bhogaśakti*).

Mayūrakhaṇḍi.—The Añjanavatī plates of Govinda III refer to it, which may have been the Rāṣṭrakūṭa capital at the time of Govinda III. Bühler identifies Mayūrakhaṇḍi with Morkhaṇḍ, a hill-fort in the Sātmālā or Ajantā range, close to Saptaśṛṅgī and north of Vaṇī in the Nasik district (*I.A.*, VI, p. 64).

Minnagar.—It was the capital of Lower Sindh in the 2nd century of the Christian era. The actual position of this place is doubtful (*C.A.G.I.*, pp. 330ff.). According to the *Periplus of the Erythraean Sea* it was the capital of Indo-Scythia. Ptolemy knew it as Binagara (McCrindle's *Ancient India as described by Ptolemy*, p. 152). Dr. D. R. Bhandarkar holds that it may be identified with Mandasor. The author of the *Periplus* mentions king Mambarus (identified by some with Nahapāṇa) whose capital was Minnagar in Ariake which is Aparāntika.

Mirāj.—It is the chief town of the Mirāj state in the southern Mārāṭhā country, Bombay, where were found the plates of Jayasiṃha II, A.D. 1024 (*E.I.*, XII, p. 303).

Miriñjī.—It may be identified with Mirāj (*E.I.*, XXIII, Pt. I, 1935, p. 30).

Mohaḍavāsaka.—It is mentioned in the Harsola grant (*E.I.*, XIX, 236). It may be identified with the modern village of Mohdasa in the Prantej taluk, Ahmedabad district.

Mukuḍasivayivā.—It is a locality in Kalyāṇa (Luders' List No. 998).

Mūlavāsara.—This village is situated about 10 miles from Dvārakā in the Okhamaṇḍala territory in Kathiawar where a stone inscription of the Mahākṣatrapa Rudradāman I, dated 200 A.D., was discovered (*Important Inscriptions from the Baroda State*, Vol. I, p. 1).

Mulguṇḍa.—It is identified with the modern village of the same name in the Gadag taluk of the Dharwar district (*E.I.*, XXVI, Pt. II, April, 1941, p. 61).

Mūṣika.—The Mūṣikas or Mūṣakas (*Mahābhārata*, Bhīṣmaparva, IX, 366, 371) were an offshoot of the northern tribe known to Alexander's historians as Mausikanos. The principality of Mausikanos comprised a large portion of modern Sind. Its capital has been identified with Alor in the Sikhur district. According to Arrian (Chinnock, *Arrian*, p. 319), the Brāhmaṇas seemed to have been very influential in this region. They are said to have been the main agents in bringing about an uprising of the people against the Macedonian invader. But Alexander took them by surprise and they had to submit to him (*C.H.I.*, I, 377). Strabo gives an interesting account of the inhabitants of this territory (H. and F. Tr. III, p. 96). In Indian literature we find frequent references to the people of Mūṣika. The Mriṣikas mentioned in the *Mārkaṇḍeya Purāṇa* (LVIII, 16) were probably the same as the Mūṣikas or Mūṣakas who, as Pargiter (*Mārkaṇḍeya Purāṇa*, p. 366) suggests, probably settled on the banks of the river Mūṣi on which stands modern Hyderabad. The Mūṣikas were probably so called because their territory lay in that portion of the northwestern trade-route which was known as *Mūṣikapatha* or red tract (Barua, *Aśoka and His Inscriptions*, Ch. III). The people called Mauṣikāra mentioned by Patañjali in his *Mahābhāṣya* (IV, 1. 4) were probably connected with the Mūṣikas.

Nandivardhana.—This may be identified with Nagardhan or Nandardhan near Ramtek in the Rampur district (*E.I.*, XXIV, Pt. VI, April, 1938). It is also mentioned in the Deoli plates of Kṛṣṇa III.

Naravana.—It is a village on the seashore in the Guhāgaḍ Peta in the Ratnagiri district. Some four miles to the north-east of Naravana stands Cindramāḍa which is the modern Cindravala (*E.I.*, XXVII, Pt. III, p. 127).

Narendra.—This village lies in the Dharwar district of the Bombay Presidency. It is situated near the high road from Dharwar to Belgaum at about 4½ miles north-west by north from Dharwar (*E.I.*, XIII, p. 298).

Nausāri.—Vide Nāgasārikā.

Navapattalā.—The district in which it was situated may have comprised the territory round the modern Nayākherā, which lies about eight miles west of Tikhāri (*E.I.*, XXV, Pt. VII, July, 1940).

Nāgasārikā.—In the Surat plates of Karkkarāja Suvarṇavarṣa we find mention of Nāgasārikā (Navasārikā) which is modern Nausāri about 20 miles to the south of Surat (vide also *Ellora Plates of Dantidurga*, *E.I.*, XXV, January, 1939, p. 29; *E.I.*, XXI, Pt. III, July, 1931; *J.B.B.R.A.S.*, 26, 250). Nausāri is the headquarters town of the Nausāri division of the Baroda State where the copperplates of Śilāditya of the year 421 were discovered (*E.I.*, VIII, 229ff.). It is also known as Navarāṣṭra, the Noagramma of Ptolemy in the Broach district (cf. *Mahābhārata*, Sabhāparva, Ch. 31).

Nāguma.—It may be identified with the modern Nagaon, about two miles south-west of Uran in the Panvel taluk of the Bombay State (*E.I.*, XXIII, Pt. VII).

Nāndipuraviṣaya.—The Añjaneri plates of Gurjara Jayabhaṭṭa III mention it, which may be identified with Nāndod, situated on the Karjan river in the Rājāpipla State (*E.I.*, XXV, Pt. VII, July, 1940). Nāndipura in the Lāṭa country is the modern Nāndod on the Narmadā (*E.I.*, XXIII, Pt. IV, October, 1935, p. 103).

Nāsika (*Nasik*).—It is mentioned in the two oldest inscriptions (20 and 22) in the caves. The people of Nāsika are described as making a grant in the inscription No. 20 and a cave also is described in the same inscription and a cave is described in the inscription No. 22 as the gift of a śramaṇa minister of Nāsika. Nāsika also occurs in the Barhut votive label No. 38. It is the same as Nāsiki or Naisika of the Purāṇas and Janasthāna of the *Rāmāyaṇa*. It is Nāsikya of the *Bṛhatsaṃhitā* (XIV. 13). It occurs in Luders' List (Nos. 799, 1109) as Nāsika, a town. According to the *Brahmāṇḍa Purāṇa* it was situated on the Narmadā. Janasthāna was within the reach of Pañcavaṭī on the Godāvarī. It came to be known as Nāsika due to the fact that here Śūrpaṇakhā's nose was cut off by Lakṣmaṇa. Nāsika is modern Nasik which is about 75 miles to the north-west of Bombay. Nasik, the headquarters of the Nasik district, lies on the right bank of the Godāvarī, about four miles north-west of the Nasik Road station. During the reign of the Sātavāhana kings of Andhra, Nāsika was a stronghold of the Bhadrayāniya school of the Buddhists (Barua and Sinha, *Barhut Inscriptions*, pp. 16, 128; cf. Luders' List Nos. 1122–1149).

The climate of Nasik is healthy and pleasant. That Nasik was situated on nine hills supports the view that it was nine-pointed. The city contains three parts: old Nasik or the Pañcavaṭī on the left bank of the river Godāvarī, middle Nasik built on nine hills on the right bank of the river Godāvarī to the south of the Pañcavaṭī, and the modern Nasik on the right bank of the river to the west of the Pañcavaṭi (*Nasik, Gazetteer of the Bombay Presidency*, Bombay, 1883, Vol. XVI, pp. 466ff.). On the right bank of the river Godāvarī, about 70 yards south-east of Umā-Maheśvara's temple, stands the temple of Nīlakaṇṭheśvara. It is strongly built of beautifully dressed richly carved trap. It faces east across the river and has a porch-dome and spire of graceful outline. The object of worship is a very old *liṅga* said to date from the time of king Janaka, the father-in-law of Rāma (*Nasik, Gazetteer of the Bombay Presidency*, Vol. XVI, 1883, p. 505).

The *Tapovana* or the forest of austerities is situated about a mile east of the Pañcavaṭī. It has a famous shrine and an image of Rāma who is believed to have lived on fruits collected by Lakṣmaṇa from this forest (*Ibid.*, 537).

The Buddhist caves at Nasik are very well known. They are known as Paṇḍuleṇas. They are situated about 300 ft. above the road level. They are excavated by the Bhadrayānikas, a Hīnayana sect of the Buddhists. There are altogether 23 excavations. The earliest is the *Caitya* cave dating from the Christian era. There are four *Vihāras*. The cave No. 1 is an unfinished *Vihāra*. The cave No. 2 is an excavation with many additions by the later Mahāyāna Buddhists. The cave No. 3 is a big *Vihāra*, having a hall 41 ft. wide and 46 ft. deep. Over the gateway the Bodhi tree, the *dogoba*, the *cakra* and the *dvārapālas* are visible. The cave No. 10 is a *Vihāra* and contains an inscription of the family of Nahapāṇa who reigned at Ujjain before 120 A.D. The pillars of the verandah contain bell-shaped Persian capitals. The hall is about 43 ft. wide and 45 ft. deep, having three plain doors and two windows. The cave No. 17 has a hall measuring 23 ft. wide by 32 ft. deep. The verandah is reached by half a dozen steps in front between the two central octagonal pillars. On the back wall there is a standing figure of the Buddha. On the right side there are four cells. There is an inscription which tells us that the cave was the work of Indrāgnidatta, son of Dharmadeva, a native of the Sauvīra country. The cave No. 17 is of a much later date. The cave No. 19 is a *Vihāra* cave dated about the 2nd century. The cave No. 23 contains the sculpture of Buddha attended by Padmapāṇi and Vajrapāṇi. There are some images of the Buddha both in the *Dharmacakramudrā* and *Dhyānamudrā*. For further details vide *the Gazetteer of Bombay Presidency*, Vol. XVI, *Nasik*, pp. 542ff.

Nidaguṇḍi.—It is a village, about four miles towards the south-southwest from Shiggaon, the headquarters of the Bankāpur taluk of the Dhārwār district, Bombay, where an inscription of Vikramāditya VI was discovered (*E.I.*, XXIII, 12ff.).

Nirguṇḍipadraka.—It may be identified with modern Nāgaravāḍā, 12 miles from Dabhoi (*E.I.*, II, 23).

Niṣāda.—The first epigraphic mention of the tribal state of Niṣāda is found in the Junāgaḍh Rock Inscription of Rudradāman who is credited to have conquered it along with east and west Malwa, the ancient Māhiṣmatī region, the district round Dwarkā in Gujarat, Surāṣṭra, Aparānta, Sindhu-Sauvīra, and other countries. This country also occurs in Luders' List (No. 965). The Citorgaḍh Inscription of Mokala of the Vikrama year 1485 states that Mokala subdued the tribal state of Niṣāda along with the Aṅgas, Kāmarūpas, Vaṅgas, Cīnas and Turuṣkas (*E.I.*, II, 416ff.). The Niṣādas are referred to for the first time in the later *Saṃhitās* and the *Brāhmaṇas* (*Taittirīya Saṃhitā*, IV, 5. 4. 2; *Kāṭhaka Saṃhitā*, XVII, 13; *Maitrāyaṇī Saṃhitā*, II, 9, 5; *Vājasaneyī Saṃhitā*, XVI, 27; *Aitareya Brāhmaṇa*, VIII, 11; *Pañcaviṃsa Brāhmaṇa*, XVI, 6. 8 etc.). The *Lāṭyāyana Śrautasūtra* (VIII, 2. 8) and *Kātyāyana Śrautasūtra* (I, 1. 12) refer to a village of the Niṣādas and a Niṣādasthapati, a leader of some kind of craft, respectively. The social duty enjoined on the Niṣādas was to kill and provide fish for human consumption (*Manu*, X, 48). According to the Pali texts they were wild hunters and fishermen (Fick, *Die Sociale Gliederung*, 12, 160, 206, etc.). Pargiter points out that they were a people of rude culture or aboriginal stock (*A.I.H.T.*, p. 290), and that they lived outside the Aryan organization. This is attested to by the *Rāmāyaṇa* story of Gūha, the king of the Niṣādas, who are described as a wild tribe (Ādikāṇḍa, Canto I; Ayodhyākāṇḍa, Canto 51). Manu explains the origin of the Niṣādas as the offspring of a Brāhmaṇa father and a Śudra mother (*Manusaṃhitā*, X, 8). At the time of the Epics and Purāṇas the Niṣādas seem to have had their dwelling among the mountains that form the boundary of Jhalwar and Khandesh in the Vindhya and Satpura ranges (Malcolm, *Memoirs of Central India*, Vol. I, p. 452). This is proved by the *Mahābhārata* (III, 130, 4), which refers to a Niṣādarāṣṭra in the region of the Sarasvatī and the Western Vindhyas, not very far from Pāripātra or Pāriyātra (*Mahābhārata*, XII, 135, 3–5). The same epic seems to connect the Niṣādas with the Vatsas and the Bhargas (II, 30, 10-11). They had their settlement in the east also (*Bṛhatsaṃhitā*, XIV, 10). According to the *Rāmāyaṇa* (II, 50, 33; 52, 11) Sṛṅgaverapura on the north side of the Ganges opposite Prayāga was the capital of a Niṣāda kingdom. It was a large town ruled by king Gūha of the Niṣādas, who was Rāma's friend. He received Rāma hospitably (Ayodhyākāṇḍa, XLVI, 20; XLVII, 9–12; cf. *J.R.A.S.*, 1894, p. 237; F. E. Pargiter, *The Geography of Rāma's Exile*). In the middle of the second century A.D. the Niṣāda country was under the suzerainty of the western Kṣatrapas (B. C. Law, *Tribes in Ancient India*, Ch. XXV). For further details, vide B. C. Law, *Indological Studies*, Pt. I, pp. 42-43.

Ossadioi.—According to some scholars like St. Martin, the Ossadioi were probably identical with the Vaśāti mentioned in the *Mahābhārata* as being associated with the Śivis and the Sindhu-Sauvīras (*Mahābhārata*, VII, 19, 11; 89, 37; VIII, 44, 49; VI, 106, 8; 51, 14). The exact geographical position of this tribe cannot be ascertained (Law, *Indological Studies*, Pt. I, pp. 33-4).

Osumbhala.—This village has been identified with the modern Umbel, seven miles south of Kamrej. One of the grants of Allaśakti, discovered at Surat, registers the donation of a field in this village (*D. R. Bhandarkar Volume*, pp. 54-55).

Pacchatri.—It is to be identified with the modern village of Pachtardi, six miles to the west of Ghumli (*E.I.*, XXVI, Pt. V, January, 1942, p. 199).

Paḍivasa.—It may be identified either with Phunda, about two miles north-east of Uran or with Panja, a village about three miles to the north of Uran in the Panvel taluk of the Bombay State (*E.I.*, XXIII, Pt. VII, p. 279).

Palāśavanaka.—It is mentioned in the Surat plate of Kīrtirāja. It may be identified with modern Palasanā, the headquarters of the Palasanā sub-division in the Surat district (*I.A.*, XXI, p. 256).

Pampā.—It is a tributary of the river Tuṅgabhadrā. It rises in the Ṛṣyamukha mountain, eight miles from the Anagaṇḍi hills (cf. *Bombay Gazetteer*, Vol. I, Pt. II, p. 369). On the bank of this river Rāma met Hanumān (*Rāmāyaṇa*, Ādikāṇḍa, Sarga I, v. 58). Lakṣmaṇa also visited it. This river was adorned with red lotuses. Its water was clear and it looked beautiful (*Rāmāyaṇa*, Kiṣkindhyākāṇḍa, Sarga I, vv. 64–66; Sarga I, vv. 1–6).

There was a lake by the name of Pampā which was also very beautiful. Its water was free from impurities (*Rām.*, Kiṣkindhyākāṇḍa, I, 1–6).

Pañcavaṭi.—It was either in Janasthāna or it bordered on it. It was visited by Sītā along with the two descendants of Raghu. Śūrpaṇakhā who was a resident of Janasthāna, encountered Rāma here (*Rāmāyaṇa*, Ādikāṇḍa, I, 47; Āraṇyakāṇḍa, XXIII, 12; *Mahābhārata*, 83, 162; *J.R.A.S.*, 1894, p. 247). Śūrpaṇakhā's ears and nose were chopped off by Lakṣmaṇa (*Rām.*, Āraṇyakāṇḍa, Sarga 21, v. 7; *Uttaracaritam*, Act I, 28). This forest was not far off from the hermitage of Agastya situated near the river Godāvarī (*Ibid.*, Sarga 13, vs. 13–19, Vaṅgavāsī ed.). It was on the Godāvarī, full of wild animals, antelopes, etc., and adorned with fruits and flowers. It was a beautiful place well-levelled and delightful. It was full of birds (*Rāmāyaṇa*, Āraṇyakāṇḍa, 15th Sarga, 1–5, 10–19). A big leaf-hut was raised here where Rāmacandra stayed for some time with Sītā and Lakṣmaṇa (*Ibid.*, 20–31).

Pañcāpasara.—This lake was situated somewhere between the Pañcavaṭī and the Citrakūṭa (*Raghuv.*, XIII, 34–47). It has been described as the pleasure lake of Śātakarṇi (*Raghuv.*, XIII, 36).

Pandhārpur.—This town is situated on the right bank of the river Bhīmā and it contains a celebrated shrine of Vithoba (Law, *Holy Places of India*, p. 43).

Palāsinī.—This is the name of a river (Luders' List, No. 965), which issues from the Mount Ūrjayat (Ūrjayanta). Some seem to identify this river with Parās, a tributary of the Koel in Chotanagpur (Law, *Rivers of India*, p. 45).

Palitānā.—It is in Kāthiāwāḍ district where two copperplates of Siṃhāditya have been found (*E.I.*, XI, p. 16).

Paṭṭadakal.—It is a village, about eight miles to the east by north of Bādāmi, the chief town of the Bādāmi taluk or sub-division in the Bijapur district, Bombay State, where a pillar inscription of the time of Kīrtivarman II was discovered (*E.I.*, III, 1ff.).

Pānāḍa.—It may be identified with Paināḍ, situated about eight miles north by east of Alibāg in the Kolaba district of the Bombay State (*E.I.*, XXVI, Pt. VI, April, 1942, p. 287).

Pārasika.—It may be some island near Thānā. Its memory is retained by one of the hills called Pārsik. According to some, it may be the island of Ormuz in the Persian Gulf (*Important Inscriptions from the Baroda State*, Vol. I, p. 66).

Pāvakadūrga.—This is to be identified with the hill fort of Pāvāgarh in the Bombay State, about 25 miles south of Godhrā and by road 29 miles east of Baroda in the Pañch Mahals district (*E.I.*, XXIV, Pt. V, p. 221).

Prābhāsa.—It is mentioned in the Nasik Cave Inscription of the time of Nahapāṇa (*c.* 119–24 A.D.). It is in Kāthiāwāḍ (cf. *Mathura Buddhist Image Inscription of Huviṣka*). It is the well-known Prabhās-Pātan or Somnāth-Pātan on the south coast of Kāthiāwār (*Gazetteer of the Bombay Presidency*, 1883, *Nasik*, p. 637). It is called Prabhāsatīrtha (Luders' List, Nos. 1099, 1131). This sacred place is mentioned in the *Bhāgavata Purāṇa* as situated on the sea-shore (X, 45, 38; X, 78, 18; X, 79, 9–21; X, 86, 2; XI, 6, 35; XI, 30, 6; XI, 30, 10). According to the *Bhāgavata Purāṇa* (VII, 14. 31), this holy place sacred to Hari is famous for the Sarasvatī flowing westwards. It was visited by Arjuna and Balarāma (*Bhāgavata*, X, 86. 2; X, 78. 18). The *Mahābhārata* (118, 15; 119, 1–3) mentions Prabhāsatīrtha. The *Kūrma Purāṇa* refers to it as one of the famous holy places of India (Ch. 30, śls. 45–48; cf. *Agni Purāṇa*, Ch. 109). The *Yoginītantra* (2. 4. 128; 2. 5. 141) also mentions it. The *Padma Purāṇa* (Ch. 133) mentions Someśvara in Prabhāsa.

Praesti territory.—The people of the territory of Oxykanos were known as Praesti corresponding to the Proṣṭhas mentioned in the *Mahābhārata* (VI. 9, 61). According to Cunningham the territory of Oxykanos lay to the west of the Indus in the level country around Lārkhāna (*Invasion of Alexander*, p. 158). Oxykanos tried to oppose Alexander but in vain (*C.H.I.*, I, 377).

Purandhar.—It is a hill-fort to the south-west of Poona, not far from Sāsvad. It contains unidentified caves which are of a type so far unknown to India (*J.R.A.S.*, Pts. 3 and 4, 1950, pp. 158ff.).

Pūrāvi.—The Pūrāvi is the river Pūrṇa on the banks of which Nausāri is situated (*E.I.*, XXI, Pt. III, July, 1931).

Raivataka Hill.—Raivata or Raivataka was near Dvārakā. It is mentioned in the *Mahābhārata* (Ādiparva, CCXIX, 7906–17) that a festival was held on this hill in which the citizens of Dvārakā took part. Pargiter is inclined to identify it with the Baradā hills in Halar (*Mārkaṇḍeya Purāṇa*, p. 289). In the Junāgaḍh Inscription of Skandagupta occurs the Raivataka hill which is opposite to Ūrjayat (See *Dohad Stone Inscription of Mahamuda* in *E.I.*, XXIV, Pt. V, January, 1938, p. 216). The Jaunpur stone inscription of Iśvaravarman Maukharī mentions it along with the Vindhya mountains (*C.I.I.*, Vol. III). Fleet has identified Raivataka with one of the two hills of Girnar and not with Girnar proper (*C.I.I.*, III, p. 64, n. 11; *I.A.*, VI, p. 239). The *Bṛhatsaṃhitā* (XIV. 19) mentions it as situated in the south-west division. In early times Raivata and Ūrjayanta might have been names of two different hills at Girnar; but in later times they came to be regarded as identical (*Bombay Gazetteer*, Vol. VIII, p. 441). The Raivataka in the *Dohat Stone Inscription of Mahamuda* refers to the hill on which there are temples and which is now known as Girnar (*E.I.*, XXIV, Pt. V, p. 222). Close to Junāgaḍh in Gujrat stands the Raivataka hill or Girnar, which is considered to be the birthplace of Nemināth, the religious preceptor of king Dattātreya. The river Suvarṇarekhā flows at the foot of this hill. There is a foot-print on the Girnar hill known as the *Gurudattacaraṇa*. The temples of Nemināth and Pārśvanath are found here. The name of Girinagara occurs in the *Bṛhatsaṃhitā* (XIV, 11). Girnār is famous in the inscriptions of Aśoka, Skandagupta and Rudradāman. To the east of Junāgaḍh there is a number of Buddhist caves. The Inscriptions of Rudradāman and Skandagupta inform us that at Girnar the provincial governors of Candragupta, Aśoka, and the Imperial Guptas lived. There is the Svayamvara lake near it. Here stands a high pinnacled temple of Neminātha on the summit of the Raivataka hill in Surāṣṭra. For further details, vide B. C. Law, *Some Jaina Canonical Sūtras*, pp. 181-182.

Rangpur.—It lies 20 miles south-east of Limbdi, the chief town of the State of the same name or three miles north-west of Dhandhuka in Ahmedabad district. For details vide *A.S.I.*, *Annual Reports*, 1934-35, pp. 34ff.

Rāmatīrtha.—It is at Sorpāraga (Luders' List, No. 1131). It is a holy reservoir in Sopara near Bassein, about 40 miles north of Bombay. Uṣabhadāta records a gift to some mendicants who lived there (*Gazetteer of the Bombay Presidency*, Nasik, Vol. XVI).

Rāmatīrthikā.—It is the headquarters of the sub-division in which Kiṇihikā was included. It may probably be identified with Rāmatīrtha, where Uṣavadāta made some gifts to the Brahmins as recorded in a Nasik cave inscription (*E.I.*, XXV, Pt. IV, October, 1939, p. 168).

Rāṣṭrikas.—Aśoka's Rock Edict V refers to the Rāṣṭrikas.

Rāyagaḍh.—It is in the Kolaba district of the Bombay State, where three copperplates of Vijayāditya were discovered (*E.I.*, X, 14ff.).

Reṭṭuraka.—It is Reṭare in the Karhād taluk in the Satara district. There are two villages of this name situated on the opposite banks of the river Krishṇā (*E.I.*, XXVII, Pt. VII, July, 1948, p. 316).

Ron.—Ron is modern Rou, the headquarters of Ron taluk in the Dharwar district of the Bombay State (*E.I.*, Vol. XX, p. 67).

Roruka.—Roruka was one of the important cities according to the *Divyāvadāna* (pp. 544ff.). It was the capital of Sovīra mentioned in the

Āditta Jātaka (*Jāt.*, III, 470). A king named Bharata of Roruva was very popular and religious. He gave great gifts to the poor, the wanderers, the beggars and the *paccekabuddhas* (*Jāt.*, III, 470–474). Sovīra has been identified by Cunningham with Eder, a district in the province of Gujarat at the head of the gulf of Cambay. The *Bodhisattvāvadāna-Kalpalatā* refers to a famous king named Rudrāyana of Roruka or Rauruka (40th pallava). King Rudrāyana of Roruka was a contemporary of Bimbisāra of Magadha and they were intimate friends. There was a trade between Rājagṛha and Roruka.

Sabarmatī.—This river flows from the Pāripātra mountain, and finds its way into the Gulf of Cambay through Ahmedabad.

Śakadeśa.—Pāṇini refers to it in his *Aṣṭādhyāyī* (4. 1. 175). The *Bṛhatsaṃhitā* mentions it as the country of the Śaka people (XIV, 21). For details vide Law, *Tribes in Ancient India*, 3–6, 77, 84, 92, 94, 157.

Śambhu (Sambos territory).—According to classical writers Sambos ruled the mountainous country adjoining the territory of the Mausikanos. There existed mutual jealousy and animosity between these two neighbours. The capital of this country was Sindimana identified with Sehwan, a city on the Indus (McCrindle, *Invasion of Alexander*, p. 404). Sambos submitted to Alexander. For further details vide B. C. Law, *Indological Studies*, Pt. I, pp. 36-37.

Samudrapāṭa.—It may be identified with Samad Piparia, four miles south of Jubbulpore (*E.I.*, XXV, Pt. VII, July, 1940).

Śarabhapura.—The Raypur Copperplate Inscription of Rājā Mahāsudevarāja refers to it (*C.I.I.*, Vol. III).

Śatruñjaya or Siddhācala.—It is the holiest among the five hills in Kathiawar according to the Jains. To the east of it stands the city of Palitana, 70 miles north-west of Surat. The Śatruñjaya temple was repaired by Bāghbhaṭṭadeva, an officer of king Kumārapāla in Gujarat. Of all Jaina temples situated on the top of the Śatruñjaya hill, Caumukha temple is the highest. Some inscriptions were found in the Jaina temples situated on the Śatruñjaya hill (*E.I.*, II, 34ff.). Śatruñjaya, also known as Siddhakṣetra, was visited by a large number of accomplished sages, such as Ṛṣabhasena. Many saints and kings attained the bliss of perfection. Here the five Pāṇḍavas with Kuntī also attained perfection. This sacred place of the Jains is adorned with five summits (kūṭas). The cave lying to north of Śrīmad-Ṛṣabha, set up by the Pāṇḍavas, still exists. Close to the Ajita-caitya lies the Anupama lake. Near Marudevī stands the magnificent caitya of Śānti. King Meghaghoṣa built two temples here. Śatruñjaya was under his rule and that of his father, Dharmadatta. For further details vide Law, *Some Jaina Canonical Sūtras*, pp. 179-180.

Sālotgi.—It is a large village six miles south-east of Indi, the chief town of the Indi taluk of the Bijapur district of the Bombay State (*E.I.*, IV, p. 57).

Sātodika.—It was a river in the Surāṣṭra country. Jotipāla, the son of the royal chaplain, who was educated at Takkasilā, became an ascetic. He attained perfection in meditation. He had many disciples and one of them went to the Suraṭṭha country and dwelt on the banks of this river (*Jātaka*, III, pp. 463ff.).

Seriva.—It is mentioned in the *Jātaka*. In the kingdom of Seri there were two merchants dealing in pots and pans. They used to sell their wares in the streets (*Jātaka*, I, pp. 111–114). According to some it has been identified with Seriyāpuṭa (a seaport town of Seriya), which is mentioned in a votive label on the stūpa of Bārhut. According to others it may be identified with Śrīrājya or the later Gaṅga kingdom of Mysore (Ray Chaudhury, *P.H.A.I.*, p. 64; Barua and Sinha, *Barhut Inscriptions*, p. 32). Barua and Sinha are right in holding that Seriyāpuṭa was like Śūrpāraka and Bharukaccha, an important port on the western coast of India and that it may be identified with Seriva (*Ibid.*, p. 132).

Seriyāpuṭa.—It is mentioned in the Bārhut inscriptions (Barua and Sinha, p. 32). It seems to be an important port on the western coast of India like Suppāraka and Bharukaccha. The merchants of Seriva reached Andhapura by crossing the river Telavāha (*Jātaka*, No. 3).

Siggāve.—It may be identified with Siggaon in the district of Dharwar (*E.I.*, VI, p. 257).

Siharagrāma—(*E.I.*, VIII, 222).—It is in southern Gujarat, and may be identified with Ser, eight miles north-east of Delvāda.

Sindhu-Sauvīra.—Pāṇini mentions Sauvīra and Suvīra in his *Aṣṭādhyāyī* (4.2.76; 4.1.148). Patañjali in his *Mahābhāṣya* also refers to it (4.2.76). The name Sindhu-Sauvīra suggests that Sauvīra was situated on the Indus and the Jhelum. That the Sauvīras are often connected with the Sindhus determines that these two peoples, who were later regarded as one and the same, were settled on the Sindhu or the Indus. They played an important part in the Kurukṣetra war. The Junāgaḍh Rock Inscription of Rudradāman (*c.* 150 A.D.) refers to the Mahākṣatrapa's conquest of Sindhu-Sauvīra along with Pūrvāparā-karāvantī, Ānūpanivrit, Ānarta, Surāṣṭra, Svabhra, Maru, Kaccha, Kukura, Aparānta and other countries. It is mentioned in the Luders' List, No. 965. The *Bṛhatsaṃhitā* mentions it (XIV, 17).

According to the *Bhagavatī Sūtra* Udayana of Sauvīradeśa was succeeded by his nephew Keśī in whose reign Vītahavya was completely ruined. He went to the extent of renouncing the world, but when the question of the succession of his son Abhi came before him, he said to himself: 'If I renounce the world after appointing Abhi to royal power, then Abhi will be addicted to it and to the enjoyment of human pleasures. He will go on wandering in this world'. This led him to renounce the world appointing his sister's son Keśī to royal power (pp. 619-20). It seems to be a case of the matriarchal system in vogue in Sauvīradeśa.

The Kṣatrapas seem to have wrested the country of Sindhu-Sauvīra from the Kuṣāṇas. After the Kṣatrapas the country probably passed over to the Guptas and later to the Maitrakas of Valabhi. In a Nausāri Copperplate grant of the Gujarat Cālukyas, Pulakeśirāja (8th century A.D.) is credited with having defeated the Tājikas, who are generally identified with the Arabas. The Tājikas are reported therein to have destroyed the Saindhavas, Kacchelas, Surāṣṭras, Cāvotakas, Gurjaras, and Mauryas before they were themselves defeated by the Cālukya king (*Bombay Gazetteer*, Vol. I, p. 109). Sovīra has been identified by Cunningham with Eder, a district in the province of Gujarat at the head of the Gulf of Cambay. Its capital was Roruka (*Jāt.*, III, p. 470). The name Sindhu-Sauvīra suggests that Sovīra was situated between the Indus and the Jhelum. A brisk trade existed between Rājagṛha and Roruka (*Divyāvadāna*, 544ff.). King Rudrāyana of Roruka and king Bimbisāra of Magadha were intimate friends. For further details, vide B. C. Law, *Indological Studies*, Pt. I, 40ff.

Sirīṣapada.—Śirīṣa may be equated with Śrīṣa (Barua and Sinha, *Barhut Inscriptions*, p. 27, Votive label No. 43). It is a village called Śirīṣa-padraka mentioned in two Gurjara inscriptions (*I.A.*, XIII).

Sirur.—Its ancient name is Sirivura. It is a village in the Gadag taluk of the Dharwar district in the Bombay State, about three miles from Ālūr, where an inscription of the reign of Jayasiṃha II was discovered (*E.I.*, XV, 334ff.).

Śivapura.—Śivapura may be identical with Śivipura, mentioned in the Shorkot inscription (*E.I.*, 1921, p. 16). Dr. Vogel takes the mound of Shorkot to be the site of the city of the Śibis. For details, vide B. C. Law, *Tribes in Ancient India*, p. 83.

Sogal.—It is a village in the Paraṣgad taluk in the Belgaum district, Bombay State (*E.I.*, XVI, p. 1).

Somanāthadevapaṭṭana.—It is situated in Kathiāwāḍ and its modern name is Verawal, where an image inscription was discovered (*E.I.*, III, 302).

Somnāth.—It is in Junāgaḍh, also known as Candraprabhāsa. It is a sacred place of the Jains. Formerly there was a wooden temple, but afterwards it was built in marble (Law, *Geographical Essays*, p. 212).

Sonnalige.—It is a part of modern Solapur (*E.I.*, XXIII, Pt. V, p. 194).

Sonne.—This river is the modern Śāstrī river flowing south of Naravana (*E.I.*, XXVII, Pt. III, p. 127).

Śrīmat-Aṇahilapura.—(*E.I.*, VIII, 219–29).—It may be identified with Aṇavāḍā in North Gujarat.

Sudarśana.—It is a lake situated at some distance from Girinagara (Girnar, Jain Girinār in south Kāthiāwāḍ). The lake originally constructed by the Vaiśya Puṣyagupta, a *rāṣṭriya* of the Maurya king Candragupta, and subsequently adorned with conduits by the Yavana king Tusāṣpha, was destroyed during a storm by the waters of the Suvarṇasikatā (Luders' List, No. 965).

Sudi.—It is the ancient Suṇḍi, a village in the Ron taluk of the Dharwar district, Bombay State. It lies about nine miles east by north from Ron town (*E.I.*, XV, 73).

Śūdra country.—According to the *Mārkaṇḍeya Purāṇa* (Ch. 57, 35) the country of the Śūdras may be located in the Aparānta region or western country. According to the *Mahābhārata* (IX, 37, 1) the Śūdras lived in the region where the river Sarasvatī vanished into the desert, i.e., Vinaśana in Western Rajputana (*Śūdrabhirān prati dveṣād yatra naṣṭā Sarasvatī*). Opinions differ as to the exact location of their territory. For further details vide B. C. Law, *Indological Studies*, Pt. I, p. 34.

Śūlika.—The Śūlikas may be identified with the Solaki and Solaṅki of the Gujarat records. Some have identified them with the Cālukyas. They are mentioned in the Harāhā Inscription of Īśānavarman Maukhari. For further details see B. C. Law, *Tribes in Ancient India*, pp. 384-385.

Sūnakagrāma.—It is in North Gujarat, and may be identified with Sunak, a village about 15 miles east-south-east from Pattan, north Gujarat, and about five miles west of Unjha railway station (*E.I.*, I, 316).

Surathā.—This river is mentioned in the *Kūrma Purāṇa* (XLVII, 30); *Varāha Purāṇa* (LXXXV) and *Bhāgavata Purāṇa* (XIX, 17). Its different reading is Surasā. It issues from the Ṛkṣa and the Vindhya mountains (vide, B. C. Law, *Geographical Essays*, p. 111).

Surāṣṭra.—The Surāṣṭras were the famous people in Ancient India. The Surāṣṭra country (Pali Suraṭṭha, Chinese Su-la-cha) is mentioned in the *Rāmāyaṇa* (Ādikāṇḍa, Ch. XII; Ayodhyākāṇḍa X; Kiṣkindhyākāṇḍa, XLI) as well as in Patañjali's *Mahābhāṣya* (1. 1. 1, p. 31). It is also mentioned in Luders' List No. 965. It is also known as Suraṭha (*Ibid.*, 1123). According to the *Padma Purāṇa* (190. 2) it is in Gurjara. The *Bhāgavata*

Purāṇa mentions it as a country (I, 10. 34; I, 15. 39; VI, 14. 10; X, 27. 69; XI, 30. 18). It is also mentioned in the *Bṛhatsaṃhitā* (XIX, 19). Rājaśekhara in his *Kāvyamīmāṃsā* (Gaekwad Oriental Series, pp. 93-94) also assigns Surāṣṭra to the western division along with Bhṛgukaccha, Ānartta, Arbuda, Daśeraka and other countries. Surāṣṭra comprises modern Kāthiāwāḍ and other portions of Gujarat. According to the *Kauṭilīya-Arthaśāstra* (p. 50) the elephants of Saurāṣṭra were the most inferior as compared with those belonging to Aṅga and Kaliṅga. According to the *Sarabhaṅga Jātaka* (*Jāt.*, V, 133), a stream called Sātodikā flowed along the borders of the Surāṣṭra country, and the sages were sent to dwell on its bank. A sage named Sālissara belonging to the Kaviṭṭhaka hermitage left it for the Suraṭṭha country where he dwelt with many sages on the bank of the river Sātodikā (*Jātaka*, III, p. 463). The prosperity of this town was due to trade (*Apadāna*, II, 359; *Milinda*, 331, 359; *Jātaka*, III, 463; V, 133). A king named Piṅgala ruled Surāṣṭra as a subordinate potentate under the Mauryas (*Petavatthu*, IV, 3; *D. R. Bhandarkar Volume*, 329ff.). The Jaina *Dasaveyāliya Cūrṇī* (I, p. 40) also refers to Suraṭṭha or Surāṣṭra which was a centre of trade in ancient times.

According to the Chinese pilgrim, Hiuen Tsang, the capital of Surāṣṭra lay at the foot of Mt. Yuh-shan-ta (Prākrit Ujjanta, Skt. Ūrjayat of the inscriptions of Rudradāman and Skandagupta and is identified with Junāgaḍ, ancient Girinagara, i.e., Girṇār). At the time of the *Mahābhārata* the Surāṣṭra country was ruled by the Yādavas. It appears from Kauṭilya's *Arthaśāstra* (p. 378) that Surāṣṭra had a Saṃgha form of government. According to Strabo (Bk. XI, section XI, i; H. & F., Vol. II, pp. 252-3) the conquests of the Bactrian Greeks in India were achieved partly by Menander and partly by Demetrios, son of Euthydemos. They gained possession not only of Patalene but also of the kingdom of Saraostos (Surāṣṭra) and Sigerdis. Ptolemy refers to a country called Syrastrene which must be identical with Surāṣṭra (modern Surat on the Gulf of Cutch). Syrastrene which extended from the mouth of the Indus to the Gulf of Cutch, was one of the three divisions of Indo-Scythia in Ptolemy's time. Syrastrene is also mentioned in the *Periplus of the Erythraean Sea* as the sea-board of Aberia which is identified with the region to the east of the Indus above the insular portion formed by its bifurcation. After the Scythian occupation Surāṣṭra seems to have passed into the hands of the Guptas (B. C. Law, *Tribes in Ancient India*, pp. 347-48). We find its decisive evidence in the Junāgaḍh Inscription of Skandagupta, *cir.* 455–480 A.D. (*C.I.I.*, Vol. III). The Udayagiri Cave Inscription tells us that Skandagupta 'deliberated for days and nights before making up his mind as to who could be trusted with the important task of guarding the land of the Surāṣṭras'. Surāṣṭra at the time of Samudragupta was ruled by the Śaka lords or chieftains (Śaka-Muruṇḍas) (cf. *Allahabad Pillar Inscription of Samudragupta*). The Surāṣṭra country came to be included in the Maurya empire as early as the reign of Candragupta for the Junāgaḍh Rock Inscription of Rudradāman refers to Candragupta's *rāṣṭriya* (Viceroy) Puṣyagupta the Vaiśya, who constructed the Sudarśana lake. It was included in Aśoka's dominions,[1] for the same inscription refers to Tuṣāspha, a Persian contemporary and vassal of Aśoka, who carried out supplementary operations on the lake. It is evident from Rudradāman's inscription that the Yavanarāja Tuṣāspha became an independent ruler of Surāṣṭra. The ancient name of Junāgaḍh indicates that the city with the hill-fort was

[1] Vide *Manshera Version of Aśoka's R.E.V.*

built by a Yavana ruler (*I.C.*, Vol. X, 87ff.). That Surāṣṭra was autonomous in Aśoka's time seems probable from Rock Edict V.[1] For further details, vide B. C. Law, *Indological Studies*, Pt. I, pp. 50–52.

Sūrpāraka (Pali Suppāraka).—It is modern Sopara or Supara in the Thana district, Bombay State, 37 miles north of Bombay and about four miles north-west of Bassim. It was the capital of Sunāparanta or Aparānta. (*Majjhima*, III, 268; *Saṃyutta*, IV, 61ff.). According to the Pali texts the people of Sunāparanta were reported as being fierce and violent. The distance of Suppāra from Sāvatthī was one hundred and twenty leagues (*Dhammapada Commy.*, II, p. 213). It is also called Sopāraga, Sopāraka, Sorpāraga, (Luders' List, Nos. 995, 998, 1095 and 1131), Saurpāraka, and Suppārika. Six Śilāhara Inscriptions in the Prince of Wales Museum refer to Sūrpāraka which is the modern Nala Sopara in the Bassim taluk of the Bombay State (*E.I.*, XXIII, Pt. VII). Sūrpāraka is mentioned in one of the inscriptions of Śaka Uṣavadāta. It was a great sea-coast emporium (*Dhammapada Commy.*, II, 210), rightly identified with Sopara of early Greek geographers. According to the *Harivaṃśa* (XCVI, 50), a sage named Rāma Jāmadagnya is credited with having built the city of Sūrpāraka. The *Mārkaṇḍeya Purāṇa* (57) mentions this city. All the *Purāṇas* agree in placing it in the west, but the *Mahābhārata* locates it in the south (Sabhāparva, XXX, 1169; Vanaparva, LXXXVIII, 8337). A ship containing 700 passengers lost her way and came to the port of Suppāra. The people of Suppāra invited them to disembark and greatly fed and honoured them (*Dīpavaṃsa*, IX, vv. 15-16). According to the *Mahāvaṃsa* (VI. 46) the port of Suppāraka situated on the west coast of India, was visited by Vijaya. Sūrpāraka seems to have been an important centre of trade and commerce where merchants used to flock with merchandise (*Divyāvadāna*, 42ff.). There was a householder named Bhava in this city who was a contemporary of the Buddha (*Divyāvadāna*, 24ff.).

Sūryapura.—It is modern Surat (*J.A.S.B.*, VI, 387). Here Śaṅkarācārya wrote his commentary on the Vedānta (N. L. Dey, *Geographical Dictionary*, p. 198).

Susaka.—It is mentioned in the Nasik inscription over which Gautamīputra is said to have ruled. It seems to mean Su or Yuetchi Śakas who probably held part of the Panjab and of the Gangetic provinces.

Sutīkṣṇa-āśrama.—It lay in the Daṇḍaka forest. The sage Sutīkṣṇa gave up his life burning himself in the sacrificial fire. This hermitage was visited by Rāma with Sītā and Lakṣmaṇa.

Svabhra.—This is mentioned in the Junāgaḍh Rock Inscription of Rudradāman I (A.D. 150). It is on the Sabarmatī (cf. *Padma Purāṇa*, Uttarakhaṇḍa, Ch. 52). It is mentioned as a country (Luders' List No. 965).

Talegaon.—It is in the Poona district. A copperplate grant belonging to the time of the Rāṣṭrakūṭa king Kṛṣṇa I, was discovered.

Tauraṇaka.—It seems to be the modern Toran on the Karjan river (*E.I.*, XXV, Pt. VII, July, 1940).

Tāladhvaja.—It is in Kāthiāwāḍ and may possibly be identified with Talaja (*I.A.*, XV, 360).

Ṭekabhara.—The Jubbulpore Stone Inscription of Vimalaśiva mentions it, which may be identified with Tikhārī, five miles south by west of Jubbulpore (*E.I.*, XXV, Pt. VII, July, 1940).

---

[1] Vide *the Manshera Version of Asoka's R.E.V*; R. K. Mookerjee, *Aśoka*, p. 140, fn. 6; H. C. Raychaudhuri, *Political History of Ancient India*, 4th ed., p. 236.

Tiḍguṇḍi.—This village is situated 20 miles north of Bijapur city in the Bijapur taluk of the Bijapur district of the Bombay State, where plates of the time of Vikramāditya VI were discovered (*E.I.*, III, 306).

Torambage.—It may possibly be identified with Tuvambe in the Kolhapur State (*E.I.*, XIX, p. 32).

Toraṇagrāma.—It is in southern Gujarat and may be identified with Torangaṃ (*J.B.B.R.A.S.*, Vol. 26).

Torkheḍe.—It is a village in the Khandesh district, where a copper-plate grant of Govindarāja of Gujarat of Śaka samvat 735 was discovered (*E.I.*, III, 53ff.).

Trayambakeśvara.—It is situated in the dense forest, and is an important Hindu holy place in the Bombay State. The river Godāvarī rises from here.

Tuppadkurhaṭṭi.—It is a village in the Navabund taluk of the Dharwar district where an inscription of the reign of Akālavarṣa Kṛṣṇa III was discovered (*E.I.*, XIV, 364ff.).

Ujjantagiri.—See Ūrjayat.

Ūnā.—This town is in the southernmost part of the peninsula of Kāthiāwāḍ in the Junāgaḍh State, where two Sanskrit inscriptions on copperplates have been discovered (*E.I.*, IX, p. 1).

Uraṇa.—It is the modern Uran (*E.I.*, XXIII, Pt. VII, p. 279).

Ūrjayat.—Ūrjayat (Ujjanta) of the Junāgaḍh Inscriptions of Rudradāman and Skandagupta may be identified with the Girnar hill near Junāgaḍh. The Kap Copperplate of Keḷadi Sadāśiva-Nāyaka refers to Ujjantagiri which is Girnar (*E.I.*, XXIV, Pt. V, January, 1938; cf. Fleet, *Gupta Inscriptions*, *C.I.I.*, Vol. III, p. 60). It is also known as Ūrjayatgiri (cf. Junāgaḍh Inscription of Rudradāman). In Luders' List No. 965 it is called Ūrjayat. This mountain which is sanctified by Śrīnemi is known as Raivataka, Ūrjayanta, etc. This mountain is situated at Surāṣṭra. Vastupāla built three temples here for the good of the world. In the temple of Satruñjaya built by Vastupāla there are images of Ṛṣabha, Puṇḍarika and Aṣṭāpada (B. C. Law, *Some Jaina Canonical Sūtras*, p. 180).

Vaḍāla.—Vaḍāla is the modern name of Bheṭalikā in the district of Pacchatri. It is a railway station on the Junāgaḍh State Railway, about seven miles north of Junāgaḍh (*E.I.*, XXVI, Pt. V, January, 1942, p. 210).

Vaḍnagar.—It is identified with the Ānandapura in North Gujarat, 70 miles south of Sidhpur.

Vaidūryaparvata.—It is the Satpura range situated in Gujarat. The hermitage of the sage Agastya was on this hill (*Mahābhārata*, Vanaparva, Ch. 88). It is so called because the costly stone of *lapis luzuli* is found here. The most important minor mountain associated with the Sahya is the Vaidūrya, which is generally identified with the Oroudian mountain of Ptolemy. It included the northernmost part of the Western Ghats, but the *Mahābhārata* suggests that it included also a portion of the southern Vindhya and the Satpura ranges.

Vallabhi.—It was a prosperous town in the country of the Gurjaras where reigned a king named Śilāditya (Law, *Some Jaina Canonical Sūtras*, pp. 183-184). The ruins of the city of Valabhi or Vallabhi were found near Bhaonagar on the eastern side of Gujarat (*A.S.W.I.*, Vol. II). In an inscription of the 5th century it has been mentioned as a beautiful kingdom of Balabhadra (*J.A.S.B.*, 1838, p. 976). A rich master-mariner lived in this city in Saurāṣṭra named Gṛhagupta who had a daughter named Ratnavatī whom a merchant's son, Balabhadra, came from Madhumatī to marry

(*Daśakumāracaritam*, p. 158). It was known to Hiuen Tsang as Fa-la-pi. The kingdom of Valabhi included the whole of the Peninsula of Gujarat and the districts of Bharoch and Surat according to Yuan Chwang (*C.A.G.I.*, pp. 363ff. and p. 697).

Vallavāḍa.—It may be identified with Vaḷayavāḍa, also called Vaḷavāḍa, the site of the present Rādhānagarī, about 27 miles to the south-west of Kolhapur (*E.I.*, XXIII, Pts. I and II).

Vaṅkikā.—This river is the Vaṅkī creek about 30 miles to the south of Nausāri (*E.I.*, XXI, Pt. III, July, 1931).

Varadākheṭa.—It is probably Warud in the Morsi taluk of the Amraoti district (*E.I.*, XXIII, Pt. III).

Vaṭapardaka (Vaṭapadrapura).—It is the ancient name of Vaṭapaṭṭana. It occurs in the Baroda Plates of Karkarāja II, dated Śaka 734. It is modern Baroda (*Important Inscriptions from the Baroda State*, Vol. I, p. 97).

Vaṭṭāra.—It may be identified with Vatar, a village about six miles north-west of Nala Sopara and four miles south-west of Agāshi in the Bassim taluk of the Bombay State (*E.I.*, XXIII, Pt. VII).

Vāghli.—It is a village six miles east or rather north-east of Chalisgāon in the Khandesh district, where a stone inscription of the Śaka year 991 has been discovered. This village has three temples: an old temple of Madhāidevī, a small ruined temple and a temple of the Mānbhāva sect (*E.I.*, II, 221ff.).

Vāhāula.—It may be identified with Vāhorā, a village about four miles south-east of Bhilodia in the Baroda State (*E.I.*, XXVI, Pt. VI, April, 1942, p. 251).

Vāluraka.—Vāluraka (Valūraka) mentioned in the Karle Cave Inscription of the time of Nahapāṇa, *c.* 119–24 A.D. appears to be the ancient name of the Karle region. Karle is situated in the Poona district of the Bombay Presidency. In Luders' List (Nos. 1099, 1100) Vāluraka is the name of a cave.

Velugrāma.—It is identified with Velgaon, three miles south-east of Kirat and 14 miles east-north-east of Palghar (*E.I.*, Vol. XXVIII, Pt. I, Jany., 1949).

Vegavatī.—The Jaina tradition associates this river with Mount Ūrjayanta in Saurāṣṭra.

Veṇākaṭaka.—The Nasik Cave Inscription of Gautamīputra Śātakarṇi mentions Veṇākaṭaka which was situated on the Veṇva river in the Nasik district.

Verāwal.—It is ancient Somanāthadeva-paṭṭana in Kāthiāwāḍ, where an image inscription was discovered (*E.I.*, III, 302).

Vindhyapādaparvata.—The *Mahābhārata* refers to it as Vindhyaparvata (Ch. 104, 1–15). The *Padma Purāṇa* (Uttarakhaṇḍa, vv. 35–38) mentions it. The Vindhya forest attached to the mountain is described in the *Daśakumāracaritam* (p. 18) as a wild wood full of terror, fit habitation for beasts and remote from the haunts of men. It is known as Quindon to Ptolemy. It forms the boundary between Northern and Southern India. The Ṛkṣa, the Vindhya and the Pāripātra are parts of the whole range of mountains now known as the Vindhya (Law, *Geographical Essays*, 107ff.). This mountain had a beautiful grotto (*kandara*) watered by the river Revā (*Mārkaṇḍeya Purāṇa*, Vaṅgavāsī Edition, p. 19). It occurs in Luders' List, No. 1123.

This mountain, otherwise known as Vijha, may be identified with the Satpura range. On a spur of this range there is a colossal rock-cut Jaina image called Bawangaj. According to modern geographers the Vindhya mountain extends eastward for a distance of about 700 miles from Gujarat on the west to Bihar on the east, taking different local names, e.g., the Bharner, the Kaimur, etc. The average elevation of this mountain is from 1,500 to 2,000 ft.; some of the peaks rising to an altitude of 5,000 ft. This mountain is not of true tectonic type. It represents the southern edge of the Malwa plateau, which got faulted in the remote geological time, resulting in the formation of the Vindhya mountain. It is believed that the Vindhya was formed of sediments derived from the Aravalli mountain.

Vinjhāṭavi.—This forest comprises portions of Khandesh and Aurangabad, which lie on the south of the western extremity of the Vindhya range including Nasik. Ariṭṭha, a minister of Devānampiyatissa, who was sent to Aśoka for a branch of the Bodhi tree, had to pass through this forest while proceeding to Pāṭaliputra (*Dīpav.*, 15. 87).

Walā.—The Maliya Copperplate Inscription of Mahārāja Dharasena II (year 152) refers to it as the chief town of the Walā estate in the Kāthiāwāḍ division (*C.I.I.*, Vol. III; *E.I.*, XIII, p. 338).

Yekkeri.—It is a village about four miles towards the north by east from Saundatti, the chief town of the Paraṣgad taluk of the Belgaum district, where a rock inscription of the time of Pulakesin II was discovered (*E.I.*, V, 6ff.).

Chapter V

CENTRAL INDIA

Acalapura.—It is a village identical with the modern Ellichpur in the Amraoti district (*E.I.*, XXIII, Pt. I, January, 1935, p. 13; *E.I.*, XXVIII, Pt. I, January, 1949).

Acāvaḍa (Accāvaṭa).—It is the Ṛkṣavat mountain where lived the banker Nāgapiya, a native of Kurara. It occurs in Luders' List (Nos. 339, 348, 581 and 1123). The Ṛkṣavat is the Ouxenton of Ptolemy. It is a part of the whole range of mountains now known by the common name Vindhya. Ptolemy describes the Ṛkṣavat as the source of the Toundis, the Dosaron, the Adamas, the Ouindon, the Namados and the Nanagouna. By the Ṛkṣvat or the Ṛkṣavant Ptolemy meant the central region of the modern Vindhya range, north of the Narmadā (Law, *Mountains of India*, p. 17; Law, *Geographical Essays*, pp. 107ff.).

Aceya.—It is about 12 miles south-west of Mandasor on the right bank of the river Seona, about a mile to the south of the Partabgarh Road.

Agar (Shajapur).—It is 41 miles by road north of Ujjain.

Airikina.—The Erāṇ Stone Inscription of Samudragupta refers to it, which has been identified with Erāṇ, a village on the left bank of the Bīṇā, 11 miles to the west by north from Khurai, the chief town of the Khurai tahsil or sub-division of the Sagor district in C.P. (*C.I.I.*, Vol. III).

Ajayameru.—The Bijholi Rock Inscription of Cāhamāna Someśvara (V.S. 1226) refers to Ajayameru. This is evidently the modern Ajmeer founded by the Cāhamāna prince Ajayadeva or Ajayarāja between A.D. 1100 and 1125 (*Ep. Ind.*, XXVI, Pt. III, July, 1941; *I.A.*, XVI, p. 163).

Ajaygaḍh.—It is a hill fort about 16 miles in a straight line south-west of Kālañjar, where two Chandella inscriptions were discovered (*E.I.*, I, 325). It is the modern name of Jayapuradūrga standing 20 miles to the south-west of the Chandel fortress of Kālañjar (*J.B.B.R.A.S.*, Vol. 23, 1947, p. 47).

Amarakaṇṭaka.—This hill is a part of the Mekhala hills in Gondwana in the territory of Nagpur in which the rivers Narmada and Son take their rise. Hence the Narmada is called the *Mekhalasutā* (*Padma Purāṇa*, Ch. VI). According to some, it is in the Rewah State on the easternmost extremity of the Maikal range, 25 miles by country road from Sahdol railway station, 3,000 ft. above sea-level. It is one of the sacred places of the Hindus (For details, vide B. C. Law, *Holy Places of India*, p. 34). The Amarakaṇṭaka is the Āmrakūṭa of Kālidāsa's *Meghadūta* (I, 17). It is also known as the Somaparvata and the Surathādri (*Mārkaṇḍeya Purāṇa*, Ch. 57). According to the *Matsyap.* this sacred hill was superior to Kurukṣetra (22. 28; 186. 12–34; 188. 79, 82; 191. 25). The *Padma Purāṇa* (Ch. 133, v. 21) mentions a holy place named Caṇḍikātīrtha at Amarakaṇṭaka.

Ambar.—It is the ancient capital of the State of Jaipur, Rajputana, about seven miles north-east of Jaipur railway station. The way from Jaipur to Ambar commands a panoramic view of hills and jungles. There are some handsome temples.

The city of Ambar, the third capital in succession of the Jaipur State, is believed to have been founded in the 10th or 11th century A.D. It is also designated as Ambāvatī which was the capital of the territory called Ḍhuṇḍa or Ḍuṇḍhāhada. Cunningham derives the name Ambar from

Ambikeśvara, the name of a large temple at Ambar (D. R. Sahni, *Archaeological Remains and Excavations at Bairāṭ*, pp. 9ff.).

Amera.—It is about one and half miles to the south of Udaipur.

Amodā.—It is a village in the Bilaspur district. An inscription has been found here incised on two massive plates (*E.I.*, XIX, 209ff.).

Amrol (Gwalior).—It is about 10 miles to the north-west of Antri, a station of G.L.R.

Anarghavalli.—It corresponds to the modern Jānjgir tahsil of the Bilaspur district (*E.I.*, XXIII, Pt. I, January, 1935, p. 3, *Peṇḍrābandh Plates of Pratāpamalla*).

Anghora.—It is two and half miles south of Kadwaha.

Añjanavatī.—It is a village in the Candur taluk, about 22 miles due east of Amraoti in Berar (*E.I.*, XXIII, Pt. I, January, 1935, p. 8).

Antri (Gwalior).—It is about 16 miles to the south of Gwalior on the old road from Delhi to Deccan, a place of Abul Fazl's murder.

Arañjara.—It is a chain of mountains in the Majjhimadesa. It is described here as existing in a great forest. (*Jāt.*, V, 134).

Aravalli.—Some have identified this range with the Apokopa. It is perhaps the oldest tectonic mountain of India. It divides the sandy desert of western Rajputana from the more fertile tracts of eastern Rajputana. The range can be traced from Delhi to Jaipur as a low hill. Farther south the range becomes more prominent. Beyond Marwara the height increases farther, the highest peak attaining the height of 4,315 ft. The main range terminates south-west of the Sirohi State. The Aravalli range is pre-Vindhyan in age. The Arbuda (Mount Abu) which is separated from the Aravalli range by a narrow valley is also pre-Vindhyan in age. (For details, vide *Imperial Gazetteers of India*, by W. W. Hunter, pp. 214-215).

Arbuda.—It is the Mount Abu in the Aravalli range in the Sirohi State of Rajputana. It is called the hill of wisdom. It contains the hermitage of the sage Vaśiṣṭha and the famous shrine of Ambā Bhavānī. According to Megasthenes and Arrian the sacred Arbuda or Mount Abu is identical with Capitalia which attaining an elevation of 6,500 ft. rises far above any other summit of the Aravalli Range (McCrindle, *Ancient India as described by Megasthenes and Arrian*, p. 147). The river called Sābhramatī has its source in the Arbudaparvata (*Padma Purāṇa*, Ch. 136). For further details, vide Law, *Some Jaina Canonical Sūtras*, pp. 184-185; *Rajputana Gazetteers*, Vol. III-A compiled by Erskine, pp. 284ff.; *The Imperial Gazetteers of India*, by W. W. Hunter, Vol. I, pp. 2ff.

Arthūṇā.—It lies above 28 miles in a westerly direction from Banswara in Rajputana (*E.I.*, XIV, p. 295).

Aśī.—It is the chief town of the sub-division in which Mahalla-Lāṭa was situated. It may be identified with Aśṭi which lies only 10 miles south-east of Belorā (*E.I.*, XXIV, Pt. VI, April, 1938, p. 263).

Aśīrgaḍh.—A strong fortress in Nimar district, C.P., 29½ miles S.W. of Khandwa (*Imperial Gazetteers of India*, Vol. I, p. 230). The Aśīrgaḍh Copper seal Inscription of Saravavarman mentions the hill-fort of Aśīrgaḍh which formerly belonged to Scindhia, about 11 miles to the north-east of Burhanpur, the chief town of the Burhanpur sub-division of the Nimar district in the Central Provinces (*C.I.I.*, Vol. III).

Avantī.—It is also called Avantikā according to the *Brahmāṇḍap.* (IV, 40. 91). The Junāgaḍh Inscription of Rudradāman I mentions Ākarāvantī (Malwa),[1] Ākara (identified with east Malwa, capital Vidiśā), Avantī

[1] Avantī is the ancient name of Malwa (cf. *Kathāsaritsāgara*, Ch. XIX).

(identified with West Malwa, capital Ujjain) along with Anūpa realm (capital Māhiṣmatī), Ānarta (North Kāthiāwāḍ), Surāṣṭra (south Kāthiāwāḍ), Śvabhra on the river Śabarmatī, Kaccha (Cutch in Western India), Sindhu (west of lower Indus), Sauvīra (east of lower Indus in Northern India), Kukura (near Ānarta in north Kāthiāwāḍ), Aparānta (North Konkan in Western India), Nishādha [1] and the Yaudheyas [1] who lived in Bijayagarh. Avantī of which Ujjayinī [2] was the capital finds mention in the Nasik Cave Inscription of Vāśiṣṭhiputra Pulumāyi as Ākarāvaṃti [3] while the Junāgaḍh Inscription of Rudradāman I speaks of two Ākarāvaṃtis, namely, Pūrva (eastern) and Apara (western). The first separate Rock Edict of Aśoka refers to Ujjayinī wherefrom the Mahāmātras were sent by the royal prince (*kumāra*). In the inscriptions of Aśoka, the Bhoja and Ṛṣṭika-Rāṣṭrika territories and their off-shoots were placed outside the territorial limit of the then Maurya province of Avantī (Barua, *Aśoka and His Inscriptions*, Ch. III). The inscriptions of Uṣavadāta of the time of the Kṣaharāta Kṣatrapa Nahapāṇa of western and southern India, when considered in relation to the inscriptions of the Śātavāhanas and the Śaka Kṣatrapas, involve a knotty chronological problem. There is no conclusive evidence to show that Ujjayinī or Avantī proper formed a dominion of Nahapāṇa. The inclusion of Ujjayinī in Nahapāṇa's territory is usually inferred from the mention of the Mālayas (Mālavas) in Uṣavadāta's Nasik cave inscription but one has yet to establish that Ujjayinī was at that time the seat of Government of the Mālavas.

As regards the location of Avantī, the *Mahābhārata* places it in western India (Avantiṣu praticyāṃ vai—Vanaparva, III, 89, 8354) and speaks of the sacred river Narmadā on which Avantī is situated. It states in the Virāṭaparva (IV, 1, 12) that Arjuna mentions Avantī along with other kingdoms in western India, namely, Surāṣṭra and Kunti. Mrs. Rhys Davids notes that Avantī lay to the north of the Vindhya mountains, north-east of Bombay (*Psalms of the Brethren*, p. 107, note 1). T. W. Rhys Davids observes that it was called Avantī as late as the 2nd century A.D., but from the 7th or 8th century onwards it was called Mālava (*Buddhist India*, p. 28). Ujjayinī, which was the capital of Avantī or western Mālava and which was situated on the river Siprā, a tributary of the Carmanvatī (Chambal), is the modern Ujjain in Gwalior, Central India (Rapson, *Ancient India*, p. 175). Avantī roughly corresponds to modern Malwa, Nimar, and adjoining parts of the Central Provinces. It was divided into two parts: the northern having its capital at Ujjayinī, and the southern having its capital at Māhissati or Māhiṣmatī.

The Avantīs were one of the most powerful of the Kṣatriya clans in ancient India. They occupied the territory which lay north of the Vindhya mountains. They were one of the four chief monarchies in India when Buddhism arose and were later absorbed into the Moriyan empire.[4] They were an ancient people as the *Mahābhārata* points out. Their dual monarchs, Vinda and Anuvinda, led Duryodhana's army in the battle of Kurukṣetra, and really speaking the Avantīs made up one-fifth of the entire Kuru host.[5] They were great warriors accomplished in battles, of firm

[1] B. C. Law, *Tribes in Ancient India*, pp. 98ff; (Niṣādas or Niṣadhas), pp. 75ff.

[2] It occurs as Ujenī, a town in Luders' List Nos. 172, 173, 210, 212, 218, 219–229, 231–237, 238, etc. In this list occurs a district called Ujenīhāra (No. 268) which is difficult to be traced.

[3] Also called Ākarāvatī (Luders' List, No. 965).

[4] *Psalms of the Brethren*, p. 107, N. 1.

[5] *Mbh.*, V, 19. 24.

strength and prowess, and were two of the best chariot-warriors.[1] They figured very prominently in the course of the whole war and performed many glorious and heroic deeds. They rendered great and useful service to the Kaurava cause both by their individual prowess and generalship, as well as by the numerous army consisting of forces of all descriptions that they led to battle. They supported Bhīṣma in the early stage of the battle.[2] They led an attack against the mighty Arjuna.[3] They fought very bravely with the mighty Irāvat, son of Arjuna. They attacked Dhriṣṭadyumna, the generalissimo of the Pāṇḍavas. They surrounded Arjuna and fought Bhīmasena.[4] Thus they fought bravely in the field until they laid down their lives at the hands of Arjuna according to some [5] or at the hands of Bhīma according to others.[6]

According to the *Matsya-Purāṇa* (Ch. 43) the Avantīs originated from the Haihaya dynasty [7] of which Kārttavīryārjuna was the most glorious ruler. There were marital relations between the royal families of the Avantīs and the ruling dynasty of the Yadus. Rājyādhidevī, a Yadu princess, was married to the king of Avantī.[8] She gave birth to two sons, Vinda and Upavinda, who are most probably to be identified with the heroic Avantī princes, Vinda and Anuvinda, whose mighty deeds in the Kurukṣetra battle are recorded in the *Mahābhārata*.[9]

The celebrated grammarian Pāṇini refers to Avantī in one of his *sūtras* (IV, 1. 176). Patañjali's *Mahābhāṣya* also refers to it (4. 1. 1, p. 36). The *Bhāgavata Purāṇa* mentions it as a city (X, 45. 31; X, 58. 30; XI, 23. 6, 23, 31). The *Skanda-Purāṇa* refers to it as a holy city (Ch. I, 19–23). The *Yoginītantra* (2. 2. 119) mentions it.

It is interesting to note that the country of Avantī, much of which was rich land, had been colonized or conquered by Aryan tribes who came down the Indus Valley and turned east from the Gulf of Cutch. It was called Avantī as late as the second century A.D. as we find in Rudradāman's inscription at Junāgaḍh, but from 7th or 8th century onwards it was called Mālava as pointed out by T. W. Rhys Davids.[10]

Avantī was one of the most flourishing kingdoms of ancient India and one of the sixteen great territories (*mahājanapadas*) of the Jambudīpa. The country produced abundance of food and the people were wealthy and prosperous.[11] The Pali language, in which the books of the Hīnayāna Buddhists have been written, was, according to some, elaborated in Avantī or Gandhāra.[12]

Avantī was a great centre of Buddhism. Several of the most earnest and zealous adherents of the *Dhamma* were either born or resided here, e.g., Abhayakumāra,[13] Isidāsī,[14] Isidatta,[15] Dhammapāla,[16] Soṇakūṭikaṇṇa,[17] and especially Mahākaccāyana.[18]

Mahākaccāyana was born at Ujjayinī in the family of the chaplain (*purohita*) of king Caṇḍa Pajjota. He learnt the three Vedas and after his father's death he succeeded him to the chaplainship. He went to the

---

[1] *Mbh.*, V, 166.
[2] *Ibid.*, VI, 16; II, 17, etc.
[3] *Ibid.*, VI, 59.
[4] *Ibid.*, VI, 102 and 113.
[5] *Ibid.*, VII, 99.
[6] *Ibid.*, XI, 22.
[7] Pargiter, *Ancient Indian Historical Tradition*, pp. 102, 267.
[8] *Viṣṇu-Purāṇa*, IV, 12; *Agni-Purāṇa*, Ch. 275.
[9] IV. 14.
[10] *Buddhist India*, p. 28.
[11] *Aṅguttara Nikāya*, IV, 252, 256, 261.
[12] Eliot, *Hinduism and Buddhism*, I, 282.
[13] *Theragāthā Comm.*, 39.
[14] *Therīgāthā Comm.*, 261–4.
[15] *Theragāthā*, 120.
[16] *Ibid.*, 204.
[17] *Ibid.*, 369.
[18] *Saṃyutta Nikāya*, III, p. 9; IV. 117; *Aṅguttara Nikāya*, I, 23; V, 46; *Majjhima Nikāya*, III, 223.

Buddha who taught him the Norm with such effect that, at the end of the lesson, he with his attendants was established in arhantship with thorough grasp of letter and meaning. It was through his effort that he succeeded in establishing Pajjota in the faith.[1] Mahākaccāyana himself being a native of Avantī worked with zeal for the diffusion of the new faith amongst his countrymen. The great success of his missionary activity in his native province is somewhat explained by the fact of his initial success in converting the ruler of the country, Caṇḍa Pajjota. He, while dwelling at Avantī, so successfully explained in detail the meaning of a stanza mainly dealing with *Kaṣiṇas* (objects of meditation) to an *upāsikā* (lay female devotee) named Kālī that she was very much satisfied with his explanation. He also explained to a householder of Avantī named Haliddikāni a stanza dealing with the question of *vedanā* (sensation), *rūpa* (form), *saññā* (perception), *viññāna* (consciousness), *dhātu* (element) and *saṃkhāra* (confections), and the householder was very much satisfied. The same devout and inquisitive householder again approached him for the elucidation of some of the knotty points of the Buddhist doctrine and he made them clear to him (*Sam.*, IV, pp. 115-116). Mahākaccāyana used to be present whenever any sermon was delivered by the Buddha on *Dhamma*. Therefore the monks used to keep a seat for him.[2] It is, therefore, clear that the followers of Buddhism in the western province of Avantī must have been very numerous and influential at the same time, showing that under the energetic ministration of the Thera Mahākaccāyana the new doctrine of peace and emancipation had spread far and wide over the province.

Mahāvīra, the great propounder of the Jaina faith, is said to have performed some of his penances in the country of Avantī. The capital of Avantī, Ujjayinī, was also visited by him where he did penance in a cemetery when Rudra and his wife tried in vain to interrupt him.[3]

One of the sacred places of the Liṅgāyat sect is situated in Avantī at Ujjayinī (Ujjenī) which is frequently visited by the Liṅgāyat itinerant ascetics.[4]

The Pradyotas were kings of Avantī. King Caṇḍa Pajjota (Caṇḍa Pradyota) was a contemporary of the Buddha. In Buddha's time the king of Madhurā was styled Avantīputta showing that on his mother's side he was connected with the royal family of Ujjayinī.[5] Ujjayinī played an important part in the political history of India. Under the Pradyotas it rose to a very high position and its power and prowess were feared even by the great emperors of Magadha. Ajātaśatru fortified his capital Rājagṛha in expectation of an attack about to be made by King Pajjota of Ujjenī. A matrimonial alliance was established between the royal families of Kauśāmbī and Avantī. Pajjota, king of Avantī, grew angry and was determined to attack Udena, king of Kosambī, knowing that he (Udena) surpassed him in glory. Pajjota got an elephant made of wood and concealed in it sixty warriors. Knowing that Udena had a special liking for fine elephants, Pajjota had informed him by spies that a matchless and glorious elephant could be found in the frontier forest. Udena came to the forest and in the pursuit of the prize, he became separated from his retinue and was made captive. While a captive he fell in love with Vāsuladattā, King Pajjota's daughter. Taking advantage of Pajjota's absence from his kingdom, he fled from his kingdom with Vāsuladattā. Udena managed

---

1 *Psalms of the Brethren*, 238-9.
2 *Dhammapada Commentary*, II, pp. 176-77.
3 Stevenson, *The Heart of Jainism*, p. 33.
4 Eliot, *Hinduism and Buddhism*, II, 227.
5 D. R. Bhandarkar, *Carmichael Lectures*, 1918, p. 53.

to reach his kingdom taking Vāsuladattā with him. He made her his queen.[1] In the 4th century B.C. Ujjenī became subject to Magadha. Aśoka, Candragupta's grandson, was stationed at Ujjain as viceroy of the Avantī country.[2] Vikramāditya, the celebrated king of Ujjain, expelled the Scythians and thereafter established his power over a great part of India. He restored the Hindu monarchy to its ancient splendour.[3] In later times some of the ruling families of Avantī made mark in Indian history. Dharmapāla of the Pāla dynasty dethroned Indrāyudha and installed in his place Cakrāyudha with the assent of the neighbouring northern powers of the Avantīs, the Bhojas and the Yavanas.[4] The Paramāra dynasty of Malwa (anciently known as Avantī) was founded by Upendra or Krishṇarāja early in the 9th century. Muñja who was famous for his learning and eloquence was not only a patron of poets but himself a poet of no mean reputation. Muñja's nephew, the famous Bhoja, ascended the throne of Dhārā which was in those days the capital of Malwa and ruled gloriously for more than forty years. Until the beginning of the thirteenth century A.D. the Paramāra dynasty of Malwa lasted as a purely local power. In this century this dynasty was superseded by chiefs of the Tomara clan who were followed in their turn by the Cauhan kings from whom the crown passed to the Moslem kings in 1401 A.D.

Avantī became a great commercial centre. Here met the three routes, from the western coast with its seaports Surpāraka (Sopārā) and Bhṛgukaccha (Broach), from the Deccan and from Śrāvastī in Kośala (Oudh). The *Periplus of the Erythraean Sea* (Sec. 48) points out that from Ozene (Ujjain) were brought down to Barygaza commodities for local consumption or export to other parts of India, e.g., onyx-stones, porcelain, fine muslins, mallow-tinted cotton, etc.

Avantī was also a great centre of learning. The Hindu astronomers reckoned their first meridian of longitude from Ujjayinī and the dramas of Kālidāsa were performed on the occasion of the Spring Festival before its Viceregal Court, *c.* 400 A.D.[5] Nine famous persons known as *Nava-Ratna* (nine gems) adorned the court of Vikramāditya, king of Ujjayinī.

Ujjayinī was built by Accutagāmi.[6] According to the Avantyakhaṇḍa of the *Skanda-Purā a* (Ch. 43), the great god Mahādeva after destroying the great demon called Tripura visited Avantipura the capital of the Avantīs, which, in honour of the great victory obtained by the god, came to be known as Ujjayinī.

This city was visited by the Chinese pilgrim, Yuan Chwang, in the 7th century A.D. According to him, Ujjayinī was about 6,000 li in circuit. It was a populous city. There were several convents but they were mostly in ruins. There were many priests. The king belonged to the Brahmin caste. Not far from the city there was a stūpa.[7]

The coins current in Ujjain have a special mark. On some of the rare coins the word *Ujeniya* is incised in Brāhmī characters of the 2nd century B.C. Generally on one side is found a man with a symbol of the sun and on the other is seen the sign of Ujjain. On some coins a bull within a fence or the Bodhi tree or the Sumeru hill or the figure of the Goddess of Fortune is seen on one side. Some coins of Ujjain are quadr-

---

[1] Cf. *Buddhist India*, 4–7, and Bhāsa's *Svapnavāsavadattā*.
[2] Smith, *Asoka*, p. 235.
[3] McCrindle, *Ancient India as described by Ptolemy*, pp. 154-55.
[4] Smith, *Early History of India*, 4th ed., p. 413.
[5] Rapson, *Ancient India*, p. 175.
[6] *Dīpavaṃsa* (Oldenberg), p. 57.
[7] Beal, *Buddhist Records of the Western World*, II, 270–271.

angular while others are round.[1] Square copper Moghul coins were struck in this city up to the time of Shah Jahan.[2] The class of round coins found at Ujjain display a special symbol, the 'cross and balls' known as the Ujjain symbol.[3] For further details vide B. C. Law, *Tribes in Ancient India*, Ch. IX; B. C. Law, *Geographical Essays*, pp. 33, 170; B. C. Law, *Ujjayinī in Ancient India*, (Gwalior Archaeological Department); B. C. Law, *Indological Studies*, I, 54.

Ābuyagrāma—(*E.I.*, VIII, 222).—It may be identified with Abu.

Āmtarī.—The Bijholi Rock Inscription of Cāhamāna Someśwara (V.S. 1226) refers to it (*E.I.*, XXVI, Pt. III, July, 1941), which may be identified with Uparamvāla-antarī. It is the name of a tract which comprises the estates of Begūn, Siṅgoli, Kadvāsa, Ratangarh, Kheḍī, etc.

Ānandapura.—It is mentioned in the Harsola grant (*E.I.*, XIX, 236). It may be identified with the modern Vaḍnagar in Baroda.

Ārthuna.—This village lies about 28 miles in a westerly direction from Banswara in Rajputana, where an inscription of the Paramāra Cāmuṇḍarāja was discovered (*E.I.*, XIV, 295).

Āvarakabhoga.—It may possibly be identified with the country round the town of Agar, north-east of Ujjain (*E.I.*, XXIII, Pt. IV, October, 1935, 102).

Badher.—It is about 10 miles by cart-track to the north-east of Shamshabad which is 31 miles by *pucca* road to the north-west of Bhilsa.

Badoh.—It is situated some 12 miles from Kulhar railway station.

Baḍvā.—It is a large village, about five miles south-west of Antah. It is in the Kotah State in Rajputana, where three Maukhari inscriptions on *Yūpas* of the Kṛta year 295 were discovered (*E.I.*, XXIII, Pt. II, April, 1935, p. 42).

Bairāṭ.—See Vairāṭ.

Baleva.—It is in Sanchor district, Jodhpur State. An inscription has been found here incised on two plates (*E.I.*, X, 76ff.).

Bamhanī.—It is in the Sohagpur tahsil of the Rewah State, Baghel-Khand, Central India. A copperplate charter has been discovered here, which is of immense value to the student of early Indian history (vide *Bhārata Kaumudī*, Pt. I, pp. 215ff.; cf. *E.I.*, XXVII, No. 24, p. 132).

Bangla.—It is about five miles to the east of the Narwar fort.

Barai.—It is about three miles from Panihar railway station (Gwalior-Shivpuri line).

Bargaon.—This village is situated at a distance of 27 miles north by west of Murwārā, the chief town of the Murwārā tahsil of the Jubbalpore district in Central Provinces (*E.I.*, XXV, Pt. VI, p. 278).

Barṇāla.—It is in the Jaipur State. It is a small village belonging to the Thakursahib of Barṇāla, about eight miles from the Lolsote-Gangapur fair-weather road, where two Yūpa inscriptions were discovered (*E.I.*, XXVI, Pt. III, July, 1941, p. 118).

Baro.—It is an ancient site, containing the remains of an ancient city extending up to the neighbouring town of Pāthār. The chief remains consist of Hindu and Jain temples (*Gwalior State Gazetteer*, I, pp. 199ff.).

Bāgh.—This village is situated in the south of Malwa, about 25 miles south-west of Dhar. It stands at the confluence of the Wāgh or Bāgh and

---

[1] R. D. Banerjee, *Prācīna Mudrā*, 108.

[2] Brown, *Coins of India*, p. 87.

[3] *Ibid.*, p. 20. Vide also B. C. Law, *Avantī in Ancient India* published in the Vikrama volume (*Scindia Oriental Institute*, 1948), pp. 281–288.

Girna streams. It lies on an old main route close to the Udaipur Ghat, 12 miles north of Kukṣī (*Gwalior State Gazetteer*, I, 196-197). To the south of this village is situated a vihāra, now much in ruins. The caves are nine in number. No inscription is found in these caves. The best images representing the Buddha or a Bodhisattva with two attendants are found in the south-western group in cave No. 2. The paintings at Bāgh may be dated the 6th century or first half of the 7th century A.D. The dagoba which is found in a few of these caves, contains no image of the Buddha. But there are images of the Buddha here and there in these caves. The architecture is not of the same type as that of the Nasik caves. The cave No. 2 known as Paṇḍaboṅkigumphā is well preserved. It is a square *Vihāra* with cells on three sides and a stūpa inside a shrine at the back. The ante-chamber has pillars in front and its walls are adorned with sculptures. The cave No. 3 is a *Vihāra*. The cave No. 4 is the finest specimen of architecture. There is a portico more than 220 ft. long supported by 22 pillars. The cave No. 5 is a rectangular excavation, the roofs being supported by two rows of columns. The roof of cave No. 6 is dilapidated. The cave No. 7 which seems to be similar to the cave No. 2, is also dilapidated. All the caves are *vihāras*, there being apparently no caitya hall or Buddhist Church attached to them.

Bāghelkhand.—The Rewah grants of Trilokyavarman show that the northern portion of Bāghelkhand was under the control of the Candellas in the 13th century A.D. (*I.A.*, XVII, 230ff.).

Bālāghāt.—It is a district in the Nagpur division of Central Provinces, where five plates of Prithivīsena II were discovered (*E.I.*, IX, 267ff.).

Bāli.—This town contains two temples, one of which is a Jaina temple containing an inscription of the 12th century A.D. It is situated about five miles south-east of Falna railway station (Erskin, *Rajputana Gazetteer*, Vol. III, p. 178).

Bārdūlā.—It is a village in the Sarangarh State, Central Provinces (*E.I.*, XXVII, Pt. VI, p. 287) where copperplates of Mahāśivagupta (year 9) have been found out.

Barṇāsā (Banāsā).—It is a river which may be the same as the river Parṇāśā (Luders' List, No. 1131).

Bāsim.—It is the headquarters of the Bāsim taluk of the Akola district in Berar, where some plates of Vākāṭaka Vindhyaśakti II were discovered (*E.I.*, XXVI, Pt. III, July, 1941).

Beṇṇakaṭa.—This district comprised the territory round the modern village called Beṇī, 35 miles to the east of Kosambā in the Gondia tahsil of the Bhander district (*E.I.*, XXII, p. 170).

Betul.—It is in the Betul district of the Central Provinces, where the plates of Saṃkṣobha of the Gupta year 199 were discovered (*E.I.*, VIII, 284ff.).

Bhaiṃsaḍā.—The Jagannātharāya temple inscriptions at Udaipur mention this village which lies near Chitor (*E.I.*, XXIV, Pt. II, April, 1937, p. 65).

Bhainsrorgarh.—At Barolli, about three miles north-east of Bhainsrorgarh in the Udaipur State in Rajputana, there is a group of beautiful Hindu temples. The chief temple, dedicated to Ghaṭeśvara, stands in a walled enclosure. There is a figure of Viṣṇu reposing on the Śeṣaśayyā or the bed of the serpent, which Fergusson considers as the most beautiful piece of purely Hindu sculpture.

Bharund.—It is a village in the Godwar district of the Jodhpur State, where an inscription has been found.

Bhābrū.—The Bhabrū Edict or the second Vairāṭ Rock Edict comes from one of the Vairāṭ hills, distant about 12 miles from the camping ground at Bhābrū (*Report of the Archaeological Survey*, Western circle, 1909-1910). The Matsya country appears to have been known in later times as Virāṭa or Vairāṭa. Vairāṭa may have included the greater part of the present State of Jaipur. Its precise boundaries cannot be determined; but they may be fixed approximately as extending on the north from Jhunjun to Koṭ Kāsiṃ 70 miles; on the west from Jhunjun to Ajmeer 120 miles; on the south from Ajmeer to the junction of the Banās and the Chambal, 150 miles and on the east from the junction to Koṭ Kāsiṃ, 150 miles or altogether 490 miles. For further details vide *Matsyadeśa and Vairāṭa*.

Bhāṇḍak.—The Nachne-ki-talai stone inscriptions of Mahārāja Prithivīsena mention Vākāṭaka which is the ancient name of the modern Bhāṇḍak, the chief town of the Bhāṇḍak Pargana in the Chanda district in C.P. (*C.I.I.*, Vol. III; cf. *E.I.*, XIV, 121ff.).

Bheraghāṭ.—It is on the Narmadā in the Jubbalpur district of the C.P. A stone inscription has been found here of the Queen Alhaṇadevī of the Cedi year 907 (*E.I.*, II, 7ff.).

Bhilaya.—It is about six miles east of Udaipur and about 18 miles from Basoda by direct route.

Bhillamāla.—The Saindhava copperplate grants from Ghumli mention it, which may be identified with modern Bhinmal, 80 miles to the north of Patan and 40 miles to the east of Mount Abu, Rajputana (*E.I.*, XXVI, Pt. V, January, 1942, p. 204). It was the ancient capital of the Gurjaras between the 6th and 9th centuries A.D.

Bhilsā.—It is situated at a distance of 535 miles from Bombay. It stands on the east bank of the Betwā river. According to Cunningham it was founded during the Gupta period. The remains consist of a series of sixty Buddhist stūpas, many of which contain relic-caskets. North-west of Bhilsā in the fork formed by the Betwa and the Besh rivers is the site of the old city of Besnagar which was a place of importance as early as the time of Aśoka. In the 4th and 5th centuries A.D. the Guptas held the town. In the 9th century it fell to the Paramāras of Malwa and in the 12th century it was held by the Cālukya kings (*Gwalior State Gazetteer*, I, pp. 203ff.). For further details vide *Vidiśā*.

Bhīmavana.—This seems to be the ancient name of the extensive forest round about the range of hills containing the great tableland called the Pathār (*E.I.*, XXVI, Pt. III, July, 1941, p. 101).

Bhinmāl.—This city is in the Jaswantpura district of the Jodhpur State where the stone inscription of Udayasiṃhadeva has been discovered (*E.I.*, XI, p. 55).

Bhitarwar.—It is 19 miles by road to the west of the Dabra railway station.

Bhumara.—The Bhumara stone pillar inscription of the time of the Imperial Guptas mentions this village which is situated nine miles to the north-west of Unchera, the chief town of the State of Nagod in Central India (*I.H.Q.*, XXI, No. 2).

Bhūravāḍī.—This village is in the Rājanagara district, C.I. (*E.I.*, XXIV, Pt. II, April, 1937).

Bihar Kotra.—It is in the Rājgaḍh State, Malwa, where an inscription was discovered (*E.I.*, XXVI, Pt. III, July, 1941, p. 130).

Bijapur.—It is in the Nimar district. It is an old hill fort in the Satpurās (Luard and Dube, *Indore State Gazetteer*, II, 259).

Bijayagaḍh.—The Bijayagaḍh stone inscription of the Yaudheyas mentions the hill fort of Bijayagaḍh, situated about two miles south-west of Byānā in the Byānā tahsil of the Bharatpur State in Rajputana (*C.I.I.*, Vol. III).

Bijolia (Bijholī).—It is a village in Mewar, about 100 miles from Udaipur. A rock inscription has been found in this village. It is a Jaina record containing salutations to Pārśvanātha and other Jaina divinities. According to Bijholī Rock Inscription of Cāhamāna Someśvara it is a fortified picturesque town situated about 112 miles north-east of Udaipur. Its position is in the midst of the uppermost tableland called Pathār in the Aravalli hills. This tableland extends from Bārolli and Bhainsarorgarh in the south to Jahāzpur in the north through Menāl, Bijholī and Maṇḍalgarh, once forming an important portion of the Cāhamāna dominions of Sāmbhar and Ajmeer (*E.I.*, XXVI, Pt. II, April, 1941). It now forms a part of the State of Udaipur. Vindhyāvallī is the ancient Sanskrit name of Vijholī or Bijholī, which is an important archaeological site with some ancient temples of unique design and elaborate sculptures (*E.I.*, XXVI, Pt. II, 84-85). It is also popularly known as Bijoliā or Bijoliyā which is derivable from Vindhyavallika.

Bonthikavāṭaka.—The Kothuraka Grant of Pravarasena II refers to Bonthikavāṭaka (*E.I.*, XXVI, Pt. V, October, 1941). It is the modern Boṭhad, about 3½ miles to the north by west and two miles to the north from Mangaon in the Nagpur district.

Buchkalā.—It is in the Bilāḍā district of Jodhpur State, where the Inscription of Nāgabhaṭṭa of the Saṃvat 872 was discovered (*E.I.*, IX, 198ff.).

Cait.—It is about five miles to the north of Karhaiya which is about 12 miles to the north of the village Devri on the Bhitawar-Harsi road.

Cammak.—The Cammak copperplate inscription of the Mahārāja Pravarasena II of the Vākāṭaka dynasty mentions Cammak in the Bhojakaṭa kingdom, which is the ancient village of Carmāṅka, about four miles south-west of Ilichpur, the chief town of the Ilichpur district in east Berar or ancient Vidarbha. This village named Carmāṅka stands on the bank of the river Madhunadī (*C.I.I.*, Vol. III).

Canderi.—It contains an old fort in the Narmar district (*Gwalior State Gazetteer*, pp. 209ff.).

Candrapura.—It may be identified with modern Candpur which lies to the south of Siwani and to the west of the Wen-Gaṅgā river (*E.I.*, III, 260).

Candrāvatī.—The ancient city has been identified by some with the Sandrabatis of Ptolemy. The remains of this city are to be seen about four miles south-west of Abu road and close to the left bank of the western Banās (*Rajputana Gazetteers*, III-A, compiled by Erskine, p. 298).

Carmanvatī.—The *Padma Purāṇa* (Uttarakhaṇḍa, vv. 35–38), the *Yoginītantra* (2. 5, pp. 139-140) and Pāṇini's *Aṣṭādhyāyī* (VIII, 2. 12) mention this river. The Carmanvatī or Chambal takes its rise in the Aravalli range, north-west of Indore, and flows north-east through eastern Rajputana into the Yamunā. It is a tributary of the Yamunā. It is associated with the Pāripātra or Pāriyātra mountain (*Mārkaṇḍeya Purāṇa*, 57. 19-20).

Cahanda.—It was the capital of the Paramāras which may probably be identified with Cāndā, the chief town of the Cāndā district of the Central Provinces, now called *Madhya Pradeśa*. (*E.I.*, XXVI, Pt. V, October, 1941, p. 182).

Cedi country.—Pāṇini mentions it in his *Aṣṭādhyāyī* (4. 2. 116). It lay near the Jumna and was contiguous to the kingdom of the Kurus. It corresponds roughly to the modern Bundelkhand and the adjoining region. The capital city of the Cedi country was Sotthivatīnagara (*Jāt.*, No. 422), which may probably be identified with the city of Śuktimatī of the *Mahābhārata* (III, 20. 50; XIV, 83. 2). The Cedi country was an important centre of Buddhism (*Aṅg.*, III, 355-56; IV, 228ff.; V, 41ff., 157ff.; *Dīgha*, II, 200, 201, 203; *Saṃyutta*, V, 436-437). According to the *Vessantara-Jātaka* Ceta or Cetiraṣṭra was 30 yojanas distant from Jetuttaranagara, the birthplace of king Vessantara (*Jāt.*, VI, 514-15).

In the early Vedic age the Cedi king must have been very powerful inasmuch as he is described in the *Ṛgveda* (VIII, 5, 37–39) as making a gift of ten kings as slaves to a priest, who officiated at one of his sacrifices. The Cedi monarch Kaśu must have been a commanding personality in Ṛgvedic times as it appears that he brought many kings under his sway. According to the *Mahābhārata* (M. N. Dutt, *Mahābhārata*, p. 83) the beautiful and excellent kingdom of the Cedis was conquered by Vasu the Paurava. His capital was Śuktimatī on the river Śuktimatī. He extended his conquest eastwards as far as Magadha and apparently north-west over Matsya. Śiśupāla, the great Cedi monarch, appears to have acquired considerable power in the Epic period (*Mahābhārata*, I, 7029). He was desirous of slaying Kṛṣṇa with all the Pāṇḍavas, but he was killed by Kṛṣṇa. Yudhiṣṭhira installed his son in the sovereignty of the Cedis.

D. R. Bhandarkar says that Ceta or Cetiya corresponds roughly to the modern Bundelkhand (*Carmichael Lectures*, 1918, p. 52). His view was accepted in the *Cambridge History of India*, p. 84. Rapson says that the Cedis occupied the northern portion of the Central Provinces (*Ancient India*, p. 162). Pargiter is of opinion that Cedi lies along the south of the Jumna (*A.I.H.T.*, 272). Some hold that Cedi comprised the southern portion of Bundelkhand and the northern portion of Jubbalpur. Cedi was also known as Tripurī (N. L. Dey, *Geo. Dict.*, 14). Sahajāti, a Cedi town, stood on the right bank of the Jumna. A deer park existed in the Pācīnavaṃsa lying to the east of Vatsa. For further details, vide B. C. Law, *Tribes in Ancient India*, Ch. VI; F. E. Pargiter, *Ancient Cedi, Matsya and Karūṣa—J.A.S.B.*, LXIV, Pt. I (1895), pp. 249ff.

Chattisgarh.—It formed an independent state under the Tummāṇa branch of the Haihayas (*E.I.*, XIX, 75ff.).

Choṭi Deori.—It is situated on the left bank of the Ken, about 16 miles to the west of Jokāhi in the Murwara tahsil of the Jubbalpur district in the Central Provinces. It is also called Māḍhā Deori on account of a number of small temples which lie buried in dense jungle. According to Cunningham all these temples were most probably Śaiva shrines (*Choṭi Deori Stone Inscription of Śaṅkaragaṇa—E.I.*, XXVII, Pt. IV, p. 170).

Ciñcāpalli.—This is the same as Chicoli which is situated on the right bank of the river Wunnā, half a mile to the south of Mangaon in the Nagpur district (*E.I.*, XXVI, Pt. V, October, 1941).

Cirwā.—It is a village situated about 10 miles north of Udaipur and two miles east of Nagda. A stone inscription has been found here incised on the door of a Viṣṇu temple. This stone inscription has been edited by B. Geiger (*W.Z.K.M.*, XXI).

Citorgarh.—It is in the Udaipur State, Rajputana (*Inscriptions of Northern India* revised by Bhandarkar, No. 570, v. 1324).

Citrakūṭa.—It has been identified by some with Citrakūṭa near Kālañjara in the Banda district. It is the modern Citrakoṭ or Caturkoṭ hill or district near Kampla in Bundelkhand. It is mentioned in the *Bṛhatsaṃhitā* (XIV, 13). It is also identified with Chitoor, the famous fort of which was captured from the Gurjara-Pratihāras by Kṛṣṇa III (vide *J.B.O.R.S.*, 1928, p. 481; H. C. Ray, *Dynastic History of Northern India*, Vol. I, p. 589, for epigraphic references). According to the Jaina *Padma Purāṇa* (summarized in Bengali by Chintaharan Chakravorti, p. 20), Rāma and Lakṣmaṇa came at the foot of the Citrakūṭa hill in the Mālava country. Here the forest was so very thick that it was difficult to find out any trace of human habitation.

Citrakūṭa.—It is one of the Ṛkṣa rivers which may have some connection with the Citrakūṭa mountain (*Mārkaṇḍeya Purāṇa*, 57. 21–25; Law, *Rivers of India*, p. 48; *Geographical Essays*, p. 110).

Curli.—It is half a mile to the south of the Tekanpur irrigation dam on the Gwalior-Jhansi road.

Ḍabok.—This village lies eight miles to the east of Udaipur in Mewar (*E.I.*, XX, p. 122).

Damoh.—The Batihāgaḍh Inscription of the Damoh district mentions Kharparas, whom Dr. Bhandarkar takes to be identical with the Khara-parikas, referred to in the Allahabad Pillar Inscription of Samudragupta (*E.I.*, XII, 46; *I.H.Q.*, I, 258; B. C. Law, *Tribes in Ancient India*, p. 356).

Daṅguna.—This is the name of a village mentioned in the Poona plates of Prabhāvatigupta (*E.I.*, XV, 39ff.). The plates record the grant of this village situated in Supratiṣṭhāhāra. It lay to the east of Vilavaṇaka, to the south of Śīrṣagrāma, to the west of Kadāpiñjana and to the north of Sidivivaraka. The ancient village of Daṅguna seems to be identical with the modern Hinganghāṭ in the Nagpur district.

Daśārṇa.—It is generally identified with Vedisa or Bhilsa region in the Central Provinces. It is mentioned in the *Mahābhārata* (II, 5–10), as well as in the *Meghadūta* of Kālidāsa (24-25). The Purāṇas associate the people of the Daśārṇa country with the Mālavas, Kārūṣas, Mekalas, Utkalas and Niṣadhas. In the *Rāmāyaṇa* (Kiṣkindhyākāṇḍa, 41, 8–10), their country is connected with those of the Mekalas and Utkalas where Sugrīva sent his monkey-army in quest of Sītā. The Daśārṇas occupied a site on the Daśārṇa river, which can still be traced in the modern Dhasan river near Saugor, that flows through Bundelkhand, rising in Bhopal and emptying into the Betwa (Vetravatī). It should be noted that the Daśārṇa country of the *Rāmāyaṇa* and the Purāṇas seems to be different from the Daśārṇa country of the *Meghadūta* (*Pūrvamegha*, 24 śl.). According to Wilson (*Viṣṇu Purāṇa*, II, 160, f.n. 3) the eastern or south-eastern Daśārṇa formed a part of the Chattisgarh district in the Central Provinces (cf. *J.A.S.B.*, 1905, pp. 7, 14). The Dosaron is the river of the region inhabited by the Daśārṇas (McCrindle's *Ancient India as described by Ptolemy*, Majumdar ed., p. 71). A Daśārṇa king named Kṣatradeva, who was a mighty hero, fought valiantly on the elephant back for the Pāṇḍavas in the great Kurukṣetra war (Karṇaparva, Chs. 22, 3; Droṇaparva, Chs. 25, 35). It is interesting to note that the warriors of the Daśārṇa king Kṣatradeva were all mighty heroes and could fight best on elephants. Pargiter thinks (*A.I.H.T.*, p. 280) that Daśārṇa was a Yādava kingdom during the period of the Kurukṣetra war. Erakaccha was a town in the Dasaṇṇa (Daśārṇa) country, as mentioned in the *Petavatthu* and its commentary (*Petavatthu*, 20; *Petavatthu Commentary*, 99–105). Daśārṇa (Dasaṇṇa) was noted for the art of making swords (*Jāt.*, III, 338; *Dasaṇṇakaṃ tikhiṇadhāraṃ asiṃ*). It is mentioned in the *Mahāvastu* (I, 34) and *Lalitavistara* as one of the sixteen *Mahājanapadas*. The people of the Dasaṇṇa country built a monastery for the Buddha who is said to have distributed knowledge among them (Law, *A Study of the Mahāvastu*, p. 9). There was a hill called Nīca in the country of the Daśārṇas (*Meghadūta*, *Pūrvamegha*, śl. 26).

Davānīgrāma—(*E.I.*, VIII, 221).—It may be identified with Davānī, seven miles north-west of Delvāda, Mount Abu.

Deogarh.—It is situated close to the south-western limit of the Lalitpur sub-division of the Jhansi district in a semi-circular bend overlooking the right bank of the Betwa (Vetravatī) river. It is 19 miles from Lalitpur and seven miles from Jakhlaun. From the former it can be approached by a motor car or a *tunga* over a fair-weather District Board road. It contains a solitary Gupta temple locally known as *S¯gaṛ Maṛh*, standing at the western edge of the elevated plain. For details vide *M.A.S.I.*, No. 70—*The Gupta Temple at Deogarh*, by M. S. Vats.

Deoli.—It is about 10 miles south-west of Wardha near Nagpur (*E.I.*, V, 188ff.).

Deolia.—It is a village 13 miles north-east of Gumli (*E.I.*, XXVI, Pt. V, January, 1942, p. 204).

Deulavāḍī.—It is identified with the modern village of Dilwārā on the Mount Abu (*E.I.*, VIII, 208ff.).

Deulā-Paṃcalā.—It is a village in the Devagrām-paṭṭala which has been identified by some with Deogavān, close to Khairha in the Rewah State. This village was granted to a Brahmin named Gaṅgādharaśarman by Yuśah-Karṇadeva (*E.I.*, XII, 205ff.).

Devadaha.—This village lies near Chitor (*E.I.*, XXIV, Pt. II, April, 1937, p. 65).

Devagiri.—Kālidāsa places it between Ujjain and Mandasar near Chambal (*Meghadūta*, Pūrvamegha, 42).

Dhanik.—It is mentioned in the Dabok (Mewar) inscription of *cir.* A.D. 725 (*E.I.*, XII). D. R. Bhandarkar identifies Dhavālappadeva, the overlord of this place, with king Dhavala of the Maurya dynasty mentioned in the Kanaswā (Kotah State in Rajputana) Inscription of A.D. 738.

Dhaṅkatīrtha.—It is the same as Dhānk in Gandal State, situated about 25 miles east of Gumli (*E.I.*, XXVI, Pt. V, January, 1942).

Dhovahaṭṭa.—The Rewah plates of the time of Trailokyamalladeva refer to it, which may be identified with Dhureti in Central India now known as *Madhya Bhārata* (*E.I.*, XXV, Pt. I, January, 1939, p. 5).

Dhureti.—It is a village about seven miles from the Rewah town (*E.I.*, XXV, Pt. I, p. 1).

Dināra.—It is about 16 miles west of Jhansi on the Jhansi-Shivpuri road.

Dīrghadraha.—It is probably Dīghi on the left bank of the Wardha about 30 miles south of Aṣṭi (*E.I.*, XXIV, Pt. VI, April, 1938, p. 263).

Diwra.—It is in the Dungarpur State, South Rajputana. An image inscription found here records that a person named Vaija erected an image at Devakarṇa (Diwra) (H. C. Ray, *Dynastic History of Northern India*, Vol. II, p. 1006).

Doṅgaragrāma.—This village is identical with Doṅgargaon, about 10 miles from Pusad, in the Yeotmal district of Berar. It is situated on a hill. There are two old temples in this village. A stone inscription of the time of Jagaddeva, dated Śaka Era 1034, has been found recording the gift of this village (*E.I.*, XXVI, Pt. V, October, 1941, pp. 177ff.).

Dudia.—It is in the Chindwara district, C.P., where four well-preserved copperplates of Pravarasena II were discovered (*E.I.*, III, 258).

Durdda.—The Bijholi Rock Inscription of Cāhamāna Someśvara (V.S. 1226) refers to Durdda, which may be identified with the modern Duddai or Dūdhai in Central India in the neighbourhood of the Cāhamāna domain in an easterly direction (*E.I.*, XXVI, Pt. II, April, 1941, pp. 84ff.).

Eracca.—In a Mahova copperplate grant dated Samvat 1230 (A.D. 1173) of the Candela Paramardi, Eracca occurs as the headquarters of a district.

Fatehābad.—It is in Ujjain, a railway station on the Rajputana-Malwa section of the Western Railway, a battlefield where the battle took place between Shah Jahan and his son Aurangzeb.

Gaṃgābheda.—The Bijholī Rock Inscription of Cāhamāna Someśvara (V.S. 1226) refers to Gaṃgābheda (*E.I.*, XXVI, 101ff.), which is evidently Gaṅgābheda at Bārolli mentioned by Tod in his *Rājasthān* (III, 1766–1768).

Gaṅgdhār.—This village, mentioned in the Gaṅgdhār stone image inscription of Viśvavarman, stands about 52 miles to the south-west of Jhalrāpatan, the chief town of the Jhalawad State in Western Malwa, C.I. (*C.I.I.*, Vol. III).

Gaonri.—It is a village three miles to the north-east of Narwal, the headquarters of Narwal Estate, 11 miles to the south-east of Ujjain on the Ujjain-Dewas road (*E.I.*, XXIII, Pt. IV, October, 1935, p. 101—*Three Copperplate Inscriptions from Gaonri*).

Gālavāśrama.—It was situated at a distance of three miles from Jaipur in Rajputana. According to the *Bṛhat-Śivapurāṇa* (Ch. I, 83) it was situated on the Citrakūṭa mountain.

Ghaṭiyālā.—It is situated 22 miles west-north-west of Jodhpur where the inscriptions of Kakkuka were discovered (*E.I.*, IX, 277ff.).

Ghosuṇḍi.—It is a village near Nagarī in the Chitorgaḍh district of Rajputana, where a stone inscription was discovered (*E.I.*, XVI, 25ff.).

Godurpura.—This village stands on the south bank of the Narmadā in the Nimar district, C.P. (*E.I.*, IX, 120).

Gohasodvā.—It is modern Gahvā, 1½ miles to the south of Añjanavatī in C.P. (*E.I.*, XXIII, Pt. I, January, 1935, p. 13).

Gośṛṅgaparvata.—It is near Niṣadhabhūmi in Central India (*Mahābhārata*, Sabhāparva, Ch. 31).

Guñji.—It is a small village, 14 miles north by west of Śakti, the chief town of a feudatory state of the same name in the Chattisgarh division of the Central Provinces. At the foot of a hill near this village there is a kuṇḍa or a pool of water, which receives the supply of water from the neighbouring hills. On one side of this pool there is a rock on which an inscription is engraved. It is about 40 miles north-west of Kirari where a wooden pillar with a record in Brāhmī characters of the 2nd century A.D. was discovered (Gunji Rock Inscription of Kumāravaradatta, *E.I.*, XXVII, Pt. I, p. 48). It was situated in a part of the country which was flourishing in the centuries before and after the beginning of the Christian era.

Gurjaratrā.—The portion of Rajputana extending from Didwāna, Siwa and Maglona came to be known as Gurjaratrā (*E.I.*, IX, p. 280) or Gurjarabhūmi.

Harṣa.—It is a hill on the top of which are found the ruins of an ancient temple. It is also called Uñchāpahar, which is near the village of Harṣanātha in the Shaikhāvatī province of Jaipur State of Rajputana, about seven miles south of Sikar and 60 miles north-west of Jaipur where a stone inscription of Cāhamāna Vigraharāja of the Vikrama year 1930 was discovered (*E.I.*, II, 116ff.).

Harsauda.—It is a village situated at a distance of a few miles from the town of Carwa in the district of Hoshangabad in C.P. (*I.A.*, XX, 310). Harṣapura may be identified with Harsauda where a stone inscription has been found in the ruins of a temple.

Holi.—This village is in the Girvā district (*E.I.*, XXIV, Pt. II, April, 1937).

Jajā-bhukti.—Jajā-bhukti or Jejā-bhukti or Jejāka-bhukti or Jejā-bhuktika is the old name of Bundelkhand (*E.I.*, I, 35; cf. *Madanpur Stone Inscription of Kalacuri Jājalladeva*, Cunningham, *A.S.R.*, Vol. X, plate xxxii).

Jābālipura.—It is in the Jodhpur State, Rajputana. A stone inscription found here records the construction of a Jaina *vihāra* containing an image of Pārśvanātha on the fort of Kāñcanagiri belonging to Jābālipura (i.e., modern Jalore) (*E.I.*, XI, 54ff.). This ancient town contains two monuments of archaeological interest, namely the Topkhānā in the heart of the town and the fort which crowns a hillock about 1,000 ft. high (*A.S.I.*, *Annual Reports*, 1930–1934, p. 50).

Jetuttara.—It has been identified with Nāgarī, a locality 11 miles north of Chitore (N. L. Dey, *Geographical Dictionary*, p. 81). It is evidently the Jattararur of Alberuni, the capital of Mewar (Alberuni's *India*, I, p. 202).

Kagpur (Kākapura).—It is popularly known as Gadhla-Kagpur. It lies on the Bhilsa-Pachar road and it is 17 miles north of Bhilsa. It is identified by Jayaswal with the capital of the Kākas of the Allahabad Pillar Inscription. It is of great archaeological interest (*J.B.O.R.S.*, XVIII, pp. 212-213).

Kakandakuṭu.—It may be identified with Khuṭunda, about six miles to the east of Deori (*E.I.*, XXVII, Pt. IV, p. 171).

Kaṇaswa.—It is in the Kotah State of Rajputana.

Kaṅkhal.—It is in Mount Abu, Rajputana (No. 454, V. 1265—*Inscriptions of Northern India*, revised by D. R. Bhandarkar).

Kapiladhārā.—It is otherwise known as Mandākinī, the holy reservoir at Bijholī near the Mahākāla temple (*E.I.*, XXVI, Pt. III, July, 1941, p. 101).

Karīkatin.—It resembles Karitalāi situated about 30 miles to the east. It is represented by Khurai, four miles to the south of Deori Māḍhā, (*E.I.*, XXVII, Pt. IV, p. 171).

Kasrawad.—It is a town in the Nimad district of the Holkar State in Central India, situated on the southern bank of the river Narmadā. Some of the antiquities found here are the perforated pottery, pottery cones, etc. Seventy miles north of Kasrawad lies Ujjain. For details, vide *Annual Report, Arch. Surv., Gwalior*, 1938-39; *I.H.Q.*, March, 1949.

Kaviḷāsapura.—It is identical with the modern village of the same name near Nulegrāma in the Hukkeri taluk of the Belgaum district (*E.I.*, XXI, p. 11; XXIII, p. 194).

Kālisindh.—See *Nirbbindhyā*.

Kāman.—It is in the Bharatpur State in Rajputana, where a stone inscription has been found out. It may be identified with Kāmyaka (*E.I.*, XXIV, Pt. VII, July, 1938, pp. 329 and 332).

Kāṃvā.—It is modern Kāmā, about two miles east of Bijholī (*E.I.*, XXVI, Pt. III, July, 1941).

Kāntipura.—It is identified by Cunningham with Kotwal, 20 miles north of Gwalior (*Skanda Purāṇa*, Ch. 47; *A.S.R.*, Vol. II, p. 308).

Kāritalāī.—It is a village in the Muḍwara sub-division of the Jubbalpore district of the Central Provinces, where a stone inscription of the reign of the Cedi Lakṣmaṇarāja was discovered (*E.I.*, II, 174ff.). It is a small village 29 miles north by east of Murwara. It seems to be of great antiquity. There are several old temples (*E.I.*, XXIII, July, 1936, p. 255).

Kāyathā.—It is a village situated in the Anarghamaṇḍala. It corresponds to the modern Kaitā, about 14 miles almost due west of Peṇḍrabandh and about four miles beyond the southern limit of the Jānjgir tahsil, Bilaspur district (*E.I.*, XXIII, Pt. I, January, 1935, p. 3).

Keslā.—This village may be taken to correspond to ancient Kailāśapura. It is near Mallār, about eight miles to the south-east containing ruins of an old temple (*E.I.*, XXIII, Pt. IV, p. 120).

Khaḍumvarī.—It appears to be the modern Khaḍipura about six miles south-east of Bijholī (*E.I.*, XXVI, Pt. III, July, 1941).

Khajurāho (Khajraho).—It is in the Chatarpur State, Bundelkhand, C.I., about 100 miles to the south-east of Jhansi (No. 300, V, 1215, *Inscriptions of Northern India*, revised by D. R. Bhandarkar). A stone inscription is said to have been discovered in the ruins at the base of the Lakṣmaṇa temple at Khajurāho and an inscription is carved on the left door-jamb of the temple of Jina in this place (*E.I.*, I, 123–35; 135-36; *J.A.S.B.*, XXXII, 279).

This place has been referred to by the Chinese pilgrim Hiuen Tsang who says that there were a number of monasteries and about ten temples in this village. There is a colossal Buddha image inscribed with the usual creed in characters of the 7th or 8th century A.D. Its importance lies solely in its magnificent series of temples, which fall into three main groups: the western, northern, and south-eastern. The western group consists mainly of Brahmanical temples, both Śaiva and Vaiṣṇava. The northern group contains one large and some small temples, all Vaiṣṇava. The south-eastern group consists mainly of Jaina temples. Almost all the temples are constructed of sandstone and are in the same style. The oldest temple in the western group is the Caunsat Yoginī. The temple of Kandarya Mahādeva is the finest. (For further details, vide B. C. Law, *Holy Places of India*, pp. 34–37).

Khalārī.—It is a village about 45 miles east of the town of Raipur in the Central Provinces where a stone inscription of the reign of Harivarmadeva of the Vikrama year 1470 was discovered (*E.I.*, II, 228ff.).

Khandesh.—Here a great Śvetāmbara Jaina teacher flourished named Ammadeva, who converted many people to Jainism (*E.I.*, XIX, 71).

Kharaparika.—Kharapara, mentioned in the Bāṭihāgaḍh Inscription of the Damoh district, C.P., may probably be identified with it (*E.I.*, XII, p. 46; *I.H.Q.*, I, p. 258).

Khejdia Bhop.—This village is in the Mandasor district where many Buddhist caves were discovered. (For details, vide *A.S.I.*, *Annual Report*, 1916/17, Pt. I, pp. 13-14).

Khoh.—The Khoh Copperplate Inscription of Mahārāja Hastin mentions it. It is situated about three miles south-west of Ucaharā, the present capital of the native state of Nagaudh in the Bāgelkhand division of C.I. (*C.I.I.*, Vol. III).

Kirari.—It is a village in the Chattisgarh division of the Central Provinces, where a Brāhmī inscription on a wooden pillar was discovered (*E.I.*, XVIII, 152).

Kirāḍu.—It is in ruins near Hāthmā, about 16 miles north-north-west of Bāḍmer, the principal town of the Mallāṇi district, Jodhpur State, where was found the Stone Inscription of Ālhaṇadeva (*E.I.*, XI, p. 43).

Kirīkaikā.—It is a village on the west of Ujjayinī mentioned in the Depālapur Copperplate Inscription of Bhoja, some lands of which were granted by Bhoja to a Brahmin hailing from Mānyakheṭa (*I.H.Q.*, VIII, 1932).

Koni.—It is a small village on the left bank of the Ārpā, about 12 miles south by east of Bilaspur, the chief town of the Bilaspur district in the Chattisgarh division of the Central Provinces where an Inscription of Kalachuri Prithvīdeva II was discovered (*E.I.*, XXVII, Pt. VI, p. 276).

Kothuraka.—This village is mentioned in the Kothuraka Grant of Pravarasena II as the donated place. It was situated in the territorial division of Supratiṣṭha. It lay to the west of the Umā river, to the north of Ciñcāpalli, to the east of Bonthikavāṭaka, and to the south of Maṇḍukigrāma. Its site seems to be occupied by Mangaon on the right bank of the river Wunnā, about 2½ miles north by west of Jāmb in the Nagpur district (*E.I.*, XXVI, Pt. V, October, 1941).

Kudopali.—This village is in the Bargarh tahsil of the Sambalpur district, C.P., where plates of the time of Mahābhavagupta II were found buried in the ground (*E.I.*, IV, 254ff.).

Kumbhī.—It is on the right bank of the Herun river, 35 miles north-east of Jubbalpur. An inscription has been found here incised on two copperplates (*J.A.S.B.*, 1839, Vol. VIII, Pt. I, pp. 481ff.).

Kuraragharaparvata.—It was in Avantī. Mahākaccāyana once dwelt here. A lay female disciple named Kālī came to him and asked him to explain in detail the meaning of a stanza. He did so to her satisfaction (*Aṅguttara*, V, pp. 46-47).

Kure.—It is modern Kurhā, three miles to the north-west of Añjanavatī (*E.I.*, XXIII, Pt. I, January, 1935, p. 13).

Kuruspāl.—It is a village situated about a mile from Nārāyaṇapāla and 22 miles from Jagdalpur, the capital of the Bastar State, where the two Inscriptions of Dhārāṇa-mahādevī of the time of Someśvaradeva were discovered (*E.I.*, X, 31ff.).

Laghu-Bijholī.—At present it is known as Choṭī Bijolia and is about three miles west of Bijholī (*E.I.*, XXVI, pp. 102ff.).

Lambeva.—It may be identified with Limbu in the Narasimpura State (*E.I.*, XXVI, Pt. II, April, 1941, p. 78).

Lodhia.—It is a small village in the Saria pergana of the Sarangarh State, C.P. (*E.I.*, XXVII, Pt. VII, July, 1948, p. 316).

Lohanagara.—It is the headquarters of an ancient division, which may be represented by Loṇī, about nine miles south-west of Warūḍ (*E.I.*, XXIII, Pt. III, July, 1935, p. 84).

Lohari.—It is a village in the Jahazpur district of the Udaipur State. A stone inscription has been found here engraved on a pillar in the temple of Bhūteśvara.

Madanpur.—It is in Saugor district, C.P. (*Inscriptions of Northern India*, revised by D. R. Bhandarkar, No. 684, V. 1385). In the village of Madanpur some stone inscriptions were discovered on the pillars of a *maṇḍapa* of an old temple. This village is situated 24 miles to the south-east of Dudahi and 30 miles north of Saugor (Sagor) (*A.S.R.*, Vol. X, pp. 98-99).

Maddukabhukti.—It may possibly be identified with Mhow, the well-known cantonment near Indore (*E.I.*, XXIII, Pt. IV).

Mahalla-Lāṭa.—It seems to mean the larger Lāṭa. It may be represented by Lāḍki or Ghāṭ-Lāḍki in the Morsi taluk of the Amraoti district, about 18 miles north by west of Belorā (*E.I.*, XXIV, Pt. VI, p. 263).

Mahauda.—It is identified with the village Mahod, about 25 miles south of Satajuna (*E.I.*, IX, 106).

Mahādvādaśaka-maṇḍala.—It must have comprised Udayapur and Bhilsā in the Gwalior State as far as Rājaśayana to the south in the Bhopal State (*E.I.*, XXIV, Pt. V, p. 231).

Mahānāla.—The Bijholī Rock Inscription of Cāhamāna Someśvara (V.S. 1226) refers to Mahānāla (*E.I.*, XXVI, Pt. III, July, 1941), which may be equated with Menāl, vividly described by Tod in his *Rājasthān* (Vol. III, pp. 1800–5).

Makkarakaṭa.—It was a forest in Avantī, where Mahākaccāyana lived in a leaf-hut and where the disciples of Lohicca approached him. He gave them a discourse on *dhamma* (*Saṃyutta*, IV. 116-117). According to the commentator it was a town (*nagara*) (*Sāratthappakāsinī*, P.T.S. II. 397).

Maksi (Ujjain).—It is to the north of Dewas on the Bombay-Agra Road.

Malhār.—It is in the Central Provinces, where a Stone Inscription of Jājalladeva of the Cedi year 919 was discovered (*E.I.*, I, 39).

Mallāla.—It is modern Mallār, 16 miles south-east of Bilaspur, C.P. (*E.I.*, XXVI, Pt. VI, April, 1942, p. 258).

Mallār.—It is a large village, 16 miles south-east of Bilaspur, the headquarters of the Bilaspur district, C.P., where the copperplates of Mahāśivagupta have been discovered (*E.I.*, XXIII, Pt. IV, October, 1935, p. 113; *E.I.*, XXVI, Pt. II, April, 1941).

Maṃḍalakara.—It is the modern Māṇḍalgarh in the State of Udaipur (*E.I.*, XXVI, Pt. III, July, 1941, p. 101).

Maṇḍala.—This town was also called Maheśmatipura (*J.A.S.B.*, 1837, p. 622). It was the original capital of the country on the upper Narmadā which was afterwards supplanted by Tripurī or Tewār, six miles from Jabbalpur. According to Cunningham Maheśmatipura on the upper Narmadā may be identified with Maheśvarapura of Hiuen Tsang (*C.A.G.I.*, pp. 559-60).

Maṇḍapa.—It is the modern town of Maṇḍu in Dhar State (*E.I.*, IX, 109).

Mandākinī.—Cunningham identifies this Ṛkṣa river with the modern Mandakin which forms a small tributary to the Paisundi (Paisuni) in Bundelkhand and flows by the side of the Mount Citrakūṭa (*A.S.I.R.*, XXI, 11). According to the *Bhāgavata* (V. 19. 18) and *Vāyupurāṇas* (45. 99), this river is the Gaṅgā (Ganges).

Mandāra.—This sacred place is on the Vindhya mountain on the southern side of the river Jāhnavī (*Varāha Purāṇa*, 143. 2). Here stands a hermitage known as the Samantapañcaka (*Ibid.*, 143, 48).

Mansiagarh.—It is about 1½ miles to the south of Bhicor which is some 30 miles west of Singholi.

Matsyadeśa.—It is one of the *mahājanapadas* of India (*Aṅg.*, I, 213; IV, 252, 256, 260; cf. *Padma Purāṇa*, Ch. 3; *Viṣṇudharmottaramahāpurāṇa*, Ch. 9). The people of this country acquired some importance in the Vedic age, but at the time of the *Rāmāyaṇa* they lost their importance. It is mentioned in the *Śatapatha Brāhmaṇa* (XIII, 5. 4. 9) that a Matsya king is mentioned among the great ancient Indian monarchs who acquired renown by performing the horse-sacrifice. The Matsyas are mentioned along with the Uśīnaras, Kuru-Pañcālas, and Kāśī-Videhas (*Kauṣītaki Upaniṣad*, IV, 1). They were connected with the Śālvas, a Kṣatriya tribe in their neighbourhood (*Gopatha Brāhmaṇa*, 1. 2. 9). The relation of the Matsyas with the Śālvas is also attested by the *Mahābhārata* (Virāṭaparva, Ch. 30, pp. 1-2). In later times the Matsyas were associated with the

Cedis and the Śūrasenas. In the Kurukṣetra battle they occupied a pre-eminent position both because of the purity of their conduct and custom and through their bravery and prowess. The Matsyas or the Macchas witnessed the dice-play of the king of the Kurus with the Yakkha (demon) Puṇṇaka (*Jāt.*, VI, *Vidhurapaṇḍita Jātaka*).

According to the *Manusaṃhitā* (II, 19-20; *ibid.*, VII, 193) the Matsya country formed a part of the Brahmarṣideśa (the country of the holy sages), which included the eastern half of the State of Patiala and of the Delhi division of the Punjab, the Alwar State and the adjacent territory in Rajputana, the region which lies between the Ganges and the Jumna and the Muttra district in the United Provinces (cf. Rapson, *Ancient India*, pp. 50-51). In ancient times the whole of the country, lying between the Aravalli hills of Alwar and the river Jumna, was divided between Matsya on the west and Śūrasena on the east with Daśārṇa on the south and south-east border. The Matsyadeśa included the whole of the present Alwar territory with portions of Jaipur and Bharatpur. Vairāṭa was also in the Matsyadeśa (Cunningham's Report, *A.S.I.*, Vol. XX, p. 2). The Matsya country seems to have been known as Virāṭa or Vairāṭa in later times. According to Hiuen Tsang who visited Vairāṭa in the 7th century A.D., the kingdom of Vairāṭa was 3,000 li or 500 miles in circuit. It was famous for its sheep and oxen, but produced few fruits or flowers. According to him Vairāṭ was 14 or 15 li in circuit, and its people were brave and bold, and their king was famous for his courage and skill in war (Cunningham, *Ancient Geography*, pp. 393 and 395).

Virāṭanagara is also called Matsyanagara (*Mahābhārata*, IV, 13, 1). It was the royal seat of the epic king Virāṭa, the friend of the Pāṇḍavas. There was a fight between king Virāṭa and the Trigarttas with the result that the king was captured by them, but was rescued by Bhīma, the second Pāṇḍava (M. N. Dutt, *Mahābhārata*, Virāṭaparva, Chs. X, XXII, XXXI). It was in the Matsya kingdom that the Pāṇḍava brothers remained *incognito* for a year. They then disclosed their identity and a marriage was celebrated between Abhimanyu, son of Arjuna, and Uttarā, daughter of king Virāṭa (*Mahābhārata*, Ch. LXXII).

The present town of Vairāṭ is situated in the midst of a circular valley surrounded by low bare bed hills which have all along been famous for their copper mines. It is 105 miles to the south-west of Delhi, and 41 miles to the north of Jaipur. The soil is generally good, and the trees, especially the tamarinds, are very fine and abundant. Vairāṭ is situated on a mound of ruins about one mile in length by half a mile in breadth. The old city of Vairāṭ is said to have been deserted for several centuries until it was repeopled most probably during the reign of Akbar.

The Matsyadeśa, when independent, seems to have had the monarchical constitution. It was probably annexed at one time by the neighbouring kingdom of Cedi and finally absorbed into the Magadhan empire (Raychaudhuri, *Political History of Ancient India*, 5th ed., pp. 66ff.; V. A. Smith, *Early History of India*, 4th ed., p. 413; R. D. Banerjee, *Bāṅgālār Itihāsa*, p. 158). For the modern history, vide *Imperial Gazetteers of India*, Vol. XIII, 382ff. See also *Vairāṭa*.

Mau.—It is in the Jhansi district, where a Stone Inscription of Madanavarmadeva was discovered (*E.I.*, I, 195).

Mayūragiri.—In the Barhut votive label (No. 28) occurs Mayūragiri, which is the Mayūraparvata referred to in the *Caraṇavyūhabhāṣya*. In Luders' List (Nos. 778, 796, 798, 808, 860) occurs the name of a place called Moragiri (Mayūragiri). Some have placed it in Madhya Pradeśa (C.P.).

Mayūrakhaṇḍi.—According to some it may be identified with the village called Markaṇḍi on the bank of the Waingaṅgā, 56 miles south-east of Cāndā in C.P. (*E.I.*, XXIII, Pt. I, January, 1935, p. 13). Markaṇḍi was a flourishing place in the time of the Rāṣṭrakūṭas and may have been the ancient Mayūrakhaṇḍi mentioned as a place of royal residence in several grants of Govinda III.

Māhissati (*Māhiṣmatī*).—It was the capital of south Avantī. The Māhiṣakas were the same people as Māhiṣmakas mentioned in the *Mahābhārata* (Aśvamedhaparva, LXXXIII, 2475). They were the inhabitants of Māhiṣmatī or Māhissati, which seems to have been situated on the river Narmadā between the Vindhya and Rikṣa and can be safely identified with the modern Mandhātā region. According to the *Purāṇas* (*Matsya*, XLIII, 10–29; XLIV, 36; *Vāyu*, 94, 26; 95, 35) Māhiṣmatī was founded by a prince of Yadu lineage. It was visited by Balarāma. Here Kārtavīrya defeated Karkoṭaka's son. Here Rāvana was imprisoned by Kārtavīryārjuna. It was founded by Māhiṣmān and was the capital of Kārtavīryārjuna (*Bhāgavata*, IX, 15. 22; *Matsya*, 43. 29, 38; *Viṣṇu*, IV, 11. 9, 19). For further details, vide Law, *Tribes in Ancient India*, pp. 386-387.

Mālava country.—The Mālava country evidently meaning the region round Ujjayinī and Bhilsā (modern Malwa) is mentioned in a number of later epigraphic records, e.g., Sagartal Inscription of the Gurjara-Pratihāras, the Paiṭhān Plates of Rāṣṭrakūṭa Govinda III, etc. The Nasik Cave Inscription of Uṣavadāta (Ṛṣabhadatta) the Śaka, son-in-law of the Kṣatrapa Nahapāṇa, refers to the Mālava occupation of the Nagar area near Jaipur in Rajputana (*E.I.*, VIII, 44). The Mālava country is mentioned in the Tewar Stone Inscription of the reign of Jayasiṃhadeva of the Cedi year 929 (*E.I.*, II, 18-19). The Daṇḍanāyaka Anantapāla, a feudatory of Vikramāditya VI, is said to have subdued the Sapta Mālava countries up to the Himalayan mountains (*E.I.*, V, 229). The Mālavas, mentioned in the Allahabad Pillar Inscription, were in occupation of a province called Vagarcāl in the south-eastern portion of the Jaipur State. They appear to have occupied Mewar and Kotah of south-eastern Rajputana and the parts of Central India adjoining them (*I.A.*, 1891, p. 404). The Pathari Pillar Inscription of Parabala bears testimony to the existence of a Rāṣṭrakūṭa family in Malwa during the first half of the 9th century A.D. (*E.I.*, IX, 248).

It is difficult to locate exactly the Mālava territory. In Alexander's time the Mālavas were settled in the Punjab. Smith thinks that they occupied the country below the confluence of the Jhelum and the Chenab, i.e., the country comprising the Jhang district and a portion of the Montgomery district (*J.R.A.S.*, 1903, p. 631). According to McCrindle, they occupied a greater extent of territory comprising the modern Doab of the Chenab and the Ravi and extending to the confluence of the Indus and the Chenab (Akesines), identical with the modern Multan district and portions of Montgomery (*Invasion of India*, App. note, p. 357). Some have located them in the valley of the lower Rāvī. Mo-la-po, visited by the Chinese pilgrim Hiuen Tsang, may be identified with Mālavaka or Mālavaka-āhāra, mentioned in a number of the Valabhi grants as included in the kingdom of the Maitrakas of Valabhi. The Mālava kingdom of Mahāsenagupta and Devagupta, referred to in the Madhuvan and Banskhera Inscriptions of Harṣavardhana, was probably identical with Pūrva-Mālava, which lay between Prayāga and Bhilsā. This country, according to Hiuen Tsang, was 6,000 li in circuit. The soil was rich and fertile. Shrubs and trees were numerous. Fruits and flowers were abundant. The people were of remarkable intelligence, virtuous and docile. There were some *saṅghārāmas* and *deva* temples (Beal, *Buddhist Records of the Western World*, II, 260ff.). For further literary details, vide B. C. Law, *Tribes in Ancient India*, Ch. VIII.

Māndhātā.—It is an island on the left bank of the Narmadā, attached to the Nimar district of the C.P. An inscription has been found here incised on two plates (*E.I.*, III, 46ff.; *Ibid.*, XXV, Pt. IV, October, 1939). Near this island on the south bank of the Narmadā, stands the well-known holy place of Amareśvara to which the third epigraphic record of the reign of Arjunavarman relates. Three plates were found near the temple of Siddheśvara at Māndhātā (*E.I.*, 103).

Māṇḍukigrāma.—This village is mentioned in the Kothuraka Grant of Pravarasena II (*E.I.*, XXVI, V, 155ff.). It is identified with modern Māṇḍagaon, two miles to the north of Mangaon, in the Nagpur district. According to tradition, Māṇḍagaon is named after a sage Māṇḍa, who is said to have done penance on the Wunnā river in the Nagpur district (*Wardhah District Gazetteer*, 1906, p. 250).

Morājharī.—This is another name of Vindhyavallī (Bijholī). The Bijholī Rock Inscription of Cāhamāna Someśvara (V.S. 1226) records that this village was donated to Pārśvanātha by a Cāhamāna prince (*E.I.*, XXVI, Pt. II, April, 1941, pp. 84ff.).

Mount Abu (*Arbudādri* or *Arbuda mountain*).—Here on the wall of the temple of Neminātha two of the Inscriptions of Somasiṃha are engraved (*E.I.*, VIII, 208ff.). Mount Abu is situated in the Aravalli range in the Sirohi State of Rajputana. It is as high as 5,650 ft. There are five Jaina temples and two of them are the most beautiful. The image of Lord Ṛṣabha was installed in a temple by Vimala Sāh, who saw many temples of God Śiva with eleven thousand worshippers on Mount Abu which once contained the hermitage of the sage Vaśiṣṭha and the famous shrine of Ambā Bhabānī. There is a lake on this mountain. According to Megasthenes and Arrian, the sacred Arbuda or Mount Abu, which is identical with Capitalia, rises far above any other summit of the Aravalli range (McCrindle, *Ancient India*, p. 147). Formerly this mountain was called Nandivardhana. Later it was named Arbuda, being the habitat of the serpent Arbuda. There are twelve villages around it. Here flows a river named Mandākinī. Here stand such sacred places as Acaleśvara, Vaśiṣṭhāśrama and Śrīmātā. On the top of this mountain Kumārapāla of the Cālukya dynasty built the temple of Śrīvīra. For further details vide Law, *Some Jaina Canonical Sūtras*, pp. 184-185.

Murumurā.—It is in the Dhamtari tahsil, Raipur district, where two stone inscriptions were discovered (*A.S.I.*, *Annual Report*, 1916-17, Pt. I, p. 21).

Naddula.—It is modern Nadol in the Jodhpur State of Rajputana (*E.I.*, IX, 62, 64).

Nandipura.—It is the modern Nandod on the Narmadā (*E.I.*, XXIII, Pt. IV).

Nandivardhana.—The Kothuraka Grant of Pravarasena II mentions it (*E.I.*, XXVI, Pt. V, October, 1941, 155ff.). This place is considered to be the earlier capital of the Vākāṭakas before the foundation of Pravarapura by Pravarasena II. It has been identified with Nagardhan or Nandardhan near Ramtek in the Nagpur district of the Central Provinces (*E.I.*, XV, 41; *E.I.*, XXIV, Pt. VI, p. 263; *E.I.*, XXVIII, Pt. I, January, 1949). This place which is described as a holy *tīrtha*, retained its ancient name down to the time of the Bhonslas. It is also mentioned in the Deoli plates of Kṛṣṇa III (*E.I.*, V, 196).

Naravara.—It is the ancient Narapura situated in the Kishengarh territory at a distance of about 15 miles from Ajmeer (*E.I.*, XXVI, Pt. III, July, 1941, p. 101; *J.R.A.S.*, 1913, p. 272 f.n.).

Narmadā.—It is the most important river of Central and Western India. It is known as the Namados according to Ptolemy. The *Padma Purāṇa* (Svargakhaṇḍa, 6th Ch., V, 15), *Bhāgavata Purāṇa* (V, 19, 18; VI, 10, 16; VIII, 18, 21) and *Yoginītantra* (2. 5, p. 139) mention it. According to the *Matsya Purāṇa* (Ch. 193) the place where this river falls to the sea is a great place of pilgrimage called the Yāmadagnitīrtha. Bhṛgutīrtha is situated on this river. Here the sage Bhṛgu performed austerities (*Matsya*, 193, 23–49). Kanyātīrtha is also situated on this river (*Matsya*, 193-194). This river rises from the Maikal range and flows more or less in a south-westerly direction forming the natural boundary between Bhupal and Central Provinces. Some hold that it rises in the Amarakaṇṭaka mountain and falls into the Gulf of Cambay. Thereafter the river runs through Indore and flows past Rewa Kantha of Bombay and meets the sea at Broach. As the river takes its course in between the two great mountain ranges of Vindhya and Satpurā, it is fed by a large number of tributaries. Before it enters Indore it is joined by some tributaries. This river is also known as the Revā, Samodbhavā, and Mekhalasutā. The Narmadā and the Revā form a confluence a little above Māndlā to flow down under either name. Kālidāsa in his *Raghuvaṃśam* (V. 42–46) makes it flow through forests of the *jambu* and *raktamāla* trees. This is poetic effulgence. According to the *Daśakumāracaritam* (p. 197) the shrine of the goddess dwelling in the Vindhya mountain existed on the bank of the river Revā. According to the *Mahābhārata* (Ch. 85, 9; cf. *Kūrmap.*, 30. 45–48; *Agnip.*, Ch. 109; *Saurap.*, 69. 19) the Narmadā formed the southern boundary of the ancient kingdom of Avantī.

The *Jātaka* (II. 344) refers to the crabs found in this river. The ospreys found on its bank were caught and killed by a bird-catcher (*Jāt.*, IV. 392).

Narod.—It is also called Ranod, an old decayed town in the State of Gwalior, where a stone inscription was discovered (*E.I.*, I, 351; Luard, *Gwalior State Gazetteer*, p. 271).

Narwar.—Cunningham identifies this town with Padmāvatī which, according to the *Purāṇas*, was one of the cities held by the Nāgas. Coins and inscriptions bearing the name of Gaṇapati who is mentioned as a Nāga King in Samudragupta's Allahabad Pillar Inscription, have been found here (*I.A.*, XII, 80, Nos. 2 and 4; Cunningham, *A.S.R.*, II, 314; Luard, *Gwalior State Gazetteer*, p. 272). This place is traditionally supposed to be the home of Rājā Nala of Naiṣadha whose romantic love for Damayantī, related in the *Mahābhārata*, is familiar to all.

Navapattalā.—It may be identical with Nayākherā lying about eight miles west of Tikhārī (*E.I.*, XXV, Pt. VII, p. 311).

Nāḍol (296, V, 1213), Osia (No. 384, V, 1236) and Phalodi (850, V, 1535) are in the Jodhpur State, Rajputana (*Inscriptions of Northern India* revised by D. R. Bhandarkar).

Nāndsā.—This village is situated in the Sahārā district of the Udaipur State. It is about 36 miles to the east of the railway station of Bhilwara and about four miles to the south of Gaṅgapur, a town in the jurisdiction of the State of Gwalior. Here two inscriptions on the *Yūpa* of a Mālava king were discovered (*E.I.*, XXVII, Pt. VI, p. 252).

Nārāṇaka.—It may be identified with Narain in the Sāmbhar Nizamat in the State of Jaipur, 41 miles west of Jaipur city and 43 miles north-east of Ajmeer (*E.I.*, XXVI, Pt. III, July, 1941, p. 101).

Nāthadvāra.—On the right bank of the Banās river, about 30 miles north by north-east of Udaipur city and 14 miles north-west of Maoli railway station, this place is situated as one of the most famous Vaiṣṇava shrines in India. It contains an image of Kṛṣṇa. This image was later placed by Vallabhācāryya in a small temple at Mathurā and was afterwards removed to Govardhana.

Nicatgiri.—It is called Bhojapura hills, the low range of hills in the kingdom of Bhopal that lies to the south of Bhilsā as far as Bhojapura (Kālidāsa's *Meghadūta*, I, v. 26).

Nirbbindhyā.—This river is mentioned in Kālidāsa's *Meghadūta* (I. 28-29) as lying between Ujjain and the river Vetravatī (Betwa). The *Vāyu Purāṇa* mentions it as Nirbbandhyā (XLV, 102). Really speaking, this river lay between Vidiśā and Ujjayinī, i.e., between the Daśārṇa (Dhasan forming a tributary of the Vetravatī) and the Śiprā. It is identified with the modern Kālisindh which forms a tributary of the Carmanvatī (*Journal of the Buddhist Text Society*, V, p. 46). The Kālisindh flows north from the Vindhya range to join the Chambal on the right. As the Kālisindh is probably the Sindhu of Kālidāsa's *Meghadūta*, the identification of the Nirbbindhyā with the Newaj, another tributary of the Chambal, seems to be more reasonable (*Thornton's Gazetteer*, *Gwalior*, Bhupal).

Niṣadha.—This country to which Pāṇini refers in his *Aṣṭādhyāyī* as Naiṣadha (4. 1. 172) seems to have been situated not very far from Vidarbha, the country of Nala's Queen Damayantī. Wilson[1] thinks that it was near the Vindhyas and Payoṣṇī river and that it was near the roads leading from it across the Ṛkṣa mountain to Avantī and the south as well as to Vidarbha and Kośala. Lassen places it along the Satpura hills to the north-west of Berar. Burgess also places it to the south of Malwa (*Antiquities of Kathiawar and Kacch*, p. 131). The *Mahābhārata* mentions Giriprastha as the capital of the Niṣadhas (III, 324, 12). The *Viṣṇu Purāṇa* (IV, Ch. 24, 17) refers to the nine kings of the Niṣadhas, while the *Vāyu Purāṇa* mentions the kings of the Niṣadha country who held sway till the end of the days of Manu. They were all the descendants of king Nala and they lived in the Niṣadha country.[2] Nala, the king of the Niṣadhas, was a skilful charioteer and knew much about the nature of horses (*Naiṣadhīyacarita*, sarga 5, śl. 60).

Osia or Osiām.—This small village is situated thirty-two miles north-north-west of Jodhpur in the midst of a sandy region. It contains temples (*A.S.I.*, *Annual Report*, 1908/9, pp. 100ff.).

Padmāvatī.—It is modern Narwar, Gwalior district of Madhya-Bhārata (C.I.) (*E.I.*, I, 147–52). Here the celebrated poet Bhavabhūti was born (*Mālatī-Mādhava*, Act I). According to some this town was situated at the confluence of the two rivers, Sindhu and Pārā (Pārvatī), in Vidarbha. It has been identified with modern Vijayanagar, which is a corruption of Vidyānagar, 25 miles below Narwar or Nalapura. According to V. A. Smith Padmāvatī was the capital of Gaṇapati Nāga. It is now called Padam Pawāyā, 25 miles north-east of the city of Narwar which is included in the Scindhia's dominions (*C.H.I.*, p. 300; *Annual Report*, *A.S.W.C.*, 1914-15, p. 68). According to the *Skanda Purāṇa* (Avantīkhaṇḍa, I, Ch. 36, 44), Padmāvatī is another name for Ujjayinī (N. L. Dey, *Geographical Dictionary*, p. 143; *A.S.R.*, Vol. II, pp. 308–18; *J.A.S.B.*, 1837, p. 17). Padmāvatī is also known as Padmapura.

Parsadā or Parsadi.—It is a village in the Balodā Bazar tahsil of the Raipur State, C.P. (*E.I.*, XXIII, Pt. I, January, 1935, p. 3).

---

1 *Viṣṇu Purāṇa*, Vol. II, pp. 156–90.

2 *Vāyup.*, Ch. 99, 376.

Pathāhri.—It is an important town of the Bhopal State, where a Pillar Inscription of Parabala of the Rāṣṭrakūṭa family (dated V.S. 917) was discovered (*E.I.*, IX, 248ff.).

Paṭṭan.—It is a substantial village with a population of 1,500 souls in the Multai tahsil of the Betul district, C.P. It lies about 10 miles south of Multai on the Multai-Amraoti road (*E.I.*, XXIII, Pt. III, July, 1935, p. 81—*Paṭṭan Plates of Pravarasena II*).

Pauni.—It is an old town situated on the right bank of the Waingaṅgā, about 32 miles south of Bhaṇḍārā, the headquarters of the Bhaṇḍārā district of the Madhya-Pradeśa (C.P.), where the Inscription of the Bhāra king Bhagadatta was discovered (*E.I.*, XXIV, Pt. I, p. 11).

Pawaya.—It is at the confluence of the Sindh and Pārvatī rivers, about 40 miles to the south-west of Gwalior. It is identified as the ancient town of Padmāvatī of Bhavabhūti and one of the three capitals of the Nāgas (*A.S.R.*, 1915-1916).

Payoṣṇī.—The *Mahābhārata* (Vanaparva, LXXXVIII, 8329-35) and the *Mārkaṇḍeya Purāṇa* (Canto LVII, 24) mention this river which was separated from the Narmadā by the Vaidūrya mountain. According to the *Mahābhārata* (CXX, 10289-90), it was the river of Vidarbha. The river Payoṣṇī flowed through the countries inhabited by the two tribes called Tamaras and Hamsamārgas according to the *Matsya Purāṇa*. Cunningham identifies this river with the Pahoj, a tributary of the Jumna between the Sindh and Betwa (*A.S.R.*, VII, Plate XXII). This identification seems to be untenable.

Pārā.—The *Mārkaṇḍeya Purāṇa* (Canto LVII, 20) refers to this river in Madhya-Bhārata (C.I.). It is called Parā according to the *Vāyu Purāṇa* (XLV, 98). It is the modern river Pārvatī which rises in Bhupal and falls into the Chambal which is the largest tributary of the Jumna (Pargiter, *Mārkaṇḍeya Purāṇa*, p. 295; Cunningham, *A.S.R.*, II, 308).

Pāripātra Mountain.—It is, according to Baudhāyana's *Dharma-sūtra* (1, 1, 25), the southern limit of Āryāvarta. According to the *Skanda Purāṇa*, it is the farthest limit of Kumārīkhaṇḍa, the centre of Bhārata-varṣa. The mountain seems to have lent its name to the country with which it was associated. Pargiter identifies the Pāripātra mountain with that portion of the modern Vindhya range, which is situated west of Bhupal together with the Aravalli mountains (Law, *Mountains of India*, pp. 17-18; Law, *Geographical Essays*, 115ff.).

Peṇḍrābandh.—It is a village in the Balodā Bazar tahsil of the Raipur State, C.P., where the plates of Pratāpamalla of the Kalacuri year 965, were discovered (*E.I.*, XXIII, Pt. I, January, 1925, p. 1).

Pīparḍulā.—This village lies about 20 miles from Ṭhākurdiyā, the findspot of a grant of Pravararāja, and it is only a few miles from the western borders of Sāraṅgarh State, Chattisgarh, C.P. This village is mentioned in the Pīparḍulā Copperplate Inscription of king Narendra of Śarabhapura (*I.H.Q.*, Vol. XIX, No. 2).

Pipliānagar.—It is a village in the Shujalpur Pargana, Gwalior State, where a copperplate inscription has been found. It was issued by Arjuna-varman on the occasion of his coronation from the fort of Maṃḍapa (*J.A.S.B.*, V. 378).

Pokṣara.—It is the same as Puṣkara, seven miles from Ajmeer, Rajputana, occurring in Luders' List, No. 1131. It is also called Pokhrā. It is considered very sacred by the Hindus (vide *Puṣkara*).

Potodā.—It may be identified with Potal in the Hindol State (*E.I.*, XXVI, Pt. II, April, 1941, p. 78).

Prārjunas.—They are mentioned in the Allahabad Pillar Inscription. They may be located somewhere near Narsiṃhagarh in C.I. Vincent Smith (*J.R.A.S.*, 1897, p. 892) places the Prārjunas in the Narasiṃhapur district of the C.P., but a more plausible location is Narasiṃhagarh in C.I. (*I.H.Q.*, Vol. I, p. 258), inasmuch as three other tribes which are coupled with the Prārjunas, namely, the Sanakānikas, Kākas and Kharaparikas, seem to have occupied regions more or less within the bounds of Central India. The author of the *Bṛhatsaṃhitā* locates them in the northern division of India. The Allahabad Pillar Inscription of Samudragupta refers to a host of tribes including the Prārjunas who obeyed the imperial commands and paid all kinds of taxes. Some hold that the Prārjunas have some connection with the name of the epic hero Arjuna, but this is doubtful.

Pūrṇa.—This river which retains its ancient identity, is mentioned in the *Padma Purāṇa* (Ch. XLI). It rises from the Satpura branch of the Vindhya range and meets the Tāptī a little below Burhanpur.

Puṣkara.—It is modern Pokhar in Ajmere. It is a holy place (*Skanda Purāṇa*, Ch. I, 19–23). Puṣkara which is seven miles north of Ajmeer, is a celebrated place of pilgrimage of the Hindus. It contains a tank the water of which is very holy. According to Hindu tradition the greatest sinner by simply bathing in it goes to heaven. There are five principal temples at this place, those dedicated to Brahmā, Sāvitrī, Badrināråyaṇa, Varāha and Śiva. The *Brahma Purāṇa* (Ch. 102) refers to Sāvitrītīrtha which is situated on a hill frequently visited by Hindu pilgrims. The *Padma Purāṇa* (Uttarakhaṇḍa, vv. 35–38) mentions it. The town is picturesquely situated on the lake with hills on three sides (*Rajputana District Gazetteers—Ajmer-Merwara*, by Watson, pp. 18–20). The *Bṛhat-saṃhitā* (XVI, 31) and the *Yoginītantra* (2. 4; 2. 6) mention it.

Puṣkaraṇa (Pokharan).—It is the same as Pokhraṇa which has been located by H. P. Śāstrī in Marwar in Rajputana. It is situated on the borders of Jaisalmere State (*A.S.I.*, *Annual Reports*, 1930–34, p. 219). King Candra, mentioned in the Meharauli Iron Pillar Inscription (*C.I.I.*, Vol. III, pp. 141ff.), has been identified by H. P. Śāstrī with king Candra-varman of the Allahabad Pillar Inscription and with the king of the same name of Pokhrāṇā. The mighty king Candra is said to have 'in battle in the Vaṅga countries, turned back with his breast the enemies who uniting together came against him'. Some have identified Pokhrāṇā or Puṣkaraṇa with a village of the same name on the Damodar river in the Bankura district of West Bengal, some 25 miles east of the Susunia hill containing the record of Candravarman (Ray Chaudhuri, *P.H.A.I.*, 4th ed., 448; S. K. Chatterjee, *The Origin and Development of the Bengali Language*, II, 1061; *I.H.Q.*, I, Pt. II, 255). Candravarman, king of Puṣkaraṇa in Raj-putana in the 4th century, was contemporary with Samudragupta and was the brother of Naravarman, mentioned in the Mandasor Inscription of 404-05 A.D. Both the brothers were the kings of Malwa (*E.I.*, XII, 317). Puṣkaraṇa is a well-known town in Marwar (*I.A.*, 1913, pp. 217–19; Tod, *Annals of Rajasthan*, 2nd ed., Vol. I, p. 605). For an account of the two inscribed pillars discovered by the Archaeological Department of the Jodhpur State at Puṣkaraṇa, vide *A.S.I.*, *Annual Reports*, 1930–34, pp. 219-220.

Rahatgadh.—It is a town 25 miles west of Sagor, the headquarters of the district of the same name in the Gwalior State, where stands a fort. The earliest of the Inscriptions of Jayavarman II has been found in this fort (*I.A.*, XX, 84).

Ratanpur.—It is in the Central Provinces, 16 miles north of Bilaspur in the Bilaspur district, where an Inscription of Pṛthvīdeva II on a black stone was discovered within the fort at Ratanpur (*E.I.*, I, 45; cf. *E.I.*, XXVI, Pt. VI, April, 1942, pp. 256ff.).

Rājim.—The Rājim Copperplate Inscription of the Rājā Tīvaradeva mentions Rājim, a town on the right bank of the Mahānadī river, about 24 miles to the south-west of Raypur, the chief town of the Raypur district in the Central Provinces (*C.I.I.*, Vol. III; cf. *E.I.*, XXVI, Pt. II, April, 1941). It is also called Devapura of the *Padma Purāṇa*. According to the Rājim Stone Inscription of the Nala king Vilasatuṅga, it is a well-known holy place, 28 miles south by east of Raipur situated on the eastern bank of the Mahānadī at the junction of the Pairi with that river. A fair is held here for a fortnight from the full-moon day of Māgh in honour of the god Rājīvalocana (*E.I.*, XXVI, Pt. II, p. 49).

Rājorgaḍh.—It is a village in the Alwar State of Rajputana, about 28 miles south-west of the town of Alwar (*E.I.*, III, 263).

Rāmnagar.—It is in the Mandla district, C.P. (*Inscriptions of Northern India*, revised by D. R. Bhandarkar, No. 1017, V, 1724).

Rāmṭek (Rāmagiri).—It is the headquarters of a tahsil of the same name in the Nagpur district of the Central Provinces (*E.I.*, XXV, Pt. I, p. 7). It is situated 24 miles north of Nagpur. Here Śambuka of the *Rāmāyaṇa* practised penances as assumed by Mirashi and Kulkarni in their article on the Rāmṭek Inscription of the time of Rāmacandra published in *E.I.*, XXV, Pt. I.

Rāṇipadra.—It may be identified with Rāṇod, an old decayed town in the Gwalior State, about halfway between Jhansi and Guna (*E.I.*, XXIV, Pt. VI, p. 242), 45 miles due south of Narwar (*E.I.*, Vol. I, p. 351).

Rāyapura.—It is a large village in the State of Koṭhi about 30 miles to the north of the Satna railway station and about 30 miles to the south-east of Kālañjar (*J.B.B.R.A.S.*, Vol. 23, 1947, pp. 47-48).

Rāyatā.—This village in the estate of Begūn is situated about 11 miles south-east of Bijholī (*E.I.*, XXVI, Pt. III, July, 1941).

Revaṇā.—This village seems to be identical with the modern Randholapura, about four miles north-east of Bijholī. It was donated to Pārśvanātha by Prince Someśvara (*E.I.*, XXVI, Pt. III, July, 1941, p. 101).

Revatī.—It is a small river flowing by the side of the Pārśvanātha temple at Bijholī (*E.I.*, XXVI, Pt. III, July, 1941). It is named after the Revatī-kuṇḍa.

Revā.—It is a river mentioned in the Mandasor Stone Inscription of Yaśodharman and Viṣṇuvardhana (Mālava year 589). The Bhāgavata-purāṇa also mentions it (V, 19, 18; IX, 15, 20; X, 79, 21). The pale mass of waters of this river flows from the slopes of the summits of the Vindhya mountain according to this inscription (*C.I.I.*, Vol. III). The *Meghadūta* of Kālidāsa also mentions it (Pūrvamegha, 19).

Ṛkṣavat.—Ṛkṣavat is the ancient name of the modern Vindhya mountain. It is called by Ptolemy Ouxenton. Ptolemy describes this mountain as the source of the Toundis, the Dosāran and the Adamas. According to Ptolemy, the Dosāran is said to have issued from the Ṛkṣa. By the Ṛkṣa he meant the central region of the modern Vindhya range north of the Narmada (Law, *Mountains of India*, p. 17).

Śailapura.—In the Barhut Votive label (No. 41) occurs Śailapura (Barua and Sinha, *Barhut Inscriptions*, p. 16).

Sakrāi.—It is a village in the Śekhāvāṭi Province of the Jaipur State in Rajputana, 14 miles north-west of Khaṇḍelā. It is a sacred place of the Hindus noted for its temple of the goddess Śākambharī on the bank of the rivulet called Śarkarā, where a stone inscription was discovered (*E.I.*, XXVII, Pt. I, p. 27).

Sallaimāla.—It is now represented by the two villages, Salora, 2½ miles to the west, and Amlā, which lies about five miles to the south-west of Añjanavatī, C.P. (*E.I.*, XXIII, Pt. I, January, 1935).

Salonī.—This village granted by Puruṣottama may be identified with Saraoni which lies about a mile and a half south by west of Koni (*E.I.*, XXVII, Pt. VI, p. 280).

Samudrapāṭa.—It is probably Samand Pipāria, four miles south of Jubbalpur (*E.I.*, XXV, VII, p. 311).

Satājunā.—It is the village Satājunā about 13 miles south-west of Mandhātā (*E.I.*, IX, 106).

Satyavāna.—This mountain stands in the midst of the Ṛkṣa and the Mañjumān (*Padma Purāṇa*, 140).

Sābhramatī.—This river consists of seven streams. The two holy places called the Nandītīrtha and Kapālamocanatīrtha stand on this river (*Padma Purāṇa*, Ch. 136). This river joins the river Brahmavallī (*Ibid.*, Ch. 144).

Śākambhari.—It was a site in Jaipur State. The ruins at Sāmbhar were explored in 1936–1938 (D. R. Sahni, *Archaeological Remains and Excavations at Sāmbhar*).

Sāmoli.—It is in the Udaipur State of Rajputana.

Sāñcī.—The ancient name of Sāñcī was Kākanāda (*C.I.I.*, Vol. III, 31; Luders' List No. 350). It is noted for its ancient Buddhist *stūpas.* A large number of votive inscriptions from the Sāñcī stūpas are available (*E.I.*, II, 87ff.). Sāñcī is situated 20 miles north-east of Bhupal in Central India. (For details, vide Cunningham, *Bhilsa Topes*, p. 183.) The Sāñcī Stone Inscription of Candragupta II mentions Sāñcī village which is situated about 12 miles to the north-east of Dewangunj in the sub-division of the native state of Bhupal in Central India (*C.I.I.*, Vol. III). There is a difference of opinion as to the date of construction of the Topes at Sāñcī. For details, vide *Excavations at Sāñcī* by M. Hamid, *A.S.I.*, *Annual Report*, 1936/37 (1940); *The Monuments of Sāñchī* by Sir John Marshall and Alfred Foucher, 1940.

Sāncor.—It is the principal town of the district of the same name in the Jodhpur State (*E.I.*, XI, p. 57).

Sārangaḍh.—It is in the Chattisgaḍh division of the Central Provinces, 32 miles south of Raigaḍh (*E.I.*, IX, 281ff.).

Sevāḍi.—It is a village in the Bali district, Goḍwār province of the Jodhpur State (*E.I.*, XI, p. 304).

Shergaḍh.—It is a deserted town in the Kotah State, Rajputana. It is about 12 miles to the south-west of the railway station of Atru where two inscriptions have been found (*E.I.*, XXIII, Pt. IV, October, 1935, p. 131).

Śiprā.—This river has its origin in the lake called Śiprā, situated to the west of the Himalaya mountain and falls into the southern sea (*Kālikā Purāṇa*, Ch. 19, pp. 14, 17). It is mentioned in the *Meghadūta*, (Pūrvamegha, 31). It has been immortalized by Kālidāsa as a historical river on which the city of Ujjayinī was situated (cf. *Raghuvaṃśa*, VI, 35). This is a local river of the Gwalior State which flows into the Chambal (Carmanvatī), a little below Sitaman. It is fed by two tributaries (Law, *Rivers of India*, p. 40). The *Harivaṃśa* (clxvii, 9509) mentions this river. According to the Pauranic list it is said to have issued from the Pāripātra mountain. The Avantyakhaṇḍa of the *Skanda Purāṇa* points out that the Śiprā in Avantī was known as *Uttaravāhinī*, i.e., flowing down to the north. When the waters of the river Revā covered the earth, the Vindhya mountain saved the earth. The three rivers, Revā, Carmanvatī and Kṣātā sprang from the Amarakaṇṭaka hill near the Vindhya. The Kṣātā split open the Vindhya and flowed to Mahākālavana, i.e., Ujjayinī to meet the Śiprā near Rudrasarovara. The confluence of the two rivers Śiprā and Kṣātā was known as the Kṣātāsaṅgama which is an important place of pilgrimage (*Skanda Purāṇa*, Ch. 56, 6–12, pp. 2868-69, Vaṅgavāsī ed.). The Jaina *Āvaśyaka-Cūrṇi* (p. 544) also mentions this river.

Siroha.—It is about three miles north-west of Narwar.

Sirpur.—It is a small village situated on the right bank of the Mahānadī in the Mahāsamunda tahsil of the Rāipur district in the Central Provinces. It is 37 miles north-east of Rāipur and 15 miles from Ārang. It was once the capital of Mahā-Kośala and was then known as Śrīpura (*E.I.*, XI, p. 184).

Śrīmālapaṭṭana.—It is the well-known Bhinmal, the capital city of the ancient province of Gurjaratrā, situated about 50 miles west of Mount Abu (*E.I.*, XXVI, Pt. III, July, 1941). It is called Śrīmāla according to the *Skanda Purāṇa*.

Śrīmārga.—Śrīmārga occurs in the Bijholī Rock Inscription of Cāhamāna Someśvara (V.S. 1226), where it appears to have been used as a variant of Śrīpatha or Śrīpathā, identified by Fleet with modern Bayāna in the Bharatpur State (*E.I.*, XXVI, Pt. II, April, 1941, pp. 84ff.).

Śrīpura.—It is modern Sirpur in the Raipur district, C.P. (*E.I.*, XXII, 22; vide *Śirpur*).

Sunārpāl.—It is a village about 10 miles from Nārāyaṇapāla in the Bastar State, where a stone inscription of Jayasiṃhadeva was discovered (*E.I.*, X, 35ff.).

Sunika.—A new charter of Mahāsudevarāja of Śarabhapura mentions this village at Dhakaribhoga (*I.H.Q.*, XXI, No. 4).

Supratiṣṭha.—It was the headquarters of the Āhāra which seems to have comprised the territory, now included in the Hingaṇghāṭ tahsil in the Nagpur district (*E.I.*, XXVI, 157-58). This Āhāra is also mentioned in the Poona plates of Prabhāvatīgupta (*E.I.*, XV, 39ff.).

Śvetā.—This river originates from the Sābhramatī (*Padmapurāṇa*, Ch. 137).

Talahārī.—It seems to have comprised the country round Mallār in the Bilaspur tahsil (*E.I.*, Vol. XXVII, Pt. VI, p. 280). Its ancient name seems to have been Taradamśakabhukti mentioned in an old copperplate grant of Mahāśivagupta Bālārjuna found near Mallār.

Talevāṭaka.—It is modern Talegaon about 10 miles south by west of Añjanavatī (*E.I.*, XXIII, Pt. I, January, 1935, p. 13).

Tāpī (Tāptī).—This is undoubtedly the river Tāptī but strangely enough it is nowhere mentioned in the Epics, not even in the Bhīṣmaparva list of the *Mahābhārata* (Luders' List, No. 1131). The *Bhāgavatapurāṇa* (V. 19, 18; X. 79, 20) and the *Padmapurāṇa* (Uttarakhaṇḍa, vv. 35–38) mention this river, which has its source in the Multai plateau to the west of the Mahadeo hills and flows westward forming the natural boundary between the Central Provinces and the north-western tip of Berar. It passes through Burhanpura and crossing the boundary of the Central Provinces, it enters the Bombay Presidency to meet the sea at Surat. It is fed by a number of unimportant tributaries. According to the *Viṣṇupurāṇa* (II, 3, 11) this river rises from the Rikṣa hills. It was visited by Balarāma (*Vāyu*, 45. 102; *Brahmāṇḍa*, II, 16. 32).

Ptolemy speaks of the Nanagounas river which must be the Tāptī. The name Nanagounas cannot be traced in the Indian sources. Ptolemy in course of his coastal description locates the mouth of this river at the same altitude as the modern town of Sopārā (Souppārā), some 33 miles north of Bombay at a great distance from the actual mouth of the Tāptī. Ptolemy locates the sources of the Nanagounas in the eastern part of the Vindhya. The Tāptī does not rise in the Vindhya (J. Ph. Vogel, *Notes on Ptolemy*, *B.S.O.A.S.*, XIV, Pt. I, p. 84).

Ṭekabharā.—It may be identical with Tikhārī, five miles south by west of Jubbalpore (*E.I.*, XXV, VII, p. 311).

Temarā.—It is a small village adjoining Kuruspal in the Bastar State of the Central Provinces (*E.I.*, X, 39ff.).

Terambi.—It may be identified with Terahi, five miles to the south-east of Rāṇod (*E.I.*, XXIV, Pt. VI, p. 242).

Tewār.—It is a village about six miles to the west of Jubbulpore in the Central Provinces, where a stone inscription of the reign of Jayasiṃhadeva of Cedi year 928 was discovered (*E.I.*, II, 17ff.).

Thākurdiyā.—This village lies six miles from Sāraṅgarh in Chattisgarh, C.P. (*E.I.*, XXII, p. 15).

Ṭiharī.—It is modern Tehri, about five miles to the east of the river Jāminī, a little below the line connecting Chattarpur with Lalitpur and about 30 miles to the north of Suraī, all within Bundelkhand (*J.B.B.R.A.S.*, Vol. 23, 1947, p. 47).

Timisa.—It is the ancient name of the hills west of Añjanavatī in C.P. (*E.I.*, XXIII, Pt. I, January, 1935, p. 13).

Tosaḍḍa.—This village may be identified with Tusdā near Dumarpalli about 30 miles to the south-east of Arang (*E.I.*, XXIII, Pt. I, January, 1925, p. 20).

Tripurī.—It lies six miles from Jubbalpur (*E.I.*, XXI, 93). It is modern Tewar near Jubbalpur. It is mentioned in the *Brihat-saṃhitā* as a city (XIV, 9).

Tumain.—It is a large village in the Guṇa district of the Gwalior State about 10 miles to the south-east of Pachar railway station (*E.I.*, XXVI, Pt. III, July, 1941, p. 115).

Tumbavana.—It is mentioned in six of the votive inscriptions of the great stūpa at Sāñcī and in the Tumain inscription of Kumāragupta and Ghaṭotkacagupta, dated GE. 116 (*E.I.*, XXVI, Pt. III, July, 1941). The *Bṛhatsaṃhitā* of Varāhamihira (XIV, 15) refers to it. It is identified with Tumain, six miles to the south of Tukneri railway station and about 50 miles to the north-west of Eran (ancient Airikiṇa).

Tummāna.—It is also known as Tumān which lies about 45 miles north of Ratanpur in the Bilaspur district (*E.I.*, XXVII, Pt. VI, p. 280).

Tuṇḍaraka.—It may be identified with the present Tuṇḍrā about six miles south of Seori Nārāyaṇa on the Mahānadī and about 35 miles west of Sārangarh. It is now included in the Balodā Bazar tahsil of the Raipur district (*E.I.*, IX, p. 283).

Udaipur.—Here stands the Jagannātharāya temple, where inscriptions have been found (*E.I.*, XXIV, Pt. II, April, 1937).

Udayagiri.—It is noted for the rock cut temples excavated in an isolated sandstone hill. The Udayagiri cave inscription of Candragupta II mentions this well-known hill with a small village of the same name on the eastern side, about two miles to the north-west of Bhilsā, the chief town of the Bhilsā tahsil or sub-division of the Isāgaḍh district in the dominions of Scindhia in Central India (*C.I.I.*, Vol. III). According to some, this hill stands 4½ miles north-west of the Bhilsa railway station. This ancient site in Bhilsā is situated between the Betwā and the Besh rivers, four miles from Bhilsā. It contains caves which are twenty in number. The region in which this hill is situated, was formerly known as Daśārṇa or Dasaṇṇa of the early Buddhist canon. Dasaṇṇa is generally identified with the region round modern Bhilsā. The hill of Udayagiri is about 1½ miles in length, its general direction being from south-west to north-east. Vedisagiri where Mahendra, son of Aśoka, stayed with his mother in a monastery before his departure for Ceylon, might probably be the same as this Udayagiri hill. The Cave No. 5 is the most important of the Udayagiri caves from the sculptural point of view. It contains the scene of Varāha inscription. The Cave No. 6 contains the sculptural representations of the two *Dvārapālas*, Viṣṇu, Mahīṣamardinī, and Ganeśa. The Udayagiri caves contain twelve inscriptions of which the four are the most important. The inscription in the Cave No. 6 discloses that the Sanakānikas occupied this region (vide D. R. Patil, 'The Monuments of the Udayagiri hills', published in the *Vikrama Volume*, ed. by Dr. R. K. Mookerji, 1948, pp. 377ff.; Luard, *Gwalior State Gazetteer*, I, p. 296).

Udayapura.—It is in the State of Gwalior. A stone inscription has been found in Udayāditya's Śiva temple built here (*I.A.*, XVIII, 344ff.). The great Nīlakaṇṭheśvara temple was built at Udayapura by Udayāditya (*J.A.S.B.*, IX, 548).

Ujjain.—Patañjali in his *Mahābhāṣya* refers to it (3. 1. 2, pp. 67-68). The *Yoginītantra* (2. 2. 119) mentions it. Ujjayinī (Ujjenī) is mentioned in the Minor Rock Edict II of Aśoka. Ujjayinī, which was the capital of Avantī or Western Mālava, was situated on the river Śiprā, a tributary of the Carmanvatī (Chambal). It is the modern Ujjain in Gwalior, Central India. It was built by Accutagāmi according to the *Dīpavaṃsa* (p. 57). According to the Chinese pilgrim Hiuen Tsang, it is about 6,000 li in circuit. There are several tens of convents mostly in ruins. There are some three hundred priests, who study the doctrines of the Hinayanists and the Mahayanists. The king belongs to the Brahmin caste, who is well versed in the heretical books and who does not believe in the true law (Beal, *Buddhist Records of the Western World*, Vol. II, pp. 270-71). The dramas of Kālidāsa were performed on the occasion of the spring festival before the viceregal court of Ujjayinī, *circa* 400 A.D. (Rapson, *Ancient India*, p. 175). Astronomers reckoned their meridian of longitude from here (McCrindle, *Ancient India as described by Ptolemy*, p. 154). In the *Periplus of the Erythraean Sea* (Sec. 48) this city is called Ozene wherefrom every commodity for local consumption is brought down to Barygaza (Bhṛgukaccha). It was a great centre of trade, which lay at the junction of at least three main trade routes.

King Bimbisāra of Magadha had a son by a courtesan of Ujjayinī named Padumavatī (*Therīgāthā Commy.*, p. 39). Mahākaccāyana was born here in the family of king Caṇḍapajjota's chaplain, who learnt the three Vedas and succeeded his father in his office. Mahāvīra, the founder of Jainism, practised penances here. In the 4th century B.C. Ujjayinī became subject to Magadha. Aśoka was stationed here as viceroy in the early part of the 3rd century B.C. Aśoka's son Mahinda was born here while his father was the viceroy. Vikramāditya the celebrated King of Ujjayinī, who is usually identified with Candragupta II (*circa* 375 A.D.), is said to have expelled the Scythians and established his power over the greater part of India.

Popular literature of India of comparatively modern age is full of many amusing and interesting stories relating to King Vikramāditya of Ujjayinī and the nine Gems who adorned his court. The tradition, on the whole, suggests that Ujjayinī became a great centre of Sanskrit learning under its liberal royal patronage.

According to the *Daśakumāracaritaṃ* (p. 31), Puṣpodbhava made friendship with a merchant's son named Candrapāla and entered Ujjayinī in his company. He brought his parents to this great city.

According to the inscription found incised on two plates in the vicinity of Ujjayinī, Vākpatirāja at the request of Āsinī, the wife of Mahāika, granted the village of Sembalapuraka to Bhaṭṭeśvarīdevī at Ujjayinī (*I.A.*, XIV, 159ff.).

The Ujjayinī coin has a distinct place of its own among the ancient Indian copper coins. Punch-marked and cast coins are found here dating from the third century B.C. to the first century A.C. In the excavations at Ujjayinī clay medals and seals are also found dating from the second century B.C. to the second century A.C. Some potteries have been found here dated from the second century B.C. to the fifth century A.C. A stone casket has also been discovered (*cir.* 2nd century B.C.).

At Ujjayinī the temple of Mahākāla, one of the twelve most famous Śaiva temples in India, was built. The *Saurapurāṇa* (Ch. 67, I) refers to Mahākāla at Ujjayinī. It is also one of the holy places of the Liṅgāyat sect. The Liṅgāyat itinerant ascetics wander over India frequenting especially the five Liṅgāyat sees. As for the Hindu shrines Kālidāsa knew about the great temple of Kārttikeya on the Mount Devagiri. For further details vide B. C. Law, *Tribes in Ancient India*, Ch. LX; B. C. Law, *Ujjayinī in Ancient India* (Gwalior Archaeological Department).

Umā.—This river which is mentioned in the Kothuraka Grant of Pravarasena II, is identified with the river Wunnā in the Nagpur district (*E.I.*, XXVI, Pt. V, October, 1941, 155ff.). It formed the eastern boundary of the donated village of Kothuraka.

Umvaraṇigrāma (*E.I.*, VIII, 220).—It is in South Rajputana, and it may be identified with Umarṇī, seven miles south-south-west of Delvāḍā.

Un.—It lies to the south of the Narmadā close to the Bombay-Agra road at a distance of 60 miles from Sanawad Station. It is in the Nimar district of Indore State containing some temples (*A.S.I.*, Annual Report, 1918-19, Pt. I, p. 17).

Upaplavya.—It was a city in the kingdom of king Virāṭa wherefrom the Pāṇḍavas transferred themselves on completion of their exile. (*Mahābh.*, IV, 72, 14). It was to this city that Sañjaya, the messenger of the Kurus, was sent by Dhṛtarāṣṭra (*Ibid.*, V, 22, 1). Nīlakaṇṭha, the commentator on the *Mahābhārata*, points out that Upaplavya was a city near Virāṭanagara, but its exact site is uncertain (Nīlakaṇṭha on the *Mahābh.*, IV, 72, 14). It does not appear to have been a capital of the Matsyas, as told in the *Cambridge History of India* (p. 316) but only one of the towns in the Matsya country.

Uttamādriśikhara.—This appears to be the ancient name of the uppermost tableland popularly called the Uparamāla extending from Bārolli and Bhainsaror in the south of Jahāzpur in the north (*E.I.*, XXVI, Pt. III, July, 1941, p. 101).

Vadapura.—It was also known as Vaḍnagar. The town of Ānandapura situated at 117 miles to the north-west of Vallabhi has been identified by St. Martin with Vaḍnagar (*C.A.G.I.*, 565; cf. *Important Inscriptions from the Baroda State*, Vol. I, p. 78).

Vaḍauvā.—It is modern Baḍauvā, about three miles south of Bijholī (*E.I.*, XXVI, 102ff.).

Vairāṭa.—Vairāṭ or Vairāṭanagara was the capital of the Matsya country which lay to the south or south-west of Indraprastha and to the south of Śūrasena (*Ṛgveda*, VII, 18, 6; *Gopatha-Brāhmaṇa*, I, 2. 9, *B.I. series*). Vairāṭanagara was so called because it was the capital of Virāṭa, the king of the Matsyas. It is the headquarters of a tahsil in the Jaipur State, now accessible by a fine metalled road connecting Delhi with Jaipur, a distance of 52 miles. Traditionally it can be identified with Virāṭapura, the capital of Virāṭa, the king of the Matsya country, at whose capital the five Pāṇḍava brothers and Draupadī passed the thirteenth year of their exile. When they disclosed their identity, Abhimanyu, the son of Arjuna, married Uttarā, the daughter of king Virāṭa (*Mahābh.*, lxxii). The town of Vairāṭa is situated in the midst of a circular valley surrounded by low hills, famous for their copper mines. It is 105 miles to the south-west of Delhi and 41 miles north of Jaipur. It is situated on a mound of ruins about one mile in length by half a mile in breadth or upwards of two and half miles in circuit, of which the town of Vairāṭa does not occupy more than one-fourth.

The ancient remains of Vairāṭ are dealt with in the *Archaeological Survey Reports*, Vols. II and VI (vide also *Progress Report of the Archaeological Survey of India, Western Circle*, for the year ending 31st March, 1910, written by Dr. D. R. Bhandarkar who visited Vairāṭ during the year 1909-10).

The present town of Vairāṭ stands in the midst of a valley about five miles in length from east to west, by three or four miles in width which is surrounded by three concentric ranges of hills, the outermost being the highest and the innermost the lowest. The Jaipur-Delhi road enters the valley through a narrow pass at the north-west corner and the area is drained by two rivulets, the Vairāṭ Nala which runs northward to join the Bāngaṅgā river and the Bandrol Nala on the south. Vairāṭ is famous for the Vairāṭ version of the Rūpnāth and Sahasrām edicts of Aśoka discovered by Carlleyle at the foot of the hill known as the Bhīmjī-kī Duṅgrī on a large rock. This hill is situated about a mile to the north-east of the town of Vairāṭ. A large cavern is found here which is believed to have been the abode of Bhīma, the second Pāṇḍava brother.

Vairāṭ contains a Jaina temple which is situated in the neighbourhood of the tahsil and consists of a sanctum preceded by a spacious Sabhāmaṇḍapa and surrounded by a broad circum-ambulatory passage on three sides (For details vide D. R. Sahni, *Archaeological Remains and Excavations at Bairāṭ*, pp. 16-17).

The top of the Bījak-kī-pahārī affords a picturesque view of the entire valley of Vairāṭ, with the Bhīmjī-kī-Duṅgrī hill and the monuments around it on the north and a perfectly level plain which surrounds the lofty town on all sides. Vairāṭ is no doubt famous for an Aśokan edict which is the only known edict of Aśoka, inscribed on a stone-slab (*Śilī-phalaka*) as distinguished from a stone-pillar (*Śilā-thamba*). This edict provides definite proof of Aśoka's faith in the Buddhist religion and his consequent exhortation to monks and nuns and to laymen and laywomen to listen to and to study the seven select passages from the Buddhist scriptures, for which he himself felt a special preference, as being most conducive to the continued prosperity of the Law of Piety promulgated by the Buddha.

By excavating the ancient site of Vairāṭ many archaeological remains of the Maurya period and immediately later have been found out. The principal monuments brought to light are numerous remnants of two Aśoka pillars similar to the other known memorial pillars of that emperor, a temple of an entirely new type, and a monastery erected by Aśoka himself. The best preserved portion of the monastery was that on the east side where a double row of six to seven cells has remained. Portable antiquities recovered from these cells included pottery, jars of different shapes and ornamented with various patterns. Some punch-marked coins of silver and some Greek and Indo-Greek silver coins have also been discovered. The discovery of a piece of cotton cloth throws interesting light on the kind of clothing used in the 1st century A.D. Among the portable antiquities found at the site mention may be made of a terracotta figurine of a dancing girl or *yakṣī* having no head and feet. The left hand rests on the hip while the right arm is laid across the chest to support the left breast. The figure is almost naked. Similar figures are found on railing pillars of about the 1st century B.C. at Mathurā. The circular temple discovered at the site is found to be a most interesting structure contemporaneous with the Aśoka pillars. It was destroyed by a big fire. Daya Ram Sahni has pointed out that an interesting feature of the excavations at Vairāṭ is the total absence among the finds of anthropomorphic representations of the Buddha of any form or material, which is in full accord with the view that the Buddha image was not evolved until about the 2nd century A.D. (D. R. Sahni, *Archaeological Remains and Excavations at Bairāt*, published by the Department of Archaeology and Historical Research, Jaipur State, pp. 19ff.). Vide also *Matsyadeśa*.

Vaṇikā.—It may be identified with the village of Benkā, 15 miles north-west of Alwar (*E.I.*, XXIII, IV, October, 1935, p. 102).

Varadākheṭa.—It is probably Warūḍ in the Morsi taluk of the Amraoti district about 12 miles south of Pattan (*E.I.*, XXIII, Pt. III, July, 1935, p. 84).

Varalāika.—It is the name of a tank near Bijholī whose embankment is strewn over with ancient temples now in ruins (*E.I.*, XXVI, Pt. III, July, 1941, p. 101).

Varatu.—This river may be identified with the river Varatroyi (*E.I.*, XXVI, Pt. V, January, 1942, p. 204), far to the east and north of the village of Deolia.

Vasantgaḍh.—It is in the Shirohi State of Rajputana, where the stone inscription of Pūrṇapāla was discovered (*E.I.*, IX, 10ff.). It is a very ancient place. Up to the end of the 11th century it was known by the name of Vaṭa, Vaṭakara and Vaṭapura. An old fort situated on a hill is found here. For details vide *Rajputana Gazetteers*, Vol. III-A, compiled by Erskine, pp. 302ff.

Vaśiṣṭhāśrama.—This hermitage was situated on the Mount Abu in the Aravalli range. Kālidāsa in his *Raghuvaṃśa* locates the hermitage of Vaśiṣṭha in the Himalayas (*Raghuv.*, II, 26). It was visited by Viśvāmitra. It was beautiful, full of sages, and adorned with various kinds of flowers, creepers and trees. (*Rāmāyaṇa*, Ādikāṇḍa, Sarga 51, vv. 22-23). Vaśiṣṭha is said to have created out of his fire-pit a hero named Paramāra to oppose Viśvāmitra while he was carrying away his celebrated cow Kāmadhenu. Paramāra was the progenitor of the Paramāra clan of the Rajputs. Dilīpa and his wife desirous of having a son started for this hermitage (*Raghuvaṃśa*, Sarga 1, v. 35).

Vaṭapadraka.—It is situated in the Kośīra-Nandapuraviṣaya. This village may be identified with modern Baṭapadaka about 14 miles from Barḍūla. The headquarters of Nandapuraviṣaya may be identified with the two adjoining villages in the Bilaspur district, C.P. (*E.I.*, XXVII, Pt. VII, July, 1948, pp. 289ff.).

Vaṭapura.—It is modern Vaḍur about a mile east of Kurha in C.P. (*E.I.*, XXIII, Pt. I, January, 1935, p. 13).

Vaṭāṭavi—Among the forest-kingdoms (*āṭavikarājyas*) may be mentioned Vaṭāṭavī and Sahalāṭavī (*E.I.*, VII, 126; Luders' List, No. 1195).

Vaṭuvāri.—It may be roughly identified with the Indian State of Chirkhari (*J.B.B.R.A.S.*, Vol. 23, 1947, p. 47).

Vāṭodaka.—The Tumain inscription of Kumāragupta and Ghaṭotkaca Gupta dated G.E. 116, mentions it, which is probably modern Badoh, a small village in the Bhilsa district of the Gwalior State, about 10 miles to the south of Eran (*E.I.*, XXVI, Pt. III, July, 1941, p. 117).

Vedisa (*Vidiśā*).—Vidiśā was a famous city in early times immortalized by Kālidāsa in his *Meghadūta*. The Vaidiśas were the people of Vidiśā[1] also called Vaiśyanagar which was an old name of Besnagar. According to the *Rāmāyaṇa* (Uttarakāṇḍa, Ch. 121) this city was given to Śatrughna by Rāmacandra. The *Garuḍapurāṇa*[2] describes it as a city full of wealth and happiness (*sarvasampatsamanvitaṃ*). It contained various countries (*nānājanapadākīrṇaṃ*), jewels (*nānāratnasamākulaṃ*), big mansions and palaces, prosperous and pompous (*śobhāḍhyam*). It was an abode of many religions (*nānādharmasamanvitaṃ*).

Vidiśā or Vedisa (Skt. Vaidiśa, Vaidaśa) is the old name of Besnagar, a ruined city situated in the fork of the Bes or the Vedisa river and the Betwa (Vetravatī),[3] in the kingdom of Bhopal, within two miles of Bhilsa. According to the *Purāṇas* Vaidiśa was situated on the banks of the river Vidiśā which took its rise from the Pāripātra mountain.[4] The ancient city of Vidiśā, mentioned in the Luders' List (Nos. 254, 273, 500, 521–24, 712, 780, 784, 813, 835 and 885), identified with Bhilsa in the Gwalior State, was situated at a distance of 26 miles north-east of Bhopal. It lay at a distance of fifty *yojanas* [5] from Pāṭaliputra.[6]

According to the Pāli legend of Aśoka the way from Pāṭaliputra to Ujjayinī lay through the town of Vedisa.[7] There is every reason to believe that Vidiśā was included in the kingdom of Avantī.[8] In *Mārkaṇḍeya-purāṇa* we have mention of Vidiśā as one of the Aparanta neighbours of Avantī. It is definitely known that the dominions of Puṣyamitra, the founder of the Śuṅga dynasty, extended to the river Narmadā and included Vidiśā, Pāṭaliputra and Ayodhyā.[9] But even if Avantī was included in the Śuṅga empire, Ujjayinī must have yielded place to Vidiśā as the viceregal headquarters.

Vidiśā was the capital of Eastern Malwa.[10] According to Bāṇa's *Kādambarī* a king of great valour named Śūdraka ruled Vidiśā, whose commands were obeyed by all the princes of the world. It remained as the western capital of Puṣyamitra and Agnimitra of the Śuṅga dynasty.[11] According to the *Meghadūta* (vv. 25-26) it was the capital of the Daśārṇa country[12] which was one of the sixteen *janapadas* of Jambudvīpa.[13] From the Vindhyapāda the cloud messenger was to proceed to the country of Daśārṇa in the direction of which lay the well-known capital city of Vidiśā on the Vetravatī. The Daśārṇas who figure in the *Mahābhārata*[14] as one

---

1 *Meghadūta*, I, 24, 25 and 28.

2 Bombay Ed. published by Sadashib Seth, ch. 7, śls. 34-35.

3 *Meghadūta*, Pūrvamegha, 25 śl.

4 Law, *Geography of Early Buddhism*, p. 3.

5 One *yojana*—about seven miles.

6 *Mahābodhivaṃsa*, 98-99.

7 *Samantapāsādikā*, p. 70; *Ujjeniṃ gacchanto Vedisanagaram patvā.*

8 Law, *Ujjayinī in Ancient India*, Gwalior Archaeological Dept. publication, p. 4.

9 Raychaudhuri, *Political History*, 4th Ed., p. 308.

10 Bhandarkar, *Carmichael Lectures*, 1921, p. 85.

11 *Cambridge History of India*, p. 523.

12 *Mahābhārata*, Ādiparva, CXIII, 4449; Vanaparva, LXIX, 2707-8; Udyogaparva, CXC–CXCIII; Bhīṣmaparva, IX, 348, 350, 363; cf. *Mārkaṇḍeyapurāṇa* 57, 52–55; *Meghadūta*, I, 24, 25 and 28.

13 *Mahāvastu*, I, 34; *Lalitavistara*, Lefmann Ed., p. 22: *Sarvasmin Jambudvīpe ṣoḍaśajanapadeṣu.*

14 Karṇaparva, ch. 22. 3; Bhīṣmaparva, chs. 95, 41, 43; Droṇaparva, chs. 25, 35.

of the tribes who fought with the Pāṇḍavas in the great Kurukṣetra war, occupied the site on the river Daśārṇa which can still be traced in the modern Dhasan river[1] that flows through Bundelkhand rising in Bhopal and emptying into the Betwa river or the Vetravatī.[2] There were two countries by the name of Daśārṇa: western Daśārṇa (*Mahābhārata*, ch. 32) representing eastern Malwa and the kingdom of Bhopal; and eastern Daśārṇa (*Mahābhārata*, ch. 30) forming a part of the Chattisgaḍh district in the Central Provinces (*J.A.S.B.*, 1905, pp. 7, 14). The *Mārkaṇḍeya Purāṇa* (57. 21–25) refers to the Daśārṇa river which gave its name to the country through which it flowed.[3] The modern Dhasan (also known as the Dushān river) with which it has been identified near Saugor, flows between the Betwā (Vetravatī) and the Ken, an important tributary of the Yamunā below the Vetravatī known to Arrian as the river Cainas. The same Purāṇa (57. 19-20) mentions Vidiśā and Vetravatī[4] among other rivers issuing from the Pāripātra mountain. The river Vidiśā[5] must be connected with the town Vidiśā on the Vetravatī, which was one of the five hundred rivers flowing from the Himalayas as mentioned in the *Miliṅda-Pañho.*[6] The temple of Bhailaswāmī which was situated on the Vetravatī at Bhilsa in the Gwalior State, 34 miles from Bhopal and eight miles from Sāñchī, must have given rise to the name of the Bhilsa town.[7] According to Pargiter Vidiśā was one among many small kingdoms into which the Yādavas appear to have been divided.[8] There was a place called Kārpāsigrāma[9] (occurring in three inscribed labels on the railing of the Sāñchī Stūpa I) in the neighbourhood of Vidiśā and certainly within Ākarāvantī noted for cotton and cotton industries.

Since the time of Aśoka it became an important centre of Buddhism and later on of Vaiṣṇavism. It came into prominence for the first time in Buddhism in connection with the viceroyalty of Aśoka. The importance of Vidiśā, the chief city of Daśārṇa, was due to its central position on the lines of communication between the seaports of the western coast and Pāṭaliputra, and between Pratiṣṭhāna and Śrāvastī.[10] Vidiśā (Vedisa-nagara or Vessanagar) was a halting place on the Dakṣiṇāpatha.

Vidiśā was famous for ivory work.[11] One of the sculptures at Sāñcī was the work of the ivory-workers of Vidiśā.[12] The *Periplus* mentions Dosarene as famous for ivory.[13] This city was also famous for sharp-edged swords.[14]

The sixteen Brahmin pupils of Bāvari visited Vedisa among other places.[15] The *Skanda Purāṇa*[16] refers to Vidiśā as a *tīrtha* or holy place

---

[1] It is connected with the Rikṣavanta (Ouxenton)—Law, *Geographical Essays*, p. 108.

[2] Law, *Tribes in Ancient India*, p. 375.

[3] Cf. Mahābhārata, II, 5–10.

[4] The water of this river was good for drinking purpose. Its waves rippled in joy indicated by their murmuring noise (*Meghadūta*, V. 26; cf. *Jāt.*, IV, p. 388). This river flows into the Yamunā. It was much used and many tooth-sticks were found in it left by the bathers after ablution (*Jāt.*, No. 497). Between this river and Ujjayinī lay the river Nirvindhyā (Law, *Geographical Essays*, p. 114; Thornton's Gazetteer, Gwalior, Bhopal; *Meghadūta*, I. 28-29; cf. *Bhāgavatapurāṇa*, IV, 14-15).

[5] *Mārkaṇḍeyapurāṇa*, LVII, 20.

[6] Trenckner Ed., p. 114; *Himavantapabbatā pañcanadī-satāni sandanti.*

[7] *E.I.*, XXIV, Pt. V, January, 1938, p. 231.

[8] *Ancient Indian Historical Tradition*, p. 273 and f.n. 7.

[9] Lüders' List Nos. 260, 515; Law, Ujjayinī, p. 8.

[10] *C.H.I.*, p. 523. [11] *Ibid.*, p. 632. [12] *Ibid.*, p. 643.

[13] Schoff, *The Periplus of the Erythraean Sea*, pp. 47, 253.

[14] *Jātaka*, III, 338; Dasaṇṇakaṃ tikhiṇadhāraṃ asiṃ.

[15] *Suttanipāta*, vs. 1006–1013. [16] Vaṅgabāsī Ed., pp. 2767-68.

which should be visited after visiting Someśvara. There were 18 donors belonging to Vidiśā, who contributed substantially towards the construction of Buddhist religious edifices at Bhilsa.[1] In the Bārhut Stūpa the Votive label on the Pillar No. 1 shows that it was the gift of Cāpādevī, wife of Revatimitra, a lady from Vidiśā.[2] There are also references to the gift of Vaśiṣṭhī, the wife of Veṇimitra from Vidiśā;[3] the gift of Phagudeva from Vidiśā; the gift of Anurādhā from Vidiśā;[4] the gift of Āryamā from Vidiśā;[5] and the gift of Bhūtarakṣita from Vidiśā.[6]

The Nīlakaṇṭheśvara temple at Udayapur in Bhilsa has been referred to in the *Udayapura praśasti* which is engraved on a slab of stone.[7] The Vedisagirimahāvihāra which is said to have been built by Aśoka's wife Devī for the residence of her son,[8] was probably the first Buddhist religious foundation which was followed by the erection of Stūpas at Sāñcī, five and a half miles south-west from Bhilsa. Mahinda the son of Aśoka by Devī stayed in this monastery for a month.[9] He came here to see his mother who welcomed her dear son and fed him with food prepared by herself.[10] He went to Ceylon from Vedisa mountain.[11] Vedisa also contained a monastery called Hatthāḷhakārāma.[12]

Vidiśā is well-known for its topes which include (1) Sāñchī Topes, five and a half miles to the south-west of Bhilsa; (2) Sonāri Topes, six miles to the south-west of Sāñchī; (3) Satdhāra Topes, three miles from Sonāri; (4) Bhojpur Topes, six miles to the south-south-east of Bhilsa; and (5) Andher Topes, nine miles to the east-south-east of Bhilsa.[13] Revatimitra was probably a member of the Śuṅga-Mitra family stationed at Vidiśā.

The inscription on a stone column at Besnagar, discovered by J. H. Marshall, the then Director General of Archaeology in India, records the erection of a column surmounted by *Garuḍa* in honour of Kṛṣṇa-Vāsudeva by the Greek ambassador Heliodoros, son of Dion, when he had been crowned twelve years.[14] Heliodoros, an inhabitant of Taxila, was sent by the Greek king Antialcidas to the court of king Kautṣīputra-Bhāgabhadra who was apparently reigning at Vidiśā. Although a Greek he was called a Bhāgavata, who, according to V. A. Smith, is credited with a long reign of thirty-two years.[15] On this column he caused to be incised some teachings of his new religion which he probably embraced at Vidiśā. These teachings are contained in the two lines engraved on the other side of the column. The Bhāgavata of the *Purāṇas* may be the corrupt form of Bhāgabhadra who was a Śuṅga prince reigning at Vidiśā, probably as *Yuvarāja*, just as one of his predecessors Agnimitra was during the reign of his father Puṣyamitra, as we learn from Kālidāsa's *Mālavikāgnimitra*. Bhāgavata, i.e., Bhāgabhadra has been assigned by V. A. Smith to *circa*

---

1 Luders' List, Geographical Index for references.

2 Barua and Sinha, *Barhut Inscriptions*, p. 3—*Vedisā Cāpādevāya* (*Cāpadevāya*) *Revatimitabhāriyāya paṭhamo thabho dānam*.

3 Barua and Sinha, *Barhut Inscriptions*, p. 35—*Vedisā Vāsiṭhiyā Velimitabhāriyāya dānaṃ*.

4 *Ibid.*, p. 14—*Vedisā Phagudevasa dānaṃ*; *Vedisā Anurādhāya dānaṃ*.

5 *Ibid.*, p. 17—*Vedisa Ayamāya dānaṃ*.

6 *Ibid.*, p. 20—*Vedisāto Bhūtarakhitasa dānaṃ*.

7 *Epigraphia Indica*, I, 233.

8 *Thūpavamsa*, p. 44.

9 *Dīpa*, VI, 15; XII, 14; 35; *Samantapāsādikā*, I, 70, 71; cf. *Mahāvaṃsa Commy.*, p. 321.

10 *Mahāv.*, ch. 13, vs. 6–11; *Dīpa*, ch. 6, 15–17; ch. 12, v. 14.

11 *Mahābodhiv.*, 116; *Thūpv.*, 43.

12 *Mahābodhivaṃsa*, p. 169.

13 Cunningham, *Bhilsa Topes*, p. 7.

14 *Archaeological Survey Report*, I, 1913-1914, Pt. II, p. 190.

15 *Early History of India*, 4th Ed., p. 214.

108 B.C.[1] The attention of J. H. Marshall who examined the ancient site of Vidiśā was drawn to a stone-column standing near a large mound, a little to the north-east of the main site, and separated from it by a branch of the Betwā river. The shaft of the column is a monolith, octagonal at the base, sixteen sided in the middle, and thirty-two sided above with a garland dividing the upper and middle portions. The capital is of the Persepolitan bell-shaped type with a massive *abaçus* surmounting it, and the whole is crowned with a palm-leaf ornament of strangely unfamiliar design. This column has been worshipped by pilgrims from generations to generations. Marshall thinks that the column was many centuries earlier than the Gupta era.[2] King Bhāgabhadra mentioned in the inscription was the son of a lady belonging to Banares (*Kāśīputrasa*). Fleet has taken *Kāśīputrasa* to mean that he was the son of a lady of the people of Kāśī, or the son of a daughter of a king of Kāśī.[3]

The Śākyas took shelter at Vidiśā being afraid of Viḍūḍabha.[4] Aśoka halted at the city of Vidiśā, while he was on his way to Ujjayinī to join the post of Maurya viceroy (*uparājā*) of Avantī.[5] Here he married Devī, who was endowed with signs of great persons and a young daughter[6] of a banker named Deva belonging to Vidiśā. According to the *Mahābodhivaṃsa* (pp. 98, 110) she was honoured as Vedisamahādevī and was represented as a Śākya princess. Devī was taken to Ujjayinī where she gave birth to a son named Mahinda and two years later, a daughter named Saṃghamittā.[7] Devī stayed at Vidiśā but her children accompanied their father when he came to Pāṭaliputra and seized the throne. Saṃghamittā was given in marriage to Agnibrahmā, a nephew of Aśoka (*bhāgineyyo*—sister's son),[8] and a son was born to them called Sumana. Dr. Barua rightly points out that the Sanskrit legends and the inscriptions of Aśoka are silent on this point.[9] Vedisamahādevī was by his side at the time of Aśoka's coronation.[10] Dr. Barua thinks that the Vidiśā residence of Devī favours the idea of having separate family establishments for individual wives at different towns.[11]

The Besnagar inscription testifies to the existence of diplomatic relations between the Greek king of Taxila and the king of Vidiśā.[12] The *Raghuvaṃśa* (XV. 36) says that the two sons of Śatrughna named Śatrughātin and Subāhu, were put in charge of Mathurā and Vidiśā. Avīkṣit, son of Karandhama, the ruler of Vaiśālī, had a great conflict with the king of Vidiśā and was captured. Karandhama rescued his son. Pargiter holds that the *Mārkaṇḍeyapurāṇa* (121–131) makes this conflict grow out of a *svayamvara* at Vidiśā.[13] About the time of Karandhama, the ruler of Vaiśālī, Parāvrit, king of the Yādava branch, placed his two youngest sons at Vidiśā and not in Vedeha.[14]

---

1 *J.B.B.R.A.S.*, Vol. XXIII, pp. 104–106.

2 *J.R.A.S.*, 1909, pp. 1053–56.

3 *J.R.A.S.*, 1910, pp. 141-142.

4 *Mahābodhivaṃsa*, p. 98.

5 *Samantapāsādikā*, I, p. 70.

6 *Mahāvaṃsa Commy.*, I, p. 324—*Vedisagirinagare Devanāmakassa seṭṭhissa ghare nivāsaṃ upagantvā tassa seṭṭhissa dhitaraṃ lakkhaṇasampannaṃ yobbanappataṃ Vedisadeviṃ nāma kumārikaṃ disvā tāya paṭibaddhacitto mātāpitunaṃ kathāpetvā taṃ tehi dinnaṃ paṭilabhitvā tāya saddhim saṃvāsaṃ kappesi.*

7 *Mahābodhivamsa*, 98-99; *Thūpav.*, 43.

8 *Mahāvamsa*, V, p. 169.

9 *Aśoka and His Inscriptions*, pp. 51-52.

10 *Ibid.*, p. 53.

11 *Ibid.*, p. 53.

12 *Cambridge History of India*, p. 558.

13 *Ancient Indian Historical Tradition*, p. 268, f.n. 4.

14 *Ibid.*, pp. 268-69. The *Mārkaṇḍeyapurāṇa* (Canto CXXII, vs. 20-21) makes this point clear by relating that when Vaiśālinī, the daughter of the Vaidiśa king named Viśāla, was waiting for the proper moment at her *svayamvara*, Karandhama's son

It is with the kingdom of Vidiśā that the Śuṅgas are especially associated in literature and inscriptions.[1] The *Mālavikāgnimitra* refers to the love of Agnimitra, king of Vidiśā and a viceroy of his father Puṣyamitra,[2] for Mālavikā, a princess of Vidarbha (Berar) living at his court in disguise. There was a war in 170 B.C. between Vidiśā and Vidarbha in which the former was victorious. Mādhavasena, a cousin of Yajñasena and a partisan of Agnimitra, was arrested and kept in custody of Yajñasena's warden when the former was on his way to Vidiśā. This led the Śuṅga monarch Agnimitra to ask Vīrasena to attack Vidarbha. Yajñasena was defeated and the kingdom of Vidarbha was divided between the two cousins.[3] After ruling Vidiśā as his father's viceroy, Agnimitra was his successor as suzerain for eight years.[4] The king at Vidiśā was the son of Kāśī, i.e., a princess from Benares.[5] The Śuṅgas ruled originally as feudatories of the Mauryas at Vidiśā.[6] Both Puṣyamitra and Agnimitra belonged to Vidiśā.

The Purāṇas preserve a tradition which avers that when the Śuṅga rule ended, one Śiśunandi began to rule Vidiśā. They lead us to think that the residual power of the Śuṅgas lingered at Vidiśā side by side with the suzerainty of the Kāṇvas. It is generally assumed that at first Vidiśā and subsequently Ujjayinī became the official headquarters of Candragupta II.[7]

In ancient Vidiśā copper *kārṣāpaṇa* was the standard money from slightly before the rise of the Mauryas to at least the beginning of the Gupta supremacy, i.e., for upwards of 600 years.[8] Punch-marked coins were found at Besnagar (ancient Vidiśā) which had its own individual marks on its coinage. They contained strata reaching down to the 4th century A.D.[9] The *kārṣāpaṇas* found at Besnagar seem to have been struck on a river bank. A zig-zig sign appears on them denoting a river bank.[10] Dr. Bhandarkar opines that owing to the enhancement of the price of copper the weight of copper *kārṣāpaṇas* was reduced at some periods in the ancient town of Vidiśā.[11]

Vediśagiri.—It was a mountain on which the Vediśagiri-mahāvihāra was built by Mahinda's mother. According to the *Samantapāsādikā* (p. 70) Mahinda stayed here and from this place he went to Tambapaṇṇi.

Vetravatī (Pali Vettavatī).—This river is mentioned in the *Mārkaṇḍeya Purāṇa* (pp. 20, 57) and also in the *Milinda-Pañha* (p. 114). It is doubtless identical with Vetravatī mentioned in Kālidāsa's *Meghadūtaṃ* (Pūrvamegha, śl. 25). It is modern Betwa which rises near Bhupal and flows into the Jumna. According to the *Purāṇas* it issues forth from the Pāripātra mountain. Bāṇa points out in his *Kādambarī* that this river flows through Vidiśā (Ed. M. R. Kale, Bombay, p. 14). The temple of Bhailaswāmī was situated on the banks of it at Bhilsā in the Gwalior State, 34 miles from Bhopal and eight miles from Sāñcī. It must have given rise to the name of Bhilsa town.[12] The city of Vetravatī was on the bank of the river of that name.[13] Close to the city of Vetravatī on the bank of the river

---

named Avīkṣita carried her off. The same *Purāṇa* further relates that Avīkṣita was captured. All the kings in company with king Viśāla entered the Vaidiśa city cheerfully, taking him bound.

1 *J.R.A.S.*, 1909, pp. 1053–56.
2 *Mālavikāgnimitra*, Act V, 20.
3 Law, *Indological Studies*, Pt. I, p. 50.
4 *C.H.I.*, p. 520.
5 *Ibid.*, p. 522.
6 *Ibid.*, p. 522.
7 Raychaudhuri, *Political History*, 4th ed., p. 468.
8 Bhandarkar, *Carmichael Lectures*, 1921, p. 88.
9 *Ibid.*, p. 185.
10 *Ibid.*, pp. 100-01.
11 *Ibid.*, p. 161.
12 *E.I.*, XXIV, Pt. V, January, 1938, p. 231.
13 *Jātaka*, IV, 388.

Vetravatī there lived a Brahmin, who was greatly proud of his birth but his pride was humbled.[1]

Veyaghana.—This is represented by Waigaon, three miles south of Añjanavatī.[2]

Vidarbha.—It is modern Berar. The people of Vidarbha are referred to by Daṇḍin in his *Kāvyādarśa* (I, 40). The people of this place, according to the *Purāṇas*,[3] were the dwellers of the Deccan (*Dakṣiṇāpathavāsinaḥ*) along with the Pulindas, Daṇḍakas, Vindhyas and others. Patañjali in his *Mahābhāṣya* (1. 4. 1, p. 634) mentions Vaidarbha. The *Yoginītantra* (2. 4) has a reference to it. The *Bhāgavata Purāṇa* mentions it as a country (IV. 28, 28; IX. 20, 34; X. 52, 21, 41; X. 84, 55). The *Brihatsaṃhitā* (XIV. 8) also mentions it. According to the *Mahābhārata* Vidarbha was the kingdom of Damayantī, Nala's queen. In the Vidarbha country lived one Puṇyavarmā, the jewel of the Bhoja royal family, who was a partial incarnation of virtue. He was powerful, truthful, self-disciplined, glorious, lofty, and vigorous in mind and body. He disciplined his people and made masterpieces his model. He caressed the wise, impressed his servants, blessed his relations and distressed his foes. He was deaf to illogical discourse and insatiable in the thirst for virtue. He was a penetrating critic of ethical and economic compendia. He controlled all functionaries watchfully and encouraged the conscientious by gifts and honours. He filled the life of a man with worthy deeds.[4] Kālidāsa in his *Mālavikāgnimitram* (Act V, 20) tells us that the Śuṅga dynasty was founded along with the establishment of a new kingdom at Vidarbha. Agnimitra's minister refers to the kingdom as one established not long ago (*acirādhiṣṭhita*) and compares its king to a newly planted tree (*navasaṃropanaśithilastaru*). The king of Vidarbha is represented as a relation of the Maurya minister and a natural enemy of the Śuṅgas.[5] During the reign of Bṛhadratha Maurya there were two factions in the Magadhan empire, the one headed by the king's minister and the other by his general. The minister's partisan Yajñasena was appointed governor of Vidarbha. He declared his independence and commenced hostilities against the usurping family when the general usurped the throne. Kumāra Mādhavasena, a cousin of Yajñasena and a partisan of Agnimitra, was arrested and kept in custody by Yajñasena's warden when the former was on his way to Vidiśā. This led the Śuṅga monarch Agnimitra to ask Vīrasena to attack Vidarbha. Yajñasena was defeated and the kingdom of Vidarbha was divided between the two cousins,[6] the river Varadā forming the boundary between the two states. Vidarbha was conquered by the son of Queen Gautamī Balaśrī according to the Nasik cave inscription (Raychaudhuri, *P.H.A.I.*, 4th ed., 309ff.; B. C. Law, *Indological Studies*, Pt. I, p. 50). For further details vide Law, *Tribes in Ancient India*, pp. 49, 100, 123, 174 and 389.

Vilāpadraka.—It may be identified with the village of Bilaṇḍi about 11 miles S.S.E. of Shergadh. Some have identified it with the village of Bilwāro situated about 25 miles east of Shergaḍh (*E.I.*, XXIII, Pt. IV, October, 1935, p. 135).

Vindhyavallī.—It is the ancient name of Bijholī. It is also popularly known as Bijoliā or Bijoliyā (*E.I.*, XXVI, Pt. III, 101).

---

[1] *Jataka*, IV, pp. 388ff.
[2] *E.I.*, XXIII, Pt. I, January, 1935.
[3] *Matsyap.*, 114, 46–48; *Vāyu*, 45, 126; *Mārkaṇḍeya*, 57, 45–48.
[4] *Daśakumāracaritam*, p. 180.
[5] H. C. Raychaudhuri, *Political History of Ancient India*, 4th ed., p. 309.
[6] *Mālavikāgnimitram*, ed. S. S. Ayyer, pp. 14ff.

Vodhagrāma (*E.I.*, X, 78-79).—It is in Satyapuramaṇḍala, south Rajputana, and may probably be identified with Bodan.

Vyāghreraka.—It is to be identified with the modern Bāghera, about 47 miles to the south-east of Ajmeer (*E.I.*, XXVI, Pt. III, July, 1941).

Wadgaon.—It is in the Warorā tahsil of the Cāndā district where the plates of Vākāṭaka Pravarsena II were found (*E.I.*, XXVII, Pt. II, p. 74).

Yaudheya.—The Yaudheyas were a republican tribe as old as the age of Pāṇini, the celebrated grammarian (Pāṇini's *Sūtras*, 5. 3. 116-117). They maintained their tribal organization as late as the fourth century A.D. about which time they are referred to in the Allahabad Pillar Inscription of Samudragupta along with other republican tribes, e.g. the Mālavas, Ārjunāyanas, Madrakas, Ābhīras and others. They were also known as such in the sixth century A.D. as we learn from the *Bṛhatsaṃhitā* of Varāhamihira (XIV. 28).

But the earliest reference to the tribe is probably made in Pāṇini. In *na prācya Bhargādi Yaudheyādibhyaḥ* (IV. I. 178) the term 'Yaudheyādi' includes the two tribes, the Yaudheyas and the Trigarttas. Elsewhere in the *sūtras* (V. 3. 117), the Yaudheyas, counting of course the Trigarttas with them, are referred to as forming an *Āyudha jīvisaṃgha* or a tribal republican organization depending mainly on arms, i.e., a warrior tribe. But the historical tradition of the tribe goes still earlier. The Purāṇas[1] refer to the Yaudheyas as having been descended from Uśīnara. The *Harivaṃśa*, too, connects the Yaudheyas with the Uśīnaras (*Harivaṃśa*, Ch. 32; cf. also Pargiter, *Mārk. P.*, p. 380). Pargiter thinks that King Uśīnara established separate kingdoms on the eastern border of the Punjab, namely, those of the Yaudheyas, Ambaṣṭhas, Navarāṣṭra, and the city of Kṛmila; and his famous son Śivi Auśīnara originated the Śivis in Śivapura (*A.I.H.T.*, p. 264). That the Yaudheyas were settled in the Punjab is also proved by their association with the Trigarttas, Ambaṣṭhas, and Śivis. In the *Mahābhārata* (Droṇa Parva, Ch. 18, 16; Karṇa Parva, Ch. 5, 48) the Yaudheyas are described as being defeated by Arjuna along with the Mālavas and Trigarttas. In the Sabhā Parva (Ch. 52, 14-15) they along with the Śivis, Trigarttas and Ambaṣṭhas are represented as having assembled and paid their homage to Yudhiṣṭhira. Elsewhere in the Great Epic (Droṇa Parva, Ch. 159, 5) the tribe is mentioned along with the Adrijas (= the Adraistai of the Greeks ?), Madrakas and Mālavas (*Yaudheyānadrijān rājan Madrakān Mālavānapi*).

The *Bṛhatsaṃhitā* places the Yaudheyas along with the Ārjunāyanas in the northern division of India. They may have been connected with the Pandonnoi or Pāṇḍava tribe mentioned by Ptolemy as settled in the Punjab (*Ind. Ant.*, XIII, 331, 349). Yaudheya appears as the name of a son of Yudhiṣṭhira in the *Mahābhārata* (Ādi Parva, Ch. 95, 76).[2]

Cunningham[3] identifies the Yaudheyas with the Johiya Rajputs and the country of the Yaudheyas with Johiyabar (= Yaudheya-vara) the district round Multan, on the strength of the evidence derived from the coins of the Yaudheya clan.[4] The Johiyas, he points out, are divided into three tribes; and he finds a strong confirmation of his identification in the fact that in the coins of the Yaudheya clan there can be traced the existence of three different tribes.

---

1 *Brahmāṇḍap.*, III, ch. 74; *Vāyup.*, ch. 99; *Brahmap.*, ch. 13; *Matsyap.*, ch. 48; *Viṣṇup.*, ch. 17, etc.

2 Raychaudhuri, *P.H.A.I.*, 4th ed., p. 457.

3 *A.G.I.*, pp. 281-282.

4 Allan, *Coins of India*, p. cli.

The Yaudheyas are also mentioned in the Junāgaḍh Rock Inscription of Rudradāman,[1] where the Śaka king boasts of having 'rooted out the Yaudheyas'. They are known from the Bijayagaḍh Stone Inscription (*C.I.I.*, Vol. III, pp. 250-51) to have occupied the Bijayagaḍh region of the Bharatpur State.[2] It probably shows that this powerful clan by this time extended their influence very far to the south, otherwise they would not have come into collision with the Śaka Satrap. But the tide of Scythian invasion could not sweep away this tribal republic which survived at least up to the time of Samudragupta. In the Allahabad Pillar Inscription of this powerful Gupta monarch the Yaudheyas are included in the list of the tribal states of the western and south-western fringes of Āryāvarta, which paid homage to Samudragupta.[3] According to some the Yaudheyas occupied an area which may be roughly described as the eastern Punjab.[4] For further details vide B. C. Law, *Indological Studies*, Pt. I, 56ff.

Yekkeri.—This village is situated about four miles towards the north by east from Saundatti, the chief town of the Parāsgaḍh taluk of the Belgaum district (*E.I.*, V, p. 6).

---

1 *E.I.*, Vol. VIII, pp. 36ff.

2 Paleographically the inscription is of an early date, the characters being of the so-called Indo-Scythic form. The leader of the Yaudheya tribe who is referred to in the inscription has been styled as Mahārāja and Mahāsenāpati. Cf. *J.R.A.S.*, 1897, 30.

3 Cf. Ray Chaudhuri, *P.H.A.I*, 4th ed., p. 457.

4 Motichandra, *Geographical and Economic Studies in the Mahābhārata*, p. 94.

INDEX

Note: *Ūrṇāvatī* printed in page 127 should be read after *Upavattanaśālavana* in page 132.